10-21-92   $375.00   (5 vols)

# GREAT EVENTS
# FROM
# HISTORY II

# GREAT EVENTS FROM HISTORY II

Human
Rights
Series

**Volume 2**
1937-1960

*Edited by*

FRANK N. MAGILL

**SALEM PRESS**
Pasadena, California     Englewood Cliffs, New Jersey

**Library of Congress Cataloging-in-Publication Data**
Great events from history II. Human rights series / edited by Frank N. Magill.
    p.    cm.
  Includes bibliographical references and index.
  1. Human rights—History—20th century—Chronology. I. Magill, Frank Northen, 1907-

K3240.6.G74  1992
341.4′81′0904—dc20
ISBN 0-89356-643-8 (set)         92-12896
ISBN 0-89356-645-4 (volume 2)         CIP

PRINTED IN THE UNITED STATES OF AMERICA

# LIST OF EVENTS IN VOLUME II

## LIST OF EVENTS IN VOLUME II

# GREAT EVENTS
# FROM
# HISTORY II

# JAPANESE TROOPS BRUTALIZE CHINESE AFTER THE CAPTURE OF NANJING

*Category of event:* Atrocities and war crimes
*Time:* December, 1937, to February, 1938
*Locale:* Nanjing, People's Republic of China

*After having captured the Nationalist Chinese capital city of Nanjing, three divisions of Japanese troops were allowed to kill, rape, loot, and burn*

*Principal personages:*
> IWANE MATSUI (1878-1948), the overall commander of the expeditionary force that captured Nanjing, later executed for war crimes
> PRINCE YASUHIKO ASAKA (1887-1964), the commander succeeding Matsui at Nanjing; presided over the atrocities but was not prosecuted
> AKIRA MUTO (1892-1948), the officer who ordered troops into Nanjing and was in closest contact with the atrocities; later executed for war crimes committed elsewhere
> KINGORO HASHIMOTO (1890-1957), the officer who ordered the sinking of the USS *Panay* and other vessels; later sentenced to life imprisonment
> CHIANG KAI-SHEK (1887-1975), the president of China and military commander in chief who rejected negotiations

## Summary of Event

Japan had begun absorbing parts of China in 1895 with the annexation of Taiwan, followed by Manchuria in 1932, Jehol Province in 1933, and Inner Mongolia in 1935. In the latter three, a pattern was established of local Japanese field commanders initiating military action, whereupon the Tokyo higher command would debate but finally back up their actions, and then the Chinese Nationalist government under Chiang Kai-shek would submit to a local settlement to avoid major confrontation. The Japanese attitude toward the Nationalist government and the Chinese people came to be contemptuous. In July, 1937, an accidental clash occurred outside Beijing and, when the Chinese did not back down, the Japanese army was forced to choose between withdrawal and full military assault. Dismissive of Chinese military capability, they chose the latter course, hoping that a quick defeat would topple Chiang, neutralize China, and free Japanese troops for expected confrontations with the Soviet Union.

The key to rapid conquest was Shanghai, the gateway to the Yangtze valley and central China. Once taken, the passage to Nanjing, the Nationalist capital 170 miles inland, would be easy. Chiang committed the cream of his officer corps and best-trained troops to the battle for Shanghai, losing the majority of them in a suicidal stand against naval and air bombardment that began in August and lasted into November.

With the Japanese forces bogged down in street fighting, the higher command formulated a strategy that would outflank the Shanghai fortifications and expedite the drive on Nanjing, which many in the Japanese army and government expected to be the final campaign. The overall commander of the expeditionary force was General Iwane Matsui, a slight, tubercular man pulled out of retirement by the emperor himself. He had been a pan-Asian idealist earlier and, although he advocated the drive on Nanjing, there is nothing to indicate that he held any enmity toward the Chinese, whose language he spoke fluently. The flanking forces he drove toward Nanjing, however, were hard to control. Indications of their mood were shown in the bombing, strafing, and looting of cities and villages along the way.

Many in the Japanese high command, including Matsui, believed that negotiations for a cease-fire should have been initiated before attacking Nanjing. Chiang had indicated willingness to negotiate, although at the same time he issued orders that Nanjing was to be defended to the last, despite its indefensible position and its lack of military value. In any case, Japanese moderates were overridden and no terms were offered. The assault began on December 9, with a creeping artillery and air barrage that shattered all resistance by December 13. On December 17, with the Nanjing atrocities already beginning, Chiang, who had moved his government inland, issued his historic address rejecting all negotiations and calling for a people's war to the bitter end.

As the attack on Nanjing began, General Matsui was removed from personal supervision of field operations and confined to theater command. Emperor Hirohito's uncle, General Prince Yasuhiko Asaka, was appointed to the Nanjing operation. His headquarters issued secret orders to kill all captives, referring presumably to the Chinese troops trapped in the besieged city. Under him were the field commanders whose troops perpetrated the Nanjing outrages: Lieutenant General Kesago Nakajima of the Sixteenth Division, General Heisuke Yanagawa of the Nineteenth Corps, Lieutenant General Hisao Tani of the Sixth Division, and Colonel Akira Muto, in charge of billeting troops, who moved troops from encampments safely outside Nanjing into the city, where the holocaust took place.

The Chinese never formally surrendered the city. Their retreat was unplanned and disjointed, leaving about seventy thousand troops trapped inside. About three-fourths of the city's population of one million fled, with Japanese firing on boats in the Yangtze, killing thousands as overloaded junks capsized. Many people were trampled in the confusion. As the Chinese authorities departed, they turned over supplies and effective authority to a self-appointed committee of twenty-seven foreign residents—American, British, German, and Danish missionaries, academics, and businesspeople—who established a safety zone of about two square miles in the northwest part of the city. Working tirelessly to protect a refugee population that reached a total of one-quarter million, they protested to Japanese authorities without result and restrained countless acts of individual brutality by their sheer presence, although they were never formally recognized by the Japanese. It was their diaries, letters, reports, film, and reminiscences that provided the four-thousand-page record of the atrocities in Nanjing for history and for the Allied war crimes trials.

Systematic looting began as soon as Japanese troops reached the city. Evidence of command complicity lay in the organized nature of the looting and the fact that army trucks were used. Later, even refugees were stripped of their pitiful possessions. Arson was likewise systematic, with thermite strips efficiently used to burn whole sections of what had been one of the loveliest cities in China. Tricked by notices promising good treatment, disarmed Chinese soldiers, and later virtually all males of military age, were bound and murdered by machine gun or bayonet. Many were staked and used for bayonet or sword practice. Prisoners were roasted over fires, doused with kerosene and set on fire, burned with chemicals, disemboweled, or buried up to the neck before torture.

Rapes occurred more and more frequently and increasingly flagrantly, often on the street in broad daylight. Pregnant women, girls as young as nine, and women as old as seventy-six fell victim. Women were gang-raped, were raped and then murdered, or had their children murdered. Women were rounded up and kept for months in sexual bondage at camps.

The grisly statistical totals for the seven weeks between December, 1937, and February, 1938, when the carnage finally subsided, are difficult to determine since official sources are often biased and the eyewitnesses were unaware of the bigger picture. Many died unrecorded, given the difficulties of wartime records in China. A high estimate of the death toll is 300,000; the true number is almost certainly more than 150,000. There were more than twenty thousand rapes. The overall economic loss is impossible to fix. Japanese army warehouses were filled with looted valuables. Some officers, including Nakajima, retained small fortunes in plunder, but most was sold to defray army expenses. A study on a limited sample of individuals estimated that the average farmer lost the equivalent of 278 days of labor and the average city dweller lost 681 days. Nanjing would take more than a year to begin economic revival.

On December 12, as Nanjing was falling, Japanese forces under Colonel Kingoro Hashimoto bombed and sank an American gunboat, the USS *Panay*, twenty-five miles upriver from Nanjing. Lifeboats were strafed and the craft was machine gunned from a nearby Japanese gunboat. Two American tankers, two British gunboats, and two British-flag steamers were also bombed. Four American crew members were killed, and sixty were wounded; two British crew members and countless refugees were also killed. Hashimoto, an ultranationalist zealot, had done this on his own initiative in defiance of standing policy to avoid provoking the West. In contrast to the Nanjing outrages, the Japanese government apologized officially and privately and offered indemnities, which were accepted by the United States and Great Britain with little protest.

## Impact of Event

The attitude of the Japanese army and government at first was to ignore the events at Nanjing, treating them as a matter for the army and accepting the army's bland fictions minimizing the horror. Later, however, Nanjing veterans on leave boasted openly of their depredations. In December, newspapers had even reported a grotesque sort of contest between two lieutenants racing to see who could cut down the most Chinese with their swords, referring to the race as "fun." The authorities were forced to suppress virtually all mention of atrocities. Japanese school texts, even decades later, avoided the subject, and prominent officials have asserted that it never happened.

The Imperial Japanese Army almost never punished a soldier for excesses (punishment was reserved for lack of aggressiveness), so punishment had to wait for the war's end. Matsui, who had scolded his subordinates for their complicity (they laughed at him), retired after Nanjing, built a temple, and held services for the dead of Nanjing. Even though he was less guilty than most, he offered no defense and so was the only prominent officer executed specifically for the Nanjing atrocities at the Tokyo war crimes tribunal. Muto was executed for war crimes in the Philippines, Hashimoto was given a life sentence, and Prince Asaka, protected by his royal connections, escaped prosecution.

Nanjing had a crucial effect on the course of the war. Japan might have won the war either with an acceptable offer of terms or with an immediate drive past Nanjing into the interior. Instead, the brutal tactics at Nanjing clearly failed to shock the Nationalists into negotiating and allowed them time to reorganize to carry on the war. This left the Japanese with the sole alternative of creating collaborationist governments, which were divided and subject to the same independent field commands that had produced the Nanjing incident. Japan's actions in China cost it any credibility in negotiations with the United States. The breakdown of these negotiations produced the impasse that made Pearl Harbor possible.

The atrocities in Nanjing had a consciousness raising effect on world, and particularly on American, public opinion. Newspapers in the United States began reporting on the sinking of the USS *Panay* almost immediately. Reports on the larger disaster at Nanjing came more gradually, but were regular after December 30. Photographs were taken by foreigners, and even by the ingenuous Japanese, of horrible scenes. Chinese shops that processed the film smuggled out duplicate prints. There was even motion picture footage taken by the Reverend John Magee of the carnage, footage that was later used by the isolationist America First organization to frighten Americans into staying out of war. So many, however, were moved to anger and sympathy that the film was withdrawn.

Nanjing was one of the great atrocities of World War II. Never quite overshadowed by the more massive but impersonal Holocaust, it remained the benchmark for personal savagery and exemplified the dilemma posed by the rights of noncombatants in any profound nationalistic or ideological conflict.

## Bibliography

Abend, Hallett. *My Life in China, 1926-1941.* New York: Harcourt Brace, 1943. Abend is a veteran journalist from *The New York Times* with top connections among

Chinese, Japanese, and American figures and long experience in the Far East. Episodic and personal, this book offers unparalleled insights into the *Panay* incident but little on Nanjing, since Abend was not there. There are detailed biographical insights into selected individuals.

Bergamini, David. *Japan's Imperial Conspiracy.* New York: William Morrow, 1971. A controversial effort to prove circumstantially that Hirohito was more involved with Japanese aggression than most histories show. The atrocities in Nanjing set the book's theme and are covered minutely. In twelve hundred pages, there are vast amounts of anecdotal material on World War II in the East and a bibliography to match.

Butow, Robert J. C. *Tojo and the Coming of the War.* Princeton, N.J.: Princeton University Press, 1961. More than a biography of Tojo Hideki, this book delineates the military-bureaucratic environment that produced the decision to go to war with the United States. A classic, and a foundation for subsequent scholarly works on the political history of Japan's part in World War II. Excellent bibliography and index.

Chamberlin, William H. *Japan over Asia.* Garden City, N.Y.: Blue Ribbon Books, 1939. A contemporary attempt to assess Japanese strategy in Asia, written for the general public. The author was a *Christian Science Monitor* correspondent with four years' experience in Japan and China. Balanced by efforts to understand "oriental psychology" and the impact of the worldwide growth of fascism.

Coox, Alvin D., and Hilary Conroy, eds. *China and Japan: A Search for Balance Since World War I.* Santa Barbara, Calif.: ABC-Clio, 1978. Predominantly analytical. Discusses the emperor's role in the war. The Nanjing atrocities are seen as a watershed in the "pure military" line toward China. Some of the articles later became major works.

Crowley, James B. *Japan's Quest for Autonomy: National Security and Foreign Policy, 1930-1938.* Princeton, N.J.: Princeton University Press, 1966. The major monograph on diplomacy, bureaucracy, and military decision making. Particularly good for Sino-Japanese relations behind the scenes, in which Nanjing becomes only a part of a larger picture composed of hard decisions, misperceptions, lost opportunities, and situational imperatives. A thorough and scholarly work covering territory not dealt with elsewhere at the time.

Eastman, Lloyd. "Facets of an Ambivalent Relationship: Smuggling, Puppets, and Atrocities During the War, 1937-1945." In *The Chinese and the Japanese: Essays in Political and Cultural Interactions*, edited by Akira Iriye. Princeton, N.J.: Princeton University Press, 1980. A thoughtful and intriguing glimpse behind the obvious national hatreds at the fraternization, trade, and other cooperative ventures between the two sides. Offsets the brutality of Nanjing with instances of mutual accommodation. Eastman makes no apology for the widely observed Japanese arrogance.

Hsue, Shu-hsi. *The War Conduct of the Japanese.* Shanghai: Kelly and Walsh, 1938. This comprises hastily compiled essays on Japanese atrocities in China. Exceedingly detailed, it is designed as an archive for war crimes charges and to inform public opinion. Based on International Safety Zone Committee sources and international publications.

Morley, James W., ed. *The China Quagmire: Japan's Expansion on the Asian Continent, 1933-1941.* New York: Columbia University Press, 1983. Part of the seven-volume Japanese *Taiheiyo senso-e no michi*, translated with additional chapters and commentary. Reflecting a Japanese academic (liberal) view, it accepts all of the occurrences at Nanjing but tends to dwell on the decisionmaking context of the war as a whole.

Wilson, Dick. *When Tigers Fight: The Story of the Sino-Japanese War, 1937-1945.* New York: Viking Press, 1982. Probably the best-balanced condensed military history of the war, it contains astute judgments of all the major military leaders of both sides. It is heavily anecdotal, with a preference for extensive quotes, but is written in an accessible style. This is the best work to start with on this subject.

*David G. Egler*

**Cross-References**

Legal Norms of Behavior in Warfare Formulated by the Hague Conference (1907), p. 92; Armenians Suffer Genocide During World War I (1915), p. 150; Soldiers Massacre Indian Civilians in Amritsar (1919), p. 264; Japan Withdraws from the League of Nations (1933), p. 474; Nazi War Criminals Are Tried in Nuremberg (1945), p. 667; The United Nations Adopts a Convention on the Crime of Genocide (1948), p. 783; China Initiates a Genocide Policy Toward Tibetans (1950), p. 826; China Occupies Tibet (1950), p. 837; The Statute of Limitations Is Ruled Not Applicable to War Crimes (1968), p. 1457; Lieutenant Calley Is Court-Martialed for the Massacre at My Lai (1970), p. 1555; Khmer Rouge Take Over Cambodia (1975), p. 1791.

# THE CONGRESS OF INDUSTRIAL
# ORGANIZATIONS IS FORMED

*Category of event:* Workers' rights
*Time:* 1938
*Locale:* Pittsburgh, Pennsylvania

*The formation of the CIO in 1935 served to broaden the basis of social democracy in the United States and expand workers' rights*

> *Principal personages:*
> JOHN L. LEWIS (1880-1969), the leader of the United Mine Workers
> DAVID DUBINSKY (1892-1982), the president of the International Ladies Garment Workers Union
> SIDNEY HILLMAN (1887-1946), the Lithuanian-born needle trades leader and leader of the Amalgamated Clothing Workers
> CHARLES E. HUGHES (1862-1948), the chief justice of the Supreme Court who presided over the decision on the constitutionality of the Wagner Act
> FRANKLIN D. ROOSEVELT (1882-1945), the president of the United States from 1933 to 1945

## Summary of Event

At the American Federation of Labor (AFL) convention in 1935, John L. Lewis spoke in favor of industrial, as opposed to trade, union organization. Even though Lewis was denied support for this initiative by the AFL's Executive Council, the signal to organize industrial labor took shape. Following the convention, Lewis, along with other key industrial leaders including David Dubinsky of the International Ladies Garment Workers Union (ILGWU) and Sidney Hillman of the Amalgamated Clothing Workers (ACW), officially formed the Committee for Industrial Organizations on November 9, 1935. Encouraged by rank-and-file rebellions of mass-production workers against AFL tactics and industry civil rights abuses, the CIO began to make significant headway in an attempt to organize industrial America, especially mass-production workers. The group reorganized as the Congress of Industrial Organizations in Pittsburgh, Pennsylvania, late in 1938.

To further its goals, the new organization immediately reinstated the concept of confrontational politics with management. Sit-down strikes, which were seen previously as a tactic of the Industrial Workers of the World (IWW), were offered to the worker as a vehicle to control union activity and influence negotiations with industry at the same time. Late in 1935, rubber workers in Akron, Ohio, organized to prevent worker layoffs and to speak out against an extended workday forced upon them by management. On January 29, 1936, Firestone workers in Akron carried out a sit-down strike. Within two weeks, the tactic spread to the Goodrich and Goodyear rubber plants in the area. In all, ten thousand Akron rubber workers organized to challenge the power of industry and government. In the process, the workers reorganized their AFL union into the United Rubber Workers (URW) and affiliated with the CIO. Following the success at Akron, CIO organizers pushed their way into other mass-production industries, including steel (Steel Workers Organizing Committee), mining (United Mine Workers), and transportation (United Auto Workers).

In spite of these initial successes, industry was still able to counter labor's newfound solidarity. The 1930's were witness to some of the most turbulent strikes in American labor history. Anti-union employers used labor spies and strong-arm methods. They hired agents to seek out trade-unionizing activity and to plant seeds of distrust among the workers themselves in an attempt to check CIO organizing efforts. Some violated the law in the process, and most were not above using the law to further their own ends. Legal injunctions in many cases thwarted labor organizing activities.

A Senate subcommittee under Robert M. La Follette exposed many of the anti-union practices that violated workers' civil liberties between 1933 and 1937. A public preview of committee reports disclosed that more than two thousand American companies had been engaged in labor espionage during that period. Provocateurs hired by the Pinkerton and Burns detective agencies had infiltrated key trade-union organizing efforts. Infiltration transgressed into the steel, rail, and auto industries with complete disregard of the legal and constitutional rights that had previously characterized official labor-management relations. Industrial espionage was not the only weapon which was used to combat trade unionism. Industrial warfare was also implemented by management, spreading fear throughout the labor community. In many locales, workers were violently denied their right to organize. When the La Follette Civil Liberties Committee reconvened in 1937, it was startled to learn of the extent to which management was prepared to fight trade unionism. Corporations such as Republic Steel and the Youngstown Sheet and Tube Company had amassed significant arsenals to fight unions. Machine guns, rifles, ammunition, gas guns, and tear and sickening gas were stockpiled to prosecute the war against the worker. According to committee reports, these two companies alone had enough arms to fight a small war.

Propaganda was another management technique used to confront trade unionism. The goal was to win public support by labeling organizing activities as alien and violent by design. The Mohawk Valley Formula was one example of a formal program to denounce union activists as dangerous lawbreakers and communists. Local committees "loyal" to American values were organized to protect plants and communities against outside agitators and disloyal employees. A major industry weapon was the threat to move a company out of a community if workers successfully organized. Countervailing responses by labor against employer intimidation often took on militant characteristics. The number of strikes throughout the period rose dramatically. By 1937, almost two million workers had been involved in a strike. In defense of civil liberties, trade unionists called for the support of all workers to rally around the cause of labor.

A key issue at this point was the enforcement of the Wagner Act. Introduced successfully in 1935 by Senator Robert Wagner of New York, the act was an official notification that government supported collective bargaining. The Roosevelt Administration went on record in support of the right of workers to organize. Recognition of the right of the worker to attempt to gain a larger share of the national income represented a shift from previous laissez-faire policies that had rested so heavily in management's corner. Unfair labor practices of the past were no longer to be tolerated. It was not, however, the government's intention to alienate industry. President Roosevelt declared that the law's purpose was to promote a better relationship between labor and management for the betterment of all.

At its core, the Wagner Act, or the National Labor Relations Act as it officially was called, suggested freedom and civil liberty, that is, the right to organize. Any employer interference in this activity was expressly prohibited. Employers could not deny to any worker the right to organize for the purpose of bargaining collectively. The law further stated that those representatives elected by the majority of workers would have exclusive bargaining rights for all employees. The government's enforcing arm was the National Labor Relations Board (NLRB). The board was to determine the bargaining units, supervise employee representative elections, hear complaints against unfair labor practices, and petition the courts to enforce such determinations. As such, the NLRB served in a judicial capacity, not a mediating capacity. Management as a whole labeled the new law unconstitutional and many corporations openly defied it.

On April 12, 1937, the Supreme Court rendered a decision as to the constitutionality of the Wagner Act. In the case of *NLRB v. Jones and Laughlin Steel Company*, the right of labor to organize for the purpose of collective bargaining was sustained: "Employees have a clear right to organize and select their representatives for lawful purposes." Chief Justice Hughes maintained in the five-to-four decision that "as the respondent has to organize its business and select its own officers and agents . . . [the] union was essential to give laborers opportunity to deal on an equality with their employer. . . ." Continued labor strife showed that enforcing the law at times proved to be difficult, but public opinion increasingly supported trade unionism for the remainder of the decade. The CIO was a major player in consolidating a working-class indentity and molding public opinion to support the rights of workers. The CIO helped to build a platform for labor to redress the inequality which had previously been tipped in favor of industry.

## Impact of Event

The CIO encouraged industrial workers to unite in support of labor's right to bargain collectively against low wages in a period of economic depression and poverty. CIO activists helped move public opinion toward the recognition of workers' rights in American industrial society. Arbitrary and discriminatory management practices that had survived in the past were no longer to be tolerated by the CIO. Collective bargaining formally established seniority and grievance procedures.

The CIO did not win all of its objectives immediately; many corporations remained openly hostile to trade unionism. As a result, the union adopted a new form of its most volatile weapon, the strike. The sit-down technique, as it came to be known, was implemented to force industry to come to the bargaining table. Traditional striking in the form of the picket line made strikers vulnerable to attack by police or private forces hired by employers. By taking control of the industrial plant—sitting down—strikers could get management recognition more readily. Industry was not fond of having police battle with strikers so close to expensive machinery. Between 1935 and 1937, there were almost nine hundred sit-downs involving one-half million workers at 150 companies across the nation. The sit-down enhanced the power of labor to demand recognition, and industrial unionism was firmly established.

The sit-down strike that vaulted the CIO into the public limelight occurred at the General Motors plants at Flint, Michigan. This was the bastion of General Motors, and GM was at the pinnacle of mass-production industry in the United States. Instead of walking off their jobs, workers went to their work stations and stayed there. This tactic won the CIO recognition as the bargaining agent for the auto workers.

Because the CIO had successfully organized unskilled workers, it managed to bring together a greater mix of people. Minorities, who had previously lacked an equal means of expression, became a recognized part of industrial America. The inclusion of immigrants, blacks, women, and other minorities helped to blur previous lines of color, gender, and skill in such a manner as to establish for the union a more egalitarian public image and point of view. The long-term effects of the founding of the CIO were profound and lasting; to ignore organized labor now meant political as well as economic instability. The CIO made collective bargaining the concern of society as a whole. Membership in the trade unions, particularly in industrial mass production, continued to grow throughout the decade. By 1941, it had topped the one million mark. At the same time, the NLRB had handled thirty-three thousand cases involving more than seven million workers. By providing representation and insisting on worker rights, the CIO helped to broaden the basis of social democracy.

## Bibliography

Auerbach, Jerold S. *American Labor: The Twentieth Century.* Indianapolis: Bobbs-Merrill, 1969. Anthology touching upon trade unions as economic and legal institutions and the thoughts and activities of labor leaders. Its main focus, however, is on the conditions, culture, and outlook of organized and unorganized workers. Many first-person accounts make this book useful for research. Indexed.

Bernstein, Irving. *Turbulent Years: A History of the American Worker, 1933-1941.* Boston: Houghton Mifflin, 1969. A general history of American labor in the era between World Wars I and II. Concerned with the development of unionism and collective bargaining in American industry and of public policy relating to collective bargaining during the New Deal era. Includes bibliographical notes and index.

Dulles, Foster Rhea. *Labor in America: A History.* New York: Thomas Y. Crowell, 1966. Seeks to give a general and comprehensive account of the rise of American labor since colonial days. Emphasis is placed on national organization during the 1930's, including the rise of the CIO and the merger of the CIO and the AFL. Includes bibliographical notes and index.

Foner, Phillip. *From the Founding of the American Federation of Labor to the Emergence of American Imperialism.* Vol. 2 in *A History of the Labor Movement in the United States.* New York: International Publishers, 1985. Explores the history of American labor during the era from the late nineteenth to the early twentieth centuries. Foner's wide-ranging research has turned up many otherwise unexplored aspects of labor in the United States such as women's and black issues. Indexed.

Green, James R. *The World of the Worker: Labor in Twentieth Century America.* New York: Hill & Wang, 1980. Focuses on notable labor leaders such as John L. Lewis and Sidney Hillman. The main emphasis is placed on the relationship between leaders and workers. Gives a valuable description of the conflict over power and authority. Includes bibliographical essay and index.

Keeran, Roger. *The Communist Party and the Auto Workers' Unions.* Bloomington: Indiana University Press, 1980. Explores the role of communists in the history of auto workers' unions in the period 1919-1949. Valuable in that it refutes some commonly held ideas about communists and labor. Also discusses the identification of communists, the reliability of communist sources, and oral history as part of methodology. Indexed.

Walker, Thomas J. E. *Pluralistic Fraternity: The History of the International Workers Order.* New York: Garland, 1991. A groundbreaking study of the issue of the Communist Party control of the IWO from its roots at the turn of the twentieth century to its eventual demise in 1954. This analysis stands out in its investigation of how the Communist Party and people broadly sympathetic to it managed to create a worker's fraternal organization based on the social, political, and cultural status of many immigrant and first-generation Americans of the 1930's, 1940's, and 1950's. Includes bibliography and index.

*Thomas Jay Edward Walker*

## Cross-References

Massachusetts Adopts the First Minimum-Wage Law in the United States (1912), p. 126; Ford Offers a Five-Dollar, Eight-Hour Workday (1914), p. 143; The International Labour Organisation Is Established (1919), p. 281; Steel Workers Go on Strike to Demand Improved Working Conditions (1919), p. 293; The Wagner Act Requires Employers to Accept Collective Bargaining (1935), p. 508; Social Security Act Establishes Benefits for Nonworking People (1935), p. 514; HUAC Begins Investigating Suspected Communists (1938), p. 550; Roosevelt Outlaws Discrimination in Defense-Industry Employment (1941), p. 578; Autoworkers Negotiate a Contract with a Cost-of-Living Provision (1948), p. 766.

# HUAC BEGINS INVESTIGATING
# SUSPECTED COMMUNISTS

*Categories of event:* Political freedom and accused persons' rights
*Time:* 1938
*Locale:* Washington, D.C.

*HUAC searched for communists and fascists within the government and elsewhere for thirty-seven years before quietly expiring in the wake of the Watergate scandal*

*Principal personages:*
MARTIN DIES (1901-1972), the first chair of the Un-American Activities Committee
SAMUEL DICKSTEIN (1885-1954), a New York congressman and tireless foe of anti-Semitism
J. EDGAR HOOVER (1895-1972), the longtime director of the Federal Bureau of Investigation (FBI)
J. PARNELL THOMAS (1895-1970), a HUAC member, later chair of HUAC

## Summary of Event

The House Committee on Un-American Activities (HUAC) investigated Communist Party members, native fascists, and other proponents of so-called foreign "isms" in five different decades. For the first seven years of its life (1938-1945), HUAC served as a special committee chaired by Martin Dies (D-Tex.). Established as a regular, standing committee of the House of Representatives in 1945, HUAC reorganized in 1969 and served the last six years of its life as the House Committee on Internal Security (HCIS). For the entire thirty-seven year period, the committee remained committed to what its members and staff called a politics of exposure.

The two congresspeople who led the fight to establish HUAC, Martin Dies and Samuel Dickstein (D-N.Y.), could scarcely have had more different priorities. Dickstein was predominantly troubled by native Nazi and other far-right movements, notably Fritz Kuhn's German-American Bund and William Dudley Pelley's Silver Shirts. Explicitly anti-Semitic, such groups looked to Hitler's Germany for inspiration. They goose-stepped, rallied, flew swastikas, and advocated violence against Jews and other so-called lesser races. To root out native fascism, Dickstein proposed an investigation of all organizations found operating in the United States for the purpose of diffusing within the United States slanderous or libelous un-American propaganda of religious, racial, or subversive political prejudices, especially that which would incite the use of force or violence. From 1933 to 1938, the House rebuffed Dickstein's repeated calls for such an investigation.

With little interest in anti-Semitism but a great interest in subversion by communists and other leftists, Martin Dies saw the possibilities in the sort of investigation that Dickstein advocated. Backed by conservative leadership in the House and assured of the support of the southern bloc, Dies proposed a similar investigation of the extent, character, and objects of un-American propaganda activities in the United States; the diffusion within the United States of subversive and un-American propaganda that attacked the form of government guaranteed by the Constitution; and all other questions that would aid Congress in any necessary remedial legislation. Dickstein himself became the most fervent advocate of Dies's resolution, and in May, 1938, with the support of both conservatives and those who wanted to attack anti-Semitism, the House overwhelmingly approved Dies's resolution. HUAC was born.

Martin Dies conceded that it would be difficult to legislate effectively in this matter but promised nevertheless to bring "the light of day . . . to bear upon" un-American activities and to allow public sentiment to do the rest. Under his leadership, the committee membership—Arthur D. Healy (D-Mass.), John J. Dempsey (D-N.M.), Joe Starnes (D-Ala.), Harold G. Mosier (D-Ohio), Noah M. Mason (R-Ill.), and J. Parnell Thomas (R-N.J.)—acted on this directive. Samuel Dickstein had only a Pyrrhic victory. He was not appointed to the committee and soon became a critic of Dies's nearly exclusive focus on the left.

Where Dickstein stood against Hitler and anti-Semitism, Dies stood against Franklin D. Roosevelt and the New Deal. During Roosevelt's first term, a clear majority of the House and Senate were willing to accept the administration's innovative social and economic program to combat the Great Depression. In the second term, a congressional rebellion began, with New Deal Democrats facing increased opposition from a coalition of Republicans and conservative southern Democrats. HUAC's birth represented one of a handful of victories for this anti-New Deal coalition.

Dies and his conservative supporters were critical of the New Deal's limited accomplishments. The depression was simply not going away. Unemployment remained high, production continued to lag, and in 1937 the economy tumbled downward once again—a recession, in other words, in the midst of depression. Roosevelt's second-term emphasis on urban-based issues, the so-called Second New Deal, also alienated congressional conservatives, many of whom, because of the seniority system, chaired powerful committees in the House and Senate. Dies's own benefactors included the ultra-conservative vice president, John Nance Garner of Texas, and Speaker of the House William Bankhead of Alabama. Dies, Garner, and Bankhead were further alarmed by the sit-down strikes of 1935-1936; the efforts of Senator Robert Wagner (D-N.Y.) and others to obtain antilynching legislation in 1936-1937; Roosevelt's court-packing scheme of 1937 and attempt to purge the Democratic party of obstructionists by calling for the defeat of anti-New Deal Democrats in the 1938 primaries; and what was generally perceived to be a marked ideological shift by the White House to the left.

President Roosevelt faced not only an informal yet quite formidable conservative coalition but also nearly unanimous congressional antipathy toward further meddling with the separation of powers doctrine or the fundamental institutions of Congress, the courts, and the states. Congressional conservatives were determined to halt the expansion of the New Deal and to reverse what HUAC would later describe, in 1942, as the "creeping totalitarianism" of the executive's "effort to obliterate the Congress of the United States as a co-equal and independent branch of government."

When HUAC began functioning in August, 1938, the conservative bloc in Congress was already strong enough to grind the New Deal to a halt. Dies used the new committee to go on the offensive. His strategy was direct. Targeting the New Deal's programs, personnel, and constituency in a series of well-publicized hearings, Dies intended to expose and neutralize what J. Parnell Thomas, the senior Republican member of the committee, called "the four horsemen of autocracy"—fascism, Nazism, Bolshevism, and New Dealism. Equating the modest social and economic reforms of the Roosevelt years with un-Americanism, Dies and Thomas recognized no distinction between the New Dealers' efforts to tinker with the system and the more radical plans of communist revolutionaries to overthrow the government and abolish capitalism.

HUAC launched well-publicized hearings on the National Labor Relations Board, the Bureau of Indian Affairs, and the Federal Theater Project, among other New Deal agencies; compiled dossiers on people from lowly civil servants all the way up to Eleanor Roosevelt; and spread allegations about communist infiltration of the Congress of Industrial Organizations and other groups that supported the Roosevelt Administration. In August, 1938, alone, *The New York Times* devoted more than two hundred column inches of space to the Dies Committee's spectacular charges.

During the World War II years, Dies and Thomas pushed for a stringent federal employee loyalty program. Although HUAC never ignored native fascist groups, the focus on communism and the New Deal remained intact. In 1942, Dies sent a list of 1,124 allegedly subversive federal employees to Attorney General Francis Biddle and Federal Bureau of Investigation (FBI) Director J. Edgar Hoover. Nearly every one of them was accused of communist associations. When subsequent investigations led to the firing of only four employees, Dies charged a cover-up. The Roosevelt Administration's incompetence and negligence in confronting the domestic communist threat, he argued, raised the specter of the administration's complicity, unwitting or otherwise, in an international communist conspiracy. "The New Deal," Thomas said, carrying the assault one step further, "is either for the Communist Party, or is playing into the hands of the Communist Party."

Such charges did not stick, and HUAC labored in relative obscurity during the last of the war years. Dies himself gave up the fight. Citing poor health and a desire to return to private business, he chose not to stand for reelection in 1944, and his committee expired at the end of the Seventy-eighth Congress, only to be recreated in January, 1945, as a regular, standing committee of the House—the result, ironically, of a parliamentary maneuver by John E. Rankin (D-Miss.), one of the most outspoken anti-Semites ever to serve in the House.

## Impact of Event

Martin Dies and his committee refined many of the methods and techniques later identified with McCarthyism. HUAC, in its early days, mined the communists-in-government issue, worked to legitimize the idea of guilt by association, championed the veracity of excommunist witnesses, and worked diligently to open a direct pipeline to the FBI and other executive agencies concerned with internal security. Dies himself, as one historian observed, named "more names in a single year than Joe McCarthy did in a lifetime."

Ultimately, HUAC derived its power from its incredibly voluminous files, consisting of derogatory information on the political associations of at least several hundred thousand American citizens; its access to FBI informants and symbiotic relationship with FBI officials; and its ability to compel testimony under threat of imprisonment. During the Cold War era, assumptions about the seriousness of the threat posed by communists on the home front put the law on HUAC's side, enabling the establishment and maintenance of pervasive blacklists of the sort that Dies could only dream about. These blacklists were first institutionalized in the entertainment industry. HUAC's interest in Hollywood had in fact dated from 1938, when its chief investigator advised the press that Shirley Temple had once inadvertently served the interests of the Communist Party. In 1947, J. Parnell Thomas, then HUAC chair, formed a secret alliance with the FBI and its director, J. Edgar Hoover. By 1950, the blacklists were spreading with startling speed to the nation's teachers, lawyers, doctors, newspaper reporters, carpenters, and plumbers.

It was also during Thomas' tenure as chair that HUAC broke its most spectacular case, against former State Department official Alger Hiss. Against the backdrop of the Cold War, the Hiss case provided HUAC with the ammunition needed to make a credible attack on the integrity of New Deal programs and personnel. It also gave HUAC and its imitators, notably Senator Joseph R. McCarthy's Permanent Subcommittee on Investigations, enough power to plunge the nation into a protracted four-year search for communists in government.

## Bibliography

Bentley, Eric. ed. *Thirty Years of Treason: Excerpts from Hearings Before the House Committee on Un-American Activities, 1938-1968*. New York: Viking, 1971. At times hilarious and at other times sobering, this volume remains the best introduction to the things said and done in HUAC's name.

Carr, Robert K. *The House Committee on Un-American Activities, 1945-1950*. Ithaca, N.Y.: Cornell University Press, 1952. This is the first scholarly study of the committee. It remains valuable for its systematic and remarkably objective coverage of HUAC's activities during the early Cold War years.

Dies, Martin. *Martin Dies' Story*. New York: Bookmailer, 1963. The memoir of the man who set the committee's tone and tact.

——————. *The Trojan Horse in America*. New York: Dodd, Mead, 1940. Dies's summary of the subversive threat posed by communists and native fascists.

Gellermann, William. *Martin Dies*. New York: John Day, 1944. The only biography to date of the committee's first chair.

Goodman, Walter. *The Committee: The Extraordinary Career of the House Commit-tee on Un-American Activities.* New York: Farrar, Straus & Giroux, 1968. Written in a lively, journalistic style, this is the standard history of HUAC's first thirty years. Goodman criticizes both the committee, for its inquisitorial and sensa-tionalist style, and the investigated, for their dissident politics and confrontational posturing.

Navasky, Victor. *Naming Names.* New York: Viking, 1980. This self-described moral detective story investigates HUAC in Hollywood and the difficult choices faced by those who received committee subpoenas.

O'Reilly, Kenneth. *Hoover and the Un-Americans: The FBI, HUAC, and the Red Menace.* Philadelphia: Temple University Press, 1983. Based on thousands of FBI and other government agency files obtained under the Freedom of Information Act, this book explores the on-again/off-again relationship between the FBI and HUAC. Particular emphasis is placed on the ways in which HUAC publicized information from FBI files on dissident individuals and groups.

Weinstein, Allen. *Perjury: The Hiss-Chambers Case.* New York: Alfred A. Knopf, 1978. The author was the first to gain access to the voluminous FBI files on this famous case. He concluded that the new evidence proved that Alger Hiss was indeed guilty as charged. Some commentators have argued that this book finally closed HUAC's biggest case. Others have argued that the author of *Perjury* ig-nored the new evidence from government files and instead relied almost exclu-sively on Whittaker Chambers' memoir, *Witness* (1952).

*Kenneth O'Reilly*

## Cross-References

"Palmer Raids" Lead to Arrests and Deportations of Immigrants (1919), p. 258; Mussolini Seizes Dictatorial Powers in Italy (1925), p. 395; Corporatism Comes to Paraguay and the Americas (1936), p. 533; The Congress of Industrial Organizations Is Formed (1938), p. 545; Roosevelt Approves Internment of Japanese Americans (1942), p. 595; The House Committee on Un-American Activities Investigates Holly-wood (1947), p. 701.

# THE FIRST FOOD STAMP PROGRAM BEGINS IN ROCHESTER, NEW YORK

*Categories of event:* Humanitarian relief and nutrition
*Time:* 1939
*Locale:* Rochester, New York

*The first food stamp plan established by the United States Department of Agriculture began as an experiment on May 16, 1939, in Rochester, New York*

*Principal personages:*

GEORGE D. AIKEN (1892-1984), a Republican senator from Vermont who tried legislatively to establish a food stamp program after administrative termination in 1943

CHRISTIAN ARCHIBALD HERTER (1895-1966), a Republican member of the House of Representatives from Massachusetts who tried legislatively to establish a food stamp program after administrative termination in 1943

ROBERT M. LA FOLLETTE, JR. (1895-1953), a Progressive senator from Wisconsin involved in the unsuccessful attempt to establish a food stamp program after administrative termination

HENRY A. WALLACE (1888-1965), the United States secretary of agriculture at the time of the creation of the first food stamp program

## Summary of Event

In May, 1939, eleven million people in the United States were receiving federal food assistance through direct commodity donations. At that time, various groups were searching for methods of increasing consumption of grapefruit and other surplus foods. In January, 1939, at a meeting in Chicago of the National-American Wholesale Grocers Convention, a plan developed by the grocers had been presented that proposed the issuance of "scrip" vouchers to unemployed people and those with low incomes. The vouchers would permit recipients to purchase designated foods and foodstuffs at retail grocery stores at prices 50 percent below normal. The federal government would make up to grocers the difference between the amount actually charged and the normal price. The cost to the government was estimated at $1.4 billion. In addition to providing reduced-price food to the needy, the plan was proposed to help wipe out agricultural surpluses.

The plan was submitted to the National Food and Grocery Conference Committee, composed of representatives from all areas of the food industry, from manufacturers to retailers. The United States Department of Agriculture explored this proposal, and at a meeting of the committee on March 13, 1939, department representatives announced an experimental food stamp plan. This plan would distribute certain surplus food items through regular channels of trade. The plan was to be tried in six cities with populations of more than fifty thousand. This was a cautious approach to the paradoxical dual problems of hunger and food surpluses. Earlier in the New Deal and the Depression, such a program might have been rushed into on a nationwide scale.

The impetus to try a food stamp or coupon approach in lieu of direct commodity distribution was based on the following assumptions. First, it reflected a desire to match more closely the kinds, varieties, and amounts of foods being made available to low-income families to the actual needs of such families. Second, the food stamp approach was thought to provide more assurance that federal subsidies actually increased food consumption rather than partially replacing previous food expenditures. Third, planners believed that there were inherent advantages in utilizing regular commercial food distribution channels rather than food banks or charities.

The plan called for the issuance of food stamps to needy persons receiving, or certified for, public aid. Each such client would be permitted to purchase a minimum value (varying according to size of family) of one type of stamp that could be used to purchase any food product. In addition, clients would receive, free of charge, another type of stamp in an amount equal to 50 percent of the value of those purchased. These supplemental stamps would be redeemable only for certain food commodities. This feature of the plan sought to guarantee that the free stamps would increase consumption, especially of surplus commodities. According to United States Department of Agriculture Secretary Henry A. Wallace, who addressed a meeting of the National Food and Grocery Conference Committee in Washington, D.C., on March 13, 1939, the plan aimed at increasing the domestic consumption of surplus food commodities. Issuance of the stamps would create demand for commodities which were surplus not because the need for them did not exist but because the persons who needed them most could not afford them. Records of various public health services and studies by the Bureau of Home Economics indicated widespread malnutrition and undernourishment, particularly of children, in every state. These same studies estimated that millions of people in the United States spent an average of $1.00 or less a week for food. Such low expenditures translated into low prices and surpluses for farmers and into diets for low-income families that were less than the minimum necessary to maintain adequate standards of health. The proposed plan was designed to raise average spending on food to $1.50 a week per person for those eligible to participate in the program. The plan was heartily endorsed by the National Food and Grocery Conference Committee.

The first food stamp plan established by the United States Department of Agriculture began as an experiment on May 16, 1939, in Rochester, New York. It subsequently was extended to five additional experimental areas: Montgomery County, Ohio; King County, Washington; Jefferson County, Alabama; Pottawatomie County, Oklahoma; and Des Moines, Iowa. Secretary of Agriculture Wallace stated that the stamp plan would apply at first only to food but that it might be extended to other goods, cotton products in particular, if it proved to be successful and if satisfactory arrangements could be made with retailers. Wallace also stated that measures such as the stamp plan, with the government subsidizing expanded consumption, were not the most desirable solution to the problem of making abundance work for the American people. He hoped that other solutions ultimately would be found.

The first food stamp program was established through the broad authority contained in Section 32 of Public Law 74-320, passed in 1935. Section 32 permanently appropriated an amount equal to 30 percent of United States Customs receipts from all sources each year for the secretary of agriculture, to be spent on three purposes: encouragement of agricultural exports, encouragement of domestic consumption of agricultural commodities, and reestablishment of farmers' purchasing power. Specifically, Section 32 provided that the funds were to be used "to encourage the domestic consumption" of agricultural commodities or products. The secretary of agriculture was given authority to pay benefits to low-income people to further the three stated purposes.

The food stamp plan was first administered by the Federal Surplus Commodities Corporation and later by the Surplus Marketing Administration and its successor organizations, the Agricultural Marketing Administration and the Food Distribution Administration of the United States Department of Agriculture. The United States was divided into four regions, each with a regional director who was given considerable discretionary powers to carry out program policy and procedures.

## Impact of Event

As measured by the number of participants, the food stamp plan reached its peak in May, 1941, when approximately four million people participated. New geographic areas were brought into the plan after 1941, but it never operated on a nation-wide basis. As measured by the number of geographical areas served by the plan, the peak was reached in August, 1942, when 1,741 counties—about half of the counties in the country—and eighty-eight cities were included. These areas contained almost two-thirds of the population of the United States, according to the 1940 census. During the forty-six months that the plan was in operation, the additional food purchasing power provided to participants by the federal government was $260 million.

Surveys and studies indicated that the plan did increase food consumption levels among participating groups. The early plan, however, was believed to have been greatly abused. The Department of Agriculture estimated that 25 percent of all benefits were misused. Some of the same types of abuse were repeated in later food stamp programs. For instance, some blue stamps reportedly were traded for liquor and tobacco and some grocers would buy them for cash at a discount, an activity now known as trafficking.

The plan was discontinued in early 1943, when World War II wartime conditions had greatly reduced unemployment and greatly increased demands upon United States food supplies, thereby removing part of the rationale for the program. Inasmuch as the program was predicated on the existence of surplus foods, the program was terminated as such surpluses turned to scarcity during the early years of United States involvement in World War II. The program had been established administratively and never had been explicitly authorized by Congress.

Immediately following termination, two bills were introduced to establish a food stamp, or food allotment, program legislatively: House Resolution 2997, by Representative Christian Archibald Herter (R-Mass.), on June 18, 1943, and Senate Bill 1331, by Senators George D. Aiken (R-Vt.) and Robert M. La Follette (Progressive-Wisc.), on July 8, 1943.

An amendment to establish a food stamp program, incorporating the thrust of S. 1331, was proposed in the Senate on February 10 and 11, 1944, by Senators Aiken and La Follette. The amendment was defeated by a vote of twenty-nine to forty-six. Hearings on the bill itself had been concluded on January 26, 1944, by a subcommittee of the Senate Committee on Agriculture and Forestry.

A two-color-stamp plan was formulated in an attempt to ensure that the federal subsidy actually was used for additional food purchases and to control the kinds of food participants could purchase with the free additional coupons. Participating families were required to exchange an amount of money representing estimated normal food expenditures for orange stamps of the same monetary value. Along with these orange stamps, participants were provided, without cost, with additional blue stamps, which could be used to buy designated surplus foods. In this manner, the plan attempted to concentrate the additional purchasing power on surplus foods, that is, foods for which there were marketing difficulties. In 1939, a significant portion of the nation's food supply could be classified in the surplus category. When the program was first begun, the surplus commodities on the blue stamp list were butter, eggs, white and grain flour, cornmeal, oranges, grapefruit, dried prunes, and dried beans. At one time or another, the list also included rice, hominy grits, peaches, pears, apples, raisins, peas, tomatoes, snap beans, cabbage, onions, pork, and lard.

Foods were designated as blue-stamp (surplus) food each month by the secretary of agriculture, and a list of those designated foods was sent to participating retail merchants. Participating retailers were required to post a notice of these monthly designations in their stores as a means of informing participants of the foods that could be purchased with the blue stamps. It was intended that this posting also would bring these foods to the attention of other customers and thereby encourage increased purchases of the surplus foods among higher-income families not participating in the plan.

Both the orange and the blue stamps were printed in two denominations—twenty-five cents and one dollar—and were like postage stamps in design. In fact, an engraver's plate for an old postage stamp was designed and used for food stamp purposes. The stamps were issued in books, and the design of the books was that of regular postage stamp books.

Participating areas were required to use public funds to establish a revolving fund to purchase the orange stamps from the department of agriculture. The revolving fund subsequently was replenished from the proceeds received from the sale of these orange stamps to participants.

## Bibliography

Batchelder, Alan B. *The Economics of Poverty*. New York: John Wiley & Sons, 1971. In Chapter 7, entitled "Transfer Programs Now Operating," there is a short discussion of the food stamp program reactivated in the early 1960's. This book notes that when the food stamp program was reactivated and counties first shifted from the surplus commodity to the food stamp program (a county could not participate in both), the number of participants dropped sharply even though food stamps appeared more attractive, in that they gave their recipients a range of choice that was denied to surplus commodity recipients. The answer to this anomaly was that there were many families with incomes insufficient to purchase food stamps.

Gaus, John M., and Leon O. Wolcott (with a chapter by Verne B. Lewis). *Public Administration and the United States Department of Agriculture*. Chicago: Public Administration Service for the Committee on Public Administration of the Social Science Research Council, 1940. This book includes an excellent three-page description of the food stamp plan and how the plan evolved out of a proposal developed by the National-American Wholesale Grocers.

Harrington, Michael. *The New American Poverty*. New York: Holt, Rinehart and Winston, 1984. This book contains several references to the food stamp program, noting, in Harrington's words, that "Food stamps have been a triumph." Harrington praises the food stamp program for establishing uniform national levels of nutritional assistance.

Haveman, Robert. *Starting Even: An Equal Opportunity Program to Combat the Nation's New Poverty*. New York: Simon & Schuster, 1988. This book contains numerous, fairly up-to-date references (including statistics presented in table form) to food stamps. The focus of government aid has shifted to Aid to Families with Dependent Children (AFDC) and food stamps plus Medicaid. The book includes discussion of proposed reforms for the food stamp program.

U.S. Congress. Senate. Committee on Agriculture, Nutrition, and Forestry. *The Food Stamp Program: History, Description, Issues, and Options*. Washington, D.C.: Government Printing Office, 1985. This report includes an excellent five-page description, "The Food Stamp Plan—The Earlier Program: 1939-43," which includes a detailed discussion of how the program was administered, the problems it encountered, and evaluations of its successes and failures.

*Gregory P. Rabb*

## Cross-References

Nevada and Montana Introduce the Old-Age Pension (1923), p. 373; Social Security Act Establishes Benefits for Nonworking People (1935), p. 514; Social Security

Act Provides Grants for Dependent Children (1935), p. 520; The Marshall Plan Provides Aid to Europe (1947), p. 706; Borlaug Receives the Nobel Prize for Work on World Hunger (1970), p. 1515; A U.N. Declaration on Hunger and Malnutrition Is Adopted (1974), p. 1775; Soviet Farmers Are Given Control of Land and Selection of Crops (1989), p. 2471.

# STALIN REDUCES THE RUSSIAN ORTHODOX CHURCH TO VIRTUAL EXTINCTION

*Category of event:* Religious freedom
*Time:* Summer of 1939
*Locale:* Union of Soviet Socialist Republics

*The long Bolshevik campaign against religious practice and belief in the Soviet Union reduced the Russian Orthodox Church to institutional near-extinction by the late summer of 1939*

Principal personages:

JOSEPH STALIN (1879-1953), the general secretary of the Communist Party of the Soviet Union

ADOLF HITLER (1889-1945), the dictator of Germany who made the Soviet-German pact of August 23, 1939

SERGIUS (1867-1944), the senior prelate of the Russian Orthodox church between 1927 and 1944

ALEKSI (1877-1970), the metropolitan of Leningrad from 1933 through the siege of Leningrad in World War II, head of the Russian Orthodox church from 1945 to 1970

## Summary of Event

When the Bolsheviks came to power in Russia in 1917, they began to act on their atheist convictions, which held that all religion was opium, a spiritual gin which capitalist exploiters used to drug the workers into submission. They decreed the separation of church and state, nationalized church lands and assets, cancelled the status of the Russian Orthodox church as a legal entity, discontinued state subsidies to religious bodies, deprived church marriages and baptisms of official standing, and banned organized religious education of the young. In 1922, in the midst of famine, the Bolshevik regime ordered the church treasures confiscated, ostensibly to finance relief for the starving. Believers and international religious bodies, among them the Holy See, offered to ransom the Russian Orthodox church's sacramental objects, but the Bolshevik regime pressed ahead. Soviet press accounts reported some fourteen thousand bloody fights as priests and parishioners tried to guard their churches. Many churches were closed and priests and hierarchs arrested. Tikhon, the patriarch (religious leader) of Moscow, was placed under house arrest. With government support, a Renovationist, or Living Church, movement was organized and split the church for a time.

On April 7, 1925, Patriarch Tikhon died. His death plunged the Russian Orthodox church into a rolling crisis of leadership. By 1927, ten out of eleven prelates successively named to act as head of the church were in prison or in exile, and most of the bishops were in similar straits.

The man who emerged as acting head of the church was Metropolitan Sergius. Arrested more than once, Sergius was released from prison in March of 1927 and issued a declaration of loyalty to the Soviet Union on July 24 of that year. Sergius' action in support of a godless and hostile state outraged many believing Orthodox people in the Soviet Union as well as many Soviet exiles abroad. Sergius justified his declaration as necessary to preserve the church.

The forced industrialization and collectivization drives that were launched in 1928 led to another crisis for the church. Troops and Communist Party workers fanned out into the countryside. Peasant resistance to them produced violence, the slaughtering of livestock, and the destruction of food stores. More than five million people were said to have died in this man-made famine. Peasants defended their churches and priests with scythes and pitchforks against soldiers and Communist militants determined to deal harshly with the vestiges of Orthodox reaction. The campaign changed the face of the Russian countryside, which has been dotted ever since with the shells of churches serving as granaries, overcrowded dwellings, storehouses, and workshops, with their rusting and disintegrating cupolas standing hollow against the sky.

A third great wave of church closings began in 1936 and gathered momentum over the next three years. This was the period of the great purges. The terror of the prison camp complex of the Gulag Archipelago in Siberia was felt in every corner of the land. An estimated nineteen million Soviet citizens died in the purges, and the police (NKVD) became the largest employer in the Soviet Union, responsible for one-sixth of all new construction. With restraint and normal living swept away, church closings on a large scale resumed, and the arrest of priests and the incarceration of bishops accelerated.

By mid-1939, Metropolitan Sergius lived in Moscow virtually alone, cut off from any regular contact with the churches still functioning in the country. There were only four active bishops in all of Russia. Metropolitan Aleksi of Leningrad was the second, Aleksi's suffragan, Nikolai of Peterhof was the third, and Metropolitan Sergi, who later defected to the Germans, was the fourth. All four prelates lived from day to day in the expectation of arrest.

The numbers of open churches and functioning priests were very small. Soviet official sources and foreign scholars confirm that there were no open churches at all in more than one-third of the provinces of the Russian federated republic. One-third of the provinces of the Ukraine had no functioning churches, and an additional three Ukrainian provinces had only one open church each. According to Friedrich Heyer, the German troops that occupied Kiev in 1941 found only two churches in that diocese; sixteen hundred churches had been functioning before the 1917 Revolution. Three priests were serving in those two churches, one at the edge of the city of Kiev and one in the countryside. In the Ukrainian province of Kamenets-Podolski, the Germans found one aged priest holding services. A mission team which followed German troops into the area south of Leningrad found two priests reduced to complete impoverishment. It is probably a fair estimate that in 1939 two hundred to three hundred churches were functioning in the Soviet Union, and no more than three hundred to four hundred priests were conducting services.

Describing the situation through the 1930's in the diocese of Rostov-on-Don, Nikita Struve observed that the archbishop, Serafin, was exiled to the far north, where he soon died. His vicar, Nicholas Ammasisky, was sent to the steppes to graze a flock of sheep. He was arrested a second time and shot, but miraculously recovered from his wounds. The former cathedral was transformed into a zoo.

In Odessa, according to Dimitry Pospielovsky, where there had once been forty-eight churches, Stalin allowed one to remain open. Apparently the great eye doctor, Academician Filatov, had treated Stalin and asked, as a return favor, that one church be allowed in the city. Stalin, however, made no promise to spare the priests. Each Sunday, and later just at Easter, a priest would appear from the congregation and celebrate the liturgy, only to disappear into the NKVD dungeons the following day. After all the priests who dared martyrdom had disappeared, there remained a few deacons who could perform the entire rite except for the eucharist. They likewise disappeared and were replaced by psalmists, who in turn were liquidated. There remained only laypeople, who prayed as best they could in the church.

In the summer of 1939, then, the Russian Orthodox Church teetered on the edge of institutional destruction.

## Impact of Event

In the late summer of 1939, an event occurred that was unrelated to Stalin's repression of the Russian Orthodox church but which profoundly affected its situation. Signed on August 23, 1939, the Molotov-Ribbentrop Pact opened the door to Soviet annexation of Eastern Poland in September of 1939 and of the Baltic states and Romanian Bessarabia and Northern Bubovina in 1940. The annexations brought the Russian Orthodox church millions of faithful parishioners and thousands of active parishes, functioning churches, and priests. The church also acquired monasteries, nunneries, seminaries, and other resources.

On June 22, 1941, Hitler's armies attacked the Soviet Union and swept forward on a thousand-mile front stretching from the Baltic Sea to the Black Sea. Behind German lines, thousands more Orthodox churches were able to open their doors and start serving believers living in pre-1939 Soviet territories, most of whom had long been denied the opportunity to worship in a functioning church.

As soon as Hitler attacked, Metropolitan Sergius publicly rallied believers to the defense of the Motherland. When German forces were advancing on Moscow, however, Stalin ordered Sergius evacuated, and the head of the Russian church was sent by train to Ulyanovsk, a small provincial city seven hundred kilometers east of the capital. Sergius was able to open some churches in that region and consecrated a few bishops, thereby reconstituting diocesan life along the Volga. By the spring of 1942, there were about a dozen Orthodox prelates of episcopal rank.

On September 4, 1943, Stalin received Sergius and two other metropolitans in the

Kremlin. Stalin authorized the opening of more churches, convents, seminaries, and theological academies, as well as allowing more bishops and the elevation of a new patriarch. Four days later, nineteen bishops assembled and elected Sergius as patriarch. By this time, Red Army forces were pushing the Germans back, and Stalin's motives in his more supportive religious policy probably revolved around the need for reliable leadership over the thousands of Orthodox parishes which had been established under the German occupation. Stalin probably also perceived an advantage in tapping Russian pride and religious patriotism as Soviet rule was being reestablished in the lands overrun by Hitler. The Russian Orthodox church emerged from the war with about fourteen thousand churches.

The travails of Orthodox believers in the Soviet Union did not end with the country's victory in World War II. Nikita Khrushchev launched another antireligious assault in the 1959-1964 period, but even Khrushchev's onslaught did not reduce the Russian Orthodox church to the desperate straits of 1939. Under Mikhail Gorbachev, the church was permitted to reopen thousands of parishes, scores of monasteries and nunneries, and a substantial number of seminaries and theological training schools. A new law of freedom of conscience was promulgated. While religious believers continued to encounter problems and difficulties of various kinds, Soviet people found the opportunity to worship, teach children religion, engage in charitable work, and perform other religious functions and duties to an extent not witnessed since the Bolshevik Revolution of 1917.

## Bibliography

Alekseev, Wasilli, and Theofanis G. Stavrou. *The Great Revival: The Russian Church Under German Occupation.* Minneapolis, Minn.: Burgess, 1976. In specialized publications written in Russian and French, Alekseev presented firsthand and eyewitness accounts of the desperate straits through which the Russian Orthodox church was passing in 1939 and the church revival experienced in German-occupied territories during World War II. Alekseev and Stavrou present these and other valuable materials to English-speaking readers here.

Anderson, Paul B. *People, Church, and State in Modern Russia.* New York: Macmillan, 1944. This classic and insightful work was written by the dean of American scholars on religion in the Soviet Union. Anderson played a central role in drawing the Russian Orthodox church into ecumenical cooperation after World War II. Index.

Bourdeaux, Michael. *Patriarch and Prophets: Persecution of the Russian Orthodox Church Today.* London: Macmillan, 1969. This is essentially a collection of vividly written documents on the life of the Russian Orthodox church. It has interesting materials on the situation of the church in 1939, including an understanding description of Metropolitan Aleksi's predicament in Leningrad at that time. Bourdeaux is the founder and head of Keston College in Kent, England, the pioneering center for the study of religion in communist lands. Index.

Ellis, Jane. *The Russian Orthodox Church: A Contemporary History.* London: Croom

Helm, 1986. This work focuses on the then-present situation of the Russian Orthodox church and the rise and repression of Orthodox dissent. It is therefore not a good source book for the agony and recovery of the church before and during World War II. It is, however, the most recent comprehensive description of churches, clergy, convents, theological education, and other aspects of Orthodox church life. Bibliography and index.

Fletcher, William C. *A Study in Survival: The Church in Russia, 1927-1943.* New York: Macmillan, 1965. Written by one of the most prolific and highly respected American scholars on religion in the Soviet Union, this little book carries the story of the Russian Orthodox church's travails through the turnaround which followed Stalin's reception of Metropolitan Sergius in 1943. Bibliography and index.

House, Francis. *The Russian Phoenix: The Story of Russian Christians,* A.D. *988-1988.* London: SPCK, 1988. This thin volume was written by an Anglican cleric who has followed Russian church affairs for more than half a century. House worked in the General Secretariat of the World Council of Churches and participated in the negotiations which brought the Russian Orthodox church into the council. House is urbane, empathetic, well informed, accessible, and quick to read. Appendix and index.

Pospielovsky, Dimitry. *The Russian Church Under the Soviet Regime, 1917-1982.* 2 vols. Crestwood, N.Y.: St. Vladimir's Seminary, 1984. Called by some reviewers the best history of Russian Orthodoxy in the Soviet period, this readable work describes with understanding and authority the repression of the late 1930's and the turnaround during World War II. Documentary appendices and index.

Struve, Nikita. *Christians in Contemporary Russia.* Translated by Lancelot Sheppard and A. Manson. New York: Charles Scribner's Sons, 1967. A highly sensitive and deeply informed account, Struve's book gives poignant and illuminating vignettes of religious life in the Soviet Union in 1939. It also covers later periods very well. Index.

Timasheff, Nicholas S. *Religion in Soviet Russia, 1917-1942.* New York: Sheed and Ward, 1942. This work conveys Timasheff's tough-minded and sharply informed understanding of the realities of the situation of the Russian Orthodox church before and during World War II. This is considered to be a classic work.

*Nathaniel Davis*

## Cross-References

Armenians Suffer Genocide During World War I (1915), p. 150; Bolsheviks Deny All Rights to the Russian Orthodox Church (1917), p. 202; Lenin and the Communists Impose the "Red Terror" (1917), p. 218; Lenin Leads the Russian Revolution (1917), p. 225; Stalin Begins Purging Political Opponents (1934), p. 503; Khrushchev Implies That Stalinist Excesses Will Cease (1956), p. 952; The Moscow Human Rights Committee Is Founded (1970), p. 1549; Soviets Crack Down on Moscow's Helsinki Watch Group (1977), p. 1915; The United Nations Votes to Protect Freedoms of Religion and Belief (1981), p. 2146; Gorbachev Initiates a Policy of *Glasnost* (1985), p. 2249; Muslims Riot Against Russians in Kazakhstan (1986), p. 2298.

# SOVIETS MASSACRE POLISH PRISONERS OF WAR IN THE KATYN FOREST

*Category of event:* Atrocities and war crimes
*Time:* 1940-1943
*Locale:* The Katyn Forest, near Smolensk, Union of Soviet Socialist Republics

*In the early spring of 1940, the Soviets executed more than four thousand Polish prisoners of war in the Katyn Forest*

*Principal personages:*

WINSTON CHURCHILL (1874-1965), the prime minister of Great Britain (1940-1945 and 1951-1955)

JOSEPH GOEBBELS (1897-1945), the Nazi minister of propaganda

FRANKLIN D. ROOSEVELT (1882-1945), the thirty-second president of the United States (1933-1945)

JOSEPH STALIN (1879-1953), the first secretary of the Communist Party of the Soviet Union (1922-1953)

## Summary of Event

On August 23, 1939, the Soviet Union and Nazi Germany signed an agreement that set the stage for the outbreak of World War II in Europe. The agreement, in part, provided the basis for the dismemberment of Poland. Shortly thereafter, on September 1, 1939, German armed forces attacked Poland, and on September 17, the Soviet army moved into eastern Poland and occupied its assigned portion of Polish territory. Under the weight of the German onslaught and the Soviet invasion, Polish resistance collapsed, and the remnants of Poland's government fled the country.

Immediately after the termination of hostilities in Soviet-occupied Poland, Soviet authorities began the forced deportation of approximately 1.2 million Poles to areas within the Soviet Union. In addition, the Soviets captured more than two hundred thousand members of the Polish armed forces. These prisoners were joined by thousands of Polish reservists arrested at home as well as by soldiers who had initially escaped to Lithuania and Estonia only to be taken by the Soviets after the Baltic states fell under Soviet control. In the final count, approximately 250,000 members of the Polish armed forces, including about ten thousand officers, were placed in more than one hundred major Soviet prison and labor camps.

The international situation changed dramatically on June 22, 1941, when Germany launched a surprise attack on the Soviet Union. Soon thereafter, the Soviets and the Polish government-in-exile, located in London, reestablished diplomatic relations and agreed that the Soviets would grant amnesty to those Poles being held in the Soviet Union. Simultaneously, the new Polish embassy in the Soviet Union took steps to organize a Polish army on Soviet soil composed of those members of the Polish armed forces who were being held as prisoners of war by the Soviets. Eventually, after these former prisoners had been assembled by the new Polish military command in the Soviet Union, it became clear that approximately fifteen thousand soldiers remained missing, including some eight thousand officers. Indeed, only two of the fourteen general officers and six of the three hundred high-ranking Polish staff officers captured by the Soviet Army reported. Moreover, it was not just professional officers who were missing: Hundreds of reservists, including doctors, lawyers, educators, and journalists, were also missing. Investigations by Polish authorities revealed that the missing individuals had been held at three camps: approximately sixty-five hundred men at Ostashkov, four thousand at Starobelsk, and five thousand at Kozelsk. In late April and early May, 1940, troops from the Soviet Union's People's Commissariat of Internal Affairs (the NKVD) had removed in small groups all but 448 of the prisoners from the three camps. Investigations revealed that the men from Kozelsk had been taken by rail to a point immediately west of Smolensk, but there they had disappeared. Indeed, of the approximately fifteen thousand men originally held in these three camps, only the 448 survived. Polish requests for information concerning the missing soldiers were addressed to Soviet officials but were met with evasive and contradictory responses. Nevertheless, between the summer of 1941 and the spring of 1943, the Poles continued to attempt to ascertain the fate of the missing soldiers.

Meanwhile, in late February, 1943, German field police discovered the mass graves of several thousand individuals, apparently Polish officers, in the Katyn Forest about ten miles west of Smolensk. Prior to the German capture of the area in 1941, the Katyn Forest had been controlled by the NKVD. This information was transmitted to Berlin, where Nazi officials recognized the propaganda value of this discovery and moved to capitalize upon the opportunity. Consequently, on April 13, 1943, German radio announced that Soviet authorities had executed thousands of Polish prisoners of war. The Germans quickly followed this announcement by inviting a series of specially chartered international groups to examine the site and report their conclusions. Three investigatory commissions were formed under German sponsorship. First, an international commission was formed, drawing distinguished specialists in the field of forensic medicine from twelve European countries other than Nazi Germany. On April 28, 1943, the members of this commission began their three-day investigation of the grave sites in the Katyn Forest. While there, they examined 982 corpses already exhumed by German authorities and 9 that had been hitherto untouched and were randomly selected by the commission. During their investigation, the members of the group had complete freedom to move throughout the area and enjoyed the full cooperation of the Germans at the site. Simultaneously, the Germans invited a medical delegation from the Polish Red Cross in German-occupied Poland to conduct a second investigation in the Katyn Forest. Without the knowledge of the German authorities, the Polish underground infiltrated the Polish Red Cross group. The Polish team remained at the site for five weeks, during which it, like the international commission, was given full German support as well as freedom of movement around the site, including authority to photograph whatever it wished. Finally, a specially formed German medical team was sent to Katyn. In addition to these three teams, journalists from Germany, German-occupied Europe, and neutral European states visited the Katyn Forest, as did German-sponsored Polish and Allied prisoner-of-war delegations.

The German authorities, the various medical commissions, and the other visitors to the area found more than four thousand corpses buried in eight six-to-eleven-foot-deep mass graves. In addition to the bodies actually found, some analysts have speculated that there may be more than three hundred more undiscovered Polish corpses in the forest. In any case, all but twenty-two of the bodies were clad in Polish uniforms and were piled face down in layers. Many, especially the younger men, had had their greatcoats tied over their heads with ropes connected tightly to their hands, which were tightly bound behind their backs. As a result, any movement of the hands would serve to tighten the ropes that secured the greatcoats at the neck. In addition, many bore bayonet wounds. All, however, had been shot through the head in a similar manner. Finally, the individual graves of two Polish general officers, in uniform, were also located in the forest.

Based upon a variety of evidence collected at the site, the three German-sponsored commissions independently reached similar conclusions. They agreed that the Polish prisoners had been executed and buried about three years prior to their exhumation. In other words, they had been murdered in the spring of 1940. Since this was more than a year prior to the German invasion of the Soviet Union in June, 1941, and since the Katyn Forest was under the control of the NKVD at the time of the killings, the conclusion of the commissions was that Soviet authorities had killed the Polish prisoners. The conclusions of the three German-sponsored commissions were confirmed and further supplemented by additional evidence supplied by the families of the dead soldiers and by the survivors of Camp Kozelsk. This additional material clearly established that the Polish soldiers found in the forest were the missing prisoners from Camp Kozelsk. Finally, the fact that the Germans fully cooperated with the investigators at the Katyn Forest site and subsequently attempted to preserve the evidence of the atrocity suggested that the Nazis were not the murderers.

Meanwhile, the Soviet Union denied the German accusations and charged that the Nazis had themselves committed the crime. On April 15, 1943, two days after the initial German radio broadcast announcing the discovery of the mass graves, the Soviets stated that the Polish prisoners had been seized by invading Nazis during the summer of 1941 and, subsequently, the Nazis had executed them. After the capture of the Smolensk region, the Soviet authorities organized a special Soviet commission to investigate the Katyn Forest murders. The Soviet team was composed exclusively of Soviet medical experts; no international medical experts were asked to participate. Predictably, given the official title of the Soviet investigatory team, "The Special Commission for Ascertaining and Investigating the Circumstances of the Shooting of Polish Officer Prisoners by the German-Fascist Invaders in the Katyn Forest," the Soviet team concluded that the Germans had murdered the Poles between September and December of 1941. The Soviets claimed to have found nine documents on the bodies bearing dates after May, 1940. In view of the fact that most of the bodies had been previously and extremely carefully searched by the German-sponsored commissions, most observers discounted these so-called finds as fabrications.

Following World War II, the Katyn Forest atrocity was inconclusively examined at the Nuremberg Trials, and later, in considerable detail, from 1951 to 1952 by a committee of the U.S. House of Representatives. Notwithstanding continued Soviet denials of guilt and assertions that the Germans were responsible, virtually all analysts outside the Communist countries concluded that the Soviets had killed the Polish prisoners found in the Katyn Forest. Finally, in 1990, fifty years after committing the atrocity, the Soviets acknowledged that the NKVD had murdered the men.

Two questions remained, however, even after the establishment of Soviet guilt for the Katyn atrocity. First, what happened to the more than ten thousand Poles held at Camps Starobelsk and Ostashkov? Apparently these men were also killed by the NKVD, although their exact fate remained unclear. Second, why were 448 men from Kozelsk, Ostashkov, and Starobelsk allowed to live? It would seem that the NKVD selected those individuals who appeared to be pro-Communist, were susceptible to Soviet propaganda, or who, by virtue of their background, were deemed worthy of selection for survival.

## Impact of Event

Nazi Propaganda Minister Joseph Goebbels immediately recognized the significance of the Katyn Forest discovery and took special efforts to make certain that Germany derived the fullest propaganda dividends from the Soviet atrocity. For example, the German-controlled media in Poland provided extensive coverage of the Katyn Forest investigations. The Nazi media argued that Jewish Bolshevism was responsible for the atrocity. Hence, the Poles were told that they must look to the Germans for protection against the ruthless Soviets. Moreover, the extensive daily coverage, extending from April 14 to August 4, 1943, coincided with the Nazi massacre of the Warsaw ghetto, the latter extending from mid-April to mid-May, 1943.

In addition to attempting to influence Polish public opinion, the Germans intended to use the atrocity to split the Allied cause. There, however, the Germans unwittingly assisted Moscow in the latter's policy objectives. Immediately following the German announcement of the discovery of the mass graves in the Katyn Forest, on April 15, 1943, the Polish government-in-exile in London decided to call upon the International Red Cross to conduct a full investigation. The following day, the British press reported this decision. On April 17, a spokesperson for the Polish government-in-exile confirmed the decision and, that same day, the Poles formally made their request to officials of the International Red Cross in Geneva, Switzerland. Meanwhile, in Berlin, acting upon a British press story predicting the Polish request to the Red Cross, but prior to the formal request itself, Goebbels decided to embarrass the Poles by issuing a second German request to the International Red Cross to investigate the atrocity. The timing of the German request was designed to coincide with the Polish request, thereby making it appear that the London Poles and Berlin were acting in concert. Thus, the German request was handed to the representatives of the International Red Cross in Geneva less than one hour prior to the Polish appeal. For its part, the International Red Cross responded that it would conduct an investigation provided that the Soviet Union joined with the Poles and Germany in requesting such an investigation. The Soviet Union, of course, did not agree to join in the request.

The appearance of Polish-German cooperation in requesting the investigation provided Soviet leader Joseph Stalin with an opportunity to cut his ties with the London Poles in favor of his own Moscow-sponsored Union of Polish Patriots, which had been formed a few weeks earlier. Thus, not only did the Soviets fail to request an investigation by the International Red Cross, but on April 19, 1943, the Soviet media also denounced members of the Polish government-in-exile for collusion with the Nazis in perpetuating the so-called Nazi-fabricated allegations that the Soviet Union was responsible for the Katyn atrocity. This theme was in turn repeated by the pro-Soviet media outside the Soviet Union. The free Polish media responded that the Polish government-in-exile was merely seeking answers to questions as to what had happened in Katyn Forest.

Nevertheless, on April 21, 1943, Stalin informed British prime minister Winston Churchill and U.S. president Franklin Roosevelt that the Soviets had decided to sever relations with the Polish government-in-exile in London. Churchill and Roosevelt responded by appealing to Stalin not to risk the unity of the Allied cause by breaking relations with the London Poles, while Churchill appealed to the Polish leaders in London to drop the entire matter. Notwithstanding British and American appeals, however, on April 26, 1943, the Soviets notified the Polish ambassador in Moscow of the Soviet government's decision to break relations with the Polish government-in-exile in London. Subsequently, despite the fact that the London Poles, under pressure from the British, withdrew their request to the International Red Cross for a neutral investigation the day after the severance of Soviet-Polish relations, the Soviet Union remained firm in its decision to break relations.

Clearly, Stalin had decided to use the Polish government-in-exile's response to the German announcement of the Katyn discovery as his excuse to dispose of the independent Polish authorities in London in favor of the Soviet-backed Poles. Indeed, the latter would ultimately serve as a central component in the satellite regime erected by the Soviet Union in postwar Poland. Thus, the massacre of more than four thousand Polish prisoners of war by the Soviet NKVD in the Katyn Forest and the disappearance and presumed execution of another ten thousand Polish prisoners not only deprived Poland of a significant element of the prewar Polish elite but also was ultimately used to advance successfully Soviet objectives in postwar Eastern Europe.

## Bibliography

Lauck, John H. *Katyn Killings: In the Record.* Clifton, N.J.: Kingston Press, 1988. A comprehensive overview of the events leading up to the massacre and the various investigations that followed, especially the hearings of the select committee of the

U.S. House of Representatives.

Lotarski, Susanne S. "The Communist Takeover in Poland." In *The Anatomy of Communist Takeovers*, edited by Thomas Hammond. New Haven, Conn.: Yale University Press, 1975. An article examining the establishment of the post-World War II Soviet satellite regime in Poland.

Mackiewicz, Jozef. *The Katyn Wood Murders*. London: World Affairs Book Club, 1951. An often personalized early examination of the atrocity.

Stahl, Zdzislaw, ed. *The Crime of Katyn: Facts and Documents*. London: Polish Cultural Foundation, 1965. A documentary source containing a wide range of material concerning the massacre, with a foreword by the former commander in chief of the Polish forces in the Soviet Union.

Tucker, Robert C. *Stalin in Power*. New York: W. W. Norton, 1990. An informative insight into Joseph Stalin and his regime from 1928 to 1941, including a brief but significant discussion of the Katyn Forest massacre.

U.S. Congress. House of Representatives. Select Committee on the Katyn Forest Massacre. *The Katyn Forest Massacre*. 7 parts. 82d Congress, 1st and 2d Sessions, 1951-1952. Washington, D.C.: Government Printing Office, 1952. An extensive record of the 1951-1952 hearings before the select committee of the U.S. House of Representatives investigating the Katyn Forest massacre.

Zawodny, J. K. *Death in the Forest*. South Bend, Ind.: University of Notre Dame Press, 1962. The most comprehensive, readable, balanced examination of the Katyn Forest massacre and its implications.

*Howard M. Hensel*

## Cross-References

Legal Norms of Behavior in Warfare Formulated by the Hague Conference (1907), p. 92; Lenin and the Communists Impose the "Red Terror" (1917), p. 218; Lenin Leads the Russian Revolution (1917), p. 225; Stalin Begins Purging Political Opponents (1934), p. 503; Roosevelt Approves Internment of Japanese Americans (1942), p. 595; Soviets Take Control of Eastern Europe (1943), p. 612; Nazi War Criminals Are Tried in Nuremberg (1945), p. 667; The United Nations Sets Rules for the Treatment of Prisoners (1955), p. 935; The Statute of Limitations Is Ruled Not Applicable to War Crimes (1968), p. 1457; Congress Formally Apologizes to Japanese Internees (1988), p. 2392.

# HO CHI MINH ORGANIZES THE VIET MINH

*Categories of event:* Political freedom and indigenous peoples' rights
*Time:* May, 1941
*Locale:* Northern Vietnam

*In May, 1941, Ho Chi Minh formed a broadly based nationalist organization known as the Viet Minh to mobilize the Vietnamese people to achieve national independence*

### Principal personages:
HO CHI MINH (1890-1969), a Soviet-trained Vietnamese Communist organizer with extensive contacts in Europe, China, and Southeast Asia

TRUONG CHINH (1907-1988), a pro-Chinese Vietnamese who became secretary-general of the Indochinese Communist Party in 1941

LE HONG PHONG (1902-1941?), a Soviet-trained Vietnamese agent of the Comintern whose arrest opened the way for Ho Chi Minh's emergence as the chief policymaker for the Indochinese Communist Party

VO NGUYEN GIAP (1912-    ), a history teacher who had special responsibility for Viet Minh military development and tactical policies

PHAM VAN DONG (1906-    ), a close associate of Ho Chi Minh who supported the decision to found the Viet Minh in 1941

## Summary of Event

At its plenary meeting in November, 1939, the Indochinese Communist Party (ICP) approved a new policy under which Japanese military expansionism and French colonial power in Indochina were identified as equally dangerous to the Vietnamese people. Both Japan and France thus became legitimate targets of Communist Party operations. To gain support for those operations, the ICP leadership approved in principle a policy which, instead of emphasizing divisions within Vietnamese society and seeking the support of disadvantaged and powerless people, emphasized the unity of all Vietnamese people, whatever their class status, in the face of the threat posed by external enemies—in this case, the French and Japanese. This approach, known as the "united front" strategy, had been endorsed by the Communists at various points earlier in the 1930's. In late 1939, however, adoption of this political strategy took on a new urgency: War had begun in Europe, and Japan's military expansion into Chinese territory continued apace. In the view of some ICP strategists, changing international circumstances presented an opportunity for the Communist Party to unify the Vietnamese people on the basis of shared nationalist conviction and thereby to assure the Communists of control over the process of obtaining Vietnam's political independence.

Many sections of the Vietnamese population were receptive to the Communists' criticism of foreign rule. Despite intermittent attempts by the colonial administration to regulate French industry in Indochina, harsh employment conditions persisted. Hundreds of thousands of Vietnamese peasants were dragooned into work on French rubber, coffee, and tea plantations in southern Vietnam. Brutalities at the hands of both French and Vietnamese overseers, poor food, and minimal medical care led to high death tolls and the need for continuous recruitment and relocation of workers from northern and central Vietnam. At the same time, northerners were pressed into employment in French-owned industrial enterprises. Men were drafted into work in coal and phosphate mines while women worked in spinning and textile factories. In both cases, pay was pitifully low, hours were long (often up to fifteen hours per day), and working conditions were dangerously unsafe, again resulting in high rates of work-related injuries and deaths. In addition, many former agricultural laborers employed in French businesses during the industrial expansion of the 1920's were left jobless as global markets contracted in the 1930's; thousands were left with neither jobs in industry nor lands to till. One of the Communists' objectives in forming the Viet Minh front in 1941 was to harness for the Communist-led independence movement the anti-French resentment engendered by such developments.

Among the Communist leaders who recognized the potential utility of this approach was Nguyen Ai Quoc, who later became known as Ho Chi Minh. Ho had participated in the founding of the French Communist Party and the Communist Parties of Thailand and Malaya, and he was involved in the reorganization of the ICP itself in 1930. After a period in political eclipse, Ho regained influence within the ICP between 1939 and 1941. His reemergence coincided with the failure of other Party leaders to orchestrate anti-French protests in September and October, 1939, and with the crushing of Communist-led insurrections in southern Vietnam in November and December, 1940. These failures resulted in waves of arrests of Communist activists and key leaders such as Le Hong Phong, the senior Comintern representative in Vietnam, and others who had directed the uprisings. More than two thousand Party members were arrested in late 1939, and French records show that in only four provinces in southern Vietnam more than fifty-six hundred arrests were made in late 1940. Many suspects were executed, while others were imprisoned. Some leaders were exiled to Poulo Condore island, southeast of Saigon in the South China Sea, where they are reported to have been treated inhumanely, as common for political prisoners at the time.

By the middle of 1940, the French colonial administration in Indochina had been placed under the authority of the pro-German French government at Vichy. The Indochina administration entered into a de facto cooperative relationship with the Japanese, who wanted access to Indochina's airfields and rice supplies. The Communists' assessment of the twin dangers presented by Japanese militarism and French colonialism thus appeared more valid in early 1941 than when it had first been stated in November, 1939. In these circumstances, Ho Chi Minh convened the ICP's Eighth Plenum in northern Vietnam in May, 1941, to launch a program for widening popular participation in the Communist-directed independence movement.

Three fundamentally important decisions were reached at the May, 1941, Party conference. First, a new Party leadership was chosen, including Truong Chinh, who was named secretary-general of the ICP. The promotion of Truong Chinh, who was a student of Chinese Communist leader Mao Tse-tung and his ideas on revolutionary mass action, illustrated the shift in ICP policy toward greater popular participation in the independence struggle. Second, the conference resolved to create a Communist military force. Two key leaders present at the meeting, Pham Van Dong and Vo Nguyen Giap, are believed to have received some military training from the Chinese Communists and to have been given special responsibility for organizing secret military training courses for Communist supporters in Hanoi and in the Tonkin delta area. Finally, a new broad-based umbrella organization was created by the ICP in May, 1941. This new institution, which was separate from but dominated by the Communist Party, was known as the Vietnam Independence League, or Viet Minh. It was composed of a number of "national salvation organizations," distinct political units for specific groups such as peasants, women, youth, students, and Catholics. Each constituent unit made contributions to the Viet Minh's "self-defense squads," and each was overseen through a network of Communist Party members. Although ICP leaders created the Viet Minh as a vehicle for unifying the Vietnamese people under Communist Party control, most ordinary people who joined the Viet Minh did so because they supported its goal of achieving Vietnam's independence from foreign powers.

## Impact of Event

In the period just after May, 1941, recruitment to the new Viet Minh affiliates was severely inhibited by both French and Japanese security forces active in Indochina and by the emergence of rival Vietnamese political parties, some of which were sponsored by the French or Japanese. Intrigues, arrests, and assassinations became almost commonplace as different intelligence agencies and political parties competed for political influence over the Vietnamese people.

Over time, however, the Viet Minh was able to take advantage of the growing political and economic dissatisfactions that accompanied the tense Franco-Japanese cooperation in Vietnam during World War II. For example, the new organization provided a mechanism for the mobilization of Vietnamese women, long excluded from mainstream political activity by both traditional Vietnamese political culture and by French colonial rule. The Viet Minh included women as members, established a Women's Association for National Salvation as an affiliate, encouraged the involvement of female textile workers in the Communists' industrial strike strategies, and to some extent welcomed women's participation in armed propaganda and combat units. Some women were active in the latter roles at least as early as July, 1941. The founding of the Viet Minh and its inclusion of Vietnamese women thus marked a significant development in the broadening of popular participation in national resistance politics.

Beginning in 1943, the Viet Minh began to garner adherents in much greater numbers. At another clandestine ICP conference held in February, 1943, the Party leadership approved additional steps to expand the activities and membership of the Viet Minh. Pro-Japanese student unions in Hanoi and pro-French ethnic minority populations in the uplands of central and northern Vietnam were the targets of intense recruitment efforts. The Viet Minh's greatest early successes came in response to the disastrous consequences of an emerging food crisis, especially in northern and central Vietnam. French policy required that increasing amounts of rice produced in Vietnam be sold to Japanese forces or stockpiled in government warehouses, rather than allowed onto domestic markets for consumption by Vietnam's own population. Even as rice shortages worsened in 1944, French policy authorized the conversion of stored rice to fuels for vehicles. The massive food shortages of 1944-1945 are believed to have resulted in more than one million Vietnamese deaths. The Viet Minh responded both with isolated armed raids on rice storehouses and with intensified propaganda that portrayed the famine as the fault of French economic and military policies.

In part because of the success of these efforts, the Viet Minh was able to accelerate recruitment, to build "base areas" in north central Vietnam, and, in 1944, to create the nucleus of a Communist-directed guerrilla army. By the middle of 1945, the Viet Minh's military wing numbered around five thousand active combatants, supported by between 150,000 and 200,000 village defense forces and auxiliary personnel. Following Japan's surrender to the Allies in August, 1945, Ho Chi Minh activated these forces and the Viet Minh's urban networks to seize power in many Vietnamese cities. On September 2, 1945, Ho Chi Minh declared the founding of the Democratic Republic of Vietnam. Like the Viet Minh, the new government was designed and managed by the Indochinese Communist Party to win broad popular support for the pursuit of Vietnamese independence under Communist rule.

## Bibliography

Chen, King C. *Vietnam and China, 1938-1954.* Princeton, N.J.: Princeton University Press, 1969. This work examines the range of contacts made by Communist and non-Communist Chinese with Vietnamese political and military groups during the early years of the Viet Minh. It is most useful for its focus on the movements and activities of key leaders, including Ho Chi Minh.

Khanh, Huynh Kim. *Vietnamese Communism, 1925-1945.* Ithaca, N.Y.: Cornell University Press, 1982. A comprehensive, detailed treatment of the growth of the Vietnamese Communist movement and its links to international communism. Chapter 5 focuses on the Communists' responses to the German victory over France in 1940 and on the formation of the Viet Minh.

Lockhart, Greg. *Nation in Arms: The Origins of the People's Army of Vietnam.* Sydney: Allen & Unwin, 1989. Emphasizes the military dimension of the Vietnamese Communist movement. Chapter 3 discusses the early 1940's, while a helpful appendix discusses the influence of Chinese Communist military thinking upon the Vietnamese.

Marr, David G. *Vietnamese Tradition on Trial, 1920-1945.* Berkeley: University of

California Press, 1981. A learned and lively treatment of the origins of modern Vietnamese political culture, this work remains one of the best-documented, most sophisticated scholarly examinations of the conditions which made the emergence of the Viet Minh possible.

Smith, Ralph. *Viet-Nam and the West.* Ithaca, N.Y.: Cornell University Press, 1971. A knowledgeable presentation of the relationship between political culture and modern nationalism in Vietnam. Chapter 7 deals with the revolutionary period and places the founding of the Viet Minh in the context of modern radical politics in Vietnam.

*Laura M. Calkins*

## Cross-References

Japanese Troops Brutalize Chinese After the Capture of Nanjing (1937), p. 539; HUAC Begins Investigating Suspected Communists (1938), p. 550; The French Quell an Algerian Nationalist Revolt (1945), p. 651; The Nationalist Vietnamese Fight Against French Control of Indochina (1946), p. 683; Vietnamese Troops Withdraw from Cambodia (1989), p. 2459.

# ROOSEVELT OUTLAWS DISCRIMINATION IN DEFENSE-INDUSTRY EMPLOYMENT

*Categories of event:* Racial and ethnic rights; workers' rights
*Time:* June 25, 1941
*Locale:* Washington, D.C.

*President Franklin D. Roosevelt's executive order outlawing racial discrimination in defense-industry employment and the March on Washington Movement that led to it were U.S. civil rights landmarks*

*Principal personages:*

ASA PHILIP RANDOLPH (1889-1979), the organizer of the March on Washington Movement

FRANKLIN D. ROOSEVELT (1882-1945), the president of the United States who issued Executive Order 8802, forbidding discrimination in defense-industry employment

ELEANOR ROOSEVELT (1884-1962), the president's wife and a well-known champion of the rights of African Americans

WALTER WHITE (1893-1955), the secretary of the National Association for the Advancement of Colored People

FIORELLO HENRY LA GUARDIA (1882-1947), the mayor of New York City

JOSEPH L. RAUH, JR. (1911-      ), a young government lawyer responsible for drafting the executive order

PAUL V. McNUTT (1891-1955), the chair of the War Manpower Commission under whose control the FEPC was placed

## Summary of Event

In one sense, the 1930's marked the nadir of the plight of African Americans in the post-emancipation era. Cotton overproduction and the New Deal programs to reduce acreage resulted in thousands of black sharecroppers and tenant farmers in the South being driven from the land. Equally bleak was the situation in urban areas. Typically the last hired and first fired, black workers were probably the group hardest hit by the Great Depression. The defense build-up beginning in 1939 resulted in only minimal gains for blacks. In 1940, for example, there were only 240 African-American aircraft workers out of a total of 100,000, and those 240 were mostly janitors. For the most part, whites received the higher paying new jobs in the defense industries while blacks filled the lower paying, less desirable service jobs whites vacated.

There were also, by the late 1930's, signs of growing support for black rights. Agitation by far-left political groups, the rise of the Congress of Industrial Organizations, the intellectual attack upon racism by social scientists, pro-civil rights

Supreme Court decisions, and the increasing black vote in northern cities all indicated support for the cause. Perhaps most important was the increased militancy found among the nation's blacks. Asa Philip Randolph sought to channel this militancy by launching the March on Washington Movement (MOWM) to pressure President Franklin D. Roosevelt into outlawing racial discrimination by defense industries. Randolph had taken the lead in unionizing the black workers on the Pullman cars of the nation's railroads. In 1937, his Brotherhood of Sleeping Car Porters, an affiliate of the American Federation of Labor, had succeeded in gaining recognition from the Pullman Company and winning impressive benefits for its members.

On January 15, 1941, Randolph first publicly called for a march by blacks upon Washington, D.C., to demand an end to racial discrimination in defense employment and in the military services. In March, his new March on Washington Committee issued a formal call for the march to take place on July 1, 1941. His strategy was that such a protest, by publicizing the gap between America's professed ideals and its practice, would force Roosevelt to act. "The Administration leaders in Washington," Randolph proclaimed, "will never give the Negro justice until they see masses— ten, twenty, fifty thousand Negroes on the White House lawn!"

All but one of Randolph's demands could be met by executive orders: withholding defense contracts from manufacturers guilty of discrimination; authorizing government seizure of recalcitrant plants; abolishing "discrimination and segregation" in the armed forces and federal government departments; ending discrimination in federally funded vocational training programs; and requiring the United States Employment Service to make nondiscriminatory job referrals. The only demand that would require congressional action was amendment of the National Labor Relations Act of 1935 to deny collective bargaining rights to unions that excluded blacks. These goals did not differentiate the MOWM from other civil rights groups. Many black leaders, such as Walter White, the secretary of the National Association for the Advancement of Colored People (NAACP), were disturbed by, and even suspicious of, the MOWM's organizational structure and tactics. First, the MOWM consciously aimed to mobilize the black masses and did not rely for its support upon the black middle class. Second, the MOWM sought to force concessions through direct action instead of via behind-the-scenes negotiations. Third, the MOWM excluded whites from all participation. Randolph feared the danger of communist infiltration if whites were allowed to participate, and he was convinced that it was time for blacks to take the lead in efforts in their own behalf. Since "no one will fight as hard to remove and relieve pain as he who suffers from it," Randolph took the position that "Negroes are the only people who are the victims of Jim Crow, and it is they who must take the initiative and assume the responsibility to abolish it."

Randolph's threat to lead a march of 50,000-100,000 blacks on Washington, D.C., on July 1, 1941, put the Roosevelt Administration in a quandary. Roosevelt's fear was that the march would result in serious violence, which would not only damage the image of the United States abroad but also impair the nation's unity at a time when war appeared imminent. His response was a mix of concessions and arm-twisting to induce Randolph to call off the march. The Office of Production Management (OPM) stepped up its efforts to get defense contractors to hire more blacks; Roosevelt himself in mid-June issued a public statement along the same lines. To pressure Randolph, Roosevelt announced that he could "imagine nothing that will stir up race hatred and slow up progress more than a march of that kind." He even had his wife, Eleanor Roosevelt, whose championship of black rights had won for her the warm affection of the black community, intercede with Randolph and warn that the march would be a "very grave mistake" that might result in a dangerous "incident" and thus "set back the progress which is being made."

Randolph's intransigence forced Roosevelt to make further concessions. On June 18, Roosevelt named Mayor Fiorello Henry La Guardia of New York City, a man known for his sympathy for black aspirations, to head a committee to work out a plan that Randolph would accept. The task of drafting an executive order formalizing the government's concessions was assigned to a young lawyer in the Office of Emergency Management, Joseph L. Rauh, Jr., who would later become one of the country's leading civil liberties and civil rights lawyers. Negotiations with Randolph finally resulted in a bargain. On June 25, 1941, Roosevelt issued Executive Order 8802, forbidding discrimination in hiring by government agencies and defense contractors on the basis of race, creed, color, or national origin and establishing a Fair Employment Practices Committee (FEPC) to investigate complaints and "take appropriate steps to redress grievances." In return, Randolph called off the march. Randolph had not gained all he had asked for, as Roosevelt balked at ending segregation in the armed forces, but won what he regarded as his "main objective." The threatened march was mostly bluff, since Randolph privately had grave doubts whether he could carry out the plan.

World War II resulted in substantial employment gains for blacks. The resulting improvement in black economic status laid the basis for black advances in other areas. There is a question of how much of those gains resulted from Executive Order 8802 and the Fair Employment Practices Committee and how much from the worsening labor shortage resulting from the war. The FEPC's chairs—Mark Ethridge, the publisher of the *Louisville Courier Journal*; Malcolm S. MacLean, the president of Hampton Institute; Catholic educator Monsignor Francis J. Haas; and former newspaperman Malcolm Ross—were staunch Roosevelt loyalists who shied from politically embarrassing the president. The situation was aggravated by the FEPC's placement under the control of agencies with different priorities. The FEPC was located first in the Office of Production Management and then in the War Production Board. At the end of July, 1942, Roosevelt placed the FEPC under the new War Manpower Commission, whose chair was former Indiana governor Paul V. McNutt. McNutt's hostility to the FEPC resulted in the agency's near strangulation. After several FEPC members resigned in protest, Roosevelt intervened. On May 23, 1943, he issued Executive Order 9346, reaffirming the ban against discrimination in government contracts on the basis of race, color, creed, or national origin, reorganizing and strengthening the FEPC, and making the FEPC an independent agency—subject only to the authority of the president—within the Office of Production Management.

## Impact of Event

Although this new set-up gave the agency more autonomy than before, the FEPC continued to be of limited effectiveness. The FEPC lacked the funds or personnel to do much and could act only upon a formal complaint. Even if its investigation found a complaint justified, the FEPC, lacking statutory authority, could not require compliance with its orders. It had to rely upon moral pressure and the backing of other government war agencies. Its ultimate sanction, cancellation of a war contract, was an empty threat given the administration's commitment to avoiding interference with war production. Only one-third of the eight thousand complaints filed with the FEPC were resolved successfully, and only one-fifth of those from the South. Compliance orders were ignored by thirty-five of the forty-five affected companies and unions. The FEPC faced continuous sniping from southern Democrats in Congress. In the summer of 1945, the FEPC's opponents in Congress succeeded in cutting its appropriation in half and ordering its termination by June 30, 1946.

Randolph attempted to maintain the MOWM as an active organization, but his calls for mass demonstrations and civil disobedience to challenge Jim Crow were too militant for most black leaders. Although the NAACP's Walter White had cooperated with the MOWM up to the issuance of Roosevelt's executive order, a widening schism developed between Randolph and the NAACP leadership by mid-1942. As the MOWM lost its momentum, direction of the battle for civil rights was resumed by more traditional organizations such as the NAACP and the Urban League. The late 1950's, however, would see the rise of a new black mass movement modeled upon the MOWM.

The termination of the FEPC involved no more than a temporary setback for the supporters of equal opportunity in employment. New York, in 1945, became the first state to adopt laws against employment discrimination. President Harry S. Truman established a Fair Employment Board within the United States Civil Service Commission in 1946 and a Government Contract Compliance Committee in 1951. President Dwight D. Eisenhower issued an executive order in 1955 barring discrimination in federal employment. President John F. Kennedy issued, in 1961, Executive Order 10925, prohibiting discrimination in government contracts and government employment and requiring government contractors to take affirmative action to insure against discrimination. Title VII of the Civil Rights Act of 1964 prohibited discrimination in private employment against any person on the basis of race, color, religion, national origin, or sex and created the Equal Employment Opportunity Commission (EEOC), with power to investigate and reconcile complaints. The Equal Employment Act of 1972 authorized the EEOC to enforce Title VII by filing suit in the federal courts. The goal of the leading civil rights organizations switched from guaranteeing equal opportunity for individuals without regard to race to demanding preferential treatment, even quotas, for racial minorities. This policy, sometimes referred to as reverse discrimination, has sometimes been accepted by the federal bureaucracy, Congress, and the courts.

## Bibliography

Anderson, Jervis. *A. Philip Randolph: A Biographical Portrait.* New York: Harcourt Brace Jovanovich, 1973. A popular biography which relies heavily upon interviews with Randolph and persons who knew him. The text is divided between Randolph's union work and his civil rights activities.

Burstein, Paul. *Discrimination, Jobs, and Politics: The Struggle for Equal Employment Opportunity in the United States Since the New Deal.* Chicago: University of Chicago Press, 1985. A perceptive analysis covering the forces responsible for congressional legislation against discrimination in employment. Coverage begins in the early 1940's.

Dalfiume, Richard M. "The 'Forgotten Years' of the Negro Revolution." *Journal of American History* 55 (June, 1968): 90-106. A landmark article showing how World War II was a watershed in the struggle for black rights.

Garfinkel, Herbert. *When Negroes March: The March on Washington Movement in the Organizational Politics for FEPC.* Glencoe, Ill.: Free Press, 1959. A detailed organizational history of the March on Washington Movement. Based on the files of the Brotherhood of Sleeping Car Porters (including the records of the MOWM and the National Council for a Permanent FEPC), extensive research in the black press, and a large number of personal interviews.

Harris, William H. *Keeping the Faith: A. Philip Randolph, Milton P. Webster, and the Brotherhood of Sleeping Car Porters, 1927-37.* Urbana: University of Illinois Press, 1977. The fullest account of Randolph's success in building the Brotherhood into a union powerful enough to win recognition from the Pullman Company.

Kesselman, Louis C. *The Social Politics of FEPC: A Study in Reform Pressure Movements.* Chapel Hill: University of North Carolina Press, 1948. An analysis of the pressure groups, for and against, involved in the fight over continuing and making permanent the wartime FEPC.

Pfeffer, Paula F. *A. Philip Randolph, Pioneer of the Civil Rights Movement.* Baton Rouge: Louisiana State University Press, 1990. A thoroughly researched and documented study that focuses upon Randolph's activities in the area of civil rights rather than upon his work as a union leader. Illuminating on how Randolph's strategies provided the blueprint for the Civil Rights movement of the late 1950's and early 1960's.

Polenberg, Richard. *War and Society: The United States, 1941-1945.* Philadelphia, Pa.: J. B. Lippincott, 1972. The best overall treatment of the American home front during World War II. Includes a brief but illuminating examination of the impact of the conflict upon black status and rights.

Ruchames, Louis. *Race, Jobs, and Politics: The Story of FEPC.* New York: Columbia University Press, 1953. Although based upon the then-available public record, this work remains the fullest account of the wartime FEPC—its organizational structure, activities, and troubles with Congress.

Sitkoff, Harvard. *The Depression Decade.* Vol. 3 in *New Deal for Blacks: The Emergence of Civil Rights as a National Issue.* New York: Oxford University Press, 1978. An illuminating study of the forces in support of black civil rights that were gaining momentum by the late 1930's, including the rising militancy among blacks that found expression in the MOWM.

*John Braeman*

## Cross-References

Truman Orders Desegregation of U.S. Armed Forces (1948), p. 777; The Civil Rights Act of 1957 Creates the Commission on Civil Rights (1957), p. 997; The Equal Pay Act Becomes Law (1963), p. 1172; Congress Passes the Civil Rights Act (1964), p. 1251; The Supreme Court Bans Employment Tests with Discriminatory Effects (1971), p. 1617; Congress Passes the Equal Employment Opportunity Act (1972), p. 1650; The Supreme Court Rejects Racial Quotas in College Admissions (1973), p. 1697; The Supreme Court Upholds an Affirmative-Action Program (1979), p. 2029.

# THE ATLANTIC CHARTER DECLARES A POSTWAR RIGHT OF SELF-DETERMINATION

*Categories of event:* Indigenous peoples' rights and political freedom
*Time:* August 12, 1941
*Locale:* Placentia Bay, Newfoundland, Canada

*The Atlantic Charter, agreed to by Franklin D. Roosevelt and Winston Churchill at their first wartime meeting, committed their countries to a peace recognizing the right of self-determination*

> *Principal personages:*
> FRANKLIN D. ROOSEVELT (1882-1945), the thirty-second president of the United States (1933-1945), an anticolonialist
> WINSTON CHURCHILL (1874-1965), the British prime minister
> SIR ALEXANDER CADOGAN (1884-1968), the British permanent undersecretary of state for foreign affairs and author of the first draft of the Atlantic Charter
> SUMNER WELLES (1892-1961), the U.S. undersecretary of state who incorporated the views of Roosevelt and Churchill into the Atlantic Charter's final draft

## Summary of Event

Although the Atlantic Charter did much to extend its impact, the idea of national self-determination was already a century and a half old by 1941. The idea holds that each nationality should be free to determine its own political arrangements, including establishing its political independence if desired. The concept of self-determination emerged from the romantic nationalism that developed in the first half of the nineteenth century and was used to justify a variety of revolutions and national unification movements in Europe and elsewhere. Historically, the idea was viewed in generally favorable terms by the United States government, which saw it as consistent with the anticolonialist nature of American foreign policy.

In World War I, the principle of national self-determination figured implicitly in several of President Woodrow Wilson's Fourteen Points, in which form it was accepted by the Allies as a war aim. It also shaped aspects of the peace settlement, notably in the creation of new states in Central and Eastern Europe out of the former Russian, German, and Austro-Hungarian empires. Its application, however, was far from consistent, especially outside Europe. The idea nevertheless contributed to the stirrings of colonial populations in Asia and Africa.

The desire to declare public support for the principle of self-determination was not the primary reason for the meeting that produced the Atlantic Charter. That meeting was primarily motivated by wartime circumstance. By mid-1941, the war in Europe was almost two years old. Great Britain had held out against Adolf Hitler's initial onslaught and had been joined by the Soviet Union after the German invasion of June 22, 1941. The United States was not yet a formal party to the war, though President Franklin D. Roosevelt had made no secret of his belief that the defeat of Germany and its Axis allies was necessary to protect American interests in the world. He had drawn closer to Great Britain and had extended to the British a variety of material aid, most notably under the Lend-Lease Act, a step that some felt had brought the American economy into the conflict. British prime minister Winston Churchill hoped that the United States would become a full-fledged belligerent. President Roosevelt probably believed that American entry would be necessary to defeat the Axis; at the very least, he hoped that American public opinion would support further measures that would aid Hitler's enemies.

It was against this background that Roosevelt and Churchill arranged to meet for the first time in the summer of 1941. The place and time of the meeting was a closely-guarded secret. On August 9, 1941, the USS *Augusta*, carrying the president, rendezvoused in Placentia Bay, off the coast of Newfoundland, with HMS *Prince of Wales*, on board which was Churchill. Over the next three days, the two men covered a range of topics: implementation of lend-lease arrangements, closer cooperation in the Atlantic, and how best to deal with the threat of Japanese expansion in Asia among them. The president, however, was determined that the conference would also result in a joint statement of war aims that would make clear to the American people and to the rest of the world the differences that existed between the values of the democracies and those of the Axis powers.

Although Churchill was not convinced of a pressing need for such a declaration, he was willing to go along and in fact took the initiative. Sir Alexander Cadogan, the British permanent undersecretary for foreign affairs, drew up a draft statement that Churchill revised before inviting Roosevelt's comments. Roosevelt's Wilsonian sentiments about self-determination were well known to the British, and the draft included statements endorsing the concept. Subsequent drafts followed, with much of the work falling to Sumner Welles, the U.S. undersecretary of state. A number of points proved controversial, but not those dealing with self-determination. Churchill made clear his view that the British Commonwealth's commitment to eventual colonial self-government (if not independence) made the principle inapplicable to the British Empire. Roosevelt did not press the point. The greatest difficulties came in trying to reconcile Roosevelt's desire for postwar free trade with Britain's commitments to imperial preference and in phrasing a reference to postwar security that would not frighten American isolationists.

Eventually, an eight-point joint declaration of war aims was hammered out, one that was in many ways reminiscent of the Fourteen Points of the previous war. The document was made public on August 14, 1941, and immediately came to be known as the "Atlantic Charter." Six of the points were devoted to topics other than self-determination. Both powers declared that they sought no territorial gains from the war and that they looked forward to a world in which all nations would have access to trade and prosperity, in which there would be freedom of the seas, and in which there would be fewer arms, less fear, and a new system of international security. Two of the charter's points dealt directly with the issue of self-determination: There would be no territorial changes contrary to the wishes of the peoples concerned, and the right of people to choose their own form of government was affirmed. In adhering to the charter, Roosevelt indicated the United States' intention to shape the postwar world, even though the country was not yet a belligerent.

The immediate reaction to the Atlantic Charter was positive in both countries, but there was also an element of disappointment. In Britain, it had been hoped that something more dramatic, such as full-fledged American entry into the war, would be announced. The charter itself seemed slightly anticlimactic. In the United States, the charter's principles were widely approved, but public opinion did not shift significantly in favor of American entry into the war, as Roosevelt had hoped it would.

Over the course of the war, however, the Atlantic Charter proved to be a document of immense importance in defining Allied goals. After the United States entered the war in December, 1941, Churchill made another voyage across the Atlantic. That meeting laid the groundwork for military cooperation and also for the proclamation of the Declaration of the United Nations of January 1, 1942. Those signing the statement agreed to embrace the principles announced in the Atlantic Charter and also agreed not to make a separate peace with the enemy. Twenty-six nations signed the original declaration, a number that subsequently doubled. The Atlantic Charter—including the principle of self-determination—now officially described the war aims of the Allies.

The charter's self-determination provisions were, however, open to varying interpretations and provided the substance for much debate within the alliance. The British maintained that the provisions applied primarily to the European countries overrun and occupied by the Nazis and that they did not apply to the British Empire. In the United States, the Atlantic Charter contributed to an increasing anticolonialist trend in public opinion. The U.S. State Department showed a growing willingness to see the concept of self-determination as applicable outside Europe—certainly to the colonies of the Axis powers and possibly to those of the Allies as well. The Soviets took a public stand in favor of self-determination everywhere, although their commitment was clouded by their clear expectation of beneficial territorial rearrangements in Eastern Europe and Asia. Overseas, supporters of independence or "home-rule" movements in Asia and Africa were inspired by the Atlantic Charter and desirous of using it as a lever against their colonial masters. In short, the charter was a source of disagreement on the Allied side even as it remained a common point of reference to which all pledged allegiance. It was in this context that the last meeting of the "Big Three" of Roosevelt, Churchill, and Stalin took place at Yalta in February, 1945. The three issued a joint Declaration on Liberated Europe that called for free elections and application of the principles of the Atlantic Charter.

The Atlantic Charter's eighth point had called for a new system of international security. This began to take shape in the form of the infant United Nations (U.N.), created at a San Francisco conference in April-June, 1945. Grounding itself in the

Declaration of the United Nations of 1942, the new organization embraced the principles of the Atlantic Charter. The organizing conference gave rise to a lively debate on the issue of self-determination, with predictable differences of opinion arising. The United Nations Charter ultimately allowed for a system of international trusteeship (involving administration by member nations under U.N. auspices) where the colonies of the Axis powers were concerned. Article 73, regarding non-self-governing territories, stated that self-government through free political institutions should be the goal of all countries with colonies or trust territories. This represented a compromise between the British and American positions. The United States foresaw the need to maintain, for strategic reasons, some of the former Japanese colonies in the Pacific, while the British were as reluctant as before to embrace a definition of self-determination that would apply to the Empire. Independence was not ruled out, but self-government short of independence would also be acceptable. As the war drew to a close, there remained an ambiguity about the principle of self-determination that would continue into the future.

## Impact of Event

The absence of a comprehensive treaty after World War II complicates any attempt to evaluate the Atlantic Charter's impact on the peace it was intended to shape. Nevertheless, it is evident that the charter's principles exerted a powerful influence on the postwar world, particularly in terms of self-determination. One example of this is provided by the functioning of the U.N. trusteeship system. Unlike the League of Nations' mandate system after World War I, U.N. trusteeship has overseen the transition to independence for numerous former colonies.

The foreign policies of the United States and other signatories to the charter showed varying degrees of commitment to the principle of self-determination. The Atlantic Charter remains an official statement of U.S. foreign policy, and the United States has often supported the emergence of former colonies as independent states. On the other hand, the onset of the Cold War in the immediate postwar period often caused ideological considerations to influence policy. The decision of President Harry S. Truman's administration to support the restoration of French colonial rule in Indochina and elsewhere, for example, put American policy on the side of colonialism in Southeast Asia and laid the foundation for eventual American involvement in the Vietnam War. The Soviet Union's failure to live up to the Atlantic Charter in its actions in Eastern Europe was even more blatant.

The long-term impact of the Atlantic Charter's endorsement of self-determination has been most visible in Asia and Africa. World War II weakened the European colonial powers militarily, and the Atlantic Charter contributed to the development of a climate of opinion hostile to colonialism that was one of World War II's most important legacies. The charter itself was often cited by those leading movements as diverse as the Viet Minh in Indochina and the Congress Party in India. The three decades following the war witnessed one of the most sudden and massive transfers of political authority in world history. In Africa alone, some fifty-one newly independent countries emerged from the former colonial empires. Many would eventually have achieved independence without the Atlantic Charter; however, by committing the victors of World War II to the principle of self-determination, the Atlantic Charter provided unique encouragement to those seeking to throw off outside control. It invested them with the moral force of the victorious crusade against Nazi racism and challenged the Allied Powers to live up to their own pronouncements.

## Bibliography

Chamberlain, M. E. *Decolonization: The Fall of the European Empires.* New York: Basil Blackwell, 1985. A short but reliable overview of the process of decolonization that followed World War II. Credits the Atlantic Charter with contributing to the worldwide growth of anticolonialist opinion and providing a moral weapon for nationalist movements. Bibliography and index.

Churchill, Winston. *The Grand Alliance.* Vol. 3 in *The Second World War.* Boston: Houghton Mifflin, 1950. Contains Churchill's personal account of the drafting of the charter. Gives a sense of the wartime context, although tending to downplay the differences of viewpoint involved. Contains a photocopy of the first draft with Churchill's comments and prints the text of the entire document. Index.

Cobban, Alfred. *National Self-Determination.* Chicago: University of Chicago Press, 1947. An eminent historian's discussion of the concept of self-determination, written during wartime. Stresses the need for the great powers to remain united. Footnotes and index, but no bibliography.

Dallek, Robert. *Franklin D. Roosevelt and American Foreign Policy, 1932-1945.* New York: Oxford University Press, 1979. The standard account of Roosevelt's foreign policy. Places the Atlantic Charter in the context of Roosevelt's efforts to support the British while preparing American public opinion for intervention. Bibliography and index.

Hannum, Hurst. *Autonomy, Sovereignty, and Self-Determination.* Philadelphia: University of Pennsylvania Press, 1990. Not about the Atlantic Charter itself, but provides an interesting treatment of self-determination from the perspective of international law. Sees the desire for self-determination as a major source of conflict in the late twentieth century. Nine case studies illustrate the influence of the concept in the post-World War II world. Bibliography and index.

Louis, William Roger. *Imperialism at Bay: The United States and the Decolonization of the British Empire, 1941-1945.* New York: Oxford University Press, 1978. Essential to understanding the self-determination aspects of the Atlantic Charter in the context of wartime diplomacy. Brings out the divergent British and American interpretations and the relationship between the charter and the eventual development of the United Nations. Extensive footnotes and index but no bibliography.

Welles, Sumner. *Where Are We Heading?* New York: Harper & Brothers, 1946. The best firsthand account of the drafting of the charter, by the man who produced the final draft. Makes it clear that other points were more controversial at the time than self-determination. Index but no bibliography.

Wilson, Theodore A. *The First Summit: Roosevelt and Churchill at Placentia Bay, 1941.* Boston: Houghton Mifflin, 1969. Well researched; the fullest account of the meeting and the drafting of the charter. Sees Roosevelt as not regarding the self-determination clause as applying to the British Commonwealth. Bibliographical essay and index.

*William C. Lowe*

## Cross-References

The Baltic States Fight for Independence (1917), p. 207; Finland Gains Independence from the Soviet Union (1917), p. 212; Ireland Is Granted Home Rule and Northern Ireland Is Created (1920), p. 309; The Statute of Westminster Creates the Commonwealth (1931), p. 453; Ho Chi Minh Organizes the Viet Minh (1941), p. 573; The United Nations Adopts Its Charter (1945), p. 657; The Nationalist Vietnamese Fight Against French Control of Indochina (1946), p. 683; India Gains Independence (1947), p. 731; Algeria Gains Independence (1962), p. 1155; Basques Are Granted Home Rule but Continue to Fight for Independence (1980), p. 2079; Sikhs in Punjab Revolt (1984), p. 2215; Namibia Is Liberated from South African Control (1988), p. 2409; Kashmir Separatists Demand an End to Indian Rule (1989), p. 2426.

# THE INTERNATIONAL LEAGUE FOR
# HUMAN RIGHTS IS FOUNDED

*Category of event:* Civil rights
*Time:* 1942
*Locale:* New York, New York

*The International League for Human Rights (ILHR) was among the first and most influential of the international nongovernmental organizations concerned with human rights*

Principal personages:

ROGER NASH BALDWIN (1884-1981), the principal founder of the ILHR

HENRI LAUGIER (1888-1973), a cofounder of the ILHR, the director of cultural relations in Charles de Gaulle's French wartime government

HENRI BONNET (1888-1978), a cofounder of the ILHR, a member of the League of Nations secretariat, and the French ambassador to the United States from 1944 to 1955

CHARLES HABIB MALIK (1906-1987), a cofounder of the ILHR, later the president of the U.N. General Assembly and chair of the U.N. Commission on Human Rights

JEROME JOSEPH SHESTACK (1925-    ), the chair of the ILHR after 1972 and the United States representative to the U.N. Commission on Human Rights

## Summary of Event

Although probably less well known than either Amnesty International or the International Commission of Jurists, the International League for Human Rights (ILHR) is one of the most important nongovernmental organizations concerned with human rights. The league is not only older than either of the other two organizations but also distinct from them in that it is uniquely devoted to the full range of human rights issues. While Amnesty International is concerned primarily with torture and political prisoners and the International Commission of Jurists with human rights and international law, the ILHR takes the wide-ranging Universal Declaration of Human Rights, adopted by the United Nations in 1948, as its platform.

The ILHR traces its origins to a citizens' league created in France in 1902 to monitor and criticize the French government in the aftermath of the Dreyfus affair and the rise of French anti-Semitism. This *Ligue Française pour la Defense des Droits de L'Homme et du Citoyen* soon became interested in broader international human rights issues and grew to more than two hundred thousand members by the eve of World War I. The *Ligue* fostered the formation of similar organizations throughout Europe and the French colonial possessions of Tonkin, Martinique, and French Guiana. An international federation affiliating all these organizations, the *Federa-*

*tion Internationale des Droits de L'Homme,* was founded in 1922 under the auspices of the French *Ligue.*

Roger Nash Baldwin, one of the principal founders of the American Civil Liberties Union in 1920, visited Paris in 1927 and was permitted to attend meetings of the French *Ligue* as a foreign observer. Baldwin's interest in civil rights and liberties became increasingly international in focus, and he maintained contact with the *Ligue* throughout the rest of the interwar period. With the fall of France in World War II, the French *Ligue* was disbanded. Shortly thereafter, Baldwin encouraged the reconstitution of the organization in the United States. For this purpose, he gathered together a group of French émigrés and other interested individuals, among them Henri Laugier, Henri Bonnet, and Charles Malik, in November of 1941. From this meeting emerged the new International League for the Rights of Man, incorporated under the laws of the state of New York in 1942. The league was to change its name formally in 1976 to the International League for Human Rights.

The reconstitution of the league in 1942 was propitious in that it occurred in the wake of Franklin Roosevelt's declaration of the "Four Freedoms," concerning the freedoms of speech and worship and the need for international economic prosperity and disarmament; the Anglo-American Atlantic Charter, which called for a new international order to preserve peace in the postwar world after the destruction of Nazism; and the United Nations Declaration of early 1942, in which twenty-six countries pledged themselves to reestablish a collective security organization after the demise of the League of Nations. Baldwin's International League regarded the proposed United Nations as the principal organization through which the league could exert its influence and promote its interests. Working in cooperation with other nongovernmental organizations, the league directed most of its early efforts at lobbying the drafters of the United Nations Charter to ensure that the relationship between international human rights and world peace would be recognized explicitly. The league's efforts helped lead to seven specific references to human rights in the U.N. Charter, the establishment of the U.N. Commission on Human Rights, and the drafting of the commission's Universal Declaration of Human Rights in 1948.

The International League continued to emphasize working within the United Nations system in the postwar era. The league was given consultative status with the Economic and Social Council (ECOSOC), the International Labor Office (ILO), and the United Nations Educational, Scientific and Cultural Organization (UNESCO). It conducted lobbying activities in the U.N. General Assembly, the Commission on Human Rights, and other U.N. organizations to promote the adoption of human rights declarations and covenants. In the 1950's and 1960's, the league paid particular attention to the issue of decolonization, since it viewed the colonial system as a chief violator of human rights. By the 1970's, the league had become disillusioned with the United Nations and its apparent inability to make much of an impact on human rights. The league believed that, despite considerable pressure from nongovernmental organizations, the U.N. Commission on Human Rights and its subcommission on the prevention of discrimination and the protection of minorities had failed to make effective use of their powers to investigate and make recommendations concerning human rights violations. Bureaucratic and procedural stonewalling kept most complaints about abuse and repression from reaching the stage of open discussion and recommendation by the commission. Moreover, the human rights commission attempted to restrict the consultative role and, thereby, the activist influence of nongovernmental organizations in the United Nations. The league perceived that human rights had become too closely linked to political relations between member states for the United Nations to deal effectively with allegations of abuse and repression. Under its chair, Jerome Shestack, the league pursued an increasing proportion of its activities outside the United Nations. The league expanded its efforts to conduct investigations of human rights abuses, send fact-finding missions to repressive nations, observe political trials, promote letter-writing campaigns, issue reports, and sponsor conferences on human rights. Still, the research and findings of league investigations continued to be an important source of information for the United Nations, which conducted almost no factual research of its own.

The expanded efforts and more formally organized and structured nature of the modern International League for Human Rights stood in marked contrast to the character of the early league. In many respects, the early league was patterned on the model of the early American Civil Liberties Union (ACLU). Both organizations were influenced strongly by the policies and personality of Roger Baldwin. The early ACLU deliberately was created and maintained as a small, private, and informally organized association. This corresponded with Baldwin's social philosophy and operational ideology, drawn from nineteenth century concepts of noblesse oblige and private charitable service. Recruitment to the early ACLU was based on an "old-boy" network of individuals known to and trusted by people already in the organization. The early ACLU emphasized discreet lobbying activities and a faith in the rule of law and the judicial process as the primary venue in which to promote civil libertarian interests. "Members" of the association existed only as a source of financial contributions to sustain the professional and legal activities of the organization's staff. The early International League was modeled after the early ACLU; it operated initially as a small, private, and informally organized group and, in many ways, as a social organization for Baldwin and his associates. It was with the increasing importance in world affairs of international human rights issues in the decades after World War II that the league became more formally organized and expanded its efforts first within and later outside the United Nations.

The structure of the International League distinguished it from other human rights nongovernmental organizations. The league was a confederation of affiliated national civil-libertarian associations, an arrangement very much in keeping with the ideology and structure of the old French *Ligue.* The International League's affiliates were not simply chapters or sections of the league in different countries. Instead, they were established and functioning civil liberties groups working for the furtherance of human rights in their own nations. The league established its headquarters in New York City and counted among its affiliates the American Civil Liberties

Union, the National Council of Civil Liberties in Great Britain, the Canadian Civil Liberties Association, the New Zealand Democratic Rights Council, and the Japanese Civil Liberties Union. The structure of the International League clearly reflected its belief that the principal protection of human rights must come through the implementation of national law.

## Impact of Event

The International League for Human Rights is a nongovernmental, nonpartisan political organization. It does not seek or accept funds from any government and relies wholly on voluntary contributions. Without state sponsorship, the league maintains the independence needed to pursue effectively its interests as an international human rights nongovernmental organization (NGO). This is of particular importance since, by their very nature, human rights NGOs play an adversarial role with respect to governments. Violations of human rights are committed primarily by governments; international human rights NGOs thus generally oppose and clash with states.

The importance of the adversarial role played by NGOs with respect to governments is perhaps the best argument for the continued existence of such organizations as the ILHR. The rights of individuals, as opposed to states, cannot be guaranteed either by states themselves or by international governmental organizations (IGOs). Friendly governments will be reluctant to accuse each other of human rights violations, since this might damage their relations and compromise their respective strategic and economic interests. Conversely, accusations of human rights abuses and repression by unfriendly states can be dismissed easily on the grounds that they may reflect purely political motives rather than humanitarian concern. As the creations of states, IGOs are subject to the same problems.

The International League for Human Rights continues to serve as an adversarial human rights NGO. As an activist association, the ILHR functions as a consultative and educational organization. At times, it has both prompted and restrained government action in the interests of human rights. The ILHR has concerned itself with such issues as the treatment of prisoners, torture, visa restrictions, family reunification, legal discrimination, religious intolerance, labor and minority rights, national independence movements, electoral fraud, and the death penalty. With such wide-ranging interests, the ILHR ranks as one of the most important human rights NGOs. The league has contributed significantly to the shaping of public debate about international human rights and has helped to influence the foreign policies of many governments that have reflected an increasing concern over human rights issues.

## Bibliography

Archer, Peter. "Action by Unofficial Organizations on Human Rights." In *The International Protection of Human Rights*, edited by Evan Luard. New York: Praeger, 1967. Examines in detail the activities of the ILHR in conjunction with the United Nations as well as league campaigns outside the United Nations in the 1960's.

Article references and a good bibliography.

Armstrong, J. D. "Non-Governmental Organizations." In *Foreign Policy and Human Rights: Issues and Responses*, edited by R. J. Vincent. Cambridge, England: Cambridge University Press, 1986. Excellent overview of the role of NGOs in the field of international human rights. Although Armstrong focuses primarily on Amnesty International and the International Red Cross, the ILHR is examined briefly. Good article references and bibliography.

Buergenthal, Thomas, ed. *Human Rights, International Law, and the Helsinki Accord*. Montclair, N.J.: Allanheld, Osmun, 1977. Examines the programs of the ILHR and its attempts to conduct more directly its human rights activities outside the United Nations. Good index and bibliography.

Drinan, Robert. *Cry of the Oppressed: The History and Hope of the Human Rights Revolution*. San Francisco: Harper & Row, 1987. Excellent general survey of human rights issues and organizational activities. Examines briefly the organization and policy of the ILHR. Index and bibliography.

Lador-Lederer, J. *International Group Protection*. Leiden, The Netherlands: A. W. Sijthoff, 1968. Although somewhat dry and legalistic, a detailed and well-argued account of the organizational structures and functions of NGOs, including the ILHR. Excellent index and bibliography.

Robertson, A. H. "Implementation System: International Measures." In *The International Bill of Rights*, edited by Louis Henkin. New York: Columbia University Press, 1981. Examines critically the role of NGOs, including the ILHR, as important sources of information and policy recommendations for the United Nations. Article references and a bibliography.

Wiessbrodt, David. "International NGOs." In *Human Rights in International Law: Legal and Policy Issues*, edited by Theodor Meron. Vol. 2. Oxford, England: Clarendon Press, 1984. Examines the important influence exerted by NGOs on the foreign policies of individual nations. Briefly discusses the ILHR in this context. Excellent article references, index, and bibliography.

*Douglas A. Lea*

## Cross-References

The American Civil Liberties Union Is Founded (1920), p. 327; The United Nations Adopts Its Charter (1945), p. 657; The United Nations Adopts the Universal Declaration of Human Rights (1948), p. 789; The United Nations Sets Rules for the Treatment of Prisoners (1955), p. 935; Amnesty International Is Founded (1961), p. 1119; The U.N. Covenant on Civil and Political Rights Is Adopted (1966), p. 1353; The Helsinki Agreement Offers Terms for International Cooperation (1975), p. 1806; The United Nations Issues a Declaration Against Torture (1975), p. 1847; The United Nations Issues a Conduct Code for Law Enforcement Officials (1979), p. 2040; A Paraguayan Torturer Is Found Guilty of Violating the Law of Nations (1980), p. 2106.

# ROOSEVELT APPROVES INTERNMENT OF JAPANESE AMERICANS

*Categories of event:* Civil rights; racial and ethnic rights
*Time:* February 19, 1942
*Locale:* Washington, D.C., California, Oregon, Washington, and Arizona

*The forced removal and internment during World War II of approximately 110,000 Japanese Americans living on the Pacific coast was one of the gravest violations of civil liberties in United States history*

*Principal personages:*

MAJOR GENERAL ALLEN W. GULLION (1880-1946), the Army's chief law enforcement officer as provost marshal general

MAJOR KARL R. BENDETSEN (1907-1989), Gullion's aide and a key figure in pushing for evacuation of Japanese Americans

LIEUTENANT GENERAL JOHN L. DEWITT (1880-1962), the commander of the Army's Western Defense Command

EARL WARREN (1891-1974), the California state attorney general

JOHN J. MCCLOY (1895-1989), the assistant secretary of war

HENRY L. STIMSON (1867-1950), the secretary of war who gave his support to the internment and removal

FRANCIS B. BIDDLE (1886-1968), the United States attorney general

FRANKLIN D. ROOSEVELT (1882-1945), the thirty-second president of the United States; issued Executive Order 9066 authorizing Japanese-American removal

DILLON S. MYER (1891-1982), the director of the War Relocation Administration

## Summary of Event

At the time of the Japanese attack on Pearl Harbor, December 7, 1941, there were approximately 110,000 Japanese Americans living on the Pacific coast of the United States. Roughly one-third of those were the issei—foreign-born Japanese who had migrated before the exclusion of Japanese immigrants in 1924 and were barred from United States citizenship. The rest were the nisei—their United States-born children who were U.S. citizens and for the most part strongly American-oriented. The government had in place plans for the arrest of enemy aliens whose loyalty was suspect in the event of war. In the immediate aftermath of Pearl Harbor, approximately fifteen hundred suspect Japanese aliens were rounded up. Those not regarded as security risks were, along with German and Italian aliens, restricted from traveling without permission, barred from areas near strategic installations, and forbidden to possess arms, shortwave radios, or maps. The attack on Pearl Harbor, however, gave new impetus to the long-standing anti-Japanese sentiment held by many in the Pacific coast states. The result was loud demands from local patriotic groups, newspapers, and politicians for removal of all Japanese Americans. Leading the clamor was California state attorney general Earl Warren, who warned that their race made all Japanese Americans security risks.

Within the military, the lead in pushing for the roundup of Japanese Americans on the Pacific coast was taken by Major General Allen W. Gullion, the Army's chief law enforcement officer as provost marshal general, in a bid at bureaucratic empire building. His key lieutenant in pushing this program was his ambitious aide, Major (later Colonel) Karl R. Bendetsen, chief of the Aliens Division of the provost marshal general's office. Lieutenant General John L. DeWitt, the commander of the Army's Western Defense Command, was an indecisive and easily pressured man with a history of anti-Japanese prejudice. At first, DeWitt opposed total removal of the Japanese Americans. By early February, 1942, however, he added his voice to the calls for such action. "In the war in which we are now engaged," DeWitt would rationalize, "racial affinities are not severed by migration. The Japanese race is an enemy race." He warned in apocalyptic terms about the dangers raised by "[t]he continued presence of a large, unassimilated, tightly knit racial group, bound to an enemy nation by strong ties of race, culture, custom and religion along a frontier vulnerable to attack."

Those views were shared by his civilian superiors. The decisive figure was Assistant Secretary of War John J. McCloy, who in turn brought Secretary of War Henry L. Stimson to support total removal. Attorney General Francis Biddle and most Justice Department officials saw no necessity for mass evacuation, but Biddle yielded to the War Department on the issue. Most important, President Franklin D. Roosevelt, from motives of political expediency as much as from any anxiety over possible sabotage, gave his full backing to the military program. On February 19, 1942, Roosevelt issued Executive Order 9066, authorizing the military to designate "military areas" from which "any or all persons may be excluded." Congress followed by adopting legislation in March making it a criminal offense for anyone excluded from a military area to remain there.

No one appeared to have given much thought to what would be done with the evacuees. At first, the military simply called upon the Japanese Americans living in the western parts of California, Oregon, and Washington, and in the strip of Arizona along the Mexican border, to leave voluntarily for the interior of the country. Resistance by interior communities to the newcomers led the Army to issue, on March 27, 1942, a freeze order requiring Japanese Americans to remain where they were. The next step was the issuance of orders requiring Japanese Americans to report to makeshift assembly centers pending transfer to more permanent facilities. By June, 1942, more than one hundred thousand Japanese Americans had been evacuated. The evacuees were transferred from the assembly centers to ten permanent relocation camps in the interior, each holding between ten and eleven thousand persons, administered by the newly established War Relocation Authority (WRA). The camps were surrounded by barbed wire and patrolled by armed military guards. The typical camp consisted of wooden barracks covered with tar paper, and each barrack was subdivided into one-room apartments—each furnished with army cots, blankets, and a light bulb—to which a family or unrelated group of individuals was assigned. Toilets and bathing, laundry, and dining facilities were communal. Religious worship (except for the practice of Shinto) was allowed. Schools were later opened for the young people. Although the evacuees grew some of their own food and even undertook small-scale manufacturing projects, most found no productive outlets in the camps for their energies and talents. The WRA promoted the formation of camp governments to administer the day-to-day life of the camps, but those governments lacked meaningful power and rapidly lost the respect of camp populations.

Conditions were at their worst, and the resulting tensions at their height, at the Tule Lake, California, relocation center, which became a dumping ground for those from other camps regarded as troublemakers. The upshot was terror-enforced domination of the camp by a secret group of pro-Japan militants.

A nisei recalled poignantly the scene of the evacuees being taken off to a camp: "The sight of hundreds of people assembled with assorted baggage, lined up to board the buses at the embarkation point, with rifle-bearing soldiers standing around as guards, is still imprinted in memory. And I can still remember the acute sense of embitterment. . . ." Life in the camps, said another, held evils that "lie in something more subtle than physical privations. It lies more in that something essential [is] missing from our lives. . . . The most devastating effect upon a human soul is not hatred but being considered not human."

At first, Dillon S. Myer, the director of the WRA from June, 1942, on, regarded the relocation centers as simply "temporary wayside stations." In 1943, the WRA instituted a program of releasing evacuees against whom there was no evidence of disloyalty, who had jobs waiting away from the Pacific coast, and who could show local community acceptance. By the end of 1944, approximately thirty-five thousand evacuees had left the camps under this release program. The Roosevelt Administration had, by the spring of 1944, recognized that there was no longer any possible military justification for the continued exclusion of the Japanese Americans from the Pacific coast. To avoid any possible political backlash, however, the Roosevelt Administration waited until after the 1944 presidential election to announce the termination of the exclusion order and allow nearly all of those still in the relocation centers to leave at will. Many of the evacuees, fearful of a hostile reception on the outside, continued to cling to the camps. In June, 1945, the WRA decided to terminate the camps by the end of the year and later imposed weekly quotas for departure, to be filled by compulsion if required.

## Impact of Event

The evacuation and internment was a traumatic blow to the Japanese-American population. Since evacuees were allowed to bring with them only clothes, bedding, and utensils, most sold their possessions for whatever they could get. Only slightly more than half of the evacuees returned to the Pacific coast, and most found their homes, businesses, and jobs lost. Japanese Americans suffered income and property losses estimated at $350 million. Of even longer-lasting impact were the psychological wounds. Internment dealt a heavy blow to the traditional Japanese family struc- ture by undermining the authority of the father. Many nisei, eager to show their patrio- tism, volunteered for service in the United States military. The Japanese-American One Hundredth Infantry Battalion and 422d Regimental Combat Team were among the Army's most-decorated units. On the other hand, more than five thousand nisei were so embittered by their experiences that they renounced their United States cit- izenship. Thousands more would carry throughout their lives painful, even shame- ful, memories from the years spent behind the barbed wire.

Defenders of civil liberties were appalled at how weak a reed the U.S. Supreme Court proved to be in the war crisis. The first challenge to the treatment suffered by the Japanese Americans to reach the Court involved Gordon Hirabayashi, a student at the University of Washington who had been imprisoned for refusing to obey a curfew imposed by General DeWitt and then failing to report to an assembly center for evacuation. Dodging the removal issue, the Court on June 21, 1943, unanimously upheld the curfew. Refusing to second-guess the military, the Court found reason- able the conclusion by the military authorities that "residents having ethnic affilia- tions with an invading enemy may be a greater source of danger than those of a different ancestry." On December 18, 1944, a six-to-three majority in *Korematsu v. United States* upheld the exclusion of the Japanese from the Pacific coast as a sim- ilarly reasonable military precaution. The Court, in the companion case of *Ex parte Endo* handed down the same day, however, barred continued detention of citizens whose loyalty had been established. The ruling's substantive importance was nil, because it was handed down one day after the announcement of the termination of the order barring Japanese Americans from the Pacific coast.

The Supreme Court has never formally overruled its *Hirabayashi* and *Korematsu* rulings. Later decisions, however, transmuted *Korematsu* into a precedent for apply- ing so-called "strict scrutiny" to classifications based upon race or national origin— that is, that such classifications can be upheld only if required by a compelling gov- ernmental interest. Pressure from the Japanese-American community led Congress in 1981 to establish a special Commission on Wartime Relocation and Internment to review the internment program. The commission report concluded that the intern- ment was not justified by military necessity, but had resulted from race prejudice, war hysteria, and a failure of political leadership. At the same time, petitions were filed in federal courts to vacate the criminal convictions of resisters to the evacua- tion. The climax was the unanimous decision by a three-judge panel of the Ninth Circuit Court of Appeals in 1987—which the government declined to appeal to the Supreme Court—vacating Gordon Hirabayashi's curfew violation conviction on the ground that the order had been "based upon racism rather than military necessity." In 1988, Congress voted a formal apology along with $1.25 billion in compensation to surviving internment victims.

## Bibliography
Collins, Donald E. *Native American Aliens: Disloyalty and the Renunciation of Citizenship by Japanese Americans During World War II.* Westport, Conn.: Greenwood Press, 1985. An in-depth examination of conditions in the relocation camp at Tule Lake, California. Attempts to explain the forces responsible for the renunciation of United States citizenship by more than five thousand nisei.

Conn, Stetson, Rose C. Engelman, and Byron Fairchild. *The United States Army in World War II: Guarding the United States and Its Outposts.* Washington, D.C.: Office of the Chief of Military History, Department of the Army, 1964. In their chapter "Japanese Evacuation from the West Coast," Conn and his coauthors were the first to exploit the rich body of records in the National Archives documenting the decisionmaking process culminating in Japanese-American removal. They found that the evidence failed to support the argument that military necessity required mass evacuation; they were the first to reveal the key roles played by Gullion and Bendetsen. All later accounts have built upon this pioneering work.

Daniels, Roger. *Concentration Camps U.S.A.: Japanese Americans and World War II.* New York: Holt, Rinehart and Winston, 1972. A handy survey that succinctly covers the history of anti-Japanese feeling on the Pacific Coast, the decision for evacuation, the constitutional issues before the Supreme Court, and camp life.

_____. *The Decision to Relocate the Japanese Americans.* Philadelphia, Pa.: J. B. Lippincott, 1975. The first fifty-five pages detail step-by-step the decisionmaking process culminating in the decision for mass evacuation of the Japanese Americans. The author concludes that political pressures were at least as important as considerations of military security. Appended are selections from the documentary record, drawn largely from the National Archives.

Drinnon, Richard. *Keeper of the Concentration Camps: Dillon S. Myer and American Racism.* Berkeley: University of California Press, 1987. A hostile biography of Myer, director of the War Relocation Authority for most of its existence (and later commissioner of the Bureau of Indian Affairs). Accuses Myer of racism.

Grodzins, Morton. *Americans Betrayed: Politics and the Japanese Evacuation.* Chicago: University of Chicago Press, 1949. Grodzins raised the first major public challenge to the military-necessity rationale; he blamed the evacuation upon "vehement racial animosity." His lack of access to the official documentary record led him to exaggerate the role of West Coast-based special-interest groups.

Irons, Peter. *Justice at War.* New York: Oxford University Press, 1983. The first quarter of the 367 pages of text reviews the steps leading up to the Japanese-American internment, with a heavy emphasis on the racist motivation. The major focus, though, is on the legal battle before the Supreme Court (and among the justices). Irons found evidence indicating that government lawyers deliberately withheld from the Court evidence refuting the military-necessity rationale.

Kitano, Harry H. L. *Japanese Americans: The Evolution of a Subculture.* Englewood Cliffs, N.J.: Prentice-Hall, 1976. The author, a Japanese American who was interned as an adolescent, blames what he terms the "*enryo* syndrome" (*enryo* being the Japanese word meaning restraint, shyness, or submissiveness) for the passivity shown by most of the evacuees.

tenBroek, Jacobus, Edward N. Barnhart, and Floyd W. Matson. *Prejudice, War, and the Constitution.* Berkeley: University of California Press, 1954. Still worth consulting for its detailed examination of the legal and constitutional aspects of the evacuation. The work, however, exaggerates DeWitt's role as initiator of the removal; even more dubiously, the authors accept that DeWitt "honestly" believed that the Japanese Americans on the Pacific coast were a security threat. They add as their personal opinion that the claim of military necessity was "unjustified."

Thomas, Dorothy S., and Richard S. Nishimoto. *The Spoilage: Japanese-American Evacuation and Resettlement During World War II.* Berkeley: University of California Press, 1946. This work, along with its companion volume by Thomas, *The Salvage: Japanese-American Evacuation and Resettlement* (1952) was a product of the University of California's Japanese America and Resettlement Study set up in early 1942. Project leaders have been criticized for agreeing, in return for government cooperation, not to say anything about the camps during the war. The first book is a study of the nisei who renounced their United States citizenship; the second volume consists of life histories of evacuees who were resettled in the Midwest and East.

*John Braeman*

## Cross-References

Japan Protests Segregation of Japanese in California Schools (1906), p. 81; The Immigration Act of 1921 Imposes a National Quota System (1921), p. 350; A U.S. Immigration Act Imposes Quotas Based on National Origins (1924), p. 383; Japan Withdraws from the League of Nations (1933), p. 474; Japanese Troops Brutalize Chinese After the Capture of Nanjing (1937), p. 539; A Japanese Commander Is Ruled Responsible for His Troops' Actions (1945), p. 662; Congress Formally Apologizes to Japanese Internees (1988), p. 2392.

# THE CONGRESS OF RACIAL EQUALITY FORMS

*Categories of event:* Civil rights; racial and ethnic rights
*Time:* Spring, 1942
*Locale:* Chicago, Illinois

*The Congress of Racial Equality (CORE), more than any other civil rights group, was responsible for the widespread use of Gandhi's nonviolent direct-action protest techniques in the Civil Rights movement in the United States from the 1940's through the 1960's*

*Principal personages:*

JAMES FARMER (1920-    ), a founder of CORE, and later its director

BAYARD RUSTIN (1910-1987), an early Quaker member of CORE, known as the organizer of the 1963 March on Washington

ASA PHILIP RANDOLPH (1889-1979), the organizer of the first civil rights March on Washington planned for 1941

MAHATMA GANDHI (1869-1948), the Indian political leader who developed and used nonviolent direct-action protest against British rule in India

## Summary of Event

African Americans began protesting racial discrimination in the United States before the Civil War, with the main objectives of eliminating racial discrimination and segregation and living in American society on an equal footing with other citizens. Controversy within the African-American community about what tactics to use and strategies to follow accompanied the protests.

At the end of the nineteenth century, the position of African Americans in U.S. society was declining. Racial prejudice flared. Disenfranchisement, lynchings, "Jim Crow" or segregation laws, and exclusion on the basis of race from the skilled trades were their lot. The early twentieth century saw mounting oppression and discrimination and an increasing frequency of race riots in both the North and the South. In general, this spurred accommodation, rather than protest, among African Americans.

Two other strategies for dealing with racial tensions developed in the early twentieth century. Booker T. Washington and his followers advocated "separatism" as a means of overcoming racism and living in U.S. society. Another group, the National Association for the Advancement of Colored People (NAACP), began attacking racial discrimination in the courts. One of the most powerful and longest-lived civil rights groups in U.S. history, the NAACP was founded in 1909 by black radicals, white progressives, and socialists, under the leadership of W. E. B. Du Bois. It had as its purpose the fight for black constitutional rights, particularly that of integration. As a rule, the NAACP employed legalistic methods of fighting for civil rights, that is, active propagandizing, legal activity, and lobbying for legislation against racial discrimination and segregation.

During World War I, a massive migration of African Americans to the North took place, as the northern cities offered a greater availability of jobs. Living conditions, however, were extremely poor. When the war ended, widespread unemployment resulted, and race riots took place. A new militancy arose among many blacks during this period. The NAACP thrived on this militancy as it fought against lynchings, disenfranchisement, and segregation, particularly in housing and schools. By the 1920's, the NAACP's legalistic approach was seen as conservative by those who advocated physical resistance to white mob violence and those who advocated racial separatism.

During the 1930's, white American attitudes toward African Americans began to change greatly, as humanitarian interest developed in improving conditions among the underprivileged. An increasingly large black vote in northern cities also drew the attention of Anglo politicians to black welfare. This was a period when interest focused on economic problems among the black community. The conservative NAACP continued its fights for integration, especially in the schools, and the vote for blacks. The NAACP emphasized legal argument as a tactic. A few other black protesting groups, however, used boycotting and picketing during this decade.

During and after World War II, a new, liberal respect for non-Anglos began to grow in the United States. During the early 1940's, the NAACP continued its legal battle against discrimination and segregation. Alongside the NAACP, two new movements—with a new approach—arose, the March on Washington Movement and the Congress of Racial Equality (CORE).

The March on Washington Movement was born in 1941, when African-American railroad workers, led by A. Philip Randolph (then president of the Brotherhood of Sleeping Car Porters) threatened to march on Washington, D.C., unless President Franklin Delano Roosevelt integrated U.S. defense industries and the military services. Randolph proposed that blacks from across the nation gather in Washington and march *en masse* to the Lincoln Monument. He also urged similar small-scale local marches. Calling for the march in July, 1941, Randolph cautioned against violence, which he argued would be more harmful than helpful. Such enthusiastic support for this march developed that Roosevelt issued an executive order in June, 1941, establishing a federal Fair Employment Practices Committee. Randolph called off the march.

The March on Washington Movement continued to exist for a short while afterward. In an address to it in September, 1942, Randolph advocated that nonviolent direct action, similar to that used by Mahatma Gandhi in India, be used by all-black groups to combat racial discrimination and segregation. He outlined a plan for forming small blocks of blacks ready to mobilize by the millions to march on Washington or to conduct simultaneous smaller marches across the nation. The movement was important, first, because it was an all-black organization that advocated mass action by urban ghetto dwellers to solve economic problems and, second, because it laid the groundwork for the nonviolent direct action movement of the 1960's.

The Congress of Racial Equality (CORE), however, was the group that made non-violent direct action a widespread and effective civil rights protest technique. CORE grew out of the Chicago Committee of Racial Equality, which met in Chicago in the spring of 1942. The Fellowship of Reconciliation (FOR), an almost entirely white Quaker pacifist group, had established a "cell" of about a dozen people at the University of Chicago in October, 1941. Many of the cell's members wanted to apply Gandhi's nonviolent direct action techniques to the United States' racial problems. FOR authorized James Farmer, a FOR staff member, to form in 1942 what later was named the Chicago Committee of Racial Equality. The group's first six members were Farmer and George Houser (another FOR staff member), Bernice Fisher, Homer Jack, Joe Guinn, and James R. Robinson. The group contained blacks and whites as well as Protestants and Catholics, but all members were pacifists.

CORE wrote two statements in 1942 outlining its basic commitment to interra-cial, nonviolent direct action and setting down the principles according to which its direct action demonstrations later would proceed. The "CORE Statement of Pur-pose" proclaimed goals of eliminating segregation and racial discrimination in pub-lic accommodation, housing, and other areas, through one method only—interracial nonviolent direct action. It denounced violence as a method of opposing racial dis-crimination, even if the protester is physically attacked, because CORE members believed social conflicts could not be resolved by means of violence. Among accept-able forms of protest, they identified negotiation, mediation, demonstration, and picketing. The "CORE Action Discipline" explained their belief that nonviolent di-rect action should be combined with goodwill toward the discriminator. Although it underwent some revision, this "CORE Action Discipline" remained the group's of-ficial statement of principle and philosophy until the 1960's. CORE's protest tech-nique was a combination of Gandhi's approach and the "sit-in," the latter of which had developed from "sit-down" strikes similar to Gandhi's that had been used in the United States in the 1930's.

During its first year of existence, the Chicago Committee worked to eliminate racial discrimination at a Chicago roller rink and at an apartment dwelling, as well as at the University of Chicago hospital, medical school, and barbershop. According to Farmer, the first sit-in was directed against the Jack Spratt restaurant in Chicago in May, 1942. It was successful in ending segregation of seating.

Local committees of CORE formed in Denver, Colorado, and Syracuse, New York, among other large cities, as Farmer and another early CORE member, Bayard Rustin, lectured on race relations for FOR in late 1942 and early 1943. An independent fed-eration of local committees was formed at a planning conference organized by Ber-nice Fisher and the Chicago Committee. It was held in Chicago in June, 1943, under Farmer's leadership. Nine local committees sent representatives, and they decided to affiliate under the name of the Committees of Racial Equality. In 1944, the national federation adopted the name Congress of Racial Equality and appointed Farmer as its national chairman and Fisher as the national secretary-treasurer.

## Impact of Event

CORE influenced the progress of the Civil Rights movement in the United States in a variety of ways. It was the black protest group that used nonviolent direct-action protest techniques, such as sit-ins, more than any other. Beginning with its first sit-in in a Chicago restaurant, CORE organized pivotal events in the history of the civil rights protest. In April, 1947, CORE and FOR staged a "Journey of Reconcilation" across the upper South to test the integration of interstate bus transport. This was the first example of what was later called a "Freedom Ride," a nonviolent direct-action protest technique. In the mid-1950's, the attack on segregated public accommodations and transportation intensified. In May and June, 1961, the "Freedom Rides" brought CORE to national attention and made it the principal national exponent of nonviolent direct action protest and the principal national black civil rights protest group. CORE was also involved in organizing the March on Washington on August 27, 1963. This march originally intended to call attention to increasing black unemployment, but it also took on the goal of pressuring the administration to pass the Civil Rights Act of 1964. It was at this huge, peaceful rally of 250,000 people on the steps of the Lincoln Memorial in Washington, D.C., that Martin Luther King, Jr., gave his famous "I Have a Dream" speech.

CORE also was responsible for spreading nonviolent direct action protest to other leaders and groups. The Reverend Martin Luther King, Jr., one of the major figures in the Montgomery, Alabama, bus boycott beginning in 1955, was greatly influenced by CORE's ideology. In the late 1950's, the use of nonviolent, direct-action protest increased markedly. This was partly a result of King's personal appeal and his founding of the Southern Christian Leadership Conference in 1957, which advocated Gandhian nonviolence. Nonviolent direct action reached its peak in the student sit-ins of 1960. These began with the February, 1960, sit-in by four North Carolina Agricultural & Technical State College students at a lunch counter in Greensboro, North Carolina. This event is regarded as the beginning of the Civil Rights Revolution. This sit-in was the most significant single event that encouraged and gave form to mass protest in the Civil Rights movement. These college students formed the Student Nonviolent Coordinating Committee in 1960 and took their philosophy from King, but they called on CORE for assistance in training protesters and organizing sit-ins. As college sit-in groups multiplied in the South after 1960, direct-action techniques won success and became the favored tactics among civil rights protest groups.

Early in its work, CORE's major fight was against racial segregation in places of public accommodation (entertainment facilities, restaurants, and housing), and it made significant gains. Then, around 1961, CORE began organizing African Americans from the ghettos in order to improve conditions. By 1963, jobs, housing, and education were perceived by CORE, as by all civil rights organizations, as the major areas of activity. Another of CORE's major campaigns was to increase black voter registration in the South; it began working in Louisiana on a voter registration program in November, 1962. Unfortunately, this resulted in the brutal murders of two

CORE voter registration workers and another student in Philadelphia, Mississippi, in the "Freedom Summer" of 1964.

As of the mid-1970's, CORE had achieved a large amount of progress in civil rights for African Americans in the United States. Like most groups, however, it was not producing results fast enough to keep up with rising expectations. The future of this historically significant protest group was entirely uncertain. CORE, the group that had pioneered the use of nonviolent direct-action techniques in the civil rights arena in the 1940's, was defunct by 1980.

## Bibliography

Blumberg, Rhoda Lois. *Civil Rights: The 1960s Freedom Struggle.* Boston: Twayne, 1984. A very useful history of the civil rights protest from the mid-1950's into the late 1960's. Gives a helpful brief chronology bringing together major events in the Civil Rights movement. Much specific information on CORE's activities alongside the activities of other civil rights organizations. Chapter 2 gives a concise history of racial discrimination and protest from the early twentieth century to the mid-1950's.

Farmer, James. *Freedom, When?* New York: Random House, 1965. A very personal and didactic narrative by one of the founders of CORE, in which he reminisces about its philosophy, background, formation, and activities. Includes a brief biography of Farmer. The book's major drawbacks are that it is not written strictly chronologically or indexed.

Meier, August, and Elliott Rudwick. *CORE: A Study in the Civil Rights Movement, 1942-1968.* New York: Oxford University Press, 1973. This massive tome, exhaustively researched and documented, details the history and assesses the accomplishments of CORE from its founding in 1942 through its internal ideological schisms, acceptance of Black Power, and loss of vitality in the late 1960's.

Meier, August, Elliott Rudwick, and Francis L. Broderick. *Black Protest Thought in the Twentieth Century.* 2d ed. Indianapolis, Ind.: Bobbs-Merrill, 1971. This highly recommended collection of primary writings comparing and contrasting the approach to protest by various twentieth century black organizations provides illuminating excerpts of writings by leaders in CORE and other groups. Has a superb introduction describing the character and historical evolution of black protest and placing CORE within its historical and philosophical context.

Rustin, Bayard. *Down the Line: The Collected Writings of Bayard Rustin.* Chicago: Quadrangle Books, 1971. A chronological collection of essays written by a man who was at the front ranks of the Civil Rights movement. Includes personal accounts and reports of such landmarks as the Montgomery bus boycott, and the Freedom Rides. Contains essays he wrote for CORE and FOR publications and other selections from the 1940's to the 1970's.

*Martha Ellen Webb*

**Cross-References**

Black Leaders Call for Equal Rights at the Niagara Falls Conference (1905), p. 41; CORE Stages a Sit-in in Chicago to Protest Segregation (1943), p. 618; CORE Stages the "Journey of Reconciliation" (1947), p. 718; Truman Orders Desegregation of U.S. Armed Forces (1948), p. 777; *Brown v. Board of Education* Ends Public School Segregation (1954), p. 913; Parks Is Arrested for Refusing to Sit in the Back of the Bus (1955), p. 947; The SCLC Forms to Link Civil Rights Groups (1957), p. 974; The Civil Rights Act of 1957 Creates the Commission on Civil Rights (1957), p. 997; Greensboro Sit-ins Launch a New Stage in the Civil Rights Movement (1960), p. 1056; Martin Luther King, Jr., Delivers His "I Have a Dream" Speech (1963), p. 1200; Three Civil Rights Workers Are Murdered (1964), p. 1246; Congress Passes the Civil Rights Act (1964), p. 1251; Congress Passes the Voting Rights Act (1965), p. 1296.

# ETHIOPIA ABOLISHES SLAVERY

*Category of event:* Civil rights
*Time:* August 27, 1942
*Locale:* Ethiopia

*The Ethiopian government decided to abolish slavery in order to gain international respectability*

*Principal personages:*
> HAILE SELASSIE I (1892-1975), the emperor of Ethiopia (1930-1936 and 1941-1974), committed, theoretically, to the abolition of slavery
> SHEWA MENELIK II (1844-1913), the emperor of Ethiopia (1889-1913); opposed the slave trade but actually caused it to increase through his expansionist policies
> BENITO MUSSOLINI (1883-1945), the Italian fascist premier who conquered and occupied Ethiopia

## Summary of Event

The abolition of slavery by the imperial government of Ethiopia was a protracted and ambiguous process involving both domestic and international factors. The principal catalysts were the League of Nations, the Italian invasion and occupation from 1935 to 1941, Emperor Haile Selassie, and an undulating political economy within Ethiopia.

Ethiopia is a hybrid nation, geographically situated between Negroid and Caucasoid peoples. Ethiopians are descendants of immigrants from Saudi Arabia, the earliest inhabitants of the high plateau, and the Negroid people of the south, west, and east. The people are predominantly, within a linguistic context, Amharic and Tigreanic speakers, related to Semitic language groups. There are about one hundred other linguistic groups. About half of the Ethiopian population belongs to the Coptic Christian Church. The remaining population is mostly Muslim, with a fairly small number of rural people practicing animism. The total population in 1991 was approximately 30 million.

The Amharas, Tigreans, Gallas, Somalis, and Danakils are different from Negro Africans. They are dark brown in complexion and have caucasian features, in particular, narrow noses and "straight" hair. It is not entirely clear what role color or complexion played in social status and in slavery. In all probability, color prejudice was important in determining servile status of people. Nevertheless, the political economy, in the original sense of that term, in Ethiopia enveloped several socio-economic fundamentals.

Historically, Ethiopian emperors had partial control over the country; the princes and nobles, or *ras*, were landowners who were able to exploit much of the land under a system called *gabar*, which was a form of serfdom. *Gabar* was a system both of rents and of tribute to landlords and local nobles.

Slavery was an important economic component of social life. It harmonized with a configuration of ancient traditions benefiting both the local aristocracy and small farmers. Those who owned land inevitably owned human beings who worked on large fruit and coffee plantations, in the gold mines in the Adowa region, and, especially in northern Ethiopia, in subsistence households producing cereals and pulses and raising livestock.

Ethiopian imperial officials wanted to create a centralized and modern state which could present itself to the world as a "civilized" country. Emperor Menelik II despised the slave trade in particular, because it depicted Ethiopia as a backward country. Menelik undertook to limit or abolish the slave trade through imperial decrees before 1907, but without measurable results. His opposition to the slave trade figured in civil strife between 1907 and his demise in 1913. The slave trade was a curious issue for the government to challenge, as it simultaneously refused to admit or oppose the institution of slavery which made the slave trade possible.

*Ras* Tafari became head of government in 1916, as regent of Empress Zauditu, Menelik's daughter. He did little to limit the growth of the slave trade or the institution of slavery. Slavery was a manifestation of local landlord prerogatives and, therefore, any real effort by central government to challenge slavery would have quickly encouraged state disintegration.

*Ras* Tafari, the future Emperor Haile Selassie, was one of three regents who tried to gain admission of Ethiopia to the League of Nations. The United Kingdom, Italy, and other members of the League opposed Ethiopia's entry because the slave trade and slavery were still practiced in Ethiopia. Slave raids were especially offensive to the British, since slave raiders crossed into British colonies. The United Kingdom's long-standing opposition to the slave trade was a major reason for its interest in questioning the independence status of Ethiopia. The British government believed in the "white man's burden" of "civilizing" what it perceived to be backward cultures. British territorial ambitions, in any case, should not be discounted. After many pledges to abolish the slave trade and slavery, Ethiopia was admitted to the League of Nations in 1923, with France as its main supporter.

The imperial government of Ethiopia passed a law in 1923, to satisfy the League of Nations' insistence that Ethiopia abolish slavery, prohibiting slave raiding across international borders. Another imperial proclamation on March 31, 1924, declared that slaves born into slavery after the date of the proclamation should be freed upon the death of their master; however, the ex-slaves must remain with the family for seven years. This law and others were powerless in actually liberating slaves.

The several proclamations were aimed at an international audience, namely, the member states of the League of Nations. Ethiopia was trying to maintain its independence within a sea of European colonialism. It is incorrect to claim that Ethiopia abolished slavery in 1924. It did not: It only made public gestures in that direction. The reality of attaining abolition would be arduous and protracted.

Haile Selassie became emperor in 1930 after the death of Zauditu. He began to transfer more political authority from local, hereditary potentates to the imperial government in Addis Ababa. Emperor Haile Selassie accepted a Briton as his adviser on slavery, Frank de Halpert. De Halpert directed the antislavery bureau and guided antislavery legislation. In 1931, an imperial edict required the registration of slaves and the manumission of slaves upon the master's death. Haile Selassie vowed that slavery would end in fifteen or twenty years. De Halpert did not believe that the emperor was truly committed to abolishing the slave trade or slavery; he resigned as adviser to the emperor on antislavery matters in 1933.

Italians represented themselves as civilizers and Ethiopians as slavers and barbarians. This explanation was used to justify Italian aggression against the Ethiopian empire in 1935. Italy took control of Ethiopia in 1936 and announced the liberation of 400,000 slaves in areas under its military control. Despite the Italians' claim, slavery continued to exist in areas under their control. The Italian government paid Ethiopian workers but did not pursue a consistent program to liberate slaves.

Italian occupation, however, did have a salutary effect on the political economy of Ethiopia. The *gabar* system of tenancy was at least damaged by allowing many tenant farmers to escape an oppressive serfdom which differed little from outright slavery. Italian rule, in short, undermined serfdom and weakened the institution of slavery itself. In no way, however, should it be construed that blatant military aggression by the Italians was designed to do anything other than satiate Benito Mussolini's desire to create an Italian empire. Italian occupation simply eroded a servile labor system and served the needs of the Italian propaganda apparatus. The Italians built roads and generally improved the infrastructure of their controlled areas, but Ethiopia was never under complete Italian military control.

After the Allies invaded Ethiopia, Haile Selassie had little choice but to reinforce his earlier attempts to abolish the slave trade and finally to end slavery itself. The British were not prepared to restore Haile Selassie to his throne unconditionally. The emperor had to prove to them that he was going to rid Ethiopia of slavery. Haile Selassie had consistently demonstrated his disdain for slavery but was timid in confronting the political risks involved with an outright assault on the practice.

On November 11, 1941, Haile Selassie abolished the *gabar* form of tenancy. This was an important step toward the abolition of slavery. The *gabar* system of tenancy was a kind of extortion, including a tithe to the emperor, forced requisitions of grain or firewood, porterage, and other forms of labor obligations.

On August 27, 1942, Emperor Haile Selassie issued the proclamation to abolish slavery in Ethiopia. It repeated the two main anti-slavery measures of the 1930's. The proclamation accepted the 1926 convention's definition of slavery as any form of servile labor against the will of the individual, and it called for the immediate abolition of the legal status of slavery. The death penalty was allowed (but unlikely) for transporting slaves and for participating in the slave trade. The weakness of the proclamation was that it placed the responsibility for enforcement of the law on local courts, courts that were controlled by slaveowners, the nobility, and smallholders. Alternative forms of punishment included forty lashes, a $10,000 fine, or a maximum of twenty years in a local jail.

## Impact of Event

The 1942 proclamation was a landmark in Ethiopian history. Its goals, however, took a long time to achieve in practice. Haile Selassie did not seriously alter the political economy of Ethiopia as it pertained to slavery or any other major component of the body politic. He did start a process toward realization of human rights. It is not too farfetched to compare Haile Selassie's accomplishments with those of U.S. president Abraham Lincoln. Lincoln issued the Emancipation Proclamation, but how effective was it? In the short term, it was ineffective, but in time the institutions of slavery and sharecropping were extinguished. Nevertheless, in both cases a process of liberation and enfranchisement was begun.

Reports of slave raiding in the 1950's were plentiful. The Annual Report of the Anti-Slavery Society for 1954-1955 told of escaped slaves from Ethiopia fleeing to the Sudan, with their masters in hot pursuit. Ethiopians and Europeans were still engaged in a flourishing slave trade in the 1960's between Ethiopia and Saudi Arabia. There was continued ambiguity in the socioeconomic situation in Ethiopia as it pertained to slavery. A raised consciousness about human rights and individual liberties in Africa gave some hope that countries might soon understand the significance of respecting the dignity and individual liberties of human beings. In the Ethiopian case, the 1942 proclamation was an incipient step taken toward abolishing slavery and morally challenging the legitimacy of it.

Much more can be done and must be done in behalf of servile laborers. The question of the status of servants in Africa, even fifty years later, needed clarification before the vestiges of slavery could be eradicated. The 1942 proclamation was a simple prescription for a highly complex social issue. The approach taken was, perhaps, the only one available. The path to abolition of slavery in Ethiopia was to abolish its legal status in the hope that reality would then follow.

## Bibliography

Derrick, Jonathan. *Africa's Slaves Today.* New York: Schocken Books, 1975. Examines the custom of human slavery in its various forms. This is both a fascinating and an exhaustive study. Slavery in twentieth century Africa is described as indistinct from other forms of labor.

Manning, Patrick. *Slavery and African Life: Occidental, Oriental, and African Slave Trades.* New York: Cambridge University Press, 1990. A contextual view of the various factors which helped to shape the forms of the slave trade. African slaves were found in many unlikely places. The nineteenth century notion, carried into the twentieth century, that slavery was benign is powerfully debunked by the cruelty of the trade.

Marcus, Harold G. *The Life and Times of Menelik II: 1844-1913.* Oxford, England: Clarendon Press, 1975. Describes the expansion of Ethiopia to the south and east. These conquests drastically enlarged the supply of slaves and aided Ethiopia in maintaining itself as an independent state in the midst of European colonization.

Miers, Suzanne, and Richard Roberts, eds. *The End of Slavery in Africa.* Madison:

University of Wisconsin Press, 1988. The book's approach is sociological and some-what apologetic for slavery in Africa. It gives a panoramic sketch of slavery in Africa.

O'Callaghan, Sean. *The Slave Trade Today.* New York: Crown, 1961. An eyewitness account of slavery in Ethiopia and other African countries during the 1950's. The author witnessed a slave auction in Saudi Arabia. This personal account is valu-able for its passionate description of the brutal business of the slave trade.

Roberts, A. D., ed. *The Cambridge History of Africa, 1905-1940.* New York: Cam-bridge University Press, 1986. Pages 720-741 give a solid account of the domestic and foreign relations of Ethiopia. While the survey is rather sketchy, it reveals ar-cane bits and pieces of modern Ethiopian history. A good and quick background for any general reader interested in Ethiopia.

Robertson, Esmonde M. *Mussolini as Empire Builder: Europe and Africa, 1932-1936.* New York: Macmillan, 1977. Covers Mussolini's invasion of Ethiopia and highlights his justification for conquest, the liberation of slaves. In truth, Italy wanted to repay Ethiopia for its ignominious military defeat at Adowa in the 1895-1896 Italo-Ethiopian war.

Sawyer, Roger. *Slavery in the Twentieth Century.* New York: Routledge & Kegan Paul, 1986. An account of slavery throughout the Third World and Europe. It defines and illustrates numerous forms of servile labor, including the exploitation of women and children.

Ullendorff, E., ed. and trans. *My Life and Ethiopia's Progress, 1892-1937: The Auto-biography of Haile Selassie I.* London: Oxford University Press, 1976. A worth-while book, even though self-serving. Haile Selassie's views clash with reality.

*Claude Hargrove*

## Cross-References

International Agreement Attacks the White Slave Trade (1904), p. 30; "Palmer Raids" Lead to Arrests and Deportations of Immigrants (1919), p. 258; The League of Nations Adopts the International Slavery Convention (1926), p. 436; The United Nations Adopts the Universal Declaration of Human Rights (1948), p. 789; The United Nations Amends Its International Slavery Convention (1953), p. 902; Con-gress Passes the Civil Rights Act (1964), p. 1251; The U.N. Covenant on Civil and Political Rights Is Adopted (1966), p. 1353; The Helsinki Agreement Offers Terms for International Cooperation (1975), p. 1806; Carter Makes Human Rights a Central Theme of Foreign Policy (1977), p. 1903.

# SOVIETS TAKE CONTROL OF EASTERN EUROPE

*Categories of event:* Political freedom and indigenous peoples' rights
*Time:* 1943-1948
*Locale:* Eastern Europe

*Between 1943 and 1948, the Soviet Union established a satellite zone in Eastern Europe within which it dramatically altered political boundaries and established Soviet-dominated totalitarian political systems*

*Principal personages:*
> JOSEPH STALIN (1879-1953), the general secretary of the Communist Party of the Soviet Union
> FRANKLIN D. ROOSEVELT (1882-1945), the thirty-second president of the United States (1933-1945)
> WINSTON CHURCHILL (1874-1965), the British prime minister (1940-1945 and 1951-1955)

## Summary of Event

The Soviet takeover of Eastern Europe was the product of a protracted series of events extending from 1943 to 1948. Soviet actions were grounded in Moscow's definition of its regional interests, as interpreted by Kremlin leaders during and immediately after World War II. At a minimum, the Soviets hoped to ensure that Eastern Europe would never again be used as a base for hostile action against the Union of Soviet Socialist Republics. At maximum, the Soviets hoped to control the region actively, thereby permitting them to draw upon the region's economic resources and strategic geographical characteristics, thus strengthening the defense of the Soviet Union and promoting its postwar economic recovery. Active control over Eastern Europe would also provide the Soviets with a base for possible future expansion into other areas of Europe.

The Soviet leadership based its specific objectives in Eastern Europe on this general definition of its regional interests. As their first objective, the Soviets insisted upon de facto and, if possible, de jure international acceptance of their annexation of Latvia, Lithuania, Estonia, portions of Finland, the eastern portion of pre-1939 Poland, Bessarabia, and Northern Bukovina which had occurred during the Nazi-Soviet Non-Aggression Pact period (August 23, 1939-June 22, 1941). Second, they hoped to establish a postwar Poland within reconfigured boundaries, governed by a regime acceptable to, and optimally subservient to, the Soviet Union. Third, the Soviet leaders sought to establish acceptable and again, if possible, subservient regimes in Rumania and Bulgaria. Fourth, Moscow wanted to incorporate the easternmost portion of prewar Czechoslovakia, the Carpatho-Ukraine, into the Soviet Union.

Beyond these areas immediately contiguous to the pre-1939 Soviet Union, Moscow sought, at a minimum, to establish buffer states in postwar Czechoslovakia, Hungary, Yugoslavia, and Albania. Moscow intended that these states be governed by friendly regimes but also influenced to some degree by the Western powers. At a maximum, the Soviets hoped that these states could be transformed into satellites similar to the type Poland, Rumania, and Bulgaria were intended to be. With respect to defeated Germany, the Soviets sought to divide East Prussia between the Soviet Union and postwar Poland, further compensate Poland for the loss of its prewar eastern territories with prewar German Silesia and Pomerania (up to the Oder and Neisse Rivers), and establish a Soviet occupation zone in a portion of the remaining German territory. Finally, of peripheral importance in the hierarchy of Moscow's European objectives, the Soviets were alert to any opportunities that might develop in Europe that could enhance their position on the continent.

The Soviets formulated a multifaceted policy in their effort to attain these objectives. Their actions were, in turn, reinforced by the Red Army as it gradually advanced into Eastern and Central Europe. By the conclusion of the European war, the Soviets were in physical possession of those territories which they sought to dominate in the postwar era.

The first component of Soviet policy was Moscow's persistent effort to obtain British and American approval of, or at least acquiescence to, its self-proclaimed dominant role in determining the postwar character of Eastern Europe. Toward that end, one of the first steps was taken at the Teheran Conference in November, 1943. Here, U.S. President Franklin Roosevelt, British Prime Minister Winston Churchill, and Soviet leader Joseph Stalin agreed to define Poland's eastern boundary along the lines insisted upon by the Soviet Union and to redefine Poland's other boundaries at the expense of prewar Germany (establishing Poland's new western boundary along the Oder and Neisse Rivers). Following the Teheran Conference, the Western powers progressively accepted the Soviet position that Poland's postwar government should, at least, not be objectionable to the Soviet Union. Meanwhile, as the Red Army advanced into Eastern Europe, the Soviet Union reinforced its claim to postwar regional dominance via the armistice terms concluded with Rumania in August, 1944, Bulgaria in September, 1944, and Hungary in January, 1945. These terms gave the Soviet military predominance in politico-military affairs in the affected states.

In an effort to delimit the proportion of Soviet versus Western influence in southeastern Europe, Churchill visited Moscow on October 9, 1944, and concluded the so-called percentages agreement with Stalin. Under the terms of the agreement, the Soviet Union was to have ninety percent predominance in Rumania versus the West's ten percent. In Greece, the percentages were to be reversed. In Bulgaria, the Soviets were to have seventy-five percent predominance, with the West having twenty-five percent. Finally, in Yugoslavia and Hungary, the Soviet Union and the West would share equally. While Churchill apparently interpreted this arrangement as a mechanism for determining the orientation of the foreign and defense policies of the relevant states, Stalin viewed the delimitation to mean that the Soviet Union would, in the totalitarian manner of the Stalinist system, determine all aspects of domestic and foreign affairs within its future satellites.

The Yalta Conference further formalized the establishment of Soviet control over Eastern Europe. On one hand, the three Great Powers agreed to assist the liberated Europeans to establish democratic, broadly based provisional governments and to hold free elections as early as possible. In practice, however, it was the Soviet Union that determined when the proposed elections would be held and which elements of society were eligible to participate. Indeed, with respect to Poland, the Soviets obtained Western agreement that the core of Poland's postwar government would be composed of individuals selected by Moscow. Moreover, throughout Eastern Europe, the proposed elections would be held in the shadow of the Red Army. As to the location of Poland's western boundary, the British and Americans favored the eastern Neisse River, whereas the Soviets preferred the western Neisse. By establishing the western Neisse as the boundary, Poland would acquire territory which had long been ethnically German and, as such, some six to seven million Germans would be displaced. From Moscow's perspective, however, the western Neisse was preferable because of geostrategic considerations, the opportunity it would provide to resettle Poles in new lands, and the implication that Polish acquisition of these territories would further cement ties between postwar Poland and the Soviet Union against any future resurgent German regime seeking to recover these lost territories. The boundary question was left vague at Yalta, but the Soviets, British, and Americans agreed to the western Neisse line at the Potsdam Conference in July, 1945, pending a final solution at a general peace conference. The three powers also agreed at Potsdam that Danzig and the southern portion of East Prussia would be placed under Polish administration, with the Soviet Union acquiring the northern portion of East Prussia. In short, through a series of agreements among the wartime allies, the Soviet Union obtained the acquiescence, if not enthusiastic endorsement, of the British and Americans to the establishment of a Soviet sphere of influence in Eastern Europe.

The second element of the Soviet effort to establish control over Eastern Europe, implemented simultaneously with the first, was the wartime isolation and elimination of those elements in Eastern Europe who presented a possible challenge to postwar Soviet domination. For example, with respect to Poland, as early as the spring of 1940 the Soviets killed some fifteen thousand captured Polish army officers and buried them in mass graves in the Katyn forest near Smolensk. This atrocity deprived Poland of many who might have made valuable contributions to the restoration of a postwar independent Poland. Similarly, during the war the Soviet Union isolated the "official" Polish government-in-exile, located in London. Instead, the Soviets sponsored their own Committee of National Liberation. As Soviet forces moved onto Polish soil, Soviet officials transferred local administration to this body rather than to representatives of the "London Poles." As for the latter, they were increasingly encouraged to break with the government-in-exile and join the Soviet-sponsored provisional government. Finally, the Soviets further reduced the prospect of postwar indigenous Polish resistance to the Soviet satellization of Poland by refusing to assist the Polish underground uprising which took place in Warsaw between

August 1 and early October, 1944. Soviet forces remained inert as the Germans crushed the resistance and destroyed the city of Warsaw.

Following the war, the Soviets completed their takeover of Eastern Europe by placing their candidates in positions of dominance within all the postwar Eastern European governments. Although the specific pattern of takeover varied with each country, depending upon the individual political climate, in general the Soviets followed a similar approach in the seizure of power. First, the indigenous Communist elements joined forces with the non-Communist parties to form a "patriotic" or "national" front. Second, often the left-wing elements merged with the Communist Party to form a new, broader, leftist party. Third, the right-wing and centrist parties were increasingly isolated, often with some of their leaders being brought to trial and others being forced abroad. Fourth, as the governmental structures, particularly the security operations, became increasingly dominated by Communists, elections were held with a single list of candidates. Following these elections, new Communist governments were formed and individuals not acceptable to Moscow were purged. The remaining monarchies of Eastern Europe were abolished and the postwar governments either ratified Moscow's pre-1941 territorial acquisitions or formally ceded new territory to the Soviet Union, as was the case with Czechoslovakia's cession of the Carpatho-Ukraine.

The timing of these takeovers and the sequence of events varied among the Eastern European countries. In Yugoslavia and Albania, the Communists dominated from the time of liberation as a result of their partisan struggle against German occupation. In Bulgaria and Rumania, the non-Communists were ousted from the coalition government during the spring and summer of 1945 and, by 1947, the takeover was complete. The Polish Communists dominated their postwar government from the liberation onward but did not complete their takeover until early 1947. Finally, in Czechoslovakia and Hungary, the process was completed in 1948.

## Impact of Event

The Communist takeovers throughout Eastern Europe led to the establishment of socioeconomic and political systems patterned after the Stalinist totalitarianism of the Soviet Union. The characteristics of that system were a monopoly over all political power by the Communist Party which, in all cases, represented only a very small minority of the population; an all-pervasive, coercive secret police which, along with the military, monopolized all combat weapons; large-scale use of the mass media as an instrument for popular socialization along lines desired by the ruling party; and abolition of a market economy based upon free enterprise and private ownership in favor of a centrally planned economy, state ownership of industry, and collectivized agriculture. In the largest sense, the boundaries between the public and private spheres were effectively erased, with all aspects of life becoming matters of state concern.

The human impact of such a transformation was enormous, even for people already reeling from nearly a decade of war. For example, in the countryside, millions of farmers, many of whom had only recently benefited from the breakup of large estates and the land redistribution and resettlement policies initially sponsored by the Communists during the takeover process, were now forced into state-controlled collective farms. Those who resisted were sent to forced labor camps or killed. In industry, trade unions, often only recently introduced, were transformed into instruments through which the regime could enforce worker discipline. Workers were severely punished for tardiness, slackness, or disruptiveness. With respect to professionals, such as engineers, doctors, and teachers, the regime used a mixture of incentives and threats to secure cooperation. The educational process was of particular interest to the new regimes. Political messages were regularly but often subtly blended with other elements of the curriculum and reinforced after school hours by the activities of officially sponsored youth organizations. Predictably, intellectual freedom was severely curtailed, with draconian penalties enforced against those expressing "reactionary" or "counterrevolutionary" ideas. Finally, to one degree or another, the Communist regimes in all the Eastern European countries persecuted the church, recognizing that religion represented a powerful challenge to the official ideology and that, institutionally, the churches presented a dangerous challenge to monopolistic rule by the Communist Party. Leading church officials in many countries were arrested and tried for conspiracy against the state.

In the Atlantic Charter of 1941, President Roosevelt and Prime Minister Churchill had stated their opposition to territorial changes without the consent of the peoples affected and their support for the principle of democratically elected governments. Contrary to this, vast areas of Eastern Europe were permanently transferred to the Soviet Union or divided among the states of Eastern Europe, with millions of people displaced and without any regard for the wishes of the peoples concerned. Similarly, despite the desire of the Eastern Europeans for genuine postwar freedom and democracy after suffering the horror of total war and Nazi persecution, Eastern Europe fell victim to Soviet-dominated totalitarian dictatorships that trampled on human rights. The spirit of resistance, however, continued to flicker in the hearts of the Eastern Europeans and, over the next forty years, it would periodically burst forth, only to be ruthlessly crushed by the Communist authorities. At the end of the 1980's, resistance yielded the successive overthrow of some of the Communist regimes of Eastern Europe, and the region entered a new era of history.

## Bibliography

Black, C. E., and H. C. Helmreich. *Twentieth Century Europe: A History.* 4th ed. New York: Alfred A. Knopf, 1972. An excellent general overview of the development of Europe from 1900 to 1972, with six chapters dedicated exclusively to the twentieth century history of the Soviet Union and the states of Eastern Europe.

Brzezinski, Zbigniew K. *The Soviet Block: Unity and Conflict.* 2d ed. Cambridge, Mass.: Harvard University Press, 1967. An examination of the establishment and evolution of the Soviet bloc in Eastern Europe as it passed through a series of phases from 1945 to 1965.

Feis, Herbert. *Churchill, Roosevelt, Stalin: The War They Waged and the Peace They Sought.* Princeton, N.J.: Princeton University Press, 1967. A detailed examination of the wartime diplomacy of the Soviet Union, the United States, and Great Britain from the outset of the Grand Coalition in 1941 to the conclusion of the war in Europe in the spring of 1945.

——————————. *Between War and Peace: The Potsdam Conference.* Princeton, N.J.: Princeton University Press, 1960. A continuation of Feis's definitive study, *Churchill, Roosevelt, Stalin* (see above), covering Grand Coalition diplomacy from the spring through the summer of 1945.

Hammond, Thomas T., ed. *The Anatomy of Communist Takeovers.* New Haven, Conn.: Yale University Press, 1975. An anthology of histories of communist takeovers, with nine excellent chapters dedicated to the post-World War II takeovers in Eastern Europe.

Korbel, Josef. *The Communist Subversion of Czechoslovakia: 1938-1948.* Princeton, N.J.: Princeton University Press, 1959. A history of the communist takeover in Czechoslovakia, tracing the process from the prewar period to the final takeover in 1948.

Seton-Watson, Hugh. *The East European Revolution.* 3d ed. New York: Praeger, 1956. A sequel to Seton-Watson's monumental study of Eastern Europe prior to World War II (*East Europe Between the Wars,* 1962), covering the postwar period of the communist takeovers and their aftermath through the death of Stalin in 1953.

Ulam, Adam B. *Expansion and Coexistence: Soviet Foreign Policy, 1917-73.* 2d ed. New York: Praeger, 1974. One of the basic histories of Soviet foreign policy from the Revolution of 1917 to the mid-1970's, with two chapters dedicated to the Soviet Union's wartime diplomacy.

*Howard M. Hensel*

## Cross-References

The Baltic States Fight for Independence (1917), p. 207; The Atlantic Charter Declares a Postwar Right of Self-Determination (1941), p. 584; The Berlin Wall Is Built (1961), p. 1125; The Brezhnev Doctrine Bans Acts of Independence in Soviet Satellites (1968), p. 1408; Soviets Invade Czechoslovakia (1968), p. 1441; The Helsinki Agreement Offers Terms for International Cooperation (1975), p. 1806; Poland Imposes Martial Law and Outlaws Solidarity (1981), p. 2152; Gorbachev Initiates a Policy of *Glasnost* (1985), p. 2249; Hungary Adopts a Multiparty System (1989), p. 2421; Solidarity Regains Legal Status in Poland (1989), p. 2477; Poland Forms a Non-Communist Government (1989), p. 2500; Ceausescu Is Overthrown in Romania (1989), p. 2546; Soviet Troops Withdraw from Czechoslovakia (1990), p. 2570; Lithuania Declares Its Independence from the Soviet Union (1990), p. 2577.

# CORE STAGES A SIT-IN IN CHICAGO
# TO PROTEST SEGREGATION

*Category of event:* Racial and ethnic rights
*Time:* May-June, 1943
*Locale:* Chicago, Illinois

*CORE's first sit-in demonstrations in Chicago in 1943 were intended to change the attitudes of business owners and thus differed from the sit-ins of the 1960's; they were, however, important precedents for the later sit-in movement*

*Principal personages:*
> JAMES FARMER (1920-    ), a principal founder of the Congress of Racial Equality (CORE) and a key organizer of the 1943 sit-ins
> BAYARD RUSTIN (1910-1987), an influential civil rights activist affiliated with CORE and the Fellowship of Reconciliation (FOR)
> GEORGE M. HOUSER (1916-    ), a white civil rights activist in FOR and CORE, one of the organizers of the 1943 sit-ins

## Summary of Event

Still in its first year when it launched the 1943 sit-ins in Chicago, the Congress of Racial Equity (CORE) had more enthusiasm for Gandhian nonviolent methods than experience with them. The Chicago Committee of Racial Equality that developed into CORE was founded in 1942, chiefly by James Farmer, Bernice Fisher, Homer Jack, George M. Houser, Joe Guinn, and James R. Robinson, all students in Chicago. This biracial group was headed by Farmer, one of two African Americans among the major founders. Farmer was a theology student whose father was a professor at Wiley College in Texas, and he was deeply interested in Christian pacifism. As a staff member of the Fellowship of Reconciliation (FOR), like Houser, Farmer wanted to apply Gandhian and Christian ideals to society with a view toward creating harmony and mutual respect among all races and classes.

This kind of social vision informed those who experimented with the sit-in technique in Chicago. In retrospect, Farmer has written, their early efforts there were idealistic. They hoped to change the minds of the restaurant owners and were "childishly literal-minded." They were not insistent that they be given access to public facilities on the basis of law but tried to convince their resisters that access would be good for business.

The 1943 sit-ins were months in the making. CORE's earliest efforts to combat racial discrimination in Chicago were undertaken on a broad front: the university barber shop (which refused in November, 1942, to cut Bayard Rustin's hair), the medical school and the hospital, even the roller rink. By the end of 1942, CORE's attention was increasingly focused on restaurants that refused to serve blacks. Two such restaurants were the Jack Spratt Restaurant near CORE Fellowship House and Stoner's Restaurant, a downtown establishment in the Loop that served chiefly an upper-middle-class clientele.

CORE first learned of racial discrimination at Stoner's in October, 1942, when three of its members (one of them black) were refused service by the owner himself. During the following five months, CORE gathered information at these two restaurants, attempting to comply with the Gandhian strategy that called for careful investigation to determine whether there was undeniable evidence of discrimination before proceeding to direct action. Interracial test groups were sent both to Stoner's and to Jack Spratt's. Sometimes the groups were served, but after a long period of waiting. On some occasions, they were served food that was overly salted or laced with broken eggshells. By December, 1942, CORE was sufficiently convinced of discrimination to spend a full week distributing to customers leaflets that pointed out the evidence and asked customers to protest against it as they paid their bills.

Some Chicago residents began to question CORE's pressure on Stoner's Restaurant, and as a result Houser and other CORE leaders decided to survey dozens of other Loop restaurants to determine whether Stoner's policy was typical or an exception to prevailing practices. The study showed that virtually all Loop eating establishments operated on a nondiscriminatory basis. CORE published the results in a pamphlet entitled "50 Loop Restaurants That Do Not Discriminate." CORE distributed this pamphlet to various groups, both white and black, and sent a copy to Stoner's management. Further efforts to desegregate the restaurant by test groups failed, and by January, 1943, Houser, Farmer, and other CORE officials were debating the possibility of direct action.

In March, 1943, CORE leaders considered staging what it called a sit-down, in which participants would occupy seats until served, at Stoner's. They decided against it after considering the logistical difficulties involved in a small group's efforts to gain meaningful attention in a two-hundred-seat restaurant. The project was delayed until June to coincide with CORE's first national convention, which would bring several direct action groups into Chicago and thus provide enough people to increase the chances of success. In May, however, CORE led a smaller sit-in operation at Jack Spratt's.

The sit-in at Jack Spratt's involved twenty-one CORE members, most of them white. The group entered the restaurant at the dinner hour on May 14, 1943, and refused to eat until the blacks among them were served. Police officers were called, but they found they could do nothing to disperse the participants in the sit-in. Within two hours, the management of Jack Spratt's decided to serve all of the group, and in that sense the sit-in was a success. It was not clear whether such a demonstration would work at the larger Stoner's Restaurant, but the experience at Jack Spratt's encouraged CORE to follow through with the plans for a June sit-in there.

The sit-in at Stoner's Restaurant involved more than three times the number of participants. Some sixty-five people, sixteen of them African American, sat in at Stoner's during the evening meal on Saturday, June 5. Around 4:30 P.M. white demonstration participants entered the restaurant in groups of two, three, and four. They were readily seated. When the first of the two interracial groups entered shortly after 5:00 P.M., the six blacks and two whites were ignored when they requested seats. After a half-hour wait, they were taken to a table and served. Houser reported that one of the white participants was kicked in the leg by the restaurant owner as the group passed.

As the first interracial group was seated, the second entered. Its nine African Americans and one white person were refused service and threatened, but they stood near the entrance for more than ninety minutes. The police were called three times but saw no cause for making arrests since the group was orderly. After the third call, the police officers instructed the restaurant owner not to call again unless there was a compelling reason. Encouraged by expressions of sympathy from some of the restaurant staff, the interracial group stood quietly, refusing to budge. Other customers in the restaurant expressed support, and several of the black employees threatened to quit if the group was not served. CORE members pledged to stay all night if necessary.

Eventually, the deadlock was broken when an elderly white woman who was not involved with CORE invited one of the black women in the group to sit at her table. The white CORE participants who were already seated followed her example and invited the unseated group to join them. When only two were left standing, one of the hostesses approached them and invited them to follow her to a small table at the center of the restaurant. With that, applause broke out across Stoner's Restaurant. For several minutes, a spontaneous demonstration of support changed the tense atmosphere to one of relief.

## Impact of Event

The CORE-sponsored sit-ins of May and June, 1943, in Chicago, were less dramatic and received far less press coverage than the sit-ins of the early 1960's. Their historic significance has, however, been recognized. Considered the first sit-in of the modern Civil Rights movement in the United States they served as examples for later sit-ins conducted by the National Association for the Advancement of Colored People (NAACP) and for the massive wave of sit-ins triggered by an incident at Woolworth's lunch counter in Greensboro, North Carolina, in February, 1960.

To the leaders of the 1943 sit-ins, the results were gratifying. Virtually no violence resulted, and the response from white people who observed the demonstration was generally very supportive. CORE leader Houser considered it a "well executed nonviolent demonstration for racial justice." The racial discrimination of Stoner's Restaurant continued unevenly throughout the war years, but by 1946 interracial groups were served without resistance.

For CORE, the experience confirmed the viability of the Gandhian methods to which it was committed. The Gandhian model called for investigation, early efforts at negotiation, firm expression of determination, personal spiritual preparation, and, if necessary, nonviolent direct action. CORE followed those steps meticulously in

Chicago and was reinforced in its belief in the effectiveness of such an approach. James Farmer, the best known of the early CORE leaders, was convinced that the 1943 sit-ins strengthened CORE's resolve and heightened its influence. The sit-in at Stoner's coincided with CORE's first national convention, bringing groups from nine cities together; out of this convention grew the beginnings of national organizational affiliation known collectively as the Congress of Racial Equality (1944). The broadened organization's "Statement of Purpose and Action Discipline" clearly committed it to nonviolent direct action and the elimination of all racial discrimination and segregation. The Chicago experience was one of the specific examples of success to which the organization could point in future years and from which it could draw inspiration.

CORE soon began to sponsor training workshops to promulgate the principles of nonviolence and to train people in its techniques. Regional organizational subdivisions linked the national office with local affiliated committees. In that way, CORE retained a democratic structure while offering guidance and personnel for various campaigns. The Chicago experience continued to provide a point of reference demonstrating that collective nonviolent action could produce results.

## Bibliography

Broderick, Francis L., and August Meier, eds. *Negro Protest Thought in the Twentieth Century.* Indianapolis: Bobbs-Merrill, 1965. This compendium of major documents on African-American protest efforts includes valuable information on the founding of CORE and its early nonviolent direct action campaigns. James Farmer's philosophy of nonviolent social change is reflected, as are incidents at Stoner's Restaurant that led to the first CORE sit-in in 1943. Contains vivid summaries of the historical setting and an index.

Farmer, James. *Freedom, When?* New York: Random House, 1965. An insightful study by one of CORE's principal founders. Farmer's account is uniquely valuable for providing insight into the motivations, dreams, problems, and experiences of the mostly young activists who spearheaded racial desegregation in the United States. He describes conditions of blacks before the Civil Rights movement of the 1960's and analyzes his own and others' goals, the emergence of black nationalism, and the continuing need for reform. Farmer avoids a sanguine or idealistic vision of the future, projecting instead a long struggle for freedom. Includes a table of contents.

Hentoff, Nat. *Peace Agitator.* New York: Macmillan, 1963. A. J. Muste was a ubiquitous influence on pacifism, nonviolence, and social reform movements in the United States for several decades. The value of Hentoff's study is its focus on Muste's outreach in shaping people like James Farmer and eventually Martin Luther King, Jr.—to the extent that Muste's arguments against violence and war contributed to their nonviolent methods of social change. Scholarly in tone, the book is not documented but has numerous quotations and a detailed index.

Houser, George M. *Erasing the Color Line.* 3d rev. ed. New York: Fellowship Publications, 1951. Originally published in 1945, this personal account by Houser complements Farmer's and Peck's. Beginning with descriptions of the problems faced by African Americans, he presents specific analyses of challenges faced in restaurants, service shops, swimming pools, housing situations, and prisons. Houser also discusses discrimination in employment and ends with his views on nonviolence. His accounts of racial discrimination include many tangible examples of nonviolent protest. This short booklet is without notes or bibliography, but has a table of contents and frequent chapter subdivisions to guide the reader.

Meier, August, and Elliott Rudwick. *CORE: A Study in the Civil Rights Movement.* New York: Oxford University Press, 1973. The most comprehensive and thoroughly researched of the books on CORE, this survey is a detailed account of its background, founding, and development. A scholarly book, it includes detailed references to primary and secondary material and analyzes objectively the successes and failures of CORE from its beginning in 1942 until the onset of its decline in the late 1960's. It is especially valuable for noting the Gandhian philosophy and techniques of CORE from 1942 to the 1960's. Contains elaborate notes, a useful note on sources, and an index.

Peck, James. *Freedom Ride.* New York: Simon & Schuster, 1962. Although chiefly about the 1947 "Journey of Reconciliation" and the 1961 freedom rides, Peck's account is indispensable for an insider's perspective on the nature and distinctive challenges of CORE's early efforts to counter racism and segregation in the United States. Many accounts of jailings, beatings, and moments of hope and discouragement are included. His account is not scholarly in the conventional sense and contains no notes or bibliography.

Schmeidler, Emilie. *Shaping Ideas and Actions: CORE, SCLC, and SNCC in the Struggle for Equality, 1960-1966.* Ann Arbor, Mich.: University Microfilms International, 1983. An analytical study focusing on three of the major activist organizations of the Civil Rights movement. Lacking in sufficient historical detail on specific campaigns, it nevertheless provides useful analyses of the protest models of CORE and other civil rights organizations and helps the reader understand their differences and similarities. CORE's pre-1960 direct action campaign, including the Chicago sit-ins and the "Journey of Reconciliation," are seen as important to the organization's self-image and social effectiveness as a Gandhian direct action entity. Contains notes and table of contents.

*Thomas R. Peake*

## Cross-References

Gandhi Leads a Noncooperation Movement (1920), p. 315; Roosevelt Outlaws Discrimination in Defense-Industry Employment (1941), p. 578; The Congress of Racial Equality Forms (1942), p. 601; Race Riots Erupt in Detroit and Harlem (1943), p. 635; CORE Stages the "Journey of Reconciliation" (1947), p. 718; Truman Orders Desegregation of U.S. Armed Forces (1948), p. 777; The SCLC Forms to Link Civil

Rights Groups (1957), p. 974; The Civil Rights Act of 1957 Creates the Commission on Civil Rights (1957), p. 997; Greensboro Sit-ins Launch a New Stage in the Civil Rights Movement (1960), p. 1056; Congress Passes the Civil Rights Act (1964), p. 1251.

# ZOOT-SUIT RIOTS EXEMPLIFY
# ETHNIC TENSIONS IN LOS ANGELES

*Category of event:* Racial and ethnic rights
*Time:* June 3-8, 1943
*Locale:* Los Angeles, California

*The zoot-suit riots made it clear that the two primary causes for the polarization of the Mexican-American and Anglo communities in Los Angeles were overt racism and tradition*

*Principal personages:*

CAREY McWILLIAMS (1905-1980), a prominent editor and chair of the Sleepy Lagoon Defense Committee

JACK TENNEY (1898-1970), the chair of the Tenney Committee, which investigated the Sleepy Lagoon case and the zoot-suit riots

FLETCHER BOWRON (1887-1968), the mayor of Los Angeles during the zoot-suit riots

EARL WARREN (1891-1974), the governor of California (1943-1953), later chief justice of the United States

JOSE DIAZ (?-1943), a Mexican-American youth who was murdered at the Sleepy Lagoon swimming hole in East Los Angeles

## Summary of Event

The events that culminated in the zoot-suit riots of 1943 cannot be traced to only one or two sources. A close examination of the social and political climate of Los Angeles in the early 1940's reveals that a combination of factors was responsible for the riots. All these factors, however, reflect the city's attitude toward minorities in general and, more specifically, the Mexican-American population of Los Angeles.

Fully expecting a sea attack from Japan after Pearl Harbor, military and civilian authorities in Los Angeles took a hard look at the activities of all minorities in the city. First, all Japanese were moved inland, away from the shoreline. This fear of subversive activities among the Japanese was extended to all minorities by a series of books that were widely read and discussed by people in Los Angeles in 1943. The paranoia generated by books such as Martin Dies's *The Trojan Horse in America* (1940) and Harold Lavine's *Fifth Column in America* (1940) led to the creation by the California State legislature of a joint senate-assembly committee to investigate communist, fascist, Nazi, and other foreign-dominated groups. The Mexican-American community became one of the objects of this growing fear of foreigners in 1942, when the Joint Fact-Finding Committee on Un-American Activities in California launched an investigation of the Sinarquistas, an anti-Communist society that had tried to influence politics in Mexico and was charged with perpetrating subversive activities in the barrios of Los Angeles. The hearings of this committee, which continued from 1940 until 1945, contributed to the city's xenophobic response to the Mexican-American community during the entire decade.

Another factor that cast Mexican Americans in a suspicious light was the American public's obsession with juvenile delinquency. Between 1942 and 1943, the Los Angeles press presented a highly distorted view of delinquency, focusing primarily on the activities of Mexican gangs. Many of these gangs adopted the *pachuco* lifestyle, which was essentially a generational rebellion against both Mexican and American cultures. Not only did these gangs adhere to traditionally violent methods of settling disputes, but they also tried to underscore their identity by adopting the then-modern "zoot suit" form of dress. This bizarre fashion acquired insidious overtones as a result of a series of "Li'l Abner" comic strips entitled "Zoot-Suit Yokum" that appeared in newspapers nationwide between April 11, 1943, and May 23, 1943. In these strips, Al Capp attached conspiratorial machinations to the wearers of zoot suits, thereby labeling them as a potential threat to the American way of life. Essentially, then, the zoot suiters in Los Angeles came to be thought of in Los Angeles as the antithesis of everything that "real" Americans, like the servicemen, police, and politicians in the area, stood for.

The gang rivalry that occasionally erupted culminated in an incident that, with the help of the press, accentuated the criminality of Mexican-American youth. According to police accounts, a clash between the Belvedere gang and the Palo Verde gang in East Los Angeles on August 1, 1942, resulted in the slaying of a young Mexican-American named Jose Diaz, whose body was found beside a swimming hole called the Sleepy Lagoon. On January 13, 1943, seventeen reputed gang members were convicted of manslaughter and assault, even though the fact of a murder had never been established and a murder weapon had never been produced. All these convictions were overturned in 1944 because of the efforts of a fact-finding committee formed by magazine editor Carey McWilliams. Nevertheless, the publicity generated by the trial convinced many members of the Anglo community that the "Mexican problem" was a genuine menace to their welfare.

As a result of the Sleepy Lagoon case, Mexican-American youth became the focus of a widespread police investigation. During hearings that were begun in 1942 by the Tenney Committee, members of the police and sheriff's departments expounded the police theory that crime was a matter of race. In 1943, the Los Angeles County Grand Jury recommended that all delinquent and "pre-delinquent" Mexican-American youth be placed in special facilities. The 1943 grand jury also proposed denying juvenile court jurisdiction for participants in zoot suit gang offenses. By encouraging the police to redouble their efforts to control the Mexican-American gangs, this court action increased the resentment of the Mexican-American community. By this time, many Mexican Americans were convinced that the Los Angeles Police Department and the Anglo community in general had embarked on a systematic campaign to destroy their way of life.

The hostility between the Anglos and the Mexicans that had been enflamed by the press, city officials, and the police erupted into violence. On June 3, 1943, several off-duty police officers entered the Mexican district to look for zoot suiters who had attacked a group of sailors there. Because the police failed to apprehend the culprits, two hundred sailors cruised the Mexican district in a fleet of taxicabs on the following night, stopping periodically to beat lone zoot suiters. The sailors were followed by the police, who arrested the youths that had been singled out by the sailors. These outbreaks of violence continued from June 5 to June 8. On June 8, the Los Angeles City Council passed an ordinance making the wearing of zoot suits a misdemeanor. The riots ended after downtown Los Angeles was placed off-limits to military personnel on June 9.

An investigation by the Tenney Committee was begun immediately following the riots. The committee charged that the riots had been started by Communists who had sought to indoctrinate the zoot-suit-wearing *pachucos*. The committee's findings were refuted by Carey McWilliams. Speaking before the Committee on Un-American Activities in California, McWilliams placed the blame on the sailors who had been dating the girlfriends of the zoot suiters. He also contended that the riots were caused by racial prejudice, a point that was echoed by the African-American press.

## Impact of Event

Ironically, the zoot-suit riots were, to a great extent, a blessing in disguise for the minority communities of Los Angeles. To prevent a recurrence of the June confrontation, the Navy command in Los Angeles and Southern California and Mayor Fletcher Bowron of Los Angeles closely examined the conditions plaguing the city's minorities. Since the Navy had trouble determining the exact cause of the zoot-suit riots, it concentrated on the problems facing the African-American community. In a report dated July 29, 1943, both the Navy and various city officials agreed that discrimination against blacks was indeed being practiced in the areas of transportation, recreation, and housing. Even though the purpose of this study was to prevent a riot among black sailors, it set the stage for the activities of other civic committees by stating that discrimination was a serious problem in Los Angeles.

It was not until 1944 that a serious attempt was made to probe the cause of the zoot-suit riots. An investigative committee chaired by Carey McWilliams attempted to bring about a "return to sanity in Los Angeles." As a result of the meeting, Governor Earl Warren formed a citizens' committee to investigate the origin of the riots. Warren's committee concluded that not all Mexicans were zoot suiters and that the origin of the riots stemmed from the outbreak of juvenile delinquency in Los Angeles. The report and recommendations of the citizens' committee eventually led to the formation of the quarter-million-dollar Youth Project, which, in conjunction with the California Youth Authority, became one of the most effective means of handling juvenile delinquency in the city's history.

The Mexican-American community in Los Angeles benefited more directly from the formation of a legion of community organizations. By 1947, the Welfare Planning Council had affiliated these organizations to produce the Community Relations Conference of Southern California. Still active more than forty years later, this con-

ference assumed a pivotal role in ending racial segregation in public housing projects and in Los Angeles' fire department. The conference also helped the police
department establish a human relations course.

Of deeper significance than the creation of committees was the rehabilitation of
the image of individual young people of Mexican descent. Many Anglo-Americans
realized as they never had before that Americans of Hispanic descent had to be
brought into the mainstream of American life. In addition, many older Mexican
Americans who had previously rejected the *pachucos* saw that a reconciliation between the generations was needed to prevent another outbreak of violence. Conversely, many younger Mexican Americans realized that they had to make an aggressive effort to earn the approval of their elders by behaving in a manner that was
socially acceptable.

## Bibliography

Adler, Patricia Rae. "The 1943 Zoot-Suit Riots: Brief Episode in a Long Conflict."
In *An Awakened Minority: The Mexican-Americans*, edited by Manuel P. Servin.
Beverly Hills, Calif.: Glencoe Press, 1974. This article is the definitive account of
the zoot-suit riots. In addition to providing a day-by-day report of the riots themselves, the author clarifies both the causes and the effects of the violence.

Himes, Chester B. "Zoot Riots are Race Riots." *Crisis* 34 (July, 1943): 200-201.
This eyewitness account of the riots is valuable because of the author's detailed
observations. The article is enhanced by the inclusion of photographs. The author's lack of objectivity, however, tends to reduce his credibility.

Mazón, Mauricio. *The Zoot-Suit Riots*. Austin: University of Texas Press, 1984. This
fascinating book explores the psychological factors that contributed to the zoot-
suit riots. The chapter entitled "The 'Zoot-Suit Yokum' Conspiracy" is particularly effective because of the inclusion of panels from the comic strip. The author's failure to provide specific details concerning the riots themselves is a major
drawback.

Redl, Fritz. "Zoot Suits: An Interpretation." *Survey Midmonthly* 73 (October, 1943):
259-262. Even though the author does not mention the zoot-suit riots, he does a
fine job explaining the lure that zoot suits had for young people during the 1940's.
He also demonstrates what the wearing of zoot suits meant to minority groups at
that time.

Servin, Manuel P. "The Post-World War II Mexican-American 1925-1965: A Non-
achieving Minority." In *An Awakened Minority: The Mexican-Americans*, edited
by Manuel P. Servin. Beverly Hills, Calif.: Glencoe Press, 1974. This historical
survey of the Mexican-American residents in the United States focuses on the
difficulties that this minority group has had in assimilating into society. The article ends by assessing the damage that the zoot-suit riots did to the reputation of
Mexican Americans in the following decades.

Tuck, Ruth. *Not with the Fist: Mexican-Americans in a Southwest City*. New York:
Harcourt, Brace, 1946. Although somewhat dated, this history of the Mexican-

American community in Los Angeles explains the reasons for the polarization of the Mexican Americans and the Anglos that contributed to the zoot-suit riots. The impact of the zoot-suit riots is discussed in the last chapter, entitled "The Minority Citizen."

*Alan Brown*

## Cross-References

Roosevelt Approves Internment of Japanese Americans (1942), p. 595; Race Riots Erupt in Detroit and Harlem (1943), p. 635; Truman Orders Desegregation of U.S. Armed Forces (1948), p. 777; Eisenhower Sends Troops to Little Rock, Arkansas (1957), p. 1003; Civil Rights Protesters Attract International Attention (1963), p. 1188; African Americans Riot in Watts (1965), p. 1301; Race Rioting Erupts in Detroit (1967), p. 1376; Race Riot Breaks Out in Miami, Protesting Police Brutality (1980), p. 2101.

# SUPREME COURT RULES THAT STATES CANNOT COMPEL FLAG SALUTES

*Categories of event:* Civil rights and religious freedom
*Time:* June 14, 1943
*Locale:* United States Supreme Court, Washington, D.C.

West Virginia State Board of Education v. Barnette, *the decision ruling that states could not compel flag saluting, was a victory for the Jehovah's Witnesses*

> *Principal personages:*
> ROBERT JACKSON (1892-1954), an associate justice in the Supreme Court and author of the majority opinion in the *Barnette* case
> HARLAN FISKE STONE (1872-1946), the chief justice of the United States and member of the majority in the *Barnette* case
> FELIX FRANKFURTER (1882-1965), an associate justice in the Supreme Court and a dissenter in the *Barnette* case
> HUGO L. BLACK (1886-1971), an associate justice in the Supreme Court and member of the majority in the *Barnette* case
> FRANK MURPHY (1890-1949), an associate justice in the Supreme Court and member of the majority in the *Barnette* case
> WILLIAM O. DOUGLAS (1898-1980), an associate justice in the Supreme Court and member of the majority in the *Barnette* case
> CHARLES TAZE RUSSELL (1852-1916), the founder of the Jehovah's Witnesses

## Summary of Event

In 1872, in the state of Pennsylvania, a new American religious sect was born that, in time, spread around the globe. Its founder was Charles Taze Russell, who became the first president of the Watch Tower Bible and Tract Society. The members of the new sect were called by a variety of names, including Russellites and Bible Students. In time, however, they came to be known as Jehovah's Witnesses.

Members of the sect became unpopular with many Americans because of both their religious beliefs and their aggressive door-to-door proselytizing. Jehovah's Witnesses believed that they alone were God's chosen people, and they believed that the clergy of other faiths were working for Satan. While they did not spare Protestant and Jewish clergy, they reserved the worst of their epithets for the Roman Catholic hierarchy. Many people who opened their doors to Jehovah's Witnesses' knocks became quite irate when they heard their religions and their clergy maligned. Even when the Witnesses were clearly unwelcome, they would return repeatedly.

Besides being offended by their proselytizing tactics, many people questioned whether Jehovah's Witnesses were loyal Americans. Witnesses were willing to obey the laws of the United States or any other government under which they lived, as long as the laws were not contrary to what they believed to be God's law. Because they believed that God had no interest in World War I, Jehovah's Witnesses refused to serve in the American military and, consequently, went to prison. Witnesses in Germany experienced a similar fate. Both sides in the war perceived Jehovah's Witnesses as unpatriotic and disloyal.

As events in Europe in the 1930's increased the possibility that the United States might once again be involved in a world war, local communities sought to inculcate patriotism and penalize nonconformity. Such was the case in Minersville, Pennsylvania. Pursuant to state law, the school board in that town sought to encourage patriotism in public school children by making a flag salute ceremony, including the Pledge of Allegiance, a required part of the school day. Believing the flag salute to be the equivalent of worshiping a graven image, which is prohibited in the Old Testament, Jehovah's Witnesses' children refused to participate on religious grounds. The penalty for their refusal was expulsion.

The Jehovah's Witnesses sought a decision from the federal courts exempting them on religious grounds from participation in the flag salute ceremony. They were successful in the lower federal courts, but the school board appealed to the United States Supreme Court. In 1940, in the case of *Minersville v. Gobitis*, the Supreme Court, with only one justice dissenting, reversed the lower courts and upheld the right of a school board to require patriotic exercises, such as the flag salute ceremony, of all students regardless of their religious beliefs. Justice Felix Frankfurter, writing for the majority, noted that the purpose of the flag salute was the promotion of national unity, since the flag is a symbol of that unity. He considered this a matter of educational policy with which courts should not interfere. Persons were free to hold whatever religious beliefs they chose, but their beliefs did not entitle them to exemption from public policies of general application.

Following the *Gobitis* decision, such patriotic ceremonies became increasingly common in the public schools of the nation, forcing hard choices on Jehovah's Witnesses with children in the public schools. Many chose to follow their religion rather than the law, and their children were expelled from school. In some instances, after expulsion the children were treated as delinquents, taken from their families, and placed in institutions. Also in the aftermath of the *Gobitis* decision, Jehovah's Witnesses increasingly became victims of violence. Violence against them had existed before the Supreme Court decision, but it increased afterward. At various times, as they sought to promulgate their religion, they were attacked by mobs, had dogs turned loose on them, and had rocks and boiling water thrown at them.

In the midst of this wave of violence, one event occurred which offered the Witnesses some hope in the legal arena. In another Supreme Court case involving Jehovah's Witnesses, although not the flag salute controversy, three justices who had been with the majority in *Minersville v. Gobitis* took the highly unusual step of saying that they had reconsidered the matter and now believed that case to have been incorrectly decided. That was almost an invitation to the Witnesses to try again.

They had their opportunity in *West Virginia State Board of Education v. Barnette*.

Relying on the *Gobitis* opinion for its authority, the State Board of Education adopted a resolution ordering that the flag salute become a regular school activity. The Witnesses again sought judicial vindication of their rights when some of their children were expelled for refusing to salute the flag. This time the decision was in their favor. The chief justice was Harlan Fiske Stone, who had been the lone dissenter in the *Gobitis* case. By this time, however, he could count on the support of three additional justices who had indicated that they had changed their minds: Hugo L. Black, William O. Douglas, and Frank Murphy. Only one more vote was needed for a majority. Justice Robert H. Jackson, who had been appointed to the Court by President Franklin D. Roosevelt in 1941, provided that vote. Chief Justice Stone assigned Justice Jackson the task of writing the opinion of the Court.

Justice Jackson viewed the controversy from a different perspective than did the justices in the *Gobitis* majority. To them, the question was whether the religious beliefs of the Jehovah's Witnesses exempted them from the compulsory flag salute. To Justice Jackson, the question was whether the state had the authority to compel children to salute the flag in the first place. He did not consider the controversy to revolve around the free exercise of religion but rather around the First Amendment guarantee of freedom of speech. He saw no need to determine whether the religious convictions of the Witnesses exempted them from the requirement to salute the flag if the state lacked the authority to make the flag salute a legal duty.

In Justice Jackson's opinion, the First Amendment guarantee of freedom of speech deprived the state of authority to compel the flag salute because the freedom of the individual to speak implies the freedom of the individual not to speak what he does not believe. Jackson denied that patriotism needed to be propped up by compulsory ceremonies. He further denied that the Court was invading the sphere of competence of school boards. Through the due process clause of the Fourteenth Amendment, the First Amendment's guarantee of freedom of speech placed limitations on what states and their instrumentalities, such as school boards, may do. He asserted that it was the responsibility of the Court to see that limitations imposed by the Bill of Rights were not exceeded. In this case, the West Virginia State Board of Education had exceeded one of these limitations. The compulsory flag salute was unconstitutional.

Justice Frankfurter, an Austrian Jew and naturalized citizen who had written the majority opinion in *Minersville v. Gobitis*, was now in the position of having to write a dissent. Clearly uncomfortable with the possibility of being perceived as one who sanctioned the persecution of unpopular minorities, he reminded the majority that he himself was a member of "the most vilified and persecuted minority in history." Frankfurter asserted that he would have voted with the majority if his personal opinion were all that mattered. As a judge, however, he could not permit his personal opinion to control his vote. He continued to consider the flag salute an educational exercise, one which did not interfere with anyone's freedom of speech. He noted that Jehovah's Witnesses, children and parents, were free to use their right of free speech to denounce the flag salute and everything it stood for. If any law attempted to prevent that, Frankfurter said that he would be the first to vote that it was unconstitutional. He continued to believe, however, that a compulsory flag salute ceremony was a legitimate educational measure within the scope of school officials' authority.

The Supreme Court's interpretation had changed. In *West Virginia State Board of Education v. Barnette*, decided on Flag Day, June 14, 1943, the Court overruled *Minersville v. Gobitis*, decided three years earlier.

## Impact of Event

The impact of *West Virginia State Board of Education v. Barnette*, through its overruling of *Minersville v. Gobitis*, was to remove the legitimacy which the Court had previously conferred on compulsory flag salute exercises. Since the decision was rendered on freedom of speech grounds rather than the right to free exercise of religion, persons could choose not to participate in the flag salute even if they held no religious beliefs prohibiting their participation. It was, however, those such as the Jehovah's Witnesses, who refused to salute the flag for religious reasons, who were the primary beneficiaries of the decision.

The Supreme Court's *Barnette* decision, in combination with other factors, resulted in decreased persecution of Jehovah's Witnesses. Court decisions of themselves are merely words on paper. To have any practical consequences, they must be enforced, which the Court itself cannot do. In the period following the *Barnette* decision, the Department of Justice conscientiously sought to enforce it without engaging in widespread prosecutions. United States attorneys would talk with school officials who continued the compulsory flag salute and try to get them to end the practice. The threat of prosecution as a real possibility usually brought compliance.

Also contributing to the decreased persecution of the Jehovah's Witnesses was the fact that the nation was at war. The flag salute controversy had been going on for a long time, but by 1943 most Americans had more on their minds than a few children who would not salute the flag. For those who needed someone to hate, Adolf Hitler fit the bill far better than children of the Jehovah's Witness sect.

Beyond Jehovah's Witnesses and others who would not salute the flag, the *Barnette* decision had only minor impact until 1989. Since the decision had been based upon the First Amendment guarantee of freedom of speech, it was no help to religious groups seeking exemptions from general laws having an adverse impact on the practice of their religions. Ordinarily, persons seeking such exemptions were not successful.

In 1989 and 1990, the flag again became the center of constitutional controversy, although the controversy was of a different nature. In 1989, no one was being forced to salute the flag, but a man burned an American flag as a form of political dissent in the state of Texas. He was subsequently convicted of violating a state law which prohibited desecration of the flag. When he appealed his conviction, the Texas Court of Criminal Appeals considered his burning of the flag a form of political expression and interpreted the *Barnette* decision as suggesting that speech could not be curtailed to preserve the flag's symbolic value. The Supreme Court of the United States, in a very controversial decision, affirmed the holding of the Texas Court of Criminal Appeals that the state legislation was unconstitutional. The unpopularity of the decision was sufficient to result in talk of amending the Constitution to permit government to punish flag desecration. Those opposed to amendment argued that the Bill of Rights had never been amended since becoming a part of the Constitution in 1791, and they cautioned against breaking that tradition. As an alternative, Congress enacted ordinary legislation prohibiting flag desecration. In 1990, the Court held the law enacted by the United States Congress to be in violation of the First Amendment's guarantee of freedom of speech but barely mentioned the *Barnette* decision. Nevertheless, it would be difficult to deny that Justice Jackson's opinion in the *Barnette* case influenced the view that patriotism might take a variety of forms and that no form had value unless it was freely chosen and could be freely exercised without fear of government.

## Bibliography

Dilliard, Irving. "The Flag-Salute Cases." In *Quarrels That Have Shaped the Constitution*, edited by John A. Garraty. Rev. ed. New York: Harper & Row, 1987. This brief account of the flag salute cases was written specifically for the general reader. It is quite well done. Although its primary focus is on the justices of the Supreme Court, it does not neglect the plight of the Jehovah's Witnesses.

Jackson, Robert H. *Dispassionate Justice: A Synthesis of the Judicial Opinions of Robert H. Jackson*. Edited by Glendon Schubert. Indianapolis: Bobbs-Merrill, 1969. Includes Justice Jackson's majority opinion in *West Virginia State Board of Education v. Barnette* as well as discussion of Jackson's position in other Jehovah's Witnesses cases.

Manwaring, David Roger. *Render unto Caesar: The Flag Salute Controversy*. Chicago: University of Chicago Press, 1962. Having begun as a doctoral dissertation, this is a very thorough case study of the flag salute controversy. It discusses the parties to the cases, the opinions of Supreme Court Justices, public reactions to the decisions, and the impact of the decisions. Does not include bibliography but is thoroughly documented.

Penton, M. James. *Apocalypse Delayed: The Story of Jehovah's Witnesses*. Toronto: University of Toronto Press, 1985. A useful history of the Jehovah's Witnesses by a Canadian historian who was himself a fourth generation Jehovah's Witness until being expelled for heresy. His work is fair and scholarly. Includes some discussion of the flag salute controversy. Contains bibliography and index.

Simon, James F. *The Antagonists: Hugo Black, Felix Frankfurter, and Civil Liberties in Modern America*. New York: Simon & Schuster, 1989. Using an engaging writing style to reach a general audience, the author focuses on the above-named justices, emphasizing their human qualities and their competition for leadership on the Supreme Court. He devotes several pages to their conflict in the flag salute controversy. Indexed, well researched and documented, but no bibliography.

Stroup, Herbert Hewitt. *The Jehovah's Witnesses.* New York: Columbia University Press, 1945. Although criticized for carelessness in documentation, Stroup nevertheless provides useful information on the beliefs and practices of the Witnesses. Includes bibliography and index.

*Patricia A. Behlar*

## Cross-References

Bolsheviks Deny All Rights to the Russian Orthodox Church (1917), p. 202; The American Civil Liberties Union Is Founded (1920), p. 327; Stalin Reduces the Russian Orthodox Church to Virtual Extinction (1939), p. 561; The Declaration on the Rights and Duties of Man Is Adopted (1948), p. 755; The United Nations Adopts the Universal Declaration of Human Rights (1948), p. 789; Soviet Jews Demand Cultural and Religious Rights (1963), p. 1177; The U.N. Covenant on Civil and Political Rights Is Adopted (1966), p. 1353; The United States Grants Amnesty to Vietnam War Draft Evaders (1974), p. 1769; The United Nations Votes to Protect Freedoms of Religion and Belief (1981), p. 2146.

# RACE RIOTS ERUPT IN DETROIT AND HARLEM

*Category of event:* Racial and ethnic rights
*Time:* June 20 and 21, 1943; August 1, 1943
*Locale:* Detroit, Michigan, and Harlem, New York City

*Race riots in Detroit and Harlem vividly demonstrated the contradiction between the United States' fight for freedom abroad and the denial of basic freedoms to African Americans at home*

*Principal personages:*

EDWARD J. JEFFRIES, JR. (1900-1950), the mayor of Detroit at the time of the riot

HARRY F. KELLY (1895-1971), the Republican governor of Michigan during the riot

FIORELLO HENRY LA GUARDIA (1882-1947), the popular and progressive mayor of New York during both Harlem riots (1935 and 1943)

THURGOOD MARSHALL (1908- ), the counsel of the National Association for the Advancement of Colored People in 1943

FRANKLIN D. ROOSEVELT (1882-1945), the U.S. president during racial confrontation in both cities

## Summary of Event

World War II involved the complete mobilization of the United States' economy to produce the materials necessary to defeat the Axis powers. One consequence of this national mobilization was the migration of millions of African Americans from the rural South to the industrial centers of the North in search of high-paying factory jobs vacated as whites were inducted into the armed forces. In addition to economic betterment, blacks hoped to escape the harsh legacy of Jim Crow relations that characterized the South, a system that effectively maintained segregation of the races through outright intimidation (for example, lynchings) and negated black political power by preventing blacks from voting through legal mechanisms such as the poll tax. As they migrated northward, blacks hoped to make a better life for themselves and their children.

Unfortunately, there was little real change for blacks upon their arrival in Northern cities. Some white workers resented their arrival and participated in "hate strikes." In addition, few cities were prepared to handle the influx of tens of thousands of blacks over such a short period of time. With domestic production oriented primarily to the war effort, there was increased competition between blacks and whites over scarce amenities. Some blacks sought escape from the bleak conditions confronting them by enlisting in the service, only to suffer further injustice. The armed forces remained strictly segregated throughout World War II, with blacks excluded from the marines and coast guard and relegated to the navy's mess section.

It is against this backdrop that the riots in Detroit and Harlem must be understood. Detroit, the reputed "Arsenal of Democracy," experienced racial disturbances prior to the June, 1943, riot. The most notable occurred when blacks were forcibly prevented from moving into the Sojourner Housing Project in 1942 by police armed with guns and tear gas. Ongoing racial antagonism culminated in the June, 1943, riot.

The genesis of the riot can be found in events occurring late in the evening of June 20 at the Belle Isle municipal park. Minor clashes between blacks and whites took place throughout the day. The bloody riot that would eventually leave thirty-four people dead (twenty-five of them black, seventeen killed by the police) was precipitated by two rumors. The first held that a black man had raped a white woman at the amusement park and that blacks had begun to riot. Shortly afterward, a rumor began at a popular black night club that some white sailors had killed a black woman and her baby by throwing them off of the bridge that connected Belle Isle to Detroit, and that the police had begun to beat blacks.

The actual rioting began early in the morning of June 21. Police reported stabbings, store windows being smashed, looting, and indiscriminate interracial beatings of pedestrians and passengers in cars and public transportation. At the riot's end, in addition to the thirty-four dead, more than one thousand had been injured. Detroit suffered more than $2 million in property losses and lost 100 million work hours in war production, according to one account. Detroit Mayor Edward J. Jeffries, Jr., conceded that much of the loss of life and property could have been prevented had federal troops been requested earlier from President Franklin D. Roosevelt, especially considering that the Detroit Police Department was approximately one-third understaffed because of the draft. It was with the arrival of federal troops that order was finally restored in Detroit very late in the evening of June 21.

In the riot's aftermath, Michigan Governor Harry F. Kelly appointed a committee to investigate the causes of the riot. The committee found no evidence of foreign subversives instigating the riot; it blamed the riot on the militancy of the black press and black leaders. The panel exonerated the Detroit Police Department (which was less than one percent black) of any wrongdoing. Jeffries' administration rejected repeated calls for a grand jury inquiry into the causes of the riot and the subsequent actions undertaken by the police to quell the riot.

Black leaders such as James J. McClendon, president of the Detroit Chapter of the National Association for the Advancement of Colored People, as well as the black press, refuted the committee's findings. They charged that the police had not been fair in their treatment and protection of blacks during the riots. They also maintained that the police generally failed to protect blacks from attacks by whites, even assisting white attackers in some cases, and that police had authorized a "shoot to kill policy" for black rioters. Black leaders also accused the city administration of Detroit of failing to act on previous committee reports specifying needed improvements for blacks in Detroit, especially regarding housing and education. The committee pointed out the hypocrisy of the United States fighting Nazi and Japanese racism abroad while condoning and maintaining it at home.

As was true for the Detroit riot, the precipitating event of the Harlem riot of 1943 was a rumor. On Sunday night, August 1, 1943, a white New York police officer wounded a black army private, Robert Bandy, who had intervened on behalf of a black woman being questioned by the officer at a Harlem hotel. A rumor began to circulate that a black soldier had been shot and killed by the police.

The rumor fell upon a receptive audience. As in Detroit, the residents of Harlem, the majority of whom were black, faced job discrimination. For example, the aircraft industries in nearby Long Island refused to hire blacks even though newspaper advertisements clamored for workers needed by that industry. The complete lack of black faculty in permanent teaching positions at any of the city's four municipal colleges was a sore point to the community. A critical shortage of housing confronted residents, and existing housing in Harlem was dilapidated. Even so, New York Mayor Fiorello Henry La Guardia had recently authorized a semipublic housing development for lower Manhattan that would be all white. Added to this were continual accounts of police brutality and verbal harassment suffered by Harlemites, especially black servicemen. Thus, the tinderbox that was Harlem needed only the Bandy incident to ignite it.

Blacks immediately took to the streets, with white property being the primary focus of the rioters. Residents initially confined themselves to breaking the windows of white merchants; only later did looting occur. Almost none of the interracial clashes that characterized the Detroit riot occurred. When the riot ended at daybreak on August 2, the damage totaled six deaths (five blacks and one white), five hundred injuries, $5 million worth of property damage, 550 arrests, and 1,450 stores either damaged or destroyed. Further destruction probably was prevented by Mayor La Guardia's prompt and effective leadership at the scene of the riot, pleas for calm by recognized black leaders who toured the area in sound trucks countering the rumor about the Bandy shooting, and the dispatching of biracial military police teams to Harlem.

A committee was empaneled to investigate the riot. Again, no evidence was found of foreign instigation of the event. In marked contrast to the Detroit administration, La Guardia acknowledged that the black community had legitimate grievances and pledged steps to remedy them.

## Impact of Event

The race riots in Detroit and Harlem represented the most destructive of the almost 250 racial battles that occurred in forty-seven cities throughout the United States in 1943. Such disturbances had immediate effects on the country during the war as well as a long-term impact on race relations in the postwar era.

In New York, La Guardia did not duplicate the mistakes he made after the Harlem riot of 1935. After that riot, La Guardia had refused to release the investigatory report and, more important, did not implement any of its recommendations. Many contend that the seeds of the 1943 riot were sown during the mayor's inaction in 1935. In the wake of the 1943 riot, the City-Wide Citizens Committee on Harlem was formed to articulate black needs. It achieved limited success in obtaining jobs for blacks and in keeping black concerns before the general public.

In Detroit, the findings of the governor's committee intensified the already strained relations between blacks and whites. The panel overemphasized the militancy of black leaders and the stridency of the black press, while minimizing the serious discrimination affecting the black community. Social, economic, and political conditions in Detroit would continue to deteriorate, ultimately setting the stage for the United States' most extensive urban riot in the summer of 1967.

The 1943 riots had relatively little impact on the Roosevelt Administration. Roosevelt treated the riots as local problems. In his view, treating race relations as a national problem presented three problems. First, and most obvious, Roosevelt feared that elevating race relations to national stature risked alienating powerful Southern Democratic leaders. Second, Roosevelt believed that publicizing racial problems would detract from national unity. Third, he was convinced that it would divert attention away from what he considered the nation's most pressing priority—winning the war.

Thus, Roosevelt refused the recommendation of one of his presidential advisers that he establish a President's Committee on Race and Minority Groups. The proposed committee would study the nation's racial situation and eventually make its findings known to the public. In hopes of further defusing the problem, Roosevelt refused even to discuss the riots in his fireside chats.

This is not to suggest that the riots had no effect on the nation. The riots were a visible testimony and ugly reminder of the wide chasm that existed between the expressed ideals of the United States—freedom, democracy, justice and equality—and the reality of the black experience in America. Blacks were painfully aware of the irony of fighting to liberate peoples in Europe and Asia while they themselves endured oppression at home. Thus, in spite of the riots, by war's end blacks remained segregated in the armed forces and were still being lynched, still suffering discrimination in every facet of American life, and still being denied the right to vote.

During the 1960's, riots once again descended upon Detroit and Harlem. Just as for the riots of 1943, discrimination and lack of meaningful opportunities contributed to the unrest. In spite of a heroic civil rights movement, the passage of landmark federal legislation, and the commitment of billions of dollars to effect change, the nation's black communities continued to suffer from such ills as lack of investment, poor housing and schools, drug abuse, gang violence, and single parenthood. Given these conditions, some believe that the nation's cities will again witness an outbreak of race riots, possibly even more severe than those that plagued Detroit and Harlem in the 1940's and 1960's.

## Bibliography

Dalfiume, Richard M. "The 'Forgotten Years' of the Negro Revolution." In *The Negro in Depression and War*, edited by Bernard Sternsher. Chicago: Quadrangle

Books, 1969. Very well-done piece in which Dalfiume argues that the roots of black militancy in the 1960's began to take hold in the 1940's. Easily understood and enlightening discussion of white discrimination against blacks during the 1940's. Useful analysis of Roosevelt's ambivalence regarding race relations and a good bibliography.

Lee, Alfred M., and Norman D. Humphrey. *Race Riot*. New York: Octagon Books, 1968. This is probably the most widely cited work concerning the Detroit race riot. It is a chronology of events leading up to the riot, listing all pertinent people and places. Includes a critical assessment of the investigatory committee's final report.

Marshall, Thurgood. "The Gestapo in Detroit." *Crisis* 50 (August, 1943): 232-233. Angry and defiant in tone, this short essay represents the black response and rejection of the report of the governor's committee charged with investigating the Detroit riot. Essential reading regarding the disturbance, for it views the events from a black vantage point.

Shapiro, Herbert. "Wartime Violence." In *White Violence and Black Response: From Reconstruction to Montgomery*. Amherst: University of Massachusetts Press, 1988. An outstanding summary of the black situation in America during World War II, especially within the military and the labor movement. Contains probably the most extensive and best bibliography related to the Detroit and Harlem riots.

Shogan, Robert, and Tom Craig. *The Detroit Race Riot: A Study in Violence*. Philadelphia: Chilton Books, 1964. A good general overview of the factors that led to the riot as well as the actual riot itself. Contains supplementary information about the riot gleaned from government memoranda obtained through the Freedom of Information Act.

Sitkoff, Harvard. "Racial Militancy and Interracial Violence in the Second World War." *Journal of American History* 58 (December, 1971): 661-681. A first-rate analysis of the plight of blacks, especially soldiers, in the United States during World War II. Contains a brief discussion of events in Harlem and Detroit. Indispensable reading for an understanding of the national context in which the Detroit and Harlem riots occurred.

White, Walter. *A Man Called White: The Autobiography of Walter White*. New York: Viking Press, 1948. This highly readable account of racism and discrimination in America in the twentieth century, by one of the leaders of the NAACP, contains separate chapters on the Detroit and Harlem riots. The latter is especially interesting as it is a firsthand account of the event and White's general impressions as he witnessed it.

*Craig M. Eckert*

## Cross-References

Roosevelt Outlaws Discrimination in Defense-Industry Employment (1941), p. 578; The Congress of Racial Equality Forms (1942), p. 601; CORE Stages a Sit-in in Chicago to Protest Segregation (1943), p. 618; Zoot-Suit Riots Exemplify Ethnic

Tensions in Los Angeles (1943), p. 624; Truman Orders Desegregation of U.S. Armed Forces (1948), p. 777; *Brown v. Board of Education* Ends Public School Segregation (1954), p. 913; The Civil Rights Act of 1957 Creates the Commission on Civil Rights (1957), p. 997; Eisenhower Sends Troops to Little Rock, Arkansas (1957), p. 1003; The Council of Federated Organizations Registers Blacks to Vote (1962), p. 1149; The Twenty-fourth Amendment Outlaws Poll Taxes (1964), p. 1231; Congress Passes the Voting Rights Act (1965), p. 1296; The Kerner Commission Explores the Causes of Civil Disorders (1967), p. 1370; Congress Extends Voting Rights Reforms (1975), p. 1812.

# CITIZENS RESCUE DANISH JEWS FROM GERMANS

*Category of event:* Atrocities and war crimes
*Time:* October, 1943
*Locale:* Denmark

*When German Gestapo and SS troops sought to apprehend seven thousand Danish Jews, thousands of Danes hid their fellow citizens and helped them to escape to neutral Sweden*

Principal personages:
MARCUS MELCHIOR (?-1969), a rabbi of the Copenhagen Synagogue who warned his congregation to go into hiding
PEDER HANSEN, a Danish fisherman who, along with many others, risked his life in many trips transporting Jews from Denmark to Sweden
AAGE BERTELSEN (1901-1957), a teacher at the Christianshavn High School; he and his wife risked their lives many times and eventually had to go into hiding themselves
WERNER BEST (1903- ), personal representative of Hitler in Denmark and virtual German dictator of Denmark
GEORG DUCKWITZ, a maritime attaché in the German legation in Copenhagen and head of shipping operations in Denmark
CHRISTIAN X (1870-1947), the popular king of Denmark who took an unequivocal stand for the protection of Denmark's Jewish citizens

## Summary of Event

Denmark was unique among the occupied countries of Europe during World War II. The German occupation was less brutal than in Poland or Norway, for example. The Danes, realizing the futility of standing up to a German Blitzkrieg, put up only token resistance in April of 1940, when Germany sent a naval task force and one armored division against the Danish army of fourteen thousand. The Nazi regime considered the Danes to be an Aryan race and wished to make a "model protectorate" of Denmark to show German "generosity" to the world. Propaganda films showed the Danes going about their lives in a somewhat normal fashion. The Danish government, including the king, was kept in place, with considerable liberty to conduct normal affairs of government as if the German Wehrmacht and Gestapo were not there. There did exist, however, a small Danish resistance movement, whose members were dealt with harshly by the Gestapo whenever they were apprehended.

This uneasy truce lasted three years. Although news was limited, Danes knew what was happening in surrounding countries, but as long as they were left alone, they thought they could survive. What finally aroused the Danes to action was Hitler's decision to go after the seven thousand Danish Jews as he had persecuted Jews all over Europe. The Danes saw this as an attack on their countrymen and the beginning of a more repressive policy toward Denmark. Consequently, an aroused and united Denmark rose to the challenge.

In September, 1943, the Germans made plans to round up all Danish Jews and ship them to Theresienstadt Concentration Camp in Terezin, Czechoslovakia. From there they would be sent to extermination camps in German-occupied Europe. Gestapo and Schutzstaffel (SS) raids were scheduled for the Jewish New Year, Rosh Hashanah, when Jews would be home. The date was the night of Friday, October 1, 1943.

Georg Duckwitz, a German government official who had lived in Denmark since 1928, risked his life to warn Danish political leaders of the impending raid. They in turn warned the Jewish community. On the night of September 30, 1943, in an impassioned plea before his Copenhagen congregation, Rabbi Marcus Melchior warned all Jews to go into hiding immediately.

Word of the impending raid spread quickly throughout Copenhagen and elsewhere in Denmark. Christian police, mail carriers, shopkeepers, workers, students, teachers, and taxi drivers took time off work to warn their Jewish friends and acquaintances. Students ran through the streets, entering cafes and searching for Jews to warn. Friends, relatives, and many complete strangers volunteered their homes and apartments as places of refuge for their fellow citizens.

On Sabbath night, October 1, 1943, the horror of coordinated Gestapo raids descended on Denmark. There was a total of 284 victims, mostly the old and sick who had not been warned or could not get away. The other seventy-two hundred Jews found hiding places scattered throughout Denmark. The danger for them was by no means over. Denmark is a small, open country with flat land and few natural hiding places.

Sweden publicly announced its willingness to accept an unlimited number of Jews from Denmark, but there remained the obvious problem of getting all those people past German guards to vessels which could carry them past German patrol boats to the safety of Sweden. Finding transportation to a coastal site where they could clandestinely find a way to Sweden proved very difficult for many.

An example of this problem was the plight of two hundred Danish Jews who had found refuge in Bispebjerg Hospital. German troops surrounded the hospital, set up checkpoints, and examined all incoming and exiting ambulances. While the Gestapo were trying to decide whether to order a search of the hospital, they were suddenly caught off guard by a funeral cortege of twenty to thirty taxis leaving the chapel with refugees.

Aage Bertelsen was a schoolteacher who, with the help of his wife and a team of neighbors, managed to help five hundred Jews on their way. His house was identified by its blue curtains and operated almost in the open as a way station for Jews seeking to flee the country. Another group operated out of a Scandinavian bookstore in Copenhagen and had control of about twelve fishing vessels. The rear room of the bookstore served as a temporary rendezvous point for embarking refugees.

Gestapo raids continued, and eventually 425 Jews were sent to Theresienstadt. The smuggling of Jews continued. The Danish resistance located fishermen and others willing to transport Jews to Sweden and set a modest price for passage. Word of mouth identified the principal contact points: the bookshop, Bispebjerg Hospital, the Rockefeller Institute, the Elsinore Sewing Club, "the house with blue curtains" in Lyngby, and the Danish-Swedish Refugee Service.

The risk was great for all involved, and it cost money to operate boats. Nevertheless, fishing boats, pleasure craft, and merchant vessels clandestinely left one at a time over a period of several days to transport to a safe haven most of the entire Jewish population of Denmark.

## Impact of Event

One of the most important and immediate effects of an entire nation joining together to help the persecuted Jews was the sudden growth of the Danish resistance movement. Prior to 1943, the numbers involved in the resistance were small, and members were not very effective in their use of sabotage against the Germans. Beginning in October, 1943, many thousands joined the resistance and thousands of others cooperated with them. By the end of the war, there were fifty-six thousand members of the Danish underground.

The underground had direct contact with the Allies in London. Its sabotage groups carried out 2,160 major operations against rail lines, 785 against factories working for the Germans, 431 against German military installations and depots, and 167 against ports, shipyards, and ships. The railroad sabotage was so effective that in 1944 the train that crossed Jutland, Germany's main line of communication with its military forces in Norway, took ten days to cross rather than the normal five hours. In these and other operations, eighty-eight Danes lost their lives and seven hundred were wounded.

The Germans knew that the Danish police had cooperated with the rescue of Jews and had done nothing to prevent sabotage against the Germans. On September 19, 1944, the Germans seized all police stations in Denmark. They arrested two thousand Danish police officers and sent them to concentration camps. Another five thousand, however, eluded the Germans and joined the underground. For nearly a year, there were no police in Denmark, but the crime rate was exceptionally low because of the self-policing of the Danish people. Serious offenses were handled by the organized resistance movement. The result of all this was a spirit of national unity. The Danes had risen to the challenge and triumphed in the midst of great adversity.

Denmark was unique in saving so many of its Jewish citizens. No other occupied country came even close in terms of percentages. More than 98.5 percent of Danish Jews were still alive at the war's end. Other nations also rescued many Jews. Holland, for example, managed to hide eighteen thousand Jews for a period of years, a very sizable proportion of the twenty-five thousand who tried to evade arrest.

The concerted effort in Denmark, however, was most remarkable. Denmark had a long tradition of acceptance of Jews as equal members of society. The Danish Parliament in 1690 rejected the idea of establishing a typical Jewish ghetto in Copenhagen, calling the ghetto concept "an inhuman way of life." In 1814, all forms of racial and religious discrimination were outlawed in Denmark. Churches throughout Denmark had repeatedly taught the Biblical admonition to treat all people with respect since they were created in the image of God. That tradition from Danish culture was drawn on in the time of crisis. On Sunday, October 3, 1943, as German soldiers were attempting to round up Danish Jews, Danish Christians heard their pastors strongly condemn such actions as contrary to scripture and Christian love. The Danish church declared its "allegiance to the doctrine that bids us obey God more than man." The Holocaust demonstrated the depths of human evil committed against other human beings, but the Danish example also demonstrated the deeds of kindness and concern performed by those who believe that the image of God is still discernible in human beings.

## Bibliography

Flender, Harold. *Rescue in Denmark*. New York: Simon & Schuster, 1963. A readable narrative of the rescue of Danish Jews by their fellow citizens. The personalities and activities of each of the main groups involved in the rescue are detailed. Includes a photograph section.

Friedman, Philip. *Their Brothers' Keepers*. New York: Holocaust Library, 1978. Of interest to those wanting to compare the Danish experience in World War II with that of neighboring countries where Jews also were rescued. Includes only one chapter on Denmark, and accepts too uncritically some of the stories it reports.

Meltzer, Milton. *Rescue: The Story of How Gentiles Saved Jews in the Holocaust*. New York: Harper & Row, 1988. Written in a simpler style for young adults, but readable and comprehensive. Based on eyewitness accounts, diaries, letters, memoirs, and interviews.

Petrow, Richard. *The Bitter Years: The Invasion and Occupation of Denmark and Norway, April, 1940-May, 1945*. New York: William Morrow, 1974. A factually oriented scholarly comparison of the World War II experiences of Denmark and Norway. Particularly significant since both countries are Scandinavian. The form of resistance pursued by the Danes was quite different from the actions of the Norwegians. The distinct geographic and political conditions are also addressed. Two lengthy and tightly written chapters deal with the rescue of Danish Jews.

Rittner, Carol, and Sondra Myers, eds. *The Courage to Care: Rescuers of Jews During the Holocaust*. New York: New York University Press, 1986. From the award-winning film, *The Courage to Care*. Mostly first-person narratives of rescue in various occupied countries. Includes many photographs.

Yahil, Leni. *The Holocaust: The Fate of European Jewry, 1932-1945*. New York: Oxford University Press, 1990. A thorough and scholarly analysis of the historical repercussions and meaning of the Holocaust. The result of twenty years of research, this may well be the most authoritative history of Hitler's war against the Jews. Originally published in Israel and later translated into English. Includes a section on the Danish Jewish experience.

*William H. Burnside*

## Cross-References

Legal Norms of Behavior in Warfare Formulated by the Hague Conference (1907), p. 92; Nazi Concentration Camps Go into Operation (1933), p. 491; Nazi War Criminals Are Tried in Nuremberg (1945), p. 667; Israel Is Created as a Homeland for Jews (1948), p. 761; The European Court of Human Rights Is Established (1950), p. 849; Eichmann Is Tried for War Crimes (1961), p. 1108.

# FRENCH WOMEN GET THE VOTE

*Categories of event:* Voting rights and women's rights
*Time:* 1944
*Locale:* France

*French women were granted the right to vote in 1944, a century and a half after the revolution of 1789 that proposed equality for all French people*

*Principal personages:*
CHARLES DE GAULLE (1890-1970), the liberator of France in 1944 who brought French women the vote
LUCIE AUBRAC (1912- ), a Resistance leader who represented the women of the French underground to General de Gaulle in Algiers
JACQUES DUCLOS (1896-1975), a Communist leader in the French National Assembly who favored votes for women

## Summary of Event

The emancipation of French women, symbolized by the extension of the voting franchise in 1944, was the result of the national struggle for survival in World War II. Emancipation of French women was not, however, a new idea.

Suffrage for French women was delayed by the determined opposition of the French Senate and by provincial and religious prejudice. These were the antifeminine suffrage arguments that dominated efforts to include women in the franchise throughout the years of the Third Republic (1875-1940). Arguments in the Senate against the female vote represented centuries of prejudice and were encapsulated nearly perfectly by a senator who said, "The woman of the Latin race does not think, does not feel, does not develop like the woman of Anglo-Saxon or Germanic race. Her position in the home is not the same." Perhaps this was too extreme for most senators, but they were ready enough to argue against woman suffrage on other grounds. If women had the vote, that would include prostitutes, and that would be indecent. If women had the vote, they would mix freely with men in the polling booths, and that, too, would be indecent. Above all, women, being religious, would vote for the clerical parties and threaten the existence of the lay republic. Ironically, it was France's Radical Party, progressive on most issues but staunchly anticlerical, that was most adamantly opposed to votes for women.

Attempts to promote woman suffrage failed in 1901, in 1910, and again in 1919. This was the pattern of political action on votes for women during the years of the Third Republic, the product of traditional attitudes and values that sought women's idealization on one hand and their repression on the other. Edmond About observed, "We want above all to keep women faithful to their husbands. So we hope that the girl will bring to the world an angelic provision of ignorance which will be immune to all temptations." Feminine innocence, purity, and timidity were virtues; achievement was not. A female journalist recalled her youth as one of constant repression, and a host of nineteenth century writers averred that if there was to be education for girls, it must differ from that provided for boys. Such values as these were as old as France itself, but as far as the political liberation of French women was concerned, their impact was greatest in the period between the revolution of 1789 and the actual granting of votes to women in 1944.

In 1789, both male and female revolutionaries wanted revolutionary principles applied to men and women equally. The Marquis de Condorcet wrote that "anyone who votes against the rights of another, whatever their religion, their color, or their sex, has from that moment abjured his own." Olympe de Gouges, a pamphleteer and playwright, complained, "I put forward a hundred propositions; they are received; but I am a woman; no one pays any attention."

These appeals were ignored, and a half-century later French women still were paid half the wages of men and denied the rights to sit on juries, hold public office, vote, or be educated. Their legal status was oppressively restrictive, and married women had almost no legal rights at all. Slight improvement was made during the Third Republic. Teacher-training colleges for women were established (1879), as was a regular system of secondary education (1880). The Paris medical faculty excluded women until 1868, however, and the Sorbonne excluded them until 1880. The first French woman received a law degree in 1884, but by 1913, men still outnumbered women at French universities nine to one.

Changes for the better in the legal position of women were equally slow in coming. A married woman could open a post-office savings account in her own name—and use it without her husband's consent—only after 1895. A married working woman could not keep ownership and use of her wages until 1907. Women could not be legal guardians of children until 1927, and it was 1920 before a woman could join a trade union without her husband's consent. Divorce remained illegal altogether in France until 1884, and women could divorce their husbands for cause only since the early 1900's. Challenges to such slow progress were present, but they were few and ineffective in the nineteenth century. A handful of protofeminist journals were published, backed by luminaries such as Victor Hugo, and occasionally women, notably the novelist George Sand, were able to live emancipated lives.

In time, France experienced feminist and suffragist movements that paralleled those in the United States and England, but without either the intensity or success. Before and after World War I, suffragist leaders were unable to put much pressure on French men to rectify the inferior status of women. French feminism expanded in activity in the 1920's and 1930's but remained largely philanthropic and reformist. It is reckoned that the strong influence of the Catholic church over women was the reason. Repression of women remained intact, virtually an article of faith for French men, until the outbreak of war in 1939.

World War II accomplished what neither idealism nor revolution had been able to. The humiliating defeat and occupation of France by Germany led many French men and women to the conviction that sweeping social and political changes must be part of a reconstructed France. In 1943, from his base in Algiers, Free French leader General Charles de Gaulle issued a call for a dramatically reformed France to be raised out of the ashes of the Third Republic once France had been liberated. Regarding women, he said, "The women of France must more than ever in the past assume a larger share in the affairs of the state. They must have the vote and be eligible to election in various posts. France needs them." The pronouncement was endorsed by the Resistance, whose manifesto of March, 1944, called for universal suffrage as part of the France to come. The law giving women the vote was also passed in March, 1944, by the Committee of National Liberation. The law read, "The women will be electors and eligible in equal right to men, and will take part in every election that takes place after the liberation of the country."

The Communist Party as well as de Gaulle's *Movement Républicain Populaire* (MRP), which was heavily Catholic, favored the change and worked to effect it in the months after liberation. Each department drew up new polling lists that included women, and women took an active role in the work. It took time, since there had been no elections in France since 1936. The elections were spread over the spring months of 1945, beginning in February, and by the end of the year a new National Assembly was in place, elected in part by women and including thirty-three women members.

The emancipation of French women paralleled the liberation of France in 1944. Indeed, the efforts of French women in resisting the German occupiers, opposing the collaborationist Vichy regime, and aiding the Allies in the liberation were largely the reason for emancipation. The Allied armies landed in Normandy on June 6, 1944, and liberated Paris in August. Along the way, women took on roles that they had never had. By October, one hundred women from the ranks of nurses, factory workers, and shopgirls, among others, had been appointed municipal councillors in Paris. A woman doctor was appointed to the post of executive secretary in the Ministry of Public Health, and other women were given jobs in the foreign office and Ministry of Colonies. Women were appointed as aides to the mayors of two arrondissements, and a committee of housewives controlled food prices and distribution in Les Halles, the central Paris food market. Juries trying collaborators included women, and the promise was made, soon to become law, that women's salaries would attain parity with men's.

Women had fought courageously for France as part of the Resistance and often had been imprisoned, tortured, or killed for their efforts. They had hidden fugitives, carried arms and messages, spied, and occasionally fought with arms, in the Maquis and other organizations. It was the consensus of journalists from around the world, writing on the events of 1944-1945 in France, that the women of France had earned their own liberation, symbolized by the granting of the vote, fully as much as had the people of France generally.

**Impact of Event**

The immediate effect of votes for French women was of small significance. The two chief fears of those who opposed female suffrage, that French women would either bring communists to power or vote Catholic, were not realized. Subsequent research indicated that in the elections of 1945, 85 percent of women voted in the manner of their husbands, the other 15 percent being largely composed of widows and unmarried women. All political candidates in 1945 sought the "female vote," but it clearly did not exist. Gaining the vote in and of itself did not immediately alter the position of women in French society.

With the vote gained, however, French women had opened the door to change for the future. By 1949, thirty-nine female deputies sat in the National Assembly, and two had served as vice presidents of the Assembly. Each of the major political parties had women in positions of leadership, including Geneviève de Gaulle, niece of the general, in the MRP. Two women were appointed judges in the national courts. Moreover, women had won important social benefits. The promise of equal wages, hours, and benefits made in 1944 had been kept, and social insurance was extended to include pregnant women, who received an allowance adjusted to the cost of living for every month of pregnancy, an extra ration card, and at the birth of their children, the cost of delivery.

In time, legislation in the Assembly responded to women's needs. Abortion was legalized, and the phrase "head of the family"—meaning the man—was deleted from the law on parental authority. The number of women in higher education increased dramatically, as did the number in the work force. By the 1980's, 72 percent of all French women between the ages of 25 and 49 held jobs outside the home, representing 43 percent of the total work force.

As time went on, women became more politically active, despite the comment in 1981 of the newly formed Ministry for Women's Rights that women remained absent from politics and were not integrated into the political system. After 1970, women were regularly named to cabinet posts. Two females were candidates for the presidency of the Fifth Republic in 1981, and Pierre Mauroy's cabinet in 1982 contained five women. Simone Weil, a veteran of the Resistance, became the first female member of the European Parliament, and in 1991, President François Mitterrand named Edith Cresson, an engineer, economist, and stalwart of the Socialist Party, to replace Michel Rocard as premier.

Votes for women in France were no more dramatic in immediate impact than in the United States or England. In the long run, however, gaining the vote led to a positive alteration in the relationship of French women to the society of which they were a part.

## Bibliography

Duchen, Claire. *Feminism in France: From May '68 to Mitterand.* London: Routledge & Kegan Paul, 1986. Includes an introduction to suffragists before World War II and to the mentality of French women in the context of both gaining the vote and applying its potential political power in subsequent years. Useful index and bibliography.

McMillan, James. *Housewife or Harlot: The Place of Women in French Society, 1870-1940.* New York: St. Martin's Press, 1987. This work is largely about the evolution of suffrage in the years of the Third Republic and is extremely useful for background to the events of 1944-1946. Index and bibliography.

Thomson, David. *Democracy in France Since 1870.* Oxford, England: Oxford University Press, 1964. A standard history of the period, this volume is useful for its inclusion of texts from the Resistance Manifesto of 1944 and the constitution of 1962. The index is adequate, and the bibliography is extensive, if slightly dated.

Wright, Gordon. *France in Modern Times: From the Enlightenment to the Present.* 4th ed. New York: W. W. Norton, 1987. A standard text in modern French history, this volume provides details for all aspects of French society and culture. Useful index and bibliography.

Zeldin, Theodore. *France, 1848-1945.* Vol. 2 in *The Oxford History of Modern Europe.* Oxford, England: Clarendon Press, 1973. This volume explores in careful detail the social, political, and cultural development of France over the period indicated and includes an in-depth analysis of the role of women in French society. Extensive index and no bibliography.

*Robert Cole*

## Cross-References

The Pankhursts Found the Women's Social and Political Union (1903), p. 19; Finland Grants Woman Suffrage (1906), p. 70; Women's Institutes Are Founded in Great Britain (1915), p. 167; Parliament Grants Suffrage to British Women (1918), p. 247; Sanger Organizes Conferences on Birth Control (1921), p. 356; The Minimum Age for Female British Voters Is Lowered (1928), p. 442; The U.N. Convention on the Political Rights of Women Is Approved (1952), p. 885; Congress Passes the Equal Employment Opportunity Act (1972), p. 1650; *Roe v. Wade* Expands Reproductive Choice for American Women (1973), p. 1703; Italy Legalizes Abortion (1978), p. 1988.

# THE FRENCH QUELL AN ALGERIAN NATIONALIST REVOLT

*Category of event:* Revolutions and rebellions
*Time:* May 8, 1945
*Locale:* Sétif, Algeria

*A series of political and social developments led to the outbreak of mass violence in eastern Algeria, hastening the process of its decolonization under French rule*

*Principal personages:*

FERHAT ABBAS (1899-    ), the president of the Algerian provisional government-in-exile in 1958

ABD EL-KADER, MESSALI HADJ (1898-1974), a radical nationalist and one-time member of the French Communist Party

CHARLES DE GAULLE (1890-1970), the head of the French government in 1945

MAURICE VIOLETTE, the governor general of Algeria from 1925 to 1927; coauthored the Blum-Violette proposals

## Summary of Event

The people of the predominantly Muslim town of Sétif, located in the Department of Constantine, Algeria, gathered on May 8, 1945, for a V-E Day celebration of the end of World War II. Some eight thousand people, many young children among them, gathered at the mosque near the town's railroad station. Violence directed against the French colonialists broke out, leading eventually to more than ten thousand deaths.

The incident in Sétif was a symptom of tension that had existed between the French and the Algerian Muslims since before World War II. Although it was not manifested in violence prior to the Sétif revolt, Algerian nationalism centered on personalities representing three major trends of thought. The first group, led by Messali Hadj, was violently anti-French and demanded total independence from French rule. After the Sétif incident, when his Algerian People's Party (PPA) was banned, Hadj persisted and created a new Movement for Triumph of Democratic Liberties (MTLD) with essentially the same demands. The second group, led by Ferhat Abbas and his Friends of the Manifesto and Liberty (AML, founded in 1944), pursued assimilationist politics with a goal of Algerian autonomy within the French system. After the AML was banned in the aftermath of Sétif, Abbas too formed a second movement, the Democratic Union of the Algerian Manifesto (UDMA). The most direct influence on the Muslim masses, however, was exerted by the third group, the religious leaders.

The *colons* (Algerian Europeans), both French and others, resisted pressure from both the Algerian moderates, who demanded French citizenship through assimilation, and the radicals, who demanded independence. The *colons* allied themselves with powerful elements of the French government, bureaucracy, and military and controlled the Algerian government through influence, finance, and the press.

The major French response to the early assimilationist demands of the educated Algerians was the Blum-Violette proposals of 1936, which would have extended citizenship initially to a few thousand Muslims. Even this modest effort at conciliation was obstructed by the determined opposition of the *colons.*

The Algerian economy mainly served the *colon* interests. Commercially cultivated farmlands in the northern plains were controlled by *colons.* These lands had yields almost ten times as high per acre as the infertile lands to the south, to which the Muslims had been driven beginning in the early 1900's. The *colons* exercised similar control over railroads, shipping, and other industrial enterprises. The plight of the Muslim farmers was complicated by high population growth and the gradual subdivision of their lands in the south. They depended for their meager livelihood on raising sheep and crops on their own land or sharecropping on *colon* farmlands in the north.

Political agitation prior to Sétif, led by Ferhat Abbas' AML, added to tension. The AML, which came to be dominated by Messali's followers, succeeded in having a resolution for complete independence adopted at the AML congress in March, 1945.

The political atmosphere in Algeria had been charged with expectation for change since the landing of the Anglo-American forces in Algeria in 1942. That atmosphere was influenced by the apparently anticolonial tone of the Atlantic Charter, signed in 1941. Muslim sentiments were further aroused by the establishment of the Arab League, a symbol of Arab unity, in 1945.

On the eve of the Sétif incident, the AML, which feared the possibilities stemming from the policy of confrontation advocated by the Communist Party of Algeria, publicly attacked that policy. During May Day parades one week prior to the Sétif incident, there had been clashes, resulting in casualties, between the police and demonstrators in Algiers and other cities. There was no police intervention during Sétif's May Day parade.

The local AML leaders agreed to act responsibly during Sétif's V-E Day celebration on May 8 as well, promising to respect a police ban on political slogans. They planned to lay a wreath at the local war memorial and then disperse. On reaching the center of town, however, some people in the crowd brought out small British, American, and French flags amid shouts of "long live Messali," "long live free and independent Algeria," and "down with colonialism." At least one mann waved the green-and-white Algerian national flag. The commissioner of police, with only a few officers at his disposal, reluctantly decided to intervene. In the ensuing scuffle a spectator was shot, possibly by a panic-stricken police officer.

By noon, the rumor of what some saw as a holy war spread east as well as north to the Babor Mountains. During the night, armed Muslims rampaged through the isolated villages and farms, cutting power lines, breaking into railroad carriages, and setting fire to public buildings. Guelma, a major town about 165 miles to the east, was encircled by a mob on May 9. Encouraged by events in Sétif, Muslim mobs went out of control and committed atrocities on helpless Europeans of all ages, sometimes mutilating the victims' bodies. The prefect of Constantine called on Yves Chataigneau, the governor general, to send in the army. Violence continued for five days, spreading to settlements such as Sillegue, El Ouricia, La Fayette, Chevreul, Perigotville, and Kerrata. More than one hundred European men, women, and children were killed, one-third of them petty government officials, symbols of French presence in Algeria.

The army, called in after five days, restored order in Constantine. Rather than bringing the culprits of the mob violence to justice and punishing the guilty, a policy of reprisal was adopted and hastily put into operation. The governor general gave the orders for repression, so Charles de Gaulle, head of the French government, was presumably kept informed and must have had some responsibility for the army actions.

The retaliatory army actions meant to protect and perhaps avenge the Europeans have been described as a veritable massacre. Martial law was declared in Constantine. An army of about ten thousand Senegalese and Legionnaires was given almost a free hand to clean up an area roughly between the cities of Sétif and Guelma extending north to the coast. This force rounded up hundreds of Muslims, summarily executing anyone suspected of any crime as well as anyone found without the identity brassard prescribed by the army. Interrogations using third-degree methods were often held in public. Indiscriminate aerial and naval bombardments added to the death tolls, especially those of the innocent. On a single day, the French Air Force P-39 and B-26 airplanes flew three hundred sorties. Such repeated punitive operations destroyed many *machtas,* or Muslim settlements, particularly between Guelma and the coast. French naval units from the Gulf of Bongui repeatedly shelled the coastal settlements at close range.

Arms were distributed to the Europeans as an added measure to ensure their safety. The Europeans quickly formed vigilante groups and roamed the countryside meting out their own justice. More than two hundred Muslims were shot in Chevreul. Victims of the vigilantes were often old men, women, and children. The victims' bodies were sometimes mutilated and their homes were often destroyed.

Estimates of the death toll ranged from a few hundred to nearly fifty thousand. Official European casualties were eighty-nine dead and 150 injured. French army officers involved gave a moderate estimate of between six thousand and eight thousand Muslim dead. The Algerian national press put the figure at fifty thousand dead, and *The New York Times* estimated about eighteen thousand Muslims dead. One plausible explanation for these wide discrepancies was the large number of Muslims who fled their villages once the army action started, thus depleting their ranks temporarily.

Apart from the activities of the vigilante groups, the army made wholesale arrests of suspects, some of whom were only remotely connected to Sétif and the mob violence there. These arrests posed a major threat to Muslims' personal freedom.

Ferhat Abbas, who visited the governor general to congratulate him on the allied victory over Germany, was arrested inside the governor general's mansion. His AML was banned soon afterward. Messali Hadj's party bore the brunt of the arrests. Of about forty-five hundred arrested in the aftermath of the Sétif incident, about one hundred were given the death penalty, and sixty-four were given life sentences.

France, along with the rest of Europe, was busy with victory celebrations, and major French newspapers played down the extent of violence in Constantine. De Gaulle himself dismissed the events as insignificant.

## Impact of Event

Tension built upon the inferiority of Muslim wealth and status within the colonial system erupted into violence in Sétif. The official inquiry committee on Sétif, which never published a final report, mentioned in its provisional report the resentment toward an unjust system felt by those Muslims who returned to Algeria after working in more egalitarian environments outside the country. Their resentment found a sympathetic reception among others.

The repression led to expression by poets and politicians alike. Poet Kateb Yacin, who was then sixteen years old, spoke about his first feelings of nationalism. Ben Bella, the revolutionary leader who was returning to Algeria after serving with the French army, was aghast at the sight of the bloody repression. Hardly any nationalists believed any longer that changes in the colonial system could be accomplished through reform.

In terms of long-run political consequences and human rights in Algeria, no result of the violence in Sétif was as important as the resolve of groups of young men to fight colonialism by every means at their disposal. Insecurity of life and property and violation of personal freedom became common experiences for many after the outbreak of revolution in November, 1954. Torture as a means of eliciting information from suspects became such common practice that at one point in 1957 a proposal was made to approve its use by the French army.

The French tried to stem the growing tide of Algerian nationalism by granting some political rights. In addition to allowing French citizenship to limited numbers who did not have to relinquish their rights under Koranic laws, a privilege that had been granted to a few beginning in 1944, the French gave voting rights to women, recognized Arabic as another official language along with French, and brought the tribes in the southern high plains under civilian rule for the first time. In September, 1947, dual electoral colleges were introduced for the Algerian assembly, one for the numerically far inferior French citizens and another for Muslim French subjects. Artificial parity between the two in representation, however, allowed the French to maintain official control, vitiating the purpose of representation. Confidence in French goodwill further eroded after the 1948 assembly elections, in which widespread official use of gerrymandering and other kinds of fraud resulted in a landslide victory of official candidates over the nationalists. The governor general, appointed by the French Ministry of Interior, retained the ultimate control over administration.

The Bandung Conference of nonaligned nations called upon France in April, 1955, to implement Algeria's right to independence. American official policy under President Dwight Eisenhower was to avoid antagonizing France, a North Atlantic Treaty Organization (NATO) ally. Upon John F. Kennedy's ascent to the U.S. presidency, U.S. military aid to France was reduced to a fraction of its 1953 volume. France sought to maintain its former ties with Algeria after an initial period of readjustment. For example, France gradually absorbed about one million Algerian workers into its expanding economy during the 1960's and 1970's. The revolt at Sétif thus marked the initial stage of Algerian revolution, starting the period of resistance to France's massive efforts to retain Algeria within its political system.

## Bibliography

Behr, Edward. *The Algerian Problem.* Westport, Conn.: Greenwood Press, 1976. A readable eyewitness account of the period from the Algerian revolution to Algeria's independence. Valuable because of the author's personal involvement with personalities and events. Keeps political and military developments in proper balance, mainly treating growth of Algerian nationalism following the failure of the French policy of assimilation. Includes a short bibliography almost entirely composed of French publications; photos, map, no index.

Bourdieu, Pierre. *The Algerians.* Boston: Beacon Press, 1962. Written by a respected French sociologist during the revolution, this book contains comparative studies on economic and social status of the Muslims and the Europeans, including the French, in Algerian society. Provides insight to understanding Muslim discontent in the French colonial system. Includes index, diagrams, and bibliography.

Clark, Michael K. *Algeria in Turmoil: A History of the Rebellion.* New York: Praeger, 1959. An early account of the revolution by an American journalist openly sympathetic to the French cause. Contains valuable details regarding Sétif in part 1. Maps, index, and bibliography.

Gordon, David C. *The Passing of French Algeria.* Oxford, England: Oxford University Press, 1966. An account of the revolution written from the neutral British perspective. Like the books by Behr and by Horne, this volume treats the nationalist cause with understanding. Mainly a political analysis of the Algerian crisis. Bibliography and index.

Grimal, Henri. *Decolonization.* Boulder, Colo.: Westview Press, 1978. A comparative approach to the decolonization process on a global basis following World War II. Treatment of British, French, Belgian, and Dutch cases of decolonization brings out their differences. Discussion of Algeria short but balanced. Contains valuable documents, index, and bibliography of English and French publications.

Halpern, Manfred. "The Algerian Uprising of 1945." *The Middle Eastern Journal* 32 (April, 1948): 191-201. Exclusively on Sétif and its immediate aftermath. Brings out much of the mob violence and retaliatory operations. Discusses causes of the Sétif insurrection according to local sources; does not anticipate the revolution of 1954.

Horne, Alistair. *A Savage War of Peace.* Harmondsworth, England: Penguin, 1987. One of the best works on the military aspect of the revolution by a British historian. Inspired and almost poetic, yet extremely detailed, account of the political and social context of the revolution. Includes maps, charts, chronology of events, detailed bibliography, and rare photos. The first three chapters are useful for those interested in Sétif.

*Asit Kumar Sen*

## Cross-References

The Young Turk Movement Stages a Constitutional Coup in Turkey (1908), p. 98; The Defense of India Act Impedes the Freedom Struggle (1915), p. 156; Soldiers Massacre Indian Civilians in Amritsar (1919), p. 264; The Atlantic Charter Declares a Postwar Right of Self-Determination (1941), p. 584; The Nationalist Vietnamese Fight Against French Control of Indochina (1946), p. 683; Brazil Begins a Period of Intense Repression (1968), p. 1468; The Argentine Military Conducts a "Dirty War" Against Leftists (1976), p. 1864; Biko Is Murdered by Interrogators in South Africa (1977), p. 1887; Palestinian Civilians Are Massacred in West Beirut (1982), p. 2164; Demonstrators Gather in Tiananmen Square (1989), p. 2483.

# THE UNITED NATIONS ADOPTS ITS CHARTER

*Categories of event:* Peace movements and organizations; international norms
*Time:* June 25, 1945
*Locale:* San Francisco, California

*The Charter of the United Nations proclaimed respect for human rights as a basis for lasting international peace and order and made promotion of rights a fundamental legal obligation of states*

*Principal personages:*

WINSTON CHURCHILL (1874-1965), the prime minister of Great Britain during World War II, a principal architect of the United Nations

ANTHONY EDEN (1897-1977), the British foreign secretary and a leading British spokesperson at San Francisco

FRANKLIN D. ROOSEVELT (1882-1945), the president of the United States and coauthor of the Atlantic Charter

JOSEPH STALIN (1879-1953), the dictator of the Soviet Union from 1924 until his death

EDWARD R. STETTINIUS (1900-1949), the U.S. secretary of state and head of the American delegation to the San Francisco conference

## Summary of Event

After World War I, isolationists in the United States refused to permit ratification of the Versailles peace treaty or American entry into the League of Nations. When World War II broke out, many Americans, including President Franklin Delano Roosevelt, came to believe that isolationism had in part contributed to the aggression of the Axis Powers, as had a lack of democracy and human rights in those countries. Roosevelt was determined not to repeat the mistake of his predecessors: If the world was going to be made safe for human rights and democracy, he thought, it was going to require continuing U.S. involvement in world affairs. He thus wanted the United States to join and to participate fully in international security and other organizations, in order to help create and sustain a newly liberal, postwar world. Even before the United States entered the war in 1941, Roosevelt ordered the State Department to begin planning for a new world security organization that would have as one of its primary purposes the promotion of democracy, human rights, and fundamental freedoms. Roosevelt hoped that by making the new United Nations, which was designed to replace the failed League of Nations, reflect American and liberal values, public opinion both in the United States and abroad would better support the organization.

For the same reason and primarily at Roosevelt's request, principles of human rights and fundamental freedoms also were written into wartime declarations such as the Atlantic Charter (1941) and the first Declaration of the United Nations (1942). Those public declarations helped shore up American and allied domestic support for the war effort but they also tied postwar planning to a set of liberal assumptions about the causes of war and ideals about how to maintain peace that were not shared by every state fighting the Nazis. The Soviet Union, for example, continued to espouse a collectivist ideology not at all in sympathy with the emphasis on individual rights promoted by the United States and other Western democracies. Nevertheless, as the United States emerged from the war as the world's dominant power, Roosevelt's thinking about the underlying importance of human rights and public opinion supporting that idea made itself felt in planning for the United Nations. Moreover, the wartime rhetoric and declarations of the Allies concerning liberation, democracy, and human rights raised popular expectations in other countries. Ordinary people everywhere, from the cities of Nazi-occupied Europe to the rice paddies of Japanese-controlled Asia, heard on their radios how the Allies intended to replace aggression and genocide with a just postwar order in which human rights and basic freedoms were respected everywhere. It was against that background of rising popular demands and expectations for self-government and human rights, born of occupation and mass suffering during the war and with images of the Nazi death camps and genocide fresh in mind, that hundreds of diplomats and politicians came together in 1944 and 1945 to draft the U.N. Charter.

Two conferences were held to draft the U.N. Charter, the constitution of the new international security organization. The first was held at Dumbarton Oaks in Washington, D.C., in late 1944. Only the four major allies (China, Great Britain, the United States, and the Soviet Union) participated at that first conference. Of the four, only the United States displayed any interest in making promotion of human rights a major purpose of the United Nations. The Americans argued that old ways of trying to establish and secure international peace (the balance of power and spheres of influence) had mostly failed and that lasting peace and security could be sustained only if individuals and nations were guaranteed basic human rights. Led by Edward Stettinius, the American delegation argued that countries such as Nazi Germany, fascist Italy, and imperial Japan had not respected the rights of other nations partly because they did not respect the human rights of their own populations. The Americans pointed to the lack of respect for human rights in fascist countries and to the war crimes, atrocities, and genocide of the Axis Powers as evidence that international security in the future had to be linked to democracy and respect for the rights of individuals. The U.S. delegation wanted this idea reflected in the U.N. Charter. China, heavily dependent on U.S. aid to fight the Japanese, tended to follow the American lead, but neither the Soviets nor the British were as easily convinced. The Soviet leader, Joseph Stalin, had put millions to death, and the British under Winston Churchill expressed concern that too much talk of democracy and basic rights for everyone might pose a threat to the integrity of their empire, especially in India. Faced with growing American power, eventually both the Soviets and the British conceded the point about human rights being a basic goal of the United Nations, though they did so only in the most general terms.

At the founding conference of the United Nations, held in San Francisco from

April to June, 1945, the idea of basing security on respect for human rights gained support from numerous small countries, many of which had been recent victims of German, Italian, or Japanese aggression. With the support of these small countries, the United States was able to pressure the other major powers into accepting a strengthening of human rights provisions in the charter. These provisions still remained quite general, reflecting continuing differences in the definition of human rights and the emphasis given to the rights and role of the individual in society in the West and in the Soviet Union. On the other hand, a promise was made that human rights would be spelled out in more detail and further protected in a universal declaration and covenant, to be drafted later.

Individuals in many countries believed the human rights sections of the charter were its most important component, but the same was not true of governments. Even in those countries such as the Western democracies, where many human rights already were well protected and respected, governments in 1945 were primarily concerned with economic reconstruction and recovery from the war. Thus, while many individuals and private lobby groups, some of which had attended the San Francisco conference as observers, enthusiastically welcomed the human rights references in the charter, the attitude of governments ranged from careful rhetorical support to indifference in the face of what seemed to be more urgent economic and social problems and to outright ideological hostility or cynical acceptance. That difference in attitude and emphasis between individuals and governments was inescapable, given the inherent tension on human rights questions caused by individuals claiming rights against the state. It was all the more remarkable, therefore, that an assembly of government officials representing fifty-one countries with a wide variety of social, political, and economic systems should have agreed to enshrine the promotion of human rights as a fundamental obligation of membership in the United Nations.

## Impact of Event

In the short run, including reference to promotion of human rights in the U.N. Charter had little to no impact on the lives of ordinary people. The references remained very general, and there was no way to force governments to live up to the obligations on human rights they undertook by joining the United Nations. Furthermore, the effort to create an international consensus in support of human rights very quickly broke down as the Cold War developed: Each side tended to define human rights as best represented and respected by their already existing social, economic, and political system. As a result, little progress was made at the governmental level on arriving at additional agreements or in developing effective machinery to enforce and protect human rights. By the mid-1950's, human rights forums and programs undertaken within the United Nations had become one more arena of Cold War and, more generally, interstate conflict.

On the other hand, the inclusion of human rights in the U.N. Charter helped inspire individuals and groups in many countries to begin making demands for social, economic, or political justice against their governments. Sometimes individuals acted alone, sometimes in groups, often citing the U.N. Charter as the basis for demands that their government live up to obligations as a member of the United Nations and the community of states. Frequently, such individuals paid high prices for their actions, including torture and death. The groups to which they belonged were sometimes declared illegal and suppressed. Over time, however, a network of human rights organizations developed to demand that governments adhere to their U.N. Charter obligations, and more recently, governments themselves have begun to add their voices to the chorus calling for universal respect for human rights.

With that development, the real long-term significance of the human rights provisions of the charter became clear. First, internationalization of human rights in the charter and in later treaties has accelerated a process of erosion of the state claim to absolute sovereignty and has aided individuals, groups, and concerned states in making strong legal claims against governments that violate basic human rights. Second, the community of states now accepts, at least in law, that lasting international peace may be erected only on a foundation of stable, humane, and representative government. The human rights provisions of the U.N. Charter thus represent the historical development wherein liberal ideas about justice and order based on individual rights have largely won out over state-centered approaches. After a century of conflict with totalitarian and collectivist systems and theories on both the right and the left, the idea of human rights and democracy now represents a worldwide movement and inspires frequent emulation.

## Bibliography

Claude, Inis, L. *Swords into Ploughshares: The Problems and Processes of International Organization.* 4th ed. New York: Random House, 1984. Single best account of the development of international organization in the twentieth century. Well written and accessible to all readers. Several appendices and an index.

Cranston, Maurice. "Are There any Human Rights?" *Daedalus* (Fall, 1983): 1-18. Most useful as a general introduction to the problem of international definition of human rights, with an emphasis on the natural rights tradition.

Farer, Tom. "Human Rights and the United Nations: More than a Whimper, Less than a Roar." *Human Rights Quarterly* 9, no. 4 (November, 1987): 550-586. Standard summary account of the U.N. record on human rights flowing out of the charter. Useful as an introduction to the complex organizational structures of the U.N. human rights network. Charts.

Henkin, Louis. *The Age of Rights.* New York: Columbia University Press, 1990. This volume by a leading expert on international law places international concern with human rights in historical and intellectual perspective. Well documented and well written. Index.

Hoffmann, Stanley. *Duties Beyond Borders: On the Limits and Possibilities of an Ethical International Politics.* Syracuse, N.Y.: Syracuse University Press, 1981. A leading liberal theorist and commentator on world politics examines the complex problems which arise when human rights become a subject of international attention. Written in the style of a long essay rather than a text or reference, it addresses the issues in a highly accessible manner.

Merton, Theodor. *Human Rights Lawmaking in the United Nations.* Oxford, England: Clarendon Press, 1986. Discusses human rights developments in the United Nations which later flowed from the charter. Technical but thorough, with several annexes and an index. Not recommended for the general reader.

Russell, Ruth B. *A History of the United Nations Charter.* Washington, D.C.: Brookings Institution, 1958. Primarily a reference work but still the best and most readable treatment of the drafting of the U.N. Charter. Comprehensively documented with a full index and appendices.

*Cathal J. Nolan*

## Cross-References

The Paris Peace Conference Includes Protection for Minorities (1919), p. 252; The League of Nations Is Established (1919), p. 270; The League of Nations Adopts the International Slavery Convention (1926), p. 436; Nazi Concentration Camps Go into Operation (1933), p. 491; The Atlantic Charter Declares a Postwar Right of Self-Determination (1941), p. 584; The United Nations Adopts a Convention on the Crime of Genocide (1948), p. 783; The U.N. Convention on the Political Rights of Women Is Approved (1952), p. 885; The United Nations Drafts a Convention on Stateless Persons (1954), p. 918; The United Nations Sets Rules for the Treatment of Prisoners (1955), p. 935; The United Nations Adopts the Abolition of Forced Labor Convention (1957), p. 985; The United Nations Adopts the Declaration of the Rights of the Child (1959), p. 1038; The U.N. Covenant on Civil and Political Rights Is Adopted (1966), p. 1353; The U.N. Principles of Medical Ethics Include Prevention of Torture (1982), p. 2169; The United Nations Adopts the Convention on the Rights of the Child (1989), p. 2529.

# A JAPANESE COMMANDER IS RULED
# RESPONSIBLE FOR HIS TROOPS' ACTIONS

*Categories of event:* Atrocities and war crimes; accused persons' rights
*Time:* October 29, 1945-February 23, 1946
*Locale:* Manila, the Philippines

*The Yamashita case set the precedents that commanders are responsible for their troops' actions and that captured soldiers are not protected by the U.S. Constitution even after hostilities end*

Principal personages:

TOMOYUKI YAMASHITA (1885-1946), the Japanese general who attempted to defend the Philippines from Allied invasion in World War II

DOUGLAS MACARTHUR (1880-1964), the supreme commander of the Allied Powers in the Pacific at the time of the Yamashita trial

RUSSEL B. REYNOLDS, the U.S. Army major general in charge of the Sixth Service Command based in Chicago and the president of the commission that tried Yamashita

## Summary of Event

General Tomoyuki Yamashita, the "Tiger of Malaya," had a distinguished career before World War II that became even more distinguished during the war. The most brilliant of his achievements was a ten-week campaign down the Malay Peninsula that led to the fall of Britain's "invincible" fortifications at Singapore on February 15, 1942. Despite Yamashita's success and immense popularity in Japan after this event, General Hideki Tōjō, Japan's prime minister, sent Yamashita into virtual exile in Manchuria. The reason for Tōjō's animosity is unknown, but it may have resulted from Yamashita's reputation as a moderate and his opposition to beginning the war. In 1929, Yamashita had gone so far as to suggest that the Japanese army should be reduced to a size adequate only for defense.

In October, 1944, new rules in Tokyo sent Yamashita to command the Fourteenth Army Group in the Philippines. By that time, the Japanese situation in the Philippines was desperate. Ten days after Yamashita arrived, American troops landed at Leyte, and Yamashita had little choice but to retreat to the mountains of Luzon. Allied naval victories and air supremacy cut off Japanese supplies and communications, placing the Japanese in a hopeless situation. Upon hearing a radio broadcast from Japan announcing defeat, Yamashita ordered his troops to surrender unconditionally and surrendered himself on September 3, 1945. General Douglas MacArthur, in Tokyo, appointed a commission of five U.S. Army generals to try Yamashita for war crimes as quickly as possible. Why MacArthur was in such a hurry remains a mystery, but he pressed for speed throughout the trial.

On October 29, 1945, Yamashita's trial opened. The charge against him was that troops under his command had committed atrocities. These were of three kinds. In the first category were atrocities committed in Manila during February of 1945, just before the Americans took the city. The troops in Manila were naval forces placed under Yamashita's tactical command in January, 1945; they remained under the administrative command of the navy. Although Yamashita ordered them to abandon the city twice, the admiral in Manila chose to obey a naval order to stay and destroy the harbor facilities. This decision doomed the troops, and they knew it. About twenty thousand soldiers ran berserk, raping and pillaging until American artillery destroyed central Manila at point-blank range.

A second group of atrocities occurred outside Manila, mainly in the district commanded by Colonel Masatoshi Fujishige. Fujishige was proud of the fact that there were no rapes in his area, but he did order the destruction of villages in an attempt to stop guerrilla actions. He stated that he ordered his troops to kill anyone who opposed them, including women and children. In defense of this policy, he told how a child had thrown a hand grenade at him. He said the policy was his, and that he had not reported his actions.

The defense wanted to remind the commission of the case of American brigadier general Jacob H. Smith, who had ordered his troops to conduct a punitive expedition against Philippine guerrillas in 1901. Smith had said, "I want no prisoners. . . . The more you kill and burn, the better you will please me." Everyone over ten years old was to be killed. A court-martial for breach of discipline sentenced Smith merely to be reprimanded by his superior. No such allusions were allowed, however, as the commission specifically warned the defense lawyers not to present any cases of misconduct by American troops.

A third category of offenses was the mistreatment of prisoners of war in violation of the Geneva Convention of 1929 requiring that prisoners receive the same rations as their captors. Many witnesses testified that they received insufficient food, but it was fairly easy for the defense to establish that Japanese soldiers were no better fed because of the American blockade and poor transportation. The prosecution concentrated on the so-called "Palawan Incident" of December 14, 1944, in which a local Japanese commander had 142 American prisoners killed. Yamashita did not take command until three weeks after this incident occurred, but the prosecution argued that he should have known about it and done something about it.

In general, the defense contended that Yamashita knew nothing of these incidents and could have done nothing about them had he known. By the time he took command, communications were so bad that he was isolated from the troops he nominally commanded. His lawyers argued that he was being tried for who he was rather for than anything he did. There was no proof that he ordered any atrocities or knew of them. The prosecution argued that he must have heard about some atrocities, because there had been so many.

Conduct of the trial by General Russel Reynolds bore only faint resemblance to normal courtroom proceedings. The commission, none of whose members were lawyers, ignored rules of evidence and law by allowing hearsay testimony, unsupported affidavits by absent witnesses—despite an act of Congress prohibiting them—and propaganda films to be submitted as evidence. They cut short defense cross-examination for the sake of speed and threatened the defense attorneys with retribution for slowing down the proceedings with objections.

It was not much of a surprise to anyone when the commission found Yamashita guilty on December 7, 1945, and sentenced him to hang. The defense lawyers feared that MacArthur would order Yamashita's execution before the U.S. Supreme Court could agree to hear the case. MacArthur did refuse a suggestion to delay the execution and announced his intention to proceed on the grounds that the Supreme Court had no jurisdiction over him, but the secretary of war ordered him to delay the execution.

Yamashita's appeal noted that the Commonwealth of the Philippines was not an occupied territory like Germany or Japan, and that he should be tried in civilian courts. His attorneys also said that the unusual circumstances of war had passed with the surrender of Japan, making military courts unnecessary. Their strongest argument was probably that the trial had been conducted in an improper manner.

Unlike the Nuremberg trials, the Yamashita trial was not in the hands of an international tribunal. It was the sole responsibility of the United States, and U.S. law applied. Eight justices of the Supreme Court heard the case and gave their opinions on February 4, 1946. Six of them declared in the majority opinion that the military commission did have the right to try Yamashita, because the war was not technically over until a treaty was signed. They dismissed the case against the irregularities in procedure by saying that it was up to the military authorities to review the case and make any corrections. Justice Frank Murphy and Justice Wiley Rutledge dissented strongly. Both delivered scathing denunciations of the commission and the "vacuity" with which it handled the case. They also agreed that Yamashita was being punished for who he was and not for anything he had done.

President Harry Truman denied an appeal by the defense attorneys. Yamashita was hanged on February 23, 1946.

## Impact of Event

Even at the time of Yamashita's trial and execution, many people saw the dangers of the precedent being set. In his dissenting minority opinion, Justice Murphy said:

In my opinion, such a procedure is unworthy of the traditions of our people or of the immense sacrifices that they have made to advance the common ideals of mankind. The high feelings of the moment doubtless will be satisfied. But in the sober afterglow will come the realization of the boundless and dangerous implications of the procedure sanctioned today. No one in a position of command in an army, from sergeant to general, can escape those implications. Indeed, the fate of some future president of the United States and his chiefs of staff and military advisers may well have been sealed by this decision.

Justice Rutledge ended his dissenting opinion with a quotation from Thomas Paine: "He that would make his own liberty secure must guard even his enemy from oppression; for if he violates this duty he establishes a precedent that will reach himself."

The fate of no U.S. president has been sealed by the Yamashita decision, but it has caused considerable embarrassment for some. During the war in Vietnam, several opponents of U.S. policy suggested that the various atrocities committed by U.S. troops were the responsibility of their commanders, up to and including the commander in chief.

Bertrand Russell and Ralph Schoenman conducted the International War Crimes Tribunal in 1967 and 1968 in an attempt to convince the world that the United States was guilty of war crimes in Vietnam. The hearings in Stockholm came to nothing because the proceedings were biased, but accusers based their contention that President Lyndon Johnson was responsible for atrocities in Vietnam on the Yamashita precedent. One historian of these events wrote, "While collective guilt, like the notion of original sin, may have a place in theology, it is not part of Anglo-American jurisprudence. Here guilt is always personal, and if all are guilty then in effect nobody is guilty." The Yamashita case introduced another principle into American jurisprudence. Someone, preferably the highest-ranking person, must pay even if all are guilty.

## Bibliography

Kenworthy, Aubrey Saint. *The Tiger of Malaya: The Story of General Tomoyuki Yamashita and "Death March" General Masaharu Homma.* New York: Exposition Press, 1953. The author was one of the military police officers assigned to guard Yamashita. He attempts to provide a dispassionate account of his contacts with Yamashita and of the trial but appears sympathetic to his subject. Describes his visit to Yamashita's widow after the execution. Most useful for the many photographs. No footnotes.

Lael, Richard L. *The Yamashita Precedent: War Crimes and Command Responsibility.* Wilmington, Del.: Scholarly Resources, 1982. Short, useful account of the case, with details of the arguments that went on between the Supreme Court justices before their decision. Contends that MacArthur and other leaders were not "black-hearted villains" but merely "made questionable decisions." Fully documented, with a bibliography and index.

Potter, John Deane. *The Life and Death of a Japanese General.* New York: New American Library, 1962. Popularized account of Yamashita's trial. Presents him as a victim.

——————. *A Soldier Must Hang: A Biography of an Oriental General.* London: F. Muller, 1963. Essentially the same as *The Life and Death of a Japanese General.*

Reel, A. Frank. *The Case of General Yamashita.* Chicago: University of Chicago Press, 1949. Reel was one of Yamashita's defense lawyers. This is one of the more useful books on the topic, as it gives a firsthand account of the trial. The organization is confused, however, and the book is written in an anecdotal style. No reference features or illustrations, but a valuable appendix containing the Supreme Court decision and dissenting opinions in full.

Swinson, Arthur. *Four Samurai: A Quartet of Japanese Army Commanders in the Second World War.* London: Hutchinson, 1968. Brief accounts of Yamashita and three other Japanese generals of World War II. The author makes some attempt to use Japanese sources but offers little information about Yamashita that is not available in the other sources listed here.

Taylor, Lawrence. *A Trial of Generals: Homma, Yamashita, MacArthur.* South Bend, Ind.: Icarus Press, 1981. Despite the catchy title, there is little in this book about MacArthur's involvement with the case. Lael's book is much better for an account of the events and their significance by a nonparticipant. Index, bibliography, and photographs.

Yamashita, Tomoyuki. *Before the Military Commission Convened by the Commanding General, United States Army Forces, Western Pacific: United States of America vs. Tomoyuki Yamashita.* 34 vols. Manila, 1945. The proceedings of the trial and, therefore, the ultimate source for information on the trial itself. Its size makes it difficult to use for any but the most interested and determined reader.

*Philip Dwight Jones*

## Cross-References

Legal Norms of Behavior in Warfare Formulated by the Hague Conference (1907), p. 92; Japan Withdraws from the League of Nations (1933), p. 474; Japanese Troops Brutalize Chinese After the Capture of Nanjing (1937), p. 539; Nazi War Criminals Are Tried in Nuremberg (1945), p. 667; Eichmann Is Tried for War Crimes (1961), p. 1108; Lieutenant Calley Is Court-Martialed for the Massacre at My Lai (1970), p. 1555.

# NAZI WAR CRIMINALS ARE TRIED IN NUREMBERG

*Category of event:* Atrocities and war crimes
*Time:* November 20, 1945-October 1, 1946
*Locale:* Nuremberg, Germany

*The Nuremberg Trials of twenty-two Germans accused of war crimes resulted in the conviction of nineteen of the defendants and provided thorough documentation of Nazi crimes against humanity*

*Principal personages:*
ROBERT H. JACKSON (1892-1954), the chief American prosecutor
GEOFFREY LAWRENCE (1902-1967), the president of the tribunal
HERMANN GÖRING (1893-1946), the designated successor of Adolf Hitler until April, 1945, and the creator of the Gestapo
ALBERT SPEER (1905-1981), the minister of armaments who relied on slave labor to increase war production
WILHELM KEITEL (1882-1946), the chief of Hitler's high command between 1938 and 1945
ALFRED ROSENBERG (1893-1946), the chief Nazi ideologue and Reich minister
HANS FRANK (1900-1946), the governor general of Poland after 1939, whose diary recorded Nazi crimes
ERNST KALTENBRUNNER (1903-1946), the head of the Reich Main Security Office who was responsible for the administration of the "final solution" after January, 1943

## Summary of Event

The war that Adolf Hitler launched in 1939 was not simply another military conflict involving territorial and economic disputes growing out of traditional international conflicts. Rather, it was an attempt by the Nazi leadership to exploit or exterminate a large number of religious and ethnic groups in Europe classified as "racially inferior." By 1942, the Allied leaders had decided that Nazi crimes demanded retribution. The next year, the Allies formed a United Nations war crimes commission to collect evidence of the activities of war criminals. After reconquering Kharkov in 1943, the Soviet army tried and executed several German officers for committing war crimes against the Soviet population. The Moscow Declaration of 1943 stated that after the conflict, Germans accused of war crimes would be returned to the countries in which their crimes had been committed and that major Nazi war criminals would be placed before an international tribunal.

Much of the responsibility for designing the mechanism and procedure that would eventually result in the Nuremberg tribunal rested on American shoulders. The U.S.

secretaries of war and state initiated plans for a trial. They faced the opposition of the U.S. secretary of the treasury, Henry Morgenthau, and the British leaders Winston Churchill and Anthony Eden, who demanded the summary execution of Nazi war criminals. In October, 1944, Joseph Stalin expressed his support of a trial, and by January, 1945, U.S. president Franklin D. Roosevelt had also become convinced of the necessity of a judicial process. After Roosevelt's death, President Harry Truman appointed Robert H. Jackson, an associate justice of the U.S. Supreme Court, as "Chief of Counsel for the prosecution of Axis Criminality." Jackson worked out the details for the trial in collaboration with other Allied representatives in London. On August 8, 1945, the Charter of the International Military Tribunal was issued in London, providing the legal basis for the prosecution of Nazi war criminals.

Nuremberg was selected as the site for the trial. The city was able to provide the essential facilities, since its palace of justice had survived Allied air attacks. In addition, Nuremberg had a symbolic significance, since it had hosted yearly Nazi Party rallies. A tribunal of eight judges was created, representing the United States, Great Britain, France, and the Soviet Union and presided over by the British judge, Geoffrey Lawrence. Only the four senior judges were permitted to vote on sentences and on guilt or innocence. Each of the four Allied countries provided a prosecuting team in charge of specific tasks. Twenty-two Nazi leaders, including both civilian and military officials, were indicted. The defendants faced either all or a combination of the following four major charges: crimes of conspiracy, crimes against peace, crimes against the rule of war, and crimes against humanity. In addition, six organizations were charged. These included the Gestapo, the Schutzstaffel (SS), the Nazi party leadership corps, the Reich Cabinet, the Sturm Abteilung (SA), the general staff, and the military high command. Based on a massive amount of documentation that came primarily from Nazi sources, the prosecution presented its case between November 20, 1945, and March, 1946. The defense was faced with the difficult task of having to refute documentary evidence that frequently had been created by the various defendants themselves. On October 1, 1946, the judges rendered their verdicts, pronouncing twelve death and seven prison sentences. Three of the defendants were freed. Three organizations, the SA, the Reich Cabinet, and the military high command, were found not to be criminal organizations, while the SS, the Nazi party leadership corps, and the Gestapo were found guilty of a variety of crimes. Hermann Göring escaped execution by committing suicide, and nine other war criminals were hanged on October 16, 1946.

The written and oral record of the trial revealed a shocking history of Nazi crimes against Jews, Gypsies, Poles, Russians, and numerous other segments of European society defined as inferior by the Nazis. Most of the individuals tried and convicted at Nuremberg represented major criminal organizations that carried out these crimes. Göring, Hitler's designated successor until late April, 1945, and the creator of the Gestapo in 1933 in Prussia, was the leading surviving representative of the Nazi hierarchy. Although he held a number of official titles, as plenipotentiary for the

Nazi Four Year Plan he had been responsible for the brutal exploitation of Europe for Nazi economic gains. In addition, in the summer of 1941 he had delegated to Reinhard Heydrich the task of preparing a plan for the "final solution" of the Jewish problem that resulted in the infamous Wannsee conference in Berlin in January, 1942. Albert Speer, the minister for armaments, played a key role in increasing German military production after 1942 by exploiting European slave labor. Perhaps as many as four million workers from Eastern Europe perished in German factories and work camps.

Nazi war crimes and crimes against humanity expanded exponentially after the invasion of Poland in 1939 and particularly after the attack on Russia in June, 1941. Beginning in 1939, thousands of Germans suffering from mental and physical defects were murdered by medical technicians. After the conquest and partition of Poland, Hans Frank was appointed governor general of that country. His diary reveals the full horror of German occupation that affected both Jews and Poles. The Nazis made every effort to exterminate the Polish intellectual and cultural elite. Before the invasion of Russia, the chief of the German high command, Wilhelm Keitel, agreed to issue orders to the troops that authorized the extermination of captured Soviet commissars. As a result of the neglect of the German army, millions of Soviet prisoners of war perished in German camps. The total of Poles, Russians, and other Eastern Europeans who died as a result of starvation, shootings, and physical exertion may have reached nine million. In addition, 40 percent of Europe's Gypsies were murdered in extermination camps.

Ernst Kaltenbrunner, the head of the Reich Main Security Office, represented the SS organization at Nuremberg. After assuming office in early 1943, Kaltenbrunner became responsible for the Nazi police and extermination forces. The most notorious Nazi crimes against humanity involved the systematic murder of six million Jews. Beginning with the invasion of Russia, SS security forces executed thousands of Jews in Eastern Europe. By the spring of 1942, extermination camps with gas chambers were in operation. Jews were rounded up in all parts of Europe and sent to extermination camps in Eastern and Central Europe, particularly the Auschwitz-Birkenau complex. The commander of that extermination camp vividly described the brutal process during the Nuremberg Trials. On April 18, 1946, the defendant Hans Frank declared that a thousand years would not erase German guilt for these crimes.

The tribunal clearly appreciated the nature of these crimes. Nineteen of the twenty-two defendants were found guilty.

## Impact of Event

The most immediate impact of the Nuremberg Trials was the punishment of at least some leading Nazis and German military leaders for crimes committed by the Third Reich. Although the Soviet Union, which under Joseph Stalin committed crimes against both peace and humanity, was represented on the tribunal, the indisputable fact remained that most of the Nuremberg defendants deserved punishment. Subsequent trials by the American military authorities between December, 1946, and March, 1949, resulted in the conviction of one hundred fifty additional war criminals ranging from industrialists to medical doctors. After West Germany regained much of its autonomy in the mid-1950's, German courts continued legal proceedings against war criminals. In 1958, the West Germans established a special investigative center in Ludwigsburg in order to bring war criminals to trial. Seven years later, the German statute of limitations for murder was extended.

The trial produced an immense amount of documentation of German military and civilian war crimes. It clearly demonstrated to the German public and the world the full extent of Nazi war crimes. In an effort to atone for German crimes against European Jews, Konrad Adenauer, the West German chancellor after 1949, concluded an agreement with representatives from Israel that provided for sizable German payments to that state. Unfortunately, Gypsies and former slave laborers from Eastern Europe had much less success in obtaining compensation from the German state. In addition, before its demise as an independent state in 1990, the German Democratic Republic (East Germany) refused to accept any responsibility for crimes committed during the Third Reich.

The long-term impact of the Nuremberg Trials has been much less spectacular. In 1946, the General Assembly of the United Nations passed a resolution that accepted the principles of international law produced by the Nuremberg Trials. In addition, article seven of the United Nations charter called for an international court of law. The United Nations, however, was unable to produce an acceptable code of crimes against peace and security. By 1953, the United Nations special committee gave up its efforts to establish an international criminal court to enforce Nuremberg's legal principles.

Unfortunately, the Nuremberg principles could neither deter violations of human rights nor prevent an increasing number of genocides around the world, including those in Kampuchea and Burundi. A typical example of the failure of Nuremberg to prevent state racism was the system of apartheid established in South Africa after 1947.

The Nuremberg Trials have been cited by a variety of partisan spokespeople defending opposite views. For example, during the Vietnam War, General Telford Taylor, a former U.S. prosecutor of Nazi war criminals, suggested that United States actions in Vietnam violated Nuremberg principles. This view was echoed by a "war crimes trial" organized in Stockholm, Sweden, by Bertrand Russell, the famous British philosopher. At the same time, spokespeople for President Lyndon B. Johnson argued that the United States was enforcing in Vietnam the Nuremberg principles against aggression.

On a positive side, U.S. Supreme Court Justice Robert Jackson maintained that he was greatly influenced by his experience at Nuremberg. He claimed that he voted to abolish state-enforced school segregation in the American South in 1954 because he had seen at first hand the results of race prejudice. If nothing else, Nuremberg will remain as a constant reminder of the inhumanity of Nazism.

## Bibliography

Biddiss, Michael. "The Nuremberg Trial: Two Exercises of Judgment." *Journal of Contemporary History* 16 (December, 1981): 597-615. An excellent, short review of the major issues of the trial that concludes that the trial helped reveal the real nature of Nazism. The author's notes and his evaluation of the trial's value for historians are helpful for further research.

Bosch, William J. *Judgment on Nuremberg: American Attitudes Toward the Major German War-Crime Trials.* Chapel Hill: University of North Carolina Press, 1970. Reviews American reaction to the Nuremberg Trials by examining various political, religious, and professional segments of American society. Concludes that, in general, American public opinion supported the trial, although some, including John E. Rankin of Mississippi and Senator William Langer of North Dakota, thought that Jews and Communists benefited most from Nuremberg. The list of periodical articles is particularly helpful.

Conot, Robert E. *Justice at Nuremberg.* New York: Harper & Row, 1983. Based on a large variety of primary sources including papers of Francis Biddle and Robert Jackson, this work is valuable for the detailed biographies of the defendants and other participants in the trial. The author stresses the impact the trial had on Jackson during the United States Supreme Court decision to desegregate schools in 1954 and argues that the world cannot afford to ignore the lessons of the trial.

Davidson, Eugene. *The Trial of the Germans: An Account of the Twenty-two Defendants Before the International Military Tribunal at Nuremberg.* New York: Macmillan, 1966. Based on Nuremberg Trials documents and secondary sources only. The author did not have access to the Biddle papers. The defendants are presented within such broad categories as "party," "big business," and "navy." This organization is at times questionable, particularly when Kaltenbrunner is presented together with Keitel and Alfred Jodl. Includes bibliography, notes, and an index.

Gerhart, Eugene C. *America's Advocate: Robert H. Jackson.* Indianapolis: Bobbs-Merrill, 1958. A highly laudatory biography of Jackson, focusing both on his role as United States Supreme Court justice and chief American prosecutor at Nuremberg. One-third of the book is devoted to Jackson's role at the Nuremberg Trials. Unlike many other scholars, the author enthusiastically praises Jackson's performance at Nuremberg.

Göring, Hermann, defendant. *Trial of the Major War Criminals Before the International Military Tribunal, Nuremberg, 14 November 1945-1 October 1946.* 42 vols. Nuremberg: International Military Tribunal, 1947-1949. This is the official trial record in English. Includes the text of the trial and eighteen volumes of supporting documents. Most of the documents came from the prosecution, not the defense. Essential for any serious examination of the trial. Available in most major university libraries.

Lawrence, Geoffrey. "The Nuremberg Trial." *International Affairs* 2 (April, 1947): 151-159. Interesting comments about the trial by the president of the tribunal. Describes the internal operations and activities at Nuremberg and offers interesting appraisals of both defendants and prosecutors. Argues that the British deputy chief prosecutor, David Maxwell Fyfe, was the most effective prosecutor at the trial. Points out that no defendant was hanged for the crime of planning an aggressive war.

Smith, Bradley F. *Reaching Judgment at Nuremberg.* New York: Basic Books, 1977. Based on thorough research and relying heavily on the Francis Biddle papers, this volume offers a fascinating insight into internal deliberations of the tribunal. Although the author questions some verdicts and procedures, he praises the tribunal's performance. Smith notes that class bias, ideological preferences, and personal dislikes of defendants or their lawyers influenced the judges on the tribunal.

Tusa, Ann, and John Tusa. *The Nuremberg Trial.* New York: Atheneum, 1984. The most reliable survey of the trial, based on a thorough use of published and unpublished primary sources and interviews. Particularly valuable for the detailed discussion of the defense case of each accused, which takes up half of the book. Although well-balanced on the whole, a British bias surfaces on occasion. Maintains that the American arguments and methods "lacked intellectual clarity and forensic sharpness."

Woetzel, Robert K. *The Nuremberg Trials in International Law.* London: Stevens and Sons, 1960. The author, a professor of public law and government at Fordham University, appraises the trial from a legal perspective. Points out some serious shortcomings of the trial but concludes that the International Military Tribunal represents a crucial stage in the evolution of "international criminal law." The bibliography and index are helpful.

*Johnpeter Horst Grill*

### Cross-References

Nazi Concentration Camps Go into Operation (1933), p. 491; The United Nations Adopts a Convention on the Crime of Genocide (1948), p. 783; Eichmann Is Tried for War Crimes (1961), p. 1108; The Statute of Limitations Is Ruled Not Applicable to War Crimes (1968), p. 1457; Lieutenant Calley Is Court-Martialed for the Massacre at My Lai (1970), p. 1555; Barbie Faces Charges for Nazi War Crimes (1983), p. 2193; Israel Convicts Demjanjuk of Nazi War Crimes (1988), p. 2370; Iraq Invades and Ravages Kuwait (1990), p. 2600.

# PERÓN CREATES A POPULIST POLITICAL ALLIANCE IN ARGENTINA

*Categories of event:* Civil rights and workers' rights
*Time:* February 24, 1946
*Locale:* Buenos Aires, Argentina

*Juan Perón was elected president of Argentina by a coalition of labor and nationalist military, ending more than a decade of conservative rule*

*Principal personages:*

JUAN PERÓN (1895-1974), the three-term president of Argentina (1946-1952, 1952-1955, and 1973-1974) who built a political alliance of military colleagues, organized labor, and the mass of Argentina's poor

EVA PERÓN (1919-1952), the second wife of Juan Perón and, as Evita, a fiery orator

RAMÓN S. CASTILLO (1873-1944), the president of Argentina from July, 1940, until overthrown by a military coup in 1943

ROBERTO ORTIZ (1886-1942), the president of Argentina from 1938 to 1940; attempted to implement democratic reforms

## Summary of Event

Argentina's last constitutionally elected president before World War II, Hipólito Irigoyen, was overthrown by a military coup in September, 1930. For the next sixteen years, a coalition of conservative political leaders would rule the country by fraud and fear. Political rights were restricted, and elections were rigged in favor of the government's candidates.

Throughout the 1930's, which came to be known as "The Decade of Infamy," labor legislation was ignored or unenforced, and many workers believed that their rights to safe working conditions and impartial arbitration were not being upheld. The election of Roberto Ortiz in 1937 brought hope for better relations between labor and the government. The *concordancia*, as the ruling conservative coalition was called, allowed only token opposition, but President Ortiz had made an effort to institute political reforms by overturning dishonest elections in Buenos Aires. Ortiz resigned because of deteriorating health, and Vice President Ramón Castillo took power. Castillo soon demonstrated that he had no sympathy for the right of the people freely to choose their elected officials or for the rights of labor.

Argentina's working class had grown and changed since the early days of the century, when most workers were immigrants employed in meat-packing plants or in the ports. Local manufacturing had become more important as Argentina's dependence on agricultural exports declined during the worldwide depression of the 1930's. The governments of the 1930's encouraged expansion of local industry. This led to a shift in employment opportunities away from agriculture and toward industry, creating a larger urban working class.

When new elections were scheduled in 1943, one of the issues was Argentina's response to the United States' pressure to enter World War II on the side of the Allies. The biggest domestic issue, however, was the continuation of government by fraud, since Castillo had hand-picked an archconservative political boss from the interior as his successor. The lack of meaningful suffrage was a growing burden to the many Argentines who wanted their vote to count. This would lead to a political opposition that brought disparate groups together.

Many Argentines were willing to support a military coup against the government of Castillo, believing that the new regime would be an improvement. The soldiers struck on June 4, 1943. Under the leadership of a secret lodge, known as the Group of United Officers (GOU), a new military government was established with General Pedro Ramírez as president. One of its first laws called for government control of the press and broadcast media. This control was given to Juan Perón, assistant to General Edelmiro Farrell. Perón would use his position to create a power base in the new government. At a rally for earthquake victims in the provincial city of San Juan in 1944, Perón met Eva Duarte, then a young radio personality who would become his wife.

Perón became a powerful force for change in the new military government. He took a relatively insignificant post as head of the Department of Labor and used it to address the grievances of workers and the poor. Perón's increasing influence in the government led to the creation of an independent Secretariat of Labor and Social Welfare, from which he granted benefits and rights hitherto denied the lower classes in Argentina.

Labor leaders, many workers, and the masses of the poor came to see Perón as the key figure in their search for dignity and human rights. The income of workers had declined in the 1930's and, as urban employment grew, shantytowns, called *villas miserias*, of tin-roofed huts sprang up around the city of Buenos Aires. Thanks to Perón, workers in 1943 got a 40 percent wage increase and the legal right to organize and negotiate. By 1944, workers were getting paid holidays, the government had negotiated more than two hundred agreements between workers and employers, and benefits were extended to two million workers. The key to getting the government to grant workers' demands was obedience to Perón. Organized labor and Juan Perón were becoming an important political coalition.

Perón's power in the government increased. When General Farrell took over as president, Perón became vice president in addition to his duties as minister of war and secretary of labor and social welfare. Perón had his opponents. Liberals, along with representatives of the United States, suspected him of sympathy with fascist regimes during World War II. Students were upset with the continuation of military regimes. Some in the military were offended by Perón's alliance with Eva Duarte (known as Evita). This opposition led President Farrell to force Perón's resignation in October, 1945, so that he could not use his influence to gain the presidency in the following year's elections.

Perón was detained and taken to an island in the Río de la Plata. When word of his arrest reached working-class suburbs, strikes were called and a march to the center of Buenos Aires began. Hundreds of thousands of workers marched on October 17, cheering their support for Perón. Middle-class Argentines, always dressed in suit and tie, would mockingly refer to these people as the "shirtless ones" after enthusiastic followers of Perón waved their shirts as banners. The people in the street that day were giving their support to someone who had promised to uphold their right to organize. The power of their numbers overwhelmed security, and President Farrell was forced to bring Perón to address the throng. Perón happily received their cheers and would later claim the "shirtless ones" as his special people. The political realignment of workers was nearly complete. Their leader was now Juan Perón.

Perón voluntarily stepped down from his positions in the government, only to declare his candidacy for the presidency. He received the support of the newly formed Labor Party as well as a splinter group from the middle-class Radical Party. Among Perón's supporters were military colleagues of the now-disbanded GOU. In addition, the Catholic church approved of Perón's call for religious instruction in the schools and supported his candidacy indirectly. In February, 1946, in one of the most open and honest elections ever held in Argentina, Perón received nearly 54 percent of the vote and was inaugurated as president in June of that year.

The coalition that elected Perón was fragile. As president, Perón attempted to strengthen his power over these groups. Benefits for labor continued as the real wages of industrial workers increased by 20 percent between 1945 and 1948. In 1947, the government took control of a private charity which eventually became the María Eva Duarte de Perón Social Aid Foundation. Headed by the first lady, this foundation constructed schools, funded hospitals, and aided the poor and the orphans. "In the New Argentina the only privileged ones are the children," stated one of the Twenty Truths of the official Peronist doctrine.

Juan Perón and Evita came to be adored by millions of Argentines. They called him "Argentina's first worker," and the paid holidays he enacted were called Saint Perón days. Evita received adulation as well, especially from women, who were given the vote in 1947, largely through Evita's insistence.

The capstone of Perón's political power, arising from the alliance of labor, women, nationalist military, and even many of the middle class, came in March, 1949, when a new constitution was promulgated. This constitution guaranteed social justice for workers and stipulated that they had the right to work, fair pay, good conditions in the workplace, dignity, and health. It also permitted a sitting president to succeed himself. This last provision paved the way for Perón's reelection in 1951. He would remain in office until ousted by a military coup in 1955. Reelected almost twenty years later, he returned to office in October, 1973. He died in office in July, 1974.

## Impact of Event

The first presidency of Juan Perón was a turning point because it offered new hope for human rights for the people of Argentina. The coalition of labor and the government under Perón brought increased living standards, political freedom, protection from abuse, and a sense of dignity to the working class. Conditions would soon change, however, as it became apparent that Perón saw these policies not as ends in themselves but as means to increased power for himself.

The relationship between labor and government had long been one of opposition and denial of many labor rights. Perón co-opted labor in Argentina and used it to gain power. He also gave labor a voice in government. Juan Bramuglia, a lawyer for the railroad union, was foreign minister in Perón's administration, and Angel Borlenghi, from the Confederation of Commercial Employees, became minister of the interior. Even after Perón's downfall, organized labor remained an arbiter in national politics.

Many workers still consider Perón's administration as the most sympathetic to their problems and the most helpful in bringing improvements to their lives. Perón's concept of social justice, or *justicialismo*, brought benefits to Argentina's working class. New schools, hospitals, and hundreds of thousands of low-cost apartments were built. A National Mortgage Bank was funded to increase home construction, and by 1951 more than 200,000 houses were built.

Women in Argentina also benefited from the policies of the Perón administration. Evita established a feminine branch of the Peronist Party and pushed successfully for voting rights for women. Hostels were built for women who needed shelter. At the end of Perón's first administration, there was talk of making Evita his running mate. Political opposition and her illness led her to withdraw.

Perón also provided Argentina's working class with a sense of pride. Model vacation resorts were constructed, and workers, many for the first time, could afford to take family vacations to the mountains or the beach. Perón preached about the dignity of work and pushed for a transformation of Argentina from an economy dominated by wealthy landowners to an industrializing society.

Perón's administration became increasingly authoritarian by the early 1950's. There were accusations that opponents were arrested arbitrarily and even tortured. Opposition newspapers were harrassed and, for a time, the prestigious newspaper *La Prensa* was closed by the government.

Perón's legacy is difficult to evaluate. He was an authoritarian leader who controlled the labor movement for his own purposes but made organized labor a political power. He ignored human and political rights of his opponents, shutting down newspapers, closing unions, and arresting politicians, but he extended voting rights to women and was elected in honest and open elections. There is agreement among his supporters and enemies, however, that Juan Perón's election to the presidency on February 24, 1946, changed Argentina forever.

## Bibliography

Alexander, Robert J. *Juan Domingo Perón: A History*. Boulder, Colo.: Westview Press, 1979. Alexander provides an excellent short account of Perón's career. His interpretation reflects extensive travel to the region and interviews with many of the participants, including Perón.

Barager, Joseph R., ed. *Why Perón Came to Power: The Background to Peronism in Argentina.* New York: Alfred A. Knopf, 1968. The essays in this book trace the background of Perón and his rise to power. Part 2 of the book focuses on the years 1945 and 1946, with essays specifically on Perón and the labor movement, the events of October 17, 1945, and the election of February, 1946.

Crowley, Eduardo. *Argentina: A Nation Divided, 1890-1980.* London: C. Hurst, 1984. Eduardo Crowley is an Argentine writer who brings a native perspective to the story of Perón. He quotes from many pamphlets of the era. Anecdotes help bring the people alive.

Fraser, Nicholas, and Marysa Navarro. *Eva Perón.* New York: W. W. Norton, 1980. Biographies about Eva Perón often have been biased and polemical. This study goes beyond the myths and looks at the woman who was both loved and hated. The authors make extensive use of interviews and bring out the complex personalities of both Evita and Juan Perón.

Hodges, Donald C. *Argentina, 1943-1976: The National Revolution and Resistance.* Albuquerque: University of New Mexico Press, 1976. Hodges updates the history of Perón's early years in power by continuing the story after his downfall. Some of the unusual sources used by Hodges include interviews with Peronist leaders in exile. The strength of this book is its ability to describe the variations within the Peronist movement that began to tear it apart when Perón returned to power in the 1970's.

Page, Joseph A. *Perón, A Biography.* New York: Random House, 1983. An easily readable book. Page uses many sources but has focused on the many diplomatic sources available to him in Washington. This book emphasizes Perón's foreign policy and the view of United States administrations.

Rock, David. *Argentina, 1516-1982.* Berkeley: University of California Press, 1985. A comprehensive history of Argentina from its founding as a Spanish colony. Attempts to give the reader the broad scope of history. Chapters 7 and 8 deal specifically with the period of Perón, although Rock's perspective is political and economic.

*James A. Baer*

## Cross-References

The Wagner Act Requires Employers to Accept Collective Bargaining (1935), p. 508; Corporatism Comes to Paraguay and the Americas (1936), p. 533; The U.N. Convention on the Political Rights of Women Is Approved (1952), p. 885; Castro Takes Power in Cuba (1959), p. 1026; The Argentine Military Conducts a "Dirty War" Against Leftists (1976), p. 1864; Argentine Leaders Are Convicted of Human Rights Violations (1985), p. 2280; Voters in Chile End Pinochet's Military Rule (1989), p. 2540.

# THE WORLD HEALTH ORGANIZATION PROCLAIMS HEALTH AS A BASIC RIGHT

*Category of event:* Health and medical rights
*Time:* July 22, 1946
*Locale:* United Nations, New York City

*In 1946, the World Health Organization's constitution declared that "the enjoyment of health is one of the fundamental rights of every human being"*

*Principal personages:*
>G. BROCK CHISHOLM (1896-1971), a psychiatrist who served as WHO's first secretary-general (1948-1953)
>PIERRE MARIE DOROLLE (1899-    ), a French physician and deputy director-general of WHO (1950-1973)
>TRYGVE LIE (1896-1968), the secretary-general of the United Nations (1946-1953)
>PAUL-HENRI SPAAK (1899-1972), the president of the United Nations General Assembly (1946)

## Summary of Event

The World Health Organization (WHO) was born between the end of World War II and the Korean conflict. World War II set the stage for decolonization, as the war weakened the major European colonial powers and Japan demonstrated to colonized countries that European powers could be defeated. The formal advent of the nuclear age, with the dropping of atomic bombs on Hiroshima and Nagasaki in August, 1945, and the Korean conflict in 1950 further destabilized the old international power system. The system that emerged was one with two superpowers, the United States and the Soviet Union. Europe and Japan were being rebuilt, largely with American aid, and the new technologies of the era began to have a global impact. The world's attention, given such turbulence, was not on health issues. Nevertheless, WHO proclaimed that its prime objective was to raise the standard of health care for all persons.

This idea's institutional ancestry begins in 1851, when the first International Sanitary Conference convened in Paris. Physicians and diplomats, representing twelve countries, met for the first time to discuss health problems and draw up the first international convention on health rules to promote uniformity in quarantine procedures. The convention was well ahead of its time and was not ratified.

The next major international efforts concerning health and health care came with the founding of the Health Organization of the League of Nations in 1923 and the International Office of Public Health in 1909. These organizations helped in healing the wounds left by World War I and in creating a better world through potent new health care weapons such as penicillin. The International Office of Public Health continued to operate after the League of Nations' collapse during World War II. These preliminary global health systems evolved into the World Health Organization in 1946.

In 1945, fifty nations attending the San Francisco Conference created and adopted the United Nations Charter. It was also decided, on June 26, to establish a world health body. The International Health Conference held in New York City (June 19-July 22, 1946) approved the creation of WHO. An interim commission ran WHO until it formally came into existence on April 7, 1948.

WHO was to be the medical body of the United Nations. It was to direct and coordinate everything related to international health issues, assisting governments in strengthening their national health services and providing emergency and technical assistance as needed. Some of the other goals and functions stipulated in its constitution were to educate all peoples (the general public as well as health care providers) about health issues; to foster and promote work (applied and research) to eradicate diseases, especially those of epidemic, endemic, or social natures; to advocate and advance maternal and child health; and to promote mental health.

WHO was designed to be a decentralized umbrella organization with six regional offices, operating independently within the larger framework of the United Nations. WHO was to establish regional centers which would conduct research and collect health data. The cancer research center in Lyon, France, is one such center designed to operate independently. The Center for Disease Control in Atlanta, Georgia, was established as a joint effort with WHO to collect data on influenza and other communicable diseases. WHO also works with other U.N. agencies, such as the Food and Agriculture Organization, on topics of mutual concern.

Article 1 of the WHO Constitution states that attainment of the best possible health care by all peoples is a basic human right. The constitution also states that "the enjoyment of health is one of the fundamental rights of every human being." WHO intended to promote these rights through education, through restructuring and training government agencies and service providers at the national level, and by providing comprehensive services (for example, technical assistance, standardized diagnostic procedures, environmental hygiene and sanitation research and assistance, and conferences on various topics).

The major innovations of the WHO Constitution, reinforced by specific articles in the Universal Declaration of Human Rights (adopted on December 10, 1948), were that for the first time health was defined as a universal human right, and furthermore, by expanding the definition of health to cover all aspects of health-related well-being (including food, housing, and clothing), responsibility for well-being was placed squarely on the shoulders of individual governments. Maternal and child welfare, as well as social security for the unemployed, the elderly, the sick, and the widowed, were also included. The constitution also stated that health is connected to international politics, in that health is necessary for the attainment of peace and security. Initially, this statement in the WHO Constitution was ignored while WHO established its fundamental activities and organized the necessary frameworks and networks to achieve its prime directive. Short-term needs of the developed and less developed countries, especially concentrated disease eradication programs for smallpox and malaria, were the initial action areas.

Not all has run smoothly for WHO. For example, the definition and categorization of human rights in the U.N. Charter do not include health as a human right. This right is listed in Article 25 of the Universal Declaration of Human Rights, but it has never been given high priority. The basics of what constitute human or natural rights form the context of many debates within the United Nations, especially when these rights clash with traditional values and ways of life. Such debates also occur within WHO and its various agencies, on topics such as population control and family planning. This lack of consensus over the meanings of "human rights" and "health as a human right" has created problems in the implementation and coordination of WHO's goals and activities.

One example of such difficulties concerns the World Health Assembly (WHO's major body) and how it forms policy regarding health standards. If a policy becomes a "regulation," it is difficult to monitor. Another difficulty is that regulations are binding on each member state, unless a state expresses some reservations or rejects the regulation. WHO has no authority to enforce its regulations. Another type of policy, less binding and stringent than a "regulation," is a "recommendation." Recommendations are more common than regulations because reservations and rejections are avoided. Recommendations are more likely to promote consensus among WHO's members. Many cultures in Africa, for example, continued to practice female circumcision even in the 1990's. This practice is part of their interpretation of Islam and is connected to the proper place of women in society, to the marriageability of females, and thus to the establishment of the family. If WHO passed a recommendation to abolish female circumcision, then member states could choose to ignore it without jeopardizing their WHO membership or feeling that Western or Christian ideas about the "proper" treatment of women were being imposed on them. WHO and the United Nations as a whole must tread softly in the areas of cultural differences, which both organizations, constitutionally, must uphold.

## Impact of Event

In spite of such problems, WHO has made considerable progress. Smallpox has been wholly eradicated. Global birth rates are beginning to decrease in the 1990's, in part because of the WHO-sponsored family planning programs which are one leg of its larger program in family health. WHO, in conjunction with other agencies and groups, has been trying actively to improve the quality of the environment. To this end, international reference systems have been established which study, monitor, and gather data on community water supplies, waste disposal, air and water pollution, and radiation protection. Between 1966 and 1970, six widespread air pollutants received intensive international study in order to establish criteria and guidelines for air quality. To promote international scientific cooperation, a network of 191 regional and international reference centers were set up in more than thirty countries between 1966 and 1970. The medical research programs overseen by WHO are engaged in ongoing efforts to control communicable diseases, the newest of which in the early 1990's was Acquired Immune Deficiency Syndrome (AIDS); to prevent nutritional disorders, which can cause permanent brain damage in infants and children and contribute to high infant and maternal death rates; to study cancer and cardiovascular diseases, which are on the rise in South America as well as in other parts of the world; and to study the incidence, treatment, and causation of mental disorders. In a 1970 survey, WHO found that both syphilis and gonorrhea were increasing globally. Gonorrhea in particular showed a dramatic increase in teenagers. Cholera was also on the increase and spread to new areas. WHO increased its aid, and cholera research intensified, especially in the areas of vaccines, detection, and treatment of cases and carriers. By September, 1970, WHO's malaria eradication program had improved living conditions for about 80 percent of almost two billion people in 145 targeted countries and territories. With WHO funds, fellowships are provided to train and educate people; specifically targeted are medical officers in key positions in governments.

In spite of its wobbly beginnings, WHO has become the global symbol of international health care through efforts such as those listed above. Increasingly, as countries recognize that primary health care, at a minimum, is essential to a country's economic well-being as well as its future, more countries will come to define health care as a basic human right. This definitional shift must occur within each country before WHO can begin to achieve this ultimate goal. In 1977, WHO set a new goal: "Health for all by the Year 2000."

## Bibliography

Berting, Jan, et al., eds. *Human Rights in a Pluralist World.* Westport, Conn.: Meckler, 1990. A collection of papers delivered at two international conferences on human rights in concert with the United Nations' fortieth anniversary of the Universal Declaration of Human Rights. Papers discuss the achievements, problems, and difficulties in defining and implementing "human rights." College-level reading; references are provided.

Chandler, William U. "Investing in Children." In *State of the World, 1986,* edited by Lester R. Brown. New York: W. W. Norton, 1986. Discussion of the efforts of WHO, UNICEF, and other United Nations agencies in concert with local governments to improve child health through improved basic health care, nutrition, and sanitation. This book is part of a World Watch Institute series which covers a different topic each year. College-level reading; references are provided.

Henderson, Donald A. "Smallpox: Never Again." *World Health* (August/September, 1987): 8-11. WHO launched a concerted and collaborative effort in 1967 to eliminate smallpox globally. This is good discussion of this time-limited, focused approach. In May, 1980, the Thirty-third World Health Assembly declared smallpox eradicated. The malaria eradication program, however, did not work. A history of the programs is provided. College-level reading.

Lambo, Thomas A., and Stacey B. Day, eds. *Issues in Contemporary International Health*. New York: Plenum Press, 1990. Good selection of readings on international health issues. Authors of the various articles are experts but write for the lay reader. College-level reading, with references at end of each article.

Rushwan, Hamid. "Female Circumcision." *World Health* (April/May, 1990): 24-25. Discussion of various types of genital mutilation practiced in various African countries. WHO has been trying to eliminate this practice since 1976.

Senderowitz, Judith, and John M. Paxman. *Adolescent Fertility: Worldwide Concerns.* Population Bulletin 2. Washington, D.C.: Population Reference Bureau, April, 1985. Good demographic analysis of global teenage fertility patterns. Issued in concert with the International Youth Year. Covers laws, access to information, behavioral patterns, and programs. Population Reference Bureau publications cover many topics and are a good neutral source of information. College-level reading with references.

"Thailand's Mr. Contraception." *Time* 117 (March 23, 1981): 67. Short, easy-to-read article on how one man improved health care, via contraception availability, in his country by utilizing local resources.

*Dixie Dean Dickinson*

## Cross-References

The United Nations Children's Fund Is Established (1946), p. 689; The United Nations Adopts the Universal Declaration of Human Rights (1948), p. 789; The United Nations Adopts the Declaration of the Rights of the Child (1959), p. 1038; The Organization of African Unity Is Founded (1963), p. 1194; The Proclamation of Teheran Sets Human Rights Goals (1968), p. 1430; The United Nations Declares Rights for the Mentally Retarded (1971), p. 1644; A U.N. Declaration on Hunger and Malnutrition Is Adopted (1974), p. 1775; The U.N. Declaration on the Rights of Disabled Persons Is Adopted (1975), p. 1841; WHO Sets a Goal of Health for All by the Year 2000 (1977), p. 1893; An International Health Conference Adopts the Declaration of Alma-Ata (1978), p. 1998; The World Health Organization Adopts a Code on Breast-Milk Substitutes (1981), p. 2130; The U.N. Principles of Medical Ethics Include Prevention of Torture (1982), p. 2169; The United Nations Adopts the Convention on the Rights of the Child (1989), p. 2529.

# THE NATIONALIST VIETNAMESE FIGHT AGAINST FRENCH CONTROL OF INDOCHINA

*Category of event:* Revolutions and rebellions
*Time:* November, 1946-July, 1954
*Locale:* North Vietnam

*Viet Minh forces defended the independence of Vietnam against French forces that were seen as a vestige of colonial influence*

> *Principal personages:*
> Ho Chi Minh (1890-1969), the president of the Republic of Vietnam, committed to the idea of Vietnamese independence
> Vo Nguyen Giap (1912- ), a Vietnamese patriot and the commander of Ho Chi Minh's military arm, the Viet Minh
> Jean Sainteny (?-1978), a French negotiator, who developed the blueprint for the recognition of the Republic of Vietnam
> Georges Thierry d'Argenlieu (1889-1964), the French high commissioner for Indochina at the end of World War II

## Summary of Event

In September of 1945, while the eyes of the world were focused on the Japanese surrender in the Pacific, Ho Chi Minh proclaimed the Republic of Vietnam. After nearly one hundred years of oppressive French domination, Ho Chi Minh believed the United States would enforce the ideals President Franklin D. Roosevelt put down in the Atlantic Charter of 1941: the return of self-government to nations that had been forcibly denied this right. Ho and other Vietnamese Nationalists did not realize that Vietnam had been used as a bargaining chip by the United States in several wartime political maneuvers. In 1942, President Roosevelt had guaranteed the Free French that they would be able to retain all of their overseas possessions, including Vietnam. This promise had been offered as an inducement to encourage greater efforts by the French military forces. In 1943, Roosevelt had countered this promise and proposed a trusteeship for postwar Indochina, claiming that the French had mismanaged the people and resources of the area. Still later in the war, in 1945, Roosevelt tried to bargain with the leader of the Nationalist Chinese, Chiang Kai-shek, by offering him control of Vietnam and any other countries in Indochina. The Chinese turned down the offer because of the difficulty of trying to govern a nation that would not conform to Chinese rule. So, in 1945, the fate of Vietnam was still undecided.

During the war, Vietnam had been occupied by the Japanese with French approval. France's credibility concerning Japan was called into question as a result of this, and at the Potsdam Conference the decision was made to allow neutral allied nations to oversee Japanese disarmament in Vietnam. The British were to supervise in the south and the Chinese were in charge of northern disarmament. The French high commissioner (governor) for Indochina, Admiral Georges Thierry d'Argenlieu, was to coordinate between the areas.

The new Republic of Vietnam had no military institutions to protect its claim of independence and no political organization that represented the nation as a whole. In 1945, the new republic was led by Communist-styled cadres, known as the Viet Minh. These cadres were organized politically by Ho Chi Minh and militarily by Vo Nguyen Giap, Ho's trusted assistant. Within days of the landing of the British forces, conflict broke out between the Viet Minh, the French, and the British.

The British officer in charge, General Gracey, ordered to remain neutral, was unquestionably in favor of French rule in the area. A product of the British colonial system, Gracey did not believe that the Vietnamese were capable of self-government, nor that they should ever be allowed to threaten the control of their masters. As soon as rioting broke out in Saigon, he released French legionnaires from their Japanese prisons and armed them with British weapons.

Fearing the return of French rule, the Viet Minh continued rioting and increased attacks against French units as well as against the British. In Saigon, the fighting was fierce at times and atrocities against civilians were committed by both sides. The British, fearing increased involvement, turned over their weapons and supplies to the French and left the country.

In the north, Vietnamese-Chinese relations went somewhat more smoothly. General Lu Han's troops were not up to the caliber of the British units. The soldiers were starving, ill-equipped, and often tubercular, more interested in ransacking the towns and countryside of Vietnam for food, clothing, and medicine than in French-Vietnamese politics. Ho Chi Minh feared the incursion of Chinese troops more than he feared the French and British, as China had been attempting to overrun Vietnam for one thousand years. He feared that the Potsdam Agreement had given China political gains in Southeast Asia that it had been unable to attain militarily. Because of this fear, Ho Chi Minh made no effort to prevent French attempts to negotiate a deal with China to override the Potsdam design and give France the control of all of Vietnam.

On February 28, 1946, a French-Chinese agreement was reached. The Chinese would remove their troops from North Vietnam, to be replaced by an equal number of French. In return, France gave up all claims to the Kwangchowan region of China (held by France since 1880). France also agreed to sell the Yunnan railroad to Chiang Kai-shek's nationalist government and to designate Haiphong as a free trade port for China.

Ho, glad to be rid of the Chinese, was not yet ready to settle for the return of French domination. Vietnam, to Ho and his followers, was now an independent republic, and he encouraged Giap to step up recruitment and training of more cadres of Viet Minh to ensure the protection of the country. The French, unable to stabilize both halves of the country, allowed a French diplomat, Jean Sainteny, to attempt negotiations with Ho.

The Sainteny-Ho agreement was completed on March 6. France guaranteed the recognition of Vietnam as an independent state within the French Union (Laos, Cambodia, and Vietnam). In return, Ho agreed to allow twenty-five thousand French troops to remain in the country for a period of five years to protect French interests.

As each side stepped up its attempts to control the area, one situation became clear. The key to success was going to be in the countryside. The rural villages and peasant farm holdings were going to be needed as base camps. The average villager, desiring neutrality, was caught between the two opposing forces.

By day, the villagers were victims of French recruitment and commissary officers. Fear for their lives or those of their families and the threat of losing the family farm, more than a committed belief in the right of the French to control Vietnam, caused peasant farmers to join the French forces. The French began to control the countryside around the major cities of Vietnam.

By night, the countryside of Vietnam belonged to the cadres of the Viet Minh. The cadres were small, self-sufficient units that survived alone in the jungle. Usually without adequate weapons or supplies, they depended on local villages for support as well as additional recruits for Giap's army. Several nights a week, they moved into the villages and conducted classes in nationalism, communism, anti-French tactics, and basic reading and writing skills. They targeted the youth of these villages as the source of future independence guerrillas and a present spy network against the French.

Most of the peasants philosophically believed in independence, but they had no stomach for more warfare. Laboring to feed their families and to preserve their small plots of land, they became trapped in an untenable position. Harangued, threatened, beaten, and sometimes tortured and killed, the peasants of Vietnam were pulled into a conflict that the Sainteny-Ho agreement was supposed to prevent. Before the agreement could be signed officially in Paris, President Charles de Gaulle sent one thousand additional troops to Saigon. Ho Chi Minh appealed to Giap to redouble his military recruiting and training efforts. Colonial business people, planters, and state officials published strong complaints against the agreement. They cabled Paris with their complaints and turned to the local governor, Admiral d'Argenlieu, with their fears.

D'Argenlieu, committed to the policy of French colonialism in Vietnam, did not wait for orders from Paris. He violated the March agreement and declared the Republic of Cochin China (South Vietnam), in the name of France. Ho, in Paris for the official signing of the Sainteny Accords, was discredited as an impotent political upstart by d'Argenlieu's actions and returned to Vietnam having failed to achieve recognition of Vietnam's independence.

Complaints from colonists in Vietnam put political pressure on the French cabinet to claim economic rights to both the north and south of Vietnam. Fearing the loss of what little recognition he had gained for his country's right to political autonomy, Ho returned to Paris in October. Pressured by French intransigence, Ho agreed to and signed a draft of an accord known as the Fontainebleau Agreement, a vague attempt to give joint rule over North Vietnam to both the French and the Vietnamese. Because of unstated lines of authority concerning the policing of cities and collection of customs, the draft led to frustration and dissatisfaction for both sides. The confusion caused by the Fontainebleau Agreement can be argued as the direct cause of the French-Indochina war.

Fighting broke out November 20, 1946, when a French patrol boat apprehended Chinese smugglers in the waterways of Haiphong Harbor. A Vietnamese patrol, observing the French apprehension of the Chinese smugglers and unsure of exact lines of authority, considered the act as one more indication of French unwillingness to allow the republic to control itself. The Vietnamese approached and overtook the French boat and arrested the three crewmen. Fighting broke out in the city of Haiphong as soon as the French became aware of the arrests.

Throughout the day of November 20, French tanks entered the city of Haiphong and overran Vietnamese barricades. The Viet Minh cadres responded with mortar fire. A cease fire was called the next day, and both sides began appealing to Paris for direction. Ho appealed to the French government to honor the signed accords. He was ordered to cede French control of the city and ports of Haiphong. When he refused, the battle resumed.

The French attack on Haiphong utilized the gamut of military technology of the day: infantry, tanks, artillery, air strikes, and naval bombardment. The underequipped Viet Minh responded with mortar fire and guerrilla raids. Entire neighborhoods of flimsy houses in the poorest sections of town were demolished, and thousands of Vietnamese refugees poured out of the city. The official French reports at the time stated that six thousand civilians had been killed as they fled the area. Later, the figures were reduced to read that no more than several hundred had died.

The fighting spread to the city of Hanoi and lasted through most of December. On December 19, at 9:00 P.M., Vo Nguyen Giap declared virtual war on the country of France and Ho Chi Minh called on the people of Vietnam to rise up and to defend Vietnamese independence and unification. Ho Chi Minh continued to appeal to the Western powers to stop French aggression throughout the month of December. While not agreeing with the French policies, Europe and the United States refused to step in. The war between France and Vietnam lasted eight years.

## Impact of Event

French colonialism was to have widespread effects throughout Europe, China, and the United States. Unable to receive the aid and support needed to break French control of Vietnam, Ho Chi Minh reverted to seeking assistance from Communist China and Russia. This action placed Vietnam in the middle of Cold War politics and on a direct line of confrontation with the United States.

Vietnam paid a heavy price for Ho Chi Minh's dream of independence. More than three million Vietnamese were killed between 1946 and 1976, as fighting shifted from a war against France to internal strife between North and South Vietnam. This figure may not be totally reliable, but error would seem to lie on the side of underestimation and not overestimation of the truth. Thousands of children, along with women and soldiers, were burned and maimed as a result of bombings, mines, and enemy raids on villages. The civilians of Vietnam were all soldiers in the eyes of their enemies, and their elimination was often condoned as a way to prevent future generations of resistance fighters.

Without sufficient medical supplies or technology, the Vietnamese victims have been condemned to a lifetime of suffering and nonproductivity. Added to the physical damage to their bodies is the hidden chemical threat. The use of hundreds of thousands of gallons of defoliant and other chemicals has imparted the legacy of fear, fear of cancer and birth defects that will not cease with the passing of this generation.

The physical human damage to the Vietnamese people was tremendous, but so was the fiscal damage. Thirty years of war prevented industrialization from occurring in this nonindustrial country. Added to this poor economic base has been the devastation of the farmland, which left the country at times unable to feed its citizens adequately.

Vietnam's wars for independence officially ended in 1974, but world recognition had still not been achieved by 1991. An economically devastated and war-torn land, Vietnam struggled for acceptance in world trade and for economic assistance to rebuild industry, farmland, and educational institutions. One of the major drains on the economy continued to be medical: dealing with the permanently disabled soldiers and civilians whose condition resulted from the two wars and coping with the aftereffects of chemicals such as Agent Orange.

## Bibliography

Boettcher, Thomas D. *Vietnam: The Valor and the Sorrow.* Boston: Little, Brown, 1985. This text can be considered as one of the basic overviews of the Vietnam war. While the emphasis is on American political and military involvement in the area, there is a cursory overview of the French colonial period and the French war. There is no consideration given to the history of Vietnam prior to the late eighteenth century. Contains pictures, chapter notes, and an index.

Fairbank, John King, Edwin O. Reischauer, and Albert M. Craig. *East Asia.* Boston: Houghton Mifflin, 1983. Possibly the best text for an overview of the entire Vietnamese-Chinese-European experience prior to 1950. The emphasis is on political, social, and military developments in specified periods. Contains a complete list of references and an index.

Hayslip, Le Ly, with Charles Jay Wurts. *When Heaven and Earth Changed Places.* New York: Doubleday, 1989. A personal account of what it was like to live in Vietnam under the rule of both the French and the American armies. The emphasis is on the peasant families and how they were controlled by the Viet Cong. Offers no references.

Karnow, Stanley. *Vietnam, A History: The First Complete Account of Vietnam at War.* New York: Viking Press, 1983. Possibly the definitive history of both the

French and the American involvements in Vietnam. The book, while highly researched and detailed, does not relate the history of the country prior to the eighteenth century. Excellent photographs. Provides chapter notes, sources, and an index.

Troung, Tang Nhu, with David Chanoff and Doan Van Toai. *A Vietcong Memoir: An Inside Account of the Vietnam War and Its Aftermath.* San Diego: Harcourt Brace Jovanovich, 1985. A personal account of how and why Ho Chi Minh gained the hearts of the Vietnamese people. Emphasis is on the author's experiences with French rule and why many Vietnamese were willing to work against it. Contains a glossary of names and an appendix of Vietcong documents. No other reference material is listed.

*Celia Hall-Thur*

## Cross-References

Ho Chi Minh Organizes the Viet Minh (1941), p. 573; The Atlantic Charter Declares a Postwar Right of Self-Determination (1941), p. 584; Four Students Are Killed at Kent State by the National Guard (1970), p. 1532; Lieutenant Calley Is Court-Martialed for the Massacre at My Lai (1970), p. 1555; Khmer Rouge Take Over Cambodia (1975), p. 1791.

# THE UNITED NATIONS CHILDREN'S FUND
# IS ESTABLISHED

*Categories of event:* Children's rights and humanitarian relief
*Time:* December 11, 1946
*Locale:* United Nations, New York City

*The United Nations Children's Fund was created to meet the basic needs of children around the world and to foster maternal and child development*

*Principal personages:*
FIORELLO LA GUARDIA (1882-1947), the director-general of the United Nations Relief and Rehabilitation Administration (UNRRA)
TRYGVE LIE (1896-1968), the secretary-general of the United Nations (1946-1952)
MAURICE PATE (1894-1965), the first executive director of UNICEF

## Summary of Event

The United Nations International Children's Emergency Fund (UNICEF) was created in 1946 by the United Nations as an emergency measure to cope with the consequences of the premature termination of the United Nations Relief and Rehabilitation Administration (UNRRA). The latter was created in October, 1943, to undertake relief work as Allied armies liberated Axis-occupied territories at the end of World War II. The UNRRA did much good work toward accomplishing its monumental task, but a number of flaws hurt the organization, not the least of which was its poor image in the U.S. Congress. The UNRRA was abruptly terminated in 1946. Unfortunately, reconstruction of Europe was far from complete. To make things worse, the winter of 1946-1947 was one of the worst ever experienced in modern Europe. On December 11, 1946, the U.N. General Assembly responded to this crisis and created, by unanimous decision, the United Nations International Children's Emergency Fund, with a life of three years.

The new organization had the good fortune of recruiting as its first executive director a man of enormous talent, drive, and dedication to its humanitarian mission, Maurice Pate, who proceeded to assemble a staff equally committed to the task. The results were little short of spectacular. UNICEF focused initially on Europe, where an estimated twenty million children were in jeopardy in fourteen countries, and launched a relief operation of vast proportions, providing food, medicine, clothing, and other desperately needed supplies.

By 1950, European reconstruction and recovery were well under way, and UNICEF's relief program reached completion. Elsewhere in the world, though, an even larger number of children were in dire straits. With decolonization, many nations became independent and, in many respects, were set adrift, with millions of children in a state of utter destitution. In December, 1950, the U.N. General Assembly extended

UNICEF's life for another three years and gave it the mandate to shift its emphasis from emergency assistance to long-term child development programs in underdeveloped countries. This was a challenge incomparably more difficult than that found in Europe.

By 1953, it was clear that, with growing decolonization and more new nations joining the ranks of the underdeveloped, the problem was bound to escalate. The General Assembly therefore made UNICEF a permanent agency of the United Nations and changed the organization's name to the "United Nations Children's Fund"; however, the original acronym, which by then had become world-famous, was retained.

UNICEF was given a semiautonomous status within the United Nations. It is governed by its own executive board of forty-one nations, selected in rotation for three-year terms from the U.N. membership. This board meets annually to determine UNICEF's program and allocate available funds. It has its own staff, part of which works at the U.N. headquarters in New York City. The larger part of this staff is deployed among UNICEF's more than 110 regional and field offices around the world.

The organization is headed by its executive director, who is appointed by the U.N. secretary-general. Throughout UNICEF's history, the executive director has played a strong leadership role and has been responsible for the quality of the agency's contribution. Maurice Pate, the first executive director, served for nineteen years and died in office in January, 1965. His successor, Henry R. Labouisse, was equally respected for his dedication to UNICEF's cause and for his skill as a leader and a diplomat. He retired on December 31, 1979, and was succeeded by James P. Grant, whose tenure would prove just as distinguished. The directors have succeeded in imparting to the UNICEF staff their high standards of integrity and service.

UNICEF's activities are funded exclusively by voluntary contributions, which come primarily from U.N. member countries. UNICEF also raises funds from the private sector. An important source of revenue is the sale of greeting cards; such sales amounted to $43 million during 1988-1989.

National committees for UNICEF have been organized in many countries. These are private volunteer organizations established to help UNICEF and make it better known. Many celebrities have contributed their talents to UNICEF and the national committees. Entertainer Danny Kaye provided perhaps the foremost example of this dedicated support. Other UNICEF goodwill ambassadors have included Peter Ustinov, Liv Ullmann, Harry Belafonte, Audrey Hepburn, and Jane Curtin. Singer Julio Iglesias appeared in February, 1991, in a gala concert for UNICEF in Houston and raised $100,000 for children who had suffered during the Persian Gulf War. In 1989-1990, the U.S. Committee for UNICEF volunteers raised a record $28.2 million.

The publicity provided by national committees is an important factor in the widespread popular support enjoyed by UNICEF. Governments impressed by such support are more inclined to work with UNICEF and help it financially.

UNICEF has circumvented the perennial inadequacy of its budget by endeavoring to make local residents practice self-help and by insisting that local governments, even in the most destitute countries, devote a larger portion of their resources to the well-being of their countries' children. (When confronted with the task of achieving development, governments are easily tempted to build roads, power plants, or modern industry rather than provide better medical care or primary education for children.) For every $1 spent by UNICEF, local governments contribute more than $2.50.

UNICEF has been very effective in enlisting the assistance of volunteers in recipient countries and in acquiring the invaluable support of nongovernmental organizations, whose skills, labor, and knowledge of local situations are potent sources of success in implementing programs and ensuring that assistance reaches the people who need it most. Furthermore, UNICEF works closely with other U.N. agencies such as the World Health Organization, the United Nations Development Program, the United Nations Educational, Scientific, and Cultural Organization (UNESCO), and the World Bank. These agencies, in fact, use some of their own resources to implement UNICEF-initiated activities.

High on UNICEF's agenda is mother and child health, one of the organization's prime concerns from the time of its inception. It has founded numerous health centers to provide maternal and child health services and teach the rules of elementary hygiene. UNICEF has also undertaken an effort to curb maternal mortality. Each year, an estimated one-half million women die of causes related to pregnancy and childbirth; the UNICEF program aimed for a 50 percent reduction in these maternal deaths by the year 2000. UNICEF also helps women by providing prenatal care, strengthening women's social roles, and providing better access to education.

In cooperation with the World Health Organization, UNICEF undertook a staggering campaign of universal immunization against preventable childhood diseases such as diphtheria, whooping cough, tetanus, polio, tuberculosis, and measles, the largest child-killer. Another extremely effective campaign focused on controlling diarrheal diseases, an important cause of infant mortality, by means of a simple, inexpensive, and effective oral rehydration procedure. UNICEF also engaged in a more complex long-term effort to combat acute respiratory infections, which in the 1980's accounted for 25 to 30 percent of the fifteen million child deaths each year. UNICEF also undertook a program focused on preventing the spread of AIDS among children.

A different area of UNICEF's concern has been the availability of clean water and effective sanitation. In 1990, an estimated one billion people were still without access to safe drinking water, and two billion (excluding China) lived in communities without sanitation services. UNICEF aimed at global, comprehensive remediation of these problems.

Hunger and malnutrition are even more challenging problems. They are rooted in economic underdevelopment and poverty, often accompanied by ignorance. UNICEF has instituted infant-growth monitoring programs to detect early signs of malnutrition, and it has promoted breast-feeding to reduce infant mortality related to the improper use of infant formulas.

Beyond health and nutrition, UNICEF is involved in numerous programs. An estimated one hundred million children in the developing world receive no schooling of any kind. In cooperation with UNESCO, UNICEF is therefore promoting and supporting access to basic education. UNICEF also attends to the needs of homeless and abandoned children and provides emergency relief and rehabilitation to young victims of disasters.

## Impact of Event

The creation of UNICEF made an important contribution to the international protection of children. By means of effective fieldwork, consciousness-raising, education, and substantial fund-raising activities to finance its social-justice work, UNICEF has saved millions of lives and considerably improved the living conditions of even larger numbers of children and their families. It is now an essential factor of social development. In 1965, UNICEF was awarded the Nobel Peace Prize. This award was hailed as well-deserved recognition for the organization's remarkable accomplishments.

The campaign to provide clean water for everyone in the world made clean water available to more than one hundred million additional people a year from 1981 to 1990. In UNICEF's drive for global immunization, international cooperation has been rewarding; even in some civil wars, belligerents have agreed to interrupt their fighting to enable medical teams to reach villages in war zones and proceed with inoculations. By 1988, 68 percent of the children in the developing world had received three doses of diphtheria, whooping cough, tetanus, and polio vaccine by their first birthdays. Coverage with antituberculosis vaccine had reached 75 percent. At the end of 1987, almost one in three episodes of child diarrhea was treated with UNICEF's oral rehydration therapy. In 1989 alone, the use of this therapy saved an estimated 750,000 children.

UNICEF has succeeded in keeping the cause of children at the center of global consciousness. The strength of public support for its programs and the effectiveness of its child survival strategies have led many countries and private donors to increase their voluntary contributions. In 1989, UNICEF's total income amounted to $667 million from all sources. Twenty-five years earlier, it was only $33 million. The United States Congress alone approved a record $75 million for UNICEF for fiscal 1991. Nevertheless, in the context of the magnitude of the problems confronting UNICEF—children in urban slums, homelessness, abandoned children, abused or exploited youths, the spreading impact of war and civil strife leading to traumatized children, and a crying need for social rehabilitation—the funds available to UNICEF remain comparatively modest.

On September 30, 1990, seventy-one presidents and prime ministers came together for the first World Summit for Children at the U.N. headquarters in New York City. This assembly wrote the World Declaration on the Survival, Protection, and Development of Children and a plan of action for implementing the declaration. The summit's actions represented the kind of global support and commitment for which UNICEF had long been working, and it promises to give children a brighter future.

## Bibliography

Bennett, A. LeRoy. *International Organizations.* 5th ed. Englewood Cliffs, N.J.: Prentice-Hall, 1991. Chapter 14, "Promoting Social Progress," introduces UNICEF and the many U.N. agencies with which it works. Other chapters explain the U.N. context within which UNICEF operates and the politics involved. Very useful to supplement materials exclusively focused on UNICEF. Provides bibliographies.

"The Best Mankind Has to Give." *UN Chronicle* 26 (September, 1989): 40-51. Reviews developments in the thirty years since the Declaration on the Rights of the Child was proclaimed by the U.N. General Assembly. Discusses UNICEF's efforts in implementing this declaration and developments in UNICEF strategy. Outlines the grave problems still facing children.

Black, Maggie. *The Children and the Nations.* New York: UNICEF, 1986. Chronicles UNICEF's story in the context of social development and international cooperation. Very informative. Shows the widespread impact of UNICEF. Prepared on the occasion of the fortieth anniversary of UNICEF.

Grant, James P. *The State of the World's Children, 1991.* New York: Oxford University Press, 1991. Makes a clear presentation of UNICEF's goals for the year 2000. Includes the World Declaration on the Survival, Protection, and Development of Children issued by the 1990 World Summit for Children, the Plan of Action for Implementing the World Declaration, and the full text of the Convention on the Rights of the Child.

Labouisse, Henry R. "For the World's Children: UNICEF at 25." *UN Chronicle* 8 (April, 1971): 48-60. Excellent survey by the dedicated and effective second executive director of the organization. Reviews UNICEF's accomplishments and examines the challenges of the years to come. Contains much useful information about UNICEF.

*Thursday's Child* 1 (Winter, 1990): 1-25. The articles in this quarterly published by the U.S. Committee for UNICEF give a down-to-earth presentation of the problems faced by children around the world. Extensively and strikingly illustrated, the articles provide case studies showing what UNICEF accomplishes and citing relevant facts and figures.

"UN Children's Fund." *Yearbook of the United Nations: Events of 1986* 40 (1990): 809-823, 1261-1262. Summarizes the activities of UNICEF for 1986 and presents a breakdown of programs by region and by type of activity. A drawback of this publication is that volumes are normally published four to five years after the events they chronicle.

*UNICEF: Annual Report, 1990.* New York: United Nations, 1990. Very informative. Detailed (and illustrated) presentation of the activities of UNICEF during the preceding year; includes analyses of resources and expenses and gives a good idea of how UNICEF's program is carried out.

Weiss, Thomas George. *International Bureaucracy: An Analysis of the Operation of Functional and Global International Secretariats.* Lexington, Mass.: Lexington Books, 1975. Discusses the functioning of the secretariats of international organizations, the problems encountered, and remedies available. Chapter 5 presents a case study, focused on UNICEF, showing the excellent performance of its staff. Includes a thorough bibliography on international administration.

*Jean-Robert Leguey-Feilleux*

## Cross-References

Japan Protests Segregation of Japanese in California Schools (1906), p. 81; Students Challenge Corporal Punishment in British Schools (1911), p. 109; The Children's Bureau Is Founded (1912), p. 131; The World Health Organization Proclaims Health as a Basic Right (1946), p. 678; The United Nations Adopts the Declaration of the Rights of the Child (1959), p. 1038; Head Start Is Established (1965), p. 1284; The Supreme Court Endorses Busing as a Means to End Segregation (1971), p. 1628; Congress Passes the Child Abuse Prevention and Treatment Act (1974), p. 1752; A U.N. Declaration on Hunger and Malnutrition Is Adopted (1974), p. 1775; Congress Enacts the Education for All Handicapped Children Act (1975), p. 1780; WHO Sets a Goal of Health for All by the Year 2000 (1977), p. 1893; An International Health Conference Adopts the Declaration of Alma-Ata (1978), p. 1998; The United Nations Adopts the Convention on the Rights of the Child (1989), p. 2529.

# SPAIN IS DENIED ENTRANCE
# INTO THE UNITED NATIONS

*Categories of event:* Political freedom and civil rights
*Time:* December 12, 1946
*Locale:* United Nations Interim Headquarters, Flushing Meadows, New York

*The General Assembly of the United Nations denied Spain membership in disapproval of its authoritarian and Fascist-oriented regime headed by dictator Francisco Franco*

### Principal personages:

FRANCISCO FRANCO (1892-1975), the dictator of Spain from 1936 until his death in 1975

JOSÉ ANTONIO PRIMO DE RIVERA (1903-1936), a charismatic leader and martyr of the Falange

BENITO MUSSOLINI (1883-1945), the Fascist dictator of Italy during Spain's Civil War and World War II

ADOLF HITLER (1889-1945), the Nazi dictator of Germany during Spain's Civil War and World War II

## Summary of Event

General Francisco Franco consolidated a military dictatorship in Spain after his armed forces prevailed in a three-year civil war against the Second Spanish Republic in 1939. Franco's totalitarian regime was born of a military insurrection against Spain's legal government. It was able to survive until Franco's death in 1975 by repressing the Spanish people through the denial of their human rights. The principal components of the regime's support were the army, the Falange, and the Roman Catholic Church. The military perceived an obligation to intervene to save the nation from the anarchy that plagued Spain's Second Republic. Franco's ironclad rule protected Spain from the chaos he believed was inherent in democracy.

The Falange was Spain's Fascist party, equally opposed to capitalism, communism, and democracy. Profoundly conservative and reactionary, it advocated the creation of a national socialist state. The Roman Catholic church sanctioned Franco's rebellion and became a part of the state. Franco's victory saved the church from the violent anticlericalism that had erupted during Spain's Second Republic. These three pillars of the Francoist state were profoundly conservative, authoritarian, antidemocratic, and intolerant of the convictions of the Spaniards who supported the Republic and were on the losing side of Spain's civil war.

When the General Assembly voted to deny Spain membership in the United Nations, it was applying diplomatic pressure on Franco. It wanted him to relinquish power to a provisional government that would respect the civil rights of all Spaniards and give them the opportunity to choose their government freely. The United Nations condemned Franco's regime not only because it was undemocratic and totalitarian but also because it was founded with the support of the Axis powers. Franco's forces won the Spanish Civil War with the help of Adolf Hitler's Nazi Germany and Benito Mussolini's Fascist Italy.

Franco's rule was imposed on the Spanish people by armed force; it did not derive its authority from the consent of the governed. It was antidemocratic and inspired by the totalitarian ideologies of the Allies' enemies in World War II, Nazism and Fascism. Franco himself abhorred representative forms of government. According to his understanding of Spanish history, Spain's glorious imperial past under the Catholic sovereigns, Ferdinand and Isabella, was destroyed by the introduction of representative government and universal suffrage in the nineteenth century. Self-serving party politics and the conspiracies of freemasonry and Marxism caused Spain's decline as a military and colonial power in this view. Franco believed that Spain faced a communist threat when he committed himself to overthrowing the Second Republic in 1936.

Franco replaced Spain's republican form of government with a totalitarian state in which he exercised absolute power. As head of state and head of the government, he functioned as prime minister and president. He was commander-in-chief of the armed forces and leader of the only political party, the Falange. Franco ruled without a constitution and therefore without the rule of law. Franco declared that his regime was responsible only to God and history.

Franco's disregard for human rights was evident from the beginning of his rule. Supporters of the Spanish Republic had no rights. Franco's regime pursued its opponents relentlessly in a large-scale campaign of repression during and after the civil war. The Law of Political Responsibilities, retroactive to October, 1934, even though enacted in February, 1939, decreed that anyone who had supported the cause of the Republic in any way, even if passively, could be subject to up to fifteen years of imprisonment. The law also targeted any member of a trade union, a masonic lodge, or a republican or left-wing party and any supporter of Basque or Catalan nationalism. More than 270,000 Spaniards were in prison by the end of 1939. Prison populations did not return to pre-civil war levels for more than a decade.

The average citizen found Franco's campaign of repression to be arbitrary and ruthless. Most of the Spanish people supported the Republic, so the insurgents decided that they had to administer a campaign of total terror to frighten the population into submission. Even a vague allegation could result in arrest or even death. Franco's side saw prominent Republicans and leftists as incurable and believed execution was a reasonable solution. People who supported the Republic, even if they had managed to survive the war and imprisonment, still had to face persecution well into the 1950's. Franco did not want those who opposed him to have access to power or wealth. Former Republicans were silenced, but they were not persuaded that they had been wrong.

When Allied victory in World War II seemed assured, Franco attempted to mask his regime's violation of human rights by revoking the Law of Political Responsibilities and issuing the Charter of the Spanish People in 1945. It purported to be a bill of rights, although the freedoms proclaimed in the charter were severely undermined on several levels. The charter only ensured such freedoms as those of expression, association, and assembly when they did not endanger the principles of the state and did not harm Spain's spiritual, national, or social unity. Liberty was further limited by the issuance of countermanding laws and decrees. Any right proclaimed in the charter could be revoked in states of emergency. The average Spaniard knew that no more freedom was available than there had been at the height of the repression after the civil war.

Freedom of expression could only be had in private conversation. The regime until 1966 censored all printed matter prior to publication, with the exception of Catholic and Falange materials. Books were banned and theaters were closed. Many topics were forbidden by the regime, including the regime itself, the succession of Franco, political and social agitation, offenses against morals, and any information that would place Spain in an unfavorable light. The government strictly controlled the press, to the extent of determining circulation and allocating newsprint. Freedom of information was not possible under such conditions. Few gave any credence to the news available from newspapers, television, and radio. The media conveyed only what the government wanted the population to know.

The regime limited freedom of association and assembly. No organization could be formed that proclaimed goals contrary to government-endorsed values. Trade unions were illegal, as were strikes. Spanish workers were forced to join the syndicate established by the state for their trade or profession. Spaniards could join only the one legal political party in the country, the Falange. This created much frustration among workers. Politics was the only channel available to seek the redress of grievances, but it served the interests of the state and not those of the worker.

The right to free assembly was also severely restricted. Any gathering of more than twenty people not sponsored by the church or the Falange required government authorization. If the government wanted to harass a known opponent of the regime, the police would raid the residence when a family reunion was in progress because they could claim that more than twenty people were together without government authorization.

While freedom of conscience was theoretically recognized, only Roman Catholicism enjoyed official protection. Other faiths could be practiced only privately. Franco persecuted Spain's thirty thousand Protestants. Protestant congregations could not own or administer church buildings and could not establish schools or evangelize.

The nature and organization of the judicial system seriously endangered human rights. In addition to being government-appointed, judges were required to swear an oath of loyalty to Franco, jeopardizing the sound and impartial administration of justice. Military courts exercised broad jurisdiction in ordinary penal law and prosecuted political crimes. Activity in opposition to the regime was classified as military rebellion. The police could arrest a suspect without a warrant. Although there was a seventy-two-hour limit on detention, illegal detention could not be appealed.

A police-state atmosphere dominated the court system. If a person was apprehended by the police, family and friends could not prevent detention. The accused had no access to a lawyer while in police custody. Only after preliminary legal proceedings were finished could the accused consult a lawyer. Depositions could be obtained through threats and violence.

The United Nations, organized by the victorious Allies after World War II, abhorred the existence of a Fascist regime like that of Franco after the defeat of Fascism had cost so many Allied lives. Exiled Republicans anticipated that the Allies would overthrow Franco's dictatorship after defeating Nazi Germany. Some believed that World War II would not be won until all Fascist regimes had been destroyed.

Although they deplored Franco's oppression of the Spanish people, the Allies did not intervene militarily. They limited themselves to isolating Spain diplomatically after World War II, hoping to pressure Franco out of power. The General Assembly's resolution in December, 1946, reaffirmed the Allies' previous condemnations of Spain in San Francisco, Potsdam, and London. It not only barred Spain from membership in the United Nations but also banned Spain's participation in all international agencies associated with the United Nations. Member states were asked to recall their ambassadors to Spain. Finally, the resolution declared that the United Nations would consider other measures if Franco's regime were not replaced by a government that represented the will of the Spanish people within a reasonable amount of time.

**Impact of Event**

Unfortunately, diplomatic pressures applied by the United Nations did not weaken Franco's hold on Spain. The United Nations' policy of ostracism was counterproductive. Franco refused to change his regime, confident that the Western democracies would eventually value Franco's staunch anticommunism. He was not mistaken. When the Western democracies determined that the Soviet Union was a threat to their interests, they recognized Spain's strategic value for the defense of Western Europe and softened their condemnation of his regime. Spain's diplomatic isolation decreased largely because of the Cold War. By 1951, most countries had returned their ambassadors and were encouraging Spain to participate in various international agencies. The United States valued Franco as an ally in the battle against Soviet expansionism and signed an accord with Spain in 1953 agreeing to provide economic and military assistance in exchange for air and naval bases.

Those who had supported the Republic, whether still resident in Spain or in exile, felt abandoned after the European democracies' failure to intervene against Franco's dictatorship. Just as aid to the Republic had been less than forthcoming during the civil war, the United States and its allies in Europe would do nothing once World War II was over to eliminate the last Fascist state on the continent. The average Spaniard could see no end to Franco's dictatorship, and in fact Spaniards would have to wait forty years to have the yoke of dictatorship lifted from them.

The General Assembly's resolution against Spain's membership in the United Nations was fully reversed in December, 1955, when Spain was finally admitted along with fifteen other nations. Although the nature of Spain's totalitarian government had not changed, the United Nations had adjusted its policy. U.N. leaders had come to believe that the United Nations should be a universal, worldwide body that offered admission to all nations regardless of their political philosophy. Governments with unacceptable practices would be more likely to change within the United Nations than outside of it. Spain was admitted with virtually no opposition. Nevertheless, a residue of dislike for Franco's rule persisted in Europe. Spain was refused membership in the North Atlantic Treaty Organization (NATO) because its government was not democratic. It also was barred from membership in the European Economic Community (EEC). Spain's diplomatic isolation did not end completely until after Franco's death. After Spain completed its transition to democracy in 1978, objections to Spain's membership in NATO and the EEC disappeared. Spain was admitted into NATO and the EEC in 1986.

## Bibliography

Carr, Raymond, and Juan Pablo Fusi Azipurua. *Spain: Dictatorship to Democracy.* Boston: Allen & Unwin, 1979. A thorough overview of all aspects of Spain's history from 1939 to 1978, including the philosophy and institutions of Francoism; changes in the economy, society, and culture during the Franco period; the crisis of the last years of the regime; and the transition to democracy. Includes an index, a chronological table of events, a glossary of political terms, and a list of main actors.

Gallo, Max. *Spain Under Franco: A History.* New York: E. P. Dutton, 1974. A history of Franco's regime from 1938 to 1969. Evident anti-Franco bias does not detract from valuable insights into the nature of the regime. Includes a thorough bibliography (mostly of material in French and Spanish), index, and genealogy of the Spanish royal family.

Gilmour, David. *The Transformation of Spain.* London: Quartet Books, 1985. Deals mainly with the transition to democracy in Spain. Opens with a very useful introduction to the nature of Francoism and the structure of the dictatorship. Includes bibliography, index, and glossary of political and other organizations in Spain.

Hills, George. *Franco: The Man and His Nation.* London: Robert Hale, 1967. Combines a biography of Franco with Spain's history from the beginning of the twentieth century into the 1960's. Thorough treatment of Spanish foreign relations during and after World War II. Biased against the Left. Includes index. Lists sources and provides an extensive bibliography, much of it in Spanish.

International Commission of Jurists. *Spain and the Rule of Law.* Geneva: Author, 1962. Useful detail on judicial and legal structure of Franco's rule with a chapter on civil rights. Detailed description of laws meant to protect the regime from the opposition. Appendices with the texts of fundamental laws and excerpts from a political trial. Accessible to the layperson.

Payne, Stanley. *The Franco Regime: 1936-1975.* Madison: University of Wisconsin Press, 1987. Complete history from the civil war through Franco's death in 1975.

Takes a neutral stance. Includes maps, index, and an annotated and select bibliography.

_____. *Franco's Spain.* New York: Thomas Y. Crowell, 1967. Brief history of Francoism from the civil war through the mid-1960's. Covers politics and diplomacy, the economy, social change, and cultural affairs. Includes index and annotated bibliography.

Whitaker, Arthur P. *Spain and Defense of the West: Ally and Liability.* Westport, Conn.: Greenwood Press, 1980. Reprint of 1961 edition of Council on Foreign Relations. History and analysis of Spain under Franco with focus on U.S. foreign policy. Special attention to the 1953 agreement between the United States and Spain. Includes index and annotated bibliography.

*Evelyn Toft*

## Cross-References

Corporatism Comes to Paraguay and the Americas (1936), p. 533; Perón Creates a Populist Political Alliance in Argentina (1946), p. 673; An Oppressive Military Rule Comes to Democratic Uruguay (1973), p. 1715; Allende Is Overthrown in a Chilean Military Coup (1973), p. 1725; The Argentine Military Conducts a "Dirty War" Against Leftists (1976), p. 1864; Spain Holds Its First Free Elections Since the Civil War (1977), p. 1921; Basques Are Granted Home Rule but Continue to Fight for Independence (1980), p. 2079; The National Commission Against Torture Studies Human Rights Abuses (1983), p. 2186; Argentine Leaders Are Convicted of Human Rights Violations (1985), p. 2280; Voters in Chile End Pinochet's Military Rule (1989), p. 2540.

# THE HOUSE COMMITTEE ON UN-AMERICAN ACTIVITIES INVESTIGATES HOLLYWOOD

*Categories of event:* Civil rights and accused persons' rights
*Time:* 1947
*Locale:* Washington, D.C.

*A strong anticommunist storm gathered in the United States that culminated in the purge of Hollywood's liberal community by the House Committee on Un-American Activities (HUAC)*

*Principal personages:*

MARTIN DIES (1901-1972), a Democratic congressman from Texas who chaired the House Special Committee on Un-American Activities from 1938 to 1944

J. PARNELL THOMAS (1895-1970), a Republican congressman from New Jersey who was a member of the Dies committee in 1938 and who became the chairman of HUAC in 1945

HARRY S. TRUMAN (1884-1972), the thirty-third president of the United States (1945-1953)

## Summary of Event

In 1938, child film star Shirley Temple (age nine) was accused of being a dupe of the Communist Party because she had waved at a group of communist journalists while in France. This was not an aberration; it was a logical outcome of the right- and left-wing extremism that infected the United States at the time.

During times of intense crisis, Americans have been prone to hunt for scapegoats to explain their troubles. Having correct ideas is used as a measure to prove that a person is indeed "100 percent American." Extremists on both the right and left vie to have their ideas become the moral law of the land. Purges ("witch-hunts"), flag waving, and a decreased tolerance for any form of dissent that might jeopardize the status quo are symptoms of such epochs.

Anticommunist, and generally antiforeign, sentiment rose during World War I and continued to find support into the 1920's. This sentiment was expressed in legal action against foreigners such as the Palmer Raids and several acts limiting immigration into the United States. Groups such as the Ku Klux Klan, with their message of intolerance of "foreign" or different peoples and ideas, flourished.

In 1934, Representative Samuel Dickstein proposed that a permanent committee be established to investigate what he called "un-American activities." On May 26, 1938, the U.S. House of Representatives authorized a special committee to investigate un-American activities. Martin Dies chaired the committee; he was assisted by his former clerk, Robert E. Stripling, as counsel, and by Representative J. Parnell

Thomas and others. During the first days of the committee's existence, 640 organizations, 483 newspapers, and 280 labor unions were accused of un-American activities. The patriotism of the Boy Scouts, the Camp Fire Girls, and Shirley Temple was questioned. When the committee could find no communists more substantial than such long-dead playwrights as Christopher Marlowe and Euripides, it quickly lost credibility. Nevertheless, a similar lack of knowledge about Marxism and communism continued to underlie HUAC inquests.

The Dies Committee did contribute heavily to Congress' June 1, 1939, elimination of the proposed Federal Theatre from President Franklin Delano Roosevelt's New Deal. The committee's lessons were not forgotten: Show business people were easy targets, and targeting Hollywood brought instant media attention. The Dies Committee also established the tactics that were used by HUAC, Senator Joseph McCarthy, and others after World War II: sensational press releases; secret, fabricated lists of "known" communists; attacks on anything liberal; and "proof" in the form of gossip, illogic, and association with a touch of truth.

Attacks on communism diminished during World War II, because the Soviet Union was one of the Allied Powers. As part of the war effort, *Song of Russia* (1944) and other pro-Soviet films were made at the War Department's request. *Song of Russia* was denounced in the 1947 HUAC hearings because it showed happy, smiling people in the Soviet Union.

After World War II, the U.S.-Soviet alliance dissolved. Republicans and ultraconservative groups assaulted communism anew. President Harry S. Truman announced the Truman Doctrine, an anticommunist foreign-aid effort, on March 12, 1947, to blunt Republican charges that he was soft on communism. The State Department was purged of alleged communists, and Truman established a peacetime security-loyalty program. U.S. attorney general Tom Clark compiled a list of organizations espousing communist, fascist, totalitarian, or subversive ideas to be used internally to determine which government employees should be investigated. The list was published and quickly became HUAC's primary source document.

On October 20, 1947, a subcommittee of HUAC opened its first postwar hearings. Because of prehearing publicity, more than one hundred news agencies were present, along with three major radio networks and eleven newsreel and television cameras stationed above the witness table. The committee was chaired by J. Parnell Thomas, and Robert E. Stripling served as chief counsel. Other members of note were Representatives Richard M. Nixon and John S. Wood, who became HUAC's chair in 1950. Friendly witnesses, mainly studio executives, were called the first week. During the second week, nineteen witnesses, mainly writers, were subpoenaed. Ten witnesses said that the proceedings themselves were un-American and un-Constitutional. These ten became known as the "Hollywood Ten" or the "Unfriendly Ten." (The Hollywood Ten were writers Alvah Bessie, Lester Cole, Ring Lardner, Jr., John Howard Lawson, Albert Maltz, Sam Ornitz, and Dalton Trumbo, in addition to directors Herbert Biberman and Edward Dmytryk and writer-producer Robert Adrian Scott.) The ten claimed the right to free speech as their defense for their actions. Hollywood's entertainment community loudly supported the ten's First Amendment rights. The ten were liberal, and all had had some affiliation, however cursory, with the Communist Party.

On November 24, 1947, Congress voted to cite the Hollywood Ten for contempt. Immediately, fifty top studio executives met at the Waldorf-Astoria Hotel in New York City to determine their position regarding the ten. Eric Johnson, the president of the Motion Picture Association of America, read the Waldorf Declaration: The Ten would be suspended without pay, and from that point forward, no studio would "knowingly" employ anyone associated with the Communist Party.

A congressional investigatory committee has two primary functions: to secure information needed to create legislation and to oversee the executive branch's activities. These committees have no direct legislative or judicial functions. HUAC in effect performed both functions, and in so doing castrated the civil rights of subpoenaed witnesses. Witnesses were not allowed to meet or cross-examine their accusers, no exclusionary rules regarding hearsay evidence were used, and witnesses were not allowed due process. Eight of the ten were writers, but the committee produced no evidence that they had written anything that was subversive or that called for the violent overthrow of the U.S. government. The committee never documented any evidence of communist infiltration of the movie industry, and even if it had, membership in the Communist Party was not illegal. Nevertheless, without judge or jury, the Hollywood Ten were tried and sentenced.

If the committee had been serious about its attempt to root communism out of the film industry, it could have succeeded. The contributions of highly paid Hollywood artists to Communist Party causes were known but not investigated. Thomas contended that he had a list of seventy-nine prominent communists in his files, but only the Hollywood Ten were prosecuted.

Thus, the subpoenaing of entertainment people was not done to support legislation (none was ever proposed). None of the witnesses were government employees, so the attorney general's list should not have been utilized. The Hollywood Ten were judged guilty because their thoughts were improper. They were convicted of contempt because they refused to answer the committee's questions the way the committee wanted them to.

In 1950, after the Supreme Court refused their last appeals, the Hollywood Ten went to jail for at least a year apiece. Ring Lardner, Jr., and Lester Cole were sent to the federal prison in Danbury, Connecticut—as was J. Parnell Thomas, who in 1948 had been convicted of a payroll scam. Lardner was made a stenographer in the classification and parole office; Thomas was made caretaker of the prison's chicken yard.

## Impact of Event

Between March, 1947, and December, 1952, some 6.6 million people were checked by Truman's security program. No espionage was discovered, but some five hundred people were dismissed from government-related jobs.

Alger Hiss was convicted in January, 1950, of perjury in a highly publicized and sensational trial. In February, the British uncovered massive espionage that eventually led to the execution of American spies Julius and Ethel Rosenberg. Senator Joseph McCarthy began his campaign for reelection by using his attack on communism as his stepping-stone to power. In June, the Korean War began, and three former Federal Bureau of Investigation agents published *Red Channels: The Report of Communist Influence in Radio and Television* (1950), which became the bible of blacklisting.

HUAC's Hollywood investigation began again in 1951. Blacklisting—for ridiculing HUAC, for being subpoenaed, or for unknowingly being on the list that Hollywood studios and professional guilds claimed did not exist—became institutionalized. A suspect person could not get work without publically naming names and recanting supposed sins, thereby receiving absolution from the committee. Informers became morally upright patriots.

Not only did Hollywood not support its own, but no one else did either. No one questioned the right of the committee to exist or to do what it was doing, not the press, not the American Civil Liberties Union, and not the Anti-Defamation League of B'nai B'rith or the Hollywood-based American Jewish Committee. Ten of the nineteen subpoenaed were Jews, as were six of the ten who were indicted.

The blacklisted went underground and set up their own networks. "Clean" writers' or fictitious names were put on scripts. Only the Hollywood community knew that Maltz wrote *The Bridge on the River Kwai* (1957) and *The Robe* (1953) or that Trumbo wrote *Roman Holiday* (1953), *Cowboy* (1958), and *The Brave One* (1956). *The Brave One* won an Oscar that no one claimed until 1975. A mystique developed around the blacklisted writers. As a result, more and more work came to them.

The blacklist had a chilling effect on social criticism. In 1947, 28 percent of all movies dealt with social issues; in 1949, only 18 percent did. By 1954, only about 9 percent of all films dealt with social problems. In 1953 and 1954, the U.S. Supreme Court made two rulings that finally protected witnesses from the abuses experienced by the Hollywood Ten and others caught up in the anticommunist sweep.

## Bibliography

Bentley, Eric. *Are You Now or Have You Ever Been: The Investigation of Show Business by the Un-American Activities Committee, 1947-1958.* New York: Harper & Row, 1972. Abridged testimonies of eighteen witnesses appearing before HUAC, 1947-1958. Testimonies of Edward Dmytryk (1947, 1951), Ring Lardner, Jr. (1947), Larry Parks (1951), Lillian Hellman (letter, 1952), and Paul Robeson (1956) are of particular interest. No references; easy to read. Photographs.

Hellman, Lillian. *Scoundrel Time.* Boston: Little, Brown, 1976. Introduction by Gary Willis. A rambling autobiographical account of the era by a prize-winning playwright, novelist, and screenwriter. Easy reading.

Kanfer, Stefan. *A Journal of the Plague Years.* New York: Atheneum, 1973. This satirical, gossipy, literate journal begins with the radicalism of the 1920's and concludes with the 1960's. The hearings are presented as farcical drama. Fun reading. Annotated references; no in-text citations. College level.

Miller, Douglas T., and Marion Nowak. *The Fifties: The Way We Really Were.* Garden City, N.Y.: Doubleday, 1977. Written by a historian and a journalist. Documented and informative but still very readable. See in particular Chapter 1 on McCarthy and Chapter 12 on Hollywood. College-level reading.

Navasky, Victor S. *Naming Names.* New York: Penguin Books, 1982. Navasky was trained as a lawyer and a journalist; he gives a factual, informative study of the era and explains why so many people became informers. Excellent source. References provided. College-level reading.

Pratt, Henry J. *The Liberalization of American Protestantism: A Case Study in Complex Organizations.* Detroit: Wayne State University Press, 1972. An academic study of Protestantism, especially the National Council of Churches. See Chapter 13 on civil rights and labor organizations' fights against charges of communism made during the McCarthy era. Well documented. College-level reading.

Schlesinger, Arthur M., Jr., and Roger Burns, eds. *Congress Investigates: 1792-1974.* New York: Chelsea House, 1975. Of particular interest here are Schlesinger's introduction, which discusses Supreme Court cases related to congressional hearings, and the article by H. Lew Wallace, "The McCarthy Era." Good background material on the era. Schlesinger is difficult to read. Good bibliography.

Schumach, Murray. *The Face on the Cutting Room Floor.* New York: William Morrow, 1964. Enlightening book on censorship in Hollywood from the silents through the 1960's. Appendix gives samples of censorship rules in other countries and Hollywood's motion-picture code. Photographs. No references. Good source on the gray list, the Hollywood underground, and the American Legion.

Vaughn, Robert F. *Only Victims: A Study of Show Business Blacklisting.* New York: G. P. Putnam's Sons, 1972. This is the actor's doctoral dissertation, covering the time period 1938-1958. Well documented and informative. Introduction by Senator George McGovern. Focuses on the sociological and psychological underpinnings of the radical right and left that fueled HUAC. Good documents in appendices.

*Dixie Dean Dickinson*

## Cross-References

Lenin and the Communists Impose the "Red Terror" (1917), p. 218; Lenin Leads the Russian Revolution (1917), p. 225; "Palmer Raids" Lead to Arrests and Deportations of Immigrants (1919), p. 258; The Ku Klux Klan Spreads Terror in the South (1920's), p. 298; The American Civil Liberties Union Is Founded (1920), p. 327; The Immigration Act of 1921 Imposes a National Quota System (1921), p. 350; Congress Establishes a Border Patrol (1924), p. 377; A U.S. Immigration Act Imposes Quotas Based on National Origins (1924), p. 383; HUAC Begins Investigating Suspected Communists (1938), p. 550.

# THE MARSHALL PLAN PROVIDES AID TO EUROPE

*Category of event:* Humanitarian relief
*Time:* 1947-1951
*Locale:* The United States and Western Europe

*Following its adoption by Congress in 1948, the Marshall Plan provided almost $12.5 billion in American aid to spur economic recovery in Western Europe*

*Principal personages:*
>GEORGE C. MARSHALL (1880-1959), the U.S. secretary of state (1947-1949) who initiated the Marshall Plan and secured its approval
>HARRY S. TRUMAN (1884-1972), the U.S. president who supported the Marshall Plan
>ERNEST BEVIN (1881-1951), the British foreign minister who was instrumental in consolidating European support for the plan
>GEORGE F. KENNAN (1904-    ), an American diplomat who headed the committee to draw up the original proposal

## Summary of Event

In the winter of 1946/1947, European nations struggled to recover from the widespread devastation of World War II. The conflict had levelled cities, destroyed thousands of factories, disrupted transportation and communication systems, and rendered machinery for extracting raw materials useless. The European standard of living had fallen drastically below that of prewar levels, even in nations that had not borne the brunt of the fighting. In the spring of 1947, two million British industrial workers were unemployed, and many others were underemployed because of shortages in raw materials. In Italy, industrial production stood at twenty percent of prewar levels. In Germany's Ruhr region, coal production had dropped to forty-five percent of its previous level, and similar declines elsewhere affected industrial production and transportation systems throughout Europe. Millions of homeless and displaced citizens strained the existing social services beyond their limits. The unusually severe European winter of 1946/1947 exacerbated the hardships brought through war. Food shortages existed in most nations and, consequently, food rationing was widely accepted. Politically, France and Italy faced growing communist and leftist movements whose popularity increased as a result of the economic hardships. European governments that had managed vast colonial regions before the war could no longer adequately manage their internal affairs.

The harsh conditions produced despondency that only increased the economic problems. Industrial workers witnessed a diminished standard of living as postwar inflation caused prices to outpace wages. Worker productivity declined. Farmers unable to purchase fertilizer and farm equipment converted their fields to pastureland, resulting in a sharp decrease in agricultural productivity.

In the United States, left untouched by the destructiveness of bombardment, the economic picture was one of prosperity and rapid growth. Despite a large postwar debt, the economy quickly responded to the release of pent-up demand for goods and services following the war. There was, however, concern within the government about the postwar settlement in Europe and particularly about the Soviet role and influence in Europe. Soviet positions on withdrawal of their forces from countries such as Iran, on the nature of Eastern European governments, and on war reparations from Germany created apprehension within the Truman Administration. Political unrest on the fringes of Europe, namely in Greece and Turkey, became America's concern after the United Kingdom took the position that it could no longer afford to aid the existing governments against communist-backed guerrilla insurgencies.

President Harry S. Truman addressed Congress on March 12, 1947, in an appeal for more than $300 million in American aid to these nations. The occasion marked the inauguration of the Truman Doctrine, which committed the United States to defend governments threatened with communist subversion throughout the world. The open-ended nature of the commitment left many in the Congress and State Department bewildered, since militarily the United States had demobilized and was in no position to make global military commitments. Within the State Department, diplomats had already begun to formulate the concept that in the looming East-West conflict, American economic power would prove to be the decisive factor.

In the same month, the newly appointed secretary of state, General George C. Marshall, led an American delegation to the Moscow Conference of Allied Leaders to negotiate the future of Germany. After weeks of futile discussions, Marshall on April 15 took the American proposals directly to Joseph Stalin, the Soviet premier. Since he had known Stalin during the war and had earned the Soviet premier's respect, Marshall believed that personal diplomacy had a reasonable chance of success. He found Stalin polite but vague and non-committal, and he left the meeting with the view that Stalin saw no need for compromise, since the Soviet leader thought time was on the communist side in Europe.

After returning to the United States, Marshall established a State Department committee on policy and planning for Europe, headed by Ambassador George Kennan, who had recently earned recognition in the inner circles of government as an expert on the Soviet Union. Within eight weeks, the committee produced a general policy statement that addressed the economic crisis in Europe. It proposed to return the European standard of living to its prewar level and to assure that the European economic system would be capable of sustained growth. The American idea was to work in cooperation with existing European governments by offering aid that would restore a measure of prosperity, not by providing direct relief to suffering people but by attacking the problems through improving the national economies. Not content to require government-to-government cooperation between the United States and other nations, the policymakers devised a procedure that would require a measure of cooperation among the European nations themselves.

On June 5, General Marshall, in a commencement address at Harvard University, delivered the essence of the Marshall Plan. Since he had the complete confidence of the president, Marshall made the proposal on his own without prior clearance. After describing the effects of war on European economies, pointing out that food and fuel shortages in European cities were severe and people there were badly undernourished, he proposed that the United States should aid all European nations, even those in Eastern Europe, provided that they presented a joint plan clarifying their needs and explaining their priorities. From the American standpoint, this proposal had the advantage of avoiding a piecemeal economic solution that evaluated the needs of each nation on an ad hoc basis. It required a degree of cooperation among European nations that Americans believed essential to long-term economic health.

In response to Marshall's proposal, Ernest Bevin, the British foreign minister, arranged a meeting of European ministers to plan a response. Nothing in Marshall's speech excluded the Soviet Union or its satellites, and at the first European planning session in June the USSR was represented by V. M. Molotov, the Soviet foreign minister. The Soviets quickly withdrew from the meeting, as the Americans, British, and French had hoped, rather than disclose details of their national economic condition and needs. After long negotiations, made more difficult by the concerns of France over the inclusion of aid to West Germany, the European nations presented a plan to the United States. Following revisions suggested by American officials, the plan became the basis for the European Recovery Act of 1948. The European Recovery Program (ERP), popularly known as the Marshall Plan, provided approximately $12.5 billion over a period of four years for European economic relief in seventeen nations. Since the American federal budget was under $100 billion at the time, this sum represented a substantial commitment. Over the nearly four years of the plan's existence, the aid provided to Europe annually amounted to 1.2 percent of the total United States Gross National Product (GNP).

Once the ERP had been formulated, the president, the cabinet, and many other officials threw their support behind it. The program provided that most food, raw materials, and machinery would be purchased in America, and thus promised a substantial increase in American exports. For this reason, the program also found widespread support among business and agricultural leaders. Many political leaders viewed it as a means of containing communism through the use of American economic strength. Their reasoning became more compelling after heavy-handed Soviet intervention and repression in Czechoslovakia in the fall of 1947. Polls taken at the time, however, showed that a majority of the American people supported the ERP on humanitarian grounds. Congress gave its overwhelming approval to the Marshall Plan on April 3, 1948.

**Impact of Event**

A measure that included such large amounts of aid and relief inevitably had a significant impact on the region, though scholars disagree about its precise contributions to Europe. Economic results varied considerably from nation to nation. During its first year, the ERP added more than ten percent to the GNP of two nations, Austria and The Netherlands, and more than five percent to the GNP in five other nations: France, Iceland, Ireland, Italy, and Norway. In those nations that suffered acute food shortages—West Germany, Austria, and the United Kingdom—more than one-third of the aid went for food supplies; in other nations, raw materials, energy, and machinery surpassed food imports. By bringing quantities of American capital and goods into Europe, the ERP contributed to a thirty-two percent rise in the GNP of the participating nations over the four-year period 1948-1951. Food rationing disappeared and the standard of living rose rapidly throughout the four years. By 1950, most European nations had exceeded their prewar agricultural production levels.

The ERP stimulated American investments and influence in Europe. American corporate investments increased more than twice as rapidly in Europe as in any other area. In addition to the large exports of machinery and supplies, the United States sent thousands of experts. A major objective was to increase the productivity of the economies through increasing their efficiency. In the American view, it was necessary to increase productive efficiency, which lagged far behind that of the United States, in order to prevent a rapid rise in inflation while external aid was stimulating economic growth.

The Marshall Plan aided people indirectly, using a systems approach, and its objectives were for the long term. By providing raw materials from America for British factories, it enabled English workers to remain productively employed. Through promoting a fourfold increase in the number of tractors in France, it contributed to the elimination of hunger in France and in other countries as well. Through providing the machinery and transportation necessary for German coal production, it assured that affordable energy was available during periods of inclement weather. By making labor more efficient, American experts helped retard inflation during a period of economic expansion, thus enabling European workers to retain their purchasing power.

From a broader policy perspective, the American consultants sought to decrease the power of industrial cartels, to increase the productive efficiency of European workers, and to promote free trade. These objectives were partially achieved, though the measure of success depended heavily on conditions in each nation. In West Germany, for example, still under American military government, breaking the power of cartels was relatively easy. The ERP was by no means the sole cause of European postwar recovery, for economies as depressed as those of Europe were almost certain to improve, given existing conditions. Most scholars agree that the ERP did provide a powerful stimulus that hastened the recovery and alleviated human suffering caused by the economic crisis. In addition, American influence furthered policies that American politicians believed were in the interest of the long-term economic health of the region.

Politically, in nation after nation, economic resurgence had the effects that American planners had desired. As hopes for prosperity became real, elections produced centrist and rightist governments at the expense of the communists and their allies. Although these governments did not invariably assure all the freedoms found in the United States, it is undeniable that they provided greater freedoms to their citizens than did the governments of Eastern Bloc nations. On the whole, they preserved freedoms of speech, religion, and the press.

In this respect the ERP contributed to the American policy of containment and to the American view of a world order that assures fundamental political and economic freedoms. In another respect, the ERP benefited both the United States and Europe by establishing a mode of cooperation that made mutual defense more palatable. The cooperation and mutual planning mandated by the ERP contributed significantly to the formation of the North Atlantic Treaty Organization in 1951. On the downside, the ERP leaders tacitly acknowledged the split in Europe between West and East and prompted the Soviet government to consolidate Eastern Europe into its own economic and defense plans.

## Bibliography

Gimbel, John. *The Origins of the Marshall Plan.* Stanford, Calif.: Stanford University Press, 1976. This analytical book traces the origins of the ERP to American policymakers and to specific postwar events. Gimbel sees the East-West conflict as a minor influence on the development and implementation of the Marshall Plan. Includes notes on unpublished sources, extensive notes on published sources, and a good index.

Hogan, Michael J. *The Marshall Plan: America, Britain, and the Reconstruction of Western Europe, 1947-1952.* Cambridge, England: Cambridge University Press, 1987. In his carefully researched and comprehensive analysis of the ERP, Hogan takes into account the arguments of its critics and concludes that it achieved its major economic and political purposes. Very extensive but unannotated bibliography. Good index.

Mee, Charles L., Jr. *The Marshall Plan: The Launching of the Pax Americana.* New York: Simon & Schuster, 1984. Mee provides a clearly written and balanced account of the formulation and adoption of the Marshall Plan, incorporating data and figures into the text. For the average reader, this book is perhaps the best introduction to the subject. Offers two useful appendices including Truman's address and Marshall's Harvard speech as well as notes, bibliography, and index.

Milward, Alan S. *The Reconstruction of Western Europe, 1945-51.* Berkeley: University of California Press, 1984. A detailed study of all aspects of the European economic recovery, the book provides numerous tables showing progress of the recovery in detail. Milward gives the background of the Marshall Plan and assesses its effects. Useful bibliography focuses on international sources. Brief index.

Pogue, Forrest C. *George C. Marshall: Statesman, 1945-1959.* New York: Viking Press, 1987. The fourth and final volume of the standard biography of Marshall, it gives an account of the formulation of the ERP. Pogue clarifies Marshall's contribution, differentiating it from the roles of other prominent diplomats and officials.

and historical context in which these individuals operated. Tygiel follows up the Robinson story by examining racial integration of all the major league teams and the subsequent issue of organized baseball's integration on the management level. He considers the Jackie Robinson "experiment" to be ongoing rather than successfully completed.

Voight, David Q. *America Through Baseball*. Chicago: Nelson-Hall, 1976. Chapter 8, "American Baseball and the American Dilemma," presents a thought-provoking critique of the so-called Jackie Robinson myth: the belief that Robinson's entry into baseball somehow fostered or signaled a golden age of racial equality.

Woodward, C. Vann. *The Strange Career of Jim Crow*. New York: Oxford University Press, 1957. A classic, highly readable account of segregation in the American South.

*Ira Smolensky*

## Cross-References

The Congress of Racial Equality Forms (1942), p. 601; CORE Stages a Sit-in in Chicago to Protest Segregation (1943), p. 618; Race Riots Erupt in Detroit and Harlem (1943), p. 635; CORE Stages the "Journey of Reconciliation" (1947), p. 718; Truman Orders Desegregation of U.S. Armed Forces (1948), p. 777; *Brown v. Board of Education* Ends Public School Segregation (1954), p. 913; The Civil Rights Act of 1957 Creates the Commission on Civil Rights (1957), p. 997; Martin Luther King, Jr., Delivers His "I Have a Dream" Speech (1963), p. 1200; Congress Passes the Civil Rights Act (1964), p. 1251; Congress Passes the Voting Rights Act (1965), p. 1296; Marshall Becomes the First Black Supreme Court Justice (1967), p. 1381; Jackson Becomes the First Major Black Candidate for U.S. President (1983), p. 2209.

# CORE STAGES THE "JOURNEY OF RECONCILIATION"

*Category of event:* Racial and ethnic rights
*Time:* April 9-23, 1947
*Locale:* Washington, D.C., Virginia, North Carolina, Tennessee, and Kentucky

*The 1947 "Journey of Reconciliation," sponsored by the Congress of Racial Equality (CORE), helped establish nonviolent direct action as CORE's identifying mark and served as a model for the Freedom Rides of the early 1960's*

*Principal personages:*

BAYARD RUSTIN (1910-1987), an influential civil rights advocate who helped organize the Journey of Reconciliation and the 1963 March on Washington

JAMES PECK (1915-    ), a white supporter of civil rights activism and one of the leaders of the Journey of Reconciliation and the later Freedom Rides of 1961

GEORGE M. HOUSER (1916-    ), one of the founders of CORE and a leader of the Fellowship of Reconciliation (FOR); a seminal figure in planning the Journey of Reconciliation

## Summary of Event

Three factors converged to bring about the 1947 Journey of Reconciliation, which was sponsored jointly by the Congress of Racial Equality (CORE) and the Fellowship of Reconciliation (FOR). The first and most basic was CORE's desire to launch a direct-action campaign that would attract national attention and thus strengthen the organization at a time when its resources were meager and its activities limited. Since its founding in 1942 by a biracial group in Chicago, CORE had been committed to nonviolent direct action on the model of Mohandas K. Gandhi in India and had sponsored sit-ins and other forms of nonviolent protest. Its budget was barely $100 per month in 1945-1946, however, and its public visibility was low. When George M. Houser became the executive secretary of CORE in 1945, a successful national campaign was one of his chief goals. A white activist in FOR when he was chosen for the new position, Houser had been involved with James Farmer and others in founding CORE and was concerned that its first three years of efforts had fallen short of his dream of making CORE a major force for nonviolent reform in the United States.

The second major cause of the journey was the United States Supreme Court decision in the *Morgan v. Virginia* case (June, 1946) that declared Virginia's policy of racial segregation on interstate motor carriers unconstitutional. When several bus companies refused to comply with the decision, Houser saw their resistance as the opportunity he had looked for. Nonviolent direct action, he believed, might help the cause of desegregated transportation while strengthening CORE's impact. Bayard Rustin, a longtime activist who had served causes such as Gandhi's liberation efforts in India and several antiwar campaigns, agreed. A founder of CORE's New York branch, Rustin was quite familiar with the organization's goals and needs. At CORE's fall, 1946, executive committee meeting, he and Houser argued that the recent *Morgan v. Virginia* decision provided a promising setting for demonstrating the potential of nonviolent direct action. Both men at the time were secretaries in FOR's Racial-Industrial Department and had the support of A. J. Muste, a widely known pacifist and FOR executive. Throughout the fall and winter of 1946-1947, Rustin and Houser gained other supporters both within and outside their organizations. By January, 1947, they were ready to take a preliminary trip along the proposed route both to gain additional partners and to finalize the details. Their original plan to extend the trip into the deep South all the way to New Orleans was abandoned because of the possibility of violent resistance. The "Journey of Reconciliation," as they called it after discussions with FOR staffers, would be confined to the upper southern states from Virginia to North and South Carolina.

The third contributing factor to the journey was interorganizational cooperation among civil rights groups, augmented by local individuals and churches. During their planning trip in January, 1947, Houser and Rustin enlisted a significant number of college students and black church members to provide housing and food for the journey participants. The National Association for the Advancement of Colored People (NAACP) had serious misgivings about the journey and refrained from active support, but it did offer its local contacts in several communities along the route. The NAACP's reluctance was caused by its fear of violent backlash if the travelers went into the deep South or possibly even the border states. CORE's decision to confine the trip to the Virginia and Carolina areas helped ameliorate this concern, but not sufficiently to convince the NAACP executive secretary, Walter White, to provide funds or active assistance.

In late March and early April, 1947, the sixteen participants in the journey engaged in intense training in Washington, D.C. Anticipating the training techniques of the 1960's, such as role-playing, lectures and discussions, and learning ways to protect oneself in case of violent resistance, they prepared.

On April 9, the group of eight whites and eight blacks left the nation's capital and headed southward through northern Virginia. Ideologically, the biracial group shared much. All the white members were pacifists—James Peck of the Peck and Peck clothing business family, George M. Houser, Homer Jack of the Chicago Council Against Racial and Religious Discrimination, New York horticulturalist Igal Roodenko, and four others of varied professional backgrounds. Two of them, Joseph Felmet of Asheville, North Carolina, and James Peck, were socialists affiliated with the Workers Defense League. Peck was editor of the league's news bulletin. The other three white participants were two North Carolina Methodist pastors, Ernest Bromley and Louis Adams, and Worth Randle, a Cincinnati biologist. Four of the black participants in the Journey of Reconciliation were also pacifists, among them Bayard Rustin, whose activist career included support for Gandhi's liberation efforts in India. Rustin was particularly controversial because of his earlier affiliation with communism, an unusual association among black leaders, but he had abandoned communism by the early 1940's. In addition to Rustin and Homer Jack, the black participants were freelance lecturer Wallace Nelson, Conrad Lynn, a New York attorney, Andrew Johnson, a student from Cincinnati, Chicago musician Dennis Banks, William Worthy of the New York Council for a Permanent FEPC (Fair Employment Practices Commission), and Eugene Stanley of A. and T. College in North Carolina.

From Washington, the group traveled to Richmond, Virginia, where the first overnight stop was scheduled. Half the group traveled on a Greyhound bus, the other half on the Trailways line. Each ticket listed every planned stopover in cities where the riders would address meetings in churches, but the planners had determined that the ultimate destination on each ticket required crossing a state line, since their specific goal was to implement the *Morgan* decision of 1946. The plan was to travel across Virginia, into North Carolina, Tennessee, and Kentucky, and then back across Virginia. The entire journey would take two weeks. Meetings were arranged chiefly by the NAACP in cooperation with local churches. Peck reported that it was exciting to begin the journey after months of anticipation and to be actually "on stage," trying to challenge resistance to the recent court decision. The underlying hope of the participants was not only to enforce a law but also to change attitudes. If idealistic, this goal was basic to those who set out on the potentially dangerous trip, usually regarded as the first Freedom Ride.

Although the journey elicited no major violent response, there were several arrests. The first was on a Trailways carrier as the group left Petersburg, Virginia. James Peck was arrested in Durham, North Carolina, along with Rustin and Andrew Johnson, during a rally in a church. Durham was a small but prosperous city with better paving, housing, and other facilities in the white sections than in the black. Peck was bothered by this and spoke out against it. He and the others were detained only briefly and then taken by car to Chapel Hill, the nearby site of the University of North Carolina. Interestingly, the Chapel Hill area was the only stop on the journey that witnessed real violence. In Cargill, a small town just outside Chapel Hill's city limits, Peck was hit by a group of taxi drivers as he stood outside his bus. Inside, four of the journey group were arrested when they tried to integrate the front seats. Released on bail, they were taken by a local white Presbyterian minister to his home for protection, but cabs full of hostile resisters wielded rocks and sticks and warned the minister that they would burn his home if he did not get the group out of town.

Other arrests occurred in Asheville, North Carolina, as the group traveled westward toward Tennessee after stopping in Greensboro. Again, Peck was arrested. The issue was the same in Asheville as in Chapel Hill, the effort to integrate the whites-only seats. Asheville happened to be the home of one of the white participants, Joe Felmet, and some of the group stayed overnight in his home. In the trial the next day, Peck and his codefendant, a black participant from Chicago named Dennis Banks, were found guilty and sentenced to thirty days on a road gang. The state's attorney and the judge who presided did not know about the *Morgan* decision and borrowed a copy of the decision from Curtis Todd, a black attorney who represented the riders. As it turned out, Banks and Peck remained in jail only a few hours and were released, but during that time, the other prisoners vented their anger at Peck, a white man supporting blacks. Eventually, the state dropped the case when its officials learned more about the 1946 court decision.

From Asheville, the Journey of Reconciliation continued into Knoxville, Tennessee, then northward into Kentucky and back across Virginia before ending in Washington in late April. Of the five arrest cases during the two-week trip, all but one were dropped. The Chapel Hill case was pursued by prosecutors, and Rustin, Joe Felmet, and Igal Roodenko served thirty days at hard labor on a road gang. Nevertheless, there were no reporters waiting to interview the participants and nothing like the intense journalistic enthusiasm that would mark the Freedom Rides fourteen years later. The Journey of Reconciliation was a pioneering effort that at the time attracted a disappointingly slight response from the press and the public.

## Impact of Event

The significance of the Journey of Reconciliation lay, in the short run, in the heightened publicity it elicited and the inspiration it gave to advocates of social change by means of nonviolent direct action. Although no reporters were waiting to interview the participants when they returned, press coverage of the various incidents during the trip was fair and rather extensive. Both Houser and Rustin were pleased with the details of press accounts and considered them positive. For the participants themselves, newspaper articles were important for their later efforts to gain support and recruit new activists. Indeed, many years later, CORE leaders used stories of the journey to teach nonviolent theory and encourage participation. James Peck was particularly encouraged by the response of people in general to the effort and noted that drivers, other passengers, and observers were sympathetic toward desegregation but were ignorant of various laws. Seeing the journey activists demonstrate nonviolent techniques, he felt, contributed to greater understanding and support.

At a deeper level, the Journey of Reconciliation was a truly paradigmatic event. Strictly speaking, it was the first Freedom Ride. What is usually termed the first Freedom Ride in popular parlance was actually modeled after the 1947 precedent in key respects. Peck, who was active in both the 1947 journey and the 1961 Freedom Rides, saw the earlier event as supremely significant in the longer process of rides by desegregationist activists, describing it as "perhaps the most unique and outstanding undertaking CORE has ever made." CORE trainers used both the concept of the journey and the methodology of nonviolent protest in preparing for the 1961 rides into the deep South.

As a factor in the history of racial and ethnic rights, the Journey of Reconciliation is somewhat analogous to the 1962 desegregation efforts in Albany, Georgia. In both cases, the immediate goals were not achieved quickly. The specific objective of the journey was to intensify grass-roots efforts to achieve a greater degree of desegregation in public transportation. That did not happen quickly, but the effort did increase public awareness of the problem and encourage many other efforts to desegregate interstate buses, trains, and other conveyances. In doing that, the 1947 journey into the upper South also demonstrated that nonviolence had much more potential than many people realized to augment legal efforts to bring about racial equality. Spiritually and intellectually, the leaders were encouraged to perpetuate the nonviolent method. Like Albany, the Journey of Reconciliation was a source of inspiration to challenge racial segregation and discrimination by concerted group action. That aspect of the journey's impact continued to have influence throughout the 1950's and into the following decade.

The judicial proceedings that occurred during and after the Journey of Reconciliation were also significant for CORE's later development. The several cases that grew out of the trip were pursued by attorneys who supported CORE's objectives and provided useful experience in using the details of local and state laws to show contradictions with Supreme Court decisions and thus to bring to bear on local problems the larger influence of federal law. This was a rather slowly developing process, since bus companies often cited state law as their guide and delayed implementing federal mandates until the courts made it clear that they applied.

CORE's finances and public visibility remained rather low even after the journey, but it was the first of several undertakings that would gradually propel the organization to higher public recognition and larger membership. FOR assisted CORE in pursuing some of the cases, including the Chapel Hill litigation in months immediately following the journey. By the 1950's, CORE was beginning to grow in several of its chapters and to equip itself for a larger role in racial desegregation litigation. Above all, the trip was a favorite topic of conversation and training programs that led eventually to the 1960's Freedom Rides that elicited widespread media coverage and support by youth across the nation. The Journey of Reconciliation was clearly a high point in CORE's history, as well as a model for the potential efficacy of nonviolent direct action.

## Bibliography

Bell, Inge Powell. *CORE and the Strategy of Nonviolence*. New York: Random House, 1968. This work traces and analyzes the development of CORE's use of nonviolent direct action from its early days until the height of the Civil Rights movement in the 1960's. Both conceptual and historical, it is useful for showing how direct action distinguished CORE from the older mainstream civil rights organizations. Contains notes, bibliography, and index.

Farmer, James. "On Cracking White City." In *My Soul Is Rested*, edited by Howell Raines. New York: Putnam, 1977. In this introductory section of Raines's valuable oral history of the Civil Rights movement, James Farmer provides perspective on the evolution of protest thought. One of the founders of CORE, Farmer had a distinctive vantage point for demonstrating the difficulties and successes of the early movement. He underscores the importance of the 1946 Supreme Court decision that declared segregated interstate bus seating unconstitutional and notes the importance of the journey as a precedent for the Freedom Rides.

Houser, George, and Bayard Rustin. *We Challenged Jim Crow! A Report on the Journey of Reconciliation, April 9-23, 1947.* New York: Fellowship of Reconciliation, 1947. This brief but valuable report lists and describes all participants in the Journey of Reconciliation, outlines the highlights of the experiences in each city, and gives brief accounts of several arrests and trials. It also includes a statement on the purposes and nature of CORE and explanations of its nonviolent theory. No notes or index.

Meier, August, and Elliott Rudwick. *CORE: A Study in the Civil Rights Movement, 1942-1968.* New York: Oxford University Press, 1973. A detailed account of the origins, development, and campaigns of CORE from 1942 to the late 1960's, when the organization began to wane. Well documented with CORE primary materials, this book is the standard account that demonstrates the periodic resurgence of the organization and explains the basic reasons for its problems after 1966. Contains a thorough list of references and an index.

Morris, Aldon D. *The Origins of the Civil Rights Movement: Black Communities Organizing for Change.* New York: Free Press, 1984. This essential background study for most civil rights activities in the South includes extensive information on all the movement centers and organizations of the period. Its value on this topic is chiefly its analysis of CORE in its early days, particularly its establishment of a base in the South during the decade following the Journey of Reconciliation. Contains notes, bibliography, and index.

Peck, James. *Freedom Ride.* New York: Simon & Schuster, 1962. This compact account is particularly valuable because its author was a leading participant in both the Journey of Reconciliation and the later Freedom Rides. A white liberal, Peck was at times injured by opponents of integration yet persisted in his civil rights activism. One sees in his work the emotions, risks, and goals of the freedom riders. Has references and an index.

Schmeidler, Emilie. *Shaping Ideas and Actions: CORE, SCLC, and SNCC in the Struggle for Equality.* Ann Arbor, Mich.: University Microfilms International, 1980. This carefully prepared doctoral dissertation examines CORE's place among the leading civil rights advocacy organizations whose principal method was nonviolent direct action. The section on CORE includes a valuable analysis of the CORE model of direct action that combined Gandhian methods and distinctive efforts to shape positive interracial attitudes. Contains reference notes, bibliography, and a table of contents.

*Thomas R. Peake*

## Cross-References

Roosevelt Outlaws Discrimination in Defense-Industry Employment (1941), p. 578; The Congress of Racial Equality Forms (1942), p. 601; CORE Stages a Sit-in in Chicago to Protest Segregation (1943), p. 618; Truman Orders Desegregation of U.S.

Armed Forces (1948), p. 777; The United Nations Adopts the Universal Declaration of Human Rights (1948), p. 789; *Brown v. Board of Education* Ends Public School Segregation (1954), p. 913; The Civil Rights Act of 1957 Creates the Commission on Civil Rights (1957), p. 997; Greensboro Sit-ins Launch a New Stage in the Civil Rights Movement (1960), p. 1056; The United Nations Issues a Declaration on Racial Discrimination (1963), p. 1212; The U.N. Covenant on Civil and Political Liberties Is Adopted (1966), p. 1353.

# JAPANESE CONSTITUTION GRANTS NEW RIGHTS TO WOMEN

*Category of event:* Women's rights
*Time:* May 3, 1947
*Locale:* Tokyo, Japan

*For the first time in Japan's modern history, Japanese women received political, social, and economic rights, under a new constitution*

*Principal personages:*

BEATE SIROTA (1923-    ), a civilian in the government section of Supreme Command Allied Powers who wrote the constitutional sections on women's rights

HUGH BORTON (1903-    ), a State Department employee and Japan expert who was the principal author of SWNCC-228

COURTNEY WHITNEY (1897-1969), a lawyer and close friend of General MacArthur; became the head of the government section on November 11, 1945

CHARLES LOUIS KADES (1906-    ), the principal drafter of the Japanese Constitution

DOUGLAS MACARTHUR (1880-1964), the commander in chief, Far East; commander in chief of U.S. Army Forces, Pacific; and supreme commander of the Allied Forces in Japan from 1945 to 1952

YOSHIDA SHIGERU (1878-1967), a career diplomat who served as prime minister during the constitution's ratification in the Japanese Diet

HIROHITO (1901-1989), the emperor of Japan who ascended to the throne in 1926; supported the constitutional rewrite and ratification process

BARON SHIDEHARA KIJŪRŌ (1872-1951), the prime minister whose unsuccessful attempts to rewrite the constitution drove MacArthur to command government sector personnel to rewrite it

## Summary of Event

On March 10, 1943, the United States State Department began to plan postwar changes for Japan. The State-War-Navy Coordinating Committee (SWNCC), formed in December, 1944, became the primary U.S. agency for formulation of policy guidelines in Japan and continued in that role until its dissolution in November, 1947. By May, 1944, "The Post-War Objectives of the United States in Regard to Japan" was formulated; it became the basis for the more detailed plan, called the "US Initial Policy" (SWNCC 150/4), which was radioed to General Douglas MacArthur, Supreme Commander of the Allied Powers (SCAP), on August 29, 1945, and received by him on August 30.

The Potsdam Declaration of July 26, 1945, had demanded Japan's immediate surrender and stated that Japan would be occupied until the government had been de-
mocratized, preferably by the people, as stipulated in the Atlantic Charter (1941).
The Japanese government rejected Potsdam, as it did not guarantee the existence of
Japan's emperor system. On August 6 and 9, 1945, atomic bombs were dropped on
Hiroshima and Nagasaki, respectively. Emperor Hirohito addressed his people over
the radio and asked that they surrender to the Allied forces and peacefully accept the
first occupation in Japan's history.

On August 30, 1945 the Eighth Army landed at Atsugi airfield (near Yokohama),
followed that afternoon by General MacArthur, who quickly established general headquarters in the Dai Ichi Building in Tokyo. President Harry S. Truman signed SWNCC
150/4 on September 6, making it official U.S. government policy, and gave MacArthur almost unconditional authority to implement U.S. policy. On September 18 and
October 22, MacArthur received more definitive orders regarding occupation policy
from the Joint Chiefs of Staff. Neither of these orders mandated constitutional reform or mentioned women's rights.

MacArthur's Civil Liberties Directive to the Japanese government, issued on October 4, stated that there would be no discrimination on the basis of race, nationality,
creed, or political opinion; gender was not addressed. This directive was supported
by the Japanese people but not by the conservative government headed by Prime
Minister Shidehara Kijūrō. On October 11, MacArthur told Shidehara to liberalize
the 1889 Meiji Constitution; emancipation of females was listed first as an objective.
This was a statement or suggestion, not a directive or order; however, Shidehara
responded by appointing Matsumoto Jōji and other cabinet ministers to rewrite the
Meiji Constitution.

Between November 27, 1944, and December 19, 1945, the SWNCC-228 and 228/1
documents mandating the reform of the Japanese constitution and government were
written, primarily by Dr. Hugh Borton, a State Department official. These documents were forwarded informally to General MacArthur and his immediate staff by
the Tokyo-based State Department political adviser, George Atcheson, Jr., on December 13, and formally sent to MacArthur on January 11, 1946, by SWNCC. They
were sent as information rather than as official directives but became the blueprint
for the American rewrite of the Japanese constitution.

In December, 1945, the Japanese Diet (legislative body) revised the election law,
granting women the rights to vote and to run for political office. Japanese suffra-
gettes had been fighting for these rights since the 1920's and had actively lobbied
both the SCAP and their government for these rights since the war's end. These
rights, however, had no constitutional protection.

The Matsumoto constitutional draft was submitted to MacArthur on February 1,
1946, and was promptly rejected by him on the grounds that the emperor system was
left largely intact and that few civil rights were accorded to the people. MacArthur
had also rejected other constitutional drafts, written by political and civilian groups,
on the same bases. Only one of these rewrites included woman suffrage; other civil

rights for women were not mentioned.

Also on February 1, a local newspaper disclosed the Matsumoto draft's inadequacies to the general public. Brigadier General Courtney Whitney, head of the government section, told MacArthur how to get a constitution drawn up legally before the Far Eastern Commission (FEC), a joint allied oversight committee, convened in late February. Once the FEC came into being, MacArthur would have to submit all work on the constitution to it for approval and face a probable Soviet veto. He wished to avoid this.

MacArthur ordered Whitney to construct a model draft. Whitney created a steering committee (Alfred Hussey, Milo Rowell, and Charles Kades, the principal drafter) to orchestrate the entire process. SWNCC-228 was divided up line by line and distributed to nine groups, consisting of one to four GS personnel each, for restructuring. Each group was to work quickly and in total secrecy. The civil rights sections were given to Beate Sirota and Harry Emerson Wildes, both civilians, and Lieutenant Colonel Pieter R. Roest. Sirota secured from local libraries copies of European constitutions, which this civil rights committee used as models. Sirota was then given the task, among others, of writing the sections on civil rights for women. The sections this twenty-two-year-old naturalized U.S. citizen (born in Vienna, reared in Tokyo) created became Article Fourteen (a Japanese equal rights amendment), Article Twenty-four (equal rights in marriage, divorce, inheritance, property rights, and choice of domicile), Article Twenty-six (equal educational opportunity), Article Twenty-seven (equal right and obligation to work), and Article Forty-four (equal rights to run for and hold political office). (Article Fifteen, universal adult suffrage, was not written by Sirota.) These rights were more sweeping and inclusive than existed in most extant constitutions. Sirota's original sections included even more rights and protections for women than those listed above, but they were eliminated by Whitney and Kades.

The entire model draft was complete and endorsed by MacArthur by February 12. The next day, the steering committee presented it to Matsumoto at Foreign Minister Yoshida Shigeru's home. The Japanese cabinet rewrote two versions of the "MacArthur Draft," as it came to be called, and submitted them to MacArthur on March 2 and 5; MacArthur accepted the March 5 draft. Emperor Hirohito endorsed that draft, and it was made public almost immediately. On June 26, both houses of the Diet began ratification debates, which lasted until October. This constitution had wide public support, but the government opposition, led by Yoshida, who had become prime minister in the July, 1946, elections, and his prewar conservative allies, kept trying to change it, especially the sections entailing women's rights. The various Japanese women's groups, organized primarily by Army Lieutenant Ethel B. Weed, along with Sirota, MacArthur, and others, fought these maneuvers. The final outcome was that few changes were made in the MacArthur Draft.

Emperor Hirohito proclaimed the new constitution to be the law of the land on November 3, 1946, the Emperor Meiji's birthday. (The date was suggested by Yoshida.) It would be called the Shōwa Constitution, after the dynastic era beginning in 1926. On May 3, 1947, the constitution officially came into effect. As of 1990, no amendments had been proposed successfully to alter this constitution.

## Impact of Event

The first postwar elections for the lower house of the Diet were held on April 10, 1947. Day-care centers were set up at election sites. Thirty-eight women won seats. This date is still celebrated as the Day of Women's Rights.

Ichikawa Fusae founded the Japanese League of Women Voters at the end of 1945. In spite of her fears of a low turnout, in the 1946 lower house elections 67.0 percent of women and 78.5 percent of men voted, and slightly lower percentages cast ballots for the upper house. By 1976, women outvoted men. Women, however, were not engaging in other political behavior to the same extent as men. In 1974, the Japanese Diet was 3.4 percent female. Even fewer women occupied political offices below the national level, such as in prefectural, municipal, town, and village assemblies. As of 1971, only 1.2 percent of high government administrative posts were held by women.

Other legislative reforms solidified some constitutional guarantees. These events were largely the result of the active Japanese women's groups organized by Weed, Weed's own work in teaching Japanese women about democracy (there are no words in Japanese for democracy or freedom; they are foreign concepts, as is liberty in the Western sense), and MacArthur's strong support for women's rights.

In 1947, the Labor Standards Act made discrimination in pay by gender illegal. Discrimination in hiring, training, promotion, work conditions, and benefits were not prohibited, providing the loopholes employers needed to discriminate against women. As of 1984, these forms of discrimination still existed.

After intense resistance from the Japanese government, the SCAP successfully pushed the creation of the Women's and Minors' Bureau in the Ministry of Labor (1947). The bureau's primary function was to protect women's rights after the occupation ended (April 28, 1952). Weed and her coalition of Japanese women's groups were instrumental in getting the SCAP to insist on this bureau's creation. The bureau was still strong and vital in 1987.

On January 1, 1948, the new civil code came into effect. In it, the constitutional guarantees of equality between the sexes in marriage, property rights, and inheritance were upheld. Nevertheless, by 1982, 40 percent of marriages were still arranged, many times by the woman's corporate employer.

The Eugenics Protection Law of 1948 was not encouraged or introduced by the SCAP. Rather, Japanese women who had worked with Margaret Sanger in New York or who had met Sanger on her two trips to Japan in the 1920's secured the right to have access to family planning information and contraceptives. Limited legal abortion was authorized. In the 1990's, securing adequate and safe contraception was still defined as a problem by Japanese women because of various regulations.

## Bibliography

Burks, Ardath W. *Japan: A Postindustrial Power.* Boulder, Colo.: Westview Press,

1984. Excellent general reference on Japan. Some material on women, but nothing extensive. College-level reading; references provided.

Curtis, Gerald L. *The Japanese Way of Politics.* New York: Columbia University Press, 1988. Contains a traditional political scientist's analysis of politics and political party structures. Minimal material on women. College-level reading.

McNelly, Theodore, ed. *Sources in Modern East Asian History and Politics.* New York: Appleton-Century-Crofts, 1967. A book of original documents concerning China, Japan, Korea, and Vietnam. Includes SWNCC-228, the 1952 peace treaty, and the Meiji and Shōwa constitutions. References and maps provided.

Morgan, Robin, ed. *Sisterhood Is Global: The International Women's Movement Anthology.* Garden City, N.Y.: Anchor Press, 1984. Contains basic demographic material on the status of women in each country listed.

Pharr, Susan J. *Political Women in Japan: The Search for a Place in Political Life.* Berkeley: University of California Press, 1981. Excellent cross-cultural study on Japanese and other women's political lives. College-level reading; references provided.

——————. "A Radical U.S. Experiment: Women's Rights Laws and the Occupation of Japan." In *The Occupation of Japan: Impact of Legal Reform,* edited by L. H. Redford. Norfolk, Va.: The MacArthur Memorial, 1977. Excellent source of material on who actually wrote the women's rights sections of the Japanese Constitution. References and documents provided.

Pyle, Kenneth B. *The Making of Modern Japan.* Lexington, Mass.: D. C. Heath, 1978. Easy reading at the college level. Some discussion of status of Japanese women. This is a good general source of information; see Chapters 12 and 13 on the occupation. References provided.

Sugisaki, Kazuko. "From the Moon to the Sun: Women's Liberation in Japan." In *Women in the World, 1975-1985: The Women's Decade,* edited by Lynne B. Iglitzin and Ruth Ross. Santa Barbara, Calif.: ABC-Clio, 1986. Excellent article on the history of Japanese women and women's activities since 1945. References at the end of each article; college-level reading.

Ward, Robert E., and Sakamoto Yoshikazu, eds. *Democratizing Japan: The Allied Occupation.* Honolulu: University of Hawaii Press, 1987. This book resulted from a joint U.S.-Japanese conference on the Allied occupation. Divergent perspectives are presented. College-level reading; references provided at the end of each article.

Warshaw, Steven. *Japan Emerges: A Concise History of Japan from Its Origin to the Present.* Berkeley, Calif.: Diablo Press, 1990. Excellent general history; not much information on women. References provided. College-level material.

*Dixie Dean Dickinson*

## Cross-References

The League of Women Voters Is Founded (1920), p. 333; Sanger Organizes Conferences on Birth Control (1921), p. 356; The Atlantic Charter Declares a Postwar Right of Self-Determination (1941), p. 584; French Women Get the Vote (1944), p. 646; The U.N. Convention on the Political Rights of Women Is Approved (1952), p. 885; The Equal Rights Amendment Passes Congress but Fails to Be Ratified (1972), p. 1656; A U.N. Convention Condemns Discrimination Against Women (1979), p. 2057.

# INDIA GAINS INDEPENDENCE

*Categories of event:* Political freedom and religious freedom
*Time:* August 15, 1947
*Locale:* India and Pakistan

*India gained its political freedom at the price of great suffering and loss of life*

*Principal personages:*

CLEMENT ATTLEE (1883-1967), the first post-World War II prime minister of Great Britain

WINSTON CHURCHILL (1874-1965), the prime minister of Great Britain during World War II; opposed independence for India and helped make possible the creation of Pakistan

MAHATMA GANDHI (1869-1948), a self-styled "holy man" whose policy of noncooperation forced the British to give up India

MUḤAMMAD IQBĀL (1877-1938), a Muslim poet, theologian, and barrister whose writings inspired the formation of Muslim Pakistan

MOHAMMED ALI JINNAH (1876-1948), the leader of the Muslim League, the person most responsible for establishing a separate Pakistan

LORD LOUIS MOUNTBATTEN (1900-1979), the last British viceroy; supervised partition of the Indian subcontinent

JAWAHARLAL NEHRU (1889-1964), the leader of the Congress Party, along with Gandhi the driving force for independence

RAM MOHAN ROY (1772-1833), sometimes called the "father of Indian nationalism," saw reformed Hinduism as the basis for a modern Indian state

## Summary of Event

Although Indian poets and philosophers had long dreamed of a united India stretching from the Himalayas to the oceans, in actuality the subcontinent for centuries was the site of warring states. Such unity as existed was imposed from the outside, such as that imposed by the British. Coming first as traders, they later turned India into a colony. The British first introduced the Western concept of nationalism, made Indians aware of their national identity, and fostered the growth of an independence movement. The British also brought the idea of white superiority—that Indians because of their color were racially inferior, their society barbarous, and their culture in an early stage of evolution.

Added to the humiliation of racial inferiority was that of economic exploitation. In order to maximize its profits, the British East India Company that first ruled India exploited Indian labor and appropriated land and raw materials. Indians found an early spokesperson for the cause of independence in the British-educated Indian patriot, Rammohun Roy. Roy advised the Indian people to copy Western methods and combine them with revived Hinduism to create an independent India. Growing resentment over continued economic exploitation as well as British disregard for Indian religious law resulted in the first open demonstration for independence, the Sepoy Rebellion of 1857.

The rebellion was suppressed. The British, however, improved the administration of India and the rights of Indians by placing India under colonial control, rather than control by the East India Company, through the Government of India Act of 1858. Even though some provincial councils were established and Indians could serve as counselors to the viceroy, the appointed British ruler in India, power remained with the British. No matter how well educated or capable, Indians remained in the lowest level of the civil service.

Economic exploitation continued but on a larger scale. The English cotton mills needed raw material, so large areas of India were turned from rice cultivation to that of growing cotton, thus endangering the food supply. The British further impoverished India by destroying its cotton industry through flooding the market with cheap British textiles that were free of tariffs. Indians were also recruited for military service at a lower pay scale than their British counterparts. Until World War I, Indians provided an effective, inexpensive police force for the British Empire. Frustrated, the Indians in 1885 founded the Indian National Congress (which later became the Congress Party) to express their desires and to make plans for achieving independence.

World War I raised Indian expectations. Even though the British assumed dictatorial control through the Defense of India Act (1915), Indians hoped that by backing the war effort they would be rewarded with greater political freedom. On the contrary, the British reasserted their control through the repressive Rowlatt Acts in 1919.

Protests resulted in the Amritsar Massacre, in which about four hundred peacefully demonstrating Indians were killed and more than one thousand wounded because of firing ordered by a British general. Indian public opinion turned further against the British, who were perceived to have approved of the action. Indians saw themselves as second-class citizens in their own land. Few were more outraged than Mohandas K. (Mahatma) Gandhi, who emerged as the leader of the Indian drive for independence. Trained in law in England, Gandhi practiced in South Africa. Offended by discrimination against nonwhites, he devised a policy of noncooperation which he used with great effectiveness in India.

Gandhi identified with the masses. He dressed in homespun, observed religious and dietary laws, and lived in humble surroundings. His followers worshipped him and called him "Mahatma," or "Great Soul." Because of his education and experience, Gandhi had the ability to unite educated Indians with the masses. The combination eventually provided the means for freeing India of foreign control.

Gandhi was joined in his drive for political independence by Jawaharlal Nehru, also from an upper-caste Hindu family. Both Gandhi and Nehru envisioned an independent India as an essentially Hindu state. This troubled the Muslim minority, concentrated in the northwest, who thought they would suffer from discrimination in such a state. The Muslims found a leader in Mohammed Ali Jinnah. Following the advice of the theologian Muḥammad Iqbāl that only a separate state could bring Muslims together in the true spirit of their religion, Jinnah resigned from the Congress Party to head the Muslim League. Its objective was the establishment of a Muslim state.

The growing religious rivalry weakened but did not stop the drive for independence. Some accused the British of covertly supporting the rivalry, continuing a "divide and rule" policy that had been effective in keeping India a colony for nearly two centuries. The accusation was not without foundation. The British in the inter-war period found their control of India increasingly to be a burden. They had a deficit trade balance with India, the Indian army with its antiquated equipment ceased to be an effective fighting force, and serving in the Indian civil service was no longer attractive to ambitious young Britons. To minimize costs, the British tended to support existing institutions and the status quo. As a result, India stagnated socially. Even though the British had introduced legislation supporting basic human rights, increasingly neither the will nor the means existed to enforce these regulations. The 495 princely states, whose rulers retained their absolute powers and lavish life-styles in contrast to the poverty of the masses, posed obstacles to enforcement.

In 1935, the British Parliament granted India a new constitution, extending the franchise and giving the separate provinces greater independence. Many maintained that India could then have been granted full independence without violence and bloodshed had it not been for the determined opposition of a small but influential group of conservative British statesmen. Among them was the wartime prime minister, Winston Churchill. Although he was a noted historian, he seemingly was blind to demands of subjugated peoples for liberation.

Part of Churchill's strategy in dealing with India was that of supporting the Muslim faction. The outbreak of World War II consequently found the Indians divided and resentful over the viceroy bringing them into the war without their consent. The Congress Party refused to back the war effort. The Muslim League, however, gave its limited support, expecting British backing for a separate state.

Hoping to retain Indian support, the British offered them the Cripps Plan, which promised full independence after the war. Remembering the betrayal after World War I, Gandhi and Nehru responded in August of 1942 with their "Quit India" demand. The British government under Winston Churchill overreacted. Gandhi and Nehru, together with their sympathizers, were imprisoned and the Congress Party was banned. The British restored order, but at the price of their right to continue to rule India.

Gandhi's hunger strikes and the threat of rioting by his loyal followers secured his release and that of most of his followers by 1944. In 1945, the British offered the Cabinet Mission Plan, which would create a federal state with considerable power in the hands of the several provinces. The Indians were firm in their demand for complete political freedom. Massive unrest was avoided because in 1945 the Churchill government was replaced by a Labour government under Clement Attlee. Sympathetic to Indian aspirations, Attlee announced that independence would be granted as soon as power could be transferred safely.

Largely because of the power given it by the wartime Churchill government, and over the bitter objection of Gandhi, the Muslim League demanded the creation of a separate Muslim state called Pakistan. The last viceroy and the person assigned the task of supervising the division of the Indian subcontinent into Muslim and Hindu states was Lord Louis Mountbatten. Mountbatten completed his onerous task ahead of schedule. The division resulted in the greatest human migration in history, as Muslims and Hindus fled to either Pakistan or India. Independence Day was enthusiastically celebrated on August 15, 1947, in both Delhi and Karachi, the capitals of India and Pakistan. Nearly a century after the struggle began, the Indians gained their independence. The dislocations of peoples and the tragic loss of life and property, however, remained a bitter legacy.

### Impact of Event

The impact on human rights of the independence of India and Pakistan was immediate, far-reaching, and controversial. Both Indians and Pakistanis gained political as well as religious freedoms in separate sovereign states. Even the British were relieved with dignity of the stigma of colonialism.

Controversy, however, remained. Religious minorities in both Pakistan and India continued to suffer persecution. With Pakistan moving increasingly in the direction of becoming an Islamic state, the question of human rights, especially for women, became acute. The constitutions, of which there were three in twenty-six years, specified that laws would contain no provisions going against the Koran. The governments, following a pattern set by the strong-willed Jinnah, who died after little more than a year in office, were often military dictatorships that committed numerous civil rights abuses. The dictatorial style of government, combined with economic exploitation and cultural differences, caused the East Pakistanis, separated from West Pakistan by more than one thousand miles, to seek independence. After a bloody civil war, the new state of Bangladesh was established in 1971 in the territory that had been East Pakistan.

Pursuit of basic human rights in India was more successful. The constitution that went into effect in 1950 guaranteed all basic freedoms. Jawaharlal Nehru, who became India's first prime minister and retained that office until his death in 1964, was determined despite formidable obstacles to enforce its provisions. His greatest accomplishments domestically were removing the stigma of caste, improving the condition of women, and fighting poverty. In foreign relations, Nehru sought to remove the last vestiges of colonialism and racism.

Untouchability was declared illegal. The custom of *sati*, or the immolation of widows, had already been abolished by the British. Hindu women now were given the vote and could aspire to all vocations or professions without discrimination. They could marry across caste lines and were allowed to divorce. They could also both inherit and control property. In his war on poverty, Nehru initiated a series of ambitious economic plans that included not only socialistic planning but changing the educational system to provide a greater emphasis on vocational, professional, and scientific training. By 1966, India had become the world's seventh most industrially advanced nation and had developed a sizable middle class. Nehru died in 1964. Despite continued religious unrest, separatist movements, border disputes, foreign invasions, and the assassination of his daughter, Indira Gandhi, and grandson, Rajiv Gandhi, who both served as prime minister, political independence and respect for basic human rights endured. India's citizens exercise their right of franchise in higher proportion than in most Western democracies.

## Bibliography

Das, Durga. *India from Curzon to Nehru and After.* New York: John Day, 1970. Durga Das is one of India's leading journalists and he writes with the clarity of a reporter. The book begins with the political awakening of India at the turn of the century, goes through independence and the Nehru era, and finally speculates about India's future. Comments on India's cultural diversity are especially interesting.

Das, Manmath Nath. *Partition and Independence of India.* New Delhi: Vision Books, 1982. Das, a member of the Congress Party and an eyewitness to partition and independence, deals with his subject in a lucid and coherent manner. He is critical of British policies and believes that they contributed greatly to the difficulties of partition and independence.

Golant, William. *The Long Afternoon: British India, 1601-1947.* New York: St. Martin's Press, 1975. As indicated by the title, this is a romanticized version of British Indian history leading up to and including partition and independence. Although he is British, the author is prone to place blame equally on the British and the Indians for what he terms "chaos." The numerous eyewitness accounts are of value; anecdotes hold the reader's interest.

Griffiths, Percival. *Modern India.* London: Ernest Benn, 1965. The author is obviously biased in favor of the British and glosses over much of what others would consider deficiencies. The chapters on the formation of the Indian constitution are the most useful part of this book.

Smith, Vincent A., Mortimer Wheeler, A. L. Basham, J. B. Harrison, and Percival Spear. *The Oxford History of India.* 3d ed. London: Oxford University Press, 1967. Probably the best concise and comprehensive history of India. It is especially of interest to those seeking more information on development of customs, religions, the rise of Muslim power, and dynasties that predate British rule and independence. The chronological tables, maps, and photographs are also useful.

Spear, Percival. *India: A Modern History.* Ann Arbor: University of Michigan Press, 1972. This is probably the most widely used college and university textbook for introductory courses on Indian history. Spear writes in a layperson's language and leaves no loose ends. He is prone to view developments such as independence more from a personal rather than a political point of view. The bibliography is annotated and cites a number of primary documents for those wishing to do further research on partition and independence.

Wolpert, Stanley. *A New History of India.* New York: Oxford University Press, 1989. Wolpert's book is of particular value to those seeking more information on developments after partition and independence. The author is critical of the government of Indira Gandhi and is pessimistic about India's future. The "priority ranking" of the bibliography should be of value to anyone doing in-depth research on India.

*Nis Petersen*

### Cross-References

The Muslim League Attempts to Protect Minority Interests in India (1906), p. 92; The Defense of India Act Impedes the Freedom Struggle (1915), p. 156; Soldiers Massacre Indian Civilians in Amritsar (1919), p. 264; Gandhi Leads a Noncooperation Movement (1920), p. 315; Women's Rights in India Undergo a Decade of Change (1925), p. 401; India Signs the Delhi Pact (1931), p. 459; The Poona Pact Grants Representation to India's Untouchables (1932), p. 469; The Indian Government Bans Discrimination Against Untouchables (1948), p. 743; The Indian Parliament Approves Women's Rights Legislation (1955), p. 924; Sikhs in Punjab Revolt (1984), p. 2215; Indira Gandhi Is Assassinated (1984), p. 2232.

# GAITÁN'S ASSASSINATION SPARKS
## *LA VIOLENCIA* IN COLOMBIA

*Categories of event:* Indigenous peoples' rights; atrocities and war crimes
*Time:* 1948
*Locale:* Colombia

*The Dance of the Millions (rapid economic expansion) led to political unrest among rural people that exploded into violence with the assassination of populist leader Jorge Eliécer Gaitán in 1948*

Principal personages:
JORGE ELIÉCER GAITÁN (1898-1948), a leftist champion of the rural poor
LAUREANO GÓMEZ (1889-1965), a Conservative Party leader and president from 1950 to 1953
MANUEL QUINTÍN LAME (1883-1967), an Indian activist who started a grass-roots movement in the 1920's
GUSTAVO ROJAS PINILLA (1900-1975), a general who seized power in 1953 at the height of the violent unrest
ALFONSO LÓPEZ PUMAREJO (1886-1959), a Liberal Party leader, president from 1934 to 1938 and 1942 to 1945

## Summary of Event

Jorge Eliécer Gaitán was the symbol of hope for the rural poor of Colombia. In a nation torn by decades of partisan strife, the assassination of this populist leader on a street in the nation's capital, Bogotá, brought a wave of revulsion against the Conservative government then in power. An enraged mob beat the assassin to death minutes after Gaitán fell. The existence of a plot behind the assassination has never been proven, but the immediate consequences of Gaitán's death were obvious. The international delegation to the Ninth Pan-American Conference, including United States Secretary of State George C. Marshall, watched with a mixture of fear and shock as violence overwhelmed their host city. The aroused masses directed their hostility against the incumbent Conservatives. Political outrage merged with urban violence to become a bloody civil war that spread into already unstable rural areas. Two hundred thousand people eventually died, and property damage was immense. *La Violencia* (the violence) swept up displaced Indians and dispossessed mestizos (a biological or cultural mixture of Indian and European) who had been struggling to survive for decades. The death of their champion darkened already dim hopes for recovery from the ravages of years of disruptive economic change.

Gaitán's death was not the sole cause of *La Violencia*. Its origins challenge even the most sophisticated analysis. Some perpetrators of violent acts were angry Liberal supporters whose frustrations from their defeat in Gaitán's presidential campaign in 1946 exploded with his assassination. Others were unbalanced types who took advantage of their nation's state of near anarchy to engage in criminal acts. A large number of the participants came from the rural poor, who attacked the Conservative government after having been driven to the margins of society by intrusive economic change.

The rapid economic expansion, or "Dance of the Millions," of the 1920's was an object lesson in economic overexpansion based on imprudent investments. Colombia found the economic means to recover from its disastrous civil war (1899-1902) and the painful loss of commercially important Panama (1903). The nation's productive coffee lands had found markets in the United States and Europe, and its petroleum potential rivaled those of Mexico and Venezuela. U.S. investors saw a bright future in the land of El Dorado, but they were mistaken. The worldwide depression of the 1930's spoiled their prognosis, and the repercussions of their massive injections of investment capital into coffee production contributed to the social and economic dislocations that spawned *La Violencia.*

By the early part of the twentieth century, the Indian population of Colombia had fared little better than the native Americans of the United States. The Chibcha civilization, located around present-day Bogotá, succumbed to Spanish conquest in the 1530's. The surviving Chibcha and other Indian groups became laborers in Spaniards' mines and on their *haciendas.* Only a few reservations, generally located in isolated zones to the south and east of the richer central mountain areas, provided havens for native communities. These reservations were segregated from the rest of Colombia and provided a subsistence living at best. By 1900, the Indian population amounted to less than 10 percent of the national total.

Under pressure from aggressive, land-hungry coffee planters in the early decades of the twentieth century, the Indians attempted to meet the challenges to their reservations and their cultural traditions. With the influx of foreign investments in the 1920's, the Dance of the Millions raced through the commercial centers of Medellín and Cali to the previously isolated mountains, where the Indians had maintained their marginal existence. State and local governments, often in collusion with the coffee interests, revised the reservation laws to open the lands for sale in the private sector. Armed with a superior knowledge of the new regulations, an eager following among certain politicians, and large capital reserves, the planters took control of what had been Indian reservation lands and, in the process, reduced the Indians to tenant farmers, wage laborers, or homeless drifters.

Indians tried to resist commercial encroachments. Native leader Manuel Quintín Lame formed a militant resistance movement in Tolima and Huila provinces in south central Colombia. Although Quintín Lame was an Indian traditionalist, he collaborated for several years with Communists to form an Indian community, San José de Indias, and to attempt to strengthen nearby reservations. His success was brief, however. In 1931, white landowners had him jailed and, after serving two years in prison, he returned to find San José de Indias destroyed and the future of the Indian people even more dismal than it had been a decade earlier.

Mestizos were a factor in Colombian history from the colonial era, and, by the twentieth century, made up probably half of the nation's population. Unlike the isolated Indians, the mestizos were direct participants in the economy, serving as laborers on the coffee plantations and working as independent peasant farmers. In the last half of the nineteenth century, mestizo peasants moved to unoccupied areas in the southern mountain region of the country and cleared land for farming. They eventually formed squatter communities along this frontier, where they used simple farming techniques to produce corn, beans, and yucca for their own consumption and coffee, tobacco, and wheat for sale in markets. They produced a significant part of the food consumed in Colombia in the late 1800's and early 1900's. Each community centered on a chapel, a market, and perhaps a school or a local government building. The peasant's lives were hard and their work was difficult, but they had a sense of ownership and independence.

Unfortunately, their lives were beginning to change in ways that brought frustration and disappointment. The expansion of the large coffee plantations soon disrupted and, in some cases, destroyed many of the peasant communities. Using their legal and political connections to full advantage, coffee entrepreneurs secured title to peasant land and forced once-independent farmers to become tenants or wage laborers, or to be expelled from the land altogether. Peasants protested such usurpations but had only minimal success in the frenzied Dance of the Millions of the 1920's. In the depression-ridden 1930's, however, peasant protests spread from local communities into an expansive but amorphous national movement. The Liberal administration of President Alfonso López Pumarejo was sensitive to this unrest and passed Law 200, the nation's first land reform legislation. This law promised to make the national government the chief protector of small properties, but the enforcement of this statute in rural areas involved land surveys, property assessments, and other complexities that the powerful estate owners blocked or delayed.

The rural poor found a new leader in Jorge Eliécer Gaitán, who carried their cause much further than had either López Pumarejo or Quintín Lame. Gaitán was a mestizo whose law degree and political ambitions elevated him above his lower-middle-class background. Gaitán was a hypnotic speaker with a charismatic personality, and his dark, rugged visage was indicative of the Indian elements in his ancestry. He appealed to the mestizo, the Indian, and the urban worker, thereby attracting a following that posed a real challenge to the nation's landed elite. His ideology was a combination of populism and socialism in which the national government was to protect the disadvantaged against the onrush of commercial expansion. Gaitán maintained his appeal to rural folk from the early 1920's until his assassination in 1948. His campaign for the presidency in 1946 aroused the hopes of the mestizo and Indian masses, and his defeat was a devastating blow. The bitter rivalry between the Gaitán wing of the Liberal Party and the victorious Conservatives erupted in sporadic violence as early as 1946, but Gaitan's dramatic death ignited an explosion of violence unprecedented in Colombian history.

## Impact of Event

The economic dislocations and human suffering caused by the "Dance of the

Millions" of the 1920's and the depression of the 1930's were greatly intensified by the epidemic of bloodshed in *La Violencia*. From 1950 to 1953, the Conservative government of President Laureano Gómez became increasingly unstable as disorder spread into rural areas. Police and military units met stalemate and even defeat in their confrontations with antigovernment guerrillas. In 1953, Gómez went into exile as a general, Gustavo Rojas Pinilla, took charge in Bogotá. The near paralysis of the national government left many rural districts without police protection. The exact causes of the violence that erupted under these conditions are too complex for easy generalization. Apparently much of the violence came out of local conflicts that varied from region to region. In the province of Boyacá it was rooted in the Liberal-Conservative animosity, in Antioquia it sprang from the struggle for control of the land, and in Tolima and the eastern plains it involved a mixture of economic and political motives. Roughly similar conditions of widespread disorder in Mexico from 1910 to 1940 had opened the way for social revolution, but in Colombia violence and disruption prevailed over organized political protest and structural reform.

The dictatorship of Rojas Pinilla generally attempted to impose military solutions in rural areas, but with little success. The army's battlefield victories were short-lived, as many guerrillas resorted to banditry in some cases in order to survive and in other cases to exact revenge. By the early 1950's, an ominous phenomenon appeared: roving groups of outlaws who plundered and murdered with no apparent motive beyond their own antisocial mentality. These unstable criminal elements inflicted a reign of terror on many defenseless rural communities.

The generations-old peasant struggle for land met another severe setback in *La Violencia*. Banditry mutated into land grabbing through violence and threats of violence. Small farmers abandoned nearly four hundred thousand parcels of land in order to protect themselves and their families. Although the fate of these farm properties is difficult to determine in every case, large estates gained considerable quantities of land in this process. Colombia lost an important part of its independent productive peasantry in these years.

The impact of the tumultuous four decades that spanned the Dance of the Millions of the 1920's and *La Violencia* of the 1940's and 1950's on the lives of Colombia's Indian and mestizo peoples gives little cause for optimism. Although the reservation Indians and the mestizo peasants of the early twentieth century did not enjoy anything approaching an idyllic existence, they were developing means of coping with the spreading commercial economy. The surge of coffee expansion in the 1920's, however, often deprived them of land, and the civil war of the 1940's and its transformation into random, criminal violence left many of them on the edge of survival. Several of the small rural communities formed by settlers a half century earlier disintegrated.

One source of hope was the 1957 formation of the National Front, a coalition of Liberal and Conservative leaders that began to search for a land reform formula to satisfy the needs of the rural masses. Unfortunately, the formula proved to be elusive. Some peasants achieved a modicum of prosperity and the National Front achieved a fragile political stability, but neither of these accomplishments could surmount Colombia's basic rural problems. In regions where violence had been most intense, many of the brutalized, the dispossessed, and the homeless became aggressive, antisocial individuals who expended their energies in outbursts of civil unrest and, during the 1970's and after, the international drug trade.

## Bibliography

Bergquist, Charles W. *Coffee and Conflict in Colombia, 1886-1910.* Durham, N.C.: Duke University Press, 1978. Historical account of the impact of the rise of coffee production on Colombian politics, especially the 1899-1902 civil war between Liberals and Conservatives.

Buitrago Salazar, Evelio. *Zarpazo the Bandit.* Edited by Russell W. Ramsey. University: University of Alabama Press, 1977. First-person account by a military intelligence operative who penetrated several bandit gangs in Tolima and Caldas in the early 1960's.

Fals Borda, Orlando. "Violence and the Break-up of Tradition in Colombia." In *Obstacles to Change in Latin America*, edited by Claudio Veliz. New York: Oxford University Press, 1970. Broad analysis of the impact of violence on previously resilient colonial traditions. One of Fals Borda's many writings on twentieth century Colombia.

Fluharty, Vernon. *Dance of the Millions: Military Rule and the Social Revolution in Colombia.* Pittsburgh, Pa.: University of Pittsburgh Press, 1957. Pioneering study of *La Violencia* that retains utility in its discussion of political events even though its conclusions on social and economic factors have been superseded by later studies.

Henderson, James D. *When Colombia Bled: A History of the Violencia in Tolima.* University: University of Alabama Press, 1985. A well-written examination of the causes and consequences of *La Violencia* in the crucial department of Tolima. Henderson explains the conflict in a national context and emphasizes its political origins.

LeGrand, Catherine. *Frontier Expansion and Peasant Protest in Colombia, 1830-1936.* Albuquerque: University of New Mexico Press, 1986. Historical analysis of the struggle for land along Colombia's frontier. LeGrand concludes that peasant farmers generally lost out to agricultural entrepreneurs even in Law 200 of 1936, which she sees mainly as a victory for the large estates.

Oquist, Paul. *Violence, Conflict, and Politics in Colombia.* New York: Academic Press, 1980. An interpretive study that employs social science methodology to explain the violence from 1946 to 1966. Oquist stresses the importance of inter-class conflict and the breakdown of the national government.

Sharpless, Richard E. *Gaitán of Colombia: A Political Biography.* Pittsburgh, Pa.: University of Pittsburgh Press, 1978. Clearly written and based on careful research. Sharpless places Gaitán within the national political and cultural trends and gives considerable emphasis to his connections in rural areas in his early career.

Zamosc, Leon. *The Agrarian Question and the Peasant Movement in Colombia: Struggles in the National Peasant Association, 1967-1981.* Cambridge, England: Cambridge University Press, 1986. A leftist sociologist's study of peasant activism in land reform since *La Violencia.* Although sympathetic to the peasants, Zamosc sees their factionalism as one of the many problems in the process of land redistribution.

*John A. Britton*

## Cross-References

Panama Declares Independence from Colombia (1903), p. 25; Intellectuals Form the Society of American Indians (1911), p. 121; The Mexican Constitution Establishes an Advanced Labor Code (1917), p. 196; El Salvador's Military Massacres Civilians in *La Matanza* (1932), p. 464; The Indian Reorganization Act Offers Autonomy to American Indians (1934), p. 497; The Declaration on the Rights and Duties of Man Is Adopted (1948), p. 755; Civil War Ravages Chad (1965), p. 1273; The Secession of Biafra Starts a Nigerian Civil War (1967), p. 1365; Brazil Begins a Period of Intense Repression (1968), p. 1468; An Oppressive Military Rule Comes to Democratic Uruguay (1973), p. 1715; Revolution Erupts in Ethiopia (1974), p. 1758; The Argentine Military Conducts a "Dirty War" Against Leftists (1976), p. 1864; Indigenous Indians Become the Target of Guatemalan Death Squads (1978), p. 1972; Presidential Candidates Are Killed in Colombian Violence (1989), p. 2465.

# THE INDIAN GOVERNMENT BANS
# DISCRIMINATION AGAINST UNTOUCHABLES

*Categories of event:* Indigenous peoples' rights; racial and ethnic rights
*Time:* 1948
*Locale:* India

*The Fundamental Rights section of the Indian constitution made the end of discrimination against untouchables a matter of national policy*

*Principal personages:*

B. R. AMBEDKAR (1892-1956), the foremost leader of untouchables in modern India, agitated for the recognition of their rights

MAHATMA GANDHI (1869-1948), the most visible leader of the Nationalist movement who took up the cause of untouchables and coined the name *Harijan* (children of God) for them

JAWAHARLAL NEHRU (1889-1964), the first prime minister of independent India, particularly concerned about raising the status of untouchables

## Summary of Event

Two hierarchies inform the conduct of social life in India. The first is based on notions of purity and pollution. The second is founded on distinctions of wealth and power. The people called "untouchables" usually have the lowest ranks in both of these hierarchical systems. In the first, traditional occupations such as removing human waste, tending cremation grounds, or disposing of animal carcasses, especially those of cows, render them perpetually impure. In the hierarchy of wealth and power, they are also at a disadvantage. Untouchables seldom own land of their own. Others who do own land are able to exploit the labor of untouchables, which keeps them poor and gives them a marginal place in the agricultural economy.

Europeans and Americans usually assume that all social categories in India, untouchability included, are "ancient and unchanging." This is a considerable distortion of the facts. Ancient legal texts such as *The Laws of Manu*, compiled in the fourth century A.D., provide a somewhat different account of how individuals might be excluded from the mainstream of society. *Manu* uses insulting terms such as *chandala* (literally, a variety of skunk cabbage) to describe individuals who have no place in the social order because they were born of irregular unions which crossed the boundaries between the priestly, warrior, merchant, and service castes. If this system were enforced, then all foreigners would be untouchable, subject to total exclusion. In addition, were this strictly observed, then the late prime minister of India Rajiv Gandhi would have been untouchable, since he was the product of a marriage between a Hindu and a Zoroastrian, a member of a foreign, casteless people. Obviously, the ancient legal theory cannot explain the practices of modern society.

Untouchability is a twentieth century concept used to describe the social and economic disabilities that tens of millions of Indians suffer as a result of their birth into one of many hundreds of low-ranked subcastes. Toward the end of the nineteenth century, British officials charged with administering the government's census of India developed the category "Depressed Classes" to describe groups that seemed to be the most deprived and socially excluded. Eventually census reports began to use the specific names of those depressed castes in a special schedule appended to the surveys. That practice gave rise to the concept that there were several hundred "scheduled castes and tribes."

Mohandas Karamchand Gandhi, known as Mahatma ("Great Soul"), tried to improve the lot of the downtrodden and took to calling them *Harijan* (literally, children of God). In doing so, he inadvertently may have insulted them. In colloquial speech, *Harijan* is a polite way of referring to someone who is illegitimate. In concrete terms, Mahatma Gandhi founded a number of ideal communities in which all members took turns at doing jobs usually assigned only to untouchables. For example, everyone was supposed to take her or his turn at cleaning toilets. Such idealism had little influence outside the small circle of the Mahatma's immediate followers.

In practice, members of low-ranked groups will rarely refer to themselves as untouchables or as *Harijan*. When identifying themselves, they will say they belong to a scheduled caste or use the proper name of their kinship group or subcaste.

The variety of terms used to describe low-status groups in India hints at the complexity of their place in society. Some are tribal groups, ethnic minorities not fully assimilated into Hindu life. Because they often live in relative isolation, tribals become aware of their degraded condition only when they have dealings with their Hindu neighbors. Untouchables experience rigorous exclusion in some areas, but in other areas they are not in the strictest sense untouchable.

As late as the early twentieth century, most notably in southern India, untouchables were forced to humiliate themselves by doing such things as announcing their presence before entering a street so as to allow the "touchables" to let them pass. Women, as a sign of their inferiority, were not allowed to cover their breasts. They could not enter most temples or public buildings. Some of these more obvious forms of discrimination were eliminated during the twentieth century, at least in the cities.

In other regions of India, depressed castes were more integrated into the life of village communities. Landholders had a patriarchal attitude toward their untouchable dependents. Powerful landlords referred to their degraded followers as "our children" and protected them from exploitation by outsiders. When working with *Harijans* in the fields, physical contact did not cause pollution. Superior castes, however, would never take food or water from their inferiors. They never allowed the depressed groups to approach them when they were eating.

Even in its mildest form, untouchability imposes a number of handicaps. The Chamars, for example, a scheduled caste of northern India numbering in the millions, have as their traditional task the removal of dead cattle. Making the best of a bad situation, Chamars often ate the cow's flesh, skinned the carcass, and prepared leather from it. Chamars were trapped in a circular dilemma. Because they were Chamars, society forced them to scavenge dead cattle. Eating the meat and selling the leather from the cows made them even more impure.

Private efforts to ameliorate the conditions of the depressed classes began in the nineteenth century. Christian missionaries began allowing untouchables into their schools. Many priests and ministers tacitly accepted the distinction between touchables and untouchables, but a few brave individuals insisted on having both clean and unclean drink from the same communion cup. Nevertheless, missionary academies were one of the few avenues to an education open to untouchables.

During the period between 1757 and 1947, the British controlled the Indian military. It recruited untouchables, usually for menial tasks, but it gave some of them the opportunity to attend army schools. Indian philanthropists, inspired by their own ideals, also provided the disadvantaged with the means to self-improvement. In Poona, Jyotirao Phule established a school for untouchables in 1851. The Maharajah of Baroda set up a school in his state in 1883 and offered scholarships for postgraduate study abroad. B. R. Ambedkar, the most important untouchable leader of the twentieth century, took advantage of several of those opportunities. His grandfather served in the army and his father also entered the military, eventually serving as a teacher in an army school for untouchables. In that way, Ambedkar had his primary schooling provided by the military. In 1913, he received a grant from the Maharajah of Baroda which financed his medical studies at Columbia University in New York City.

In 1938, the Madras legislature passed a law making it a punishable offense to discriminate against untouchables. Most of the provinces of British India, and a number of the princely states, quickly followed suit. By 1947, many statutes banning untouchability were in force. When the matter was raised in the Constitutional Assembly, the inclusion of an article in the 1948 Indian Constitution forbidding discrimination received nearly unanimous support. Prime Minister Jawaharlal Nehru used all of his influence and invoked Mahatma Gandhi's exemplary lead in providing assistance to *Harijans* to ensure the measure's inclusion.

Following the Constitution's example, many official measures were taken which were supposed to prevent further discrimination. Steps were also taken to redress previous wrongs done to the scheduled castes. These "affirmative action" measures reserved places in state legislatures, government employment, and schools for scheduled tribes and castes. In 1955, the parliament enacted the Untouchability Offenses Act which made more types of discrimination illegal and provided for stiff fines and jail terms for anyone convicted of violating its provisions.

Despite those legal measures and the constant use of eloquent political rhetoric against untouchability, discriminatory behavior has proven hard to eliminate. Although thousands of individuals have taken advantage of the protections and opportunities offered them, most of the tens of millions of untouchables remained in poverty with little hope of improving their status. Those who succeeded became an untouchable elite unwilling or unable to help the mass of their fellows.

Untouchables who acquired an education and comparative wealth continued to find it difficult to assimilate into the higher ranks of society. Even in late twentieth century India, most marriages were arranged by parents, so a close inquiry into the family background of any potential mate invariably precedes a wedding. Few men and women were willing to face their parents' or friends' disapproval. Therefore, marriages across the touchable-untouchable divide were rare, even when the untouchable spouse had a good job or education.

Government lists of untouchable castes and tribes may actually have worked against these individuals by broadcasting their inferior status. The reservation of jobs and scholarships for untouchables created a backlash among higher ranked castes that considered those measures to be reverse discrimination. They believed that the scheduled classes had received too many privileges. This led to riots and organized violence against untouchables.

## Impact of Event

Because of their poverty, untouchables found it difficult to use the courts to enforce their claims to equal treatment. Judges proved unwilling to apply rigorously laws such as the Untouchability Offenses Act. Higher courts tended to reverse convictions obtained under that and other laws or give those convicted only token fines. The number of antidiscrimination suits lodged in the courts by untouchables actually declined over the two decades following passage of the act.

The untouchable elite living in the cities experienced improvement in their lives, but the majority of the depressed classes continued to live in the countryside, where it was more difficult to escape the burdens of their inferior status. As landless laborers, untouchables were still exploited. Landlords, even petty peasants owning only a few acres, were still able to force them to work in the fields at starvation wages. They found it possible to employ untouchables during the peak work periods and then let them go during slack seasons.

In the comparatively restricted society of India's villages, everyone knew who the untouchables were. The untouchables therefore found few ways to make good a claim to higher status. Some groups tried to refuse doing the tasks, such as disposing of dead cattle or cleaning latrines, which rendered them impure, but they rarely succeeded because the majority often used violence to keep them in their place at the bottom of society. Another way of claiming status as a "clean" caste was to adopt the customs of neighboring higher-status groups. For example, some untouchables became vegetarians, a mark of priestly status. Some refused to allow widows to remarry, another type of high-caste behavior. Such steps are not always positive: Although denying women the right to remarry is an attempt to raise their neighbors' estimate of the group's rank, it also restricts the freedom of one-half of the community.

Some groups tried more radical steps, such as changing their religious affiliation. Conversions to Christianity, Islam, or Buddhism, religions which assert the equality of all believers, did not significantly improve the social position of those who converted. Ultimately, the success or failure of an effort to win recognition as a clean caste depends on the reaction of the other communities in the area. Rarely would superior groups accept such a shift. More often, they did not and continued to regard a given subcaste as untouchable.

The constitutional ban on discrimination against untouchables was one of many lofty goals which India set for itself at independence. Modern legislative measures and governmental affirmative action schemes have built on both official and private efforts to bring equality to the depressed classes. These actions have had little practical impact on the mass of untouchables as of 1991. A comparative few have been able to improve their condition dramatically. Even so, the aims of India's democracy do inspire those who seek to extend equal rights to all who experience deprivation because of untouchability.

## Bibliography

Bailey, Frederick G. *Caste and the Economic Frontier: A Village in Highland Orissa.* Manchester, England: Manchester University Press, 1957. This study documents the way in which a tribal group in the state of Orissa managed to use the wealth they acquired by making and selling moonshine to elevate their status from that of untouchable to that of "clean caste Hindu." It shows how mobility is possible, if rare, for scheduled tribes and castes.

Beteille, André. *Caste, Class, and Power: Changing Patterns of Stratification in a Tanjore Village.* Berkeley: University of California Press, 1965. This is a detailed study of the relations between castes in a village in south India. It is a complement to the essays by Bernard Cohn noted below, which focus on a village in North India. Beteille provides a very detailed description of the ways caste relations have changed since 1947.

Buhler, Georg, trans. *The Laws of Manu.* New York: Dover, 1969. Although the language of Buhler's translation is somewhat archaic, *Manu* is a concise statement of the Brahmanical (priestly) theory of social organization. By comparing *Manu* with anthropological accounts of the life of untouchables, the reader will gain a sense of the complex interplay between ancient traditions and the necessities of life in Indian society.

Cohn, Bernard S. *An Anthropologist Among the Historians and Other Essays.* Delhi: Oxford University Press, 1987. This volume by one of the most influential contemporary scholars of India contains several essays that describe the internal organization of untouchable communities and their interactions with higher-ranked castes in a North Indian village. The writing style is lively and provides more than a series of commonplace assertions about untouchables and their lot.

Galanter, Marc. *Law and Society in Modern India.* Delhi: Oxford University Press, 1989. Galanter is a perceptive critic of the differences between law and practice in contemporary India. Several of the essays in this volume focus on untouchables as well as on the problems of reverse discrimination and judicial redress of inequalities.

Isaacs, Harold R. *India's Ex-Untouchables.* New York: John Day, 1965. Isaacs' book is sometimes too impressionistic and has a tendency to generalize based on only a few cases. Nevertheless, it remains one of the most riveting journalistic accounts of the successes and failures of India's attempt to end untouchability.

Sen, D. K. *A Comparative Study of the Indian Constitution.* 2 vols. New York: David McKay, 1966. Sen's legalese is a bit dry, but the book has the merit of explicating the principles of India's constitution in comparison with those of a number of Western and non-Western countries. Sen also refers to a great deal of case law relating to the implementation of the constitution.

*Gregory C. Kozlowski*

## Cross-References

Gandhi Leads a Noncooperation Movement (1920), p. 315; Women's Rights in India Undergo a Decade of Change (1925), p. 401; The Poona Pact Grants Representation to India's Untouchables (1932), p. 469; India Gains Independence (1947), p. 731; The Civil Rights Act of 1957 Creates the Commission on Civil Rights (1957), p. 997; Congress Passes the Civil Rights Act (1964), p. 1251.

# PALESTINIAN REFUGEES FLEE
# TO NEIGHBORING ARAB COUNTRIES

*Categories of event:* Indigenous peoples' rights and refugee relief
*Time:* 1948
*Locale:* Palestine

*Four hundred thousand Palestinians were driven from their homeland after the first Arab-Israeli war in 1948, joining those who fled to safety after the U.N. vote to create a Jewish state*

*Principal personages:*

ARTHUR BALFOUR (1848-1930), the British foreign minister and author of the Balfour Declaration

COUNT FOLKE BERNADOTTE (1895-1948), the United Nations special mediator in charge of reconciling Arabs and Jews

HAJ AMIN AL-HUSSEINI (1893-1974), the British-appointed mufti of Jerusalem who became leader of the Palestine Arab Higher Command in 1935

CHAIM WEIZMANN (1874-1952), the chief Zionist delegate to the Paris Peace Conference and the first president of Israel

DAVID BEN-GURION (1886-1973), a principal leader of the Zionist movement in Palestine and Israel's first prime minister

## Summary of Event

As World War I raged in the Middle East, England and France signed the Sykes-Picot Agreement in 1916 to divide the region into British and French zones of influence. Meanwhile, the British high commissioner of Egypt, Sir Henry McMahon, carried out diplomatic contacts with Hussein ibn Abdallah, emir of the Hijaz, whereby the British promised the Arabs independence if they joined the allies against the Turks. On November 2, 1917, however, British Foreign Minister Arthur Balfour issued a declaration favoring the idea of establishing a Jewish national home in Palestine.

The Balfour Declaration stipulated that nothing would be done to harm the rights of the indigenous Arab population, at the time numbering nearly 575,000, or 92 percent of the population. Subsequent events proved otherwise. Violence was already foretold by the King-Crane Commission, dispatched by U.S. president Woodrow Wilson in the summer of 1919 to investigate conditions of the region in preparation for the Paris Peace Conference.

The Zionist delegates at the conference argued that England, not France, should be given the League of Nations' mandate to rule Palestine. Having been supported by the Balfour Declaration, the Zionists were handed their second victory when the British were given the mandate to govern Palestine and when the preamble of the mandate contained a copy of the Balfour Declaration. Article 2 of the mandate gave the British responsibility "to place the country under such political, administrative and economic conditions as will secure the establishment of the Jewish national home." Article 4 called for the establishment of a "Jewish Agency" "as a public body for the purpose of advising and cooperating with the Administration of Palestine in such economic, social and other matters as may affect the establishment of the Jewish national home." The agency was allowed "to construct or operate, upon fair and equitable terms, any public works, services and utilities, and to develop any of the natural resources of the country." In addition, Jewish militias became armed. Thus, the British were constrained by their commitment to the idea of a Jewish homeland in Palestine from protecting the civil rights and nurturing the national aspirations of the indigenous population, as mandate powers were supposed to do.

A rural, largely peasant, society long ruled by the Ottoman Turks, the Palestinians entered the twentieth century ill-equipped to cope with the problems presented by the modern world. The traditional Palestinian leadership consisted mostly of urban notables, who failed to unite and to form an effective response either to the British or to the Zionists. Palestinian political parties were divided according to family or local, rather than national, interests. Furthermore, the Palestinians found themselves isolated as the Sykes-Picot Agreement took effect and the new Arab states fell under British and French colonial rule.

The imbalance in the benefits of the British mandate became manifest in the growing ability of the Zionist movement and the Jewish Agency to create an infrastructure for a future state, especially as Jewish immigration increased in the 1930's. Palestinians and their political parties became gravely alarmed as the institutional gap between the two communities widened. The parties set aside their differences and, in 1935, formed the Palestine Arab Higher Command, headed by Haj Amin al-Husseini. The Palestinians resisted the British and the Zionist program with a long general strike, followed by the 1936-1939 revolt. The weakness of the Palestinians, the might of the British troops, and the pressure applied by surrounding Arab governments combined to defeat the revolt.

The Zionist drive to establish a Jewish state in Palestine began to bear fruit. Already the Peel Comission, sent in 1937 to investigate the sources of Palestinian unrest, recommended partition of the country. First raised in 1937, the idea of partition was revived. The United Nations authorized the creation of the United Nations Special Committee on Palestine (UNSCOP) to investigate all questions and issues relevant to the Palestine problem and to make its recommendations to the United Nations by September, 1947. When UNSCOP finally submitted its findings to the U.N. General Assembly, it recommended partition of the country into a Jewish state and an Arab state and that Jerusalem become an international city. The Palestinians rejected partition on the grounds that it violated their rights, as it violated the provisions of the U.N. Charter. They pointed out that the proposed Jewish state included 56 percent of Palestine even though Jews were not in the majority. Also, Jews owned only 10 percent of the land in the proposed Jewish state. Despite the misgivings of some and the total rejection of others, the partition was passed on November 29, 1947.

The partition resolution guaranteed, in theory, the civil, political, economic, religious, and property rights of the Arabs who were to be included in the Jewish state. It stipulated, among other things, that no discrimination of any kind would be made among the inhabitants on the grounds of race, religion, language, or sex. In practice, it sparked a new wave of violence, as a result of which nearly three hundred thousand Palestinians fled their homes to safer areas before May 14, 1948, the date the state of Israel was proclaimed. A significant event in this period was the April 9 attack on the Arab village of Deir Yassin, on the outskirts of Jerusalem, where more than 250 men, women, and children were massacred. News of the massacre spread, raising the level of fear and panic among the population. Having already lost its leadership and having no institutional support, the Palestinian civil and political authority quickly collapsed. Villagers felt defenseless, and the numbers of those fleeing to safety accelerated. The exodus left some areas with no resistance to approaching Zionist forces. Tiberias fell on April 18, Safad on May 10, and Jaffa on May 13, 1948.

The armies of the Arab states finally entered Palestine on May 15. During the ensuing war, thousands more villagers fled to safety. On May 22, the United Nations ordered a cease-fire, which was affirmed on May 29. Intermittent truce violations and outbreaks of fighting led to another U.N. Security Council-sponsored cease-fire on July 15. Count Folke Bernadotte, the U.N. special mediator, was charged with the supervision of truce arrangements. In his attempt to reconcile the two sides, Bernadotte submitted plans for a settlement advocating the refugees' right to return home. He argued that "It would be an offense against the principles of elemental justice if those innocent victims of the conflict were denied the right to return to their homes while Jewish immigrants flow into Palestine."

On November 16, with no peace in sight and with more refugees being forced out of their homes, the United Nations ordered the establishment of an armistice in Palestine. Armistice agreements between Israel and its Arab neighbors were negotiated between February and July of 1949 with the mediation of Ralph Bunche, who became U.N. special mediator after Bernadotte's assassination. By then, Israel controlled 77 percent of Palestine. Estimates of the total number of refugees range from 750,000 to 900,000. Most of them were forced under the care of the United Nations Relief and Works Agency for Palestine Refugees in the Near East (UNRWA), established on December 9, 1949.

## Impact of Event

The war of 1948 is regarded by the Palestinians as a catastrophe. They had become a shattered nation. Palestinians who remained under Israeli rule suddenly found themselves a defeated minority in their own land. Palestinian national authority was destroyed. The majority of Palestinians became stateless refugees, living in makeshift camps and depending on rations issued by the United Nations.

The Arab host countries were poor and underdeveloped. Their fledgling, and largely agrarian, economies were unable to absorb the sudden influx of refugees. The UNRWA offered food and health care, started development programs, and built schools, among other assistance programs. Once education and vocational training became available to the Palestinians, their social, economic, and political role in the region improved. Many moved to Saudi Arabia and to the Gulf emirates when these began to develop their oil economies. Palestinians served in a variety of roles, such as educators and skilled laborers. Many became wealthy, but they remained stateless, except for those who acquired Jordanian citizenship.

Their presence throughout most of the Arab world was a reminder to the Arab people as well as to various governments of the plight of the Palestinians. To the Arab people, the Palestinians became a symbol of their own lack of power and the backward conditions of the region after years of misrule. A bond would be established between the forces for social change. To the majority of Arab governments, for whom realization of the Palestinians' right to return became a humanitarian duty and a political necessity, their presence was viewed as a radicalizing factor. This shaped the relationship of the Palestinians to the Arab governments: sometimes championed and at other times barely tolerated because of their influence. For the most part, Palestinians' civil rights were neglected whether they were living in refugee camps in the surrounding Arab countries or were under Israeli rule.

The region experienced revolutionary upheavals after the creation of Israel in 1948, changing the nature of the ruling groups and radicalizing the domestic and international policies of the Arab states. The Arab-Israeli conflict remained alive and led to major wars in 1956, in 1967 (when Israel took over the West Bank and the Gaza Strip), and in 1973. Two major Israeli military operations against the Palestinians in Lebanon were carried out in 1978 and in 1982.

The Palestinian question had global repercussions as the United States and the Soviet Union supplied arms and extended, to their respective allies, economic assistance and diplomatic backing. During the era of the Cold War, the Arab-Israeli conflict remained a dangerous issue between the two superpowers. The Palestine Liberation Organization (PLO), formed in 1964, represented the Palestinians after 1967. Arab and non-Arab governments gradually recognized the position of the PLO, which was eventually granted observer status at the United Nations in the continuing effort to find a just solution to the Palestine question and to redress the loss of Palestinian national rights.

## Bibliography

Abu-Lughod, Ibrahim, ed. *The Transformation of Palestine*. Evanston, Ill.: Northwestern University Press, 1971. Written by a host of scholars, this book contains valuable articles on the demography of Palestine, land alienation, resistance to the British mandate, and regional and international perspectives on the Arab-Israeli conflict.

Flapan, Simha. *Zionism and the Palestinians.* New York: Barnes & Noble Books,

1979. A valuable account of the relationship of the Zionist movement to the Palestinians before 1948 by a well-known Israeli author. The details which Flapan provides will challenge the myths of the Arab-Israeli conflict and the creation of the refugee problem.

Hadawi, Sami. *Bitter Harvest: A Modern History of Palestine.* New York: Olive Branch Press, 1989. Impassioned but well documented, the book provides an account of the mandate years, the struggle between the two communities, the birth of the refugee problem, and the violations of refugees' human and civil rights. Valuable maps and appendices.

Hourani, Albert. *A History of the Arab People.* Cambridge, Mass.: Harvard University Press, 1991. A comprehensive history of the Arab people from the rise of Islam to the present. Places the political developments in the region and their international implications in historical perspective.

Khouri, Fred. *The Arab-Israeli Dilemma.* 3d ed. Syracuse, N.Y.: Syracuse University Press, 1985. An excellent, well-documented account of the Arab-Israeli conflict from 1947 through the 1980's, with chapters on the refugee problem, Jerusalem, and the American administrations' involvement. This book has been described as a model of objectivity.

Laqueur, Walter, ed. *The Israel-Arab Reader: A Documentary History of the Middle East Conflict.* New York: Citadel Press, 1969. An important sourcebook for students of the modern Middle East and the Arab-Israeli conflict. It contains excerpts from major works on Zionism, Israel, the Palestinians, Arab-Israeli relations, Pan-Arabism, and other topics.

Morris, Benny. *The Birth of the Palestinian Refugee Problem: 1947-1949.* New York: Cambridge University Press, 1987. A controversial issue regarding Palestinian refugees is whether they left on their own accord or as a result of their leaders' urging. Benny Morris, one of few Israeli scholars to challenge official claims and Zionist propaganda, shows in this well-documented account that Palestinians were forced out of their homes.

Quandt, William, Fuad Jabber, and Ann Mosely Lesch. *Politics of Palestinian Nationalism.* Berkeley: University of California Press, 1973. Deals with the development of Palestinian nationalism from 1915 onward and with the resistance after 1967. The authors provide maps, figures, and a table to illustrate the complexity of the subject.

Said, Edward, and Christopher Hitchens, eds. *Blaming the Victims: Spurious Scholarship and the Palestinian Question.* New York: Verso, 1988. Several authors discuss how Western scholarship dealt with important issues in the Arab-Israeli conflict. Contains chapters on the various debates about the conditions of the Palestinian exodus, particularly the claim that refugees left at their leaders' urgings.

*Mahmood Ibrahim*

## Cross-References

The Balfour Declaration Supports a Jewish Homeland in Palestine (1917), p. 235; Israel Is Created as a Homeland for Jews (1948), p. 761; The United Nations Creates an Agency to Aid Palestinian Refugees (1949), p. 814; Israel Enacts the Law of Return, Granting Citizenship to Immigrants (1950), p. 832; Palestinian Refugees Form the Palestine Liberation Organization (1964), p. 1241; Arab Terrorists Murder Eleven Israeli Olympic Athletes in Munich (1972), p. 1685; Sadat Becomes the First Arab Leader to Visit Israel (1977), p. 1943; Sadat and Begin Are Jointly Awarded the Nobel Peace Prize (1978), p. 2003; Palestinian Civilians Are Massacred in West Beirut (1982), p. 2164; The Palestinian *Intifada* Begins (1987), p. 2331.

# THE DECLARATION ON THE RIGHTS AND DUTIES OF MAN IS ADOPTED

*Categories of event:* Civil rights and political freedom
*Time:* March 30-May 2, 1948
*Locale:* Bogotá, Colombia

*In 1948, the Ninth International Conference of American States, which established the Organization of American States, adopted the American Declaration on the Rights and Duties of Man*

*Principal personages:*
GEORGE C. MARSHALL (1880-1959), the U.S. secretary of state
ALBERTO LLERAS CAMARGO (1906-1990), the director general of the Pan-American Union
RÓMULO BETANCOURT (1908-1981), a former president of Venezuela and chair of the Venezuelan delegation

## Summary of Event

From March 30 to May 2, 1948, the Ninth International Conference of American States met in Bogotá, Colombia, to consider a wide range of agenda items. Perhaps the most consequential outcomes of the conference were the signing of the charter of the Organization of American States (OAS) and the signing of the American Declaration on the Rights and Duties of Man. The latter event was significant in that it was the first international declaration on human rights, preceding the United Nations Universal Declaration of Human Rights, which was signed later the same year.

The conference was notable not only for what it achieved but also for the social and political context in which it was held. The assassination in 1948 of Liberal politician Jorge Gaitán, who had been denied a seat in the Colombian delegation to the conference, triggered rioting and accelerated the period of violence that engulfed Colombia from 1946 to 1958. The rioting put the capital city in chaos, and the turmoil spread to other cities in Colombia. While the military defended the government, the national police, according to James D. Cockroft, took arms with the anti-government Gaitán supporters. The military and the government prevailed, but not until thousands had died.

Foreign Minister Laureano Gómez was a Conservative rival to Gaitán and opened the conference as its president. The April, 1948, disturbances prompted the relocation of the conference to a more secure site in the outskirts of Bogotá. Colombians, in the midst of profound threats to their lives and security, thus hosted a conference that eventually affirmed the right to life, liberty, and personal security.

The origins of the 1948 declaration date at least as far back as the 1936 Inter-American Conference for the Maintenance of Peace, at which a proposal affirming the right to life, liberty, and freedom of religion, and the duty of states to protect those rights for all was considered but rejected. In early 1945, the American states met in Mexico City for the Inter-American Conference on Problems of War and Peace. Among the results of that conference was a call for the development of a declaration on the international rights and duties of man. In the preamble to the Inter-American Treaty of Reciprocal Assistance (the "Rio Pact" of 1947), signatories affirmed the importance of the protection of human rights but did not bind themselves to upholding them.

Responding to the call of the Mexico conference, the Inter-American Juridical Committee developed a draft resolution, the final version of which was presented to the Ninth International Conference. In the preparation of the document, much of the debate centered on the degree to which it would be legally binding. Some states, including Guatemala, Uruguay, and Brazil, sought effective enforcement mechanisms and strong language concerning human rights. The United States, among others, urged more moderate language, successfully opposing, for example, a statement on the right of resistance to oppression. On the question of the right to health, the U.S. delegation successfully inserted a statement disavowing any preference between public and private health care systems.

During the drafting of the declaration, central questions concerned whether the statement would have the force, and enforcement mechanisms, of a treaty, and whether human rights should be extensively incorporated into the Charter of the Organization of American States. Most states, including the United States, favored a nonbinding declaration with no enforcement mechanisms. On the question of the charter, most states held the view that it should be confined to matters of organizational purpose, structure, and function.

The OAS Charter does, however, make some mention of human rights, most notably in article 5(j), which states: "The American States proclaim the fundamental rights of the individual without distinction as to race, nationality, creed or sex." The preamble to the charter proclaims a desire for "individual liberty and social justice based on respect for the essential rights of man." Despite such rhetoric found in the charter, the Declaration on the Rights and Duties of Man is a more definitive statement on human rights.

Approximately three hundred officials, representing all twenty-one American states, attended the Bogotá conference to consider, among other documents, the charter and the draft declaration. The United States delegation was led by Secretary of State George C. Marshall. Marshall stayed for the majority of the almost five-week conference, indicating the priority of such matters on the foreign policy agenda of President Harry Truman. Alberto Lleras Camargo, director general of the Pan-American Union and soon to be secretary general of the new Organization of American States, was also a delegate to the conference. The subcommittee concerned with the rights and duties of man was chaired by Chile's Enrique Bernstein. Former (and later) Venezuelan President Rómulo Betancourt headed his country's delegation.

The final declaration was adopted as Resolution XXX of the Final Act of the Conference and was signed on May 2, 1948. The preamble to the declaration asserts that "all men are born free and equal" and notes the interrelationship of rights and duties: "While rights exalt liberty, duties express the dignity of that liberty." The declaration contains thirty-eight articles, twenty-eight of which proclaim the "rights" of people and the remaining ten of which describe the "duties" of individuals. Among the rights affirmed by the declaration are those to life, liberty, and personal security; to equality before the law; to religious freedom; to a family and its protection, specifically protection for mothers and children; to residence and freedom of movement; to the preservation of health; to education; to take part in the cultural life of the community; to work and to receive fair remuneration; to social security; to enjoy basic civil rights; to a fair trial; to vote; to assemble peaceably; to petition; and to protection from arbitrary arrest. Those duties spelled out by the declaration include those toward children and parents; to vote; to obey the law; to serve the community and nation; to pay taxes; to work; and to refrain from political activities in another country.

The declaration thus considers the rights and duties of humanity to be social, political, and, to some degree, economic. Many of the principles spelled out in the declaration are also contained in the constitutions of various American states, a fact that the declaration observes.

Resolution XXXI of the Final Act, which was unsuccessfully opposed by the United States, sought to create an Inter-American Court to guarantee the rights of man and thereby enhance the possibilities of implementation of the declaration. This resolution called upon the Inter-American Juridical Committee to prepare a draft statute creating the court, to be presented to the Tenth Inter-American Conference. Resolution XXXII, supported by the United States and consistent with the nascent cold war atmosphere of the post-war era, effectively endorsed the efforts of several Latin American nations to outlaw Communist parties.

The years preceding the declaration had seen a hesitant and, as it turned out, short-lived movement in several Latin American nations toward the establishment of broader political rights, at least among non-Communist parties and their members. Nowhere was this trend better exemplified than in Venezuela, which between 1945 and 1948 experimented with popular democracy under the leadership of Rómulo Betancourt and his Acción Democrática party. Venezuela's first free elections were held in 1947, and the populist Acción Democrática won a resounding victory. Peasants seeking land and all those seeking the right to a voice in government saw the election as a harbinger of a brighter future. A military coup in 1948, however, delayed the reality of Venezuelan democracy for another decade, forced many of Acción Democrática's leadership underground and into exile, and led to the brutally repressive dictatorship of General Marcos Perez Jimenez.

The American Declaration on the Rights and Duties of Man, for the precedent that it set, was a landmark statement. By the time the document was signed, however, the momentum toward meaningful civil and political rights begun in 1945 and 1946 had slowed considerably. Dictatorships in such places as Nicaragua and the Dominican Republic not only survived but, by 1948, seemed to be strengthened as well. The Somoza family dynasty in Nicaragua, launched in the 1930's, would last until the 1979 revolution. Rafael Trujillo in the Dominican Republic would control that country until 1961. Leslie Bethell notes that although many Latin American nations at the time were respectful of the right to vote in elections, in most such "democracies" the rights of reformists and leftists were severely curtailed.

It should not be surprising, therefore, that the declaration did not take the form of a more potent, and controversial, convention or treaty. Although not possessing the legal power of a convention or a treaty, the declaration did clarify hemispheric goals with respect to human rights and laid the groundwork for the United Nations Universal Declaration. As a symbolic gesture, if not a substantive one, the document was an important contribution to human rights in the inter-American system.

## Impact of Event

The human rights situation in the Americas did not improve dramatically in the years following the declaration. While the late 1950's and early 1960's appeared to be, in the words of one observer, the "Twilight of the Tyrants," the human rights situation worsened considerably under the many military governments of the late 1960's and 1970's. In any case, the commitment of the American states to the principles laid down in the declaration did not appear noticeably stronger in the years following its signing.

The Inter-American Juridical Committee chose not to pursue the matter of an inter-American court after the Ninth International Conference, deciding that such a body would be a premature addition to the inter-American system. The declaration did become the precedent, however, for several more potent documents and structures with regard to human rights in the hemisphere. The decline of dictatorship in the region by the late 1950's had created a climate more favorable to international human rights agreements. Further, a European Convention on Human Rights had been put into effect. In 1959, the Inter-American Commission on Human Rights was created under the auspices of the Organization of American States. Diplomatic pressure from the United States was successful in limiting the formal scope of the commission, but it has since become a prominent proponent of human rights throughout the hemisphere.

In 1969, the American Convention on Human Rights (the Pact of San Jose) was adopted, and in 1978 it entered into force. Its provisions make specific reference to the principles implied (and not merely stated) in the Charter of the Organization of American States and therefore comprise a much bolder statement on human rights than either the charter or the declaration. The convention, unlike the declaration, contains provisions for effective enforcement mechanisms, specifically the Inter-American Court of Human Rights and the Inter-American Commission on Human Rights. Like the declaration, the convention lists the duties of individuals as well as their rights. In any case, the declaration paved the way for the more ambitious American Convention two decades later.

The widespread democratization of Latin American governments which began in the late 1970's and continued in the 1980's brought renewed attention to the principles of the declaration, as new civilian governments, notably the Argentine, grappled with the human rights abuses of previous military regimes. The declaration cannot be held directly responsible for the transition to a more favorable human rights climate in Latin America, but the goals of that document do seem closer at hand.

## Bibliography

Ball, M. Margaret. *The OAS in Transition.* Durham, N.C.: Duke University Press, 1969. An amply documented, legalistic description of the creation of the Organization of American States which gives appropriate attention to the development of human rights in the years leading up to and following the creation of the OAS. Footnotes, index, bibliography, appendices.

Bethell, Leslie. "From the Second World War to the Cold War: 1944-1954." In *Exporting Democracy: The United States and Latin America*, edited by Abraham F. Lowenthal. Baltimore: The Johns Hopkins University Press, 1991. Insightful overview of a crucial period in U.S.-Latin American relations, noting the inconsistencies in U.S. support for democracy in the region at the time of the signing of the declaration. Footnotes, index included.

Claude, Richard Pierre, and Burns H. Weston, eds. *Human Rights in the World Community.* Philadelphia: University of Pennsylvania Press, 1989. Several of the articles in this volume are useful for placing the American Declaration and other aspects of inter-American human rights into a broader international and comparative perspective. The selection coauthored by Weston explicitly compares the inter-American system with other regional approaches. Includes bibliography and index.

Inter-American Institute of International Legal Studies. *The Inter-American System: Its Development and Strengthening.* Dobbs Ferry, N.Y.: Oceana Publications, 1966. Straightforward, legalistic presentation of international law in the Americas, with an extensive chapter devoted to human rights and representative democracy. Useful appendices and bibliography. No index.

Slater, Jerome. *The OAS and United States Foreign Policy.* Columbus: The Ohio State University Press, 1967. Examines the uses to which the United States has put the OAS, noting the positions taken with respect to dictatorship, democracy, and other facets of human rights. Critical and at times cynical toward the patterns of U.S. foreign policy. Bibliography, index included.

Thomas, Ann Van Wynen, and A. J. Thomas, Jr. *The Organization of American States.* Dallas: Southern Methodist University Press, 1963. Considers the structure, principles, and functions of the OAS, including its role in the development of an inter-American system of human rights. The chapter discussing democracy and human rights pays particular attention to the American Declaration. Appendices, footnotes, and index included.

*Robert B. Andersen*

**Cross-References**

The United Nations Adopts the Universal Declaration of Human Rights (1948), p. 789; The Organization of American States Is Established (1951), p. 879; The Inter-American Commission on Human Rights Is Created (1959), p. 1032; Brazil Begins a Period of Intense Repression (1968), p. 1468; The Inter-American Court of Human Rights Is Established (1969), p. 1503; Allende Is Overthrown in a Chilean Military Coup (1973), p. 1725; Indigenous Indians Become the Target of Guatemalan Death Squads (1978), p. 1972; Argentine Leaders Are Convicted of Human Rights Violations (1985), p. 2280; Arias Sánchez Is Awarded the Nobel Peace Prize (1987), p. 2336.

# ISRAEL IS CREATED AS A HOMELAND FOR JEWS

*Categories of event:* Immigrants' rights and indigenous peoples' rights
*Time:* May 14, 1948
*Locale:* Tel Aviv, Israel

*The independence of Israel, among the first countries to gain national liberation from colonialism after World War II, solved a two-thousand-year-old global civil rights problem*

> *Principal personages:*
> DAVID BEN-GURION (1886-1973), a leader of the Jewish community in Palestine and the first prime minister of Israel
> CHAIM WEIZMANN (1874-1952), the leader of the Diaspora Zionist movement and the first president of Israel
> ARTHUR BALFOUR (1848-1930), the British foreign minister and promulgator of the Balfour Declaration
> THEODOR HERZL (1860-1904), a founder of Zionism, regarded as the father of the state of Israel

## Summary of Event

From the human rights perspective, the founding of the state of Israel has a four-fold significance: It marked the return of a scattered people to its homeland after two thousand years of exile, it signaled the success of one of the earliest movements of national liberation in the Middle East, it offered an asylum for the survivors of the Holocaust, and it instituted a state sanctuary for all Jews threatened by anti-Semitic persecution.

After their forcible expulsion by the Romans from their native land, the Jews became the prototype of a diaspora people, one dispersed as a minority in other nations and lacking the territorial contiguity of a land of their own. Such people, exemplified also by the Armenians and Gypsies, are perpetually vulnerable and are liable to suffer legal, economic, and cultural disadvantages. The additional factor of religious animosity exacerbated the persecution of Jews in Europe from earliest times. Examples include the Crusader massacres, the expulsions from England in the thirteenth, from France in the fourteenth, and from Spain in the fifteenth centuries, and the Cossack pogroms of the seventeenth century. This in turn may explain the yearning for spiritual redemption in the land of Israel which became a central theme of Jewish religious identity throughout the ages, as summarized in the famous lines of the medieval poet HaLevi, "I am in the West but my heart is in the East," or in the conclusion of the Passover Seder, "Next year in Jerusalem." Actually, there was always a Jewish presence in Palestine, amplified by devout individuals and groups who came throughout the centuries to settle. By the mid-nineteenth century they formed an absolute majority in Jerusalem.

Nevertheless, not until the late nineteenth century did the move toward the "in-gathering of the exiles" and the formation of a Jewish state take practical form. Zionism, as the movement came to be known, offered answers to two issues raised by the historical processes by which the modern state system of Europe was taking shape. The granting of legal citizenship in many states, coupled with cultural and political boundary-setting processes, forced upon the Jews the necessity to reset their own boundaries and to define their identity in relation to their environments. At the same time, the rise of national and racial, as distinct from religious, anti-Semitism placed the new issues firmly in the context of the accumulated history of persecution. The two problems reinforced each other to prompt the formulation by a secular Jewish intelligentsia of a doctrine that was related to other European nationalisms and yet radically different from them. Whereas European nationalists based their demands on existing national territories and cultures, Zionism proposed cultural rebirth in a territory still to be resettled, and followed by renewed sovereignty.

Zionist activity took the form of encouraging, financing, and settling immigrants. Immigrants came primarily from Central and Eastern Europe, where anti-Semitism was rife, but also from Western and Middle Eastern countries. Immigration increased the Jewish population from about 50,000 in 1900 to about 650,000 by 1948, over one-quarter million of whom left Germany in the early years of the Hitler regime. In effect, the *Yishuv*, as the Palestine Jewish community was called, became a state in the making, with its own political institutions and a large degree of authority despite the lack of the sanctions available to a sovereign state. It set up such crucial services as education, health, employment, and welfare; established its own trade unions, banking, and marketing systems; and created the machinery for the rapid demographic and economic development of a society distinct from that of the Arabs. Concurrently, Zionism pursued official recognition of the Jewish right to return to Palestine. Its greatest early victory was the November, 1917, declaration submitted by Arthur James Balfour on behalf of the British cabinet: "His Majesty's Government view with favour the establishment in Palestine of a national home for the Jewish people, and will use their best endeavors to facilitate the achievement of this object." This commitment was formally confirmed in 1922 by the League of Nations as a condition of the granting of mandatory power over Palestine to Britain.

Nevertheless, in the same year the British government issued, under Arab pressure, an interpretation of the declaration limiting immigration as overtaxing the economy. The British also defined the national home not as Palestine itself but as an entity within it. The next two decades saw the steady increase of hostility between Arabs and Jews, each accusing the authorities of siding with their opponents. Hostilities culminated in 1936 in the outbreak of virtual civil war. A royal commission headed by Lord Peel issued a report in 1937 proposing, as the only viable solution, the partition of Palestine into a small Jewish state and a large Arab one. This was denounced by the Palestinian leadership as well as by radical Zionist elements. The mainstream leadership, including Chaim Weizmann of the World Jewish Agency and David Ben-Gurion of the *Yishuv* itself (later the first president and the first prime minister of Israel, respectively), endorsed the plan in principle as a recognition of the Jewish right to sovereignty.

After the failure of the partition scheme, and constrained by the ongoing violence, the British government issued a new policy in May, 1939, limiting Jewish immigration to seventy-five thousand over five years, after which such immigration would be forbidden altogether. The Arab leadership refused even this concession, demanding the cessation of all immigration and the declaration of Palestine as an Arab state. The Jews too rejected it as denial of the "right to rebuild their national home . . . and a surrender to Arab terrorism." Toward the end of World War II and even more so after the peace, the sense of betrayal was deepened by the revelation of the extent of the Holocaust and the huge numbers of death-camp survivors denied immigration elsewhere. This sense of betrayal exploded in the form of massive attempts to smuggle in immigrants and in underground activity against the military and police, which were trying to stop such illegalities. Meanwhile, the internecine warfare between Arabs and Jews intensified. Faced with a country steadily becoming ungovernable, the British decided to refer the problem to the United Nations, which nominated a special committee to study the crisis and to recommend solutions. The outcome was a new partition plan which was again rejected by the Arabs and accepted as the "indispensable minimum" by the Jews. This time, however, the proposal was not dropped but was brought before the General Assembly, which endorsed it by a majority of more than two-thirds, including the Soviet Union and the United States. The resolution terminated the British mandate as of August, 1948, at the latest and authorized the establishment, two months after the evacuation of the British armed forces, of independent Arab and Jewish states and a special international regime for Jerusalem.

The proclamation of Israeli independence was issued in Tel Aviv on May 14, 1948, on the night preceding the date fixed by the British as the termination of the mandate. In it, the Provisional State Council, forerunner of the Knesset (Israeli Parliament), announced that "the recent Holocaust, which engulfed millions of Jews in Europe, proved anew the need to solve the problem of the homelessness and lack of independence of the Jewish people . . . the state of Israel will be open to the immigration of Jews from all countries of their dispersion."

## Impact of Event

Much of the change undergone by Israel since 1948 results from efforts to realize its original goals, those of serving as a sanctuary for persecuted Jews and of providing a national center for the gathering of a dispersed people. The deluge of refugees that poured in with the opening of the gates was made up of Holocaust survivors, including those who were caught trying to enter illegally into Palestine and were kept by the British in concentration camps in Kenya and Cyprus. They were followed by Jewish refugees from the Arab countries at war with Israel. By the third year of the state's existence, its Jewish population had more than doubled. Periodically thereafter, additional waves of immigrants flooded the state, coming from countries ranging from North Africa in the early 1950's to the Soviet Union and Ethiopia in the early 1990's. There was also a constant dribble of immigrants from the affluent countries of the West. As of 1991, the Jewish population stood at about four million, more than six times its size at the birth of the state. The demographic and cultural composition of Israel has likewise changed, with Jews of "Oriental" origin—Turkey, the neighboring countries, and North Africa—becoming the majority. A massive Soviet immigration occurred in the 1980's and 1990's. This fluidity, along with the fact that the term "Jew" has more than a single meaning, explains the delay in the formulation of the long-envisaged constitution promised in the Proclamation of Independence. The proclamation itself enjoys a quasi-constitutional status, and its central commitments were put into effect by the Law of Return (1950) and its amendments. These guarantee the right of every Jew to settle in Israel as a full-fledged citizen from the moment of landing and in effect obligates the state to provide immigrants with the full range of services required for their absorption.

The coin, however, has a reverse face. Following the invasion of Israel by five Arab armies on the very first day of its independence, approximately 400,000 Palestinian Arabs fled, the majority of them to become refugees in the neighboring Arab states. The outcome was the creation of a new diaspora people and a civil rights problem waiting for its own solution.

## Bibliography

Ben-Gurion, David. *Rebirth and Destiny of Israel.* New York: Philosophical Library, 1954. Offers an insight into the formation and birth of Israel, the problems attending them, and the ideals of Israel's founders. Significant as coming from the prominent leader of the Jewish community in Palestine and the first prime minister of the new state.

Bethell, Nicholas. *The Palestine Triangle: The Struggle for the Holy Land.* New York: G. P. Putnam's Sons, 1979. A detailed analysis and interpretation of the struggle between Jews, Arabs, and the British from 1935 to the independence of Israel.

Cohen, Mitchell. *Zion and State: Nation, Class, and the Shaping of Modern Israel.* New York: Basil Blackwell, 1987. Analysis of the relationship between nation, state, religion, and class in the emergence of Israel, and of the struggles to shape the new state.

Elazar, Daniel. *Israel: Building a New Society.* Bloomington: Indiana University Press, 1986. An examination of the historical development of the Israeli polity from the pre-Zionist era to the founding of the state. Explores the basic cleavages Israel inherited when a "new society" was formed.

Hertzberg, Arthur, ed. *The Zionist Idea.* Garden City, N.Y.: Doubleday, 1959. An anthology of writings of the fathers of Zionism. Especially noteworthy is the lengthy philosophical examination by the editor of the central concepts of Zionism and its development and significance in Jewish history.

Horowitz, Dan, and Lissak Moshe. *Origins of the Israeli Polity: Palestine Under the*

*Mandate.* Chicago: University of Chicago Press, 1978. A brilliant, in-depth socio-political study of the Jewish *Yishuv*, the centrifugal and centripetal forces that activated it, and its function as a state in the making.

Laqueur, Walter, ed. *The Israel-Arab Reader.* Rev. ed. New York: Viking-Penguin, 1984. A comprehensive collection of documents relating to the formation of Israel and to the Israeli-Arab conflict. The first three sections are of particular relevance to students of the formation of Israel as a homeland for the Jewish people.

*Jonathan Mendilow*

## Cross-References

The Balfour Declaration Supports a Jewish Homeland in Palestine (1917), p. 235; The United Nations Creates an Agency to Aid Palestinian Refugees (1949), p. 814; Israel Enacts the Law of Return, Granting Citizenship to Immigrants (1950), p. 832; Eichmann Is Tried for War Crimes (1961), p. 1108; Wiesel Is Awarded the Nobel Peace Prize (1986), p. 2292; Israel Convicts Demjanjuk of Nazi War Crimes (1988), p. 2370.

# AUTOWORKERS NEGOTIATE A CONTRACT WITH A COST-OF-LIVING PROVISION

*Category of event:* Workers' rights
*Time:* May 25, 1948
*Locale:* Detroit, Michigan

*The United Auto Workers received a contract from General Motors that included an "escalator clause" that increased wages as prices increased*

*Principal personages:*

JOHN W. ANDERSON (1906-1989), the socialist president of UAW Detroit Fleetwood Local 15; campaigned for a cost-of-living clause in autoworkers' contracts

WALTER P. REUTHER (1907-1970), the president of the UAW, elected in 1946

CHARLES ERWIN WILSON (1890-1961), the president and CEO of General Motors who proposed an "escalator clause" in 1948 negotiations with the UAW in return for a long-term contract

## Summary of Event

After the end of World War II and the abolition of wartime price controls, inflation grew and the real wages of American workers fell. As rank-and-file autoworkers saw their standard of living decline, they exerted pressure on the United Auto Workers (UAW) leadership to respond to this growing problem. A 1946 conference of UAW officials, representing sixty-five thousand General Motors employees from the Flint-Lansing region, demanded an upward sliding scale of wages in every new contract.

Inspired by the new "escalator clause" won from the Sinclair Oil Company by the Oil Workers International Union, many autoworkers pushed their union to fight for a similar cost-of-living agreement in their new contract. Such a provision would guarantee wage increases whenever the cost of living increased. On March 8, 1947, in Detroit, the UAW held its national General Motors Delegates Conference. John W. Anderson, president of Fleetwood Local 15, introduced a resolution demanding that the UAW fight for a cost-of-living clause for GM workers similar to that won at Sinclair Oil. UAW president Walter Reuther prevented serious discussion by referring the resolution to the UAW's International Policy Committee, which never acted upon it.

The beginning of 1948 saw UAW locals representing more than two hundred thousand autoworkers go on record as being in favor of an escalator clause in the next contract. With the five presidents of the Flint UAW supporting the idea as a means of ensuring the basic human right of their members to a decent and stable living, it seemed as if the cost-of-living adjustment (COLA) clause would be a major union contract demand. Walter Reuther went to the Flint conference and vigorously opposed the concept, arguing that it was a radical "trick" which would cause nothing but problems for the autoworkers. Some opponents of the COLA concept suggested that it would freeze workers in the same economic position and make union wage advances more difficult, if not impossible.

John Anderson and other proponents of the cost-of-living escalator charged that Reuther and others were more concerned with the company and their own positions than in serving the rank-and-file autoworker. At the 1948 Detroit GM delegates' conference, held shortly before talks with the company were to begin, a motion to include an escalator clause in the forthcoming contract was ruled out of order by the UAW leadership. Many believed that any guarantee in a legal contract giving economic protection against the ravages of inflation would have to be won over the objections of the Reuther leadership.

With so much division within the union itself, the whole concept of tying wages to the cost of existence might well have been lost except for the unforeseen intervention of Charles Wilson, president and chief executive officer (CEO) of General Motors. Wilson saw a booming market for automobiles that could be exploited fully only with a work force that was willing to work overtime, and certainly not with one that was out on strike frequently. To take full advantage of its economic possibilities, Wilson reasoned, GM needed long-term contracts with the UAW that would ensure labor stability.

Rather than allowing Reuther and the UAW to make demands and then attempting to whittle them down, the General Motors CEO planned to present the autoworkers with a proposal which would meet the needs of his corporation while granting GM employees new rights. Wilson's innovative approach was designed to gain labor peace in the present while tying future worker wage increases to company profits.

In the 1948 bargaining sessions with the UAW, General Motors put forth a proposal that contained two new key provisions. The autoworkers' wages were to be tied to the cost-of-living index compiled by the Bureau of Labor Statistics, so that income would keep pace with inflation. Further, GM pushed the principle that all future wage increases would be tied to productivity, so that GM would gain something in exchange for any future real wage increases.

Although Reuther was opposed to many aspects of the proposal, the UAW leadership was in an awkward position for a number of reasons. The anti-union Taft-Hartley Act, passed by Congress over presidential veto in 1947, made some leaders fearful that a long, bitter strike might provoke even harsher unfavorable legislation. In addition, the cost-of-living clause was popular with many rank-and-file members and was by no means seen as the extreme or unreasonable position that Reuther attempted to paint it. Thus, the UAW leadership believed it to be prudent to avoid a strike while also wishing to pacify the opposition within the union that wanted to establish the escalator clause as the workers' protection against inflation. To further complicate matters, Walter Reuther was recovering from an assassination attempt and unable to attend personally the contract talks where Wilson made his unexpected offer.

Negotiations were intense and at times heated. On May 25, 1948, seventy-two hours before the strike deadline, agreement was reached between the United Auto Workers and General Motors Corporation. Hailed by *Fortune* magazine as "the treaty of Detroit," the new contract ensured the continued production that GM so desperately wanted and needed. The new agreement was to run for two years, which was the longest contract term in GM history up to that point even though shorter than the five years GM had hoped for. It contained "penalty clauses" designed to prevent any worker resistance to measures designed to increase worker productivity.

In return, the autoworkers received an eleven-cent boost in hourly wages and, for the first time, a cost-of-living escalator that would increase pay one cent per hour for every two-thirds of 1 percent increase in the Bureau of Labor Statistics' cost-of-living index. Wages would be adjusted automatically every three months. How this benefited GM workers became evident shortly. The thirteen-cent-per-hour wage increases at Chrysler and Ford were overtaken on July 15 as the escalator kicked in and raised GM wages an additional three cents, putting GM workers ahead of the UAW divisions that had not fought for the new arrangement. In the next twelve years, the cost-of-living clause resulted in lower wages only once, during the 1949 recession, and then the drop was only one cent per hour.

## Impact of Event

The inclusion of a cost-of-living escalator clause in the 1948 GM contract was significant in a number of important ways. By establishing the principle that working people have the right to a secure standard of living, the agreement helped to define economic protection as a human right. By linking wage increases to inflation, GM workers were freed from some of the anxiety faced by most workers in a modern economy subject to constantly rising prices.

The escalator clause meant that the average autoworker at General Motors could now plan his or her economic future with some degree of certainty, knowing the "real," or inflation-adjusted, income would not be completely decimated by economic forces beyond personal control. This added not only to workers' material standard of living but also to their emotional well-being and sense of security. In an industry cited by the Bureau of Labor Statistics as having one of the highest levels of employment instability, the achievement of some type of wage security was particularly important.

Further, the principle that labor has the human right to a secure wage was acknowledged by the 1948 GM agreement. A concept such as this went against the ingrained notion that workers had only the right to what "market forces" allowed them to earn. Thus, the cost-of-living agreement can be seen as a victory for human rights over traditionally defined property rights. At the same time, it should be noted that General Motors also prospered by the agreement, much as predicted by Charles Wilson.

The 1948 General Motors contract agreement should not be viewed as having only symbolic value. It produced wage increases and economic security that allowed a generation of autoworkers to rear their families at a higher standard of living and allowed workers' children to pursue educational opportunities denied to the workers themselves in the past. Most of all, the 1948 General Motors contract set a new standard in the United States by which workers' rights would henceforth be judged.

## Bibliography

Anderson, John. *Fifty Years of the UAW: From Sit-Downs to Concessions.* Chicago: Bookmarks, 1986. Although brief and obviously not impartial, Anderson's book manages to exhibit the spirit and beliefs of the radicals who played such a vital part in the creation of the United Auto Workers. No reference features.

Chinoy, Ely. *Automobile Workers and the American Dream.* Garden City, N.Y.: Random House, 1955. A sociological study that examines how autoworkers in the 1950's looked at their future and opportunities for advancement. Useful as an introduction to the attitudes of the rank-and-file worker. Reference notes and index

Cray, Ed. *Chrome Colossus: General Motors and Its Times.* New York: McGraw-Hill, 1980. An extremely readable and interesting account of GM from its beginnings through its "golden days" of world dominance to its crisis in the 1970's. Reference notes, bibliography, and index.

Howe, Irving, and B. J. Widick. *The UAW and Walter Reuther.* New York: Random House, 1949. Partial to but not uncritical of Walter Reuther, this volume is well written and worthwhile although a bit dated. Reference notes and index.

Preis, Art. *Labor's Giant Step: Twenty Years of the CIO.* New York: Pathfinder Press, 1972. Written by a socialist labor journalist with no pretense of objectivity, this volume is a wealth of information and detail about the inner workings of the major industrial unions. Preis was present at many of the major events described. Index.

Reuther, Victor G. *The Brothers Reuther and the Story of the UAW.* Boston: Houghton Mifflin, 1976. Told from the viewpoint of the Reuther wing of the UAW. The reader will find numerous interesting personal insights in addition to a clear statement of Reuther's position on the key issues affecting autoworkers. Appendices and index.

*William A. Pelz*

## Cross-References

Supreme Court Disallows a Maximum Hours Law for Bakers (1905), p. 36; The British Labour Party Is Formed (1906), p. 58; Massachusetts Adopts the First Minimum-Wage Law in the United States (1912), p. 126; Ford Offers a Five-Dollar, Eight-Hour Workday (1914), p. 143; The International Labour Organisation Is Established (1919), p. 281; Steel Workers Go on Strike to Demand Improved Working Conditions (1919), p. 293; Great Britain Passes Acts to Provide Unemployment Benefits (1920), p. 321; British Workers Go on General Strike (1926), p. 429; The Wagner Act Requires Employers to Accept Collective Bargaining (1935), p. 508; Social

Security Act Establishes Benefits for Nonworking People (1935), p. 514; The Congress of Industrial Organizations Is Formed (1938), p. 545; Chávez Forms Farm Workers' Union and Leads Grape Pickers' Strike (1962), p. 1161; The International Labour Organisation Wins the Nobel Peace Prize (1969), p. 1509.

# THE UNITED STATES AIRLIFTS SUPPLIES TO WEST BERLIN

*Category of event:* Humanitarian relief
*Time:* June 24, 1948-May 12, 1949
*Locale:* Berlin, Germany

*In one of the first Cold War crises, the Soviet Union blockaded Western access to Berlin, and the United States responded by undertaking a massive airlift*

*Principal personages:*

HARRY S. TRUMAN (1884-1972), the thirty-third president of the United States (1945-1953); decided that the United States would not leave Berlin

JOSEPH STALIN (1879-1953), the Soviet dictator whose attempt to pressure the West backfired and led to international embarrassment for his country

GEORGE C. MARSHALL (1880-1959), the U.S. secretary of state when the blockade began

DEAN ACHESON (1893-1971), the U.S. secretary of state who began the negotiations that ended the blockade

ERNEST BEVIN (1881-1951), the British foreign minister

LUCIUS D. CLAY (1897-1978), the American governor of occupied Germany

## Summary of Event

When Harry S. Truman became president of the United States on April 12, 1945, an adviser warned him of an impending social, economic, and political collapse in Germany and Central Europe unparalleled in history since the fall of the Roman Empire. In May, 1945, Germany surrendered, bringing the European phase of World War II to an end, and the Allies occupied the ruins of Adolf Hitler's Third Reich.

In 1945, the immediate problems of dealing with a devastated Germany obscured potential future problems among the Allies. About six million Germans had died, two million were prisoners of war, and millions were missing. German industry and agriculture were almost nonexistent. Most of Berlin's three million people lived in cellars or in ruined buildings and had no coal for heat and light. The people wandered the city, dazed from defeat and hunger.

The Allies had already agreed to divide Germany into four zones, one governed by each of Great Britain, the United States, France, and the Soviet Union. Similarly, the Allies had agreed to divide Berlin, located deep in the eastern Soviet zone, into four sectors. The Allies created a four-power Allied Control Council (ACC) to administer Germany and to work out details of occupation policy. Great Britain and the United States did not bother to get a written Soviet guarantee of highway and railroad access to Berlin, although they did work out written provisions for Western air corridors into Berlin. The American military assumed that any problems of land access could be worked out in an atmosphere of comradeship.

Wartime comradeship did not last. The United States and the Soviet Union had been at loggerheads since the Communists took power in Moscow in 1917. With World War II's end, tension mounted among the Allies, and by 1947 the Cold War was under way. Berlin became a pawn in the conflict between the great powers, and the Allies made little progress toward getting Germany back on its feet. During the winter of 1946, the Germans in the Western zones consumed an average of only nine hundred calories per day, a slow starvation diet.

In July, 1946, U.S. secretary of state James Byrnes began negotiations with the British to create a unified bizonal economic system for the German sectors; the French zone joined the system later. The West began to lay plans to revive the German economy and to reintegrate it into the West European economy. The Soviets charged that the West was violating wartime agreements and was taking unilateral actions that would lead to a divided Germany. The Soviets retaliated by putting pressure on Berlin. The Berliners in the Western sectors declared their intention to resist Soviet domination.

On the night of March 30, 1948, the Soviets issued new transportation rules that required inspection of overland traffic crossing the Soviet zone. General Lucius Clay, the military governor of the American zone, proposed to his superiors that the United States send in a military unit prepared to shoot its way through a Soviet blockade. Cooler heads prevailed, and American leaders overruled Clay. The Soviets blockaded military transportation but allowed civilian traffic to continue.

In April and May, the Soviets periodically harassed traffic but did not escalate the conflict. Moscow's aims were probably limited. The partial blockade was designed to increase Berliners' feelings of isolation and stress. On June 18, 1948, the Western powers announced their currency reform program, and on June 24, the Soviets cut off all overland traffic into the Western sectors of Berlin. The blockade had begun.

Tension was high in Washington. Truman wrote to his daughter that the United States might have to fight rather than engage in appeasement. The Berliners themselves stiffened Western resolve. They cheered city leaders such as Ernst Reuter, who called on them to defy Soviet domination at any cost.

On June 24, General Clay asked the U.S. air force to give him all available planes for an airlift. The Allies needed to bring into Berlin two thousand tons of food each day to keep the people fed. Long-term viability required twelve thousand tons of supplies per day, including coal for electric power and heat, medical supplies, clothing, and other items. The United States and Great Britain brought in only 1,404 tons in the entire month of June, but they airlifted 1,117 tons on July 8 and 1,480 tons on July 15.

On June 28, Truman told his cabinet that the United States was going to stay in Berlin—period. In July, he ordered the military to give Clay the planes he needed to supply the 2.5 million civilians in the Western sectors. British foreign minister Ernest Bevin strengthened his nation's resolve to pour its limited resources into the airlift. By July 22, the Allies had 132 planes committed to the airlift, each shuttling into Berlin twice a day.

The Allies brought more and larger planes into the airlift and began emergency construction to improve airport runways and loading facilities. In July, the daily lift averaged 2,226 tons, and by September it had reached 4,641 tons per day. The city needed 5,500 tons of basic food, light, and heat each day to survive the winter, and it needed 12,000 tons a day to maintain low economic existence.

Accidents and deaths occurred in the crowded air corridors. Planes lined up through the airways separated by only a few minutes of flying time. Pilots often flew blind into the center of Berlin, threading through towers and other obstacles. By November, 1948, planes were landing and taking off every three minutes, twenty-four hours a day. The roar of the engines strengthened the morale of the Berliners, since it was a noisy symbol of the world's commitment to a free Berlin.

The survival of the city during the winter of 1948 depended as much on the strength of the Berliners as it did on the technology of the airlift. The city survived because the people were willing to put up with hunger, dark, and cold. Electricity was on for only four of each twenty-four hours. Heat was scarce. The people cooked food in batches and often ate it cold. The food was mainly bread and cabbage soup, with a cereal and milk ration for children.

These harsh conditions did not weaken Berlin's resolve to defy Soviet pressure. Hardship brought a sense of solidarity. In November, 1948, the West Berliners created their own Free University after the Soviets cracked down on Berlin University. In late 1948, the charade of a unified city government ended, and the West Berliners created a separate government headed by Ernst Reuter. In January and February, 1949, the airlift reached its needed minimum of 5,500 tons. The Berliners were eating better than they had since the end of the war.

As spring arrived in 1949, the Western powers faced the future with confidence. They now had eight months to accumulate supplies for the next winter, and they were confident that they could keep Berlin alive until the Soviets settled on the West's terms.

The Soviets probably had no well-considered policy goals when they began to blockade Berlin, but perhaps they hoped that the West would take the easy way out and leave the city. By 1949, the blockade was a growing international embarrassment for the Soviets. The blockade also strengthened the position of those who wanted an independent West Germany. The constitution for the Federal Republic of Germany was completed in February, 1949, and was adopted in May. The Marshall Plan to aid European economic recovery was in high gear, and in April, 1949, the Western allies established the North Atlantic Treaty Organization (NATO).

Meanwhile, on January 31, 1949, Soviet dictator Joseph Stalin took the unusual step of replying to several written questions put to him by Western journalists. He said that the Soviets would raise the Berlin blockade if the West would postpone the establishment of a West German government until the four powers met to discuss all

German problems. Dean Acheson, who had just become U.S. secretary of state, regarded this as a deliberate signal that Stalin wanted to end the crisis, and he initiated secret discussions at the United Nations. Finally, the Soviets agreed that the blockade would be lifted on May 12, 1949, and the West agreed that the four-power Council of Foreign Ministers would meet on May 23, 1949, to discuss German questions.

### Impact of Event

Although the Council of Foreign Ministers soon stalemated in typical Cold War wrangling, the Soviets did not reimpose the Berlin blockade. For decades, Berlin would remain a flashpoint of conflict between the Soviet and Western Blocs, but the airlift wound down and life returned to as normal as it could be in that divided city.

Although the Berlin blockade ended without war, its human cost was great. For a year, more than two million Berliners were held hostage in one of the first Cold War crises. Seldom have so many people been terrorized for so long. Berliners had experienced war and material deprivation since Hitler's war had started in 1939, but the blockade subjected them to new levels of psychological and emotional terror. They were located deep in the Soviet zone, surrounded by the most powerful land army in the world and subjected to steady encroachment of Communist totalitarian control. Terror came from a feeling of isolation from the outside world. Berliners were imprisoned as surely as if they had been tried and convicted of crimes. The sight of planes strung out across the Western air corridors and the unceasing roar of engines was a welcome antidote to Soviet terrorism.

Berliners received one of the first lessons in modern psychological warfare. While the rest of Western Europe began to revive from war devastation, life continued on hold for the Berliners. For a year they sat in their urban prison and waited. The airlift's success was measured by its ability to supply the city with basic foodstuffs and medical supplies; restoration of long-term economic viability was impossible. Berliners wandered the quiet streets trying to accumulate their daily food rations and to maintain their morale in the dark, cold surroundings. They lived among the ruins and debris of war destruction, which they had neither the equipment nor physical energy to clear. Private transportation was nonexistent, and public transportation was limited. Friends and relatives were cut off from one another as governments drew boundary lines through the city. While other Europeans had a glimpse of returning normality, Berliners waited.

The Soviets intended to break the people's will by making them feel helpless and isolated, yet the Berliners never lost the feeling that to some extent they controlled their own destiny. Their stoic willingness to endure cold and hunger inspired the outside world to continue the lifeline into Berlin. Berliners even found positive aspects to the crisis. They regained their commitment to freedom and a feeling of pride after years of living under Nazism. They reestablished a feeling of community as they turned to each other for help. Families and friends huddled together in their bleak rooms and entertained one another in order to make the long evenings pass faster; they shared food and medicine; they eagerly revealed their discoveries of new ways to cope with shortages. Even while they were hungry, cold, and surrounded by ruins, they tried to provide their children with education and cultural life.

The blockade and airlift had many international consequences. Stalin's decision to blockade Berlin was an incredible propaganda blunder. It confirmed the view that he was a brutal dictator who would destroy innocent people to accomplish his own ends. It damaged his nation's attempt to win support in the Third World and other places. The crisis strengthened ties among the United States, England, and France. The crisis also helped to rehabilitate Germany in world opinion. While only a few years earlier many people had regarded Germans as bloody-handed militarists, now the world saw them as heroic freedom fighters.

As the Cold War began to wind down decades later, it seemed remarkable to many observers that for more than forty years the United States and Soviet Union had confronted each other with nuclear weapons and yet had never gone to war. One effect of the Berlin blockade was to teach the superpowers important lessons. Rash Soviet action had caused great embarrassment and had taught both sides to act with caution. The United States learned that the Soviets responded to policy alternatives short of war. The crisis helped build American, and Western, consensus behind Truman's containment policy, which was based on avoiding war while confronting the Soviets with massive economic, psychological, and military power.

## Bibliography

Donovan, Frank. *Bridge in the Sky.* New York: David McKay, 1968. Donovan provides a popular history of the Berlin blockade that captures the drama and human elements of the story.

Morris, Eric. *Blockade: Berlin and the Cold War.* New York: Stein & Day, 1973. Morris evaluates Berlin in the broader context of conflict between the United States and the Soviet Union and shows the importance of the city as a major focus of Cold War conflict.

Nelson, Daniel J. *Wartime Origins of the Berlin Dilemma.* Tuscaloosa: University of Alabama Press, 1978. Nelson examines the wartime diplomacy among the Allies that determined the postwar role of Germany and laid the foundation for the future crises involving Berlin.

Shlaim, Avi. *The United States and the Berlin Blockade: A Study in Crisis Decision-Making.* Berkeley: University of California Press, 1983. This excellent study, based on archival documents and important secondary sources, uses the airlift to study crisis decision-making and finds that although the West overestimated the importance of Berlin as a symbol, its leaders wisely chose options that avoided war.

Tusa, Ann, and John Tusa. *The Berlin Airlift.* New York: Atheneum, 1988. A recent study based on available archival material that provides an excellent general history of all aspects of the Berlin blockade and airlift.

*William E. Pemberton*

## Cross-References

Soviets Take Control of Eastern Europe (1943), p. 612; The Marshall Plan Provides Aid to Europe (1947), p. 706; The Berlin Wall Is Built (1961), p. 1125; The Brezhnev Doctrine Bans Acts of Independence in Soviet Satellites (1968), p. 1408; Soviets Invade Czechoslovakia (1968), p. 1441; Hungary Adopts a Multiparty System (1989), p. 2421; Poland Forms a Non-Communist Government (1989), p. 2500; The Berlin Wall Falls (1989), p. 2523; Ceausescu Is Overthrown in Romania (1989), p. 2546; Soviet Troops Withdraw from Czechoslovakia (1990), p. 2570; Gorbachev Agrees to Membership of a United Germany in NATO (1990), p. 2589.

# TRUMAN ORDERS DESEGREGATION OF U.S. ARMED FORCES

*Categories of event:* Racial and ethnic rights; civil rights
*Time:* July 26, 1948
*Locale:* Washington, D.C.

*Desegregation of the armed forces continued a process of granting equal civil rights in American life and acted as an important impetus for the desegregation of public facilities*

Principal personages:

ASA PHILIP RANDOLPH (1889-1979), an African-American labor and civil rights organizer who pushed the government for more rapid desegregation

HARRY S. TRUMAN (1884-1972), the American president (1945-1953) who signed Executive Order 9981

WALTER WHITE (1893-1955), the longtime executive secretary of the NAACP who effectively fought against lynching

## Summary of Event

At the beginning of World War II, the American armed services, reflecting larger patterns in American society, were almost completely segregated. Although African Americans had participated in every war, their numbers were small, their roles were limited, and their units were almost always segregated.

Few African-American units engaged in combat in the Spanish-American War or in World War I. Their uneven levels of performance allowed many white Army officers to retain their prejudices, thus limiting African-American troop deployment and obstructing the services' willingness to desegregate.

American success in both those wars allowed for the maintenance of a racial status quo in the military. Change effected by World War I and the industrialization of America created conditions allowing for movement toward a more egalitarian civilian life. Many African Americans moved from the rural South to the industrialized North, where their incomes and education rose dramatically. Racial relations began to change.

World War II provided the spark to ignite the Civil Rights movement. In addition to the underlying internal demographic changes, the war provided specific conditions enabling progress in civil rights. First, America went to war with the avowed intention of defeating the racism and aggression of both Nazi Germany and Imperial Japan. The *raison d'être* for American involvement was that of human rights. Second, the large African-American emigration to the North created a new voting bloc, historically Republican but newly Democratic because of the economic and political policies of the New Deal. Moreover, African Americans were concentrated in industrial states with large electoral college slates, especially important for presidential elections. Third, World War II was a protracted war in which American human resources were taxed. At the end of the war replacement personnel became harder to come by. Any policy of underenlisting or undertraining any sizable segment of the population, such as a policy segregating African Americans, led to problems of inefficiency and shortages.

The armed services remained largely segregated throughout the war, although some desegregation occurred toward the end of the war. Units from the Army's four black regiments—overstaffed with draftees—were merged with larger white ones suffering manpower shortages. In some cases, the same training facilities were made available to black and white units.

Immediately after the war, the direction bifurcated: internal armed services developments hindered significant change in the racial balance, while societal developments encouraged more rapid desegregation. Internally, as occurred after each previous war, pressures on the armed services to desegregate abated. The numbers of African Americans declined so drastically that African-American units could easily be accommodated in segregated units. Externally, the African-American emigration from the rural South accelerated during and after World War II. African-American voters increased in number. Civil rights organizations also grew in number and in political power: Over a period of six years, membership in the National Association for the Advancement of Colored People (NAACP) exploded ninefold to 450,000. Moreover, non-Southern whites grew more sympathetic to the demands for greater equality, although there were periodic race riots in the North revolving especially around the issue of jobs and the fear that African Americans would dispossess whites.

During the war, President Franklin D. Roosevelt took a few small steps to address the question of segregation. He recommended that African Americans be given more options in the Navy; he revived a 1937 War Department program to increase the numbers of African-American soldiers to their proportion in the society; and, most important, in 1941, via Executive Order 8802, he established the Fair Employment Practices Commission (FEPC). Roosevelt, much less committed to civil rights than his wife, Eleanor, was concerned primarily with winning the war and pleasing the Southern component of his political coalition.

Little was known about the civil rights orientation of Roosevelt's successor, Harry S. Truman. As a senator from Missouri, Truman had been able to win essential African-American votes by supporting the few pieces of civil rights legislation and by supporting New Deal economics. Truman, a centrist with humanitarian leanings and a respect for the Constitution, was a sharp politician but also a man moved by personal experiences. One national incident which shocked him and touched the hearts of many Americans involved a returning African-American veteran. While still in uniform, literally on his return, Sergeant Isaac Woodard was removed from a bus by a local South Carolina sheriff and beaten with a nightstick by two lawmen so badly that he was blinded.

A series of vicious attacks against and murders of African Americans in the South in 1946 led to public protests. Truman was quoted by Walter White as responding, "My God! I had no idea that it was as terrible as that. We have to do something." Reacting to these incidents, to the changing demography, to a changing world environment, and to a new world of domestic politics, Truman set out on a course that would dramatically change human rights.

Immediately after the war, Truman spoke out periodically about human rights, including statements in his State of the Union addresses in 1946 and 1948. He helped commission several internal studies of the armed forces which looked specifically at the status of African Americans. The most comprehensive study was made by the Gillem Board. In April, 1946, the board came up with a plan to expand the role of African Americans in the Army and to provide more equal facilities and opportunities. One key item was a quota of ten percent in each large unit. The board did not, however, push for integration within the smaller units. Thus, the report, reflecting the military's reluctance to change radically, was largely rejected by civil rights organizations, which favored desegregation of all facilities.

By 1947, two important conditions had changed. The Cold War was beginning in earnest, leading both the military and Truman to push for stronger, larger armed forces. Moreover, the United States began an ideological war of propaganda against the Soviet Union focusing in part on basic human rights. The international audience for this campaign was largely nonwhite. Second, the Republicans controlled both houses of Congress and Truman's chances for a presidential victory in 1948 looked bleak. He knew that he could not win without a substantial proportion of the African-American vote.

The African-American leadership pushed for more desegregation. On October 23, 1947, W. E. B. Du Bois and other radical African Americans embarrassed the administration by bringing charges against the American government before the newly formed United Nations Commission on Human Rights. Six months later, in a more mainstream development, A. Philip Randolph's Committee Against Jim Crow in Military Service threatened an African-American boycott of a new conscription law if it contained no antisegregation clause.

In response to all these pressures and frustrated by Congress' refusal to extend the FEPC, Truman took a major step when he commissioned the President's Committee on Civil Rights, a fifteen-member board composed of leading figures from the worlds of business, academia, government, and religion.

On October 29, 1947, this committee published its findings in *To Secure These Rights*, a monograph that received widespread public attention. The committee argued strongly on behalf of racial equality and prescribed deep-seated societal changes, including specific recommendations for desegregating all branches of the armed services. Truman took the report seriously, although he chose to implement it according to his own political calendar. That calendar became crowded in 1948, a presidential year that promised what looked like a certain victory for the Republicans.

Frustrated with the Republican Congress, liberal Democrats pressured Truman to push for a liberal agenda. Some even joined a committee to draft Eisenhower. Part of that frustration led to a third-party, strongly pro-civil rights Progressive candidacy of Henry Wallace, Roosevelt's former vice president. To make election matters even more complicated for Truman, some of the southern wing of the party bolted and nominated Strom Thurmond for president.

Truman obliged the liberals, knowing that he needed the industrial states for victory. A Republican convention that made a strong statement on race—specifically, the desegregation of the armed services—and the surprising success of the liberal forces led by Hubert Humphrey on the Democratic Convention floor prompted Truman to release two key executive orders on July 26, 1948.

Order 9980 called for a Fair Employment Board to provide redress for racial discrimination in federal employment. Executive Order 9981 announced the policy of "equality of treatment for all persons in the armed services without regard to race, color, religion, or national origin." A second provision called for an advisory committee to oversee that policy of equality, constituted in September, 1948, as the Fahy Committee.

## Impact of Event

Exactly what did Executive Order 9981 entail? Was it another rhetorical promise, was it a plan to implement the *Plessy v. Ferguson* (1896) principle of "separate but equal," or was it a plan to desegregate? In answer to a reporter's public question, Truman made clear that it was indeed a plan to desegregate.

In reality, the armed services did not desegregate immediately. Rather, there was uneven compliance both in time and in depth. Entrenched forces in the services resisted the orders and put up barriers to implementation.

Nevertheless, desegregation progressed, supervised by the Fahy Committee and with the prodding of African-American defense organizations. Wartime Secretary of War Henry Stimson, who opposed the idea, had been replaced by the first secretary of defense, James Forrestal, who was committed to the idea but unwilling to force it upon the service leadership. His successor, Louis Johnson, was more willing to go along with Truman in imposing it from the top.

In part, the decisions were hindered or expedited by individuals along the chain of command. The most resistant force was Kenneth Royall, secretary of the same army which had previously been the service most open to African Americans. Eventually, Truman intervened personally with Royall's successor, Gordon Gray. In the Far East, Douglas MacArthur managed to delay the policy, but it was accelerated when Truman replaced MacArthur with a more cooperative Matthew Ridgway.

Change was more forthcoming from the Air Force, largely because of the strong support of Stuart Symington, later a Democratic senator from Missouri. The Marines, which had long been lily-white, also fell into place in short time. The Navy earlier had been more accommodating to African Americans in terms of numbers, but the overwhelming percentage of those were in the food service. Slowly, the Navy began to give more equal training to African Americans in other jobs and upgraded the ranks of some of the stewards.

The war in Korea provided the final thrust for desegregation, again supported by the need for more troops to engage in combat. The remaining pockets of segregation were systematically eliminated, even under President Eisenhower, who was less committed to civil rights than was Truman. By the end of the Korean War, virtually all of the armed services were desegregated at the most basic level.

Segregation practices, however, still faced African-American soldiers and their dependents, especially in the Southern towns where many were stationed. Because local policy involved states' rights, it took longer to overcome that discrimination. These practices were not legally resolved until the Supreme Court decisions that grew out of Executive Order 9981.

The desegregation of the armed forces served as a reference point for the further desegregation of the rest of the society. Under Truman, the Justice Department argued a number of cases before the Supreme Court which systematically eroded segregation as a legal policy. The Court issued decisions making restrictive housing covenants illegal (*Shelley v. Kraemer*, 1948); banning segregation in interstate busing (*Henderson v. the U.S.*, 1950); giving rights to education (*Sweatt v. Painter* and *McLaurin v. Oklahoma*, 1950); and eventually, a year after the Korean War ended, banning segregation in public schools (*Brown v. Board of Education*, 1954).

Beyond the legal cases, an important human dynamic arose from the consequences of Executive Order 9981. Those African Americans who were integrated in the armed forces found it difficult to return to a segregated civilian life-style. Their experiences in the military acted as an impetus for them to reject the segregation of civilian life. For whites who served with African Americans on the front lines, it also became more difficult to return to a completely segregated life. Moreover, especially after World War II and then Korea, it became increasingly difficult to accept the war contributions made by African-American soldiers but then to deny them basic civilian rights afterward.

Desegregating the armed services allowed for much greater contact between whites and blacks, as well as among whites and significant numbers of Puerto Ricans and Filipinos, many of the latter also formerly in segregated units.

In retrospect, the conditions allowing for successful interracial contact as a means of breaking down prejudice were more propitious in the military than they were in the school systems. Not only was there more regimentation in the military, but the soldiers also had both a common goal and a common enemy, conditions supporting the effectiveness of contact in dissolving differences. Although contact often has surprisingly little effect in diminishing prejudice, a study on soldiers conducted at The Johns Hopkins University found that contact in the armed forces did contribute to a lessening of prejudice and discrimination.

President Truman, as was his hyperbolic wont, remarked later of Executive Order 9981, "It's the greatest thing that ever happened to America." A less effusive but similar evaluation was proffered by eminent legal and political historian Milton Konvitz: "[I]n the history of civil rights in the United States, this order ranks among the most important steps to end racial discrimination."

## Bibliography

Berman, William C. *The Politics of Civil Rights in the Truman Administration.* Columbus: Ohio State University Press, 1970. A focused, insightful, balanced account of the interplay between political pressures and civil rights policy.

Dalfiume, Richard M. *Desegregation of the U.S. Armed Forces.* Columbia: University of Missouri Press, 1969. One of the first scholarly treatises on the topic; still a good place to start.

Foner, Jack D. *Blacks and the Military in American History.* New York: Praeger, 1974. A popular, easy-to-read, surprisingly comprehensive history, though lacking in specific citations and somewhat biased.

McCoy, Donald R., and Richard T. Ruetten. *Quest and Response: Minority Rights and the Truman Administration.* Lawrence: University Press of Kansas, 1973. Solid, comprehensive research. The best single concise discussion (see Chapter 11) on this particular issue.

Nalty, Bernard C. *Strength for the Fight: A History of Black Americans in the Military.* New York: Free Press, 1986. A solid, extensively researched, thorough history.

Nichols, Lee. *Breakthrough on the Color Front.* New York: Random House, 1954. The first major work on this topic. Partly anecdotal and based on interviews; it was reportedly read by the judges before deciding *Brown v. Board of Education.*

President's Committee on Civil Rights. *To Secure These Rights.* Washington, D.C.: Government Printing Office, 1947. This original report shows a sincere concern with racial problems. Some statistics and general recommendations. Written from the perspective of mainstream America.

*Alan M. Fisher*

## Cross-References

Roosevelt Outlaws Discrimination in Defense-Industry Employment (1941), p. 578; The United Nations Issues a Declaration on Racial Discrimination (1963), p. 1212; Congress Passes the Civil Rights Act (1964), p. 1251; Marshall Becomes the First Black Supreme Court Justice (1967), p. 1381; A World Conference Condemns Racial Discrimination (1978), p. 1993; The Supreme Court Upholds an Affirmative-Action Program (1979), p. 2029; Wilder Becomes the First Elected Black Governor (1989), p. 2517.

# THE UNITED NATIONS ADOPTS A CONVENTION ON THE CRIME OF GENOCIDE

*Categories of event:* Atrocities and war crimes; international norms
*Time:* December 9, 1948
*Locale:* United Nations, New York City

*Nazi execution of millions of persons in attempts to exterminate whole races provoked the United Nations, in one of its first acts, to draft international conventional law declaring genocide a crime against humanity*

*Principal personages:*
> RAPHAEL LEMKIN (1900-1959), a Polish lawyer and longtime advocate of branding genocide as an international crime
> ELEANOR ROOSEVELT (1884-1962), the chair of the United Nations Commission on Human Rights
> CHARLES MALIK (1906-1987), the rapporteur of the Commission on Human Rights during the drafting of the convention

## Summary of Event

Although massive violations of the human right of existence have not disappeared, twentieth century civilization no longer accepts such behavior as unfortunate but normal. Willfully destroying a people is now repugnant, condemned by principles of international law. Stirred by the Nazi execution of millions of persons in attempts to exterminate whole races, the United Nations General Assembly, at its first meeting in 1946, addressed the systematic killing or harming of target groups of persons.

In a 1946 resolution, the Assembly defined genocide as the denial of the right of existence of entire human groups. It said that this act shocks the human conscience, violates moral law, and offends the spirit and aims of the United Nations. The Assembly affirmed that genocide is a crime under international law, a crime the entire civilized world condemns and the commission of which is punishable for the principals and accomplices, whether public officials or private individuals, and whether the crime was committed on religious, racial, political, or any other grounds. The Assembly initiated a study group to draft a convention on the prevention and punishment of this crime. Two years later, on December 9, 1948, the Assembly adopted the Convention on the Prevention and Punishment of the Crime of Genocide, or the Genocide Convention.

The term "genocide" was coined by Raphael Lemkin, a Polish lawyer who served as an adviser during the Nuremberg trials. He had sought as early as the 1930's to arouse interest in condemning genocide and campaigned successfully for the United Nations' adoption of the convention. The word derives from the Greek word *genos*, meaning race, tribe, descent, kin, sex, or kind, and the Latin word *cida*, meaning killing. This created word, Lemkin said, denoted destroying a nation, people, ethnic group, or other identifiable group through coordinated action directed against individuals, not as individuals but as members of an identified group. This definition was revised during the negotiation producing the 1948 convention.

Working with Lemkin on the convention's first draft were two well-known human rights supporters, Eleanor Roosevelt, U.S. delegate to the United Nations and chair of the U.N. Commission on Human Rights, and Charles Malik, Lebanon's permanent representative to the United Nations and commission rapporteur. The trio found some legal groundwork in the Charter for an International Military Tribunal (CIMT) of August 8, 1945. This document had authorized the major war crimes trials at the conclusion of World War II. The CIMT specified three types of crimes—crimes against peace, crimes in war, and crimes against humanity. Crimes against humanity included genocide. The Genocide Convention, however, went beyond the CIMT, separating such assaults from wartime. Criminal genocide, then, could be action by governments against their own nationals, in war or in peace.

In the Genocide Convention, the contracting parties confirm that genocide is a crime under international law and that they will prevent and punish it. The convention describes genocide as any of several acts committed with intent to destroy, in whole or in part, a national, ethnic, racial, or religious group. Those acts include killing group members, causing serious bodily or mental harm to group members, deliberately inflicting on the group conditions of life calculated to bring about its physical destruction in whole or in part, imposing measures intended to prevent births within the group, or forcibly transferring children of the group to another group.

The convention says clearly that genocide is a matter of international concern. This is true of conspiracy in, incitement of, and complicity in attempts to commit genocide, even if perpetrated by a government on its own territory and against its own citizens. Any contracting party can call upon the United Nations to intervene anywhere against genocide. The convention specifies that genocide shall not be considered a political crime. Someone accused of a political crime is normally not subject to extradition. The contracting parties pledge in genocide cases to grant extradition in accordance with their national laws and treaties in force, to try people accused of genocide in their own courts, or to turn the accused over to a recognized international penal tribunal should the world community create one. The convention binds the parties to enact the necessary enforcement legislation.

The United Nations achieved some success creating this convention, which came into force in 1951. The United Nations managed modestly to define the crime of genocide, symbolically denounce it, and prescribe some punishments for it. The convention prompted some member states to enact enabling legislation that defined genocide as a crime under their codes, punishable by municipal courts. Finally, the convention stipulated a procedure for punishment: competent U.N. organs, using the International Court of Justice to interpret, apply, or demand compliance with the convention.

The United Nations has had difficulty in preventing or punishing genocide. The convention lacks needed specificity for several reasons. It was the international community's first attempt at drafting rules to constrain genocide. It was also one of the first post-World War II attempts at international legislation. Moreover, several states negotiating the convention had themselves been guilty or suspected of behavior they were now calling criminal. Meanwhile, for various reasons, courts have found no opportunity to clarify through decisions in individual cases the meaning of many of the convention's articles. In addition, the convention focuses more on punishing an act of genocide than on preventing it. This makes teaching the law difficult as well. Several of these points deserve further attention.

First, the convention has wording problems. How should courts determine "intent"? Does this word rule out as "accident" any actions that might appear to constitute genocide? The phrase "in whole or in part" raises a question of how large a "part" would qualify. How, in this sense, does genocide differ from murder? What is "mental harm" in the convention's language? How would one document it? How severe need it be to qualify as genocide? What objective standards would a foreign ministry or court use to determine that a crime had occurred? At what point does the restriction against "incitement to genocide" become an infringement of other human rights, such as freedom of speech and press?

The convention does not address whether a government has the right to dispose of its political opposition without interference from the outside world. The convention's listing of acts constituting genocide is not logically exhaustive and appears to be more the outcome of the dynamics of negotiating, competing national interests, and personalities than of an intellectual exercise. This is evidenced in the convention's excluding as genocide, in effect, the destruction of political groups, as in the Soviet Union under Joseph Stalin, Indonesia in 1965, Democratic Kampuchea under Pol Pot, or Uganda under Idi Amin. This need not thwart growth in the convention's applicability. Drawing a line between political violence and ethnic violence is sometimes difficult, as in Burundi. Ethnic difficulties rapidly become politicized after a previously repressed group achieves independence. Older rivalries, suspended during a period of external control, may break out when the control lifts. Evidence of this existed in South Africa and the Balkans during the early 1990's.

Second, states' values conflict. This has frustrated application of the convention and prevented its ratification in some countries. With collective major power interests growing more common regarding matters of international peace and security, the international community may witness more willingness to take steps to stem human rights abuses, including genocide, even without host government approval. In the decades immediately after the convention's enactment, superpower rivalry contributed to states' preferring not to think about the convention's existence.

Third, states put sovereign interests above protecting human rights. Negotiators of the convention inevitably faced the same spirit that drove drafters of the U.N. Charter to include an article enshrining territorial sovereignty. This allows individual states to judge their own interests and, when they can get away with it, their own behavior. One result is that, the Genocide Convention notwithstanding, some states still may practice genocide. No matter how many governments deny directly having approved genocide within their borders, large sections of populations have been eliminated with at least tacit approval of other states. Genocide remains, then, a major form of contemporary massive massacres, with death tolls in the millions. Indeed, in the twentieth century more persons have died at the hands of their own states than have been killed in war by other states. The real issue is how free a government is to dispose of its political opposition without interference from the outside world.

Fourth, the convention names no specific court to rule reliably and effectively. United Nations members are left only whatever existing courts that are recognized by disputants governed by the convention. Hence, enforcement provisions are weak. How likely are governments to pass, or obey, legislation regarding genocide when the governments themselves are likely to be the perpetrators?

## Impact of Event

More than one hundred states had ratified the convention by mid-1991. The convention's authors hoped that they had made permanent and universal a generation's revulsion. With the law spelled out, they believed that states would hold one another in check, through either moral suasion or the threat of international embarrassment. If these failed, states party to the convention would try the accused, allow an international penal tribunal to do so, or extradite them for trial elsewhere. Any needed clarification of the convention would come from the International Court of Justice (ICJ).

The proponents' hopes faded. Several signatory states have themselves committed genocide, with no other states calling them legally to account. Continually, somewhere, one or more states appear indifferent to genocide or to genocidal massacres. Even the United Nations sometimes has been blind and deaf to such actions. The United Nations' major contribution has been to provide humanitarian relief for survivors; however, U.N. peacekeeping and observer forces have certainly also averted many massacres. The international community has not yet found the will to create either an ad hoc or standing international criminal court beyond the war crimes tribunals at the close of World War II. Numerous governmental and nongovernmental bodies have examined particular instances of genocide and repeatedly called on states to desist from or avoid engaging in the crime. When the United States finally ratified the convention in 1986, it attached two reservations, five understandings, and one declaration. These amendments had the effect of denying ICJ jurisdiction without express U.S. consent. The United States promised to extradite accused persons only if required to by specific prior treaty with the country concerned, putting U.S. combat forces outside the convention during wartime, and agreed to participate in a future international penal tribunal only if permitted by the U.S. Congress. Forty years after signing the convention, the United States finally amended its laws to comply with it.

A United Nations assessment of the convention in 1985 underscored certain weaknesses in the law by proposing an optional protocol to deal with ethnocide (systematic mistreatment or killing of an ethnic group) and ecocide (degrading the global environment in ways that seriously injure or kill human beings, as in the Persian Gulf War in 1990-1991); killing political groups and other groups not covered by the convention's definition; amending the convention to clarify what acts constitute culpable omission and the question of using superior orders as a legal defense; and clearly stating that genocide is subject to universal jurisdiction, or that any state may try someone accused of genocide. In the absence of these revisions, the international community will continue to face the reality of continued unpunished acts of genocide.

The Genocide Convention contributed to fundamental change in international law. It, the U.N. Charter, and other human rights conventions together have internationalized many human rights. Prior to World War II, such rights were deemed matters of domestic jurisdiction of each state. How a state treated its own nationals was not an international legal concern. States had no right to address each other concerning behavior such as genocide. It is no longer intervention in another state's affairs for a state to express concern about or ask for explanations of another state's human rights practices.

## Bibliography

Beres, Louis René. "Genocide and Power Politics: The Individual and the State." *Bulletin of Peace Proposals* 18, no. 1 (1987): 73-79. Normative essay arguing that despite the United States' having finally ratified the Genocide Convention in 1986, the United Nations and the world community will not effectively enforce this convention until citizens stop deifying territorially based states.

Charny, Israel. *How Can We Commit the Unthinkable—Genocide: The Human Cancer.* Boulder, Colo.: Westview Press, 1982. Clinical psychologist's evocative, accessible description of human destructiveness. Offers a wide range of conceivable explanations for this criminal behavior at individual, family, and social levels. Describes cultures, genocidal fantasy and ideology, the destabilizing character of major social change, having technical means, institutionalized discrimination, and psychological denial. Bibliography and index.

Fein, Helen. *Accounting for Genocide: National Responses.* New York: Free Press, 1979. An objective reference that thoroughly examines national preconditions of the destructive process. Suggests that the convention omits unpremeditated genocide, a type not necessarily meeting the convention's test of "intent." Heavy reading for some. Bibliography and index.

Hannum, Hurst. "International Law and Cambodian Genocide: The Sounds of Silence." *Human Rights Quarterly* 11 (February, 1989): 82-138. Detailed examination of a recent case of genocide, with particular reference to provisions of the convention and the U.N. Charter. Extensive notes.

Kuper, Leo. "The Plural Society and Civil Conflict." In *UNESCO Yearbook on Peace and Conflict Studies, 1986.* Paris: UNESCO, 1988. Updates his earlier work, examining the relationship of plural societies and civil violence to show that the greater the cleavage and inequality, and the more the disparate groups experience all aspects of life the same differential way, the more likely is genocidal conflict. Notes and bibliography.

_____. *The Prevention of Genocide.* New Haven, Conn.: Yale University Press, 1985. Probably the most conscientious author on this subject. Builds on his numerous previously published case studies of genocide, this time including domestic mass killing. Emphasizes that although state interests often inhibit U.N. action, the structure, procedures, and publicity of the United Nations can constrain potentially offending states. Bibliography and index.

Sieghart, Paul. *The Lawful Rights of Mankind: An Introduction to the International Legal Code of Human Rights.* New York: Oxford University Press, 1985. Readable handbook-style distillation of Sieghart's massive, comprehensive work, *The International Law of Human Rights* (1983). Provides the larger human rights context of genocide. Examines the historical problems giving rise to the need for human rights laws, how such laws are made, their content, and actual documents. Bibliography and index.

*Kenneth L. Wise*

## Cross-References

Armenians Suffer Genocide During World War I (1915), p. 150; Nazi Concentration Camps Go into Operation (1933), p. 491; China Initiates a Genocide Policy Toward Tibetans (1950), p. 826; China Occupies Tibet (1950), p. 837; The Iraqi Government Promotes Genocide of Kurds (1960's), p. 1050; Eichmann Is Tried for War Crimes (1961), p. 1108; Conflicts in Pakistan Lead to the Secession of Bangladesh (1971), p. 1611; Burundi's Government Commits Genocide of the Bahutu Majority (1972), p. 1668; East Timor Declares Independence but Is Annexed by Indonesia (1975), p. 1835.

# THE UNITED NATIONS ADOPTS THE UNIVERSAL DECLARATION OF HUMAN RIGHTS

*Category of event:* International norms
*Time:* December 10, 1948
*Locale:* United Nations, New York City

*The Universal Declaration of Human Rights was the first major document to provide a comprehensive and authoritative statement of international human rights norms*

Principal personages:

ELEANOR ROOSEVELT (1884-1962), the U.S. delegate to and chair of the U.N. Commission on Human Rights

JOHN HUMPHREY (1905-    ), the director of the Division of Human Rights and one of the two principal authors of the declaration

RENÉ CASSIN (1887-1976), the French delegate to the U.N. Commission on Human Rights and one of the two principal authors of the declaration

CHARLES MALIK (1906-1987), the Lebanese representative to and rapporteur of the U.N. Commission on Human Rights

P. C. CHANG (1892-1957), the Chinese representative to and vice-chair of the U.N. Commission on Human Rights

## Summary of Event

The United Nations Charter includes the promotion of human rights and fundamental freedoms among the principal purposes of the organization. It does not, however, specify their substance. One of the principal human rights contributions of the United Nations has been to forge an international normative consensus on a list of human rights. The central expression of that consensus is the Universal Declaration of Human Rights, adopted by the General Assembly on December 10, 1948.

The U.N. Commission on Human Rights, a permanent functional commission of the Economic and Social Council (ECOSOC), was given principal responsibility for drafting an international human rights covenant (treaty). The commission decided to prepare a nonbinding declaration as quickly as possible. This became the Universal Declaration. Meanwhile, work continued on the more difficult and more controversial task of producing a binding treaty. It was finally completed in 1966, when the International Human Rights Covenants were opened for signature and ratification. The Universal Declaration and the Covenants together are frequently referred to as the International Bill of Human Rights.

At its first meeting, in January, 1947, the commission appointed a drafting committee made up of its three officers, Eleanor Roosevelt (United States), P. C. Chang (China), and Charles Malik (Lebanon). In March, representatives from Australia, Chile, France, the United Kingdom, and the Soviet Union were added. During the summer, an outline (initially drafted by John Humphrey, the director of the Secretariat's Division of Human Rights and revised by the French delegate, René Cassin) was debated. By Christmas, a complete draft was circulated to governments for comment. On June 18, 1948, the full commission adopted a draft declaration.

In the fall of 1948, the Third (Social and Humanitarian) Committee of the General Assembly devoted eighty-one meetings to the discussion of the draft declaration and nearly seventy proposed amendments. This arduous process was eased somewhat by the fact that the chair of the committee was Charles Malik, the rapporteur of the Commission on Human Rights. On December 10, 1948, the committee completed its work. The full General Assembly adopted the Universal Declaration of Human Rights with none opposed and eight abstentions.

South Africa abstained because of the declaration's provisions on racial discrimination. Saudi Arabia abstained over the treatment of women's rights and the right to change one's religion. The other abstentions came from the Soviet Union and its allies, whose delegates believed that economic and social rights were not given enough emphasis. Thus although the declaration was not adopted unanimously, no states voted against it and only two believed that it went too far (and even then only in a few areas).

The Universal Declaration of Human Rights begins with the claim that "recognition of the inherent dignity and of the equal and inalienable rights of all members of the human family is the foundation of freedom, justice and peace in the world." Article 1 echoes these sentiments of the preamble, holding that "all human beings are born free and equal in dignity and rights. They are endowed with reason and conscience and should act towards one another in a spirit of brotherhood." Articles 2-28 then lay out a comprehensive set of human rights.

The Universal Declaration specifically proclaims that everyone has human rights to enjoy all rights equally, without discrimination; life; liberty and security of person; protection against slavery; protection against torture and cruel and inhuman punishment; recognition as a person before the law; equal protection of the law; access to legal remedies for violations of rights; protection against arbitrary arrest, detention or exile; an independent and impartial judiciary; presumption of innocence; protection against ex post facto laws; protection of privacy, family, and home; freedom of movement and residence; seek asylum from persecution; nationality; marry and found a family; own property; freedom of thought, conscience, and religion; freedom of opinion, expression, and the press; freedom of assembly and association; political participation; social security; work under favorable conditions; free trade unions; rest and leisure; food, clothing, and housing; health care and social services; special protections for children; education; participation in cultural life; and a social and international order needed to realize these rights.

The Universal Declaration, however, contains no implementation or enforcement mechanisms. It is only a statement of principles and aspirations, without a mechanism or program for realizing them.

The 1966 International Human Rights Covenants gave binding international legal force to the rights of the Universal Declaration and established rudimentary international monitoring procedures. They did not, however, fundamentally alter the substance of the declaration. There have also been important treaties dealing with particular human rights such as racial discrimination, women's rights, torture, and children's rights. These too are best seen as supplements to the Universal Declaration which give greater specificity to particular rights and establish international monitoring procedures. They do not significantly alter the norms laid out in the Universal Declaration.

The Universal Declaration remains the single most important statement of international human rights norms. It is widely commended by virtually all states, from all regions and all ideological perspectives—even those states which systematically violate its provisions. In recognition of its importance, most countries celebrate December 10, the anniversary of the adoption of the Universal Declaration, as Human Rights Day.

This does not mean that the Universal Declaration has always been uncontroversial. In particular, the relative weight of civil, political, economic, social, and cultural rights, which led to the abstention of the Soviet bloc states, remained a matter of intense controversy in the following decades. In fact, this issue often transformed international discussions of human rights in the 1950's and 1960's into exercises in Cold War ideological rivalry.

Nevertheless, the principle that all human rights are interdependent and indivisible, first established in the Universal Declaration, has largely prevailed. The Universal Declaration is not a list from which states may pick and choose as they see fit. Rather, it is a comprehensive set of minimum standards of domestic political behavior. The fundamental unity of all human rights, exemplified by the existence of a single Declaration containing both civil and political rights and economic, social, and cultural rights without any indication of categorical differences or priorities, has been central to the international definition of human rights since 1948.

Another complaint has concerned the alleged "Western" bias of the Universal Declaration of Human Rights. When it was drafted, most of Africa and much of Asia was under colonial rule. Only half of the commission's eighteen members, and only three of the eight members of the drafting committee, were from developing countries. One consequence was that the declaration does not recognize the right of peoples to self-determination. That was remedied by the 1966 International Human Rights Covenants, also known as the International Covenant on Civil and Political Rights. More generally, a number of critics in the Third World have argued that the Universal Declaration systematically disparages collective rights in favor of the individual rights emphasized in the West.

The most striking fact about today's list of internationally recognized human rights is the persistence of the original list presented in the Universal Declaration. Virtually all the rights in the International Covenant on Political and Civil Rights, except for the right to self-determination, were enumerated in the Universal Declaration (although often in much less detail). Furthermore, only one right in the Universal Declaration (the right to own property) is not included in those covenants. The constitutions of some two dozen Third World countries that achieved their independence after 1948 contain explicit references to the Universal Declaration of Human Rights, and many other have drawn their definition of rights from the declaration, sometimes verbatim. Virtually all states treat the Universal Declaration as an authoritative statement of international human rights norms.

## Impact of Event

Before World War II, there were few explicit international human rights norms. The Treaty of Versailles, which ended World War I, established a (very weak and incomplete) system to protect minorities' rights through the League of Nations. The Treaty of Versailles also created the International Labor Organization, which began to deal with workers' rights issues in the 1920's. The 1926 International Slavery Convention dealt with that one important human right. Such international efforts to protect individual human rights were clearly exceptions.

Until 1945, the human rights practices of states were treated as internationally protected exercises of the sovereign prerogative of states. International human rights law basically did not exist. The human rights practices of other states simply were not considered a legitimate matter for either bilateral or multilateral international action.

The Nuremberg war crimes trials of 1945 introduced the idea of crimes against humanity into international legal practice. Nuremberg, however, dealt only with the particular case of the Holocaust and Nazi atrocities. It did not address human rights violations short of genocide or the practices of states other than Germany. Furthermore, the prosecution at Nuremberg was forced to deal with the uncomfortable fact that although the Nazis were obviously guilty of great moral crimes, such crimes against humanity had not been prohibited explicitly by prewar international law.

The Universal Declaration was the United Nations' first major response to this distressing and embarrassing absence of an explicit international law of human rights. The Universal Declaration, however, forthrightly refers to itself as "a common standard of achievement for all peoples and all nations." It does not claim to create binding international legal obligations. In fact, as a resolution of the U.N. General Assembly it is technically speaking only a recommendation to states.

Many lawyers, scholars, and activists have argued that over time it has become a part of customary international law. For example, article 2 of the 1968 Proclamation of Teheran plausibly claimed that "the Universal Declaration of Human Rights states a common understanding of the peoples of the world concerning the inalienable and inviolable rights of all members of the human family and constitutes an obligation of the members of the international community." Whatever its technical legal status, the Universal Declaration of Human Rights has become a political standard of reference in the diplomacy of human rights. Numerous General Assembly resolutions have reaffirmed its centrality. It is explicity referred to as a standard in the European Convention for the Protection of Human Rights and Fundamental Freedoms and the

Charter of the Organization of African Unity. Virtually all states use the Universal Declaration as a point of reference when defending or criticizing the human rights practices of other states or their own practices.

The Universal Declaration, as already mentioned, contains no implementation or enforcement mechanism. Usually it cannot be enforced in either national or international law. Many, perhaps most, states have seriously violated its provisions for an extended period of time. Nevertheless, even those states that criticize or violate it typically treat the Universal Declaration as a definitive statement of the standards of domestic political behavior required of states that wish to be considered fully legitimate members of the international society of states. The Universal Declaration of Human Rights has become a normative standard of political legitimacy in the contemporary world, an authoritative international statement of the minimum standards of treatment that every state owes to all of its citizens.

## Bibliography

Berting, Jan, et al., eds. *Human Rights in a Pluralist World: Individuals and Collectivities.* Westport, Conn.: Meckler, 1990. Part 1 considers the Universal Declaration forty years after its formulation. The remaining parts focus principally on the relationship between individual and collective rights and varying cultural conceptions of human rights.

Humphrey, John P. *Human Rights and the United Nations: A Great Adventure.* Dobbs Ferry, N.Y.: Transnational Publishers, 1984. A sometimes engaging and always opinionated memoir of the United Nations' first director of the Division of Human Rights and author of the initial draft of the Universal Declaration.

Johnson, M. Glen. "The Contributions of Eleanor and Franklin Roosevelt to the Development of International Protection for Human Rights." *Human Rights Quarterly* 9 (February, 1987): 19-48. A look at the special contributions of Franklin Roosevelt in helping to inspire U.N. action on human rights and of Eleanor Roosevelt in bringing the Universal Declaration to fruition.

Ramcharan, B. G., ed. *Human Rights: Thirty Years After the Universal Declaration.* The Hague: Martinus Nijhoff, 1979. Chapters 1, 2, and 7 deal with the Universal Declaration and later efforts at setting international human rights norms. The remaining chapters focus on strategies and institutions for implementing these norms.

Schwelb, Egon. *Human Rights and the International Community: The Roots and Growth of the Universal Declaration of Human Rights, 1948-1963.* Chicago: Quadrangle Books, 1964. An accessible general survey of the origins of the Universal Declaration and its place in the emergence of human rights as a significant issue in international relations in the postwar era.

Tolley, Howard, Jr. *The U.N. Commission on Human Rights.* Boulder, Colo.: Westview Press, 1986. This is the authoritative work on the Commission on Human Rights. Chapter 2 briefly discusses the process of drafting in the general context of the political controversies in the commission during its early years.

United Nations Commission on Human Rights. "Universal Declaration of Human Rights." In *The Human Rights Reader*, edited by Walter Laqueur and Barry Rubin. Rev. ed. New York: New American Library, 1989. One of many sources for the text of the Universal Declaration, which deserves reading in its entirety (about five pages).

*Jack Donnelly*

## Cross-References

The Paris Peace Conference Includes Protection for Minorities (1919), p. 252; The League of Nations Is Established (1919), p. 270; The International Labour Organisation Is Established (1919), p. 281; The League of Nations Adopts the International Slavery Convention (1926), p. 436; The United Nations Adopts Its Charter (1945), p. 657; Nazi War Criminals Are Tried in Nuremberg (1945), p. 667; The U.N. Covenant on Civil and Political Rights Is Adopted (1966), p. 1353; The Proclamation of Teheran Sets Human Rights Goals (1968), p. 1430; A U.N. Convention Condemns Discrimination Against Women (1979), p. 2057; The United Nations Adopts the Convention on the Rights of the Child (1989), p. 2529.

# HUNDREDS OF THOUSANDS LEAVE EAST GERMANY FOR THE WEST

*Categories of event:* Political freedom and refugee relief
*Time:* 1949
*Locale:* Berlin, Germany

*Hundreds of thousands of people migrated to the West after the partition of Germany into the German Democratic Republic (East Germany) and the Federal Republic of Germany (West Germany)*

*Principal personages:*

KONRAD ADENAUER (1876-1967), the conservative anti-Communist, anti-Nazi chancellor of the Federal Republic of Germany

WALTER ULBRICHT (1893-1973), the Communist leader of East Germany, a loyal ally of Moscow

HARRY S. TRUMAN (1884-1972), the president of the United States (1945-1953)

JOSEPH STALIN (1879-1953), the general secretary of the Communist Party of the Soviet Union, leader of the communist world

## Summary of Event

World War II was a series of different conflicts. In Europe, it was simultaneously a continuation of a centuries-old struggle between Germany and Russia for the mastery of Central Europe, an ideological battle against fascism, and a fight by a coalition of powers to stop Adolf Hitler's aggression. German defeat brought these conflicts into conjunction. When the war ended, Stalin, as master of Russia wanted Germany prostrate and its resources used to rebuild the Soviet state.

Stalin's Western allies, the United States, Great Britain, and France, had less clear goals. Some Western leaders saw communism as being as great a danger as fascism and had joined Stalin only for political expediency, seeing Hitler as the more immediate threat. Others hoped that the wartime alliance would produce continued cooperation with the Soviet Union after the peace. Some in the West agreed with Stalin that Germany should be reduced to impotency. They believed, perhaps unfairly, that the country had been responsible for both world wars and therefore should be severely punished. Henry Morgenthau, Jr., a presidential adviser and secretary of the treasury under President Franklin D. Roosevelt, suggested in 1943 that the country be "pastoralized" so that it could never make war again. France, which like the Soviet Union had suffered brutal occupation by the Nazis, particularly desired that German aggression be curbed.

In the years following World War II, as Moscow imposed its own order on Eastern Europe with less than democratic means, Western skepticism grew concerning Stalin's commitment to European peace and independence. A civil war between communists and monarchists in Greece and the appearance of strong communist movements in France and Italy also contributed to the breakdown of the East-West coalition.

Geopolitical issues overrode even these ideological concerns. Neither Germany nor France remained strong enough to counterbalance the Soviet Union on the European continent. As early as October, 1944, British Prime Minister Winston Churchill and Stalin agreed that there should be a formula for dividing Eastern Europe. In February, 1945, at Yalta in the Soviet Union, Churchill, Stalin, and Roosevelt developed further plans which placed Eastern Europe in the Soviet sphere and Western Europe in the Anglo-American. Roosevelt died in April, 1945, a month before the war in Europe ended. After the German surrender, Churchill and Stalin met with the new U.S. president, Harry S. Truman, at Potsdam (outside Berlin). Here they decided the fate of Germany. In the midst of the conference, British voters unseated Churchill's Conservative party. Labour Party leader Clement Atlee became prime minister and replaced the venerable Churchill at Potsdam. The change did not greatly affect the negotiations in progress.

The Potsdam agreement called for the division of Germany into four parts—American, British, French, and Soviet zones. It treated Berlin separately but also divided it into four parts, even though it was situated geographically inside the Soviet zone. Furthermore, the treaty allowed the Soviets to take reparations, including machinery and produce, from their zone and from the others as compensation for the damage done to the Soviet Union under German occupation. France and other European countries occupied by the Nazis received similar, but lesser, compensations. The Soviets, in fact, removed industrial material from Germany as soon as they could, even before the agreements were in place.

The Soviet zone, the largest in area, encompassed about 40 percent of German territory, including most of eastern Prussia to the Weser river, Saxony, and Thuringia. In addition, the Germans surrendered their prewar territory east of the Oder and Neisse rivers directly to the Soviet Union, Poland, and Czechoslovakia. Both of the latter were soon to fall under the complete domination of Moscow. Furthermore, all German conquests after 1938 were restored. The French zone, 10 percent of German territory, fell along the Rhine valley. The British zone, 20 percent, lay in the north. The United States' zone, 30 percent, was located in the southwest.

Stalin interpreted the meaning of democracy in a manner vastly different from that of the Western leaders. Moscow instituted systems of government in Eastern Europe that were controlled by Communist parties through one-candidate elections. Opponents of the Moscow system were forced into silence or exile. The authorities even imprisoned or executed some. On the other hand, the West put pressure on native communists, sometimes extralegally, reducing their influence. The Communist parties, however, were rarely completely outlawed. Moreover, Washington's Marshall Plan brought rapid economic recovery to Western Europe, further reducing the communists' appeal in both Eastern and Western Europe. The two camps rapidly went their separate ways. In 1946, Winston Churchill declared that an Iron Curtain had fallen across Europe. By 1948, the wartime alliance between the Soviet Union and the West had broken down completely. The Cold War began.

The split between the former Allies had repercussions for Germany. Each occupier drew up a temporary administration modeled on its own goals and precepts of government. In 1947, the Western allies—Great Britain, the United States, and France—relinquished their own authorities and united their sections into the new Federal Republic of Germany, with a capital at Bonn. The first elections resulted in the anti-Nazi conservative Konrad Adenauer becoming the first chancellor. Berlin remained legally distinct, but the three Western sections there were also united into a free city, West Berlin.

The Soviets followed suit. They declared East Germany as the German Democratic Republic (DDR), with East Berlin as its capital and Walter Ulbricht, a Communist leader loyal to Moscow, as its prime minister. In 1948, Moscow tried to restrict access to the city even though access was guaranteed by treaty. An air lift, sponsored chiefly by the United States, caused the plan of blocking the roads to backfire. The Kremlin lifted the blockade.

The new situation struck terror into the Germans in the East. While others in the Soviet Bloc had little chance of leaving their homelands, Germans who lived in Berlin, or who could get there, could make their way to West Berlin simply by taking a subway ride. Once in West Berlin, they could join relatives or simply move themselves into the Federal Republic. The total number of Germans who had left the East for the West exceeded 1.5 million by the end of 1951. The lure of the West, especially the benefits provided by the airlift and the Marshall Plan, provided the East Germans more than enough incentive to give up all of their possessions and take a chance in the West. The bleak future which the German Democratic Republic promised also provided an impulse. In addition, the new governments of Eastern Europe expelled almost eight million more Germans whose families had lived in their countries for generations. Most of these came from German territories received as compensation by Poland, Czechoslovakia, and the Soviet Union. These migrations further divided the two Germanies. This division, perhaps more than any other condition, symbolized the Cold War.

## Impact of Event

The establishment of two Germanies was in many ways convenient for both the West and the Soviet Union. It allowed the World War II settlement to continue even after the alliance broke down. The Germans did not like this settlement, however, and the Federal Republic of Germany (West Germany) never recognized the two-Germany policy. It even took measures against the policy, such as the 1955 Hallstein Doctrine, named after Walter Hallstein, a foreign office official. The Hallstein Doctrine stated that Bonn would not recognize any country with diplomatic relations with the DDR. Exceptions were granted to the Soviet Union and some Third World countries. Later, in the 1960's, Bonn modified the doctrine in order to establish relations with Eastern Europe, but unification remained a goal for West Germany.

In contrast, the communist leaders of the DDR supported the two-Germany policy, since it served both Moscow's interest and their own. Only under this situation could they have an opportunity to govern, as it was clear that reunification would mean the end of communist power in Germany. The Sovietization of East Germany, however, produced a large amount of hostility among the populace. In 1953, a mass uprising erupted.

Escape to the West through Berlin continued. Between 1949 and 1961, another 1.5 million or more East Germans migrated to the West. In the 1950's, Western aid rebuilt Western Europe, including West Germany and West Berlin. In the meantime, the states of Eastern Europe suffered under the burden of having to help build up the devastated Soviet Union as well as their own countries. As West Berlin became a beacon of prosperity, more and more East Germans decided to forsake their homes and migrate to the West.

Stalin died in 1953. His successor, Nikita Khrushchev, soon began a program of de-Stalinization, reversing some of Stalin's policies. Some liberalization took place in the East. The example of West Berlin and West Germany prospering in Europe spurred an economic revival in the East. Compared to other socialist countries, the German Democratic Republic was a miracle in its own right, especially considering that the Soviet Union took its goods and services as reparations and that it had not received the massive aid granted to West Germany. The exceptionally rapid development of the Federal Republic, however, increased the migrations to the West to a fever pitch. While the Soviet Union and its allies could glory in technological accomplishments, such as the first earth satellite and manned space flights, or in their huge armed forces systems and intercontinental ballistic missiles (built and designed in large part by German engineers and scientists), the West continued to enjoy a consumer and societal miracle. West Germany joined the North Atlantic Treaty Organization (NATO) and the Common Market. The Federal Republic had become a world economic power. There were no lines or shortages, as there were in the East. The new era in the 1960's, under the guidance of dynamic young President John F. Kennedy in the United States, added to the lure and attraction of the West for Germans living in the East Bloc. The loss of East German citizens to the West became too much for both the Germans and the Soviets, especially since those who left were the most highly trained and skilled. On August 13, 1961, the authorities sealed the border, and in the next weeks the Soviets and East Germans erected a massive wall across Berlin which endured until 1989.

## Bibliography

Backer, John H. *Winds of History: The German Years of Lucius DuBignon Clay.* New York: Van Nostrand Reinhold, 1983. A history of General Clay's administration of the American sector in Germany. Very well researched, with detailed documentation. Illustrations, index, and bibliography.

Botting, Douglas. *From the Ruins of the Reich: Germany, 1945-1949.* New York: New American Library, 1985. A history of Germany under Allied occupation, analyzing many different aspects. Very readable and well researched. Has some material on the refugee question. Illustrations, bibliography, and index.

Clay, Lucius D. *Decision in Germany*. Garden City, N.Y.: Doubleday, 1950. Memoirs of the American general in charge of military occupation of the American zone in West Germany from 1945 to 1949. Has some comments on the refugee question, but only in the context of expellees from other countries and displaced persons in general. Also deals with the Nuremberg Trials and tension between the Soviet Union and the West. Illustrations, chronology, and index. No bibliography.

Davidson, Eugene. *The Death and Life of Germany: An Account of the American Occupation.* New York: Alfred A. Knopf, 1961. Analysis of the period of German occupation from 1945 to 1953, especially in the American zone. It deals with the refugee question and the problems caused by the Cold War. Very well researched. Puts positive light on American rehabilitation efforts. Bibliography and index.

Keesing's Research Report. *Germany and Eastern Europe Since 1945: From Potsdam Agreement to Chancellor Brandt's "Ostpolitik."* New York: Charles Scribner's Sons, 1973. The history of Germany from 1945 to 1970, based on contemporary news reports from the Keesing's archives linked together by a narrative. The first section deals with the occupation period. Contains material relating to East German refugees. Index, no bibliography.

McInnis, Edgar, Richard Hiscocks, and Robert Spencer. *The Shaping of Postwar Germany.* New York: Praeger, 1960. A survey of the German situation at the end of the 1950's. Considers the entire German question, including the refugees from the East. Gives a brief historical outline and focuses on the division by the superpowers, a comparison of the economics and politics in the two Germanies, the Berlin issue, and the dilemma of unification. Contains a chronology and maps as well as documentation and an index.

Pounds, Norman J. G. *Divided Germany and Berlin.* Van Nostrand Searchlight Book 1. Princeton, N.J.: D. Van Nostrand, 1962. Part of a series of short geographical studies published for university students in the 1960's. The author, a leading geographer of Eastern Europe, surveys the German question at one of the peaks of the Cold War, shortly after the communists built the Berlin wall. Examines the question of refugees. Bibliography and index.

Rodnick, David. *Postwar Germans: An Anthropologist's Account.* New Haven, Conn.: Yale University Press, 1948. An anthropological view of German society immediately after the war. Considers the question of the refugees, who at the time the book was written moved quite freely from East to West. Index, no illustrations or bibliography.

Ruhm von Oppen, Beate, ed. *Documents on Germany Under Occupation: 1945-1954.* London: Oxford University Press, 1955. A selection of documents concerning the Allied occupation of Germany. Contains the texts of treaties, memoranda, protocols, and decrees from all occupying powers and concerning various issues, including the refugees and reparations. Contains a map and index.

Settel, Arthur, ed. *This Is Germany.* New York: William Sloane Associates, 1950. A collection of contemporary newspaper and magazine articles on occupied Germany, written by international correspondents. "March of Millions," by Denis Martin, concerns the refugees coming from Eastern Europe and East Germany into the Western zones. No index or bibliography.

*Frederick B. Chary*

## Cross-References

Soviets Take Control of Eastern Europe (1943), p. 612; Nazi War Criminals Are Tried in Nuremberg (1945), p. 667; The Marshall Plan Provides Aid to Europe (1947), p. 706; The United States Airlifts Supplies to West Berlin (1948), p. 771; Khrushchev Implies That Stalinist Excesses Will Cease (1956), p. 952; The Berlin Wall Is Built (1961), p. 1125; The Berlin Wall Falls (1989), p. 2523.

# SPANISH BECOMES THE LANGUAGE
# OF INSTRUCTION IN PUERTO RICO

*Categories of event:* Educational rights and indigenous peoples' rights
*Time:* 1949
*Locale:* Puerto Rico

*Attempts to Americanize Puerto Ricans by imposing English as the language of instruction in elementary and secondary schools ended in 1949*

*Principal personages:*

LUIS MUÑOZ MARÍN (1898-1980), the leader of the Popular Democratic Party and first popularly elected governor of Puerto Rico

VICTOR S. CLARK (1868-1946), the president of the Insular Board of Education of Puerto Rico under the military government following the Spanish-American War

EPIFANIO FERNÁNDEZ VANGA (1880-1961), a polemicist of the Union and Popular Democratic parties and a leading opponent of instruction in English

JOSÉ PADÍN RODRÍGUEZ (1886-1963), a Puerto Rican commissioner of education who in 1934 attempted to establish Spanish as the language of instruction

JOSÉ MIGUEL GALLARDO GARCÍA (1897-1976), the commissioner of education in Puerto Rico from 1937 to 1947

## Summary of Event

When the United States occupied Puerto Rico in 1898 as part of the spoils of victory in the Spanish-American War, a prolonged struggle began over attempts to Americanize the island. Congress annexed Puerto Rico as an American territory, and resident commissioner Henry Carroll urged Washington to grant the new acquisition self-rule, as with other territories. Congress rebuffed Carroll and passed the Foraker Act of 1900, which gave the American government direct control over the island's political life. The act imposed an American governor appointed by the U.S. president, who also named other high-ranking executive, legislative, and judicial officials in the territorial government. It also empowered Congress to annul any Puerto Rican legislation. Congress took these unusual steps out of apprehension that Spanish rule and culture had not prepared the island for democratic self-rule, necessitating a reshaping of Puerto Rico's culture before it could enjoy the typical prerogatives of a territory.

American actions puzzled and appalled Puerto Ricans who had supported U.S. intervention in the war. Nationalists had hoped that American victory would liberate their homeland from Spanish rule. Although some nationalists were willing to accept a degree of political alignment with the victor, they resented the extreme domination of the island by Congress.

Educational policies set by the United States also alienated many Puerto Ricans. From the outset, American politicians decided that the island could not become a true part of the United States as long as it retained its Spanish culture. This was particularly true in regard to language. The military government at the conclusion of the war named General John Eaton and Victor S. Clark to oversee the establishment of public schools on the island. They created a free system, which made it possible for many more Puerto Rican children to attend school, but they also attempted to transplant the American pattern in its entirety, regardless of local conditions. The two Americans also decreed that teachers were to instruct in English rather than Spanish, and that the schools were not to teach any Spanish at all. This policy met with some initial enthusiasm on the island. Because of their liberation from Spanish rule, many Puerto Ricans were exuberant about the United States, and elementary school children delighted in learning American songs and reciting the Pledge of Allegiance.

Difficulties soon became obvious. Teachers proficient in English were scarce, and those recruited on the mainland often proved to be adventurers or homesick young women who abandoned their posts within a year. Many children could not understand sufficient English to learn the other academic subjects, so instructors furtively began to teach in Spanish. The aims of American-style education also conflicted with Puerto Rican culture. For example, the United States established coeducational public schools on an island where boys and girls traditionally did not study together. Middle- and upper-class families protected their daughters from contact with the opposite sex. If they received any education, it centered on domestic arts and manners. Lower-class girls received no education at all. Undergirding traditional attitudes toward female education was the bias that females lacked the intellectual ability of males.

Early American policies with regard to the new territory consequently created a political and cultural conflict almost impossible to resolve. On one hand, the United States was determined to retain the island in a form of tutelage until Puerto Ricans became fully Americanized. On the other hand, most islanders refused to abandon their Spanish language and traditions as long as the American government discriminated against them and denied them full citizenship. With neither side willing to back down, a clash ensued, with the debate over which language should be used in the public schools becoming the chief symbol of the struggle. The language issue also became embroiled in the political factionalism that beset the island.

In 1917, the U.S. Congress abolished the Foraker Act and granted citizenship to Puerto Ricans but still refused to allow self-government. At about the same time, the commissioner of education altered the policy regarding English, permitting teachers in the first four grades to instruct in Spanish while teaching English as a special subject. He reversed the status of the two languages for the more advanced students. This change attempted to address the reality of education in Puerto Rico: Many students, particularly in rural areas, attended only for three or four years before dropping out. If taught in English, they did not achieve any mastery of the language, and the linguistic difficulties prevented them from learning much in the other subjects. The new policy preserved congressional insistence that students be as able in the English language and American culture as they were in the Spanish language and Puerto Rican culture. Bilingualism and biculturalism remained primary objectives of Puerto Rican education.

Both the Teachers College of Columbia University and the Brookings Institution completed surveys of Puerto Rican education and socioeconomic conditions in the 1920's and offered opinions on the language question. Published in 1926, the Columbia findings concluded that instructors of the early elementary grades should teach in Spanish, not because Puerto Ricans opposed learning English but because more than four-fifths of them left school by the fourth grade. The Brookings analysis of 1928 reported that study of English was a magnet that attracted students to schools. It further asserted that unless the government remedied the severe shortage of rural teachers competent to instruct in English, it would create severe class divisions, with middle- and upper-class urban students learning English and poor rural populations denied this advantage.

In the meantime, Puerto Ricans who favored independence had taken up the language issue as a means of rallying support, and by the 1930's, during the Depression, discontent made the islanders more attentive to nationalists. Devastated by hurricanes in 1928 and 1932, the island's economy offered little hope. Enthusiasm for the United States waned as that country sank into economic crisis. Although Puerto Ricans could emigrate to the mainland, the Depression made employment scarce. This gave the islanders less incentive to learn English. While the Republican Union and Socialist parties advocated statehood for Puerto Rico, the Liberal Party, led by Luis Muñoz Marín, demanded independence. More extreme was the Nationalist Party of Pedro Albizu Campos, which turned to violence in 1937, staging an uprising in Ponce that killed a number of people. The Liberals attacked the school language policy, claiming that Americanization would destroy Spanish on the island and would never make Puerto Ricans anything more than second-class American citizens. A leading Liberal advocate of this viewpoint was Epifanio Fernández Vanga, who in 1931 published a compilation of articles entitled *El idioma de Puerto Rico y el idioma escolar de Puerto Rico* (the language of Puerto Rico and the school languages of Puerto Rico). In it, he argued that the United States imposed English to subvert Puerto Rican culture and maintain political control over the island. Previously tolerant of bilingualism and biculturalism, the Liberals now rejected both.

As the dispute over language grew more heated, the administration of Franklin Delano Roosevelt supported the customary American position. When José Padín Rodríguez, the new commissioner of education, changed the policy in 1934 to make Spanish the elementary-school medium, Washington resisted and the president asserted that Puerto Ricans must become proficient in English in the event they moved to the mainland. To the delight of the proindependence parties, Padín finally resigned in protest. Thereafter, the United States had difficulty in persuading any Puerto Rican educator to assume the post of commissioner between 1937 and 1948, for fear of being branded a traitor to Puerto Rico by the opposition. José Gallardo García eventually accepted the office and, under instructions from Washington, intensified the use of English. He permitted instructors to use Spanish in the first two grades but insisted on an increasing importance for English thereafter. English was the sole language permissible in high school.

The controversy intensified. In 1940, the Popular Democratic Party, headed by Luis Muñoz Marín, won control of the Puerto Rican legislature, advocating commonwealth status for the island. Five years later, Muñoz Marín and his followers in the legislature voted to make Spanish the language of instruction. The American-appointed government vetoed the bill. The next year, legislators and the governor repeated the frustrating process, but this time the legislature overrode the veto. U.S. president Harry S. Truman responded by disallowing the bill. Other nationalists sought redress through the judicial system. A private citizen sued for the establishment of Spanish as the language of instruction on the grounds that English was harmful to his children's education and culture. The Puerto Rico Teachers Association entered a similar suit.

In 1947, Congressman Fred Crawford of Michigan opened an avenue to resolve the language issue when he proposed legislation to permit Puerto Ricans to elect their own governor. When Congress approved, the islanders chose Muñoz Marín. He appointed Mariano Villaronga as commissioner of education, and Villaronga decreed Spanish as the language of instruction on August 6, 1949, although strongly advising that students also learn English. The following year, Congress allowed Puerto Rico to draw up its own constitution, and the island effectively became a U.S. commonwealth in 1952.

## Impact of Event

The new political status and the associated change to Spanish in Puerto Rican schools quieted much of the sentiment for independence on the island. After 1952, most Puerto Ricans opted either to remain associated with the United States in the commonwealth arrangement or to support statehood for the island. The militancy of the Nationalist Party and the resort to acts of terrorism, such as the attack on Blair House in 1950, no longer persuaded public opinion. In fact, after 1952 support for the Independence Party steadily declined from election to election.

The island made significant educational progress. In 1900, less than 10 percent of school-age children attended class, but attendance had risen to 65 percent by 1950. Fifty percent continued past the third grade. Great disparities still existed between the quantity and quality of schools and teachers in rural and urban Puerto Rico. All too often, rural children lacked satisfactory facilities and had to attend part-time because overcrowding dictated that the school staff operate a morning and an afternoon session. Wealthier families also tended to shelter their children from the educational problems by sending them to private schools, where English was often the language of instruction.

If the change to Spanish as the language of instruction did not solve the educational problems of Puerto Rico, neither did it end the corrosive effects of Americanization upon traditional island society. Economic opportunity in the United States continued to attract many Puerto Ricans, who consequently were anxious to study English. The high rate of investment in Puerto Rico by U.S. companies fueled rapid industrial growth and an impressive increase in both standards of living and per-capita income. The economic expansion, however, tended to benefit the Puerto Ricans who were receptive to Americanization. Knowledge of English gave them an advantage in seeking employment with the American firms.

At the same time, most of those who became proficient in the new language remained culturally tied to traditional Puerto Rico. Drawn to the economic dynamism and democracy offered by the United States, they still thought of themselves as Hispanic and Caribbean in culture. Knowledge of English did not erase the Puerto Rican roots of those who immigrated to the mainland and left them ambivalent regarding their true culture. Their Puerto Rican roots acted as obstacles to their complete assimilation into American society, and many experienced serious difficulties in adapting to their new home.

Cultural nationalism continued to surface on the island. In 1962, Commissioner of Education Cándido Olivares touched off a tumult when he threatened to deny accreditation to some Catholic schools that taught in English rather than Spanish. Parents sending students to the church schools were outraged, since many had purposely chosen such institutions to ensure that their children would learn English. Luis Ferré, the prostatehood governor of the island, immediately criticized Olivares for trying to deny parents control over the education of their offspring. At roughly the same time, a congressional commission investigated the political status of Puerto Rico and its potential for becoming a state. Senator Henry M. Jackson voiced a concern that permeated the commission: To be granted statehood, Puerto Rico would have to accept English as the official language.

In effect, the 1949 decision to make Spanish the language of instruction did not resolve the problems of bilingualism and biculturalism because the ultimate political status of the island remained to be determined. Modernization and industrialization continued to confront Puerto Ricans with ambivalent feelings about their language and culture. By the 1970's, the island and the United States had become more conciliatory regarding Americanization. Most Puerto Ricans agreed that their culture was valuable and deserved preservation. Thus, if they eventually sought statehood, it would have to be under conditions that permitted them to retain their cultural roots. In the meantime, the mushrooming Hispanic population in the United States forced many non-Hispanics to accord them linguistic and cultural tolerance, if not complete acceptance and equality.

## Bibliography

Columbia University. Teachers College. Institute of Field Studies. *Public Education*

806 *Great Events from History II*

*and the Future of Puerto Rico: A Curriculum Survey, 1948-1949.* 1950. Reprint. New York: Arno Press, 1975. Provides a dispassionate look at the state of Puerto Rican schools just before Spanish definitively became the medium of instruction. Chapter 15 deals specifically with the language issue.

Epstein, Erwin H., ed. *Politics and Education in Puerto Rico: A Documentary Survey of the Language Issue.* Metuchen, N.J.: Scarecrow Press, 1970. Contains articles, documents, and speeches outlining the difficulties inherent in preserving Puerto Rican biculturalism, given the island's political ties to the United States. The selections deal primarily with the period after 1949. Epstein is sympathetic to the Puerto Rican dilemma.

Gutiérrez, Edith Algren de. *The Movement Against Teaching English in Schools of Puerto Rico.* Lanham, Md.: University Press of America, 1987. Although primarily concerned with the rhetoric used by those who opposed English as the language of instruction, Gutiérrez includes brief historical descriptions of the conflict during its various stages. Brief but informative.

Lewis, Gordon K. *Puerto Rico: Freedom and Power in the Caribbean.* New York: Monthly Review Press, 1963. A sympathetic analysis of Puerto Rican culture and the island's struggle to survive as a colony first of Spain and then of the United States. Although it is a general survey, it does address the language issue briefly. More important, it provides the historical context for understanding the ambivalence many Puerto Ricans feel for the United States.

Osuna, Juan José. *A History of Education in Puerto Rico.* 2d ed. New York: Arno Press, 1975. Moderate in tone. Originally written as the author's thesis at Columbia University in 1923, it was later expanded in an edition published in 1949. Although it deals only with the language problem until 1948, the year before it was resolved, Osuna's work is the classic study of Puerto Rican education during the island's first half century as an American territory.

Rodríguez Pacheco, Osvaldo, ed. *A Land of Hope in Schools: A Reader in the History of Public Education in Puerto Rico, 1940 to 1965.* San Juan, Puerto Rico: Editorial Edil, 1976. This useful collection of transcribed speeches and other documents contains a chapter on the language question, along with other material on the period when the crisis was finally resolved.

Walsh, Catherine E. *Pedagogy and the Struggle for Voice: Issues of Language, Power, and Schooling for Puerto Ricans.* Critical Studies in Education. New York: Bergin & Garvey, 1991. Written from the perspective of radical social science theory, this study reviews the language debate in Chapter 1. To the author, the American imposition of English as the language of instruction was an attempt by a colonial power to subjugate the island.

*Kendall W. Brown*

## Cross-References

The United Nations Adopts the Declaration of the Rights of the Child (1959),

p. 1038; Cubans Flee to Florida and Receive Assistance (1960's), p. 1044; Congress Enacts the Bilingual Education Act (1968), p. 1402; Congress Requires Bilingual Elections to Protect Minority Rights (1975), p. 1817; The United Nations Adopts the Convention on the Rights of the Child (1989), p. 2529.

# THE GENEVA CONVENTION ESTABLISHES
# NORMS OF CONDUCT IN WARFARE

*Category of event:* International norms
*Time:* August 12, 1949
*Locale:* Geneva, Switzerland

*The Geneva Convention of 1949 established norms of conduct in warfare that addressed assistance and protection of members of the armed forces, prisoners of war, and civilians*

*Principal personages:*
JEAN HENRI DUNANT (1828-1910), the Swiss founder of the International Red Cross and joint winner of the first Nobel Peace Prize
U THANT (1909-1974), the Burmese secretary-general of the United Nations from 1962 to 1971
PAUL RUEGGER (1897-1969), the Swiss diplomat who served as president of the International Red Cross from 1948 to 1955

## Summary of Event

The unparalleled loss of life in World War II refocused efforts to establish norms of conduct in warfare, efforts that diplomats and scholars have made throughout history. The first Generva Convention of 1864 laid the groundwork for a number of subsequent conventions. Article six of the first of the Geneva "laws on war" attempted to establish the principle that "wounded or sick combatants, to whatever nation they may belong, shall be collected and cared for." A major force behind this convention was Jean Henri Dunant, the founder of the International Red Cross. The 1864 convention was a significant departure from previous agreements among states that addressed rules of state conduct in war, innovative because it moved toward the protection of individual human rights during hostilities.

During World War II, the principles contained in the original Geneva Convention and its revisions were not successful in preventing military actions against noncombatants. While existing conventions did protect several categories of persons, events during the war suggested that the original Geneva Convention required revision. The German policy of genocide against European Jews and the Allied policy of bombing civilian population centers (including the atomic destruction of the cities of Hiroshima and Nagasaki) were examples of violations of the humanitarian principles contained in the original convention. After the war, the War Crimes Tribunals in Nuremberg and Tokyo suggested to the international community that the most flagrant violations of human rights during war were not against soldiers or prisoners but rather against civilians in the form of forced labor, relocation, and torture.

Before World War II ended, there was general agreement that the protection of individual human rights would be incorporated in some fashion into the United Nations organization proposed by the Allied powers. The London Charter that established the Military Tribunals at Nuremberg identified murder, enslavement, deportation, and other actions as crimes against humanity. The United Nations Charter of 1945 declared that the advancement of human rights was a primary goal of member states. The modern concept of human rights was also contained in the United Nations' Universal Declaration of Human Rights of 1948.

In the twentieth century, the establishment of norms of conduct designed to protect civilian populations in war has been addressed primarily by the International Committee of the Red Cross (ICRC), headquartered in Geneva, Switzerland. Although the United Nations has frequently referred to the Geneva Conventions of 1949, the conventions were prepared under the auspices of the ICRC and the Swiss government. By the late 1940's, the efforts of the United Nations to establish laws of war had fallen victim to the superpower rivalry between the Soviet Union and the United States. Between 1945 and 1948, the ICRC conferred with a number of diplomats and experts about clarifying the existing conventions as well as establishing more efficient monitoring structures.

These efforts led to the Diplomatic Conference for the Establishment of International Conventions for the Protection of Victims of War, held in Geneva from April to August, 1949. The sixty-four states represented at the conference endorsed four international conventions that addressed postwar concerns about wounded combatants in the field and at sea, the treatment of prisoners of war, and protection of civilians in periods of state warfare. The overall agreement was divided into four separate conventions linked by general principles included in the preamble of each convention.

The first and second conventions were not dramatic departures from international agreements established before World War II. The 1949 convention on the amelioration of the condition of wounded, sick, and shipwrecked military personnel were in large part a restatement of the humanitarian principles contained in the 1929 Geneva Convention and the 1907 Hague Convention. In both conventions, combatants on land or sea who were unable or unwilling to engage in military operations were not to be murdered, tortured, deliberately subjected to illness, or denied medical treatment. The first two conventions also restated both the noncombatant status of medical personnel and clergy as well as the special status of vehicles and facilities marked with the distinctive symbol of ICRC.

The third convention, the Geneva Convention Relative to the Treatment of Prisoners of War, was an attempt to broaden the 1929 Geneva Convention that addressed treatment of prisoners. While many elements of the 1929 convention remained, the later conventions were significant because they attempted to grant prisoner-of-war status to a number of categories of persons who were previously denied such status. Although various articles of the convention dealt with the physical treatment of prisoners, the convention was significant because it extended prisoner-of-war status to a number of different categories of persons. Under the 1949 conventions, partisans, regular forces who profess allegiance to a state not recognized by the detaining power, and military support staff possessed the same rights under international law as regular combatants. The convention also stated that prisoners cannot be punished without a proper legal tribunal.

The fourth convention was the first international agreement on the laws of war to establish norms of conduct in the treatment of civilians. Previous conventions, including the 1864 Geneva Convention, had not specifically addressed the rights of civilians during war. Although most of the provisions in the 1949 convention were adopted by the ICRC in 1939, the outbreak of World War II prevented their adoption. The Geneva Convention Relative to the Protection of Civilian Persons in Times of War, adopted in 1949, was in large part accepted by the international community as a response to the savage Nazi wartime occupation of Europe. The Nazi practices of denial of medical care to civilians, mental and physical coercion, imprisonment of civilians as hostages, and use of civilians for medical experiments were prohibited. The fourth convention established a code of conduct for occupying powers that prohibited murder, torture, and corporal punishment of civilians in occupied territories. The fourth convention also established a system of monitoring actions of states through neutral states and the ICRC.

## Impact of Event

At first glance, the large number of nations that were parties to the 1949 conventions suggests that the principles contained in the conventions became central components of international law. Unlike domestic law, international law is based on custom and precedents. States generally tend to obey international law when it benefits their interests. Events after World War II suggest that the legal and political difficulties that hindered previous conventions also applied to the conventions of 1949. While a number of signatory states have publicly embraced the conventions over the years, it is apparent that states have not forsworn the use of armed force. Historically, the creation of standards of conduct in war has tended to lag behind both military strategy and technology. It is clear when examining the conduct of wars since 1949 that civilians continued to be subjected to the burdens of armed conflict. Because they were in large part a response to the devastation of World War II, the 1949 conventions did not address the conduct of military operations. The conventions also did not anticipate the tremendous increase in internal armed conflict and the resulting impact on civilian populations.

Most twentieth century armed conflicts after 1945 were not those between sovereign states, addressed in the 1949 conventions. Most armed conflict has been in the form of civil wars that were often supported by one or more outside states. States that were signatories to the 1949 convention frequently took the position that internal conflicts did not fall under the 1949 convention because they did not meet the convention's definition of armed conflict. There were many examples of states refusing to recognize the application of the 1949 conventions to internal armed conflicts. During the 1960's and 1970's, the government of Iraq denied the ICRC access to Kurdish populations because it took the position that the Geneva protocols did not apply to civil conflict. Despite numerous reports of civilian hardships, the Ethiopian government provided a similar explanation when it denied the ICRC access to the Eritrean populations in the 1970's.

At an individual level, the 1949 conventions did not address the difficulties involved in compelling states to follow the conventions protecting civilians. While many states have recognized the human rights of military prisoners, the welfare of civilians has often been ignored by states that publicly embrace the first three Geneva conventions of 1949. In 1971, the Pakistani government went to the International Court of Justice to secure protection for members of its armed forces that had been detained by India. During the same period, the Pakistani government failed to show similar respect for Indian or Bangladeshi civilians in war zones.

In 1970, in response to the Proclamation of Teheran, issued by the International Conference on Human Rights in 1968, United Nations Secretary-General U Thant issued a report that called for a renewed emphasis on the protection of prisoners and civilians close to battle zones. U Thant's report proposed that the ICRC expand on article three of the 1949 convention to apply protection to persons not participating in armed conflict. From 1971 to 1973, the ICRC held meetings in Geneva to prepare texts of two protocols to the 1949 conventions. By 1974, the protocols had been submitted to the Diplomatic Conference on the Reaffirmation and Development of Humanitarian Law in Geneva, and in June, 1977, they were adopted. Protocol 1 extended the coverage of the four Geneva conventions to wars of "national liberation." The broadening of the definition of armed conflict led the United States and other states to reject ratification of the protocol. Protocol 1 also prohibited methods of warfare that cause unnecessary suffering to civilian populations. Protocol 2 was an attempt to modify the rights of noncombatants in international armed conflict.

## Bibliography

Bailey, Sydney D. *Prohibitions and Restraints in War.* London: Oxford University Press, 1972. An excellent examination of the philosophical foundations of "just war" theory as well as an account of the contemporary interpretation of the 1949 Geneva Convention. A useful resource for students interested in humanitarian law or human rights in war and their relationship to arms control and disarmament. Includes notations, several appendices, and an index.

Best, Geoffrey. "The Law of War in a World of Co-existences." In *Humanity in Warfare: The Modern History of the International Law of Armed Conflict.* New York: Columbia University Press, 1980. A well-researched and thoughtful examination of the immediate postwar order and the interpretation of the law of war after 1945. Includes a chronology, notations, a comprehensive bibliography, and an index.

Coursier, Henri. *Course of Five Lessons on the Geneva Convention.* Geneva, Switzerland: International Committee of the Red Cross, 1963. A short and very detailed description of the four elements of the 1949 convention. Useful for students interested in the legal foundations and the Red Cross interpretation of the protocols. Includes notations, bibliographies, and appendices.

Draper, G. I. A. D. *The Red Cross Conventions*. New York: Praeger, 1958. A detailed account of the 1949 convention by an English professor of law. This volume is useful for students interested in the essential legal principles underlying the convention. Includes notations, the entire text of the 1949 convention, and an index.

_____. "Wars of National Liberation and War Criminality." In *Restraints on War*, edited by Michael Howard. New York: Oxford University Press, 1979. An account of the classical interpretation of the law of war and the 1949 Geneva protocols, including applicability in "just" and "unjust" warfare. Includes notations, suggested reading list, and index.

Forsythe, David P. *Humanitarian Politics: The International Committee of the Red Cross*. Baltimore, Md.: The Johns Hopkins University Press, 1977. A standard history of the Red Cross movement and the ICRC's efforts to protect human rights around the world. Includes notations, appendices, and index.

Green, Leslie C. "Human Rights and the Law of Armed Conflict." In *Essays on the Modern Law of War*. Dobbs Ferry, N.Y.: Transnational Publishers, 1985. An excellent account of the historical development of rules of armed conflict. A thorough introduction to the complex subject of human rights in international law. Includes standard notations and index.

Meron, Theodor. "The Geneva Conventions as Customary Law." *American Journal of International Law* 81 (January, 1989): 348-370. A detailed account of the influence of the 1949 convention on contemporary international law. The dispute between Nicaragua and the United States in the International Court of Justice is contrasted with the current interpretation of the convention as customary international humanitarian law. Includes extensive notations.

_____. *Human Rights Law-Making in the United Nations: A Critique of Instruments and Processes*. Oxford, England: Clarendon Press, 1986. A comprehensive examination of United Nations efforts to influence human rights worldwide. Because Meron draws extensively from United Nations sources, this volume is recommended to students interested in the United Nations interpretation of the 1949 Geneva Convention. Includes an index and several appendices.

Roberts, Adam, and Richard Guelff, eds. *Documents on the Laws of War*. Oxford, England: Clarendon Press, 1982. An extensive collection of international agreements, dating from 1856 to 1981, on international norms of conduct in warfare. All documents are introduced by excellent prefatory notes that briefly describe the agreements. An excellent source for students of international law. Includes charts, bibliography, and index.

*Lawrence Clark III*

### Cross-References

Legal Norms of Behavior in Warfare Formulated by the Hague Conference (1907), p. 92; Nazi War Criminals Are Tried in Nuremberg (1945), p. 667; The United Na-

# THE UNITED NATIONS CREATES AN AGENCY
# TO AID PALESTINIAN REFUGEES

*Category of event:* Refugee relief
*Time:* December 9, 1949
*Locale:* United Nations, New York City

*Lack of political will to solve the problems of Palestinian refugees led to the establishment of the United Nations Relief and Works Agency for Palestine Refugees*

Principal personages:
ARTHUR BALFOUR (1848-1930), the British author of the Balfour Declaration, which promised to establish a Jewish homeland
DAVID BEN-GURION (1886-1973), the prime minister and defense minister of Israel
COUNT FOLKE BERNADOTTE (1895-1948), the first United Nations mediator in Palestine
RALPH BUNCHE (1904-1971), the successor to Bernadotte as U.N. mediator
MOSHE SHERTOK (1894-1965), the Israeli foreign minister and director of the political department of the Jewish Agency

## Summary of Event

The Palestinian refugees are a primarily Arab population who have been uprooted from their homes and land by the wars and political problems that have plagued the Middle East since the partition of Palestine in 1947. Of more than one million people in Palestine at that time, approximately two-thirds were rural peasants and one-third were professionals, landlords, small traders, and artisans.

The area that is now Israel came under the control of the United Kingdom through a mandate of the League of Nations after World War I. The Balfour Declaration of 1917, designed by British foreign secretary Arthur James Balfour, promised a national home to world Jewry at an unspecified future date. The United Kingdom continued to control the area under the mandate until 1948. On May 14, 1948, the British terminated the mandate and left the newly created United Nations with the problem of creating a Jewish state amid the Palestinian Arabs. There had been U.N. discussion of the problem prior to termination of the British mandate. The United Nations decided in November, 1947, to partition Palestine into a Jewish state and a much larger Arab state.

Palestinian Arabs feared for their safety within a Jewish state. Hostilities between Israeli and Arab forces began in 1948. The initial exodus of refugees that began in November, 1947, continued until March. Middle- and upper-class Arabs fled from Jerusalem, Jaffa, and Haifa. This flight triggered exodus from rural areas as well. Arabs became increasingly unsure that the Arab forces that had intruded into Palestine would be able to protect them from Jewish forces.

In the second phase of the mass exodus, from April, 1948, until May 14, 1948— the expiration of the British mandate—two hundred thousand to three hundred thousand Arabs left. Jewish defense plans called for securing the rear of their state's territory and its main roads against subversion. During this time, Israel received somewhere near three hundred thousand Jewish immigrants, whose resettlement in Arab property coincided with the mass exodus of Arabs.

Israeli military operations against Arab forces in mid-July, 1948, created a third surge of about one hundred thousand refugees. This group went mainly to eastern Palestine, upper Galilee, Lebanon, and the Egyptian portion of the Gaza Strip. The fourth major exodus of Arabs took place in October and November, 1948, amid Israeli military operations in the Negev Desert and Galilee, when some 150,000 fled to Transjordan, the Gaza Strip, and the Hebron Hills. Israeli forces apparently had never been given a definite order to expel Arabs, but wartime uncertainties, atrocities, and Israeli cleanup operations achieved the same effect.

In the exodus as a whole, most northern Palestinians, from the areas surrounding Haifa, Acre, and Galilee, fled north into Syria and Lebanon. Those from the south— from Jaffa, Gaza, and the Beersheba district—crowded into the narrow Gaza Strip bordering Egypt. By the end of 1948, about 726,000 Arabs had fled, leaving another 150,000 in the new state of Israel. Another 200,000 to 250,000 who did not need relief found refuge in Jordan, Kuwait, Lebanon, the United Arab Republic, and Syria.

The United Nations had appointed Count Folke Bernadotte, a Swede, as a mediator in the area on the eve of the British mandate's expiration. He was to supervise a cease-fire between the Arabs and Israelis and promote a peaceful resolution of their dispute. Almost from the date of the British mandate's expiration, Bernadotte pressured the Israeli government to admit the right of return to a substantial number of refugees.

Repatriation and resettlement of refugees quickly became a major problem for the United Nations. Only Transjordan, where most of the refugees (about one-half million) took refuge, granted them citizenship. Other governments, such as those of Lebanon and Egypt, did not want to incorporate large bodies of foreigners into their systems, for political and other reasons.

There were fundamental differences of belief between the Israelis and the United Nations concerning the causes and solution of the mass exodus. Israeli foreign minister Moshe Shertok told Bernadotte in July, 1948, that war had brought the refugee problem in its wake. Bernadotte, though, reported to the United Nations in September, 1948, that he believed the exodus to have been a result of panic caused by fighting in Arab countries and by rumors of alleged or real acts of Israeli terrorism and expulsion. Bernadotte thought that the solution to the problem lay in repatriating refugees. The Israeli government, however, denied having expelled the Arabs and consequently refused to shoulder the responsibility of repatriation. The Israeli government stood ready to aid in the resettlement of refugees in neighboring countries, rather than in Israel itself.

By October, 1948, the refugee situation was critical, according to Ralph Bunche, who had become the acting mediator after Bernadotte's assassination by a Jewish terrorist group that objected to his support of the Arab refugees. Urgent measures were needed to avert starvation and other distress. Voluntary relief organizations, such as the International Committee of the Red Cross and America Friends Service Committee, and U.N. agencies such as the World Health Organization (WHO) and the U.N. International Children's Emergency Fund (UNICEF) were already active. On November 19, 1948, the United Nations created the United Nations Relief for Palestine Refugees (UNRPR) program for the purposes of coordinating relief activities and raising funds for relief operations. Relief operations themselves were left, as before, to the voluntary agencies.

A potentially far more important decision was made by the U.N. General Assembly. Basing its decision on Bernadotte's final progress report, it recognized the right of refugees to return to their land, now part of Israel, or to receive compensation for their property if they chose not to return. To attend to the problems of compensation or repatriation of refugees, the General Assembly on December 11, 1948, created the Conciliation Commission for Palestine (CCP). The CCP was to work for conciliation between the Arabs and Israel and to form plans for economic development, repatriation, and rehabilitation of refugees or for payment of compensation. Few refugees, however, had ever been ready to take compensation. On the other hand, Israel rejected all appeals for refugee resettlement in its territory or land it had subsequently annexed. This was the primary impasse necessitating a permanent U.N. agency to attend to long-term needs of refugees. The United Nations had no enforcement mechanism behind its demands.

For all practical purposes, any long-term solution to the refugee problem meant a gradual integration of refugees into the economic life of their host countries. In August, 1949, the CCP set up the U.N. Economic Survey Mission (the Clapp Mission) to survey the prospects of such a long-term solution. The Clapp Mission recommended the establishment of a new agency to attend to the long-term objectives of the refugees. This agency would formulate its own plans and execute them with proper funding and would not simply coordinate the activities of other relief organizations. Such an agency could concern itself directly with the affairs of the refugees.

The General Assembly voted to establish the U.N. Relief and Works Agency for Palestine Refugees in the Near East (UNRWA) on December 9, 1949. The UNRWA was to be a specialized organization separate from other relief agencies and headed by a director appointed by the secretary-general of the United Nations in consultation with an advisory commission comprising representatives of the United States, the United Kingdom, France, and Turkey. The agency's director was to report annually to the General Assembly on progress in the agency's mission of negotiating to obtain employment for refugees within their host countries, among other resettlement aims.

## Impact of Event

Few problems in international affairs proved as intractable as the resettlement of Palestinian refugees. The United Nations foresaw the difficulties in the way of a quick settlement of the problem when it entrusted the UNRWA first to attend to urgent relief work and then to evolve its works and rehabilitation program.

When early resolution of the problem became recognized as an unrealistic goal, the UNRWA concentrated its energies on long-term educational projects for refugees —general education for youngsters and technical, vocational, and teachers' training for adults. These projects would continue for more than forty years. More than 60 percent of the UNRWA budget was allocated to such projects, with relief and health services accounting for about 30 percent. The UNRWA depended for its smooth operation on regular financing, mostly through voluntary contributions, and peaceful conditions. Both of these conditions failed to be met on occasion, forcing the agency temporarily to suspend or curtail operations.

Refugees at first took shelter in temporary camps and housing. Many had moved out of Palestine in communities and migrated as such to towns and villages, taking refuge in mosques, churches, schools, and abandoned buildings. They settled in over-crowded, often unsanitary housing with poor ventilation and little privacy. Often, several families were housed in one room, with nothing more than sacks or similar hangings partitioning them in their corners. All activities of daily life were performed in these cramped spaces.

The physical condition of the refugees improved once housing, relief, and sanitation projects of the UNRWA were put into organized operation in different host countries. Basic rations were distributed and medical services rendered in clinics and hospitals set up by the UNRWA.

The physical loss of the refugees' homes and land has been compounded by their fear about the future. The refusal of the Israeli government to resettle the refugees in its territory has been only one side of the problem. The other side has been that the refugees are reluctant to settle permanently in their host countries for fear of losing their right to their homes. This has kept the crisis alive into a second generation of refugees. Their realization that a solution will be harder to find as time passes has added to their bitterness and frustration, which has erupted from time to time into open revolt and violence directed against the Israeli government.

The United Nations recognized the right of refugees to return to their homeland if they so wished. To deny that right would be an offense against elemental justice. The fact is, however, that most had no home to which to return. Homes were either destroyed or passed on to Israeli immigrants. Nevertheless, in the opinion of the United Nations, the mass exodus of 1947-1948 and in subsequent years did not absolve the Israeli government from the responsibility of resettling the Palestinian refugees. Similarly, the establishment of the UNRWA, in the opinion of the United Nations, did not prejudice the refugees' right of return to their homeland, which the United Nations continued to state. The problem has continued to grow, as more refugees fled from continuing war and invasion of property. The total number of refugees was near two million by 1991.

In spite of financial constraints and political uncertainties, the UNRWA has by and large fulfilled its limited mission. It has managed a situation of seemingly permanent crisis. The resolution of the crisis, which depends on political will, has lain outside the scope of its operation.

## Bibliography

Bernadotte, Folke. *To Jerusalem.* London: Hodder & Stoughton, 1951. Posthumously published diary of the principal U.N. mediator. Shows his determination to succeed in the difficult task of monitoring the cease-fire during the turbulent times between July and September, 1948. Appendices and index.

Chaliand, Gerard. *The Palestine Resistance.* Harmondsworth, England: Penguin, 1972. Although mainly dealing with Palestinian resistance efforts against Israeli authorities, this work includes an informative chapter on the refugees and the role of the UNRWA in Arab countries outside Palestine. Includes an index.

Hadawi, Sami. *Bitter Harvest: A History of Modern Palestine.* New York: Olive Branch Press, 1983. Historical account of the Palestinian problem from the expiration of the British mandate until the start of the West Bank uprising. Contains a useful chapter on refugees. The narration is charged with emotion, and is forceful yet judiciously documented. The author, an Arab activist, has firsthand experience of the refugee problem. Bibliography, index, and appendix containing important documents.

Moore, Benny. *The Birth of the Palestinian Refugee Problem, 1947-1949.* Cambridge, England: Cambridge University Press, 1987. In-depth study of the origins, development, and present status of the refugee problem, largely documented from both official and unofficial Israeli sources. Holds a different view of the origin of the refugee problem from that of Michael Palumbo (listed below), namely that it was a result of the Arab-Israeli war and later accelerated by deliberate expulsion. Contains an important note on the controversy over the number of refugees, bibliography of primary and secondary sources, maps, and an index.

_____. "Operation Dani and the Palestinian Exodus from Lydda and Ramle in 1948." *Middle Eastern Journal* 40 (1986): 82-109. A graphic account of how two towns in Palestine were attacked in July, 1948, and their people expelled. Morris exonerates the Israeli cabinet, laying the blame largely on defense forces.

Palumbo, Michael. *The Palestinian Catastrophe: The 1949 Expulsion of a People from Their Homeland.* London: Faber & Faber, 1987. A forceful narration of how the Palestinian problem arose, with a brief note on the developments during the years before World War II. According to Palumbo, displacement of Palestinians was done in a planned way to make room for a Jewish state. Contains extensive notes on primary sources, maps, sketches, and an index.

Quigley, John. *Palestine and Israel: A Challenge to Justice.* Durham, N.C.: Duke University Press, 1990. The author takes a stand on the refugee question similar to Palumbo's, but he adds emphasis on implications of the refugees' status in international law. Includes developments such as the uprising on the West Bank and suggestions on the United Nations' role in the refugees' right of self-determination. Bibliography, notes, and index.

Smith, Charles D. *Palestine and the Arab-Israeli Conflict.* New York: St. Martin's Press, 1988. A chronological history of Palestine from Roman times to Camp David and beyond. The refugee problem is put in the historical context of international politics. The author finds no possible solution to the problem. Valuable for historical perspective. Select bibliography and index.

Thicknesse, S. G. *Arab Refugees.* London: Royal Institute of International Affairs, 1949. Dated but useful survey of the refugee problem, written soon after the initial conflict in Palestine between Arabs and Israelis. In view of the difficulties of resettling refugees in Palestine, the author considers the possibility of resettlement in Jordan and other friendly Arab countries. Maps and appendix.

United Nations. *The Right of Return of the Palestinian Refugees.* New York: Author, 1978. Brief and cogent argument from the official standpoint of the United Nations, based on the rights of the refugees in international law and according to the Universal Declaration of Human Rights and other documents. Gives a brief overview of the origins of the Palestinian exodus and the role of the Conciliation Commission in attaining the refugee rehabilitation. Has a section on the legal and political obstacles of refugee return. Contains a list of U.N. resolutions from 1950 to 1977 affirming the right of return. Appendix and bibliography.

*Asit Kumar Sen*

## Cross-References

The Balfour Declaration Supports a Jewish Homeland in Palestine (1917), p. 235; The Paris Peace Conference Includes Protection for Minorities (1919), p. 252; Palestinian Refugees Flee to Neighboring Arab Countries (1948), p. 749; Israel Is Created as a Homeland for Jews (1948), p. 761; The United Nations Adopts the Universal Declaration of Human Rights (1948), p. 789; The United Nations High Commissioner for Refugees Statute Is Approved (1950), p. 855; The U.N. Convention Relating to the Status of Refugees Is Adopted (1951), p. 867; Palestinian Refugees Form the Palestine Liberation Organization (1964), p. 1241.

# U.S. GOVERNMENT ENCOURAGES NATIVE AMERICANS TO SETTLE IN CITIES

*Category of event:* Indigenous peoples' rights
*Time:* The 1950's
*Locale:* The United States

*The United States government actively encouraged Native Americans to leave reservations and to settle in cities, contributing to a rapid increase in the number of urban Native Americans*

    *Principal personages:*
        DILLON S. MYER (1891-1982), the U.S. commissioner of Indian affairs from 1950 to 1953
        GLENN L. EMMONS (1895-    ), the U.S. commissioner of Indian affairs from 1953 to 1961
        PHILLEO NASH (1909-1987), the commissioner of Indian affairs from 1961 to 1966

## Summary of Event

From the end of the eighteenth century until the 1930's, the United States government pursued a variety of policies in carrying out its constitutional responsibility for the conduct of Native-American relations. A succession of programs had as their goal the ultimate assimilation of Native Americans into the mainstream of American life. Such policies generally showed little respect for Native American culture and viewed tribes as barriers to successful assimilation. During the Franklin D. Roosevelt Administration, the direction of federal policy shifted dramatically with the passage of the Indian Reorganization Act of 1934. Tribes were again recognized as legal and important aspects of Native American life. Under the leadership of Commissioner of Indian Affairs John Collier, the Bureau of Indian Affairs (BIA) showed a new sensitivity to Native-American culture, and the pressure for assimilation lessened. This "Indian New Deal" seemed to indicate that a new era of Native-American policy was under way, one that would respect and sustain the distinctive character of Native American cultures.

This policy direction, however, proved short-lived. In the late 1940's, Congress and public opinion began to press for a return to assimilationist policies. By 1950, it was clear that major changes in federal policy were coming. Two of the most notable new initiatives were the policies of termination and relocation. The former aimed at "freeing" Native Americans from dependence on the federal government by terminating tribes as legal entities and ending the trust relationship the federal government held toward them; the latter aimed at bringing Native Americans into the mainstream of urban industrial society by encouraging them to relocate in cities. Although termination and relocation were often seen as related policies, especially by Native Americans, they were in fact distinct. Termination may have effected the more dramatic changes, such as the formal dissolution of several tribes and reservations, but the policy of relocation proved more long-lasting and had a greater impact on Native-American life in general.

A number of developments paved the way for the relocation program. Urban Native Americans were already a reality, and their numbers increased markedly during World War II. During the war, some twenty-five thousand Native Americans served in the Armed Forces, and almost twice that number left reservations for war-related work. Many members of both groups settled in urban areas after the war. There was also concern that some reservations were becoming overpopulated. In 1947, the BIA set up a modest program designed to find off-reservation employment for Hopis and Navajos. In the following year, the Hoover Commission, then investigating ways to improve the efficiency of the executive branch, recommended that a large-scale program of job training and placement be established to meet the threat of overpopulated reservations.

It was in this context that, in 1950, Dillon S. Myer became commissioner of Indian affairs. A conscientious and strong-minded administrator, Myer had been head of the War Relocation Authority during World War II. In that capacity he had overseen the camps in which Japanese Americans had been interned. He came to view reservations as similar to the internment camps that had isolated Japanese Americans from American society. At the end of the war, he had tried to foster the reentry of Japanese Americans into American life as individuals, rather than have them remain apart as a group. A similar solution seemed desirable for Native Americans, especially because Myer genuinely believed that they could never enjoy an acceptable standard of living as long as they remained on reservations. He supported both relocation and termination as means of assimilation.

In 1950, the BIA began its first general relocation program. Placement offices were opened in Aberdeen, Washington; Billings, Montana; Minneapolis, Minnesota; and Portland, Oregon. In 1952, Myer began to plan for a nationwide "Operation Relocation." Congressional funding was increased, and financial assistance was provided to Native Americans willing to relocate. Congress, however, rejected Myer's request that it also fund a vocational education program for Native Americans.

Glenn L. Emmons, a New Mexico banker, succeeded Myer at the BIA. He was an enthusiastic supporter of the relocation policy, and during his tenure (1953-1961) the program expanded and became the responsibility of a new relocation division within the BIA. Relocation offices were established on most reservations as well as in Oklahoma, to serve the nonreservation tribes there. In the early years of the program, there was a tendency toward a hard-sell approach, as Native Americans were propagandized and pressured by officials working to meet quotas assigned to them by the relocation division.

Native Americans applying for the program were typically allowed one month to prepare for the transition to urban life. They were given fifty dollars apiece to cover moving expenses, one-way train or bus tickets to relocation cities, and small sums for subsistence. (Originally, Los Angeles, Chicago, and Denver were designated as relocation cities, but the list was subsequently expanded to include Cincinnati, Oakland, San Jose, San Francisco, Cleveland, St. Louis, and Dallas.) Once at their destinations, the new urban Native Americans received help from local relocation offices in obtaining housing and employment, including a month's financial assistance (forty dollars a week for an individual or couple, more for larger families).

The BIA reported that the program was successful, and Congress increased appropriations during the late 1950's. Relocation, however, also attracted a large number of critics both inside and outside the ranks of Native Americans. To many Native Americans, relocation seemed simply another face of the hated policy of termination, an association that caused much distrust toward the program and one that caused many urban migrants to move on their own. In 1956, the Association on American Indian Affairs, a group largely made up of sympathetic non-Native Americans, issued a report that listed some forty-eight specific criticisms of the program. Many of these centered around the problems experienced by the newly arrived urban Native Americans.

Indeed, the experiences of many of those who left the reservation were too often characterized by frustration and failure. One of the basic problems was that many Native Americans were simply not prepared for life in the metropolitan United States. Coming from cultures that were often communal and cooperative, many migrants found it difficult to adjust to the impersonal and competitive character of urban life. In many cases, the BIA provided inadequate counseling and insufficient economic support for the transition. Many relocatees received minimal job training, and the employment they obtained often proved to be poorly paid or temporary. Many missed medical and other programs that had been available to them on the reservations. Program participants, in short, often found themselves becoming discouraged slum-dwellers beset by a host of social problems. Particularly noticeable among these was alcoholism. The BIA admitted in 1959 that about a third of those participating in the relocation program had returned to reservations.

Although proclaiming the program a success, the BIA did attempt to respond to criticisms. After 1957, the relocation officers on the reservations modified their sales pitches and employed a less-aggressive approach. Greater attention was paid to preparing those willing to relocate (including family members), and more of an effort was made to determine individual aptitudes for particular occupations. Medical examinations were required, and extended social support services were offered for the first year of urban residence. The effectiveness of such changes, however, became a topic for debate. While the number of urban Native Americans continued to increase—with many migrants not participants in the program—there was little evidence that Native Americans were being assimilated into the mainstream of American society.

Commissioner Emmons did try to complement the relocation program by attempting to increase employment opportunities on reservations through private industrial development. There were many legal complications, however, and investors often proved reluctant to get involved. In the end, fewer than a thousand industrial jobs were created for reservation Native Americans.

Controversy over relocation was often overshadowed by the debate engendered by the policy of termination. BIA support for the latter lessened during the late 1950's, and the policy was effectively ended during the early 1960's. Relocation remained a part of federal policy but was modified under Philleo Nash, the John F. Kennedy Administration's commissioner of Indian affairs. Nash reduced the number of relocation centers and changed the program's name and focus to one of employment assistance. In addition, the voluntary character of the program was given greater emphasis, more attention was paid to job training, and additional stress was placed on finding job placements closer to reservations. There was also greater awareness shown to the needs of the growing number of urban Native Americans who had relocated on their own.

During the 1960's, the thrust of federal policy increasingly focused on the concept of Native-American self-determination. Commissioner Nash faulted the programs of the 1950's for being imposed from above without consultation with the Native Americans involved. Self-determination—the idea that Native Americans should determine for themselves the direction of Native-American policy—became the explicit policy of the administrations of Lyndon B. Johnson and Richard Nixon and culminated in the Indian Self-Determination Act of 1975, which gave Native Americans a much greater voice in the planning and administration of federal programs.

## Impact of Event

The BIA's relocation program was intended to promote the assimilation of Native Americans into American society. It was not noticeably successful in achieving its aim. It did, however, have several important effects on Native American life.

Perhaps the most obvious effect of the relocation program was that it encouraged what became one of the most important post-World War II demographic trends in Native-American life: urbanization. In 1940, urban Native Americans numbered a mere twenty-four thousand (or about 13 percent of the total). By 1980, more than 740,000 Native Americans, almost half the total, lived in urban areas. Los Angeles, with more than sixty thousand Native Americans, had the largest Native American community in the country, although the vast majority of such residents came from outside California. This was a development without precedent in the history of Native Americans. Although the majority of urban Native Americans did not relocate under BIA auspices, the relocation program provided an important impetus. Overall, from 1950 to 1972 more than one hundred thousand Indians moved to cities under the program, and those cities with relocation offices became the main centers of Native American urbanization.

The development of a large urban population had important consequences for Native-American life. Although statistical measures of housing and income showed that urban Native Americans enjoyed a higher material standard of living than did those still on reservations, alcoholism and other social ills continued to trouble them.

Urban Native Americans, however, tended to be less tolerant of substandard conditions and more critical of government policies. It is noteworthy that many of the leaders of the more radical Native-American movements that appeared in the 1960's and 1970's, such as the American Indian Movement (AIM), were urban Native Americans.

The growth of Native American radicalism was typified by a spirit of pan-Indianism, and this was at least partially a result of urbanization. By bringing together in metropolitan areas Native Americans of diverse tribal backgrounds, the relocation program encouraged interaction among many different Native-American groups. Finding that they were subject to the same treatment and faced similar problems, many became more willing to assume a common front. It may be the crowning irony of relocation that a policy intended to bring Native Americans into the mainstream of American society instead fostered a greater sense of Native American separateness and encouraged a more active and confrontational approach to dealing with the federal government.

## Bibliography

DeRozier, Arthur. "The Past Continues: Indian Relocation in the 1950's." In *Forked Tongues and Broken Treaties*, edited by Donald E. Worcester. Caldwell, Idaho: Caxton, 1975. Sees relocation as part of the termination policy and a contributing factor to the radicalism of the 1960's and 1970's. Also provides a good sense of what the process was like for those who participated in the program.

Fixico, Donald L. *Termination and Relocation: Federal Indian Policy, 1945-1966.* Albuquerque: University of New Mexico Press, 1986. An in-depth survey of federal policy toward Native Americans over two decades. Sees termination and relocation as failed policies whose roots were very much in the Harry S. Truman Administration. Fixico believes that the BIA and Congress assumed a willingness on the part of Native Americans to assimilate into urban society that simply was not there. Endnotes, bibliography, and index.

Gundlich, James H., and Alden E. Roberts. "Native American Indian Migration and Relocation: Success or Failure?" *Pacific Sociological Review* 21 (January, 1978): 117-128. The authors attempt to evaluate the success of the relocation program by comparing the experiences of Native Americans who moved under its auspices with those who migrated to urban areas on their own. Their evidence shows that those who were part of the relocation program tended to be more successful in their adjustment.

Kvasnicka, Robert M., and Herman J. Viola, eds. *The Commissioners of Indian Affairs, 1824-1977.* Lincoln: University of Nebraska Press, 1979. Collected biographies of the various individuals who have headed the BIA. Those by Patricia K. Ourada, on Dillon S. Myer and Glenn L. Emmons, and by Margaret Connell Szasz, on Philleo Nash, are particularly useful for students of relocation policy. Each entry has endnotes and a note on sources. Index.

Olson, James S., and Raymond Wilson. *Native Americans in the Twentieth Century.*

Provo, Utah: Brigham Young University Press, 1984. A sound overall survey of Native-American life in the twentieth century, sympathetic to its subject. Useful for putting relocation and other federal policies in context. Each chapter contains a list of suggested readings. Index.

Prucha, Francis Paul. *The Great Father: The United States Government and the American Indian.* 2 vols. Lincoln: University of Nebraska Press, 1984. The definitive study of federal policy toward Native Americans. Sees relocation as complementing termination. Also available in a one-volume abridged edition. Extensive bibliographic essay and index.

Sorkin, Alan L. *The Urban American Indian.* Lexington, Mass.: Lexington Books, 1978. Provides an overview of urban social conditions as experienced by Native Americans. Argues for a single agency to manage urban programs for Native Americans and for greater federal assistance. Chapter notes and index.

Waddell, Jack O., and O. Michael Watson, eds. *The American Indian in Urban Society.* Boston: Little, Brown, 1971. A useful collection of essays that cover various urban aspects of Native-American experience. Particularly useful is James E. Officer's summary of federal policies. Officer, a former BIA official, argues that relocation and termination had quite different roots. Chapter bibliographies and index.

*William C. Lowe*

## Cross-References

Intellectuals Form the Society of American Indians (1911), p. 121; The Indian Reorganization Act Offers Autonomy to American Indians (1934), p. 497; Roosevelt Approves Internment of Japanese Americans (1942), p. 595; Government Policies Seek to End the Special Status of Native Americans (1953), p. 897; Congress Ratifies the National Council on Indian Opportunity (1970), p. 1537; Native Americans Occupy Wounded Knee (1973), p. 1709; Congress Extends Voting Rights Reforms (1975), p. 1812; Congress Requires Bilingual Elections to Protect Minority Rights (1975), p. 1817; Inuit File Claim to a Section of Canadian Territory (1976), p. 1876.

# CHINA INITIATES A GENOCIDE POLICY TOWARD TIBETANS

*Categories of event:* Indigenous peoples' rights; atrocities and war crimes
*Time:* 1950
*Locale:* Tibet and China

*China's 1950 invasion and subsequent annexation of Tibet resulted not only in Tibetans' loss of political freedom but also in a large-scale destruction of their religion and culture*

*Principal personages:*
> TENZIN GYATSO (1935-        ), the fourteenth Dalai Lama, leader of the Tibetans, forced to leave Tibet in 1959
> DENG XIAOPING (1904-        ), the Chinese leader who supported introduction of reforms in Tibet during the 1980's but was unwilling to grant any genuine autonomy
> HU YAOBANG (1915-1989), a moderate and reformist member of the Chinese Communist Party who was instrumental in causing reforms in Tibet
> MAO TSE-TUNG (1893-1976), the chair of the People's Republic of China from 1949 until his death; largely responsible for China's invasion of Tibet in 1950 and its harsh policies toward Tibetans in later years
> PANCHEN LAMA (1938-1989), the nominal ruler of Tibet after the Chinese dissolved the Dalai Lama government; openly criticized Beijing's policies toward Tibet just before his death

## Summary of Event

Until 1949, Tibet had enjoyed a semi-independent status. Tibet's international standing had been worked out at a conference in Simla, India, that was attended by Tibetan, Chinese, and British representatives and resulted in the Simla Convention of 1914. Representing a compromise between Tibet's desire to become independent and China's claim for greater control, the convention accepted China's suzerainty over the territory but granted Tibetans full control over their internal affairs, including the right to have their own army.

After a long civil war in China, Mao Tse-tung's army finally succeeded in establishing a Communist government in Beijing in October, 1949. The new government soon announced its intention to "liberate" Tibet. As a first step, and in order to force capitulation on the part of Tibet's ruler, the Dalai Lama, Mao's People's Liberation Army (PLA) soon occupied Eastern Tibet.

Having lost a major portion of its army to the PLA, Tibet appealed to the United Nations for assistance. England and India, the two key countries whose attitude eventually shaped the U.N. decision not to intervene, were engaged in normalizing their relations with Beijing, though, and declined to aid Tibet. Left to its own resources, Tibet saw no alternative but to negotiate with the Chinese. The result was the Seventeen-Point Agreement signed on May 23, 1951. Drafted by Beijing, the agreement provided for Chinese sovereignty over Tibet and gave China the right to station troops in Tibet for defensive purposes. Beijing in return promised that it would not "alter the existing political system" or "the established status, functions, and powers of the Dalai Lama," promised to pursue a "policy of freedom of religious beliefs," and promised to leave the Tibetan monasteries untouched.

Uneasy calm prevailed in Tibet. The large influx of Chinese soldiers into Tibet created some suspicion and resentment, but the Dalai Lama tried to work with the Chinese, believing that only a policy of cooperating with Beijing within the framework of the Seventeen-Point Agreement could preserve Tibet's autonomy and avoid the imposition of a Communist social, economic, and political system on Tibet. The Chinese, on their part, decided not to introduce socialist reforms at the time.

In Eastern Tibet, however, Beijing adopted a different policy. This area was outside Tibet proper and was not ruled directly by the Dalai Lama, and there the Chinese felt no hesitation in introducing revolutionary changes that disrupted the traditional Tibetan way of life. The result was a widespread uprising led by the local Khampa tribespeople. Beijing retaliated harshly when the rebels killed a number of Chinese. Several monasteries were shelled in the belief that they were rebel strongholds. Reprisals and severe punishments resulted in large-scale Tibetan casualties. Chinese settlers were brought in, further worsening relations between the local people and the Chinese.

The fear that the Chinese might do in Tibet proper what they had done in Eastern Tibet prompted the Dalai Lama to go to India in 1956, ostensibly to attend the twenty-five hundredth anniversary of the birth of Buddha, and announce from there that he might not return to Lhasa. Chinese prime minister Zhou Enlai, who also was in India at the time, gave an assurance that Tibet's autonomy under the 1951 agreement would be preserved. Mao gave additional reassurances in a speech in February, 1957, when he said that Tibet was not yet "ripe" for socialist reforms and that any reforms could be undertaken only when the Tibetans themselves decided that the time was "opportune" for them. On the basis of these assurances, the Dalai Lama returned to Lhasa in March, 1957.

The return of the Dalai Lama, however, did not ease the situation in Tibet. Many of the Khampa rebels who had been driven from their homes in Eastern Tibet moved westward and joined forces with local anti-Chinese elements. Tibet was, in fact, heading toward a crisis. It exploded in the form of a major uprising against the Chinese. The Dalai Lama, with his entourage, fled to India. The Chinese now adopted the same harsh measures they had already used in Eastern Tibet. A large number of Tibetans—their number has been estimated into tens of thousands—died at the hands of Chinese forces. About one hundred thousand fled to India and the neighboring countries of Nepal, Sikkim, and Bhutan. Beijing also decided that it could no longer delay its reforms. The Communist revolution had finally come to Tibet. The

Dalai Lama was overthrown; in his place Beijing installed the Panchen Lama, a longtime rival of the Dalai Lama. In 1965, the Chinese declared Tibet an autonomous region, which, like similar autonomous regions of the country, was under direct rule from Beijing.

Tibet suffered further destruction and humiliation during Mao's Cultural Revolution of 1966-1969. Tibet's traditional society became an easy target for the Red Guards—who poured into Tibet from outside—when Mao gave a call for the destruction of the "four olds," two of which were old culture and old customs. Some of Tibet's most sacred monasteries were destroyed, and numerous shrines and temples were turned into rubble. The local Chinese commander, General Zhang Guohua, supported by Zhou Enlai, eventually brought the Red Guards under control, but irreparable damage to Tibet's ancient culture and its priceless heritage had already been done.

The death of Mao in 1976 led to a policy of relative liberalization in China and to some changes in its Tibetan policy, especially under Deng Xiaoping, who, after a short interval of post-Mao power struggles, assumed power in China. Believing that Tibet was fully pacified, he invited the Dalai Lama to send a delegation to China in an effort to settle the Tibetan question. Led by the Dalai Lama's brother, Gyalo Thundrup, the delegation visited Lhasa, where they were given a tumultuous welcome by Tibetans. Their visit, in fact, turned into an anti-Chinese and proindependence demonstration.

Clearly realizing that the situation in Tibet was not what the local Chinese officials were reporting to Beijing, the Chinese leadership decided to make a radical departure. Hu Yaobang, the reformist general secretary of the Chinese Communist Party, went on a fact-finding mission to Tibet in 1980 and publicly recommended sweeping reforms. It is said that in private he came down harshly on China's rule in Tibet, saying that it had been no different from the West's old colonial policies.

The new reform policy aimed at both political and economic reforms, including the abolition of the hated communes in the countryside. Encouragement was given to the use and study of Tibetan language and literature; freedom of religion was assured, and the government helped rebuild some of the monasteries destroyed by the Red Guards.

Deng also tried to approach the Dalai Lama on a "let-bygones-be-bygones" basis. The Dalai Lama, on his part, hoped that Beijing would offer Tibet the same framework of "one country, two systems" that it had offered to Taiwan in 1981. The Chinese made it clear such a policy could not apply to Tibet, but they continued their dialogue with the Dalai Lama.

Tibet was once again affected by developments inside China. China's move toward a more liberalized system had been opposed by conservative forces. Prodemocracy student demonstrations in early 1987 led to the dismissal of Hu Yaobang from his position as general secretary of the Party. Deng, who at one time was Hu's mentor, now sided with the conservatives.

Events in China provided fuel to various elements in Tibet who still clamored for

Tibet's real autonomy or outright independence. They were also encouraged by the fact that during his visit to Washington in mid-September, the Dalai Lama had received a warm welcome from the U.S. Congress. Riots broke out in Lhasa on October 1, during which Tibetan flags were raised and slogans were shouted in favor of independence. Beijing's efforts to put down these riots resulted in several casualties, further fueling resentment of the Chinese. It was quite clear that Beijing's efforts to improve economic conditions and grant Tibetans relative freedom in religious matters had failed to satisfy a basic Tibetan aspiration to manage their affairs without any dictation or intervention from outside.

The Dalai Lama himself tried to break the ice in a major proposal made at the European Parliament at Strasbourg in June, 1988. He offered Beijing control of Tibet's foreign relations and the right to station Chinese forces in Tibet until Tibet became a zone of peace; in return, he wanted China to grant a genuine, unfettered autonomy to Tibet. China viewed these proposals as a demand for independence in a disguised form. Several radical elements in the Tibetan exile community, especially the Tibetan Youth Congress, criticized the Dalai Lama for giving up the goal of an independent Tibet.

Tibet's resentment continued to manifest itself in occasional protests. There had been a riot in Lhasa in March, 1988, just three months before the Dalai Lama's Strasbourg proposals. A demonstration in December, 1988, also resulted in violence. The Panchen Lama was sent to Tibet in January, 1989, by a reformist group led by Zhao Ziyang. The Panchen Lama, who had in the past cooperated with the Chinese, criticized Chinese policy as it had been pursued. He died soon after criticizing China, and his supporter, Zhao Ziyang, was himself purged after the suppression of student demonstrations at Tiananmen Square in June, 1989.

Within Tibet itself, a major riot took place in March, 1989. The Chinese, as they had in the past, took harsh steps to suppress it. Scores of Tibetans were killed, and China imposed martial law. Faced with widespread international criticism for its violation of human rights in all parts of China, Beijing finally decided to lift the martial law in Tibet on April 30, 1991. In a speech delivered in February, 1991, however, Chinese prime minister Li Peng made it quite clear that China's government remained ready to crush all "separatist activities" of the country's ethnic minorities.

## Impact of Event

The question of the basic rights of the Tibetan people has been closely linked with both internal developments in China and with China's relations with other powers. It was Mao's determination to "liberate" Tibet that first brought the Chinese army into the country. Although Mao did not try to impose the Communist system on Tibetans in those early years, he refrained only reluctantly, and he remained a strong advocate of radical changes, which were finally introduced after he succeeded in suppressing the 1959 uprising.

During the Cultural Revolution, the destructive role of the Red Guards in Tibet became an issue between the radical supporters of Mao, including his wife, Jiang Qing, who supported the Red Guards, and Zhou Enlai, who tried to put restraints on their activities. Later, Deng Xiaoping and Hu Yaobang, in accordance with some of their liberal policies, adopted a new course for Tibet. The fall of Hu Yaobang meant a setback for Tibet. Later, Zhao Ziyang, another supporter of moderate policies for both China and Tibet, tried to change Beijing's policy toward Lhasa, but his fall after the Tiananmen killings ended that prospect.

The question of Tibet's status has also been an important factor in Sino-Indian relations. India had inherited English commercial and other rights in Lhasa when India became independent in 1947. Jawaharlal Nehru, the Indian prime minister, sympathized with the Tibetan people, but he also wanted to establish a cooperative relationship with Beijing. The Chinese criticized him—often in very strong language—for sympathizing with the rights of the Tibetans, but they also used his services to deal with the Dalai Lama. India decided to welcome the Dalai Lama after he fled Lhasa in 1959 and provided shelter to him and the thousands of refugees who left Tibet as a result of the 1959 rebellion and its brutal suppression by the Chinese. New Delhi's relations with China, the course of which had been set by Nehru and Zhou in the mid-1950's with great public cordiality, now suffered. The issue of Tibetan autonomy, along with the Sino-Indian border conflict, resulted in a short war between the two countries in 1962.

Tibet was only a remote issue in Sino-American relations during the early years of the Cold War. The United States was busy in Korea and Vietnam. When President Jimmy Carter began to emphasize human rights issues in his policies, Tibet still remained in the background, as Carter saw China as a counterweight to the Soviet Union. In later years, though, the question of the rights of the Tibetan people was discussed in the American media and congressional debates. With the radical change in U.S.-Soviet relations resulting from the end of the Cold War, Beijing no longer occupied the same strategic position in Washington's calculations as it once did. President Ronald Reagan did not meet the Dalai Lama when he visited the United States in 1987, but during a later visit, President George Bush had a meeting with him, thus clearly signaling a departure from Washington's noninterventionist policy toward Tibet's aspirations. In the American media, columnists such as A. M. Rosenthal of *The New York Times* began to speak forcefully for human rights in Tibet. The U.S. Congress held lengthy hearings on the subject. Finally, the award of the Nobel Peace Prize to the Dalai Lama in 1989 put the Tibetan question in the forefront of human rights issues.

## Bibliography

Goldstein, Melvyn C. "The Dragon and the Snow Lion: The Tibet Question in the 20th Century." In *China Briefing, 1990*, edited by Anthony J. Kane. Boulder, Colo.: Westview Press, 1990. The author claims that his effort has been to explore "shades of gray" between the two extreme positions represented by Beijing and the Tibetan exiles. He credits the Chinese for introducing significant reforms in the early 1980's but admits that nothing short of genuine autonomy would satisfy Tibetan aspirations.

Grunfeld, A. Tom. *The Making of Modern Tibet.* New York: M. E. Sharpe, 1987. An excellent one-volume history of modern Tibet that provides valuable historical background as well as a dispassionate presentation of events since 1950.

*Human Rights in Tibet.* Washington, D.C.: Asia Watch/Government Printing Office, 1988. A verbatim record of the hearings conducted by the Committee on Foreign Affairs of the U.S. House of Representatives on October 14, 1987. These hearings, which provided valuable data on human rights violations in Tibet, took place shortly after the riots that broke out in Lhasa on October 1.

Moraes, Frank. *The Revolt in Tibet.* New York: Macmillan, 1960. Written by a prominent Indian journalist, the book provides a detailed account of the 1959 Tibetan uprising. The author provides an excellent analysis of the impact Tibetan events had on public opinion in India and neighboring Asian countries.

Ngawang Lobsang Yishey Tenzing Gyatso. *My Land and My People: The Autobiography of His Holiness the Dalai Lama.* Edited by David Howarth. New York: McGraw-Hill, 1962. Although obviously describing events in Tibet from the Dalai Lama's standpoint, the book remains a valuable source for understanding the impact Beijing's policies had on Tibet in the early years of its occupation.

Wu, Yuan-li, et al. *Human Rights in the People's Republic of China.* Boulder, Colo.: Westview Press, 1988. Although it contains only a brief direct discussion of human rights abuses in Tibet, the book is valuable for providing a general framework of Beijing's policies as they have been applied to all parts of China.

*Surendra K. Gupta*

## Cross-References

Japanese Troops Brutalize Chinese After the Capture of Nanjing (1937), p. 539; China Occupies Tibet (1950), p. 837; The Chinese Cultural Revolution Starts a Wave of Repression (1966), p. 1332; Carter Makes Human Rights a Central Theme of Foreign Policy (1977), p. 1903; Demonstrators Gather in Tiananmen Square (1989), p. 2483.

# ISRAEL ENACTS THE LAW OF RETURN, GRANTING CITIZENSHIP TO IMMIGRANTS

*Category of event:* Immigrants' rights
*Time:* July 5, 1950
*Locale:* Jerusalem, Israel

*The unparalleled rights guaranteed to Jews immigrating to Israel by the Law of Return reflected the designation of the country as a homeland for the Jewish people*

*Principal personages:*
DAVID BEN-GURION (1886-1973), the first prime minister of Israel, popularly considered the founder of the state
THEODOR HERZL (1860-1904), a founder of Zionism, popularly regarded as the father of political Zionism
SHABTAY ZVI (1626-1676), a self-proclaimed messiah who tried to organize a large-scale Jewish return to Palestine

## Summary of Event

The first step taken by the state of Israel after it had declared its independence was the repeal of all restrictions on Jewish immigration into Palestine. These restrictions had been the main bone of contention between the Jewish community in Israel and the country's Arab inhabitants, and between the Jews and the British authorities that had governed Palestine. Israel's proclamation of independence affirmed that Israel would be "open to the immigration of Jews from all countries of their dispersion" and that this solemn intention would be incorporated into a constitution to be drawn up in the near future. The difficulty of arriving at an acceptable definition of "Jew" and the fact that the majority of Israel's potential citizens were scattered in the Diaspora, or the dispersal of Jews from their historical homeland, prevented the adoption of a constitution conveying this intention. Nevertheless, in lieu of a formal bill of rights, the Israeli supreme court granted the proclamation a quasiconstitutional status. Moreover, on July 5, 1950, the Israeli Knesset (parliament) passed unprecedented legislation regarding immigrants' rights entitled the "Law of Return." This law stipulated that all Jews had the right to immigrate to the country and receive full citizenship immediately on arrival. In effect, this meant that the state took upon itself to supply immigrants with the full range of services necessary for their absorption. Excluded were only such Jews as were deemed by the authorities as "acting against the Jewish nation" or as constituting a threat to "public health or State security." Sometime later, an additional category was added of Jews fleeing specified kinds of criminal prosecution.

The significance of the Law of Return did not reside only in the unparalleled scope of the rights it guaranteed but also in its Zionist solution for the "Jewish problem." Despite their expulsion from their land by the Romans nearly two thousand years before, the Jews had retained almost all the attributes associated with the concept of "nation": a historical consciousness of being one people, an association with a specific territory, a common culture (including language), and the possession of, or at least the aspiration for, political independence. These factors explained the persistence of the yearning to return to the land of Israel expressed in religious prayers and rituals and in secular literature. Indeed, from time to time there were eruptions of messianic fervor and even attempts at large-scale return, the best known of which was that of the seventeenth century self-proclaimed messiah Shabtay Zvi and his followers. Zionism can be interpreted as a secular variant of such messianism. It was, however, also an expression of the spirit of the Age of Enlightenment and a reaction against other solutions proposed at the time for the Jewish problem.

The growth of the ideas of citizenship and civil rights and the incorporation of minorities into national life confronted the Jews of Europe with the need to define their relationship to the societies in which they lived. Against this background, four distinct approaches developed. One involved assimilation; Jews would merge as individuals into the general population, enjoying the same public privileges and duties while retaining their own private beliefs. This approach was summed up in a well-known dictum: "Be a Jew in your home and an ordinary human being outside it." A variant of assimilation was advocated by socialists ranging from Karl Marx to Leon Trotsky as well as by specifically Jewish socialist movements. These thinkers envisaged the transcendence of all religions and national movements under the aegis of universal social order in which Jews would no longer be distinguishable. Another solution was that of Reform Judaism. This sought to dissolve the cultural walls that isolated Jews, thereby allowing modern non-Jewish practices and ideas to enter into the closed world of orthodox Judaism and blur the distinctiveness of the Jews. Finally, there was the territorial solution that attracted many of the early Zionists, including Theodor Herzl, the Austrian journalist generally considered to be the father of political Zionism. The territorialists were prepared to forgo the Jews' ancient territorial heritage in favor of any immediately available territory, such as Uganda, Azerbaijan, or parts of Argentina, which could offer a basis for a Jewish state. The common denominator of all four approaches was the readiness to sacrifice one or another of the constituent elements of the historical Jewish identity. Zionism, in contrast, insisted that the acquisition of human rights should be the result of Jewry itself and not something granted by others at the expense of some element of Jewish identity. Contrary to the views of the assimilationists, Zionism demanded the "ingathering" of the Jews from all over the world; contrary to the reformists, it demanded the revitalization of Jewish culture; contrary to the territorialists, it insisted on a return to the land of Israel. In positive terms, Zionism's ideal was the integration of Jewry as an independent cultural and national entity living in its historical homeland and equal in all respects to the other nations of the world. Consequently, the lever acting on the fulcrum was large-scale immigration to Palestine.

From the end of the nineteenth century, and increasingly after the British had been given a mandate by the League of Nations to govern Palestine and other parts of the Ottoman Empire in 1922, Zionist groups, "the Pioneers," began to realize their vision by spearheading the formation of a Jewish homeland. This met, however, with growing opposition from Palestine's British authorities and the Arab population. After Adolf Hitler's rise to power, the right of free immigration became the focal point of dissension between the Zionists and the League of Nations powers. At the same time, the implementation of Zionism fomented Arab terrorism, which escalated in time into full-fledged civil war. Both conflicts came to a head in 1947. On November 29, 1947, the United Nations General Assembly voted by an overwhelming majority to terminate the British mandate over Palestine and to partition the country into independent Jewish and Arab states. November 30 is considered as the day when the ongoing civil war developed into Israel's war of independence.

The enacting of the Law of Return by the Knesset of the country's first elected government, headed by David Ben-Gurion, thus expressed the victory of Zionism over its alternatives in the Jewish world and over its British and Arab opponents. It also reflected the nature of the new state. Israeli immigration laws were designed to correspond to those of other Western countries. Residency permits would be issued to individuals on application, and full citizenship could be granted after a specified period. Since the state was considered to be the homeland of the Jewish people, however, all immigrant Jews were considered to be homecoming nationals. Other countries had similar regulations, but in Great Britain and the United States, for example, homecoming nationals were not considered as immigrants even if they were born abroad to nationals. The fact that most of the homecoming nationals in Israel were indeed immigrants and the first generation of their families to become citizens illustrated the unusual character of a state founded to normalize the status of a Diaspora people.

## Impact of Event

The impact of the Law of Return can be measured in terms of its immediate, intended effects as well as its long-term, unexpected ones. The former included the massive immigration to Israel and the prominent role of the state in bringing in and settling the immigrants. The latter involved the danger of fracturing the fused constituents of Jewish identity into separable attributes and the consequent raising of the question "Who is a Jew?"

Between 1948 and 1991, the Jewish population of Israel increased by more than 600 percent to reach approximately four million. Some of the newcomers, in general those from affluent countries, arrived individually on their own initiative and found relatively little difficulty in integrating into Israeli society. Nevertheless, they enjoyed housing subsidies and such privileges as release from customs on imports. Most newcomers, however, were brought in organized waves or in smaller groups with few or no possessions, no capital, and often little education relevant to a modern industrial democracy. The first wave consisted of Jews displaced by the Nazis, many of them survivors of the death camps. Having nowhere to return to, and denied entry into Western countries, most were herded into camps awaiting some resolution of their fate. Others were caught trying to smuggle themselves into Palestine and were incarcerated by the British in Kenya and Cyprus. A later wave of immigrants escaped or were expelled from Arab countries following wars between Israel and its neighbors. Later still came those escaping extreme economic hardships, as in Ethiopia, or political instability and the threat of anti-Semitism, as in Eastern Europe and the Soviet Union. Such immigrants were treated as potential citizens even before setting foot on Israeli soil and hence were already supported abroad and transported at state expense. Immediately on arrival, the state undertook to supply virtually all of their needs, including education, health care, training, employment, and settlement in different parts of the country. This further bolstered the centrality of the state in the personal life of the citizen and, for the first generation at least, created a relationship of direct dependency.

Problems arose because the Law of Return was a secular law and was passed by a secular parliament. The difficulty was that the term "Jew," which was critical to the law's interpretation, had both an ethnic and a religious meaning. In a situation in which most Jews were still in the Diaspora while most Israelis were secular and the Israeli population included non-Jews as well, the cleavage between nationalism and religion became increasingly marked. A Jew living abroad with no intention of emigrating to Israel was still considered Jewish from the religious point of view, even if the applicability of the national aspects of the association with a specific territory, and even more the aspiration to political independence in it, was questionable. Conversely, the population living in the Jewish state could certainly be considered Jewish in the national sense, but the applicability of the religious aspects of term was by no means assured. To offer only one illustration, in 1970 the Israeli supreme court ordered that the children of a naval officer married to a non-Jewess must be registered as Jews whereas by religious law they were considered Gentiles. Numerous efforts therefore were made by religious parties and bodies in Israel to amend the Law of Return so as to restrict its usage of the term "Jew" to apply solely to its orthodox religious sense. The implications of such a change for the interpretation of what Israel stood for and for the issue of the rights of immigration remained unclear.

## Bibliography

Elazar, Daniel. *Israel: Building a New Society*. Bloomington: Indiana University Press, 1986. Although not dealing directly with the Law of Return, this book provides the context needed for appreciating the law and its outcome. Especially useful is Chapter 7, "Religion and the Polity."

Gitelman, Zvi. *Becoming Israelis: Political Resocialization of Soviet and American Immigrants*. New York: Praeger, 1982. A comprehensive study, descriptive, analytical, and evaluative, of the scope and problems of immigration, absorption, and acculturation in Israel. Particularly concerned with problems relating to Jews from the United States and the Soviet Union.

Lacqueur, Walter, and Rubin Barry, eds. *The Israel-Arab Reader*. New York: Citadel Press, 1969. A collection of documents, including the Law of Return and those relating to its background and application. Of special relevance are sections covering the period from the pre-Zionist *Yishuv* settlement of Palestine to the 1950's.

Liebman, Charles, and Don-Yehiya Eliezer. *Religion and Politics in Israel.* Bloomington: Indiana University Press, 1984. An excellent study of the general topic. Of particular relevance to the Law of Return are the chapters on the meaning of "Jewish identity" for nonreligious Israeli Jews and on the institutional framework regulating the relations betwen religious and nonreligious political interest.

Rubinstein, Amnon. "Law and Religion in Israel" *Israel Law Review* 3 (1967): 380-414. A legal analysis of the Law of Return and other laws pertaining to religious practice in Israel, together with court decisions relating to their application.

*Jonathan Mendilow*

## Cross-References

The Balfour Declaration Supports a Jewish Homeland in Palestine (1917), p. 235; Nazi Concentration Camps Go into Operation (1933), p. 491; Israel Is Created as a Homeland for Jews (1948), p. 761; Eichmann Is Tried for War Crimes (1961), p. 1108; Soviet Jews Demand Cultural and Religious Rights (1963), p. 1177.

# CHINA OCCUPIES TIBET

*Categories of event:* Atrocities and war crimes; religious freedom
*Time:* October 7, 1950
*Locale:* Tibet and China

*Although the Communist Chinese claimed that Tibet had always been part of China, the military invasion and subsequent immigration of ethnic Chinese caused massive dislocations of population and culture*

*Principal personages:*

TENZIN GYATSO (1935-    ), the fourteenth Dalai Lama, spiritual leader and head of state of Tibet

MAO TSE-TUNG (1898-1976), a Chinese Communist leader and founder of the People's Republic of China

ZHOU ENLAI (1898-1976), the leading international spokesperson and prime minister of the People's Republic of China from its founding until his death

JAWAHARLAL NEHRU (1889-1964), a leader of the Indian independence movement and first prime minister of India

## Summary of Event

No two countries on earth could have been geographically and historically closer, yet ideologically farther apart, than Tibet and the People's Republic of China (PRC) in 1950. After more than a millennium of cultural and political development, Tibet had evolved into a theocracy whose head of government was regarded as divine, and China had become an atheistic Marxist state headed by one of the most powerful revolutionary figures of the century. Conflict between the two was inevitable.

Nevertheless, according to the official view of the PRC, there was no invasion of Tibet in 1950. Tibet was historically a part of China, according to this view, and the military intervention was based on humanitarian socialist principles. Although the Chinese prevailed militarily and politically in that conflict, the official Chinese view found only marginal acceptance in the world community.

Tibet did not really exist as a country before the seventh century A.D., when it was finally unified by a powerful tribal leader named Songtsen Gompo. By marrying into royal families of both Nepal and China, he consolidated his power, and as a secondary effect, introduced Buddhism to Tibet. The balance of power between ancient China and Tibet shifted many times before a treaty concluded between the nations in 821-822 A.D. established inviolable boundaries and pledged mutual sovereignty. Between the tenth and thirteenth centuries A.D., power gradually became concentrated in the Buddhist monasteries, and in 1244 A.D. Basba, the first Lama king, became ruler. In a later period (the eighteenth and nineteenth centuries), Manchurian Chinese had considerable influence in Tibet, although the exact nature of the relationship remains controversial among historians. China points to this period as a time of suzerainty of the Manchus over Tibet, supporting the claim that China and Tibet are historically one. Tibet, however, was isolated by choice from the world at large, while China had trade and diplomatic contacts with Europe and Asia. China was therefore free to color its relationship with Tibet in shades of its own choosing.

Tibet's isolation came to an end at the close of the nineteenth century. Interventionist pressure came not from China but from British India, when the Younghusband expedition of 1904 forced Tibet into accepting trade agreements with the outside world. The moderate stance of the British emboldened the Chinese to use force against Tibet for the first time in more than ten centuries. The Tibetans drove out the Chinese (Manchu) forces in 1912, and in 1913 the thirteenth Dalai Lama declared Tibet independent. This move led to border disputes with China in the eastern areas of Tibet, and an attempt to settle the disputes at the Simla Conference (1913-1914) failed when China refused to ratify a treaty agreed to by the British and Tibetan delegations. A *de facto* boundary followed the upper Yangtze River.

The thirteenth Dalai Lama died in 1933. According to Tibetan tradition, the Dalai Lama reincarnates within a few months and succeeds himself; a successor, slightly more than two years old, was chosen according to traditional principles in 1937. The new Dalai Lama began his monastic training shortly thereafter, and was lifted onto the golden throne at the age of five.

Meanwhile, civil war in China was drawing to a close. The Communists, under Mao Tse-tung, defeated the Nationalists, and the People's Republic of China was inaugurated on November 24, 1949. On January 1, 1950, the "liberation" of Tibet was announced as one of the main tasks of China's People's Liberation Army (PLA), and on September 30, 1950, Chinese Premier Zhou Enlai declared that Tibet "must be liberated." Historians view China's real interest in Tibet as military and strategic.

On October 7, the PLA invaded neighboring Tibet. The Tibetan army resisted but was overrun within a few weeks. Although the PRC maintained from the outset that it was acting to free the people of Tibet from "imperialist oppression," it has never been made clear who the imperialists were. The last group of non-Tibetan people to inhabit Tibet in significant numbers were the Manchus, and only a handful of European traders were in Tibet at the time of the invasion.

The Dalai Lama completed his formal training at the age of fifteen and was installed as head of the government on November 17, 1950. On May 23, 1951, the PRC announced the signing in Beijing of a Seventeen-Point Agreement between the two countries. The terms of the treaty were apparently arrived at through coercion and deception, as the delegation sent by the Dalai Lama was not empowered to conclude such an agreement.

The situation in Tibet remained highly unstable, but the Tibetan government did everything possible to make the best of it. The Dalai Lama himself went to Beijing and served as a vice president of the Steering Committee of the People's Republic of China. By his own account, he found many things in Marxism that he felt to be compatible with Buddhist philosophy, and his meetings with Chairman Mao were earnest and friendly. In the end, however, the deceitfulness of the Chinese and the atheistic orientation of Communism convinced him that the Chinese were intent on destroying his country as he knew it. On the point of deceitfulness, his experiences with the charming but untrustworthy Zhou Enlai were educational. On the point of atheism, Mao reminded the Dalai Lama of Communist theology in their last private meeting. "Religion is poison," said Mao. "Firstly it reduces the population, because monks and nuns must stay celibate, and secondly it neglects material progress."

Revolt broke out in Tibet's eastern region in 1956, and as it spread into the central regions Mao announced that Tibet was not yet ready for Communist reforms. As the unrest continued, the Chinese tried to assert control, but the revolt exploded in 1959. The situation deteriorated so completely that the Dalai Lama was forced to flee into northern India. About twenty thousand Tibetans followed during the first year of his exile.

India's role in the unfolding tragedy of its neighbor and spiritual cousin has been widely criticized. The government of the Hindu subcontinent made only the mildest of protests when the invasion began and failed to offer even significant moral support. Historians of the period assign much of the blame to Prime Minister Jawaharlal Nehru. Although his government did offer land for refugee settlements, the Dalai Lama was initially restrained from taking his people's case to the court of world opinion and was forbidden from engaging in political activities.

Analysts are generally in agreement that fear of China, not antipathy toward Tibet, accounted for India's rather cynical performance. India's deference toward the Chinese, however, did not prevent the outbreak of war between the two countries in 1962. Ironically, India had hoped that Tibet would be a buffer against Chinese military incursions, but it became a springboard instead.

In fairness to Nehru, it can be said that he learned from his mistake, if only too late. In fairness to his government, it can be said that India has provided much-needed assistance with land for settlements, education, and health care for its nearly one hundred thousand Tibetan refugees.

## Impact of Event

Although Tibet was a feudal society in which needed reforms had been blocked by the aristocracy and vested interests, reports from refugees and independent investigations disclose a far different picture of the "liberation" from that put forth by the Communist Chinese. According to the Legal Inquiry Committee on Tibet in its report to the International Commission of Jurists in Geneva (1960), the Chinese had violated sixteen of the thirty points of the United Nations Universal Declaration of Human Rights. Atrocities of the most egregious kind were amply documented, including summary execution, torture, rape, forcible separation of children from parents, and wholesale destruction of shrines and monasteries. In the name of reform, Tibetans were forced to work longer hours for less food, but collectivization of Tibet's agriculture proved as disastrous as China's own "Great Leap Forward." Eventually the death toll from famine ran into hundreds of thousands.

In addition to the turmoil and destruction that took place during the invasion and subsequent uprisings, Tibetans were subjected to the depredations of the Red Guards during the Cultural Revolution in China. The Red Guards were keenly interested in Tibet's shrines and monasteries, which they considered to reflect the "reactionary" side of Tibetan culture. Of approximately thirty-seven hundred monasteries operating in Tibet before the invasion, only seven hundred were spared. The International Commission of Jurists found unequivocally that the Chinese had committed genocide against Tibetans through their attempts to eradicate Buddhism.

As a result of an aggressive Chinese immigration policy, Chinese outnumbered ethnic Tibetans in the Tibetan Autonomous Region, and Chinese arts and crafts began to replace indigenous arts and crafts in that area. What remained was a thin veneer of Tibetan culture, which apparently was being maintained as a tourist attraction.

The Chinese introduced secular public education to Tibet, provided health care facilities, improved drainage, and built wells, canals, and roads. Nevertheless, the death tolls in various uprisings give some indication of the depth of Tibetan suffering under the Chinese and Tibetans' determination to regain their independence. More than eighty-seven thousand died between March of 1959 and September of 1960, and even more than that number are thought to have been killed in the 1969 uprising. An independence uprising in 1989 left as many as one hundred dead in Lhasa, Tibet's capital. The death toll since the 1950 invasion is estimated at 1.2 million.

After the Cultural Revolution, China admitted that "mistakes" had been made. China's policy became more "open," and in 1979 the first of several fact-finding missions by representatives of Tibet's government-in-exile (including the Dalai Lama's brother) was allowed to return to Tibet.

Tibet's plight gradually gained the world's attention and sympathy. The Dalai Lama, living in exile in northern India, received the 1989 Nobel Peace Prize for his efforts to gain independence through nonviolent means. His brother, Lobsang Samten, died in 1985 at the age of fifty-four. In his autobiography, the Dalai Lama writes: "In a way, despite my profound sorrow, I was not much surprised at this. His experiences as a member of the first fact-finding mission had affected him profoundly. . . . I do not think it an exaggeration to say that he died of a broken heart."

## Bibliography

Barber, Noël. *The Flight of the Dalai Lama.* London: Hodder & Stoughton, 1960. Well written and engrossing, this book combines historical background with first-person narrative by Barber, who made the arduous journey to Tibet to cover one of the great stories of the century. Includes comments by the Dalai Lama and a detailed chronology of events through 1959.

Dalai Lama. *Freedom in Exile: The Autobiography of the Dalai Lama.* New York: HarperCollins, 1990. Although it must necessarily be regarded as partisan in its outlook, this book reflects the almost universally acknowledged integrity of its author. If anything, it is too gentle in its treatment of some figures, such as Nehru. The volume provides a rich and unique perspective. Maps and photographs included.

Hopkirk, Peter. "Red Guards in Lhasa." In *Trespassers on the Roof of the World.* London: John Murray, 1982. A historical account of various visitors to "the Forbidden Land," told in human terms. Includes many photographs taken during expeditions by foreign explorers. Chapter 15 details the impact of the Red Guard on Tibetan culture.

International Commission of Jurists. Legal Inquiry Committee on Tibet. *Tibet and the Chinese People's Republic.* Geneva: Author, 1960. A collection of interviews and documents dealing with issues of genocide, human rights, progress, Tibet's status, and the Seventeen-Point Agreement.

Mitter, Jyoti. *Betrayal of Tibet.* Bombay: Allied Publishers, 1964. An Indian's view of China's expansionism and India's role in the Tibetan controversy. Highly critical of Nehru and the Indian government, it sees India's official position as creating conditions for the Sino-Indian border conflict of 1962.

Moraes, Frank. *The Revolt in Tibet.* New York: Macmillan, 1960. Covers events leading to the Dalai Lama's escape, and also examines the impact of Chinese aggression on the rest of Asia, particularly India.

Norbu, Dawa. *Red Star Over Tibet.* New Delhi: Sterling Publishers, 1987. First-person account of a native Tibetan who fled to exile in India. Excellent for insights into Tibetan culture and direct reporting of the Chinese invasion. Includes drawings and a glossary of Tibetan and Chinese terms.

Sacks, Howard C. *The Quest for Universal Responsibility: Human Rights Violations in Tibet.* Dharamsala, India: Information Office, Central Tibetan Secretariat, 1983. A slim volume, dealing primarily with legalistic questions and supported by original documents. Clear and straightforward.

Tung, Rosemary Jones. *A Portrait of Lost Tibet.* New York: Holt, Rinehart and Winston, 1980. A remarkable book, based on photographs taken in 1942 and 1943 by Ilya (grandson of Leo) Tolstoy and Brooke Dolan. Tolstoy and Dolan were on a diplomatic mission for U.S. president Franklin D. Roosevelt. The mission failed, but the photographs and text by the author, captured a Tibet which is gone forever.

*L. B. Shriver*

## Cross-References

Sun Yat-sen Overthrows the Ch'ing Dynasty (1911), p. 116; Students Demonstrate for Reform in China's May Fourth Movement (1919), p. 276; The United Nations Adopts a Convention on the Crime of Genocide (1948), p. 783; The United Nations Adopts the Universal Declaration of Human Rights (1948), p. 789; China Initiates a Genocide Policy Toward Tibetans (1950), p. 826; The European Convention on Human Rights Is Signed (1950), p. 843; Mao Delivers His "Speech of One Hundred Flowers" (1956), p. 958; Mao's Great Leap Forward Causes Famine and Social Dislocation (1958), p. 1015; Amnesty International Is Founded (1961), p. 1119; The Chinese Cultural Revolution Starts a Wave of Repression (1966), p. 1332; The United Nations Issues a Declaration Against Torture (1975), p. 1847; China Publicizes and Promises to Correct Abuses of Citizens' Rights (1978), p. 1983; The United Nations Votes to Protect Freedoms of Religion and Belief (1981), p. 2146; Tibet's Dalai Lama Is Awarded the Nobel Peace Prize (1989), p. 2535.

# THE EUROPEAN CONVENTION
# ON HUMAN RIGHTS IS SIGNED

*Category of event:* Civil rights
*Time:* November 4, 1950
*Locale:* Rome, Italy

*The European Convention on Human Rights established a comprehensive and effective system for the international protection of human rights*

*Principal personages:*

SIR DAVID MAXWELL FYFE (1900-1967), a British statesman committed to the European Movement, which sought the political, economic, and military unification of Western Europe

PIERRE-HENRI TEITGEN (1908- ), a French statesman and lawyer and member of the Council of Europe

BROC ARVID STURE PETREN (1908-1976), a Swedish lawyer, adviser to the Swedish delegation at the United Nations, and member of the European Commission of Human Rights

FERNAND DEHOUSSE (1906- ), a Belgian university professor, politician, and member of the Council of Europe

SIR HUMPHREY WALDOCK (1904-1981), the first elected president of the European Commission of Human Rights

## Summary of Event

The content of the provisions of the European Convention on Human Rights for the protection of individual rights is virtually identical to that of the United Nations' Universal Declaration of Human Rights and the International Covenant on Civil and Political Rights. The European Convention, however, goes beyond any other instrument of human rights protection in terms of the effectiveness of its procedures. For this reason, the European Convention is regarded generally as the best system for the protection of human rights established by any international organization.

Europeans in the post-World War II era had an immediate interest in the issue of human rights. Western European diplomats believed that the rise of fascism was the principal cause of World War II and the misery and devastation experienced by millions of people in that conflict. Fascist Italy and Nazi Germany made the suppression of human rights a deliberate and integral part of their policies and programs. Postwar leaders thought that the creation of an effective system to guarantee human rights and freedoms would help to inhibit the reemergence of such dictatorships. At the same time, the continued postwar existence of Joseph Stalin's regime in the Soviet Union concerned Western Europeans. Thus, the protection of human rights became linked to European efforts to defend against all forms of dictatorship and totalitarianism.

Well before the end of World War II, a concern for human rights was being expressed. The Atlantic Charter of 1941 proclaimed the "Four Freedoms," which, among other things, enunciated the freedom of speech and worship. The United Nations Declaration of 1942, the U.N. Charter of 1945, and the U.N. Universal Declaration of Human Rights of 1948 reaffirmed and expanded this earlier interest in human rights.

Western European leaders believed that such general international proclamations needed more specific application to postwar European conditions. For that reason, the Congress of Europe met at The Hague in 1948 and declared the need for a united Europe, a European charter of human rights guaranteeing freedom of expression and assembly, a court of justice to implement the charter, and the formation of a European representative assembly. In short, the construction and maintenance of an effective system to protect human rights was to become the collective responsibility of a united Western Europe. This was to be the regional counterpart of the worldwide system established by the United Nations.

The newly created Consultative Assembly of the Council of Europe directed its attention to designing such a system. The assembly's Committee on Legal and Administrative Questions met, under the chairmanship of Sir David Maxwell Fyfe, to draft proposals for the system. Assisted by the contributions of such members as Fernand Dehousse and Pierre-Henri Teitgen, the committee presented its conclusions to the Council of Europe on September 8, 1949, in the Teitgen Report. The report proposed that the member states of the Council of Europe should be obligated to guarantee collectively a list of ten human rights from the U.N. Universal Declaration of Human Rights. The report proposed also that a European commission for human rights and a European court of justice be created to examine and adjudicate cases of alleged human rights violations.

The Council of Europe appointed separate committees to study the Teitgen Report and draft a final declaration based upon the report's proposals. The committee chaired by Broc Arvid Sture Petren drew up this declaration, the European Convention on Human Rights. The convention was signed on November 4, 1950, in Rome by the foreign ministers of the member states of the Council of Europe. The principles and rights to be guaranteed were essentially the same as those proposed in the Teitgen Report, and the provisions were to be implemented by a commission and court of human rights. The convention was ratified and entered into force on September 3, 1953.

The European Convention stressed the protection of the principal civil and political rights deemed necessary in a democratic society. It was structured to allow for additional rights to be included later through protocol agreement. The convention of 1950 and the first protocol of 1952 guaranteed fourteen rights and freedoms to all individuals within the jurisdiction of the signatory states. These rights and freedoms applied to all persons, regardless of national or legal status and length of stay, within the territorial boundaries of the nations that ratified the convention. They included the right to life, freedom from torture and from inhuman treatment or punishment, freedom from slavery and servitude, the right to liberty and security of person, the right to a fair trial, protection against retroactivity of the law, the right to respect for one's private and family life, one's home, and one's correspondence, freedom of thought, conscience, and religion, freedom of expression, freedom of assembly and association, the right to marry and found a family, the right of property, the right of parents to ensure the education of their children in conformity with their own religious and philosophical convictions, and the right to free elections.

The collective guarantee of civil and political rights embodied in the European Convention on Human Rights led to interest in economic and social rights. In 1954, the Council of Europe proposed the drafting of a social charter that would enunciate and guarantee these rights. The European Social Charter was signed on October 18, 1961, in Turin, Italy. The charter's list of nineteen economic and social rights was designed to guide the policy of the Council of Europe in the social field and complement the European Convention on Human Rights. Further civil and political rights were incorporated into the European convention in later protocols. These included freedom from imprisonment on the ground of inability to fulfill a contract, freedom from discrimination on the basis of sex, freedom to impart information without interference, freedom of movement to enter or leave one's own country, and freedom from exile.

To implement the provisions of the convention, the European Commission of Human Rights and the European Court of Human Rights were established and headquartered in Strasbourg, France. An existing governmental organ of the Council of Europe, the Committee of Ministers, was also to play a part in the operation of the convention. The European commission consists of as many members as have ratified the convention and functions along the lines summarized in the Teitgen Report. It examines cases of human rights violations brought by one state against another. In 1955, the commission instituted a more important and valuable procedure by granting the right to individuals to file direct complaints against governments, including their own. Allowing individuals the right to appeal to an international organ against governments was a remarkable innovation in international law, because it upheld the rights of individuals against those traditionally held by states. The commission draws up a report of all admissible cases that have not been settled amicably and includes its opinion as to whether the facts represent a violation of the convention. This report is then sent to the Committee of Ministers of the Council of Europe, which consists of the foreign ministers of the member states. If the case is not referred to the Court of Human Rights, the committee decides whether a violation has occurred. The committee may also mandate a period of time in which a state may remedy a violation. The committee is responsible also for supervising the execution of any decisions made by the European Court of Human Rights. The court may hear cases brought before it by the European Commission, a state against whom a complaint has been made, a state making a complaint, or a state whose national is alleged to be the victim of a violation of the convention. It is the decisions that have been made by the European Court that have, more than anything else, developed the jurisprudence concerning human rights under the European Convention. No other international organization for the protection of human rights has produced a body of law that is in any way comparable.

## Impact of Event

There are limits to the impact made by the European Convention on Human Rights. As with any agreement, the convention's effectiveness depends on the extent to which the contracting parties agree to abide by its provisions. The right of individuals to bring complaints before the European Commission was made conditional on the expressed acceptance of this procedure by the state concerned. Similarly, the ability to cite a state before the European Court was made conditional on that state's agreement to accept the jurisdiction of the court. Not all the nations that ratified the convention accepted these specific procedures. Moreover, the European Convention protects only a limited number of rights and freedoms, to the exclusion of other rights not guaranteed expressly. The convention can come into effect only after it has been judged that all domestic remedies have been exhausted. For all these reasons, 90 percent of all complaints submitted are ruled inadmissible. Those that are admissible face a slow-moving bureaucratic process in the commission and court that can take up to five years to reach a conclusion.

Despite these shortcomings, the European Convention has had an important impact on human rights in Europe. The most striking and innovative feature of the convention is the new status it accorded to the individual in international law. Classic international law regulated relations between states and bestowed no rights on the private citizen. The convention's granting of the right of individual petition to the European Commission set an important precedent in international law upholding the rights of private citizens against those of the state.

The European Convention implies also a measure of international control over the actions of national governments. The commission and Court of Human Rights have the competence to examine and judge the activities of states that adhere to the convention. This European arrangement contrasts with the United Nations charter, which prohibits the United Nations from intervening in the domestic affairs of any state.

The European Convention has had an important impact on the national courts of certain states that have ratified the convention. Nations such as Belgium, Austria, and The Netherlands apply the provisions of a treaty directly to their domestic law. Thus, the rights guaranteed by the European Convention may be invoked by litigants in these states, and they may be held to prevail over any national laws and administrative decisions that contradict the convention.

Finally, the European Convention has had an impact on other parts of the world. Nations that have ratified the convention may extend its application to any overseas territories they may possess. Great Britain and The Netherlands extended the convention to their imperial possessions in the 1950's. When former colonies gained independence, many of them adopted the convention's provisions for the protection of human rights and incorporated them into their new constitutions. The European

Convention also served as the model for the convention on human rights established by the Organization of American States in 1965. Similar human rights conventions in Africa and Southeast Asia were influenced by the European model. Thus, the impact of the European Convention includes not only its direct effects in Europe but also its value as a precedent for other parts of the world.

## Bibliography

Beddard, Ralph. *Human Rights and Europe: A Study of the Machinery of Human Rights Protection of the Council of Europe.* London: Sweet and Maxwell, 1980. General account of the background and procedures of the European Convention. A brief, lucid introduction to the topic. Index and bibliography.

Castberg, Frede. *The European Convention on Human Rights.* Leiden, The Netherlands: Sijthoff, 1974. Clearly written study of the background ideas and principles of the convention. Examines also the procedures of the convention and the development of its jurisprudence through the 1960's. Somewhat dated, but still useful for the general reader and student. Index and bibliography.

Drzemczewski, A. *European Human Rights Convention in Domestic Law: A Comparative Study.* London: Oxford University Press, 1983. Excellent interpretive analysis of the ways in which member nations of the Council of Europe incorporate the provisions of the European Convention into their domestic law. Index and useful bibliography.

Jacobs, Francis G. *The European Convention on Human Rights.* Oxford, England: Clarendon Press, 1975. Well-written general survey of the background and history of the European Convention. Covers all aspects of the principles of the convention and the policies and procedures of the commission and the Court of Human Rights. Index and bibliography.

Morrison, Clovis C. *The Dynamics of Development in the European Human Rights Convention System.* The Hague: Nijhoff, 1981. Interpretive and critical examination of the work of the European Court of Human Rights. Analyzes in detail the ways in which the court has interpreted, modified, and even extended the principles and provisions of the European Convention. Index and bibliography.

Robertson, A. H. "The European Convention on Human Rights." In *The International Protection of Human Rights*, edited by Evan Luard. New York: Praeger, 1967. The best of the brief accounts of the convention. Outlines the origins, principles, and impact of the convention. Provides detailed examples of how the provisions of the convention have been applied and implemented. Article references and brief bibliography.

_____. *Human Rights in Europe.* 2d ed. Manchester, England: Manchester University Press, 1977. A more substantial and detailed survey of the subject that supplements the previous entry. Includes a thorough analysis of the procedures of the commission and court. An excellent work for the general reader and student. Index and good bibliography.

Van Dijk, P., and F. Van Hoof. *Theory and Practice of the European Convention on*

*Human Rights.* Deventer, The Netherlands: Kluwer, 1984. The most comprehensive source on the subject. A valuable and detailed examination of the procedures of the convention. The ponderous prose of the English translation is more suited to the academic reader. Index and bibliography.

Weil, Gordon L. *The European Convention on Human Rights: Background, Development, and Prospects.* Leiden: Sijthoff, 1963. Dated but useful account of the convention. Includes an analysis of the background and impact of the convention and a detailed description of its articles and protocols. No index, but a good bibliography.

*Douglas A. Lea*

## Cross-References

The Atlantic Charter Declares a Postwar Right of Self-Determination (1941), p. 584; The United Nations Adopts Its Charter (1945), p. 657; The United Nations Adopts the Universal Declaration of Human Rights (1948), p. 789; The European Court of Human Rights Is Established (1950), p. 849; The United Nations Sets Rules for the Treatment of Prisoners (1955), p. 935; The European Social Charter Is Signed (1961), p. 1137; The U.N. Covenant on Civil and Political Rights Is Adopted (1966), p. 1353; Cassin Is Awarded the Nobel Peace Prize (1968), p. 1462; The Inter-American Court of Human Rights Is Established (1969), p. 1503; The United Nations Issues a Declaration Against Torture (1975), p. 1847; The United Nations Issues a Conduct Code for Law Enforcement Officials (1979), p. 2040; A Paraguayan Torturer Is Found Guilty of Violating the Law of Nations (1980), p. 2106.

# THE EUROPEAN COURT OF HUMAN RIGHTS IS ESTABLISHED

*Category of event:* Civil rights
*Time:* November 4, 1950
*Locale:* Rome, Italy

*The European Convention on Human Rights provided for concrete human rights machinery—a European Commission and Court of Human Rights*

*Principal personages:*
WINSTON CHURCHILL (1874-1965), the former British prime minister who called for a "United States of Europe"
ÉDOUARD HERRIOT (1872-1957), the president of the French National Assembly
PAUL-HENRI SPAAK (1899-1972), the Belgian premier
RENÉ CASSIN (1887-1976), a judge on the European Court of Human Rights

## Summary of Event

The European Court of Human Rights can trace its roots in two different directions—to the support by the United Nations (UN) of human rights and to the post-World War II forces in Europe urging various forms of European integration. On December 10, 1948, the General Assembly of the United Nations proclaimed the Universal Declaration of Human Rights and asked that steps be taken to give legally binding effect to the principles articulated in the declaration. Gaining the support of U.N. member states for concrete human rights efforts would turn out to be a daunting task, but the Western European states were prepared to move ahead with a regional experiment in human rights protection.

Among the early calls for organizing Europe after World War II was a speech by former British prime minister Winston Churchill in Zurich, Switzerland, on September 19, 1946, in which he pointed out the desirability of a "United States of Europe." His view was supported by many others, such as Édouard Herriot, the president of the French National Assembly and president of the French Council for a United Europe, one of several groups working toward European unity. These groups united in organizing a Congress of Europe, with Winston Churchill as honorary president, at The Hague during May, 1948. The Congress agreed upon a series of resolutions that pointed to the past problems and divisive nature of national sovereignty in Europe, called for a European parliament that would establish a court and implement a charter of human rights, and noted that a united Europe was an essential feature for the creation of a united world.

The Hague efforts would ultimately find realization when ten Western European states signed the Statute of the Council of Europe in London on May 5, 1949. The initial organs of the Council were the Committee of Ministers, consisting of the foreign ministers of each of the member states, and the Consultative Assembly, made up of delegates selected by national parliaments on a proportional basis linked to country size and party strength in parliament. The preamble and first article of the Council's statute reflected a commitment to the ideals of the Hague resolutions, so when the Consultative Assembly convened in Strasbourg, France, during the summer of 1949, with Édouard Herriot as honorary president and Paul-Henri Spaak, the Belgian premier and dedicated European, as its formal president, it addressed such questions as paths to European unity and protection of human rights.

On November 4, 1950, the Council of Europe states, meeting in Rome, signed the European Convention for the Protection of Human Rights and Fundamental Freedoms, which drew heavily from the Universal Declaration of Human Rights. The protected rights included the rights to life, liberty, and security of person; freedom from torture, slavery, servitude, arbitrary arrest, detention, or exile; the right to a fair trial; freedom from arbitrary interference in private or family life, home, and correspondence; freedom of thought, conscience, religion, opinion, expression, assembly, and association; and the right to marry and found a family. Going a step further than the United Nations, however, the European convention provided for the machinery, pending complex ratification options open to Council of Europe member states, to protect the enumerated human rights. The machinery included a European Commission of Human Rights and a European Court of Human Rights, each with a membership equal to Council of Europe membership. Initial petitions were to be filed with the commission. If the commission decided to hear a complaint (some 98 percent of complaints would be rejected), a diplomatic settlement would be attempted. Failing to achieve a settlement, the commission could refer the case to the Committee of Ministers for a "political" settlement or to the court for a "legal" settlement. Individuals could not bring a case directly to the court; a case could only be brought by the commission or by a member state that had referred the case to the commission, whose national was alleged to be a victim, or against which a complaint had been lodged.

Why would the established Western European democracies, states likely to protect human rights anyway, be pioneers in establishing human rights machinery? Postwar European leaders had experienced war firsthand and had seen the forces of totalitarianism sweep across Europe; a number had been in internment camps and had been tortured (often by their own governments), and perhaps the time was ripe for a reaffirmation and strengthening of democratic values and human rights to prevent the past from returning. In the year between the creation of the Council of Europe and the signing of the European Convention on Human Rights, a Communist government had seized power in Czechoslovakia, a civil war had erupted in Greece, the blockade of West Berlin had unfolded, and the Korean War had begun.

The European human rights system, which became widely praised (in spite of some deficiencies) for its contributions to international law and human rights protection, nevertheless had a slow start. The convention on human rights, signed on November 4, 1950, did not go into force until September 3, 1953, following the required number of ratifications. The first election of the commission took place on May 18, 1954. The court could not be elected until January 21, 1959, following acceptance by eight states of the court's jurisdiction as compulsory. Accepting states obligated themselves to carry out decisions of the court, but the real strength of the court lay in publicity and moral suasion.

The court's first decision came in 1960 in the case of *Lawless v. Ireland*, in which an alleged member of the Irish Republican Army claimed he had been detained without trial by Irish authorities. The court noted that his arrest and detention had not been in accord with the convention but also noted that the convention allowed states to deviate from their obligations under the convention in time of war or other public emergency. Consequently, the court found in favor of Ireland.

In its second case, *DeBecker v. Belgium*, the court was asked to rule on the complaint of Raymond DeBecker, a journalist who had been prohibited from practicing his profession because of his alleged wartime collaboration with the Nazis. The court voted to strike the case from its list in 1962, after DeBecker and the Belgian government came to an informal agreement.

The court's start was slow; the court averaged about one case a year during its first decade of existence. In 1985, its one hundredth judgment was rendered. Activity in later years went as high as twenty decisions in a year. The court turned out to be relatively active, and its consideration of cases arising under the convention has been wide-ranging. Perhaps more significant, however, the work of the court has affected people's lives, examined societal norms, altered the behavior of governments, and made significant contributions to international law. It has also represented a concrete, effective regional implementation of the human rights ideals advanced by the United Nations in 1948.

## Impact of Event

The influence of the Council of Europe and its organs developed slowly. The council has generally been eclipsed by such other organizations as the North Atlantic Treaty Organization (NATO) and the European Community (the "Common Market" countries).

Nevertheless, the early work of the council in encouraging European cooperation and defining democratic values as the unsettled postwar years merged with the threatening Cold War years deserves recognition, certainly in the area of human rights. The council has won praise for its work across a broad spectrum of European cooperative efforts. The European Court of Human Rights, however, is not one of Europe's better-known institutions.

The European Court of Human Rights has nevertheless made a difference, and it has sided often with individuals in claims against states. One easily forgets what a novelty it is in international law for a citizen to be able to appeal over the head of a national government to an international tribunal. Much of the court's work deals with the mundane issues of law found anywhere—conditions of arrest and detention, vagrancy, wiretapping, or deviant behavior. Other issues seem to involve broader social questions, such as the selection of textbooks for schools or linguistic questions in linguistically divided states where language looms large in school instruction, job placement and advancement, and official dealings with the state.

Some cases are well-known and are very controversial in their impact. The case of the *Sunday Times*, for example, concerned a newspaper article discussing litigation between representatives of the victims of thalidomide and the British manufacturers of the drug. The article reviewed evidence of the manufacturer's liability and was the subject of an injunction restraining publication. The court sided with the newspaper in support of freedom of expression.

The publicity surrounding a case may cause a state to change policy and come to an agreement with a complainant, as *DeBecker v. Belgium* showed. States have changed their laws, or drafted new laws, based upon court rulings. The European Community has also been influenced by the human rights decisions of the court.

Although clearly reflecting personal achievement, the awarding of the Nobel Peace Prize in 1968 to René Cassin, a judge on the European Court of Human Rights, showed the impact of the human rights effort. Judge Cassin, one of the authors of the U.N. Declaration of Human Rights of 1948, was cited for his tireless efforts on behalf of human rights both in Europe and worldwide.

Ultimately, courts must be judged by the force of their reasoning in important cases, their record of wise jurisprudence, and the impact they have upon law generally. The European Court of Human Rights, which generally has evoked positive evaluations, may also serve as a human rights model for new U.N. efforts as well as for developing human rights structures in Africa and Latin America. One measure of its success may be the flocking of the states of Eastern Europe to join the Council of Europe in the wake of the collapse of the Soviet empire.

## Bibliography

Cassese, Antonio. *Human Rights in a Changing World.* Philadelphia, Pa.: Temple University Press, 1990. This book offers a chapter-length discussion of the European Commission and Court of Human Rights and provides a worldwide context for assessing the status of human rights in Europe. The author appears both as scholar and advocate. An appendix discusses major international human rights organizations.

Crawford, Oliver. *Done This Day: The European Idea in Action.* New York: Taplinger, 1970. An explicitly partisan and pro-European federalist book, this volume nevertheless offers a thoughtful examination of the "European Idea"—represented in both the Council of Europe and the European Community. The author provides a vivid and moving account of the people and forces working for "Europe."

Fawcett, J. E. S. *The Application of the European Convention on Human Rights.* Oxford, England: Clarendon Press, 1969. This is a rather stuffy and structured analysis of the European Convention on Human Rights as applied by its organs between 1954 and 1967. Nevertheless, the presentation gives a strong sense of public interest and organizational response to the convention on a clause-by-clause, article-by-article basis.

Merrills, J. G. *The Development of International Law by the European Court of Human Rights.* Manchester, England: Manchester University Press, 1988. An excellent, thorough, and readable study of the European Court of Human Rights. Merrills examines the mechanics and philosophy of the court's functioning as well as its contributions to the development of international human rights law. Also includes a table of cases.

Mikaelsen, Laurids. *European Protection of Human Rights: The Practice and Procedure of the European Commission of Human Rights on the Admissibility of Applications from Individuals and States.* Alphen aan den Rijn, The Netherlands: Sijthoff & Noordhoff, 1980. The European Commission of Human Rights is a crucial organ in protecting human rights that may refer cases to the European Court of Human Rights. Mikaelsen offers a detailed study of the process of applying to the commission, which rejects some 98 percent of all applications.

Mower, A. Glenn, Jr. *Regional Human Rights: A Comparative Study of the West European and Inter-American Systems.* Westport, Conn.: Greenwood Press, 1991. This book compares the backgrounds and human rights structures of the Council of Europe and the Organization of American States. Stressing the divergent experiences of Western Europe and Latin America, the author examines the economic, social, political, and human rights backgrounds of each region.

Robertson, A. H. *The Council of Europe: Its Structure, Functions, and Achievements.* London: Stevens & Sons, 1956. One of the classic works on the Council of Europe, this book examines its origins and structure with focused discussions of economic, social and cultural, human rights, legal, and other questions. The European Court of Human Rights had not yet become active, so the discussion focuses on structure and potential.

_____. *The Law of International Institutions in Europe: Being an Account of Some Recent Developments in the Field of International Law.* Manchester, England: Manchester University Press, 1961. Based on a series of lectures delivered by Robertson, this book examines different expressions of the "European idea." Robertson discusses the history of European integration, with particular focus on the Council of Europe, human rights, and the European Commission and Court of Human Rights. Extensive appendices reproduce relevant European documents.

*Forest L. Grieves*

## Cross-References

The Declaration on the Rights and Duties of Man Is Adopted (1948), p. 755; The United Nations Adopts the Universal Declaration of Human Rights (1948), p. 789; The European Convention on Human Rights Is Signed (1950), p. 843; The U.N. Convention on the Political Rights of Women Is Approved (1952), p. 885; The United Nations Amends Its International Slavery Convention (1953), p. 902; The Inter-

American Commission on Human Rights Is Created (1959), p. 1032; The European Social Charter Is Signed (1961), p. 1137; The United Nations Issues a Declaration on Racial Discrimination (1963), p. 1212; The U.N. Covenant on Civil and Political Rights Is Adopted (1966), p. 1353; Cassin Is Awarded the Nobel Peace Prize (1968), p. 1462; The Inter-American Court of Human Rights Is Established (1969), p. 1503; The Helsinki Agreement Offers Terms for International Cooperation (1975), p. 1806; Soviets Crack Down on Moscow's Helsinki Watch Group (1977), p. 1915.

# THE UNITED NATIONS HIGH COMMISSIONER FOR REFUGEES STATUTE IS APPROVED

*Category of event:* Refugee relief
*Time:* December 14, 1950
*Locale:* United Nations, New York City

*By adopting this statute, the international community reaffirmed its commitment to protect and assist persons possessing a well-founded fear of persecution*

*Principal personages:*

GERRIT JAN VAN HEUVEN GOEDHART (1901-1956), the first United Nations (U.N.) high commissioner for refugees

JOHN DONALD KINGSLEY (1908-1972), the director-general of the International Refugee Organization (1949-1952) who presided over its transfer of authority to the U.N. high commissioner's office

TRYGVE LIE (1896-1968), the secretary-general of the United Nations (1946-1952)

## Summary of Event

The creation of the Office of the United Nations High Commissioner for Refugees (UNHCR) by the U.N. General Assembly on December 14, 1950, did not mark the first effort by the international community to address the problem of large-scale refugee migrations. In 1921, the League of Nations appointed Fridtjof Nansen to the post of high commissioner for refugees for the purpose of grappling with refugee problems associated with the Bolshevik revolution in Russia. Later, Nansen extended protection and assistance to Armenians, Assyro-Chaldeans, and Turks fleeing from turmoil attending the collapse of the Ottoman Empire. Efforts by the League of Nations on behalf of refugees continued officially until the organization's dissolution in 1946.

During World War II and its immediate aftermath, several organizations were established to deal with the nearly thirty million displaced persons and refugees in Europe. Many of these people were homeless, destitute, and highly vulnerable, especially during Europe's cold winters. The United Nations Relief and Rehabilitation Administration (UNRRA), established in 1943, cared for and assisted millions of displaced persons and repatriated some six million persons before it was replaced by the Preparatory Commission for the International Refugee Organization (PCIRO) in 1947. The Intergovernmental Committee on Refugees (IGCR), first established in 1938 to deal with the Jewish refugee problem spawned by Nazi anti-Semitic policy in Germany, also briefly took responsibility in 1946 for Nansen refugees who had been under the care of the League of Nations.

In 1947, work on behalf of refugees and displaced persons in Europe was consolidated under the authority of the PCIRO and in 1948 under the fully constituted but

856

temporary mandate of the International Refugee Organization (IRO). By this time, Cold War politics were chilling international relations, and the IRO contended not only with a large number of war-displaced persons but also with new arrivals from behind the Iron Curtain. In 1946, the General Assembly of the United Nations reaffirmed the principle that no persons fearing persecution could be compelled to return to their country of origin against their will, even if their governments insisted upon their return, as many East European governments did. Thus, although the IRO was charged with exploring repatriation of refugees and displaced persons as the solution of first preference, thousands of East Europeans refused to go home, so the IRO explored possibilities of settlement in their countries of first asylum or resettlement to third countries. Under the capable leadership of its directors-general, including John Donald Kingsley, more than one million persons were resettled in third countries during the IRO's operations, mainly in the United States, Australia, Israel, and Canada. Nevertheless, by the time the IRO was liquidated and its protection function shifted to the UNHCR in 1951, there were still about 400,000 unresettled refugees under the IRO mandate.

With the IRO's mandate fast approaching its conclusion, the U.N. General Assembly on December 3, 1949, established another temporary successor agency. Wrangling over the exact nature and extent of this new agency's mandate centered on whether it should be responsible for material assistance and the very expensive resettlement operations conducted by the IRO or merely for protection of refugees until resettlement was effected by another agency. The United States, which had financed up to 70 percent of the IRO's work, wished to see expenditures for refugee operations reduced, while West European countries worried about the political and economic implications of a large and lingering refugee population in their territories. The Soviet Union and East European countries resented the creation of any agency that would protect and assist exiles from their territories and refused to become members of the UNHCR, which they viewed as a tool of Western capitalism.

The upshot of these variable pressures was the creation of an agency whose responsibilities included, first and foremost, protection of refugees. The UNHCR also was given responsibility for material assistance to refugees, but its initial budget, provided out of the regular U.N. budget, included only administrative expenses, not operational ones, and any efforts by the UNHCR to raise revenue from governments or private sources directly was subject to General Assembly approval. Under its statute, the UNHCR had no direct responsibility for resettlement of refugees; this function was later placed in the hands of the Intergovernmental Committee for European Migration. The UNHCR was given responsibility for seeking permanent solutions for refugees, which included not only repatriation and local integration but also third-country resettlement. More important, the statute's definition of the term "refugee" was sufficiently elastic to include all persons previously classified as refugees by the IRO and other persons who could show a well-founded fear of persecution if returned to their country of nationality. The definition was universal in nature, and—unlike the definition incorporated in the 1951 Convention Relating to the

Status of Refugees, which contained time restrictions—was potentially applicable whenever refugee problems might arise. Moreover, the statute stipulated that the UNHCR's work was entirely nonpolitical in nature, focusing rather on the social and humanitarian aspects of refugee situations.

Answering to the General Assembly through the U.N.'s Economic and Social Council, and working under the supervision of an advisory committee composed of governments and other interested parties, Gerrit Jan van Heuven Goedhart was named to a three-year term as the UNHCR's first high commissioner and assumed his position on January 1, 1951. Operating under the statute's initially restricted and temporary, but potentially elastic, mandate, van Heuven Goedhart aggressively carved out a permanent and effective UNHCR role not only for protecting but also for assisting refugees. He won permission from the General Assembly to seek funds for emergency assistance in 1952. In 1953, the General Assembly extended the UNHCR's mandate from three to five years, and in 1954 the high commissioner was allowed to seek funds for a "Program of Permanent Solutions." In the same year, the UNHCR won the first of two Nobel Peace Prizes.

When refugees began pouring out of Hungary as a result of the Soviet crackdown of 1956, the UNHCR was well positioned to respond to Austria's request for its intervention on behalf of Hungarian refugees. The UNHCR's success in protecting, assisting, and promoting resettlement of Hungarian refugees further heightened its prestige in the eyes of Western governments and solidified the foundation from which it has gradually, under the direction of the General Assembly and with the support of member governments, extended its good offices to refugees and other persons in need of its help throughout the world.

Measured in human terms, the early success of the UNHCR meant not only that refugees would be spared from forcible repatriation to countries that might persecute them but also that they would be provided with care and assistance until such time as they might find new and permanent homes. In addition to protection and assistance, the UNHCR provided hope for a better future to destitute and homeless people who otherwise might have died or languished in needless poverty. In time, and contrary to the initial hopes and expectations of its founders, global events dictated that the UNHCR could not remain a temporary and fragile holding operation. Hundreds of thousands of European refugees benefited from its work in the early 1950's, and as time passed millions more would benefit in every corner of the globe.

## Impact of Event

The true impact of the General Assembly's decision to create the UNHCR cannot be measured solely by its immediate effects. With a budget in 1952 of little more than $700,000 and only about 400,000 European refugees under its care, the UNHCR's birth was not an especially auspicious one. Nevertheless, and despite periodic budgetary crises throughout its history, the UNHCR matured into an agency responsible for the protection and welfare of some sixteen million refugees throughout the world. Its annual budgets regularly approached or exceeded $500 million by the

1990's, and it maintained a physical presence in about eighty countries.

As refugee situations developed in Africa and Asia during the 1960's and 1970's, the U.N. General Assembly encouraged the UNHCR to extend its protection and assistance functions to non-European contexts, despite the 1951 Convention Relating to the Status of Refugees' restriction that considered only those persons fleeing from persecution as a result of events prior to January 1, 1951, as refugees. This extension of UNHCR good offices was made easier when, in 1967, a protocol to the 1951 convention formally removed the time limitations. Thus, over the years—informally and through ad hoc procedures before 1967 and more formally and routinely since then—the UNHCR has extended its protection and assistance to refugees in Third World countries where civil war, domestic upheaval, and political persecution, often exacerbated by drought and famine, have produced refugee flows of monumental proportions.

By the late 1970's, the world was wracked by major refugee flows from Indochina, where hundreds of thousands of boat people and land refugees sought relief from repression. In Africa, millions of people fled from civil war and drought-ridden countries. These movements intensified during the 1980's. The Soviet Union's intervention in Afghanistan in 1979 and the ensuing long civil war produced more than five million refugees in the 1980's. Tens of thousands of Central Americans fled from civil conflicts in that region. The UNHCR was actively involved in all these situations, coordinating assistance with governments and private agencies, providing emergency aid to refugees, promoting refugee protection, and working with U.N. development agencies and governments to address the long-term development implications of massive refugee migrations on the social and economic infrastructures of poor host countries.

In addition, in keeping with its statute, the UNHCR has encouraged governments to pursue durable solutions for refugees. It has assisted in the successful voluntary repatriation of millions of refugees since its inception. It has promoted programs to encourage successful settlement of refugees in their countries of first asylum and, where appropriate, has encouraged governments to consider third-country resettlement.

The hallmark of the UNHCR has been its ability to adapt to changing circumstances and to cope with the often very difficult political circumstances that surround refugee situations. Having started on tenuous footing with a fragile consensus among governments, the UNHCR, under the able leadership of several high commissioners, has proven its worth as an indispensable element of the international refugee protection and assistance network.

## Bibliography

Chandler, Edgar H. S. *The High Tower of Refuge.* New York: Praeger, 1959. This book, written by a former director of the Service to Refugees of the World Council of Churches, offers an inspiring and compassionate from-the-trenches perspective about refugees and relief workers, the very constituencies for which UNHCR was created and upon which it relies to carry out its mandate. Includes photographs, an index, and a short bibliography.

Gordenker, Leon. *Refugees in International Relations.* New York: Columbia University Press, 1987. A thoughtful and balanced analysis of the global refugee problem and the role of the UNHCR. Using the notion of forced migrations as the test for defining refugees, the author discusses realistic ways in which the international community can respond to contemporary refugee emergencies and resolve long-term refugee situations. Includes a bibliography and index.

Gorman, Robert F. *Coping with Africa's Refugee Burden: A Time for Solutions.* Dordrecht, The Netherlands: Martinus Nijhoff, 1987. This book describes the difficulties encountered by the UNHCR and other bodies in meeting the assistance needs of Third World asylum countries and their local populations, whose well-being is often adversely affected by the presence of large numbers of refugees. Includes figures, tables, a bibliography, and an index.

Holborn, Louise. *Refugees, a Problem of Our Times: The Work of the UNHCR, 1951-1972.* 2 vols. Metuchen, N.J.: Scarecrow Press, 1975. This is the definitive work on the formation of the UNHCR and its first two decades of work. Highly detailed and voluminously documented, this book serves as a sequel to Holborn's work on the UNHCR's predecessor, the IRO. Includes numerous charts, tables, an index, and a bibliography.

Marrus, Michael R. *The Unwanted: European Refugees in the Twentieth Century.* New York: Oxford University Press, 1985. This painstakingly researched, comprehensive, and readable history of Europe's refugee problem traces in detail Jewish and European refugee flows and the international politics that spawned them from the late nineteenth century to the creation of the UNHCR. An excellent treatment of League of Nations and pre-UNHCR international policy responses. Includes a bibliography and an index.

Shawcross, William. *The Quality of Mercy: Cambodia, Holocaust, and Modern Conscience.* New York: Simon & Schuster, 1984. This journalistic account of the conflicting interagency mandates and governmental policies that plagued the Cambodian relief effort provides insight into the difficulties that the UNHCR and other international and private relief agencies encounter in highly politicized situations. Lacks consultation with academic sources but is strong on interviews. Contains a source section and an index.

Vernant, Jacques. *The Refugee in the Post-War World.* New Haven, Conn.: Yale University Press, 1953. This lengthy encyclopedic work meticulously catalogues the global refugee situation as it existed at the inception of the UNHCR. Early chapters summarize the refugee problem and international agency responses to it. Subsequent chapters catalog in more pedestrian fashion the legal, economic, and social status of refugees by country of reception. Includes charts, a bibliography, and an index.

Zarjevski, Yefime. *A Future Preserved: International Assistance to Refugees.* Oxford, England: Pergamon Press, 1988. This book chronicles the formation and growth of the UNHCR to the mid-1980's. It surveys refugee situations in various regions while nicely documenting how the UNHCR gradually strengthened its capacity to provide protection and assistance to refugees. Includes a bibliography and an index.

Zolberg, Aristide R., Astri Suhrke, and Sergio Aguayo. *Escape from Violence: Conflict and the Refugee Crisis in the Developing World.* New York: Oxford University Press, 1989. Three talented refugee specialists combine forces to produce a comprehensive assessment of the factors that motivate and exacerbate refugee flows in the Third World. The role of the UNHCR is ably and extensively analyzed. Exhaustively documented and footnoted. Contains an index but no bibliography.

*Robert F. Gorman*

## Cross-References

Nansen Wins the Nobel Peace Prize (1922), p. 361; Soviets Take Control of Eastern Europe (1943), p. 612; The Marshall Plan Provides Aid to Europe (1947), p. 706; The United Nations Adopts the Universal Declaration of Human Rights (1948), p. 789; Hundreds of Thousands Leave East Germany for the West (1949), p. 795; The Geneva Convention Establishes Norms of Conduct in Warfare (1949), p. 808; The United Nations Creates an Agency to Aid Palestinian Refugees (1949), p. 814; The U.N. Convention Relating to the Status of Refugees Is Adopted (1951), p. 867; The United Nations Drafts a Convention on Stateless Persons (1954), p. 918; A Hungarian Uprising Is Quelled by Soviet Military Forces (1956), p. 969; The U.N. Covenant on Civil and Political Rights Is Adopted (1966), p. 1353.

# SOUTH AFRICA BEGINS A SYSTEM OF SEPARATE DEVELOPMENT

*Categories of event:* Racial and ethnic rights; civil rights
*Time:* June 21, 1951
*Locale:* Cape Town, South Africa

*The Bantu Authorities Act, one of several key apartheid laws passed after the National Party victory of 1948, began to implement the "grand design" for separate development in the Bantu Homelands*

> *Principal personages:*
> DANIEL FRANÇOIS MALAN (1874-1959), the South African prime minister from 1948 to 1954
> HENDRIK FRENSCH VERWOERD (1901-1966), the leading theorist of separate development, native affairs minister from 1950 to 1958 and prime minister from 1958 until his death
> ALBERT LUTULI (1898-1967), the president of the African National Congress from 1952 to 1967
> JAN CHRISTIAN SMUTS (1870-1950), the prime minister from 1939 to 1948

## Summary of Event

Before the watershed election of 1948, South Africans of non-European ancestry had long experienced significant forms of legal and social discrimination. With the end of slavery in 1833, pass laws continued to require blacks (also called "Natives" or "Bantu") to carry identification cards. The Native Land Acts of 1913 and 1936 prohibited blacks from owning land in areas of white residence and designated about 13 percent of the land for blacks, who composed about 70 percent of the population. Although most segregation laws were aimed at blacks, there were also limitations on the political and social rights of Asians and so-called coloreds (people of mixed black-white ancestry). In general, Afrikaners of Dutch ancestry were more uncompromising supporters of rigid segregation than were English-speaking whites, and in the 1930's Afrikaners began to use the word "apartheid" to refer to their ideas of racial apartness or separation.

The government of the United Party under Jan Christian Smuts, in power between 1939 and 1948, did not in any way challenge the legitimacy of segregation and white domination. Still, United Party policies were considered excessively liberal by members of the National Party, the party of most Afrikaners. Although Smuts was one of the designers of the United Nations charter, his government passed a 1946 law that restricted places where Indians might reside or purchase land, and Smuts's prestige was damaged when the U.N. General Assembly approved a resolution critical of the 1946 law. Early in 1948, nevertheless, liberals were encouraged when Smuts chose Jan Hofmeyr as deputy prime minister and when he accepted H. A. Fagan's commission report that concluded that "total segregation" was entirely impractical.

In the election of 1948, the platform of the National Party denounced the Fagan Report and endorsed a policy of apartheid. A campaign pamphlet argued that black rights should be restricted to the black reserves, that most Indians should return to India, and that "the fundamental guiding principle of National Party policy is preserving and safeguarding the White race." The conservative leader of the party, Daniel François Malan, was a Dutch Reformed minister who often spoke of Afrikaner history as "not the work of men but the creation of God." The election was very close, but the National Party, in a coalition with other Afrikaner parties, did manage to win a five-seat majority in the House of Assembly, the dominant chamber of the South African parliament.

Despite this slight majority, the Nationalists moved boldly to implement their program for apartheid. On August 19, Prime Minister Malan told the parliament that this program would begin with four points: the end of black representation to the House of Assembly; the establishment of limited self-government for blacks in their reserves; the removal of colored voters from the electoral roll in Cape Province, allowing them white representatives; and the mandated racial segregation of all schools and universities. The parliament quickly passed one of many "petty apartheid laws" that made it illegal for blacks to use first-class coaches of railroad cars, and in 1949 it approved a law that prohibited marriages between persons of different races.

Smuts, until his death in 1950, led the fight against the passage of apartheid legislation, but the National coalition had the necessary votes to prevail. The African National Congress (ANC), a black organization begun in 1912, was the most conspicuous opponent of the Malan government, and it was at this time that Albert Lutuli and Nelson Mandela began to attract international attention. In its annual meeting of 1948, the ANC developed a program of action based on strikes and civil disobedience; by 1950 the ANC had decided to end all cooperation with the government. Similarly, the Anglican church, the Catholic bishops, and the South African Indian Congress all made strong denunciations of the concept of apartheid. Moral condemnation, however, did not have any visible impact on the Malan government.

During 1950, Malan was able to win the parliament's approval of three significant laws. On June 19, the parliament passed the Group Areas Act, which divided the country into specific regions to be exclusively reserved for whites, blacks, or coloreds. About the same time, the Population Registration Act provided for the systematic classification of people into one of those three racial categories (an Asian category was added later). The third law, the Suppression of Communism Act, outlawed the expression of almost any ideas that had anything in common with Marxist socialism, including any doctrine that promoted "the encouragement of feelings of hostility between the European and non-European races."

On October 18, 1950, while the parliament was in the process of making these sweeping changes, Malan added Dr. Hendrick Verwoerd to his cabinet as the minister of native affairs. A university sociologist and newspaper editor from Johannesburg, Verwoerd was an articulate defender of a "grand design of separate development" for the different ethnic groups of South Africa. Verwoerd insisted, and probably convinced himself, that his grand design was not oppressive to non-Europeans and that it would allow all South Africans to realize their aspirations with full respect for the country's pluralism of cultures and traditions. Tribalism was the key to Verwoerd's grand design, with the goal of increasing tribal autonomy within the reserves while excluding blacks from other regions, except when their cheap labor was necessary.

Verwoerd's ideas about tribal autonomy provided the theoretical justification for the Bantu Authorities Act, which passed the House of Assembly on June 21, 1951. The main intention of the legislation was to reinforce the authority of the tribal chiefs and headmen, thus endorsing the traditional basis of authority within the reserves. Each local tribe was to have a tribal council (made up of a chief and his advisers) for the administration of local affairs. The tribal councils of a region would elect representatives to a regional council, which would have executive authority over hospitals, roads, education, medical care, and other matters designated by the governor-general. Above this level, regional councils would appoint representatives to a territorial council, with the entire system under the supervision of the Department of Native Affairs. The law abolished the Natives' Representative Council, a partially elected advisory body that had existed since 1936.

Under the new system, tribal chiefs and headmen were selected from customary ruling families, but at the same time they were officially appointed by the white government and paid a small salary for carrying out their duties. As a result, tribal chiefs and headmen had the problem of keeping the confidence of both their own people and their European supervisors. The Department of Native Affairs reserved the power to remove any chief or headman considered unreliable, and Verwoerd made no secret about his determination that tribal leaders were expected to conform to official policies. In future years, the government would not hesitate to dismiss nonconformists, the most famous case being the 1952 dismissal of Lutuli because of his refusal to give up membership in the ANC. In addition to the issue of white control, the ANC opposed the Bantu Authorities Act because of its promotion of divisive tribalism. The ANC looked upon tribalism as the greatest barrier to the development of the kind of African unity necessary for a successful struggle against apartheid.

In the defiance campaign of 1952, the ANC leadership wrote to Prime Minister Malan requesting the repeal of the Bantu Authorities Act and five other "unjust laws." Malan's secretary replied that they should address their concerns to the Native Affairs Department and that the government would "make full use of the machinery at its disposal" to enforce the laws. Despite the defiance campaign and international protest, the Malan government was able to get its way in putting the 1951 law into effect. In 1953, three Bantu Authorities were introduced in the Transvaal, and two years later, the government achieved a major goal when the Transkeian General Council (called the "Bunga") voted to accept the principle of the new system. Meanwhile, the parliament continued to pass increasingly restrictive apartheid legislation, and there appeared to be no way to stop South Africa from moving further in the direction of Verwoerd's grand design for separate development.

## Impact of Event

The Bantu Authorities Act of 1951 began the implementation of separate development by promoting Bantu self-government in the reserves while preserving white control. Verwoerd understood that it was necessary to gain the support of chiefs and headmen and that this required that they be given vested interests in the system. In altruistic rhetoric, he argued that integration of the races could only result in conflict and the exploitation of non-Europeans; in contrast, the system of separate development would allow the Bantu to achieve equality and democracy within the tribal homelands. Critics noted that the fragmented reserves were in isolated areas with poor land and with few resources for economic development.

By 1953, the pillars of the apartheid system were firmly in place. Apparently the majority of white voters in South Africa approved of the direction of the National Party leadership, for in the general election of that year the National Party coalition greatly increased its majority. With its new majority, the Malan government passed three important laws that made apartheid increasingly oppressive to blacks, coloreds, and Asians. The Reservation of Separate Amenities Act of 1953 required segregation of all public facilities, including recreational areas and governmental services. The Bantu Education Act segregated educational institutions and increased governmental control of education to prevent blacks from receiving preparation for jobs reserved for whites. A third law of 1953, the Public Safety Act, authorized the police to arrest suspects without trial or judicial review, and it also allowed the government to declare a state of emergency for a period up to one year.

By the time that Verwoerd became prime minister in 1958, he had formulated a blueprint for taking apartheid to its logical conclusion. He was determined to eradicate all "black spots" in areas of white residence, forcing all blacks to live in one of the reserves. Also, building upon the foundation of the Bantu Authorities Act, he was resolved to bring order to the 260 scattered reserves. His first measure as prime minister was the Bantu Self-Government Act, which aimed at consolidating the existing reserves into eight Bantu homelands (called "Bantustans" by Verwoerd). In general, the homelands were made up of scattered pieces of land spread across three provinces. As in the 1951 law, the governing authorities were tribal chiefs and headmen, with the Bureau of Bantu Affairs retaining the veto over appointments and major decisions.

Despite internal and external condemnation, in subsequent years the National Party continued to win elections and to consolidate the apartheid system. In the 1970's, the government managed to transfer limited powers of self-government to ten tribal homelands and to confer all blacks with citizenship in one of these ethnic homelands. Since they were deemed to be citizens of the homelands, blacks of South Africa could not claim any political rights within the regions of the country that elected the national parliament. Thus, by the 1970's Verwoerd's vision for separate development appeared to be evolving in the way that he had intended; however, he had not anticipated the extent to which black poverty, alienation, and international opposition would increase over the years.

## Bibliography

Bunting, Brian. *The Rise of the South African Reich*. Baltimore, Md.: Penguin, 1964. A stimulating account that argues that the National government created a Nazi-like state after the 1948 election. If the generalizations are sometimes extreme, Bunting always presents an abundance of evidence.

Carter, Gwendolen. *The Politics of Inequality: South Africa Since 1948*. New York: Praeger, 1958. A detailed account of the first decade following the 1948 election, with excellent coverage of laws and parliamentary conflicts. The appendix has many original documents. Not recommended for beginners.

Carter, Gwendolen, Thomas Karis, and Newell Stultz. *South Africa's Transkei: The Politics of Domestic Colonialism*. Evanston, Ill.: Northwestern University Press, 1967. An excellent study of the largest of the tribal homelands of South Africa, including an analysis of the legislation that created the system of separate development. Too specialized for the general reader.

Davenport, T. R. H. *South Africa: A Modern History*. Toronto: University of Toronto Press, 1977. Probably the best general history of the country, including the various ethnic groups. The book provides a good reference for events, individuals, and movements, with exhaustive notes that refer to more specialized sources. Davenport is pessimistic about the prospects for the future.

Hepple, Kenneth. *Verwoerd*. Baltimore, Md.: Penguin, 1967. Written by a former leader of the South African Labor Party, the book presents a fascinating and fair account of a major ideologue responsible for the concept of the Bantu Authorities Act. An extremely readable book.

Ingham, Kenneth. *Jan Christian Smuts*. New York: St. Martin's Press, 1986. A good biography of South Africa's dominant figure of the twentieth century, written from a liberal perspective. Ingham is critical of Smuts's racial policies. There is little material about the period after 1948.

Lapping, Brian. *Apartheid: A History*. New York: George Braziller, 1987. An excellent and readable summary of the history of racial discrimination and apartheid from 1652 to the government of Pieter Botha, including many fascinating photographs and an annotated bibliography. Probably the best introduction to the topic.

Meredith, Martin. *In the Name of Apartheid: South Africa in the Postwar Period*. New York: Harper & Row, 1988. An interesting interpretative account of racial policies from the twilight of the Smuts era until the election of 1987, with a focus on major trends and themes. Writing just before Frederik de Klerk became prime minister, Meredith predicted that "the prospect of revolution seemed to draw inexorably closer."

Moodie, T. Dunbar. *The Rise of Afrikanerdom: Power, Apartheid, and the Afrikaner Civil Religion*. Berkeley: University of California Press, 1975. An emphasis on the religious component of Afrikaner nationalism, with many quotations from Malan and Verwoerd. Although Moodie probably minimizes the roles of economic and social forces, he has written a fascinating account of intellectual history.

Peterson, Robert, ed. *South Africa: A Modern History.* New York: Facts on File, 1979. A useful summary of the factual aspect of apartheid following the 1948 election, with a clear and concise description of major laws and events. Organized chronologically, the book is valuable as a quick reference for facts without much interpretation.

*Thomas T. Lewis*

**Cross-References**

The United Nations Adopts the Universal Declaration of Human Rights (1948), p. 789; Lutuli Is Awarded the Nobel Peace Prize (1961), p. 1143; The United Nations Issues a Declaration on Racial Discrimination (1963), p. 1212; The U.N. Covenant on Civil and Political Rights Is Adopted (1966), p. 1353; The United Nations Votes to Suppress and Punish Apartheid (1973), p. 1736; Students in Soweto Rebel Against the White Government (1976), p. 1882; Biko Is Murdered by Interrogators in South Africa (1977), p. 1887; The United Nations Imposes an Arms Embargo on South Africa (1977), p. 1937; The United Nations Issues a Declaration on South Africa (1979), p. 2008; Tutu Wins the Nobel Peace Prize (1984), p. 2244; Black Workers in South Africa Go on Strike (1987), p. 2304; Mandela Is Freed (1990), p. 2559; De Klerk Promises to Topple Apartheid Legislation (1991), p. 2606.

# THE U.N. CONVENTION RELATING TO THE STATUS OF REFUGEES IS ADOPTED

*Category of event:* Refugee relief
*Time:* July 28, 1951
*Locale:* Geneva, Switzerland

*The unanimous adoption of the United Nations Convention Relating to the Status of Refugees was a major step forward in according refugees explicit treaty-based rights*

*Principal personages:*

GERRIT JAN VAN HEUVEN GOEDHART (1901-1956), the United Nations high commissioner for refugees

KNUD LARSEN (1905-1965), the president of the Conference of Plenipotentiaries on the Status of Refugees and Stateless Persons, which adopted the 1951 convention

TRYGVE LIE (1896-1968), the secretary-general of the United Nations

## Summary of Event

Modern refugees face a terrible predicament: Having fled from persecution in their home states, they fear returning home, but as exiles they have no legal protection, no passports or visas, and no governments willing to protect them from mistreatment abroad. Unlike exiles of the past, however, who could be ruthlessly exploited or forcibly deported or extradited to their country of origin, modern refugees benefit from efforts made first by the League of Nations and later by the United Nations to give them legal protection abroad. These protections include travel documents that allow refugees to seek out new and permanent homes and guarantees against being returned against their will to their countries of origin, where they fear persecution. These efforts to protect refugees gathered steam in the late 1940's as governments tried to cope with the millions of homeless, destitute, and stateless displaced persons and refugees resulting from World War II.

On July 28, 1951, the United Nations Convention Relating to the Status of Refugees was concluded and opened for signature at the European office of the United Nations in Geneva, Switzerland. It was the product of three weeks of negotiations in which twenty-six governments and two observer states participated. Also invited to the conference as nonvoting participants were Gerrit Jan van Heuven Goedhart, the United Nations high commissioner for refugees, whose office would be made responsible for oversight and implementation of the treaty, and representatives of the International Labour Organisation and the Council of Europe. Nearly thirty nongovernmental organizations also participated as observers. The three weeks of negotiations, however, were only the culmination of years of prior concern for and action on behalf of refugees by the international community.

The Conference of Plenipotentiaries on the Status of Refugees and Stateless Persons, which was initiated by a General Assembly resolution of December 14, 1950, marked only the second time that the United Nations had convened a conference under its aegis, thus emphasizing the special importance that the United Nations attached to the resolution of refugee situations. Indeed, during its early years, concerns about how to cope with the great humanitarian needs of refugees, displaced people, and stateless persons occupied the nearly constant attention of the United Nations, which, in turn, built upon the pioneering work done by the League of Nations.

The United Nations faced two interrelated tasks: to create and sustain institutional mechanisms to assist and find solutions for refugees and stateless persons, and to provide refugees and stateless persons with legal status and protection until permanent solutions were found for them. Through the creation of temporary expedients such as the United Nations Relief and Rehabilitation Administration and the International Refugee Organization, and finally with the creation of permanent mechanisms such as the United Nations Relief and Works Agency for Palestine Refugees and the United Nations High Commissioner for Refugees (UNHCR), the United Nations gradually built an institutional capacity to respond to refugee situations.

These institutions provided both assistance and some degree of protection to refugees. Indeed, refugees and stateless persons had already gained by this time a capacity to travel with international documents, including the "Nansen Passports" issued by the League of Nations and later issued under the authority of the 1946 London Intergovernmental Agreement on Refugee Travel Documents. Similarly, League of Nations practice, under the inspiring leadership of its first high commissioner for refugees, Fridtjof Nansen, reflected the belief that, on moral and humanitarian grounds, refugees should not be forced against their will to return to their countries of origin. This principle was reaffirmed by the U.N. General Assembly in 1946, thus building a basis for a legal right of *nonrefoulement*, or the right not to be repatriated by force.

Although progress had been made in clarifying the legal status of refugees and stateless persons, it was clear that the work of the UNHCR would be reinforced by the adoption of explicit conventions. An ad hoc committee on refugees and stateless persons produced a draft convention and protocol on these subjects as early as August of 1950. Thus, when U.N. secretary-general Trygve Lie convened the Conference of Plenipotentiaries Relating to the Status of Refugees and Stateless Persons, which chose as its president Knud Larsen of Denmark, its work consisted largely of finalizing draft treaties on refugees and stateless persons. Conference participants decided that the convention on stateless persons was less ripe for action than that on refugees, so they postponed work on the former and concentrated on the latter.

The convention, which entered into force on April 22, 1954, contained a definition of the term "refugee" that was more restrictive than that contained in the UNHCR's statute. Both instruments applied to persons who did not want to return to their country of origin because of a well-founded fear of being persecuted for reasons of race, religion, nationality, political opinion, or membership in a particular social group. Under the 1951 convention, however, only those persons fleeing from events occurring in Europe or elsewhere prior to January 1, 1951, were considered to be refugees. Under the UNHCR statute, all persons fleeing from persecution were eligible for refugee status without regard to geographical or time limitations.

The more detailed elaboration of rights for refugees contained in the convention made many governments hesitant to sign it, as it might involve extensive and unknown future obligations. Still, in the final act of the conference, participating governments recommended that signatory states continue to extend welcome and protection to refugees and other persons on a cooperative and humanitarian basis. The convention time limitations, although cumbersome, did not prevent the UNHCR or governments from extending favorable treatment to those individuals not eligible under the convention. In any case, the 1967 protocol to the 1951 convention eliminated the geographical and time restrictions, allowing states party to the former to adopt a less restrictive refugee definition. The 1951 convention, with minor differences from provisions contained in the UNHCR statute, also clearly defined when a person ceased to qualify for refugee status.

Apart from the definitional issue, the 1951 convention provided that refugees should not be discriminated against because of race, religion, or country of origin and that they should be as free as a country's nationals to practice their religion and provide religious training to their children. The convention also provided that refugees should be accorded treatment as favorable as that accorded a country's nationals in regard to rights to association, access to courts, protection of artistic rights and industrial property, access to public relief and rationed products in short supply, and elementary education. It further provided that refugees should be treated no less favorably than other similarly situated aliens in connection with acquisition of property, employment, practice of a profession, housing, higher education, and freedom of movement. Refugees, in turn, are obliged to observe the laws and regulations of their host country as well as any measures adopted by it for the preservation of order and security. In practice, the latter provision often limits the ability of refugees to move freely within their host countries.

Of all the obligations incurred by states in relation to refugees, none is more important than the duty contained in article 33 of the convention, which calls upon governments to refrain from returning refugees to territories where they risk persecution. This provision of *nonrefoulement*, although not without qualification, provides refugees a protection that aliens lacking refugee status do not enjoy. Contracting states agreed to cooperate with the UNHCR, which was charged with the duty to supervise application of all the provisions of the convention, including the provision dealing with *nonrefoulement*.

With the adoption and entry into force of the 1951 Convention Relating to the Status of Refugees, governments broke new ground in extending rights and protection to refugees. Although only those governments that later became parties to the convention (or to the revisions contained in the 1967 protocol to the convention) were bound to abide by its terms, in time many nonsignatories acquiesced in practice to the humanitarian provisions that it embodied, thus affording millions of refugees protection they otherwise might not have enjoyed.

## Impact of Event

The 1951 Convention Relating to the Status of Refugees remains, in 1991, the cornerstone of refugee law. As modified by the 1967 protocol, it permits the UNHCR to extend its protection to refugees in virtually every corner of the globe. More than one hundred states are parties to either the convention, the protocol, or both. Many governments that are not parties to these legal instruments nevertheless have respected their provisions and permitted the UNHCR to afford protection and assistance to refugees residing in their territories. Many states also have incorporated the definition of refugee status contained in either the convention or the protocol into their domestic legislation, thus giving domestic effect to these international provisions. The principle of *nonrefoulement* has ripened into a general principle of international law binding on all states, whether parties to the 1951 convention or not.

This process of legal development on behalf of refugees did not begin with the 1951 convention, but it was given substantial impetus by the adoption of that agreement. The UNHCR has applied the provisions of the convention, as well as its own statute, to protect and assist millions of refugees. Recommendations of the U.N. General Assembly, conclusions of the UNHCR's executive committee, and the actual practice of states in dealing with refugees have further strengthened the status of refugees under international law and promoted protection of their rights. Ultimately, however, the convention realistically underscores that it is governments and not the UNHCR that must provide protection for refugees. The UNHCR can only gain access to refugee populations with the consent of host countries, and its efforts to promote the welfare and to protect the status of refugees can extend only so far as host states cooperate in those endeavors.

The normal legal relationship that exists between a citizen and his or her government breaks down when governments persecute citizens or abuse their human rights, forcing them to flee. The 1951 convention represents a recognition by governments that people who become refugees under these exceptional circumstances must be accorded alternative means of legal protection, since having fled abroad they no longer are able or willing to avail themselves of the protection of their country of nationality and are thus in a predicament unlike that of most aliens traveling or residing abroad. The convention recognizes that the rights of refugees must be protected until such time as they can return home freely and safely or find another state willing to grant them rights of residency or citizenship. In a world marked by substantial abuse of human rights and of consequent flows of refugees, legal instruments such as the convention, although often far from flawless in design and imperfectly implemented in practice, provide refugees a genuine means of protection and reaffirm the international community's aspiration to respect human rights.

## Bibliography

Aga Khan, Sadruddin, and Hassan Bin Talal. *Refugees: The Dynamics of Displacement*. London: Zed Books, 1986. This jargon-free and readable report for the Independent Commission on International Humanitarian Issues reviews current pressure on the existing structure of refugee law and policy. It critically assesses the repressive policies governments employ to displace people and examines how the international community might better respond to these movements. Includes an index but lacks other reference features.

Goodwin-Gill, Guy S. *The Refugee in International Law*. Oxford, England: Clarendon Press, 1983. A comprehensive legal analysis of the U.N. Convention Relating to the Status of Refugees, this book meticulously reviews existing customary and treaty law relevant to refugees and the practice of asylum at both the international and national levels. Extensive references, a select bibliography, and an index are included.

Grahl-Madsen, Atle. *The Status of Refugees in International Law*. 2 vols. Leiden, The Netherlands: Sijthoff, 1966 and 1972. These volumes by a highly respected student of international law are definitive treatments of the application and interpretation of refugee and asylum law. More for the legal specialist than the casual reader. Extensive references and bibliography. Includes subject and case indices.

Holborn, Louise. *Refugees, a Problem of Our Times: The Work of the UNHCR, 1951-1972*. 2 vols. Metuchen, N.J.: Scarecrow Press, 1975. This standard work on the formation and early work of the UNHCR also focuses on the legal status of refugees under the 1951 convention and 1967 protocol. Highly detailed and voluminously documented, this book serves as a peerless reference on the modern refugee problem and on the UNHCR's work under the 1951 convention. Includes numerous charts, tables, an index, and a bibliography.

Nanda, Ved P., ed. *Refugee Law and Policy: International and U.S. Responses*. New York: Greenwood Press, 1989. This anthology includes a dozen articles, many authored by noted legal specialists, attorneys, and academics, on various aspects of refugee and asylum law. Also included are critiques of the refugee and immigration policies of governments. Includes a bibliography and an index.

Smyser, William Richard. *Refugees: Extended Exile*. New York: Praeger, 1987. This short and highly readable book, by a former deputy high commissioner for refugees, expertly traces the development of the UNHCR and the legal aspects of the refugee problem while suggesting policies for governments to cope with new asylum and immigration pressures.

United Nations High Commissioner for Refugees. *Handbook on Procedures and Criteria for Determining Refugee Status*. Geneva: Author, 1979. This brief but useful handbook contains a copy of the 1951 convention and protocol, with interpretations used by the UNHCR to determine refugee status. Contains an index but no bibliography.

*Robert F. Gorman*

## Cross-References

The International Labour Organisation Is Established (1919), p. 281; Nansen Wins the Nobel Peace Prize (1922), p. 361; The International League for Human Rights Is Founded (1942), p. 590; The United Nations Adopts the Universal Declaration of Human Rights (1948), p. 789; The Geneva Convention Establishes Norms of Conduct in Warfare (1949), p. 808; The United Nations Creates an Agency to Aid Palestinian Refugees (1949), p. 814; The European Convention on Human Rights Is Signed (1950), p. 849; The United Nations High Commissioner for Refugees Statute Is Approved (1950), p. 855; The United Nations Drafts a Convention on Stateless Persons (1954), p. 918; The U.N. Covenant on Civil and Political Rights Is Adopted (1966), p. 1353; An African Convention Expands the Definition of Refugees (1969), p. 1491.

# JOUHAUX IS AWARDED THE NOBEL PEACE PRIZE

*Categories of event:* Workers' rights; peace movements and organizations
*Time:* December 10, 1951
*Locale:* Oslo, Norway

*Léon Jouhaux was honored for his lifelong work in support of workers' rights, international peace, disarmament, and socialism*

*Principal personages:*

LÉON JOUHAUX (1879-1954), a French labor leader and prominent figure in the International Labour Organisation

BENOÎT FRACHON (1893-1975), the French communist labor leader who was Jouhaux's rival after World War II

ROBERT SCHUMAN (1886-1963), the French premier who faced the labor crisis of 1947

GUNNAR JAHN (1883-1971), the chair of the Nobel Committee of the Norwegian Parliament

## Summary of Event

In late 1951, the Nobel Committee of the Norwegian Parliament, with Gunnar Jahn as chair, announced the selection of Léon Jouhaux as winner of the Peace Prize. Jouhaux was the first labor leader selected in the fifty years of the prize's history. The Nobel Committee, charged with choosing the individual or organization who has best served the interests of peace over the previous year, is not required to provide rationale for its choice. In most cases, the rationale is clear; in 1951, however, the choice of Jouhaux was attributed by some to his fifty years in the French and international labor and peace movements, and by others to his key role in the late 1940's in stemming the rise of French communism. Thus, the award must be viewed in the context of both achievements.

Jouhaux was born in Paris on July 1, 1879, to a working class family with a tradition of activism. His grandfather had fought in the Revolution of 1848, and his father had participated in the 1871 commune that ruled Paris briefly after the Franco-Prussian War. A promising student, Jouhaux hoped to become an engineer, but economic hardship because of a strike at his father's match factory forced him to leave school and contribute to the family budget. After working at a sugar refinery, a paper mill, a soap factory, a fertilizer plant, and the local docks, he spent a year in the military in Algeria, but his father's blindness brought him back in 1895 to join his brother and sister at the Aubervilliers match factory.

Jouhaux immediately joined the local union and in 1900 participated in his first strike, which successfully protested the use of white phosphorous, the volatile substance that had caused the elder Jouhaux's blindness, in match production. Dismissed and blacklisted as a result of the strike, Jouhaux took odd jobs and studied intermittently until, through union intervention, he was reinstated at the factory.

His commitment to union activism was cast. He spoke and organized on the local level, and in 1906 became a representative to the National Confederal Committee of the Confédération Générale du Travail (General Confederation of Labor), the CGT. In early 1909, Jouhaux was named its interim treasurer, and on July 12 he became secretary-general, a position he held for the next thirty-eight years. During his tenure, membership in the organization increased tenfold to five million.

In 1911, Jouhaux began editing *La bataille syndicaliste* (the syndicalist battle), the CGT's main organ, and attended meetings in Berlin and Paris to mediate the Franco-German dispute over the Agadir incident in Morocco. Sensing the coming war, he urged labor unions throughout Europe to unite for peace. He promoted a CGT peace program calling for arms limitation, international arbitration, and respect for nationalities. In 1914, just before the outbreak of World War I, Jouhaux sent a telegram to Germany's labor leaders appealing for cooperation.

Though antimilitarist, Jouhaux supported the French war effort and served both in the army and on the Labor Committee of the Ministry of Munitions. In April, 1916, he arranged a meeting in Paris of British, French, Belgian, and Italian trade unionists which led that summer to the Inter-Allied Trade Union Conference in Leeds, England, where Jouhaux presented a report that aggressively called for the establishment of an international labor organization.

That call was answered in 1919. The League of Nations was established, and Jouhaux was appointed to its labor committee at the Paris peace conference. He became an active and idealistic participant and was instrumental in incorporating into the Versailles Peace Treaty the constitutional basis for the International Labour Organisation (the ILO). He was chosen as a worker-representative to the ILO's governing body. While generally supportive of the final treaty, with its resolutions recognizing the importance of social and labor conditions, he was disappointed in its failure to establish an eight-hour workday and fearful that the ILO would become an instrument of the capitalist victor nations.

In 1919, Jouhaux was elected vice president of the International Federation of Trade Unions. In 1921, he led the charge against French employer-representative Robert Pinot's proposal to restrict ILO activities in investigating complaints, fearing that the resolution would strip the ILO of significant influence. He urged an ILO mission to the Soviet Union to observe labor conditions and allay Soviet suspicions of the ILO's bourgeois roots. Meanwhile, in France, communists and radicals had infiltrated the CGT and challenged Jouhaux's leadership. He responded by expelling the entire communist membership from the union in 1921.

Jouhaux's two decades in union, government, and international policymaking had tempered his extremism. During the 1920's, the focus of his peace work shifted to disarmament. From 1925 to 1928 he was a member of the French delegation to the League of Nations that drafted a proposal on arms control, and in 1927 he published a treatise on the subject, *Désarmement* (disarmament), in which he called for government ownership of arms production under the League's supervision. His 1932 address to the Conference for the Limitation and Reduction of Armaments was one of the personal highlights of his life.

In the 1930's, Jouhaux became involved with the Popular Front, believing that peace would come only with economic equality, and united with the communists to stem the rise of fascism. In 1935, a major labor issue was the adoption of an ILO resolution for the general reduction of working hours in selected industries. The following year, Jouhaux was among the signatories to the Martignon Agreement, which established the eight-hour day, paid vacations, and union rights for French workers. Meanwhile, Jouhaux continued his writing, including a book on trade unionism, and finally completed his university studies.

Adolf Hitler's power in Germany was growing steadily and many people, Jouhaux included, sensed the approaching world war. He joined with Lord Robert Cecil of the British League of Nations Union to organize unionists in an international peace campaign. In 1938, following the invasion of Czechoslovakia, he met with President Franklin Delano Roosevelt to urge the United States to intervene against Germany, but to no avail. With the outbreak of war and the occupation of France, the CGT was dissolved. Jouhaux was asked to join the French Free Forces in England, but he believed that his place was on French soil. He organized an underground movement among trade unionists and established a courier system for communicating with England. In December, 1941, he was arrested and placed in house confinement for two years, after which he was sent to Buchenwald concentration camp, where he spent twenty-five months.

After the war, Jouhaux returned to find the CGT revived and filled with communists. He was welcomed back to share the post of secretary-general with communist leader Benoît Frachon. Frachon was a miner's son who, like Jouhaux, had joined the union as a teenager and participated in the French Resistance during the war. Partnered with Frachon, Jouhaux soon realized he had little power. At the ILO's thirtieth annual conference in June, 1947, he sponsored a resolution supporting the Marshall Plan; the communist-dominated CGT vehemently opposed it. In late 1947, the union called a general strike despite Jouhaux's opposition. In November, the government of Paul Ramadier was disbanded and foreign minister Robert Schuman was asked to form a cabinet. He responded to the labor crisis by increasing cost-of-living adjustments, family allowances, and war pensions and by supporting passage of the Law for Defense of the Republic and the Right to Work. On December 10, the CGT ended its strike. Jouhaux, angered by the union's communist leadership, decided he could no longer participate. He withdrew on December 19, 1947, sacrificing a valuable retirement pension but taking with him more than a million loyal followers to form the nonpartisan CGT-Force Oeuvrière (workers' force). In so doing, he stemmed the rise of communist power in the French labor movement.

That same year Jouhaux was elected to the French National Economic Council, an advisory body established to integrate economic forces in France for European economic cooperation. In addition, from 1946 to 1951, he was a French delegate to the United Nations, where he fought for universal recognition of the right to free association. He continued his role in the ILO, the only League of Nations organization to survive World War II, and helped to define the ILO's continuing role.

Though well on in years, Jouhaux was as active as ever. He attended the Westminster Economic Conference on the future of Europe's working class in 1949 and became president of the European Movement, which established the Council of Europe as the first step toward formation of a United States of Europe. In December, 1951, he traveled to Oslo, Norway, to accept his Nobel Peace Prize.

## Impact of Event

The greatest impact of Jouhaux's Peace Prize was the implicit recognition of workers and organized labor in the international pursuit of peace. As Jouhaux noted shortly after receiving the prize, it was given not in recognition of him but of those millions he had worked beside and represented throughout his life, and not only as an honor for past deeds but as a mandate for future efforts as well.

Jouhaux's work continued until his death in 1954. He remained a leader in the ILO (which itself was awarded the Nobel Peace Prize in 1969), striving to keep the organization strong, effective, and impartial. Under Jouhaux's leadership, the focus of the labor movement's pacifist endeavors shifted to new issues. Many of the original goals—limits on working hours, improved conditions, and free association— had been adopted in member nations. Jouhaux recognized the complex network of circumstances that connected international hostilities to unemployment, economic disparity, and worker dissatisfaction. Given the large number of migrant workers in Europe, Jouhaux played a large role in the Intergovernmental Committee for European Migration during the early 1950's. The Nobel Peace Prize, and the recognition and financial award that it brought, facilitated Jouhaux's continued work.

Perhaps most striking was the impact of Jouhaux's Nobel Prize on the East-West dialogue and the Cold War. As no official reason was given for his selection, observers were free to interpret as they pleased. In a world polarized by capitalists and communists, with the United States and Soviet Union engaged in a growing rivalry, communist parties rallying for support throughout Western Europe, and the House Un-American Activities Committee investigating communist collaboration in the United States, Jouhaux's award was interpreted in many quarters as a victory for the forces of capitalism and democracy. The French Communist party responded with defiance and anger to the announcement, as did the nations of the Soviet bloc. In the United States, commentators acknowledged Jouhaux's lifetime achievement but characterized him primarily as a savior against communist infiltration. Jouhaux saw himself less as a partisan politician than as a labor leader and pacifist, but he nevertheless became a symbol of the anticommunist movement.

Just as the man was "politicized" by his Nobel Prize, so was the Nobel Prize Committee. By leaving the choice of Jouhaux open to interpretation, the Nobel Prize Committee was seen as having chosen less according to merit than according to political considerations. In his presentation speech on December 10, 1951, Jahn clearly acknowledged Jouhaux's role in the fight against communism. For many, the belief that the Committee was taking a Western viewpoint in defining peace and recognizing accomplishment was confirmed in 1953 when George Marshall, American general and architect of the Marshall Plan for European reconstruction, was awarded the Nobel Peace Prize.

## Bibliography

Alcock, Antony. *History of the International Labor Organization.* New York: Octagon, 1971. This volume of 360 pages is a systematic examination of the ILO from its origin in 1919 through 1970. Somewhat dry and journalistic in style, it is strong on Jouhaux's omnipresence in the labor movement.

Bernard, Georges, and Denise Tintant. "Léon Jouhaux: 1879-1954." *International Labor Review* 70 (September/October, 1954): 241-247. This piece consists of selected tributes to Jouhaux written and compiled shortly after his death.

Johnston, G. A. *The International Labour Organisation: Its Work for Social and Economic Progress.* London: Europa Publications, 1970. Johnston, a former ILO assistant director with a background in ethics, social theory, and government service, provides a clear, detailed profile of the organization as of 1970. The reference section is exhaustive, including documents, statistics, biographical notes, budget analyses, a chronology, and lists of members, offices, and conventions.

Lichtheim, George. *Marxism in Modern France.* New York: Columbia University Press, 1966. This slim book (200 pages) explores the historical context of French Marxism, French Marxist thought, and the movement's links to both organized labor and Soviet communism. It is academic, philosophical, and couched in the language of Marxist dialectics but provides a good, somewhat dense, view of the atmosphere at the time of Jouhaux's Peace Prize.

Lorwin, Val R. *The French Labor Movement.* Cambridge, Mass.: Harvard University Press, 1954. Insightful analysis of the development of the movement by one of the best scholars on the subject. Lorwin's anthologized articles include "France," in Walter Galenson's *Comparative Labor Movements* (New York: Prentice-Hall, 1952) and "The Struggle for Control of the French Trade-Union Movement, 1945-49," in M. Earle's *Modern France: Problems of the Third and Fourth Republics* (Princeton, N.J.: Princeton University Press, 1951).

Micaud, Charles A. *Communism and the French Left.* New York: Praeger, 1963. Micaud's is a weighty and speculative work that deals less with individuals than with groups, movements, and political maneuverings. Its strength lies in Micaud's firsthand research into the lives and opinions of French factory workers.

Werth, Alexander. *France, 1940-1945.* Boston: Beacon Press, 1966. In his long, detailed examination of France during and after World War II, Werth skillfully interweaves economic and political analysis with observation of social forces and the French national character. Included are a lengthy discussion of the anticommunist struggle and a comprehensive (primarily foreign-language) bibliography.

*Barry Mann*

## Cross-References

The British Labour Party Is Formed (1906), p. 58; Ford Offers a Five-Dollar, Eight-Hour Workday (1914), p. 143; The League of Nations Is Established (1919), p. 270; The International Labour Organisation Is Established (1919), p. 281; The United Nations Adopts Its Charter (1945), p. 657; The Marshall Plan Provides Aid to Europe (1947), p. 706; The United Nations Adopts the Abolition of Forced Labor Convention (1957), p. 985; Leftists Rebel in France (1968), p. 1425; The International Labour Organisation Wins the Nobel Peace Prize (1969), p. 1509.

# THE ORGANIZATION OF AMERICAN STATES IS ESTABLISHED

*Category of event:* Peace movements and organizations
*Time:* December 13, 1951
*Locale:* Bogotá, Colombia

*From its inception, the OAS has championed human rights by attempting to prevent warfare between member nations and condemning human rights violations within these nations*

### Principal personages:

JAMES MONROE (1758-1831), the fifth president of the United States and author of the Monroe Doctrine for hemispheric security

SIMÓN BOLÍVAR (1783-1830), the liberator of South America and visionary who called the first Pan-American conference

JAMES G. BLAINE (1830-1893), the United States secretary of state (1880, 1889-1892) who committed the United States to inter-American cooperation

ALBERTO LLERAS CAMARGO (1907-1990), the first general secretary of the OAS and onetime president of Colombia

## Summary of Event

Proposed by the Ninth International Conference of American States held in Bogotá, Colombia, in 1948, the Organization of American States (OAS) came into existence on December 31, 1951. The establishment of the OAS represented an institutional evolution of Pan-American relations, which had historic roots in both the United States and Latin America. United States president James Monroe proclaimed a unique hemispheric community in his famous doctrine of 1823. The Latin-American liberator Simón Bolívar convened the first Inter-American Congress in Panama in 1826.

At the instigation of Secretary of State James G. Blaine, the First International Conference of American States was held in Washington, D.C., from October, 1889, to April, 1890. Eighteen Latin-American nations and the United States established the International Bureau of American Republics, housed in Washington, D.C., for the collection and publication of information on production, commerce, customs, and laws of member states.

Between 1890 and 1910, four Inter-American Conferences expanded the duties of the International Bureau of American Republics, and in 1910 the bureau was reorganized and renamed the "Pan-American Union." The union was given a permanent standing and charged with preparing special reports requested by the Inter-American Conference meetings.

Between 1910 and 1948, the International Conference of American States held four regular meetings, discussing the implications of the Monroe Doctrine and policies of nonintervention for the collection of debt payment. Four extraordinary meetings of Inter-American Conferences addressed security and human rights issues arising from World War II. The more significant results of these meetings were the creation of an inter-American security system, established by the Act of Chapultepec in 1945 and the Rio Treaty in 1947, and the 1938 Resolution of the Defense of Human Rights. These actions created a defensive military alliance for the Americas and acknowledged a formal obligation by member states to respect basic human rights.

At the Ninth International Conference of American States held in Bogotá in April, 1948, the conference and the Pan-American Union were fundamentally restructured and renamed the "Organization of American States."

The founding charter for the OAS outlined the main purposes or principles of the body: to strengthen peace and security, prevent possible causes of difficulties, and ensure pacific settlements of disputes; to organize common action against aggression; to seek the solution of political, juridical, and economic problems among the members; and to promote economic, social, and cultural development through cooperative action. Also approved as a collateral set of principles, although not as part of the charter, was the American Declaration on the Rights and Duties of Man, which proclaimed the fundamental rights of the individual without distinction as to race, nationality, creed, or sex.

In terms of organization, the Pan-American Union remained the central organ of the OAS, with its director serving as the OAS general secretary. The new Inter-American Conference met every five years to set policy. The Meeting of Consultation of Foreign Ministers dealt, on an ad hoc basis, with urgent issues. The OAS charter created three specialized bodies—the Inter-American Economic and Social Council, the Inter-American Cultural Council, and the Inter-American Council of Jurists—to address the specific principles of the OAS.

Alongside the new structures, the OAS maintained a variety of special organs that had come into existence since 1890. Concerns of these various committees included health, children, women, geography and history, Indian peoples, peace, and agricultural science.

These institutional transformations reflected more than bureaucratic reorganization. With the Pan-American Union located in the United States, staffed by United States citizens, and chaired, without exception, by the United States secretary of state, the organization became referred to as the "American Ministry of Colonies." From the time of the Spanish-American War in 1898, United States policies in Cuba, Panama, Mexico, Nicaragua, and the Caribbean had angered many Latin-American nations and left them sensitive to the charge of United States manipulation.

Consequently, within the OAS charter were provisions designed to offset United States predominance and expand participation by other member states. Representatives were no longer diplomats to the United States but rather delegates specially appointed by their governments with the rank of ambassador to the OAS. Although

Washington, D.C., remained the seat of the organization, the charter specifically called for the selection of staff personnel from across the spectrum of member nations. In the most visible symbol of this change, the members elected the ex-president of Colombia, Alberto Lleras Camargo, as the first general secretary of the OAS.

Although the "Good Neighbor" policy of the United States accepted a more autonomous role for the inter-American organization, the political climate of the Cold War challenged the integrity and independence of the OAS from 1949 to 1967. During these years, while most of the Latin-American members of the OAS desired financial assistance to modernize their economies and diplomatic aid to help them find a secure niche in the postwar world markets, the United States focused its attention on Europe and Asia and returned to exercising its influence in its "sphere" to combat communist ideology while forsaking public economic assistance in favor of opening Latin-American markets to private investment. The role of the United States in the invasion of Guatemala in 1954, the Bay of Pigs incident in Cuba in 1961, and the occupation of the Dominican Republic in 1965 once again raised the question of the viability of the OAS. The organization was condemned by the political left as a tool of the United States and held in low esteem by the center and right as ineffectual both in aiding modernization in Latin America and in effectively countering communist influence.

In light of this criticism, the OAS adopted fundamental revisions of its charter at the Third Special Inter-American Conference in Buenos Aires in 1967. These provisions took effect following their ratification in 1970.

The Inter-American Conference (IAC), which was to meet every five years, was replaced by the annual meeting of the OAS General Assembly. The Meeting of Consultation of Ministers of Foreign Affairs was kept, but where before it had served as the primary policy-making body between IAC meetings, that function now shifted to the General Assembly. The council was renamed the "Permanent Council." The Inter-American Economic and Social Council was separated and elevated to equal status, the Cultural Council was likewise elevated to independent status and renamed the "Inter-American Council for Education, Science, and Culture," and the Council of Jurists was abolished, but its main working committee, the Inter-American Juridical Committee, was expanded and preserved as a separate organ of the OAS. The title "Pan-American Union" was dropped as the designation of the permanent central bureaucracy in favor of "General Secretariat" of the OAS.

The OAS, including its various committees and its written documents, has had influence in numerous human rights issues. The 1902 Convention Relative to the Rights of Aliens, the 1938 Resolution of the Defense of Human Rights, the 1948 American Declaration on the Rights and Duties of Man, and the American Convention on Human Rights, ratified in 1978, underscored the human rights concerns of the OAS. Most significant were the creation in 1960 of the OAS Inter-American Commission on Human Rights and the establishment of the Inter-American Court of Human Rights in 1979.

The commission comprises private citizens elected by the OAS. They function in their elected capacities and are not representatives of their governments. The commission's charge is to "promote respect for human rights." It investigates complaints of human rights violations in member states, a duty that often includes fact-finding visits to the countries involved. The findings and final reports of the commission are presented to the OAS General Assembly and made public.

Significantly, the commission can receive complaints from individuals, groups of persons, and nongovernmental agencies as well as from state agencies. In 1965, the commission distinguished itself by intervening in the civil war in the Dominican Republic, helping individuals to places of safety, investigating charges of human rights violations, and securing good treatment for noncombatants from all parties. One observer stated that the commission's most important role was in providing "therapeutic relief," by providing an authority to which oppressed people could turn with some hope of obtaining aid.

### Impact of Event

Throughout its evolution, the OAS has championed the principles of human rights and, within its bureaucratic limitations, has proven to be an effective agency in the promotion of those rights in the Western Hemisphere. In the broadest sense of this, the OAS labored to diminish overt interstate conflicts. From 1890 to 1948, the inter-American body adopted the principles of nonintervention, endorsed the Hague conventions on the pacific settlement of international disputes, and adopted conventions for inter-American conciliation and arbitration of disputes. Following its formal establishment in 1948, the OAS moved immediately to investigate a Nicaraguan invasion of Costa Rica and to assist in the conclusion of a negotiated settlement between the parties. Such activity is characteristic of the OAS, which has continued to work to reduce or diminish interstate conflicts.

The Inter-American Commission on Human Rights has accepted thousands of cases and conducted hundreds of investigations of human rights violations. Commission reports have catalogued and condemned torture by police, military, and government agents in Paraguay, Uruguay, Chile, Brazil, and Argentina. Commission reports on the treatment of the Miskito Indians prompted the Sandinistas of Nicaragua to grant a general amnesty for those arrested on security offenses and allow them to return to their homes. Visitations to Chile in 1973 and Argentina in 1976 called attention to human rights abuses that not only helped document the events for later retribution but also in some cases disrupted programs of torture and saved lives. In Argentina, a petition by the commission on behalf of a defense lawyer sponsoring the rights of political prisoners ultimately led to release from a harsh detention that had taken the life of a companion.

While one analyst has concluded that "the actual results of the Commission's activities, despite its noble efforts, have been marginal," others have disagreed. The concluding comment by Argentina's National Commission on Disappeared People in its 1986 report stated, "We would like to emphasize the extraordinary significance of the visit of the Inter-American Commission for Human Rights of the OAS."

In 1979, the OAS established the Inter-American Court of Human Rights to allow the commission to bring cases of human rights violations before a judicial body. The court has no means to enforce its decisions but relies upon international obligation and accountability of member states. In its first trial, in 1988, the court found the government of Honduras guilty of the violation of human rights in the disappearance of two citizens and awarded substantial financial compensation to the surviving families.

## Bibliography

Ball, Mary Margaret. *The OAS in Transition.* Durham, N.C.: Duke University Press, 1969. Heavily documented study of changes in structure and operation of the OAS since 1948.

Brown, Cynthia, ed. *With Friends Like These: The Americas Watch Report on Human Rights and U.S. Policy in Latin America.* New York: Pantheon Books, 1985. Nine case studies of human rights abuses in Latin America and United States foreign policy reaction.

Dreier, John C. *The Organization of American States and the Hemisphere Crisis.* New York: Harper & Row, 1962. By a onetime U.S. ambassador to the OAS. A basic review of OAS evolution, strengths, and weaknesses and a call to invigorate the inter-American system.

Farer, Tom, ed. *The Future of the Inter-American System.* New York: Praeger, 1979. Fourteen essays by academic experts on inter-American diplomacy. Worthy of special note is the chapter "Human Rights and the Inter-American System" by Bryce Wood.

Medina Quiroga, Cecilia. *The Battle of Human Rights: Gross, Systematic Violations and the Inter-American System.* Boston: Martinus Nijhoff, 1988. A detailed analysis of the documentary and legal structure of OAS human rights organs and an examination of OAS investigations of Cuba, Nicaragua, and Chile.

Schoultz, Lars. *Human Rights and United States Policy Toward Latin America.* Princeton, N.J.: Princeton University Press, 1981. Examination of economic, diplomatic, and military interests of American states and human rights issues, including the role and actions of the OAS.

Stoetzer, O. Carlos. *The Organization of American States: An Introduction.* New York: Praeger, 1965. Basic organizational review. Includes appendix of charter, treaties, list of organizations, and conferences.

Thomas, Ann Van Wynen, and A. J. Thomas, Jr. *The Organization of American States.* Dallas: Southern Methodist University Press, 1963. Detailed study of organizational and legal aspects of the OAS. Examination of ideological challenges to international cooperation. Includes Rio Treaty and OAS charter.

*Roger P. Davis*

## Cross-References

The League of Nations Is Established (1919), p. 270; The United Nations Adopts Its Charter (1945), p. 657; The Declaration on the Rights and Duties of Man Is Adopted (1948), p. 755; The United Nations Adopts the Universal Declaration of Human Rights (1948), p. 789; The European Convention on Human Rights Is Signed (1950), p. 843; The European Court of Human Rights Is Established (1950), p. 849; The Inter-American Commission on Human Rights Is Created (1959), p. 1032; Amnesty International Is Founded (1961), p. 1119; The Inter-American Court of Human Rights Is Established (1969), p. 1503; The National Commission Against Torture Studies Human Rights Abuses (1983), p. 2186.

# THE U.N. CONVENTION ON THE POLITICAL RIGHTS OF WOMEN IS APPROVED

*Categories of event:* Women's rights and political freedom
*Time:* 1952
*Locale:* United Nations, New York City

*The United Nations General Assembly expanded its commitments to universal political equality for women by formulating a convention on women's electoral and office-holding rights*

*Principal personages:*
TRYGVE LIE (1896-1968), a Norwegian politician and diplomat who became the first secretary-general of the United Nations (1946-1952)
HELVI SIPILA (1915-    ), the chair of the Committee on the Status of Women in 1967, when the Declaration on the Elimination of Discrimination Against Women was issued
MINERVA BERNARDINA, the chair of the Committee on the Status of Women elected in 1953

## Summary of Event

At its inception following World War II, the United Nations assumed declaratory commitments to the preservation and expansion of human rights. The charter of the United Nations listed the promotion of human rights and fundamental freedoms among the chief purposes of the new international organization, and both the preamble to the charter and its first article affirmed that such rights were held equally by men and women. Empowered by this charter, which included these general statements on the principle of political equality, the United Nations General Assembly convened its first session in 1946. The assembly was immediately confronted with the fact that some of its member states had not yet extended to their female populations political rights equal to those enjoyed by men.

To address this situation, Denmark's delegation to the United Nations presented a draft resolution, or policy proposal, to the General Assembly in late 1946. The proposal recommended that all United Nations member states permit women to run for political office and to participate in elections on an equal basis with men. The debate that followed gained some urgency when the United Nations Economic and Social Council gathered statistics indicating that, although 70 percent of United Nations member states had granted women the franchise, 20 percent had not, and 10 percent had placed special conditions and limitations on women's voting rights that did not apply to men residing in the same country.

In considering the Danish proposal, member countries differed widely on what action the United Nations should take. Some argued that Denmark's proposal was too narrow because it did not address economic or legal issues; others, including the United States, resisted the proposed resolution on the grounds that it was only a restatement of principles already contained in the United Nations charter and that therefore its passage would have no effect. There was, however, general acceptance of the view that political discrimination against women solely on the basis of gender was inconsistent with the charter's declarations on equality. On December 11, 1946, the General Assembly adopted its first resolution primarily concerned with women's enfranchisement, the "Resolution on the Political Rights of Women." This declaration called upon United Nations member states that had not granted women equal political rights to do so.

At the same time, the Economic and Social Council established the Commission on the Status of Women, a new body within the United Nations that monitored women's progress toward equality under the national laws of United Nations member states and provided information on relevant developments to the General Assembly. Following the December, 1946, resolution, the new commission faced a dilemma: Although the General Assembly could adopt prescriptive resolutions, the U.N. charter expressly precluded the organization from intervening in matters that lay within the domestic jurisdiction of member states. Thus, although the General Assembly had passed the resolution on political equality, neither the Commission on the Status of Women nor any other United Nations body could compel member states not in compliance to implement the resolution.

Nevertheless, from early 1947 the commission resolved to give the highest priority to the issue of political equality for both genders, and it developed a twofold policy strategy. Annual reviews of the legal, social, economic, and political impediments to women's equality in all United Nations member states were produced, and in 1949 the commission initiated an effort to draw up a binding international instrument under which governments would commit themselves to guaranteeing women equal rights of political participation. This initiative culminated in the promulgation of a Convention on the Political Rights of Women in 1952.

Between 1947 and 1952, however, an extended debate arose at the United Nations over the issues connected with the full enfranchisement of women. The Commission on the Status of Women consulted with a number of nongovernmental organizations such as the International Federation of University Women, the International Cooperative Women's Guild, and the World Women's Christian Temperance Union, and its reports revealed not only the extent of women's exclusion from electoral politics but also a pattern of officially sanctioned economic and racial discrimination in member states of the United Nations. Government officials from these states often confirmed the findings, arguing that special circumstances justified their policies. In 1947, for example, the Guatemalan government told the commission that enfranchisement provisions of its domestic legislation did not apply to native inhabitants of non-European origin because "their cultural level is not yet sufficiently developed." Governments responsible for administering trust and colonial territories were also reluctant to approve the enfranchisement of women in those areas. New Zealand, often commended for extending the vote to its female citizens as early as 1893, prevented women of non-European origin from voting in its trusteeship territory of the Samoan Islands.

The Belgian example of electoral restrictions on women is representative of many of the issues debated at the United Nations in the early 1950's. In Belgium, all women could vote in municipal elections, but only mothers and widows of World War I-era soldiers and female deportees of that time could vote in national elections. No similar conditions were applied to men. Belgium also refused to accept the principle of political equality in its African territories, claiming that local conditions and the "stage of development of the indigenous populations" made democratic equality impossible there.

The problems of European states' colonial possessions and the political rights of their inhabitants were never successfully addressed by the Commission on the Status of Women. In order not to impede progress toward drafting a new convention, the commission decided to decouple the question of political rights for women in signatory states from the issue of political rights for women living in dependent or colonial territories. With this compromise in place, United Nations agencies including the commission were able in 1951 to make strides toward a new, binding convention. At its fifth session in 1951, the commission recommended that a draft be prepared of an international legal instrument that would assure women in signatory states of equal political rights. This new document differed from the 1946 resolution in one important aspect: Member states of the United Nations would be requested to sign and ratify this convention, thus undertaking responsibility for upholding its provisions in all of their domestic legislation. On October 2, 1951, United Nations secretary-general Trygve Lie circulated the text of a draft convention, requesting comments and reactions from member states.

Canada, the United States, and Great Britain all argued against the proposed convention, citing its limited scope, technical questions about the wording of the draft, and the need for education about equality, not new legal requirements. Other states, such as Iceland and the Republic of China (Taiwan), fully endorsed the proposal. In the General Assembly, where the one-country, one-vote principle applied, a loose coalition of European, Asian, and American countries cast their ballots in favor of promulgating the convention, which was adopted by the General Assembly on December 20, 1952. The final draft of the convention thus approved would be binding only upon those countries that subsequently chose to accede to it. Its provisions included two articles declaring that women would be entitled to vote in all elections on the same terms as men and would be eligible for election to all publicly elected bodies. A third article required that women be entitled to hold appointed offices and to exercise all public functions established by national law on equal terms with men.

## Impact of Event

The 1952 Convention on the Political Rights of Women was of greatest importance as a symbolic statement of the principle of political equality between the sexes rather than as a catalyst for United Nations member states to overhaul their discriminatory domestic legislation or for governing states to alter the terms of their rule over territories and possessions. In 1968, the International Year of Human Rights, the Commission on the Status of Women reviewed the developments since 1952 and noted with regret that only half of the United Nations member states had ratified or acceded to the 1952 convention; a total of fifty-four countries had formally accepted the obligations it imposed. Among those states that had not signed was the United States, which based its continuing rejection of the convention on its third article. American officials argued that accession to the convention would enable women in the U.S. armed forces to engage in combat duty.

Although many countries chose not to accede formally to the 1952 convention, United Nations figures gathered in 1968 indicated that by then 120 countries, including almost all the newly independent states, had adopted domestic legislation that granted women most of the rights embodied in the convention. The exceptions to this general trend toward enfranchisement included states such as Portugal, which imposed special taxation or educational qualifications on female voters, and a number of predominantly Islamic countries, including Jordan, Kuwait, and Saudi Arabia, that barred women from voting and holding public office.

Although the formal adoption by the General Assembly of the convention in 1952 stimulated the general trend toward greater political equality for women, its significance as a precedent for subsequent human and women's rights enactments by the United Nations is of even greater importance. The 1952 convention was the first international treaty under which signatories assumed legal obligations concerning the exercise by women of domestic political rights, as well as the first instrument in which the United Nations charter's statements on gender equality were applied to a particular political problem. After its promulgation, United Nations agencies such as the Economic and Social Council and the International Labour Organisation, supplementing the pioneering work of the Commission on the Status of Women, investigated a broad array of technical, economic, and social issues of special importance for women's lives. From these investigations and continuous monitoring of marriage laws, education and employment opportunities, and family-planning and health-care regulations emerged a variety of new policy initiatives designed to protect women's positions throughout the world. Indeed, in a number of United Nations covenants and policy declarations since 1952, the basic provisions of the 1952 Convention on the Political Rights of Women have been repeated and expanded.

The clearest example of the impact of the 1952 convention upon subsequent United Nations activities emerged in the late 1960's. In 1966, the United Nations approved the Covenant on Civil and Political Rights, which incorporated the fundamental elements of the earlier convention. Most important, in November, 1967, the General Assembly approved the Declaration on the Elimination of Discrimination Against Women, which was a comprehensive statement of the many antidiscriminatory policies approved by the United Nations since the late 1940's. This document, updated and rewritten as a United Nations convention in 1979, traces its origins directly to the

1952 convention and serves as a catalog of the fields in which the United Nations has pressed for the extension of full and equal rights for women throughout the world. Although the limitations on the United Nations' power to compel its member states to implement its decisions remain in force, the organization has successfully framed statements such as the 1952 Convention on the Political Rights of Women that have had broad and lasting impacts as precedents for international legislation on basic human rights and gender equality.

## Bibliography

Carter, April. *The Politics of Women's Rights.* New York: Longman, 1988. Presents a focused discussion of the forms and consequences of political discrimination against women in the post-World War II era. Primarily concerned with the British context, but also discusses legal changes affecting women's status implemented by the European Economic Community and its European Court of Justice. Chapter 6, entitled "Can the Law Secure Women's Rights?," is particularly noteworthy.

Nash, June C. *Women, Men, and the International Division of Labor.* Albany: State University of New York Press, 1983. This general work outlines the particularities of women's political and economic status in the global context. Identifies many of the chief issues with which United Nations agencies and policy declarations have been concerned since the late 1940's and upon which debate on the promulgation of the 1952 convention focused.

Osmanczyk, Edmund Jan. *The Encyclopedia of the United Nations and International Agreements.* Philadelphia: Taylor and Francis, 1985. Provides brief but detailed entries on a variety of international organizations and enactments relevant to women's political rights. Includes entries on the history of the international movement for women's political equality and on a number of United Nations initiatives to improve women's political and economic status.

Sieghart, Paul. *The International Law of Human Rights.* New York: Clarendon Press, 1983. This general survey of international human rights legislation outlines the framework within which United Nations activities and initiatives in the field are introduced. Its discussions of the nature and limitations of international legal instruments and of the relationship between sovereign governments and international organizations are vital to an understanding of the utility of United Nations enactments.

U.N. General Assembly. *International Human Rights Instruments of the United Nations, 1948-1982.* Pleasantville, N.Y.: UNIFO Publishers, 1983. This collection contains texts of most of the major international conventions and protocols approved by the United Nations before 1982 that are related to the affirmation of fundamental human rights and women's equality.

*Laura M. Calkins*

## Cross-References

The United Nations Adopts the Universal Declaration of Human Rights (1948), p. 789; The United Nations Amends Its International Slavery Convention (1953), p. 902; The U.N. Covenant on Civil and Political Rights Is Adopted (1966), p. 1353; The United Nations Issues a Declaration on Equality for Women (1967), p. 1391; The World Conference on Women Sets an International Agenda (1975), p. 1796; Congress Votes to Admit Women to the Armed Services Academies (1975), p. 1823; A U.N. Convention Condemns Discrimination Against Women (1979), p. 2057.

# THE MAU MAU UPRISING CREATES HAVOC IN KENYA

*Categories of event:* Indigenous peoples' rights; revolutions and rebellions
*Time:* October 20, 1952
*Locale:* Central Kenya

*To cope with the Mau Mau uprising against their rule in Kenya, the British declared a state of emergency and gave security forces special powers to hunt down insurgents*

Principal personages:

JOMO KENYATTA (1889-1978), a nationalist leader, the head of the Kenya African Union, later prime minister and president of Kenya

SIR EVELYN BARING (1903-1973), the governor of Kenya from September, 1952, until 1959

FRED KUBAI (1915-    ), one of the organizers of Mau Mau; controlled "oathing" in Nairobi

BILDAD MWANGANU KAGGIA (1922-    ), one of the organizers, with Fred Kubai, of Mau Mau

DEDAN KIMATHI (1920-1957), the most famous of the Mau Mau field commanders

WARUHIU KUNGU (?-1952), a prominent Christian Kikuyu leader closely aligned with the government

## Summary of Event

The Mau Mau uprisng, aside from being one of the most serious nationalist challenges to British colonial rule in Africa, was to a large extent a conflict over land. Kenya was a British settler colony, meaning that European immigration was encouraged. The settlers, who never numbered more than 1 percent of the population, occupied much of the best land of the country, the so-called "White Highlands," beginning in the early twentieth century. Although few in number, settler farms could be quite large and accounted for the bulk of Kenya's agricultural exports. The settlers also exercised considerable power in the government. The African residents of this area, mainly the Kikuyu, provided much of the labor for the white farms, and large numbers were tenants ("squatters") on land claimed by whites. As many as one-fourth of all Kikuyu lived on white farms. The remainder were restricted to their own reserve areas. Land hunger increased as the Kikuyu population increased. By 1952, at least ninety-five thousand Africans had moved into Nairobi, where they crowded into urban "locations." Although the British government had declared in 1923 that "Kenya is an African territory" and "the interests of the African native must be paramount," Africans were in fact treated as second-class citizens and possessed few of the civil or political rights enjoyed by whites. They did not have the right to travel freely in the country or to reside in certain areas.

By the end of World War II, various segments of the population were showing signs of frustration. Educated Kenyans in general chafed at discrimination and lack of a political voice (Africans were subject to their traditional chiefs). In 1944, the Kenya African Union (KAU), representing a cross-section of Kenya's ethnic groups, was founded, overlapping to a large extent the previous Kikuyu Central Association (KCA), banned since 1940 but still active. In 1947, Jomo Kenyatta (a Kikuyu) became chair of the KAU and campaigned for greater African representation in government. A more militant element was introduced with the return of African veterans from the war. Kenyans who had served in the British military faced unemployment, discrimination, and landlessness upon their return, and many turned to political agitation. Most of the organizers of the Mau Mau uprising were ex-soldiers.

Outside the reserves, the two hundred thousand or more Kikuyu squatters in the White Highlands were becoming increasingly impoverished and were worried about their security. Over the years, more and more land had been taken away from squatter cultivation by white farmers who wished to expand their own activities and limit the squatters' independence. Wages, however, did not rise, leaving squatters working longer hours for lower wages with less access to land than previously. Thousands of British soldiers were encouraged to settle in Kenya after the war, adding to squatters' fears of displacement. Some well-publicized evictions in 1946 only served to heighten their anxiety. Squatters received little education and few social services from the government. Many were beyond the reach of their landlords or the government, forming virtually independent communities. It was these increasingly marginalized squatters who provided much of the support for Mau Mau.

In 1950, police claimed to have uncovered a "Mau Mau Association" (the origin and meaning of the term "Mau Mau" is still debated) which sought to drive the whites from Kenya. This organization was said to use secret oaths in recruiting its members, and several people were arrested for administering the oaths. The government quickly banned the organization. The Mau Mau Association to which the government was referring actually consisted of militant elements, led by Fred Kubai and Bildad Mwanganu Kaggia, of the KAU and KCA. Both organizations used oaths and ceremonies which contained vows of unity, loyalty, obedience, and secrecy. These oaths varied according to purpose and became much more elaborate and serious during the state of emergency. By the time the government banned Mau Mau, Kubai and Kaggia had spread these oaths throughout Nairobi and the Kikuyu area.

Kubai and the other militants associated with the "oathing" began collecting weapons for an armed uprising, but the government struck before they were prepared. Acts of violence had been increasing in Kikuyu areas, and in November, 1951, a white settler was killed. Kikuyu who publicly supported the government were assassinated, the most dramatic of these assassinations being that of Senior Chief Waruhiu Kungu, an outspoken opponent of violence, who was shot in his car by men disguised as police on October 9, 1952. The result of these incidents was something of a panic among the settlers, who armed themselves and demanded firm action from the government. The governor, Sir Evelyn Baring, an aristocrat who had been in the country only three weeks, obliged by declaring a state of emergency on October 20.

Although martial law was not imposed, the declaration of the state of emergency gave the military authorities wide powers. Forest zones where Mau Mau operated were declared "prohibited areas" in which the army could fire at will. Elsewhere, the army and police had the right to search houses without a warrant and detain suspects indefinitely on the basis of an accusation by a single witness. Political meetings were banned. Collective punishment, including the confiscation of cattle, was imposed on communities which helped the insurgents or did not help the authorities. Illegal possession of weapons carried a death penalty, as did administering certain oaths and aiding insurgents. Movement of Kikuyus was controlled through a passbook system, and many Kikuyus were forced to relocate to special government-controlled villages. African "locations" in Nairobi were fenced in. An attack on a European, although relatively uncommon, could result in the removal of thousands of neighboring Kikuyu. Each murder of a white settler provoked revulsion, fear, and panic in the white community, which continued to pressure the government for more decisive action. Some settlers took matters into their own hands, killing anybody suspected of being a Mau Mau follower. One consequence of the fears among the settlers was that they pressured the government to expel Kikuyu squatters from the farms and replace them with workers from other ethnic groups. Some 100,000 Kikuyu squatters were sent to the reserves, which were already overcrowded. This and many other government actions during the emergency served to provide more recruits for the insurgents.

The first action under the state of emergency was Operation Jock Scott on the night of October 20. In this sweep, most of the major African political leaders and trade unionists, including Kenyatta, Kubai, and Kaggia, were arrested. Kenyatta had had little to do with the spread of "oathing" and the increasing violence. His repeated public condemnations of the Mau Mau tactics notwithstanding, he was regarded with great suspicion by the government and as a hero by the Mau Mau fighters. Along with Kubai, Kaggia, and three others, he was convicted in 1953 of leading or being associated with Mau Mau and was sentenced to seven years of hard labor. These prominent activists were followed over the next few years by tens of thousands of others who were detained for being associated with Mau Mau. Conditions in many of the detention camps were brutal. In addition to various forms of hard labor, corporal punishment, and solitary confinement, detainees were put through "rehabilitation" programs designed to extract confessions and cure the Mau Mau of their "disease" through education. Many former guerrillas were recruited for the government forces in this way.

## Impact of Event

With the declaration of the state of emergency, Africans were forced to take sides in the conflict. Many, if not most, Kikuyu supported the aims of Mau Mau, although they often opposed its violent strategy. Large numbers of people were forced by insurgents to take oaths, and persons suspected of collaborating with the government might be killed. Tom Mbotela, vice-president of the KAU and an opponent of Mau Mau, was assassinated in 1952. In the infamous Lari massacre of March 26, 1953, insurgents killed at least ninety-seven people, mostly women and children. Lari was a settlement established by the government in 1940, on land claimed by other Kikuyu, for a group of people who were moved from the Highlands to make way for white settlers. Its inhabitants were regarded as traitors by the Mau Mau and squatters for having agreed to leave their original homes.

On the British side, there were numerous cases of torture and summary execution committed by security forces. Few of these cases were investigated, and only a small number resulted in prosecutions. Particularly notorious were the Home Guard, Kikuyu irregulars who bore the brunt of Mau Mau attacks. The biggest scandal involved the detention camps and did not come to light until very late in the emergency. The camps were found to have poor sanitation, and hundreds of prisoners died of disease. Detainees were often overworked, underfed, beaten, and kept for long periods in solitary confinement. The most notorious case was the Hola camp, which was investigated in 1959 after eleven men died after being beaten when they refused to dig a ditch.

In 1954, one of the most important Mau Mau leaders (known as "General China") was captured. Soon thereafter, in Operation Anvil, security forces swept Nairobi sector by sector, rounding up some 16,500 people, mostly Kikuyu, and severely damaging Mau Mau operations in the city. The same procedure was carried out in the countryside, with areas cordoned off and their inhabitants screened for insurgents. New passbooks, which carried photographs, were introduced and had to be carried at all times. Loyal Kikuyu were organized to police their own areas.

By 1956, the British had reduced the insurgents in the forest to manageable numbers and were removing troops from Kenya. White settlers had already begun trying to recruit Kikuyu workers again, having been disappointed with their replacements. Dedan Kimathi, a Mau Mau field commander, was captured in October, 1956, and hanged in 1957. This event marked the end of the insurgency, although mopping-up operations continued for some time. In 1956 and 1957, some of the more severe regulations under the emergency, such as the death penalty for possessing weapons, were dropped. The state of emergency was finally lifted in 1960.

Official figures list 11,503 Mau Mau insurgents killed in the fighting, although the death toll was probably higher than this. More than one thousand people were executed for murder, administering oaths, or possessing firearms. A telling statistic is that only 5,299 insurgents were captured or surrendered. Security forces lost 590, while 1,875 civilian killings were attributed to Mau Mau, of which only 32 were of Europeans. Kenyatta emerged from prison in 1961 as a hero and led his country to independence on December 12, 1963. The settlers were forced to reconcile themselves to African rule. Although Mau Mau failed in its immediate aims, there is little doubt that it served to hasten British withdrawal, not only from Kenya but from East Africa as a whole.

## Bibliography

Barnett, Donald L., and Karari Njama. *Mau Mau from Within*. London: MacGibbon & Kee, 1966. The first major account of Mau Mau to be based on the reminiscences of a prominent insurgent leader. It contains a wealth of information about the organization and activities of the movement, and about Dedan Kimathi and other leaders. Glossary, index, and short bibliography.

Edgerton, Robert B. *Mau Mau: An African Crucible*. New York: Free Press, 1989. A very readable account of Mau Mau, and thoroughly researched. The work avoids historical analyses and concentrates instead on telling a story. The organization is somewhat disconcerting but effective. Index and bibliography.

Füredi, Frank. *The Mau Mau War in Perspective*. Athens: Ohio University Press, 1989. This work critiques previous interpretations of Mau Mau and carefully differentiates Mau Mau from other forms of resistance in Kenya and from the elite politics of the KAU. Includes a long discussion of the impact of Mau Mau on the process of decolonization. Bibliography, index, and maps.

Kanogo, Tabitha. *Squatters and the Roots of Mau Mau, 1905-63*. Athens: Ohio University Press, 1987. This work focuses on the squatter factor in the origins of Mau Mau and carries its discussion through the period of the emergency. Based on extensive interviews with former squatters. Bibliography, index, glossary, and maps.

Kariuki, Josiah Mwangi. *"Mau Mau" Detainee*. London: Oxford University Press, 1975. The experiences of an insurgent who spent more than five years in detention. Includes descriptions of conditions in the camps, the screening process, and "rehabilitation" programs. Also contains an account of the "oathing" ceremony. Index, photographs, no bibliography.

Likimani, Muthoni. *Passbook Number F.47927: Women and Mau Mau in Kenya*. New York: Praeger, 1985. A collection of short stories written by a woman who lived in Nairobi during the emergency. Although fictional, the stories highlight the varied experiences of women during the Mau Mau uprising. Has a glossary.

Rosberg, Carl G., Jr., and John Nottingham. *The Myth of "Mau Mau": Nationalism in Kenya*. Stanford, Calif.: Hoover Institution Press, 1966. The first major scholarly study of Mau Mau and the first to argue that Mau Mau was not a deranged rejection of modernization, as the government preferred to believe, but rather was a nascent nationalist movement. A thorough account, in spite of the lack of access to archival materials. Index, maps, and a good bibliography.

Spencer, John. *The Kenya African Union*. London: KPI, 1985. A study of the KAU up to the conviction of Kenyatta in 1953. Highlights the struggles within the party over platform and strategy. Particularly important for the information the author has gathered on the nature of links between the KAU and Mau Mau. Based on extensive interviews. Bibliography and index.

Throup, David. *Economic and Social Origins of Mau Mau, 1945-53*. Athens: Ohio University Press, 1988. This work discusses events leading up to Mau Mau, covering much the same material as Kanogo. It also has an interesting discussion of the outlook of British officials before Mau Mau. Arrives at the conclusion that the government had lost control of the Kikuyu countryside as early as 1947. Contains a very useful biographical appendix and bibliography. Also has an index and several maps.

*T. K. Welliver*

## Cross-References

The Defense of India Act Impedes the Freedom Struggle (1915), p. 156; The Easter Rebellion Fails to Win Irish Independence (1916), p. 178; The Atlantic Charter Declares a Postwar Right of Self-Determination (1941), p. 584; The French Quell an Algerian Nationalist Revolt (1945), p. 651; The Sudanese Civil War Erupts (1955), p. 941; Riots Erupt as Katanga Province Secedes from the Congo (1960), p. 1068; The United Nations Intervenes in the Congolese Civil War (1960), p. 1074; Zimbabwe's Freedom Fighters Topple White Supremacist Government (1964), p. 1224; The Palestinian *Intifada* Begins (1987), p. 2331; Namibia Is Liberated from South African Control (1988), p. 2409.

# GOVERNMENT POLICIES SEEK TO END THE SPECIAL STATUS OF NATIVE AMERICANS

*Category of event:* Indigenous peoples' rights
*Time:* August 1, 1953
*Locale:* Washington, D.C.

*House Concurrent Resolution 108 stated a termination policy that would end the special relationship that Native American tribes had with the federal government*

*Principal personages:*

WILLIAM F. ZIMMERMAN, JR., the assistant commissioner of Indian affairs under John Collier and acting commissioner after Collier's resignation

DILLON S. MYER (1891-　　　), the commissioner of Indian affairs (1950-1953)

GLENN L. EMMONS, the commissioner of Indian affairs (1953-1961); headed the Bureau of Indian Affairs through the active years of the termination policy

JOHN COLLIER (1884-1968), the commissioner of Indian affairs (1933-1945)

RICHARD M. NIXON (1913-　　　), the president of the United States (1969-1974)

## Summary of Event

On August 1, 1953, House Concurrent Resolution 108 (HCR 108) was adopted by the Congress of the United States of America. This resolution stated that the policy of the federal government, as understood by Congress, would be to end federal control of Native American tribes as soon as possible. HCR 108 targeted specifically all American Indians in the states of California, Florida, Iowa, New York, and Texas, as well as the members of individual tribes: the Klamath, Menominee, Flathead, and Osage tribes, the Potawatomi of Kansas and Nebraska, and the Turtle Mountain band of Chippewas. With the adoption of this resolution, these tribes and individuals in them were no longer considered to have a special relationship with the federal government and would no longer receive special considerations or exemptions based on that relationship. The tribes and individuals named in HCR 108 were expected to assume the full benefits and responsibilities of being United States citizens.

The late 1940's and the new prosperity of post-World War II America marked a turning point in Native American policy. The toleration of Indian separateness and the efforts at improving Indian lives and encouraging self-determination through legislation, including the Indian Reorganization Act of 1934, began to lose ground. Once again, the advocates of forced assimilation, active throughout most of U.S. history, rose to the top in national policy-making.

Resentment had been growing toward the special relationship that Native American tribes had with the federal government. With national prosperity came increasing demands for land and resources. Various developers coveted tribal lands, some of which had been restored to tribes only within the previous decade. Some Native Americans wished to sell their share of tribal lands for immediate profit rather than maintain land as a base for future development. These lands were held in trust for the tribes by the federal government, however, and special permission was required before they could be sold. Those who sought to exploit and develop the natural resources of the United States saw these tax-free Indian lands as a wasted resource. Development by the tribes was slow, as they relied upon federal assistance to undertake various projects. Some groups, such as the Klamath and Menominee, owned valuable timberlands that were managed through the federal government to provide an income for the tribe. Others, such as the Osage, controlled the rights to oil deposits on their lands. Exploitation of these resources was done cautiously under federal control, to allow the tribes a continuous source of income. Some individuals, both within and outside the tribes, thought that immediate liquidation was more attractive in some cases. On many reservations, economic opportunities were severely restricted. Returning military personnel and employees of war industries put a strain on resources that were in some cases inadequate to support existing populations. An expanding birthrate exacerbated the problem. The Relocation Service Program was implemented to ease this situation.

Relocation policy consisted of efforts to encourage Native Americans to leave their reservations and seek employment in urban areas. Aimed initially at the Navajo population, the Relocation Service Program opened field offices in Los Angeles, Denver, and Salt Lake City in the late 1940's to serve individuals and families seeking urban employment opportunities. By the late 1950's, however, it was determined that more than half of those leaving the reservations eventually returned. Some critics argued that culture shock experienced by these Native Americans in urban areas was to blame; others claimed that not only were the participants ill-prepared to deal with white society, but also they were sent to areas that did not have adequate or suitable employment opportunities.

The first overt attempt to remove federal protection from Native American groups took place in 1947. John Collier, a longtime champion of Native American rights and commissioner of Indian affairs from 1933 to 1945, had resigned amid growing unpopularity with Congress. His assistant commissioner, William F. Zimmerman, Jr., was made acting commissioner until another appointment could be made. While Zimmerman headed the Bureau of Indian Affairs (BIA), he was subpoenaed to appear before the Senate Committee on Civil Service and present a plan for reducing expenditures. Reluctantly, Zimmerman suggested that certain tribes were ready for the removal of federal controls and services and that other tribes could be made ready in the near future if certain steps were taken to prepare them adequately to take control of their own affairs. The Senate committee then requested that the bureau draw up a list of those tribes deemed ready for termination of federal controls. The bureau presented a list of three groups: group one consisted of the tribes ready for self-determination; those in group two should be ready in ten years; and those in group three required an indefinite time for full relinquishment of government supervision. In his testimony, Zimmerman stated that the criteria used to determine the readiness of a tribe for termination were "the degree of acculturation; . . . economic resources and condition of the tribe; . . . the willingness of the tribe to be relieved of federal control; and . . . the willingness of the State to take over." All tribes listed in group one were later included in HCR 108.

In 1950, Dillon S. Myer was appointed commissioner of Indian affairs. Myer's experience included a position as director of the Japanese War Relocation Authority from 1942 to 1946. Collier accused Myer of viewing the reservations as vast concentration camps and Native Americans as prisoners. It did seem, however, that Myer was interested in "freeing" Native Americans from the reservations. He concentrated on expanding relocation efforts and also restricted Indian access to the limited credit offered by the BIA to help Native American businesspeople. His goal in this was to help his charges to understand how the white business community worked. He encouraged Native Americans to take out loans at private banks and loan organizations by permitting them to mortgage tribal lands and individual allotments held in trust by the federal government. Glenn L. Emmons succeeded Myer in 1953. Emmons shared the belief that Native American unemployment could be solved through massive relocation efforts and continued this practice.

Before the termination exercised through HCR 108, Native American tribes had a special status that included federal government protection and exemption from all federal, state, and local taxes. State laws and regulations did not apply to Native Americans living within the boundaries of reservation lands, and civil and criminal law enforcement was handled by the tribes and the federal government. Health facilities and utilities were provided by the federal government, with the Public Health Service operating most reservation facilities. Under termination, Native Americans would be subject to state regulation and taxation, as were any other citizens living within a particular state. This control extended to the enforcement of civil and criminal laws. This was a dangerous situation for Native Americans, as state and local powers were often hostile to their Indian populations. Later, Public Law 280 provided for all states to exert civil and criminal jurisdiction over tribes within their boundaries, without the consent of the tribes involved, but few states undertook what would be a costly measure. President Dwight D. Eisenhower signed Public Law 280 but protested against it, urging Congress to adopt additional legislation specifying that tribes could refuse state control. Congress never did so.

Termination did not happen overnight. Several years elapsed for some tribes between the adoption of HCR 108 and the official termination of the tribes named in it, time which was supposed to be used for careful planning for the eventual end of federal supervision.

## Impact of Event

House Concurrent Resolution 108 was the most disastrous congressional action forced upon Native Americans since the Dawes or Allotment Act of 1887, with many similar results. As had happened through land allotment, Native Americans lost valuable lands and the livelihood derived from them. Most of the tribes affected by HCR 108 did not understand fully what was going to happen to them when termination was concluded.

In 1954, when the Menominee of Wisconsin were officially terminated, the lack of adequate preparation became evident. The tribe had appeared to meet all four of the BIA's criteria for termination. The Menominee had requested more control over their own affairs, and the state of Wisconsin initially was willing to take over many of the services provided by the federal government. On paper, the Menominee appeared to be prosperous, in possession of a renewable resource, their timberlands. The assessed value of their forest, $36 million, however, could not be realized unless the forest was sold, which would destroy the Menominee economy. The tribe entered into termination believing that accepting it was the only way to receive funds that the federal government held in trust for it, funds which the tribe had won in a settlement against the Bureau of Indian Affairs for mismanaging the forest. Few Menominee even participated in formulating the final plan for termination. What followed termination was a tragedy for the Menominee.

The tribe was charged for the cost of planning its termination. It had received its settlement funds, but per-capita payments to tribal members had used up most of this money. The loss of tax-exempt status created a further drain on economic resources.

Reservation health and education facilities did not meet Wisconsin state standards and were closed down, leaving the Menominee without access to education or health care on the reservation. It became obvious that the federal government had never provided adequate facilities for its charges. Not long after termination, a tuberculosis epidemic struck the tribe, and no health facilities were available on the reservation to help fight it. An inadequate sewage system required costly renovation when it failed to meet state standards. Individuals had to pay for their own water and electricity. The state of Wisconsin was unable to provide the services needed by the Menominee, and the tribes' status quickly fell from fairly prosperous to desperately impoverished. Similar experiences occurred to other tribes terminated under HCR 108 in spite of their opposition.

This experience caused many Native Americans to realize that they needed to develop political techniques if they wanted to retain their rights. The National Congress of American Indians (NCAI), founded in 1944, was strengthened by Indian reaction to termination and became a more intertribal organization. Voting in general elections increased, and large Native American populations in some states could determine the outcome of elections. Senators and other elected officials began paying more attention to Native American needs.

In 1970, President Richard M. Nixon officially pronounced termination "morally and legally unacceptable." In 1973, the Menominee Termination Act was repealed. The rights gained by treaty in fair exchange for the original Menominee lands were restored.

Despite the recommendations of BIA personnel, including Zimmerman, who had provided the lists for termination, Congress eagerly pushed ahead in "getting out of the Indian business." Once again, legislation had to fix what damage had been done by earlier resolution. Native Americans continued to engage federal and local governments in battles for their rights.

## Bibliography

Josephy, Alvin M. *Now That the Buffalo's Gone.* Norman: University of Oklahoma Press, 1984. An interesting book that contains chapters illustrating the difficulties Native Americans have faced in retaining their rights. Chapter 4, "Cornplanter, Can You Swim?" and Chapter 6, "The Great Northwest Fishing War," are of special interest. Extensive bibliography and index.

Nichols, Roger L., ed. *The American Indian: Past and Present.* New York: John Wiley & Sons, 1971. This text consists of separate articles covering cultural and historical aspects of Native American experience. Contains chapters on the Menominee Termination Act and the experience of Native Americans in urban areas. Includes a bibliography.

Tyler, S. Lyman. *A History of Indian Policy.* Washington, D.C.: Government Printing Office, 1973. A worthwhile, extensive text on United States government policy toward Native Americans. Highly recommended for the serious student. Includes an extensive bibliography.

Washburn, Wilcomb E., ed. *History of Indian-White Relations.* Vol. 4 in *Handbook of North American Indians*, edited by William C. Sturtevant. Washington, D.C.: Smithsonian Institution, 1988. A comprehensive volume. Information is organized chronologically within chapters concerning the legal status of Native Americans, the Indian rights movement, and United States Indian policies, among other topics.

—————————. *The Indian in America.* New York: Harper & Row, 1975. A history of Native American interactions with European and American settlers, with chapters on allotment and the Indian Reorganization Act. Photographs and index.

*Patricia Alkema*

## Cross-References

Intellectuals Form the Society of American Indians (1911), p. 121; The Indian Reorganization Act Offers Autonomy to American Indians (1934), p. 497; U.S. Government Encourages Native Americans to Settle in Cities (1950's), p. 820; Congress Ratifies the National Council on Indian Opportunity (1970), p. 1537; The Blue Lake Region in New Mexico Is Returned to the Taos Pueblo (1970), p. 1573; Native Americans Occupy Wounded Knee (1973), p. 1709.

# THE UNITED NATIONS AMENDS ITS
# INTERNATIONAL SLAVERY CONVENTION

*Categories of event:* Civil rights and workers' rights
*Time:* October, 1953, and September, 1956
*Locale:* United Nations, New York City and Geneva

*The United Nations acted to expand the definition of slavery and to prohibit certain kinds of exploitation designated as similar to slavery*

*Principal personages:*
> MUHAMED AWAD (1910-1971), the chief United Nations investigator of slavery and the author of a report issued in 1971
> HANS ENGEN, a Norwegian appointed by the United Nations to collect information on slavery in 1953
> DAG HAMMARSKJÖLD (1905-1961), the secretary-general of the United Nations
> FREDERICK LUGARD (1858-1945), a British statesman and critic of all forms of slavery
> ROGER SAWYER (1931- ), a British lawyer and leader of the Anti-Slavery Society
> BARON SHACKLETON (1911-1985), a British author and member of the Anti-Slavery Society

## Summary of Event

The United Nations Charter of 1945 did not mention slavery, even though the practice of owning other humans as property continued to exist in countries such as Ethiopia, Liberia, and Saudi Arabia. Slave traders from the latter nation were reportedly sending emissaries to Nigeria, then a British colony, to offer temporary employment to Africans as household servants. Investigators found that hundreds of slaves were transported to the Persian Gulf every year. The agents told the Africans that they would get free passage to Mecca, the holy city of Islam, in return for two years' service; when the victims got to Saudi Arabia, they were arrested for entering the country without visas and handed over by the police to slave traders.

In 1948, the Declaration of Human Rights was adopted by the United Nations; the declaration prohibited "slavery and the slave trade" in all forms among member nations. Enforcement powers were lacking, though, and slavery continued to be a problem in many areas of the world. In 1950, the United Nations created an ad hoc committee on slavery with authority to send questionnaires to all states asking them to report on customs and practices "resembling slavery." The committee, made up of representatives of Chile, the United Kingdom, France, and the United States, met twice over a two-year period and sent its questionnaires to all states. Before the committee could collate the responses, the General Assembly heard an angry attack on the ad hoc committee by the delegate from Peru, a country accused by a Catholic relief agency of allowing child slavery in rural areas and coal mines. The Peruvian ambassador tried to stop the investigation, claiming that the charges against his country were unreliable and irresponsible propaganda. His appeal to stop the investigation failed to win a majority. The narrow margin of victory in the General Assembly for those favoring continuation of the survey, twenty-one to seventeen with sixteen abstentions, showed that many nations were embarrassed by allegations of exploitation within their borders and wished to drop the issue. The four members of the committee had great difficulty in agreeing upon a course of action. Eventually, they received sixty-four replies to the questionnaire; twelve nations did not respond to the survey. Despite this problem, the committee's report concluded that slavery "even in its crudest forms" still existed in the world and that the United Nations had to take a stand against it. The committee also recommended that the United Nations expand the definition of slavery to include new forms of exploitation.

The ad hoc committee recommended that the United Nations adopt the view of the League of Nations, which in 1926 had defined slavery as "ownership of another human being" and called for its abolition. That agreement, ratified by forty-five states, did not achieve its goal, however, because it had been based on voluntary consent, and no enforcement procedures had been adopted. So many violations were reported that in 1931 the League of Nations created a committee of experts on the slavery question. This committee met twice, gathered information, and called for establishing a standing advisory committee that could follow up on complaints and issue punishments for violations of the 1926 convention. The full league agreed and created a seven-member agency that would meet annually, present reports on the extent of exploitation, and enforce the 1926 agreement. This committee met several times in the 1930's but had little influence on the forced-labor systems emerging in Nazi Germany and the Stalinist Soviet Union. The fight against slavery would not be renewed until after World War II, when the United Nations dealt with the issue.

After the ad hoc committee studied the question for two years, it reported its findings. The General Assembly asked Secretary-General Dag Hammarskjöld to draft a treaty expanding on the 1926 convention. Hammarskjöld recommended that debt bondage, exploitation of women through forced marriages, and the sale of children for adoption be added to the definition of slavery. He appointed Hans Engen of Norway to prepare a summary of information received by the committee of experts. Engen's survey urged the creation of a permanent committee of experts and a supplementary convention, or treaty, to add the new categories of slavery to the earlier definition. Engen said that all governments should adopt policies to end slavery quickly but without creating social disorder. This illustrated a major problem: Most states in which forms of slavery existed were Islamic, and a means would have to be found to free slaves although the practices resembling slavery had been ordained by religious leaders and royal authorities. To prevent great social disruption, the United Nations voted to delay action on new categories. It ratified the 1926 convention on

October 23, 1953, and called for a meeting in Geneva, Switzerland, to take up Engen's proposal for expanded controls.

The supplementary convention on slavery, officially titled the Geneva Conference
of Plenipotentiaries and the Proposal for a Limited International Regime Against the
Slave Trade, opened in the late summer of 1956. Delegates from ten nations debated
a draft proposal submitted by the United Kingdom and made several significant
changes weakening the enforcement powers of the United Nations, but the conference's essential decisions expanded the forms of labor defined as slavery. The 1926
and 1953 conventions had a limited view of slavery, covering only "chattel slavery,"
meaning ownership of another human being. Three new practices "similar to slavery" were defined: debt bondage, in which a person works without wages until a
debt is repaid, a condition prevalent in India; serfdom, interpreted as bound service
to a master on land a servant does not own and cannot move away from without
permission of the landlord, a condition especially common in South American countries such as Colombia and Peru; and the selling of women into marriage without
their consent and the selling or giving of children under eighteen to another person
for exploitation. To end Islamic practices victimizing women, the delegates agreed
that governments would set "suitable minimum ages" for marriage and encourage
couples to marry in the presence of a civil or religious authority. The goal was to
assure that Muslim girls could not be married without their consent, an age-old
practice that now violated an international treaty.

The supplementary convention declared that violations of these provisions should
be made a criminal offense under the laws of each nation. The draft called for
international control of the Red Sea, the Persian Gulf, and parts of the Indian Ocean,
the last areas of the world where chattel slavery still existed. Any slave-carrying
vessel found in these zones would be considered a pirate ship, and the courts of the
capturing nation would try the suspected slave traders and administer punishment.
Islamic delegates found this idea unacceptable and forced a change. In the final
protocol, nations themselves were called upon to prevent ships and aircraft carrying
their flag from transporting slaves to other states. Slave traders would be tried in the
courts of their homelands, a provision that severely weakened the final document.

Another amendment calling for abolition of all forms of slavery "as soon as possible" was also rejected by the delegates. Instead, the final agreement called upon all
parties to set suitable deadlines for ending slavery-like practices but left the exact
time to individual states. Otherwise, delegates argued, too much "disorganization"
would result. All countries were asked to make it a criminal offense to "induce"
human beings to give themselves or anybody dependent upon them into any type of
"servile status." A final paragraph made it a crime to mutilate, brand, or mark
another person as a punishment or as a sign of ownership or "for any other reason."
On September 4, 1956, thirty-one members of the United Nations signed the convention. The United States, however, refused to ratify the new regulations, saying that it
preferred to deal with the problem of slavery through public debate and education in
the nations affected instead of interfering in their domestic affairs.

## Impact of Event

The slavery convention led to major changes in nations such as Saudi Arabia, Yemen, Muscat, Oman, and other Persian Gulf states, where an estimated one-half million slaves were said to be held in 1956. In Saudi Arabia, where only a year earlier three fugitive slaves who had escaped from King Saud's household were beheaded, steps were begun to make chattel slavery illegal, a process finished in 1962. As late as 1966, however, the United Nations Economic and Social Council debated enforcement policy over the objections of Peru, India, and Iran. Arguments in favor of more vigorous policing of abuses made little headway. Instead, council members voted to classify South Africa's system of apartheid, under which blacks were totally segregated and had no political rights, as a "slave-like practice." The council handed responsibility for overseeing the convention to the Commission on Human Rights.

In 1967, the commission created a subcommission on slavery and authorized a new study to be headed by Muhamed Awad of Egypt. Awad presented his report to the commission and made two proposals: That a new convention further redefine the meaning of the term "slavery" and that slavery be fought on a regional basis. The London-based Anti-Slavery Society found that slavery existed in many Third World nations. In Southeast Asia and India, millions of human beings lived in debt bondage, while in Peru thousands of families had been forced into serfdom by poverty and hunger. In Colombia, children under age ten worked seventy-hour weeks in coal mines, and seven-year-old girls were sold by desperately poor parents into domestic service in the homes of rich landlords. In Brazil, seven-year-old children worked twelve-hour days in sugarcane fields, and Indians in the Amazon basin were being exterminated by the thousands in a deliberate campaign to get them out of the way of "progress." In Paraguay, the Ache Indians slowly were being decimated by government forces in the northern desert because they too obstructed economic development.

Not all such tragedies took place in Third World nations. Even in Europe, children were being exploited in violation of the 1956 convention. In Spain, young children worked in shoe factories where they used toxic glues to attach soles, and in southern Italy thousands of agricultural laborers were under the age of ten. Exploitation of women existed in Thailand and Nepal, where the selling of teenage girls into prostitution was an important part of the rural economy. In Africa, young girls were still mutilated in accord with traditional religious rites, while in Mauritania, apparently the last country in the world to outlaw the practice, slavery was legal until 1980.

Beginning in 1975, a United Nations Working Group of Experts on Slavery met yearly in Geneva and continued to gather proof and hear reports on the recognized forms of slavery that still existed. It had little power except public exposure of illegal activity. The experts recognized slavery as chattel slavery, exploitation of women, debt bondage, and serfdom. All forms were to be found somewhere in the world, though the oldest type, direct ownership of another human being, was on the verge of extinction. Because of that step, the international movement against slavery was nearing an important victory, though exploitation of women and children continued unabated in many nations.

## Bibliography

Asher, Robert E., and Walter M. Kotschnig. *The United Nations and Promotion of the General Welfare.* Washington, D.C.: Brookings Institution, 1957. An account of the background and proceedings of the antislavery conventions held by the United Nations. Contains a lengthy account of the 1926, 1953, and 1956 decisions. An unbiased, dispassionate account of U.N. efforts in all areas of human rights and welfare. A useful summary of the new categories of slavery added in the 1956 supplementary convention. Includes an index and a bibliography.

Cordier, Andrew W., and Wilder Foote, eds. *Dag Hammarskjöld: Public Papers of Secretaries-General of the United Nations, 1956-1957.* New York: Columbia University Press, 1973. Contains the secretary-general's views of the slavery convention and supplement. Provides little information on the background of the issue.

Eagleton, Clyde, and Richard N. Swift, eds. *Annual Review of United Nations Affairs, 1955-1956.* New York: New York University Press, 1957. A shorter, more concise account of the Geneva meeting. Provides a useful overview of other U.N. involvement in human rights. Prior editions of the series carry brief summaries of investigations conducted in the early 1950's. A short bibliography and index.

Sawyer, Roger. *Slavery in the Twentieth Century.* London: Routledge & Kegan Paul, 1986. Written by a member of the Anti-Slavery Society, this book contains the most extensive survey of slavery as it exists in the modern world. A critical view of customs and traditions that lead to the exploitation of women and children and a fervent call for an immediate prohibition of such practices. An index and a most useful bibliography.

Winks, Robin W. *Slavery, A Comparative Perspective: Readings on Slavery from Ancient Times to the Present.* New York: New York University Press, 1972. Has several informative and useful articles on slavery throughout human history. Leading experts on every period present brief, accurate accounts of the rise and fall of slave systems in every area of the world. There are two essays on slavery in the twentieth century. Has an index and a bibliography.

*Leslie V. Tischauser*

## Cross-References

International Agreement Attacks the White Slave Trade (1904), p. 30; The International Labour Organisation Is Established (1919), p. 281; The League of Nations Adopts the International Slavery Convention (1926), p. 436; Ethiopia Abolishes Slavery (1942), p. 607; The United Nations Adopts the Universal Declaration of Human Rights (1948), p. 789; The United Nations Adopts the Abolition of Forced Labor Convention (1957), p. 985; The U.N. Covenant on Civil and Political Rights Is Adopted (1966), p. 1353.

# SCHWEITZER IS AWARDED THE NOBEL PEACE PRIZE

*Categories of event:* Health and medical rights; peace movements and organizations
*Time:* December 10, 1953
*Locale:* Oslo, Norway

*The award to Albert Schweitzer of the Nobel Peace Prize symbolized the near-universal admiration he attained through his life of devotion as a medical missionary in Africa*

*Principal personages:*

ALBERT SCHWEITZER (1875-1965), the recipient of the 1952 Nobel Peace Prize

GUNNAR JAHN (1883-1971), the president of the Nobel Committee of the Norwegian parliament

GEORGE C. MARSHALL (1880-1959), the sponsor of the Marshall Plan for European reconstruction, recipient of the 1953 Nobel Peace Prize at the same time Schweitzer's award was announced

ALFRED NOBEL (1833-1896), a Swedish engineer and inventor of dynamite who founded the Nobel Prizes with a bequest in his will

## Summary of Event

On December 13, 1953, Gunnar Jahn, the president of the Nobel Committee of the Norwegian parliament, awarded the 1952 Nobel Peace Prize to Albert Schweitzer. Traditionally, the recipient of the prize responds with a talk. Schweitzer delivered his response on November 4, 1954, speaking on "The Problem of Peace," since he was unable to be in Europe in 1953. Like Jahn's presentation, Schweitzer's talk was delivered in the auditorium of the University of Oslo.

The Nobel Prizes are awarded each year through a bequest from the will of Alfred Nobel. Nobel, a Swedish engineer, invented dynamite; as a result of this and other inventions, he became enormously wealthy. In spite of the character of his most famous invention, Nobel was devoted to peace and left money in his will to be distributed to worthy recipients in the areas of physics, chemistry, medicine, literature, and peace (economics was added in 1961). The prizes, which have been awarded each year since 1901, are under the jurisdiction of the relevant Swedish academies, with the exception of the prize for Peace, which is awarded by the Norwegian parliament. The prizes have come to be regarded as the highest tributes that persons working in the subject fields can receive.

As Jahn made clear in his address, the award to Schweitzer was made not for a single achievement but for the sum and substance of his life. Schweitzer was born in 1875 in Alsace, which had been annexed by Germany after the Franco-Prussian War of 1871. Schweitzer's family had been devoted to scholastic pursuits for several generations, and he proved no exception to the family pattern. He was a child prodigy who played the concert piano and organ before reaching his teens.

Schweitzer achieved international recognition in several disciplines while he was still in his twenties. In *The Quest of the Historical Jesus: A Critical Study of Its Progress from Reimarus to Wrede*, (1906), he summed up a century of scholarly research on the New Testament. He concluded that the Gospels provided little material for an accurate portrayal of the life and teachings of Jesus. From the available sources, Schweitzer argued, one could reasonably conclude that Jesus expected the end of the world to occur within a short time after his life. Jesus taught an "interim ethic" that was to apply only for the few years before the world came to an end. Schweitzer's conclusions aroused considerable controversy, as it was clear that he did not accept the orthodox Christian account of Jesus. Subsequently, his book was recognized as a landmark of New Testament studies. Although Schweitzer's views differed from Protestant orthodoxy, he was clearly committed to a religious point of view. As he made clear in *Civilization and Ethics* (1925), his position was based on the conviction that the key to history was the development of the spirit. By "spirit," Schweitzer meant a realization that all life was a unity. When one realized the meaning of spirit, a new ethical system would immediately become plausible.

Schweitzer termed this ethics "reverence for life." The phrase, if not the underlying rationale for it, became famous. Schweitzer meant by it that instead of concentrating exclusively on human welfare, as most ethical systems do, the interests of all life must be taken into account. This does not imply that one must always refrain from violence, even to the extent of refusing to kill an insect. The popular caricature of Schweitzer as someone who deplored swatting a pesky mosquito ignores the fact that he held that the interests of life as a whole must be taken into account, rather than simply the interests of individual living beings. In appropriate circumstances, violence could be acceptable, Schweitzer believed. In "The Problem of Peace," Schweitzer referred to the view that war has been an instrument of human progress. Although he rejected that view of twentieth century wars, his remarks suggest that he believed it to be true of the wars of certain eras.

Why did Schweitzer espouse "reverence for life"? He devoted little formal argument to establishing his view, although he drew on his wide learning in history to provide illustrations of his system. He based his view on a mystical intuition of the oneness of life. This illumination was not susceptible to rational analysis, and critics have sometimes contrasted the rationalism of Schweitzer's biblical studies with his ethical mysticism. Because he based his ethics on intuition rather than logic, his moral system has not attracted much attention from philosophers.

The real significance of Schweitzer's ethics emerged in his life. He believed that he was required to abandon his scholarly career and devote himself to work as a medical missionary. In 1913, he traveled to French Equatorial Africa, where he set up a settlement at Lambaréné. He divided the remainder of his long life between Europe and Africa, campaigning for money in Europe to support his African work. He died in Lambaréné in 1965 at the age of ninety.

The principal reason Schweitzer aroused near-universal admiration was his abandonment of an eminent scholarly career for difficult service as a medical missionary. Before moving to Lambaréné, Schweitzer had qualified as a medical doctor, and he devoted almost all of his attention when he arrived in Africa to providing medical care for the native population. He established a hospital, which he supervised himself throughout his years in the settlement. Although he still considered himself to be a Protestant pastor and preached weekly sermons, he did not spend much time on efforts to convert the natives to Christianity.

Jahn maintained that the spirit of service manifested in Schweitzer's life offered a key to world peace; it was for this reason that Schweitzer had been awarded the Nobel Prize. Schweitzer's own views about the importance of reverence for life emerged with full clarity in his acceptance speech. Schweitzer began his talk with a historical perspective on the rise of Europe. Migration and invasion had interfered with the permanent settlement of southern and eastern Europe on a peaceful basis. The conflicting interests of the various nationalities in these areas threatened the peace of Europe. The appalling massacres and dislocations of people following the two world wars made it clear that violence was no longer available as a solution. What then was to be done?

Schweitzer reviewed attempts to end war through alliances or leagues of states. Beginning in the sixteenth century, these proposals culminated in the eighteenth century with the plans of Jean-Jacques Rousseau, the Abbé de Saint-Pierre, and Immanuel Kant. Schweitzer did not reject such leagues altogether: On the contrary, he noted, the League of Nations and the United Nations had accomplished considerable good. A league of states alone was not sufficient to attain peace, though. It was essential, Schweitzer said, to transform human nature through the general adoption of reverence-for-life ethics. The realization of the oneness of life would ameliorate ethnic tensions and rivalries inimical to world peace.

Critics sometimes dismissed Schweitzer for "head-in-the-clouds" thinking, but much of his advice was down to earth. He called for the abolition of nuclear weapons, since their unparalleled destructive power threatened the collapse of civilization. He did not favor undue emphasis on self-determination of colonial peoples, since in his view national rivalries were the principal threat to peace. Instead, the civilized peoples had the duty of caring for their primitive brethren. Although one might dismiss this view as paternalistic and racist, Schweitzer's good faith was difficult to fault. The award of the Nobel Prize encapsulated the worldwide admiration he received for his life of dedicated service to others.

## Impact of Event

After the end of World War II in 1945, the peoples of the world looked forward to a new era of peace. The Axis Powers had been defeated at the cost of millions of lives and untold misery. Perhaps the world could turn from violence and develop civilization on a peaceful footing.

This hope proved unfounded. The Cold War, a struggle between the United States and its allies on one hand and the Soviet Union and its satellites on the other, soon erupted. The development of atomic weapons made the peace of the world more precarious than ever before. The Cold War became quite hot with the onset of the Korean War in 1950. In these circumstances, there was a widespread feeling of despair.

The award of the Nobel Peace Prize to Albert Schweitzer signified that perhaps a better way of attaining peace than traditional power politics could be found. Schweitzer's reverence-for-life philosophy sought to overcome conventional antagonisms through a recognition of spiritual unity.

Few proved able to accept fully either the mystical foundation or the radical implications of Schweitzer's philosophy. Schweitzer's life was nevertheless viewed with widespread admiration. His receipt of the Peace Prize met with near-total acclaim in the United States and elsewhere. *The New York Times* devoted an editorial to praising Schweitzer (November 1, 1953), while *Newsweek* (November 9, 1953), hardly a bastion of starry-eyed idealism, noted that admirers of Schweitzer considered him among the world's greatest men. *The Christian Century* (November 3, 1953), the leading voice of American liberal Protestantism, saw in Schweitzer a veritable superhero. He was an example of the heights human beings were capable of achieving.

The impact of the prize consisted of more than idealistic outpourings of support. The award gave impetus to Schweitzer's campaign against nuclear weapons. He initiated an international letter-writing campaign aimed at banning the testing and use of nuclear weapons. The campaign tried to secure the signatures of prominent people in the hope that sufficient public support would be generated to attain its goals. Schweitzer had the support of his friend Norman Cousins, the editor of the *Saturday Review*, in this endeavor.

The campaign resulted in a break in the universality of praise for Schweitzer, the first since his emergence early in the century as a New Testament critic. Many supporters of United States foreign policy viewed the disarmament campaign as a Soviet ploy: They saw in Schweitzer an unwitting tool of the Communists. His admirers sharply counterattacked, seeing in his antinuclear efforts a characteristic manifestation of his lifelong efforts at goodwill.

The prize also had a material impact on Schweitzer's activities. He expanded his medical facilities at Lambaréné, using the $33,000 he received from the Nobel Committee for the construction of a leprosarium. Although the attendant publicity stemming from the award increased even further the means at Schweitzer's disposal, he refused to modernize his equipment. Schweitzer believed it was necessary to adapt Western techniques to the mentality and customs of the natives among whom he worked. This attitude brought him some criticism, most notably from the journalist Gerald McKnight, who in *Verdict on Schweitzer* (1964) termed Schweitzer a racist and paternalist as well as a colossal egotist. Most observers found the criticism vastly exaggerated. The award of the Peace Prize enhanced the fame of an already much-admired man, and Schweitzer's few detractors were unable to dent his significance as a symbol of hope.

## Bibliography

Clark, Henry. *The Ethical Mysticism of Albert Schweitzer*. Boston: Beacon Press, 1962. A sympathetic study of Schweitzer's ethics of reverence for life. His notion of a mystical intuition of unity among all living beings is carefully explained. Clark stresses Schweitzer's early writings in his exposition. The relation between Schweitzer's ethical views and his work on Christianity is explored.

Franck, Frederick. *Days with Albert Schweitzer*. New York: Holt, Rinehart and Winston, 1959. The memoirs of an American artist and dentist who worked with Schweitzer in the hospital at Lambaréné. Franck gives a good portrayal of Schweitzer's personality and methods of work. The book provides important source material for critical evaluation of the charges brought by Gerald McKnight in *Verdict on Schweitzer*.

Jack, Homer, ed. *To Dr. Albert Schweitzer: A Festschrift Commemorating His Eightieth Birthday from a Few of His Friends*. Evanston, Ill., 1955. Jack, a leading American pacifist, has edited a collection of articles in tribute to Schweitzer. The articles discuss Schweitzer's ideas, stressing their potential as contributions to world peace. The book includes a comprehensive bibliography of Schweitzer's work to 1955.

McKnight, Gerald. *Verdict on Schweitzer*. New York: John Day, 1964. The most negative full-length assessment of Schweitzer. McKnight claims that Schweitzer's radical methods were outdated and his techniques of sanitation inadequate and primitive, and argues that Schweitzer was a racist and paternalist.

Marshall, George, and David Poling. *Schweitzer: A Biography*. Garden City, N.Y.: Doubleday, 1971. The most comprehensive biography of Schweitzer, offering extensive discussion of Schweitzer's activities and ideas. Marshall is extremely favorable to Schweitzer and devotes considerable attention to refuting McKnight and other critics. The book includes a bibliography and a critical discussion of books about Schweitzer.

Schweitzer, Albert, and C. T. Campion, trans. *Out of My Life and Thought: An Autobiography*. New York: Henry Holt, 1933. Schweitzer's autobiography. Although it deals with his life only to age sixty, it covers the principal events of his career. The dramatic story of Schweitzer's abandonment of his scholarly career for work as a medical missionary is fully described. Schweitzer depicts his hospital at Lambaréné and gives an account of the local population and their reactions to him.

Schweitzer, Albert, and W. Montgomery, trans. *The Quest of the Historical Jesus: A Critical Study of Its Progress from Reimarus to Wrede*. London: A & C Black, 1910. Schweitzer's most famous book. It summarizes a century of (mostly German) critical research on the New Testament. Schweitzer concludes that Jesus was an apocalyptic preacher who foresaw the imminent end of the world. The Gospels do not provide an adequate basis for a historically accurate life of Jesus. Schweitzer's conclusions led some to claim he was not a Christian, but Schweitzer continued to view himself as a Protestant pastor throughout his adult life.

Schweitzer, Albert, and John Naish, trans. *Civilization and Ethics*. London: A & C

Black, 1923. The most complete description of Schweitzer's ethics. Schweitzer explains his view that civilization rises through increased recognition of the spirit. Progress has been threatened by the unparalleled destruction of World War I, and conscious adoption of reverence for life is necessary. The mysticism lying at the base of his doctrine prevented the book from having much impact on professional philosophers.

*Bill Delaney*

## Cross-References

The World Health Organization Proclaims Health as a Basic Right (1946), p. 678; The United States Peace Corps Is Founded (1961), p. 1102; A U.N. Declaration on Hunger and Malnutrition Is Adopted (1974), p. 1775; The Declaration of Tokyo Forbids Medical Abuses and Torture (1975), p. 1829; WHO Sets a Goal of Health for All by the Year 2000 (1977), p. 1893; Misuse of Psychiatry Is Addressed by the Declaration of Hawaii (1977), p. 1926; An International Health Conference Adopts the Declaration of Alma-Ata (1978), p. 1998; Mother Teresa Is Awarded the Nobel Peace Prize (1979), p. 2051; Commission Studies Ethical and Legal Problems in Medicine and Research (1980), p. 2090; The U.N. Principles of Medical Ethics Include Prevention of Torture (1982), p. 2169.

# BROWN V. BOARD OF EDUCATION ENDS PUBLIC SCHOOL SEGREGATION

*Categories of event:* Racial and ethnic rights; educational rights
*Time:* May 17, 1954
*Locale:* United States Supreme Court, Washington, D.C.

*For almost sixty years, racial segregation had been established by law in the United States; the Supreme Court decision in* Brown v. Board of Education *changed race relations*

*Principal personages:*

EARL WARREN (1891-1974), a former governor of California and chief justice of the United States in 1954

THURGOOD MARSHALL (1908-      ), an attorney for the National Association for the Advancement of Colored People (NAACP)

JOHN W. DAVIS (1873-1955), the solicitor general of the United States under President Woodrow Wilson, defended segregated schools in the Brown case

## Summary of Event

Segregation of blacks and whites in the United States is the most obvious of the racial problems that have faced the nation, because black people form its largest racial minority and have been the object of laws, as well as customs, which have kept them from full participation in social and economic life. Many of the laws imposing racial segregation dealt with public schools' segregation of children based on their race.

Legal segregation began in the United States in the years following the Civil War. Since black people were declared equal citizens to whites by the Fourteenth and Fifteenth Amendments to the Constitution, a new basis for race relations needed to be worked out to replace the prewar master-slave status. Because most black people lived in the states which had formed the Confederacy, the problem of race relations was more intense in the South.

In 1896, the Supreme Court of the United States was asked to settle the question of whether forcing black people to use separate facilities was a violation of the Constitutional guarantees of equality. The case in question, *Plessy v. Ferguson*, involved street cars in New Orleans, Louisiana. In that case the Supreme Court ruled that "separate, but equal" facilities did not violate the demands of the Constitution. Based on this decision, a number of states passed laws that demanded racial segregation in almost every aspect of life, from restaurants to public schools to the ballot box, with most black people losing the right to vote.

Many African-American leaders, such as Booker T. Washington, accepted the reality of segregation and did not openly challenge the system. White political leaders, in southern and border states, found they could whip up enthusiasm for their candidacies and could win votes by making strong and emotional supports of segregation. This separation of the races was reinforced by the economic conditions of the period from 1920 to 1940, when agricultural and blue-collar industrial workers were competing for jobs. In this economic competition, race was an easily identified and easily exploited factor. Black workers were accused of accepting lower wages and of being strike breakers.

If the "separate" aspect of the *Plessy v. Ferguson* decision was honored, the "equal" was quickly forgotten. In the twenty-one states which either required or permitted segregation, salaries for African-American teachers were about one-half those for white teachers, and the amount of money spent for each black pupil was about one-fourth that spent on each white pupil. In the states of the old Confederacy and in the border states, separate schools with enrollment based on race were a universal practice. Such segregation was not uncommon in the rest of the nation. In some cases separate schools were maintained contrary to state law. Hispanics, Asians, and Native Americans were often the subjects of segregation in western states.

Although segregation was widespread, the practice was under attack by 1950. President Harry S. Truman had ordered the desegregation of facilities belonging to the federal government, and the armed forces were beginning to integrate their units. Also, five suits challenging the validity of public school segregation had been introduced before the federal courts of various districts. These cases involved the public schools of Clarendon County, South Carolina; Prince Edward County, Virginia; Topeka, Kansas; Wilmington, Delaware; and Washington, District of Columbia. These were all "class action" suits, meaning that any decision reached in them would apply not just to the people who had brought suit but also to any others in the same district who suffered the same discrimination.

All five of these cases were heard by the Supreme Court of the United States under Chief Justice Earl Warren. In order to make sure that all aspects of this sensitive and important issue were covered, the Supreme Court ordered certain aspects of the cases reargued in 1953. At this point, all five cases were consolidated and listed alphabetically. This listing meant that the first case on the docket would be *Brown*, et al. *v. the Board of Education of Topeka, Kansas*, or as it would be better known, *Brown v. Board of Education*.

The nation's oldest civil rights organization is the National Association for the Advancement of Colored People (NAACP). This group traditionally has challenged discriminatory practices through lawsuits. The chief counsel for this group who would argue the case before the Supreme Court was Thurgood Marshall. Marshall was a veteran of many court battles over racial discrimination and was anxious to demonstrate not only that segregation was unfair under the Constitution but also that the practice was psychologically damaging to African Americans, especially black children. To assist him in making this point, Marshall invited several prominent social scientists to study the situation in Topeka, Kansas, and to comment on the psychological impact of segregation. It was the opinion of this group that assigning a particular group to separate facilities identified this group as having a lower status than other people. This evaluation of having a lower status became damaging to the segregated group by lowering its members' self-esteem.

The defendants in the case assembled a team of lawyers led by John W. Davis, a corporate lawyer from New York City. Davis was a former Democratic presidential nominee and solicitor general of the United States. In his government capacity, Davis had successfully prosecuted the Ku Klux Klan and had won cases which successfully restored the right to vote to black citizens in some states. The line of defense taken by Davis was not based on racial prejudice but on the matter of states' rights, a troublesome issue which, along with slavery, had led to the Civil War almost a century before. Davis argued that the federal government generally and the Supreme Court specifically were not qualified to take over and conduct the business of state operations such as schools.

Chief Justice Earl Warren had only recently been appointed to his post by newly-elected President Dwight Eisenhower. Warren was thought to be of a conservative point of view, and many people favorable to civil rights were unsure how he would vote, especially since his record when he was governor of California gave few hints as to what his judicial opinions might be.

Both sides presented their arguments in December, 1953. On May 17, 1954, the Supreme Court ruled that "separate but equal" had ceased to be the law of the land. State-enforced racial segregation in the public schools would no longer be permitted. This ruling meant that while the school districts covered in the five combined cases should be desegregated quickly, the way was also open for all other court districts to hear suits on the same basis. The unanimous opinion of the Supreme Court, written by Chief Justice Warren, left no doubt as to the outcome of future suits. The chief justice wrote, "We conclude that in the field of public education the doctrine of 'separate but equal' has no place. Separate educational facilities are inherently unequal." This decision in *Brown v. Board of Education* may well be the most momentous and far-reaching court order in the area of civil rights in the twentieth century.

## Impact of Event

It would be no exaggeration to say the decision in *Brown v. Board of Education* completely changed the face of the United States. Although some states tried to resist the process of integration of public schools for a time, their resistance was doomed to fail. When President Eisenhower sent U.S. Army troops to Little Rock, Arkansas, in 1957 to enforce school desegregation, it became clear that the impact of *Brown v. Board of Education* would be universal. No state would be able to impose its will on the national Supreme Court.

Within ten years, many public schools had been integrated by race. After fifteen years, virtually all public schools had ended segregation. One reaction to desegregation was the creation of numerous private schools, often connected with churches, in which the student body was all white. Students in the integrated public schools found common ground, and joint achievement in extracurricular activities such as music and sports soon drew favorable public attention. For example, in 1964 three civil rights workers were murdered near Philadelphia, Mississippi. In 1980, the same town held a parade honoring Marcus Dupree, a black football player at the local high school. With the breakdown of segregation in public schools, the task of attacking race separation in other aspects of life also became easier.

The integration of public schools did not produce national heroes such as Dr. Martin Luther King, Jr. Instead, there were many heroic individuals such as the black children who walked through crowds of yelling protesters to enter the schools, the white students who violated the customs of their communities to welcome their black classmates, and community leaders such as the *Nashville Tennessean* newspaper editor who advocated peaceful acceptance of integration as the proper action.

It should not be assumed that integration of public schools solved the matter of race relations in the schools or in society at large. Issues such as busing students to other schools to achieve racial balance, employment opportunities for black teachers and administrators, "white flight" to private or suburban schools, inclusion of black history in the curriculum, and the events and ideas to be emphasized in teaching the history of the Civil War would all cause problems and debate following 1954. Indeed, some black leaders would come to call for all-black schools and colleges as a means of preserving a black culture and heritage.

Leslie W. Dunbar, a white Southern teacher, consultant, and community organizer, sums up the impact of the Supreme Court decision very well:

> I think *Brown v. Board of Education* has a very special historical claim. I guess you could say the same thing, in a way, about 1865, with the Thirteenth Amendment [which abolished slavery and involuntary servitude]. But that got ignored. Up until *Brown v. Board of Education*, in 1954, segregation had been legal. Up to *Brown v. Board of Education*, the Constitutional rights of black people *not* to be discriminated against were, to say the least, unclear. After that, they were not. From 1954 on, it was as though the Constitution had been clarified.

## Bibliography

Branch, Taylor. *Parting the Waters: America in the King Years, 1954-63.* New York: Simon & Schuster, 1988. This book won the 1989 Pulitzer Prize for its historical and personal portrayal of all the major, and many minor, characters involved in what the author calls "The King Years." This is the first volume of a series, but other volumes are not yet published.

Franklin, John Hope, and Isidore Starr. *The Negro in the Twentieth Century.* New York: Vintage Books, 1967. Franklin is the "Dean" of Afro-American history. This book gives a survey of blacks in America. Book 3, pp. 262-286, deals especially with *Brown v. Board of Education.*

Friedman, Leon. *The Civil Rights Reader: Basic Documents of the Civil Rights Movement.* New York: Walker & Company, 1968. The value of this book is found in its reprinting of original interviews and documents from the civil rights years.

Lewis, Anthony. *Portrait of a Decade: The Second American Revolution.* New York: Random House, 1964. Lewis was a reporter who covered in person the events he describes. His firsthand involvement is backed with accurate historical research.

Powledge, Fred. *Free at Last? The Civil Rights Movement and the People Who Made It.* Boston: Little, Brown, 1991. The author is a journalist, born in North Carolina, who covered the civil rights movement for the Atlanta *Journal* and *The New York Times.* Valuable because the author has interviewed participants in the movement and has allowed them to tell their own stories of these events.

Southern Education Reporting Service. *With All Deliberate Speed.* Edited by Don Shoemaker. New York: Harper and Brothers, 1957. The date of this book shows that it deals only with the early days of the civil rights movement, but it provides excellent background for understanding the situation as it existed in 1957.

Woodward, C. Vann. *The Strange Career of Jim Crow.* New York: Oxford University Press, 1974. "Jim Crow" was the nickname for discriminatory laws and practices. This book is the standard history of racial segregation. Frequent revisions have kept it up to date with legal, social, and historical trends.

*Michael R. Bradley*

## Cross-References

Black Leaders Call for Equal Rights at the Niagara Falls Conference (1905), p. 41; The Ku Klux Klan Spreads Terror in the South (1920's), p. 298; Truman Orders Desegregation of U.S. Armed Forces (1948), p. 777; Parks Is Arrested for Refusing to Sit in the Back of the Bus (1955), p. 947; The Civil Rights Act of 1957 Creates the Commission on Civil Rights (1957), p. 997; Eisenhower Sends Troops to Little Rock, Arkansas (1957), p. 1003; Greensboro Sit-ins Launch a New Stage in the Civil Rights Movement (1960), p. 1056; The Council of Federated Organizations Registers Blacks to Vote (1962), p. 1149; Meredith's Enrollment Integrates the University of Mississippi (1962), p. 1167; Civil Rights Protesters Attract International Attention (1963), p. 1188; Martin Luther King, Jr., Delivers His "I Have a Dream" Speech (1963), p. 1200; Three Civil Rights Workers Are Murdered (1964), p. 1246; Congress Passes the Civil Rights Act (1964), p. 1251; Marshall Becomes the First Black Supreme Court Justice (1967), p. 1381.

# THE UNITED NATIONS DRAFTS A CONVENTION ON STATELESS PERSONS

*Category of event:* Refugee relief
*Time:* September 28, 1954
*Locale:* United Nations, New York City

*As part of a broad effort to aid refugees, the United Nations Conference on the Status of Stateless Persons drafted a convention to improve the status of persons without legal citizenship in or nationality of any state*

*Principal personages:*
JUAN I. COOKE (1895-1957), an Argentinean lawyer and diplomat; the president of the Economic and Social Council of the United Nations in 1954
KNUD LARSON (1895-     ), the president of the U.N. Conference on the Status of Stateless Persons
DAG HAMMARSKJÖLD (1905-1961), the secretary-general of the United Nations from 1953 to 1961
FRIDTJOF NANSEN (1861-1930), the Norwegian delegate to the League of Nations who was instrumental in early efforts to aid refugees and stateless persons
ELEANOR ROOSEVELT (1884-1962), the wife of U.S. president Franklin Delano Roosevelt and a major advocate of international human rights, including those of stateless persons

## Summary of Event

In the twentieth century, the plight of refugees became a major human rights issue. Political and territorial changes caused by World Wars I and II displaced millions of people from their native countries. In addition to the human suffering endured by refugees, their presence causes economic and social strain on host countries. The United Nations Convention Relating to the Status of Stateless Persons, signed in New York in 1954, addressed a specific aspect of the world refugee problem by improving the legal status of individuals with no clearly defined nationality.

Stateless persons were defined by Article 1 of the convention as individuals who were not considered as nationals by any state under the operation of that state's laws. The condition of statelessness could be the result of many factors, such as accidents of birth or marriage, conflicts of nationality laws, political changes of frontiers, and, particularly, territorial shifts resulting from war. Stateless persons were significantly disadvantaged before the convention. While being subject to the laws and authority of host countries, stateless persons were not recognized as nationals and, therefore, did not enjoy the rights and protections of native citizens. In addition, stateless persons received no diplomatic representation and faced the possibility of arbitrary deportation.

Statelessness became a major international issue after World War I, when the Bolshevik Revolution in Russia and the restructuring of Europe following the defeat of Germany and the fall of the Austro-Hungarian Empire left tens of thousands without legally defined national status. The League of Nations first addressed the issue by establishing the Nansen International Office of Refugees in 1931. The NIOR issued travel documents to stateless refugees that became known as "Nansen passports." The problem was further addressed when the Convention on Conflicts of Nationality Laws and Statelessness was signed at The Hague on April 12, 1930. Article 15 of the 1948 Universal Declaration of Human Rights expressed the principle that every individual has the right to nationality.

The U.N. Convention Relating to the Status of Stateless Persons continued a series of United Nations efforts toward aiding refugees. World War II increased the scope of the world refugee problem, which prompted the attention of the United Nations. The process, which began in 1947 with the U.N. Commission on Human Rights, culminated first in the 1954 convention and later in the 1961 U.N. Convention on the Reduction of Future Statelessness.

The New York Convention was closely modeled after the 1951 U.N. Convention Relating to the Status of Refugees signed in Geneva, and the two evolved almost simultaneously. In fact, the U.N. Commission on Human Rights, the U.N. Economic and Social Council (ECOSOC), and the U.N. secretary-general referred to statelessness in their first recommendations that a U.N. conference be held to address the refugee problem. ECOSOC was instrumental in drafting both conventions. In 1949, following the report on statelessness submitted by Dag Hammarskjöld, the secretary-general of the United Nations, ECOSOC established the ad hoc Committee on Statelessness and Related Problems. The ad hoc committee created the Draft Convention Relating to the Status of Refugees and the Protocol on Stateless Persons. The draft relating to refugees became the basis of the 1951 Geneva Convention.

The United Nations, however, as Eleanor Roosevelt noted, had not yet established basic legal protection for nonrefugees without recognized nationality. The Geneva Convention was founded upon a specific definition of the term "refugee" that did not encompass the unique condition of statelessness. Although the Geneva Conference encouraged nations to apply its convention to the stateless, it chose not to make a binding decision concerning stateless persons. In addition, stateless persons were eventually excluded, by definition, from the direct jurisdiction of the Office of the United Nations High Commissioner for Refugees established in 1950.

Statelessness was a widespread problem in the postwar period. A 1951 survey funded by the Rockefeller Foundation revealed that approximately one million refugees were stateless, some 402,000 in Europe, another half million in Asia, Africa, and the Middle East, and about 2,000 in miscellaneous areas. Of these, about 130,000 survived in camps. One of the groups that suffered most was the refugee population of Germany, both before and after the division of Germany into two separate states in 1949. There were more than 600,000 refugees in the American, British, and French occupation zones by 1947, and the number increased to more than 970,000 by 1951. Their difficulties were not largely the result of indifference or restrictions by the occupying powers but of the confused status of Germany and the enormous problems of providing for de facto and de jure stateless persons. Many of them had fled Eastern European countries and the Soviet Union before 1939, and the dislocations of the war and its aftermath brought in more. Thousands were persons dragged into Germany by the Nazis to work in coerced labor units. Others fled the expanding Soviet power in Eastern Europe.

The lives of such people were very difficult, and in many cases their dilemma was aggravated by the fact that they did not want to return to their native states because of oppressive political conditions. The Basic Law that formed the Federal Republic of Germany (West Germany) in 1949 provided for the the right of asylum in its territory but did not clearly define "political refugee" status. Nor did the new West German state have the means to absorb all the refugees into its economy. Restrictions were applied to arrivals after June 1, 1950, and those that were admitted were often sent to refugee camps. By 1951, there were 143 such camps with a population of 56,555. All of this illustrates the fact that statelessness, whether de facto or de jure, was burdensome both to the refugees themselves and to the governments that attempted on a limited basis to respond to their needs.

After 1951, the United Nations began its efforts to extend to stateless persons some of the rights and protections given to refugees. At the request of the U.N. General Assembly, Secretary-General Dag Hammarskjöld communicated the Draft Protocol on Stateless Persons to all countries invited to the 1951 Geneva Conference Relating to the Status of Refugees. These countries were requested to comment on the draft and to indicate which provisions of the Geneva Convention they would apply to the stateless. Based on these comments, ECOSOC recommended that a new conference of plenipotentiaries be convened and charged with creating a revised protocol on statelessness to be open for signatures. On September 13, 1954, the United Nations Conference on the Status of Stateless Persons convened in New York with twenty-seven states represented by delegates and five additional countries observing. By a vote of twelve to zero with three abstentions, the conference decided to create an independent convention rather than merely a protocol to the convention on refugees. The conference approved a new convention on September 23, 1954, and on September 28, 1954, the U.N. Convention Relating to the Status of Stateless Persons was signed by sixteen countries: Belgium, Brazil, Costa Rica, Denmark, Ecuador, El Salvador, the Federal Republic of Germany, Guatemala, Honduras, Liechtenstein, The Netherlands, Norway, Sweden, Switzerland, Great Britain, and the Vatican City. Israel and Italy signed on subsequent dates. The convention came into force on June 6, 1960, when a sixth country had given it formal ratification. By 1972, twenty-six states had become parties to the convention. Although the conference lasted only eleven days, the process that led to the convention began five years before and involved numerous organizations within the United Nations.

## Impact of Event

The New York Convention significantly improved the status of stateless persons by guaranteeing them basic social, economic, and legal rights. Countries party to the convention were required to accord to stateless persons the same protection accorded to their nationals in terms of certain rights. These included freedom of religion, access to courts of law, elementary education, and social welfare programs. In other areas, such as property rights, employment, higher education, and freedom of movement, the convention guaranteed to stateless persons the same rights and privileges enjoyed by aliens in similar circumstances. Contracting states were obligated to issue travel documents to stateless persons to serve in place of national passports. In addition, the convention contained provisions concerning residence criteria, personal identity papers, and naturalization intended to meet the unique needs of those without a nationality.

Generally, the New York Convention provided stateless persons with the same rights and protection given to refugees under the 1951 Geneva Convention. In some respects, however, the convention on stateless persons was more narrow in scope. For example, provisions dealing with wage-earning employment and the right to association in the Geneva Convention required that refugees benefit from any most-favored-nation agreements to which their host countries were party. In these areas, the New York Convention guaranteed only that stateless persons receive the same treatment as foreigners in general. Some provisions of the Geneva Convention had no parallel in the stateless convention. In particular, the New York Convention did not contain provisions regarding freedom from penalties for unlawful entries and freedom from expulsion to countries of past persecution.

The convention did not provide relief for all individuals who might be considered stateless. Article 1 explicitly excluded stateless persons in specific circumstances. Moreover, the provisions of the convention were deliberately designed to aid only de jure stateless persons. Those who did not legitimately renounce the nationality and protection of their native country faced de facto statelessness. De facto stateless persons had no recourse under the New York Convention. Based on these factors, the Palestinian Arabs living in the territories occupied by Israel, for example, have not been protected by this convention as stateless people.

It should be noted that, while improving the legal status of stateless persons, the New York Convention did not reduce their numbers. The total number of stateless persons is difficult to determine. At the time of the 1961 conference, hundreds of thousands were estimated to be stateless. The 1961 U.N. Conference on the Elimination or Reduction of Future Statelessness held in Geneva and New York was charged with providing a long-term solution to the problem. The resulting Convention on the Reduction of Statelessness (1961) was based on a draft prepared by the International Law Commission in 1953. The 1961 convention, which came into force in 1975, provided legal standards concerning the acquisition, the automatic loss, and the deprivation of nationality. Particularly, the 1961 convention benefited the children of refugees who, because of the status of their parents, would otherwise be stateless at birth.

The United Nations Convention Relating to the Status of Stateless Persons affirmed that individuals without a recognized nationality had certain basic rights. The convention strengthened international law protecting refugees and was a significant expansion of the international protection of human rights.

## Bibliography

Coyle, David Cushman. "Human Rights." In *The United Nations and How It Works.* New York: New American Library, 1965. Brief and factual account of the international refugee problem as perceived in the early 1960's. Outlines the office and duties of the United Nations High Commissioner for Refugees.

Holborn, Louise Wilhelmine. *Refugees: A Problem of Our Time: The Work of the United Nations High Commissioner for Refugees, 1951-1972.* 2 vols. Metuchen, N.J.: Scarecrow Press, 1975. This massive study of the background, development, and attempted resolution of the problems of refugees and stateless persons is essential for accurate perception of this major issue. Holborn begins with the increasing scope of refugee problems that followed World War II and continues to the post-World War II period. She provides much primary material in the form of conventions, resolutions, and treaties that are included in her analysis. There is particular focus on the activities of international organizations such as the League of Nations and the United Nations Organization as well as on the direct efforts of diplomats and political leaders. Includes extensive notes, bibliography, and index.

"Questions Concerning Human Rights." In *Everyman's United Nations.* 8th ed. New York: United Nations, 1968. This chapter reviews the history and provisions of various international human rights provisions, including the 1948 Universal Declaration of Human Rights. Provides an overview of U.N. action regarding human rights concerns, including refugees and stateless persons. Appendices include the texts of the U.N. Charter and the Universal Declaration of Human Rights. Includes index.

Riphagen, Willem. "The United Nations Conference on the Elimination or Reduction of Future Statelessness." *United Nations Review* 8 (October, 1961): 16-17. Personal narrative by the president of the conference. Provides background of statelessness and U.N. efforts to solve the problem. Insightful discussion of the provisions of the Convention on the Reduction of Future Statelessness.

"Status of Stateless Persons Improved Under New United Nations Convention." *United Nations Review* 1 (November, 1954): 30-32. Outlines U.N. action to alleviate statelessness. In particular, points out similarities and differences between the New York Convention on statelessness and the Geneva Convention on refugees. Details the rights and privileges accorded to stateless persons by the convention. Informative, although clearly written from a U.N. perspective, which assumes the success of the convention.

United Nations Conference of Plenipotentiaries on the Status of Refugees and Stateless Persons. *Final Act and Convention Relating to the Status of Refugees.* Geneva: United Nations, 1951. Primary source providing the final text of the convention resulting from the conference held in Geneva in July, 1951. Translated in English and French.

United Nations Conference on the Status of Stateless Persons. *Final Act and Convention Relating to the Status of Stateless Persons.* New York: United Nations, 1954. Primary source providing the final text of the convention resulting from the conference held in New York in September, 1954. Translated in English and French.

Vernant, Jacques. *The Refugee in the Post-War World.* New Haven, Conn.: Yale University Press, 1953. An in-depth survey of the refugee problem after World War II in Europe, the Middle East, and Latin America. Examines in detail the refugee situation in various countries, including legislative action concerning refugees and the economic and social conditions of refugees. Includes bibliography, index, and footnotes.

*Thomas R. Peake*

## Cross-References

Nansen Wins the Nobel Peace Prize (1922), p. 361; Palestinian Refugees Flee to Neighboring Arab Countries (1948), p. 749; Israel Is Created as a Homeland for Jews (1948), p. 761; The United Nations Creates an Agency to Aid Palestinian Refugees (1949), p. 814; Israel Enacts the Law of Return, Granting Citizenship to Immigrants (1950), p. 832; The United Nations High Commissioner for Refugees Statute Is Approved (1950), p. 855; Pire Is Awarded the Nobel Peace Prize (1958), p. 1020; Cubans Flee to Florida and Receive Assistance (1960's), p. 1044.

# THE INDIAN PARLIAMENT APPROVES
# WOMEN'S RIGHTS LEGISLATION

*Category of event:* Women's rights
*Time:* 1955-1956
*Locale:* India

*The passage of four separate parliamentary acts, the so-called Hindu Code, between 1955 and 1956 sought to give women formal legal rights that they had not previously enjoyed*

*Principal personages:*
> JAWAHARLAL NEHRU (1889-1964), the prime minister of India who took the lead in legislating rights for Hindu women
> MAHATMA GANDHI (1869-1948), the independence leader who encouraged the participation of women in the movement
> INDIRA GANDHI (1917-1984), a prominent woman in Indian politics; daughter of Jawaharlal Nehru

## Summary of Event

Indian society historically has been patriarchal. Males enjoyed prerogatives and prestige generally denied women, although a few regions in India preserved some important matriarchal traditions. In some places, property and the family name passed from mother to daughter, but these were isolated exceptions to the rule.

*The Laws of Manu*, an ancient Indian legal text compiled in the fourth century A.D., asserts that a woman should always be controlled by men. In her youth, a father must guard her. As an adult, she must serve her husband. In her old age, her sons must protect her. In practical terms, this meant that a woman had few rights to real property. When her husband or parents died, she had no claim on their estates. Male relatives disposed of any wealth as they saw fit. If a husband decided to take on other wives, a woman had no alternative but to accept his decision. Marriages were arranged, so women had little to say about the choice of a mate.

Marriages often took place while the partners were still infants or toddlers. Although these couples did not live together as man and wife until they attained puberty, child brides were subject to all the constraints of married women. Most dramatically, if their child husbands happened to die, girls were classified as widows. Among upper-caste Indians, widow remarriage was forbidden. Child widows were doomed to miserable lives as little more than slaves in the homes of their in-laws or as burdens for their parents and brothers.

Even if widowhood came while she was an adult, a woman faced a bleak future if she did not have sons willing to support her. For that reason, especially in higher castes, widows were encouraged to become *satis*. A *sati* is literally a virtuous woman, but in this instance it meant that a new widow should volunteer to be immolated on her deceased husband's funeral pyre. In practice, relatives used the custom to get rid of unwanted female dependents. They went as far as drugging women and placing them on the pyre against their will.

An important dimension of a wife's existence was her place in what has been called the joint family system. A woman was expected to move into her husband's household. The joint family ideal was that a father and mother would live with all of their married and unmarried sons. In part, this was supposed to prevent a division of property, since all sons would be entitled to equal shares.

In practice, women's lives in joint family households could be miserable. Indian folklore, stories, and movies often depict a young bride as the victim of her tyrannical mother-in-law and the wives of her husband's older brothers. She does all the work, while being subjected to constant harassment from the other women in the family. Her husband has no sympathy for her plight. She is a Cinderella without the glass slipper. Her only pleasure seems to be to dream of the day when her sons will marry and she will dominate their wives. Although every member of the joint family was supposed to contribute and share equally, women invariably received very little recompense for their domestic labor. A widow might well be driven from her house and was certain to receive less than a rightful share of her husband's property.

Beginning in the eleventh century A.D., Muslims began to arrive in India in considerable numbers. In the thirteenth century A.D., the first of many independent Muslim kingdoms was established. Until the breakup of the Mughal empire in the eighteenth century, Muslims ruled much of the subcontinent. Especially in North India, Hindus were influenced by many Muslim customs, including the tendency to isolate women from society at large. A woman was supposed to enter her husband's home in the bridal carriage and leave it only on her funeral bier. This custom, known as *purdah*, meant that Indian women of the upper classes had to face sexual apartheid as well as the other disabilities mentioned above.

Women's place in traditional society was not totally hopeless. A strong-willed individual could use certain customs to gain security for herself. One obvious way was to forge close bonds with any sons she might have. Indeed, Indian cultures often stress the closeness of a mother's relationship to her sons. The sons could see to it that their mother was not deprived of her life by becoming a *sati* when her husband died, or forced to live in desperate poverty in her old age.

A woman traditionally received gifts from her husband's family before marriage. In poorer groups, this amounted to a few articles of clothing and household utensils. In richer families, however, such offerings could include elaborate dresses and expensive jewelry. Usually, women had the right to keep these. Often, mothers passed these articles on to their daughters. By managing this personal wealth, a woman could gain a better than average style of life.

Hindu law allowed that when a man died without sons, his wife could adopt a son who would then succeed to his father's wealth and status. Through this custom, women could gain real power in a family. Most often, a wife selected the adopted son from among her own or her husband's kin. By choosing a candidate over whom she had influence, a widow could acquire considerable authority over her late spouse's property.

In the early nineteenth century, many Indian and British social reformers took up women's issues such as marriage, divorce, and education. Ram Mohan Ray, the Bengali social critic, agitated for an end to the burning of widows and for the education of women. In 1828, the government did ban *sati* and small attempts to found women's schools began.

Other legislative reforms occurred later in the nineteenth century. For example, the British raised the age at which girls would be considered the victims of statutory rape from age ten to age twelve. This meant that girls were not forced to consummate their marriages when they were still children.

In the twentieth century, women took a very active role in the freedom struggle. Mohandas Kamarchand (Mahatma) Gandhi's wife, Kasturbai, frequently led demonstrations. The Mahatma himself gave women a prominent place in the Congress Party. While the Indian independence movement was under way, few attempts were made to address women's concerns. After 1947, however, politicians anxious to make India a truly modern, democratic state gave considerable emphasis to women's health, education, and legal rights. Between 1955 and 1956, the Indian parliament, which had at the time only twenty-five female members, passed four pieces of legislation: the Hindu Marriage Act, Hindu Succession Act, Hindu Adoptions and Maintenance Act, and Hindu Minority and Guardianship Act, which taken together as the "Hindu Code" constituted a statement of Hindu personal law.

In the Hindu Code, women were guaranteed several legal rights. In the event that a husband took a second wife, the first was entitled to sue for divorce. Several other grounds on which wives could divorce their husbands were also laid down. The Marriage Act was further amended in 1976 to allow for "no fault" divorce.

The Succession Act gave widows rights to real property. It also abolished the joint family system, which favored male heirs over females. Instead of small cash settlements or nothing at all, women now had the opportunity to hold agricultural land as well as houses in their own name.

**Impact of Event**

Taken by themselves, each of the four acts of the Hindu Code is an impressive piece of legislation that appears to give women a considerable number of legal rights. Many obstacles, however, existed to the full implementation of those laws. As of 1991, the great majority of women still lived in the countryside in villages. The numbers of women in school increased impressively in the years after 1947, but the rate of literacy among women remained far below that of men. In this situation, women often did not know what legal prerogatives they had.

In the restricted world of the villages, women had few opportunities to learn about the law and fewer still to consult with a lawyer. The law of inheritance supposedly eliminated the economic restrictions imposed on women by the joint family system, but in the countryside females had few chances to acquire the necessary cash to hire a lawyer. Males remained in control of most of a family's wealth.

Even in 1991, marriages were still arranged, and women had very little to say about when they married or who they would marry. The society still disapproved of divorce. A divorced woman was often thought to be unlucky, so her chances of remarriage were slight. Only in the best-educated and wealthiest circles was divorce or remarriage tolerated. Even there, the incidence of divorce was very low when compared to Europe or the United States.

A new crime, bride burning, appeared in the 1980's, showing that many people in India still tolerated the physical abuse, including murder, of women. The crime was most common among middle-class families in the cities of North India. It involved a husband demanding gifts, such as motorbikes, televisions, or videocassette recorders, from his wife's parents or brothers. If these "presents" were not forthcoming, the bride met with a horrible death. Even in middle-class homes, cooking was often done on kerosene stoves. Husbands found it fairly easy to fake an accidental death by throwing the flammable liquid over their wives, setting the liquid on fire, and then claiming that the stove exploded. A bride's death freed her husband to seek another wife and, perhaps, repeat the crime. At first, police were reluctant to pursue criminal investigations of such deaths, but an outcry from women's groups led to a number of arrests and convictions, so the incidence of the crime diminished.

Women's rights to property became the most hotly contested of the reforms made by the Hindu Code. Many court suits have been filed by family members seeking to reduce or eliminate a woman's share of her husband's estate. The courts often ruled against women. Even when a woman succeeded in maintaining her inheritance rights, the financial and time costs of a lawsuit left her financially and emotionally exhausted.

In the 1980's, an increasingly vocal feminist movement began making headway, especially among women in the cities. Women's groups devoted themselves to the educational and economic welfare of their poorer, less privileged sisters. In the future, the true test of the rights guaranteed by the Hindu Code will be their extension to women in the countryside and among the poorer segments of the populace.

## Bibliography

Desai, Neera, and Maithreyi Khrishnaraj. *Women and Society in India*. Delhi, India: Ajanta, 1987. This is an introductory textbook written from an interdisciplinary feminist perspective. Some of its articles are not theoretically rigorous, but the work provides a considerable amount of anecdotal evidence about the lives of women in modern India.

Dhruvarajan, Vanaja. *Hindu Women and the Power of Ideology*. Granby, Mass.: Bergin and Garvey, 1989. A study of women's lives in a South Indian village. The author treats such important issues as work, health, and education. The study provides some sense of how women's lives have and have not changed in the contemporary countryside.

Khrishnamurty, J., ed. *Women in Colonial India*. New Delhi, India: Oxford University Press, 1989. This collection of eleven essays considers many different aspects of women's lives in the nineteenth and twentieth centuries. Several articles are detailed studies of women's economic activities. Others deal with women's legal rights and wrongs as well as with general cultural attitudes toward women.

*The Laws of Manu.* Translated by Georg Buhler. New York: Dover, 1969. *Manu* puts forward ideas which women the world over will find familiar. It emphasizes that women are weaker and less intelligent by nature than males. It also stresses that women's chastity must be closely protected because, left on their own, women quickly will go astray.

Mandelbaum, David G. *Women's Seclusion and Men's Honor.* Tucson: University of Arizona Press, 1988. This is a brief study of several areas of the Indian subcontinent where *purdah*, the seclusion of women, is practiced. It highlights the ambiguity of the place of women in such systems. On one hand, they carry a family's honor in a unique way. On the other, that exalted status leads to their segregation from society at large.

Preston, Laurence V. *The Devs of Cincvad: A Lineage and the State in Maharashtra.* Cambridge, England: Cambridge University Press, 1989. This is a detailed historical study of the material base of a particular lineage of holy men from the first half of the eighteenth century to the end of the nineteenth. By indicating how important women were within the kin group and how powerful they could become through their control of adoptions, the book provides a somewhat different perspective on women in "traditional India."

Ramu, G. N. *Women, Work, and Marriage in Urban India.* Newbury Park, Calif.: Sage Publications, 1989. This sociological study deals with some of the new problems that arise for women in modern cities. It studies women who work outside the home as well as those who do not. It highlights some of the satisfactions as well as the frustrations that both sorts of women experience.

*Gregory C. Kozlowski*

## Cross-References

Women's Rights in India Undergo a Decade of Change (1925), p. 401; India Gains Independence (1947), p. 731; The Indian Government Bans Discrimination Against Untouchables (1948), p. 743; The U.N. Convention on the Political Rights of Women Is Approved (1952), p. 885; A U. N. Convention Condemns Discrimination Against Women (1979), p. 2057.

# PRESBYTERIAN AND METHODIST CHURCHES
## APPROVE ORDINATION OF WOMEN

*Category of event:* Women's rights
*Time:* May, 1955-May, 1956
*Locale:* Los Angeles, California, and Minneapolis, Minnesota

*Equality for women became an issue among members of major Protestant groups at the same time that blacks were claiming equal rights in the larger society*

*Principal personages:*
> RALPH WALDO LLOYD (1892-1986), the moderator of the General Assembly of the Presbyterian Church in the United States of America (PCUSA) while ordination for women was being discussed
> PAUL S. WRIGHT (1900-1987), the leader of the PCUSA when ordination for women was accepted
> ZACK JOHNSON (1918-1989), a leader of the fight for ordination of women in the Methodist church

### Summary of Event

One of the issues that is identified with a basic change in American life, the changing role of women, received a boost in the 1950's when the Presbyterian and Methodist churches decided to ordain women as ministers. The Supreme Court decision in *Brown v. Board of Education* (1954) and the Montgomery bus boycott were beginning to make churches centers of social debate and change. As the churches were involved in the debate over civil rights and equality for minorities, the question of equal opportunity for women also surfaced.

There were three major Presbyterian bodies in the United States in 1955. The Presbyterian Church in the United States of America (PCUSA) was composed of the descendants of the colonial Puritans and other "old family" Americans who had come together into a single church following the Civil War. Although originally there had been many ethnic divisions within this group, the basis of union within one church was a common acceptance of the teachings of the sixteenth century Protestant reformer John Calvin. The PCUSA was the largest of the Presbyterian bodies and would be the one to approve the ordination of women in 1955. A second body was the United Presbyterian Church of North America, the organizational descendant of the church founded by Scottish settlers in the eighteenth century. This group would unite with the PCUSA in 1958. The third Presbyterian group was the Presbyterian Church in the United States (PCUS), a group found almost entirely in the South and tracing its roots to the independent church formed in the Confederacy during the Civil War.

In the Presbyterian system of government, issues to be voted on at the national level originate with the governing body of a local congregation, the Session of Elders. The session of any church can write and forward an overture requesting action on any issue or idea. The overture is forwarded through the local representative assembly, or presbytery, made up of elected representatives from each congregation in its jurisdiction, and, if accepted, goes on to the annual General Assembly. If an overture is approved by majority vote in the General Assembly, it is then returned to the presbyteries for final debate. If a majority of these local representative bodies approves, it then becomes binding as church law or policy.

As the PCUSA gathered in Los Angeles in 1955 for its 167th General Assembly, several overtures were scheduled to come before the body to permit the ordination of women as ministers. The moderator who had presided over the placing of these overtures on the agenda was the Reverend Doctor Ralph Waldo Lloyd. Lloyd was president of Maryville College in Maryville, Tennessee, a church-affiliated school. Maryville College had always supported a tradition of social liberalism. The school was founded early in the nineteenth century to educate young men from the mountains of Appalachia. During the Civil War, the college was pro-Union, and blacks were admitted to study during Reconstruction. Women enrolled at Maryville College long before state-supported schools admitted them. Lloyd, a native of the Maryville area, was a firm supporter of this liberal tradition. He was very supportive of the idea of ordaining women and, in his final address to the assembly prior to the election of his successor, Lloyd pointed out that women had been accorded the right to serve on the Session of Elders in local churches in 1930. In 1955, more than three thousand women were serving as governing officials in their local congregations. Women had been admitted to these posts of leadership because the Presbyterian Church saw no theological barrier to their so serving and because, in the New Testament, women were seen occasionally in similar roles. It was Lloyd's opinion that the life of the church would be enriched by allowing women to become ministers and to bring to the service of the church their insights on life and theology.

Several prominent women in the Presbyterian church agreed with this point of view. Louise Brady pointed out that women had been accepted as missionaries for over a century, and asked "Are we to believe it is appropriate for a woman to present the gospel to African or Asian males but not to American men?" Others, such as Mary Taggart, pointed out that as elders women could exercise authority within the church, work in executive positions as heads of boards and committees, and even serve on the committee that chose the pastor for a congregation. It made no sense, she argued, for women to be allowed to serve in all church positions except one. The most telling argument was raised by Geneva Iradell, who reminded the church that its historical belief was that God called to the ministry those chosen and predestined by the Deity. "Who are we," she asked, "to deny ordination to those God has chosen?" The criteria for ordination applied to men were confession of a "call" from God, completion of theological studies, and an upright life. The same criteria, it was argued, should be applied to women.

The person elected as moderator to succeed Lloyd was the Reverend Doctor Paul S. Wright of Portland, Oregon. Wright agreed with the views of his predecessor, but not all the delegates did. The debate over the proposal was fierce at times. The committee reporting on overtures made several points in favor of ordaining women. The Presbyterian Church, for example, already ordained women as deacons and elders. In other areas of life, such as business, industry, and government, there was increasing cooperation between men and women. The Bible taught that "in Christ Jesus there is neither male nor female." Moreover, the committee concluded, there was no theological ground for denying ordination of women simply because of their gender.

Opponents of ordaining women also made several points. They pointed out that, in the New Testament, only men made up the group of twelve apostles called by Jesus to follow him. The language used in the Bible for God uses male imagery such as "Father" and "Son." Also noted were the historical instances in which female church leadership had led to cults and heresies. Finally, the opponents cited the writings of Saint Paul, who had ordered women to be silent in church.

When the vote was taken, the nine hundred delegates voted by an overwhelming margin to approve the ordination of women and to send the matter back to the local presbyteries for final ratification. During the following year, almost all these local bodies made binding the policy of ordaining women as ministers.

The governmental structure of the Methodist Church differs from that of the Presbyterian Church. Pastors of local congregations are assigned by bishops, and the elected representatives meet only once every four years in a Quadrennial Conference. This conference has authority to adopt policies without reference to the local congregations. In 1956, the Quadrennial Conference, meeting in Minneapolis, had before it about four thousand "memorials," requests for action from local congregations. More than two thousand of these dealt with the issue of ordaining women.

For some years prior to 1956, Methodist women had been permitted to be "lay supply pastors," which meant they could help on a temporary basis churches that had no pastor. This allowed women who wished to be ministers a halfway approach, but they were still barred from full ministerial rights and service. Specifically, women were barred from the "itinerancy," the rotation system of pastors in which an area bishop is required to assign a church to every ordained minister. Indeed, it was this right to assign pastors that was cited by opponents of female ordination, since bishops could then "inflict" women pastors on churches that did not want them.

Women such as Nora Neal argued that such views called into question the good judgment of bishops and showed a rather low opinion of the process of assigning pastors to churches. Further, she argued, how could the church recognize a valid ministry for a woman by allowing her to serve a church on a temporary basis but then deny that ministry by refusing to allow her to exercise it on a full-time basis? How could something be valid only half the time?

When the report of the Committee on Memorials came to the floor of the conference, it called for ordination of women. This report was countered by a minority report submitted by the Reverend James A. Chubb of Grand Island, Nebraska, which would have allowed full ministerial status for single and widowed women only. This idea was soundly rejected. The majority report was then moved by Dr. Zack Johnson of Asbury College in Wilmore, Kentucky. The debate among the Methodists mirrored the arguments presented among the Presbyterians the year before and had the same result. The majority report was adopted by a majority of 389 to 297.

## Impact of Event

Since 1955, the presence of women pastors in mainline protestant churches has become more frequent but has not become commonplace. In addition to the Presbyterian and Methodist churches, the Congregational Christian churches, the Disciples of Christ, the United Churches of Christ, and the American Baptist (northern) church accept women as ministers. In the early 1990's, there were approximately three thousand women serving as Presbyterian ministers and more than twenty-four hundred female Methodist clergy. The Presbyterian Church has elected to its highest office of leadership, the moderator of the General Assembly, such women as Thelma Adair, Isabell Wood Rogers, and Joan Salmon-Campbell, while the Methodists have had a number of female district superintendents as well as some female bishops, including Marjorie Matthews, Leontine Kelly, and Susan Morrison.

As more women have been ordained as ministers and have become pastors, some trends have emerged. Women ministers often take the lead in speaking to churches on issues related to social justice and sexual policies. As agents of change, these pastors face the risk of being labeled "women's libbers" or "pushy," but they also have the opportunity to use their perceived level of sensitivity as a positive force. Women pastors have developed a theologically sophisticated method of scriptural interpretation to deal with many portions of the Bible that reflect a male-dominated historical situation. Women pastors also find themselves in excellent positions to deal with such personal problems as those faced by women who are single parents, battered and abused wives, and families abandoned by husbands.

Problems faced by women ministers have included the reluctance of many congregations to abandon the tradition of male leadership. For this reason, many female pastors have found themselves either in small churches, where economic necessity sometimes forces the acceptance of a woman who will accept a lower salary, or on the staff of a large church, where women often serve as "associates," often dealing largely with the problems of women and the youth of the church. Another growing phenomenon has been that of "clergy couples," in which both husband and wife are ordained and either serve one congregation as copastors or are employed to serve two congregations within driving distance of their home.

As more Protestant churches have come to focus on the ideas and values of the Christian religion instead of dealing only with the literal meaning of the Bible, a new approach to the role of women has emerged, resting on the perception that the Christian God is spirit and, as spirit, cannot be restricted to male or female attributes. This understanding of the nature of the Christian God opens all leadership roles to women. Moreover, in most congregations of any church in the United States, the majority of members are women, a fact that seems to offer the opportunity of continued growth for the number of female ministers.

## Bibliography

Cameron, Richard. *The Rise of Methodism: A Source Book*. New York: Philosophical Library, 1954. This historical treatment of the early days of the founding of the Methodist church shows quite clearly the role women played in founding the movement. This historic role aided the arguments of women seeking ordination in 1956.

Gaustad, Edwin Scott. *A Religious History of America*. New York: Harper & Row, 1966. Although dated, this book is readily accessible. It is not a history of a particular denomination but is instead a history of the impact of religion on America. In detailing this impact, the role and contribution of women both as ministers and lay members of the church is described.

Hendry, George S. *The Westminster Confession for Today*. Atlanta: John Knox Press, 1960. The Westminster Confession of 1648 is still among the classic statements of faith of the Presbyterian church. This theological examination of the confession shows how the church has separated the historical circumstances from the essential message to employ a contemporary as well as a historical understanding of the reformed tradition. This has included a changing attitude toward the role of women.

Loetscher, Lefferts A. *A Brief History of the Presbyterians*. Philadelphia: Westminster Press, 1978. This short book, now available in paperback, does just what the title promises. Beginning with the European background, the author traces the growth of this group and includes a discussion of the debate over the ordination of women and the development of a racially inclusive church.

MacGregor, Geddes. *The Thundering Scot: A Portrait of John Knox*. Philadelphia: Westminster Press, 1957. This short biography of the founder of Presbyterianism in Scotland helps the reader understand the attitudes toward women and the Bible that Scots settlers brought to the United States.

Parker, T. H. L. *Portrait of Calvin*. Philadelphia: Westminster Press, 1964. This is a brief but accurate sketch of the life of the Protestant reformer John Calvin, whose teachings are the basis for all Presbyterian and Reformed churches. Those seeking ordination for women and many women Presbyterian ministers appealed to the open-minded attitude toward the Bible developed by Calvin.

Short, Roy H. *United Methodism in Theory and Practice*. Nashville: Abingdon Press, 1974. Written by a bishop in the Methodist church, this is a practical guide to understanding the operation of the church and how women as well as men go about being appointed pastors of churches.

*Michael R. Bradley*

## Cross-References

Rankin Becomes the First Woman Elected to Congress (1916), p. 190; The League of Women Voters Is Founded (1920), p. 333; The Nineteenth Amendment Gives American Women the Right to Vote (1920), p. 339; Nellie Tayloe Ross of Wyoming Becomes the First Female Governor (1925), p. 412; Franklin D. Roosevelt Appoints

Perkins as Secretary of Labor (1933), p. 486; The Equal Pay Act Becomes Law (1963), p. 1172; The National Organization for Women Forms to Protect Women's Rights (1966), p. 1327; The First Female Conservative Rabbi is Ordained (1985), p. 2262.

# THE UNITED NATIONS SETS RULES FOR THE TREATMENT OF PRISONERS

*Category of event:* Prisoners' rights
*Time:* August-September, 1955
*Locale:* Geneva, Switzerland

*The United Nations' formulation of Standard Minimum Rules for the Treatment of Prisoners committed the associated nations, at least in principle, to the acknowledgment of prisoners' rights*

*Principal personages:*
JOHAN THORSTEN SELLIN (1896-    ), the general rapporteur of the First United Nations Congress on the Prevention of Crime and Treatment of Offenders
DAG HAMMARSKJÖLD (1905-1961), the secretary-general of the United Nations
WILLIAM P. ROGERS (1913-    ), a vice chairman of the Congress on the Prevention of Crime and Treatment of Offenders

## Summary of Event

Article 1, paragraph 3 of the United Nations Charter, drafted in 1945, acknowledges the goal of "promoting and encouraging respect for human rights and for fundamental freedoms for all without distinction as to race, sex, language, or religion." It was a decade from the signing of the charter before the First United Nations Congress on the Prevention of Crime and Treatment of Offenders met in Geneva, Switzerland, from August 22 through September 3, 1955, to devise specific language on behalf of those humans with the status of prisoners. This delay is hardly surprising. For most of recorded history all over the world, little attention has been paid to the subject of prisoners' rights. Customarily, prisoners everywhere cede specific rights as a result of their convictions, but society has tended to ignore the matter of prisoners' rights. As a matter of fact, the 1955 congress approached the subject of the treatment of prisoners more from a humanitarian perspective than from a legal one.

Fifty-one nations participated in the congress, which drew heavily on the work of the International Penitentiary Commission in 1926, as revised in 1933 and noted by the League of Nations in the latter year. The Standard Minimum Rules for the Treatment of Prisoners—the resolution which the congress adopted on August 30, 1955—reflect a last revision of the Penitentiary Commission's work before the functions of this organization were transferred to the United Nations in 1951.

The rules are divided into two sections, those of general application and those applicable to special categories of prisoners. A statement of nondiscrimination against prisoners on the basis of race, color, sex, language, religion, political or other opinion, national or social origin, birth, or other status stands as a preface to the first section. The first of the general rules requires an entry in a registration book for every prisoner indicating identity, reasons and authority for commitment, precise time of commitment and release, and details of the commitment order.

The remaining rules in this section pertain to seventeen aspects of prison life: separation of categories; accommodation; personal hygiene; clothing and bedding; food; exercise and sport; medical services; discipline and punishment; instruments of restraint; information to and complaints by prisoners; contact with the outside world; books; retention of prisoners' property; notification of death, illness, transfer, and the like; removal from prison; institutional personnel; and inspection. The following paragraphs will discuss the rules pertaining to a selection of the foregoing items.

Prisoners should be separated by categories determined by reference to such matters as sex, age, criminal record, the reason for their detention, and necessities of their treatment. Many prisoners are people awaiting trial; these should be separated from convicts. In addition, civil prisoners (for example, those confined for debt) should be separated from convicted criminals, and young prisoners from adults. The congress could not precisely define for facilities in countries all over the world such terms as "young prisoners" and "adults," nor could it specify the criteria for separating prisoners according to types of offenses.

The subsection on discipline and punishment insists on firm discipline that does not restrict prisoners more than dictated by the need for safety and order. Prisoners are not to be entrusted with disciplinary duties, they are not to be punished except in accordance with regulations, and they must be informed of the offenses for which they are disciplined. Corporal punishment, detention in a dark cell, and "all cruel, inhuman, or degrading punishments" are forbidden as punishments for offenses of a disciplinary nature. Any punishments that might endanger the physical or mental health of a prisoner cannot be imposed without certification of the prisoner's fitness by a medical officer.

The participants in the congress obviously associated the need for books with the need for religious life. Thus, recreational and instructional books are to be made available to all categories of prisoners, and wherever the number of prisoners of a particular religion warrants, a qualified representative of the religion should be available for counseling and services.

The longest discussion pertains to institutional personnel, who must exhibit "integrity, humanity, professional capacity, and personal suitability." Knowing full well the difficulty in staffing prisons all over the world with such people, the congress emphasized in this section the importance to the larger community of the social service provided by prison personnel. This section discusses such matters as salaries, work conditions, education and training (including in-service training), and types of specialists needed. The director should be a qualified, full-time person who lives in or near the institution and should speak the language of the majority of the inmates; the director of a women's facility should be a woman. Close supervision by medical officers is also specified.

The rules applicable to special categories indicate the provisions necessary for prisoners under sentence, prisoners with mental disorders, prisoners awaiting trial, and civil prisoners. Although the congress termed the rules "minimum" ones, few of the world's penal institutions had attained such standards. It was decided to ask governments throughout the world to consider the adoption of the rules and to issue progress reports to the United Nations every three years.

What the congress attempted to do was to reflect the consensus of prevailing thought on the treatment of prisoners and the general management of penal institutions. Like many pronouncements by United Nations bodies, the rules are necessarily expressed in the kind of general terms that almost inevitably emanate from a group representing vastly different cultures from around the world, and this lack of specificity is a drawback. The rules were significant nevertheless because they represented acknowledgment by an international body of the parameters of prisoners' rights.

The devisers of the minimum rules represented a rather broad spectrum of humanitarian, economic, administrative, social, and psychological thought. They were not a group that could be faulted as being "soft on crime." Much of the motivation was practical: All over the world, prison experience often made offenders a greater threat to society than they had been previously.

On July 31, 1957, the Economic and Social Council (ECOSOC) of the United Nations passed a resolution urging that the Standard Minimum Rules be as widely publicized as possible and that Secretary-General Dag Hammarskjöld make arrangements to publish information on compliance as it came from various world governments. In addition, ECOSOC urged wide publicity for other recommendations made by the 1955 congress having to do with the selection and training of personnel for penal and correctional institutions, on open penal and correctional institutions, and on general principles of prison labor.

On December 20, 1971, the General Assembly reaffirmed the resolution of 1957 and drew attention to articles 5, 10, and 11 of the Universal Declaration of Human Rights, which dealt respectively with the right not to be subjected to inhuman treatment or punishment, the right to a fair and public hearing by an independent and impartial tribunal in any civil or criminal proceedings, and the right of an indicted person to be presumed innocent until proven guilty along with the right not to be subjected to retrospective criminal sanctions. On December 14, 1973, the General Assembly, by a vote of 107-0 with 20 abstentions, praised the continuing work of an ad hoc committee concerned with the Standard Minimum Rules and recommended renewed attention to their dissemination and implementation.

## Impact of Event

Many writers on prisoners' rights in the decades following the United Nations' adoption of the Standard Minimum Rules either explicitly judged the rules to have had little impact or implicitly suggested as much by their inattention to them. Disenchantment with the efficacy of United Nations efforts in general probably played a part in forming the consensus, as did a common conviction that rules written so generally as to gain the approval of representatives of many diverse nations must necessarily have few teeth in them.

It is ironic that prisoners' demands in the Attica Prison riots in New York in September of 1971 included many of the items covered in the Standard Minimum Rules, for example, the needs for a healthier diet and for adequate medical treatment. These issues were subsequently addressed, but unless one or more of the rebelling prisoners had been reading the rules, fear generated by the riots, not the recommendations of the United Nations, motivated such reforms as were achieved. Two years after the riots, G. O. W. Mueller, the director of the Criminal Law Education and Research Center at New York University, concluded that the rules "have not yet been complied with" in the United States.

Nevertheless, the Standard Minimum Rules have had an impact. They are invoked from time to time in cases involving prisoners in the United States, and nongovernmental bodies such as the International League of Human Rights and the International Commission of Jurists often refer to them. The Canadian Human Rights Act condemns discrimination on the basis of race, sex, religion, and other usual bases but adds the far less usual "conviction for an offence for which a pardon has been granted."

Among medical and health professionals, the Standard Minimum Rules have gained widespread attention. A 1972 international symposium on the medical care of prisoners in London disclosed some hopeful signs. The assertion by a professor of criminal law in Warsaw University that Poland observed the rules and had based its penal code partly on them was not seriously challenged in the subsequent discussion. The medical superintendent of Grendon Psychiatric Prison in England (which he reported as having achieved impressive results with prisoners plagued by mental disorders) insisted that England and Wales had "advanced well beyond the Standard Minimum Rules for the medical care and protection of prisoners."

The United States has seen a trend away from the traditional "hands off" policy of the courts in cases involving medical practice. Beginning in the 1970's, suits by prisoners increased greatly. By 1980, more than half the state prison systems in the United States were subject to court orders because of prison conditions or flawed decisionmaking processes. Such developments do not in and of themselves improve the lot of any prisoner. Suits often fail, and states manage to dodge or stall compliance with court orders. The process of educating governments and the general public in neglected rights of prisoners is a slow one, and it is extremely difficult to point to any individual who has unequivocally benefited from the Standard Minimum Rules, but they have increasingly become part of the atmosphere in which penologists, criminologists, and legislators work. It appears, however, that prisoners' rights are unlikely to become a major element in the social consciousness of very many people without direct experience of prison life.

## Bibliography

Clark, Roger S. "Human Rights and the U.N. Committee on Crime Prevention and Control." *The Annals of the American Academy of Political and Social Science* 506 (November, 1989): 68-84. Of the articles in this volume, which focuses on the topic "Human Rights Around the World," Clark's is most relevant to the rights of prisoners. It places the Standard Minimum Rules for the Treatment of Prisoners in the context of other standard-setting instruments of the United Nations.

Fried, John H. E. "Social and Humanitarian Matters." In *Annual Review of United Nations Affairs, 1955-1956*, edited by Clyde Eagleton and Richard N. Swift. New York: New York University Press, 1957. Fried summarizes the background of the 1955 congress and describes its work briefly. Although short on detail, this account gives a good sense of how the establishment of the Standard Minimum Rules relates to international social concerns at the time.

Luini del Russo, Alessandra. "Prisoners' Right of Access to the Courts: A Comparative Analysis of Human Rights Jurisprudence in Europe." In *Legal Rights of Prisoners*, edited by Geoffrey P. Alpert. Beverly Hills, Calif.: Sage Publications, 1980. In a book that focuses mostly on the United States, Luini del Russo's essay reviews the international approach to an important aspect of human rights protection for prisoners in the wake of the Standard Minimum Rules. The extensive notes identify many specific cases and documents.

Maguire, Mike, et al., eds. *Accountability and Prisons: Opening Up a Closed World*. New York: Tavistock, 1985. This work deals with four principal issues: prisoners' rights, grievance procedures, management and discipline, and the need for prison regime standards. Most of the essays pertain to Great Britain, but The Netherlands, Canada, and the United States also get attention. The contributors generally stress the need to move from enunciation of general principles to practical solutions of problems. Useful bibliography and indexes.

*Medical Care of Prisoners and Detainees*. Ciba Foundation Symposium, new series, vol. 16. New York: Associated Scientific Publishers, 1973. This book is especially valuable in two ways. It prints as an appendix the entire text of the Standard Minimum Rules, otherwise difficult to find even in fairly large libraries, and it discusses in detail the extent to which the considerable number of rules bearing on prisoners' health were being implemented around the world at its date of publication.

Robbins, Ira P., ed. *Theory, Litigation, Practice*. Vol. 2 in *Prisoners' Rights Sourcebook*. New York: Clark Boardman, 1980. Essentially a collection of essays focusing on American prison law, litigation, the enforcing of prisoners' rights, and related topics. Devised as a practical handbook, this volume portrays bluntly the gap between theory and practice in the United States. Essays are grouped by topic. No index.

Rudovsky, David. *The Rights of Prisoners: The Basic ACLU Guide to a Prisoner's Rights*. New York: Avon Books, 1973. This book does not concern itself with the Standard Minimum Rules. It is intended as a practical guide to the rights of

Americans under present law and an encouragement to exercise them. Contains many references to cases in federal and state courts pertaining to prisoners' rights.

*Robert P. Ellis*

## Cross-References

The International League for Human Rights Is Founded (1942), p. 590; The United Nations Adopts Its Charter (1945), p. 657; The United Nations Adopts the Universal Declaration of Human Rights (1948), p. 789; Prisoners Riot in Attica (1971), p. 1633; The United Nations Issues a Declaration Against Torture (1975), p. 1847; The United Nations Issues a Conduct Code for Law Enforcement Officials (1979), p. 2040; The U.N. Principles of Medical Ethics Include Prevention of Torture (1982), p. 2169; New York Opens "Shock" Incarceration Camps for Female Prisoners (1988), p. 2359.

# THE SUDANESE CIVIL WAR ERUPTS

*Categories of event:* Atrocities and war crimes; racial and ethnic rights
*Time:* August 18-30, 1955
*Locale:* Torit, Equatoria Province, Sudan

*The revolt of the Southern Corps of the Sudanese army against their northern officers, only months before Sudan's independence, was the first incident in a long-running civil war*

*Principal personages:*
> RENALDO LOLEYA (?-1956), a second lieutenant in the Southern Corps and leader of the mutiny
> ISMĀʿĪL AL-AZHARĪ (1902-1969), the prime minister of the Sudan during the transition to independence, 1954-1956
> SIR ALEXANDER KNOX HELM (1893-1964), the governor-general of the Sudan during the final months of British colonial rule
> IBRAHIM ABBOUD (1900-1983), the commander in chief of the Sudanese armed forces who seized power in 1958 and remained president until 1964

## Summary of Event

The civil war in the Sudan is one of the more intractable conflicts in Africa, having claimed countless lives. The conflict centered on the southern Sudan—defined as the Bahr al-Ghazal, Upper Nile, and Equatoria provinces—which is distinguishable from the rest of the country on both ethnic and religious lines. Whereas the north is largely Muslim and Arabic-speaking, at least thirty different languages are spoken by people in the southern provinces. The people of the south adhere to a variety of religions, including Christianity, and are generally darker skinned than the northerners (the majority of whom consider themselves to be Arabs), but there is no clear racial distinction.

The British ruled the Sudan from 1898 to 1956, although they did so (in theory) jointly with Egypt, in an arrangement known as the Condominium. The British were never enthusiastic about the cultural influence of Islam in the south, and from 1930 their policy aimed specifically at maintaining the distinct identity of the peoples of the south. The southern provinces were closed to northerners, except for those on government business. Greek, Syrian, and Jewish traders were encouraged to set up business in the south, while northern traders were expelled. The Arabic language, northern styles of dress, and even Arabic names were discouraged or prohibited. Christian missionaries were encouraged; Muslim proselytizing was banned. Education in the south was left to missionaries. The aim of the British was to preserve and develop southern cultures, but the result was inequality and mistrust between north and south. Southerners lagged behind northerners in education, economic development, and political experience. Northerners tended to view the south as backward and uncivilized, whereas memories of nineteenth century slave trading added to southerners' fears of the north.

In 1946, the British reversed their policy and began to reintegrate the south. By this time, nationalist political parties had emerged in the north and were demanding British withdrawal. Negotiations for the transition to independence largely bypassed the southerners, many of whom feared they were unprepared to hold their own in an independent Sudan. Mistrust in the south increased when, in 1954, the newly elected transitional government, dominated by northerners, began the process of "Sudanization" of the army, police, and administration. Most of the positions vacated by the British went to northerners: Out of eight hundred administrative posts which were "Sudanized," only six went to southerners. Even in the Southern Corps, which was entirely composed of southern troops, the higher ranks (twenty-four positions in all) were filled by northerners as British army officers departed, while only nine junior posts remained for southerners. Although the root of the problem was that there were few southerners qualified to fill higher ranks, southern soldiers tended to view it as another case of northern arrogance and discrimination.

By 1955, the situation had become dangerously polarized. Two southern members of the ruling cabinet were dismissed in May for disagreeing with the prime minister, Ismāʿīl al-Azharī, on southern affairs. Southerners of all political stripes were attempting to form their own southern bloc in Parliament, advocating a federal constitution with some autonomy for the south. The government rather clumsily attempted to head this off, and in July had one southern member of Parliament and five other men arrested and sentenced to prison, after a trial later described as "farcical" by a commission of inquiry. The day after this trial, and only sixteen miles away, a crowd protesting the dismissal of three hundred southern workers at a cotton project was fired on by soldiers and police. Six were killed by gunfire, and two others drowned trying to escape. Meanwhile, a faked telegram had been circulating in the south, purporting to be by Prime Minister Ismāʿīl al-Azharī, in which officials in the south were instructed to "persecute [the southerners], oppress them, ill-treat them according to my orders."

On August 7, authorities uncovered a mutiny plot in the Southern Corps. The conspirators were spreading the rumor that northern troops were "coming to kill Southerners." Three days later, the government airlifted northern troops into Juba, the capital of Equatoria, and civilians began to flee the city. Meanwhile, the government proceeded with plans to move Number-Two Company of the Southern Corps from Torit, Equatoria, to Khartoum, the capital of the Sudan, on August 18. When the day came, the soldiers refused to obey their orders, having heard rumors that they were to be executed in the north. Within a few hours, the base was under the control of mutineers. The mutineers killed several northern officers and looted shops in town owned by northerners. Several dozen southerners were drowned trying to flee Torit.

On August 19, Lieutenant Renaldo Loleya arrived from Juba with the (somewhat exaggerated) news that the northern troops in Juba were indiscriminately killing southern soldiers and civilians. Renaldo assumed command of the mutineers. Northerners who took refuge at the police station were rounded up by the mutineers on August 20, and several were executed. In all, seventy-eight northerners were killed at Torit. Other garrisons of the Southern Corps in Equatoria soon joined in the mutiny, as did many police, civilians, and even some government officials. Only one-quarter of those later tried and executed were actually soldiers. Northerners were attacked, and their property was looted. In Bahr al-Ghazal and Upper Nile provinces, however, authorities were able to disarm and calm the soldiers before full-scale mutiny could occur.

When Prime Minister al-Azharī asked the mutineers to surrender and promised them fair treatment, they responded by asking that the northern troops be withdrawn from Juba and the British or United Nations brought in to investigate. Al-Azharī refused to remove his only loyal troops from the region, and in fact began to send more troops south. The governor-general of the Sudan, Sir Alexander Knox Helm, who was on leave when the mutiny occurred, returned to the country on August 25. He ordered the Southern Corps to surrender, promised them safe conduct, and added his assurance that a "full and fair investigation" would be conducted. Because he was in the process of evacuating the British from the country, he refused to consider sending in British soldiers as the mutineers had requested. On August 27, the mutineers agreed to surrender, but when northern troops arrived in Torit on August 30, they found the garrison deserted, except for Renaldo and a few companions. The others had fled, fearing retribution from the northerners. All told, only 461 southern soldiers surrendered, out of a total force of some 1,400. Nevertheless, on September 6 the government declared the disturbances to be over. The Southern Corps was disbanded and its place taken by northern forces.

In all, at least 261 northerners and 75 southerners were killed in the actual uprising, according to the commission of inquiry which followed. Women and children had not always been spared. It would seem likely that many more people died in later reprisals by northern troops, as there were reports of torture, mutilation, and summary execution by northern soldiers. Of those formally convicted for participating in the mutiny, 121 were executed, including Renaldo Loleya. It is alleged by southerners that several of these mutineers were put on trial posthumously, having already been summarily executed, and that the government was trying to cover its abuses of justice by announcing their trial and execution. Southerners also accused Sir Knox Helm, who left the country on December 15, of doing nothing to fulfill his promise of safe conduct for those mutineers who surrendered.

## Impact of Event

Although more than one thousand of the Southern Corps remained at large, this did not interfere with the celebration of Sudan's independence on January 1, 1956. Over the next few years, there were scattered incidents in the south. In 1957, the army destroyed seven hundred huts in one district alone in reprisal against villagers who sheltered rebels. Southern members of parliament continued to seek a political solution to the southern problem through some sort of federation, but without success.

The situation grew worse with the overthrow, on November 17, 1958, of the elected government of the Sudan by Brigadier General Ibrahim Abboud. It was under Abboud's regime that the tense situation in the south turned into an outright civil war. Abboud's policies toward the south were little different from those of his predecessors—the basic assumption of northern leaders was that assimilation of the south into Arabic and Islamic culture would solve the problem—but he took the policies much further than had his predecessors. Abboud apparently sought to arrest many of the southern political leaders in 1960, but they were warned and chose to leave the country. Many educated southerners followed these leaders into exile. Abboud also sought to remove the influence of foreign Christian missionaries, who were regarded as the main source of the troubles. In 1960, the Sunday holiday was abolished, and a number of priests were arrested. In 1961, all religious gatherings outside churches were banned, and missionaries who left the country were prohibited from reentering. In 1962, missionaries were required to apply for a license, and finally, in 1964, all foreign missionaries were expelled from the south (although not from the north). One effect of this action was that nearly all the schools in the south were closed.

In 1962, a group of prominent southern politicians in exile founded an organization, later known as the Sudan African National Union (SANU), devoted to complete independence for the southern Sudan. In the following year, an organized guerrilla movement, popularly known as *Anya-nya* ("snake venom"), was forged in the south from the various remnants of the Southern Corps and others who had joined them in the bush. As the military campaign against the government increased in strength, the government reacted more harshly, and there were reports of atrocities on both sides. It was the ordinary people, caught in the middle, who suffered the most.

Abboud was overthrown in 1964, and the Sudan returned to civilian rule. For a time, it looked as though a compromise could be reached with the southern leaders, many of whom returned from exile, on the basis of a federal system. By this time, however, the southerners themselves were split on whether to work toward federation or independence. Meanwhile, the violence escalated in the south until hundreds of thousands of southerners had fled to neighboring countries or to the north. Finally, in 1972, President Jafir Nimeiri, who had come to power in a military coup in 1969, was able to negotiate a cease-fire with the *Anya-nya* and the exiled southern leaders. The south was granted a certain amount of autonomy, and the guerrillas were given amnesty and absorbed into the Sudanese army. The uneasy peace lasted for only eleven years, and in 1983 another mutiny, this time in Upper Nile province, resulted in the resumption of the civil war. Again hundreds of thousands of people fled the country, and millions were threatened with starvation, condemned by their leaders' inability to find a way out of the predicament.

**Bibliography**

Albino, Oliver. *The Sudan: A Southern Viewpoint.* London: Oxford University Press, 1970. A very concise work, written by a southerner who became a member of SANU. This book has been widely quoted in subsequent literature. Contains an overview of the history of the southern Sudan, a recounting of the author's own political activities before being exiled, and a chapter detailing the discrimination against the south in independent Sudan. Some references, no bibliography or index.

Alier, Abel. *Southern Sudan: Too Many Agreements Dishonoured.* Oxford, England: Atlantic Highlands Press, 1990. This contribution by a prominent southern attorney and former vice president of the Sudan is based largely on his own experiences. It includes a wealth of detail and insights into the southern question and is particularly valuable for its discussions of the 1972 accord and the post-1983 phase of the struggle. It is, however, somewhat disorganized. Index, maps, and short bibliography.

Beshir, Mohamed Omer. *The Southern Sudan.* New York: Praeger, 1968. The author, a prominent northern journalist, attempts to give a balanced account of the southern issue through 1965. The work is particularly valuable for the official documents, dating from 1930 to 1965, which are reproduced in the appendices. Also contains very useful maps of languages, ethnic groups, and spheres of missionary activity in the south. Bibliography and index.

Collins, Robert O. *Shadows in the Grass: Britain in the Southern Sudan, 1918-1956.* New Haven, Conn.: Yale University Press, 1983. This is the most detailed account of British policy toward the southern Sudan available, although it actually carries events only up to 1954. Has the advantage of being based partly on interviews with Sudanese and former colonial officials. Index, strong bibliographic essay.

Daly, M. W. *Imperial Sudan: The Anglo-Egyptian Condominium, 1934-1956.* New York: Cambridge University Press, 1991. A detailed, meticulously researched history of the later British period in the Sudan. Useful as background to the southern problem, and presents some new information on the mutiny as well as on the transition to independence. Bibliography, index, and a small map.

O'Ballance, Edgar. *The Secret War in the Sudan: 1955-1972.* London: Faber, 1977. This work, focusing on the military aspects of the conflict, is particularly valuable for having been based on interviews with Sudanese on both sides. Unfortunately, these sources are often not revealed, so the book should be treated with some caution. Contains a full chapter on the 1955 mutiny. Map, index, few references.

Wai, Dunstan M. *The African-Arab Conflict in the Sudan.* New York: Africana, 1981. A theoretical analysis of the southern problem and Sudanese politics, but organized chronologically. The author, a southerner, argues for an effective federal system in the Sudan. The work is especially useful for its glossary of principal figures and its chart of southern political movements and their leaders. Index and bibliography.

_____, ed. *The Southern Sudan: The Problem of National Integration.* London: Frank Cass, 1973. A collection of articles by both northerners and southerners, as well as non-Sudanese, on various aspects of the southern problem, including the issues of race, ethnic identity, secession, economic development, and education. Although somewhat dated, many of the conclusions are still apt. Several documents are reproduced in the appendices. Index, maps, and references.

Yangu, Alexis Mbali. *The Nile Turns Red.* Edited by A. G. Mondini. New York: Pageant Press, 1966. A collection of reports of atrocities committed by northern soldiers in the south. Accuses the Khartoum government of genocide. A highly polemical work, and should be treated with some caution. Short bibliography, no index.

*T. K. Welliver*

## Cross-References

The Iranian Constitution Bars Non-Muslims from Cabinet Positions (1906), p. 52; The United Nations High Commissioner for Refugees Statute Is Approved (1950), p. 855; Riots Erupt as Katanga Province Secedes from the Congo (1960), p. 1068; The United Nations Intervenes in the Congolese Civil War (1960), p. 1074; The United Nations Issues a Declaration on Racial Discrimination (1963), p. 1212; Civil War Ravages Chad (1965), p. 1273; The Secession of Biafra Starts a Nigerian Civil War (1967), p. 1365; Revolution Erupts in Ethiopia (1974), p. 1758; The OAU Adopts the African Charter on Human and Peoples' Rights (1981), p. 2136; The United Nations Votes to Protect Freedoms of Religion and Belief (1981), p. 2146; Hunger Becomes a Weapon in the Sudanese Civil War (1988), p. 2354.

# PARKS IS ARRESTED FOR REFUSING
# TO SIT IN THE BACK OF THE BUS

*Category of event:* Racial and ethnic rights
*Time:* December 1, 1955, to December 20, 1956
*Locale:* Montgomery, Alabama

*The Montgomery bus boycott brought the black community of a large city together to protest segregation and propelled Martin Luther King, Jr., into the national spotlight*

*Principal personages:*

MARTIN LUTHER KING, JR. (1929-1968), the coordinator of the Montgomery bus boycott and founder of the Southern Christian Leadership Conference

ROSA PARKS (1913-      ), an assistant tailor at Montgomery Fair Department Store whose arrest touched off the boycott

RALPH ABERNATHY (1926-1990), the pastor of the First Baptist Church of Montgomery

E. D. NIXON (1899-      ), an organizer of the Montgomery chapter of the NAACP, recognized by the black community of Montgomery as a challenger of racial injustice

CLIFFORD DURR (1899-      ), a white attorney and Rhodes Scholar; as a liberal on racial issues, Durr was not popular in Montgomery society

## Summary of Event

The ruling of the Supreme Court in May, 1954, in *Brown v. Board of Education* attacked the system of racial segregation in the public schools. This court decision did nothing to challenge other aspects of the racial order. President Dwight Eisenhower was anxious to attract black voters to the Republican party but did not wish to make civil rights an important issue for fear of alienating white voters. Most states in the Deep South had adopted attitudes of "massive resistance" designed to delay if not defeat the progress of racial integration.

The black community of Montgomery was concerned with improving the treatment of Negro patrons of the city bus service. City buses were segregated by city and state law, requiring white patrons to sit in the front of the bus while black patrons sat in the back. If black riders were seated toward the front because all seats behind them were filled, they could be required to give up their seats and stand if white passengers boarded the bus. This pattern of segregation was enforced by the bus drivers, who could call on the city police to make arrests to uphold the segregation laws.

During 1953, three arrests had been made of Negroes who violated the segregation ban, but E. D. Nixon, a recognized leader of the black community, had not chosen to make an issue of any of these because he believed that the people involved would not do well in court or because of personal problems in their backgrounds. Nixon wanted a plaintiff who would be beyond reproach.

On December 1, 1955, Rosa Parks boarded the Cleveland Avenue bus for her usual ride home. As the bus filled with riders, she was ordered by the driver to give up her seat and move to the rear. Not for the first time, she refused to obey an order based on upholding segregation. On prior occasions Parks had been put off the bus. This time she was arrested. Rosa Parks's decision not to obey the driver was based in part on the knowledge that a test of bus segregation laws was being sought and in part on ideas she had developed at the Highlander Folk School in Tennessee, where an emphasis on equality and interracial cooperation had given her a vision of harmony among the races. Although released from jail on bond within a few hours, Parks, in consultation with Nixon and attorney Clifford Durr, agreed to allow her arrest to become a challenge to the segregation of city buses.

As word of the planned challenge spread through the black community, several members of the Women's Political Council, an upper-class professionals' organization, got together to talk. They issued a statement asking for a one-day boycott of the buses in protest. As Nixon began calling other black leaders the next day, the boycott idea took shape. These leaders called a mass meeting of the black community and set up an organization to press their cause, the Montgomery Improvement Association (MIA). The recently installed pastor of the black Dexter Avenue Baptist Church, Martin Luther King, Jr., was elected president of the group.

King was the son of a well-known black Baptist preacher in Atlanta, so he had been brought up in the deepest religious traditions of the church. He was also very well educated, having graduated from Morehouse College and Boston University. This combination allowed King to address the common black people as a native son and also to make an appeal to intellectuals as one of them. The speech he made to the initial mass meeting at which the decision was made to undertake a long-term boycott marked King as an orator of unusual power and ability.

The black community committed itself to a long-term boycott of city buses on December 5, 1955. This method of protest would be very difficult to sustain because of its impact on the black community. The bus company would suffer financially because about eighty percent of its patrons were black, but the black community would also suffer because most blacks depended on public transportation to reach their jobs and there was no alternative to the bus company. The sponsors of the boycott faced a massive task in providing up to twenty thousand rides daily in volunteered private cars and in keeping community enthusiasm behind the boycott effort.

The first problem was attacked by setting up phone banks to coordinate rides with riders, using black churches as gathering points for rides and riders, and even having the MIA purchase a fleet of nineteen station wagons, autos which were insured by Lloyd's of London when no local agency would cover them. Hundreds of people chose to walk wherever they needed to go.

The second problem was attacked by holding regular mass meetings, sometimes as many as seven in one night to accommodate the crowds, and by using the worship services of the churches to encourage opposition to segregation. At one of the meetings an elderly woman, known as Mother Pollard, inspired those attending by announcing, "My feet is tired, but my soul is rested."

As the boycott continued, so did negotiations between the MIA and the city government. Although various alternatives were discussed, these negotiations were nonproductive because neither side wanted to compromise. MIA leaders wanted segregation ended; city officials wanted it maintained. The Montgomery police tried to hamper the boycott by arresting black carpool drivers, including King, on a variety of minor charges. The city government even had criminal indictments brought against 115 boycott leaders for conspiracy, but these events only intensified the determination of the black community. Even violence, such as the bombing of King's and Nixon's houses, had no negative effect.

While the boycott proceeded, a court case brought by the National Association for the Advancement of Colored People (NAACP) led to a ruling by a district court that segregated buses were unconstitutional. That ruling was being heard by the United States Supreme Court on appeal by the State of Alabama. Throughout the summer of 1956 and into the autumn, the opposing forces struggled in the courts and in the newspapers. Not only local but also national and international attention was given to the boycott. More than one hundred reporters visited Montgomery to write profiles of boycott leaders and stories about what one called "the unforgettable image of old black women walking in the sun."

On November 13, 1956, the Supreme Court of the United States ruled that the state and local laws of Alabama requiring segregation on buses were unconstitutional. This order was transmitted to city officials on December 20, and the next day black patrons began to ride desegregated buses.

## Impact of Event

Martin Luther King, Jr., summed up the immediate impact of the Montgomery bus boycott in a speech he gave before the final mass meeting of the Montgomery Improvement Association. King noted that Negroes had discovered they could stick together; that black leaders did not have to sell out; that threats and violence did not overcome strongly motivated nonviolence; that black churches were becoming militant; that black people had gained a sense of dignity and destiny; and that nonviolent resistance was a powerful weapon.

The boycott was both an end and a beginning for large-scale black community organization. The Montgomery Improvement Association disappeared without taking on any more massive challenges to segregation. King, Abernathy, and other leaders, however, met a few weeks later to organize the Southern Christian Leadership Conference (SCLC). This group led protests against segregation all across the South, acting as a clearinghouse for change, and also gave King a platform from which to speak to the world. The SCLC would become a major factor leading to the Birmingham demonstrations of 1963 and the March on Washington during which King gave his "I Have a Dream" speech. The Montgomery boycott also exploded a long-held white myth, the idea that Southern blacks had no objections to segregation and that all protests were caused by "outside agitators." This idea could not stand before the reality of a massive long-term boycott conceived, organized, and led by local black citizens.

Until Montgomery, the only effective tactic challenging segregation had been the legal approach used by the NAACP. After Montgomery, it was clear that boycotts, mass meetings, and demonstrations could be used along with court challenges. There was some bickering between the MIA and the NAACP over which approach worked best. Obviously, the court ruling forced the Montgomery bus company to end segregation at a time when it might have held out longer against economic pressure, but without the organization of the black community, there would have been no roused national conscience to encourage legal and legislative action.

No one can think of the civil rights movement without thinking of Martin Luther King, Jr. On December 1, 1955, King was a young, unknown minister of a black Baptist church in the Deep South. By December 20, 1956, he was an internationally recognized black leader. If Rosa Parks had not refused to give up her seat, the world might never have heard of King.

Integration of the city buses was not the last act of the drama of race relations in Montgomery. There would be violence and blood would be shed at later dates, but an irreversible step had been taken. One of the major streets in Montgomery was renamed Rosa Parks Boulevard. Appropriately, city buses traveling this thoroughfare carry the destination sign "Rosa Parks."

## Bibliography

Branch, Taylor. *Parting the Waters.* New York: Simon & Schuster, 1988. This book won the 1989 Pulitzer Prize for its historical and personal portrayal of all the major, and many minor, characters involved in what the author calls "The King Years." This is the first volume of a series, but other volumes are not yet published.

King, Martin Luther, Jr. *A Testament of Hope: The Essential Writings of Martin Luther King, Jr.* Edited by James Melvin Washington. San Francisco: Harper & Row, 1986. This collection of Dr. King's writings is arranged topically, but within each topical division the selections are placed chronologically. In addition to the well-known "Letter From a Birmingham Jail" and "I Have a Dream" are descriptions of the Montgomery situation such as "Our Struggle" and "Walk for Freedom."

_____. *The Trumpet of Conscience.* New York: Harper & Row, 1967. This slim book sums up the ideas and beliefs of Dr. King as he had come to state them a few months before his death. Although this book does not deal directly with the Montgomery bus boycott, it does provide excellent and understandable insights into the philosophy that guided that event.

Oates, Stephen B. *Let the Trumpet Sound: The Life of Martin Luther King, Jr.* New York: Harper & Row, 1982. This is a readable but thorough biography of Dr. King written from an analytical perspective which tells what happened and suggests why it happened. This book is good literature as well as good history. The chapter "On the Stage of History" deals effectively and movingly with the events in Montgomery.

Powledge, Fred. *Free at Last? The Civil Rights Movement and the People Who Made It.* Boston: Little, Brown, 1991. The author is a journalist, born in North Carolina, who covered the civil rights movement for the Atlanta *Journal* and *The New York Times.* The book is valuable because the author has interviewed participants in the movement and has allowed them to tell their own stories of these events.

Raines, Howell. *My Soul Is Rested: Movement Days in the Deep South Remembered.* New York: G. P. Putnam's Sons, 1977. This is a very readable and rewarding collection of first-person remembrances of the civil rights movement. Raines does not try to hide the personality conflicts that often plagued the movement.

Williams, John A. *The King God Didn't Save.* New York: Coward-McCann, 1970. This is a controversial book because it argues that Dr. King was chosen for leadership by the white society, and especially by the white media, because he was a safe spokesperson whose nonviolent approach offered no real threat to white domination. Valuable because it summarizes much of the criticism King received from radical Negro leaders.

Woodward, C. Vann. *The Strange Career of Jim Crow.* New York: Oxford University Press, 1974. This is the standard history of racial segregation. The phrase "Jim Crow" was the nickname for discriminatory laws and practices. Woodward frequently revised his book to keep up to date with legal, social, and historical trends.

*Michael R. Bradley*

## Cross-References

*Brown v. Board of Education* Ends Public School Segregation (1954), p. 913; The SCLC Forms to Link Civil Rights Groups (1957), p. 974; The Civil Rights Act of 1957 Creates the Commission on Civil Rights (1957), p. 997; Eisenhower Sends Troops to Little Rock, Arkansas (1957), p. 1003; Greensboro Sit-ins Launch a New Stage in the Civil Rights Movement (1960), p. 1056; Meredith's Enrollment Integrates the University of Mississippi (1962), p. 1167; Civil Rights Protesters Attract International Attention (1963), p. 1188; Martin Luther King, Jr., Delivers His "I Have a Dream" Speech (1963), p. 1200; Martin Luther King, Jr., Leads a March from Selma to Montgomery (1965), p. 1278; The Civil Rights Act of 1968 Outlaws Discrimination in Housing (1968), p. 1414.

# KHRUSHCHEV IMPLIES THAT
# STALINIST EXCESSES WILL CEASE

*Category of event:* Political freedom
*Time:* February 25, 1956
*Locale:* Moscow, Soviet Union

*In a stunning four-hour speech to the Twentieth Congress of the Communist Party of the Soviet Union, Nikita Khrushchev exposed for the first time political repression under Joseph Stalin*

*Principal personages:*
> NIKITA KHRUSHCHEV (1894-1971), the first secretary of the Communist Party of the Soviet Union (1953-1964); the successor to Joseph Stalin and the initiator of the de-Stalinization campaign
> JOSEPH STALIN (1879-1953), Khrushchev's predecessor as the leader of the Communist Party of the Soviet Union
> LAVRENTII BERIA (1899-1953), the head of the Soviet secret police and a key figure in the political repression under Stalin

## Summary of Event

Joseph Stalin's victory over his political rivals and his accession to power as the leader of the Soviet Union in 1928 marked the beginning of a quarter-century of brutal suppression of the Soviet people's political and ideological freedoms. It signaled a reversal of rather moderate and more flexible policies espoused by the Communist Party of the Soviet Union (CPSU) in the early to mid-1920's, and the initiation of forced-draft industrialization and coercive agricultural collectivization. The result was the imposition of one of the most powerful and oppressive dictatorships in modern history. "Stalinism," as this political system came to be called, rested in part on mass terror and the cult of the personality of the man behind it. The most visible victims of Stalin's autocratic rule ranged from the Soviet Union's political elites to the better-off peasants or *kulaks.*

Stalin's narrow base of support came from a byzantine network of extralegal secret police and sections of the government bureaucracy that were accorded special privileges. The tremendous centralization of administrative and coercive powers reflected Stalin's singleminded pursuit and consolidation of power without regard to human cost. No one was fully immune from the dictator's abuse of power during the successive waves of purges that were carried out in the 1930's, not even high-level members of the Politburo (Political Bureau of the Communist Party), in which Soviet political power was concentrated.

The first sign of a pattern of political excesses came most clearly during the forced collectivization drive that began in late 1929. This rural transformation, which occurred at breakneck speed, led to special hardships for the *kulaks* whose property was confiscated, but it wreaked havoc on ordinary peasants as well. Nearly 60 percent of Soviet agriculture was collectivized in a little more than one year. Entire villages were emptied, and the rural economy suffered, with harvests falling precipitously. The shortfall in 1932 produced a famine that killed one million peasants.

If the government was willing to sacrifice sections of the peasantry for its economic goals, it went even further in the political sphere. Until 1934, the victims of the Soviet secret police were largely members of the bourgeoisie, royalists and political opponents of the Bolsheviks (as the ruling Soviet Communists were originally called). Soon, however, the Communist Party itself felt the full brunt of terror. The slaughter of Party members began in earnest in 1934 following the assassination of Sergei Kirov, a member of the Politburo and Party boss in Leningrad. Although the circumstances surrounding his death remain unclear, it set off an unparalleled campaign of repression by the secret police against alleged antileadership elements within the Party.

A hallmark of the great purges was the series of show trials that reached their climax from 1936 to 1938. Arthur Koestler's novel *Darkness at Noon* (1940) offers an allegorical glimpse into the frightening fall of the Party leadership and intelligentsia. The first of the great public trials began in August, 1936; all sixteen defendants were executed, including two Party stalwarts, Grigori Zinoviev and Lev Kamenev, who had in fact been top candidates to succeed Vladimir Ilich Lenin, the founder of the Soviet state.

The purges cast an ever-widening net fanning out from Party officials to trade unionists, leading writers, scholars, scientists, and engineers, and drawing in relatives, friends, and associates, thereby threatening the whole spectrum of Soviet society. Several draconian laws were passed, repaving the way for the terror that ensued. Among them was the decree of April, 1935, making children aged twelve years or over subject to criminal charges. Laws passed in 1934 and 1937 permitted persons charged with the most serious antistate crimes to be tried secretly, in absentia, and without counsel. The number of unnatural deaths under Stalin has never been conclusively calculated, but millions of innocent men, women, and children were arbitrarily arrested, executed, or imprisoned in labor camps.

Khrushchev's speech to the Twentieth Party Congress in 1956 was a turning point in Soviet political life. It represented the first formal acknowledgment of one of the bleakest chapters in the country's history and provided encouragement to the gradual liberalization that began occurring after Stalin's death on March 5, 1953. Even before the speech by Stalin's successor, steps had been taken to undo some of the dictator's damages. Between 1953 and 1956, Khrushchev rebuilt important organs of the Party and in the process rooted out a number of Stalin's lieutenants.

The first indication of post-Stalin change was the release in April of the Kremlin doctors who had been arrested under Stalin four months earlier for "plotting" to assassinate important Soviet leaders. The plot was officially denounced as a pure fabrication, thereby thwarting Stalin's last terror episode. Soon afterwards, Lavrentii Beria, the chief of the secret police, was arrested and along with six other top police officials executed as part of a dramatic drive to tame this institutional rogue elephant.

Many people were released from prisons, and others who had been attacked as "enemies of the people" were "rehabilitated" (readmitted to history or society in a favorable light), often posthumously. Of the twelve to thirteen million people believed to have been in labor camps during Stalin's time, approximately sixteen thousand were released in the first three years after his death. Although relatively small in number, this group comprised influential people from the government and the Party, and their resumption of active political life hastened the changing of the attitudes of the elite.

From 1955, systematic reexamination was undertaken of all cases of persons previously convicted of political crimes. In anticipation of large-scale releases of prisoners, temporary judicial commissions were created and allowed to hold hearings at the camps themselves. Reliable estimates suggest that in 1956 and 1957, nearly eight million people were freed and another six million posthumously rehabilitated.

In other legal affairs, military courts that had previously had a wide jurisdiction in civil matters, especially in political crimes, were deprived of all authority over civilians except in the case of espionage. The law on state secrets was significantly relaxed and amended to include a more precise and less sweeping description of what constituted a state secret. Confessions alone were no longer acceptable as incriminating unless they were corroborated by independent evidence. The burden of proof, which under Stalin had fallen on the accused in political crimes, now shifted to the prosecutors.

In the wake of Stalin's death, a very cautious policy of encouraging greater intellectual freedom was also initiated. Censorship was maintained but relaxed; criticism of abuses, shortages, and inefficiencies of the political economy was tolerated. Writers and artists began faulting the rigidity and "formalism" under Stalin. For example, one of the country's most eminent composers, Dmitrii Shostakovich, called for greater freedom in music without suffering any consequences.

The everyday welfare of the Soviet people, which had been subordinated under Stalin to the dictates of rapid industrialization to compete with the West, was given higher priority by Khrushchev. For example, greater emphasis was placed on agricultural products and consumer goods over heavy industry. The new leader launched a highly publicized campaign to catch up with the United States in the per-capita production of meat, milk, and butter. The harsh criminal penalties to maintain labor discipline under Stalin were abandoned, and the workweek was reduced from forty-eight to forty-one hours. A minimum wage was instituted that greatly benefited the lower classes.

Although Khrushchev's speech itself was delivered in secret and never published in the Soviet Union, it was circulated in official meetings across the country, and its contents became widely known at home and abroad. Khrushchev attacked Stalin's despotic rule with detailed accounts of the dictator's personal responsibility for repression, self-glorification, and historical falsification. Stalin was portrayed as a morbidly paranoid man who exacted complete servility from his subordinates. The speech was studded with harrowing passages read from letters sent by victims languishing in prison camps.

## Impact of Event

Khrushchev's speech was electrifying, offering hope that the gradual thaw following Stalin's death would turn into a full-blown "spring." At that first Party Congress since Stalin's death, Khrushchev vowed never to resume Stalin's repressive methods of rule.

In cultural and intellectual spheres, censorship of forbidden themes began to be erased. At times, Khrushchev personally intervened in support of publishing topics that had been taboo, including, for example, Aleksandr Solzhenitsyn's novella *Odin den Ivana Denisovicha*, 1962 (*One Day in the Life of Ivan Denisovich*, 1963), set in a prison labor camp. Solzhenitsyn was even nominated for the Lenin Prize, the Soviet Union's highest literary honor, for the novella. In the theater and in literature, interrogation of the perpetrators of crimes under Stalin was portrayed more and more openly. Soviet novelists of rural life also began questioning the myth of collectivization as a purely voluntary, spontaneous, and benign movement by chronicling the harsh methods employed to enforce collectivization in the late 1920's and early 1930's. Indeed, many of the social and political criticisms of Stalinism that surfaced in later dissident writings were anticipated in the official and unofficial publications of the Khrushchev period.

One important aspect of Khrushchev's democratization effort was a huge increase in political participation. For example, a government decree required greater and more immediate attention to citizen demands. Membership in the Communist Party increased nearly 50 percent between 1957 and 1964. Greater autonomy for such organizations as trade unions and the rejuvenation of citizen committees for local government were evident. In the new environment, more independent and scholarly research in the social sciences was encouraged for the first time in thirty years.

The effects of de-Stalinization under Khrushchev reached a peak in October, 1961, at the Twenty-second Party Congress, in which a more radical version of official anti-Stalinism was sanctioned. Most important, the attack on the former leader was conducted in public, with the Soviet media providing daily coverage of speaker after speaker denouncing Stalin's excesses in detail for a full two weeks. In the impassioned atmosphere of the congress, numerous resolutions designed to chip away at the legacy of Stalin were passed, including ones to remove Stalin's body from the Lenin Mausoleum on Red Square and obliterate his name from thousands of buildings, monuments, and towns.

Khrushchev's campaign to reveal the truth about his predecessor and to begin to purge Soviet society of Stalinist remnants, however, always contained contradictions and had its share of powerful opponents. The democratization process was ultimately not allowed to blossom fully, partly because of Khrushchev's own tentativeness and partly because of a conservative reaction that weakened his position. For example, in the artistic sphere, Khrushchev at times sent out mixed signals. Although the government espoused freedom of expression in general, it frowned upon avant-garde experimentation and continued to expect artists to adhere to socialist realism.

In the religious realm, the new leader proved to be more hardline than his predecessor. The Jewish faith was circumscribed more, as was the Russian Orthodox church. The Soviet Union's internal relaxation also produced unexpected movement in a number of East European countries toward liberalization, especially in Hungary and Poland, with unrest in the latter and a full-fledged uprising in the former. This development threatened Soviet control in these countries and in turn provided ammunition for conservatives who had been opposing Khrushchev's fast-paced reforms at home.

With the ouster of Khrushchev in 1964 by his opponents in the Politburo, a ten-year period of reformation in Soviet politics was ended and a lengthy era of conservatism was ushered in under his successor, Leonid Brezhnev. Khrushchev's reformist legacy survived, however, and Soviet president Mikhail Gorbachev's policy of *glasnost* (openness) in important ways harked back to it.

## Bibliography

Breslauer, George. "Khrushchev Reconsidered." In *The Soviet Union Since Stalin*, edited by Stephen F. Cohen, Alexander Rabinovitch, and Robert Sharlet. Bloomington: Indiana University Press, 1980. Offers a balanced portrayal of Khrushchev's attempt at reformulating the terms of political participation and government responsiveness in opposition to the Stalinist legacy. Also looks at the obstacles and opportunities facing Khrushchev and how well he managed them. Index.

Cohen, Stephen F. *Rethinking the Soviet Experience: Politics and History Since 1917.* New York: Oxford University Press, 1985. An excellent and concise overview focusing on key historical events and enduring political outcomes since the Communist revolution. Extended treatment is given to the Stalin question and its aftermath. Index.

Fainsod, Merle. "Terror as a System of Power." In *The Soviet Crucible*, edited by Samuel Hendel. New York: Wadsworth, 1982. Combines theory with Stalinist practices to offer a penetrating analysis of the emergence of terror and its decline in the Soviet Union. Offers bibliography.

Khrushchev, Nikita. *Khrushchev Remembers: The Glasnost Tapes.* Edited by Jerrold L. Schecter. Boston: Little, Brown, 1990. This work constitutes the third volume of Khrushchev's memoirs. Fresh and fascinating, much of it is relevant to 1990's upheaval in the Communist world. It includes some of the most sensitive material from Khrushchev's tapes, such as his recollections of Stalinist repression, which have been published under Gorbachev's new policies.

Medvedev, Roy A. *On Stalin and Stalinism.* New York: Oxford University Press, 1979. Written by a Soviet author living in the Soviet Union, this book is unique in that it gathers information from sources not available to outsiders. Provides detailed accounts of Stalin's excesses through interviews with victims and places Stalinism in the broader political context.

Medvedev, Roy A., and Zhores Medvedev. *Khrushchev: The Years in Power.* New York: Columbia University Press, 1976. Offers a critical review of Khrushchev's rise and fall from power. Records the atmosphere of the period as it was felt by those living in the Soviet Union. Offers significant information on the top personalities involved in the government. Index.

Nove, Alec. *Stalinism and After: The Road to Gorbachev.* Boston: Unwin Hyman, 1989. In highly accessible style, the author provides a sweeping overview of how Stalinism came to be and how it was modified after Stalin's death. Provides valuable insights into the role of personalities, especially of Stalin and Khrushchev, in policy preferences. Offers a bibliography and index.

Salisbury, Harrison E. *Moscow Journal: The End of Stalin.* Chicago: University of Chicago Press, 1961. The author, a Moscow correspondent for *The New York Times* from March, 1949, to October, 1953, offers a highly readable and at times entertaining volume filled with extracts from diaries, memoranda, letters, and newspaper dispatches, including passages excised by Soviet censors at the time. Includes index.

*Deepa Mary Ollapally*

## Cross-References

Lenin and the Communists Impose the "Red Terror" (1917), p. 218; Lenin Leads the Russian Revolution (1917), p. 225; Stalin Begins Purging Political Opponents (1934), p. 503; Soviet Jews Demand Cultural and Religious Rights (1963), p. 1177; The Brezhnev Doctrine Bans Acts of Independence in Soviet Satellites (1968), p. 1408; Soviets Invade Czechoslovakia (1968), p. 1441; The Moscow Human Rights Committee Is Founded (1970), p. 1549; Solzhenitsyn Is Expelled from the Soviet Union (1974), p. 1764; The Helsinki Agreement Offers Terms for International Cooperation (1975), p. 1806; Sakharov Is Awarded the Nobel Peace Prize (1975), p. 1852; Soviets Crack Down on Moscow's Helsinki Watch Group (1977), p. 1915; Gorbachev Initiates a Policy of *Glasnost* (1985), p. 2249.

# MAO DELIVERS HIS
# "SPEECH OF ONE HUNDRED FLOWERS"

*Category of event:* Political freedom
*Time:* May, 1956
*Locale:* Beijing and Shanghai, People's Republic of China

*Mao Tse-tung's slogans of "Let a hundred flowers bloom" and "let a hundred schools of thought contend" was an invitation to China's intellectuals to criticize the Communist regime*

*Principal personages:*

MAO TSE-TUNG (1893-1976), chair and leader of the Chinese Communist Party (CCP)

LIU SHAOQI (1898-1969), the first vice chair, selected to be Mao's successor in the 1960's but purged from the CCP in 1966

DING LING (1904-1986), a CCP member and feminist writer imprisoned in the Antirightist Campaign which followed the Hundred Flowers Campaign

ZHOU ENLAI (1898-1976), the premier of China from 1954 to 1976

ZHU DE (1886-1976), the commander in chief of the People's Liberation Army

## Summary of Event

By the beginning of 1956, China had experienced three years of drastic changes in the process of transforming itself into a socialist state as outlined by the Chinese Communist Party (CCP) in the First Five-Year Plan (1953-1957). The plan was based on the Soviet model, which emphasized industrialization at the expense of the agricultural sector. Mao Tse-tung's policy of rapidly ending private enterprise in industry and agriculture faced opposition from other CCP leaders such as Gao Gang, Liu Shaoqi, and Peng Dehuai. In the agricultural sector, Mao's plan of forming advanced cooperatives similar to the Soviet collective farms saw dramatic changes in 1956. For example, in January of 1956 only 4 percent of the peasant households were members of advanced cooperatives, but by December of 1956 about 88 percent of peasant households had joined the advanced cooperatives.

For the Five-Year Plan to succeed, the CCP had to force changes on the population. The CCP and its huge bureaucracy imposed rationing on food, clothing, and other necessities. Jobs were assigned by the state and there were restrictions on residence and movement. People's lives came increasingly under bureaucratic control, which also tried to regiment art and literature. One of the early victims of the need for intellectuals to adhere to the party line was Hu Feng. He was an author and CCP member, and had seats on the executive boards of the Writer's Union and the National People's Congress. Hu's mistake was to charge that the party's use of Marxism to judge works of art was crude and would stifle creativity. Mao had him arrested and charged as an imperialist and a counterrevolutionary. In order to speed up his own agenda of land reform, Mao instituted a campaign of repression called the suppression of hidden counterrevolutionaries (1955 to 1956). This campaign demoralized thousands of intellectuals who had thought they could work with the CCP to build a better China. Consequently, the party leadership itself became bitterly divided over how to deal with the intellectuals. According to Mao's estimation, out of the five million intellectuals (high school graduates), only about 3 percent were hostile to the CCP. With this small number in mind and with his new theoretical contribution "On the Correct Handling of Contradictions Among the People" in April, 1956, Mao believed that the intellectuals could be used to build socialism.

Thus, on May 2, 1956, Mao introduced the slogan "Let a hundred flowers bloom, let a hundred schools of thought contend." This sudden and curious change of heart to encourage intellectuals to criticize the CCP by Mao, who up until a few months before was persecuting intellectuals in the suppression of hidden counterrevolutionaries campaign, resulted from his analysis of the changes that were taking place in the Soviet Union and Eastern Europe and his need to shake up the leaders of the CCP. In February, 1956, Soviet leader Nikita Khrushchev had denounced Joseph Stalin for his oppression of the Russian people and his practice of the cult of personality. Khrushchev was also in favor of peaceful coexistence rather than constant conflict and projected a more liberal regime for the Soviet Union.

Then came the Polish riots in June, followed by the Hungarian rebellion against the Soviet Union in October, 1956. Mao must have interpreted the Polish and Hungarian revolts as a sign of too much repression. He worked to provide a safety valve for China by urging the country to begin a full-fledged, "Hundred Flowers Campaign."

The opportunity for Mao to convince intellectuals to provide input into the building of China came with his conciliatory speech before eighteen hundred invited Communist and non-Communist delegates to the Supreme State Conference. By early May, 1957, almost a year after Mao had introduced the slogan of "Let a hundred flowers bloom, let a hundred schools of thought contend," the full weight of the press and other propaganda organs formally started the Hundred Flowers Campaign.

The intellectuals, once convinced that they could officially air their grievances against the CCP, did so with enthusiasm. Abuses by party cadres in the form of corruption, cruel labor practices, and foolish experiments in production were aired in closed forums attended by CCP delegates. The state-controlled press, wall posters, and street demonstrations aired public anger against the cruelty of previous campaigns and the shameless copying of Soviet systems and models. The violations of human rights and the tyranny of the communist system were condemned.

The students at Beijing University set up a "Democratic Wall" on which were plastered criticisms against the CCP. By the beginning of June, students were so incensed by the revelation of abuses by the CCP that protest movements were coordinated throughout the major cities of China. Students rioted, went on strike, ransacked files, beat up cadres, and demanded more educational freedom. One fiery student leader, Lin Xiling, a twenty-one-year-old law student at Beijing University, revealed how alleged counterrevolutionaries were brutalized when she worked in district courts. She charged that about 700,000 people had been executed based on trumped up charges and tampering of records by public-security personnel during the early 1950's.

Workers demanded better working conditions and wages with the right to form labor unions; they went on strike or work slowdowns to emphasize their needs. In defiance of rural collectivization, large numbers of peasants decided to leave the cooperatives. Taxes were also withheld by many, who charged that the communist government taxed them more than their old landlords had.

Famous scholars used the new freedom to do comparative research. Sociologist Fei Xiaotong published in June, 1957, his observations of a remote village in Jiangsu. He concluded that the villagers were less well off in the 1950's than they had been in the 1930's, because many of the economic and agricultural programs were unsuitable and forced upon the peasants by overzealous cadres.

Mao's Hundred Flowers Campaign, whose goals were to inspire the lethargic and bureaucratic CCP with the skills of those involved in the creative arts and humanities (the flowers) and to boost China into a higher stage of socialism with those skilled in the areas of science and technology (the schools of thought), had backfired. The most articulate groups, the scholars and college students who had always been identified as allies of the CCP, became its most vehement critics. They resented the dictatorship of the CCP, the corrupt and incompetent party cadres, the lack of civil liberties, and the regimentation of all aspects of life. Mao was overwhelmed by the barrage of criticisms from the very people he thought would support his liberalism. In order to strengthen his position and to stop this intellectual rebellion without making himself appear as a hypocrite, Mao made some changes in a new publication of "On the Correct Handling of Contradictions Among the People" on June 18, 1957. The revised text listed several criteria that must be taken into account in all future criticisms. Thus, it appeared that intellectuals could still criticize, but with certain conditions. The conditions for criticism included the ability to benefit social transformation and to strengthen democratic centralism and the CCP. With this move, Mao won over the support of party hard-liners such as Liu Shaoqi, Zhu De, and Peng Zhen, who were skeptical about the Hundred Flowers Campaign because it allowed outsiders to criticize the CCP, which to them was the leading force of the people. The momentum of criticism could not be changed by Mao's new requirements. Mao and the party hard-liners came down ruthlessly on dissident intellectuals by invoking the Antirightist Campaign of late June, 1957, through 1958.

## Impact of Event

More than 300,000 intellectuals were branded as "rightists," an unforgiving and scornful label which would ruin careers and obstruct any opportunities for a better life in China. For example, Fei Xiaotong was made to repudiate his Jiangsu report and was forbidden to teach, do research, or publish about Chinese society. Ding Ling, the famous feminist author, was stripped of her party membership and was banished to labor on a farm in Manchuria. She was charged with ambitions of taking over the Writer's Union and using her position to attack the CCP.

More telling was the plight of the Liang family. Mrs. Liang (her maiden name is Yar Zhi-de), a devout party member and a respected public security officer, was branded a "rightist." During the Hundred Flowers Campaign, the Changsha Public Security Bureau held nightly meetings at which everyone was urged to express feelings. Mrs. Liang had no reason to criticize the CCP, but her section head insisted that she say something to fulfill a quota. Mrs. Liang did not criticize the party, but she did say that her boss sometimes used crude language and did not follow consensus opinion in making pay raises. When the Antirightist Campaign started, her boss took revenge. He reduced her cadre rank, cut her monthly salary from fifty-five to fifteen yuan, and sent her to a farm to labor. Although her husband, Liang Ying-qiu, was an important journalist and a trusted party member, he had to divorce her to save their children. "Rightist" children could not attend good schools or have good positions in life.

Another case of a loyal party member who was discredited and branded a "rightist" was Yang Kang, who was assistant editor of the government's paper, *People's Daily*, in Beijing. Apparently, a journal which she had kept showed her admiration of certain political and economic characteristics of the United States when she was there in 1946 and 1947. This made her vulnerable under questioning. With her love and faith for the CCP shattered, she killed herself.

The Antirightist Campaign worked to "cleanse" other CCP members, cadres, and students of "rightist" wrongs by instituting the *hsia fang*—"sending down" to the farms and countryside to do productive labor. About 1.3 million cadres participated in *hsia fang*, and several million more students were forced to do physical labor under similar programs. In total, about 1.7 million people were investigated for antiparty activities. About one million party members were rebuked, put on probation, or dropped from membership.

The Hundred Flowers Campaign ended with the Antirightist Campaign, which caused untold hardships on the Chinese people. Many lives were lost, and survivors learned to distrust the government, fellow workers, friends, and even relatives.

## Bibliography

Fairbank, John King. *The Great Chinese Revolution.* New York: Harper & Row, 1986. An excellent condensed account of modern Chinese history with personal anecdotes about Chinese friends or colleagues who had suffered from the Hundred Flowers Campaign.

Harrison, James Pinkney. *The Long March to Power: A History of the Chinese Communist Party, 1921-72.* New York: Praeger, 1972. Mao's leadership of the CCP and his concept of permanent revolution is well chronicled in Chapter 22. Good statistics are provided on the different categories of purges after the Hundred Flowers Campaign.

Heng, Liang, and Shapiro, Judith. *Son of the Revolution*. New York: Alfred A. Knopf, 1983. This book covers the life of Liang Heng from the 1950's to the 1980's. Although the bulk of the book is on the Cultural Revolution of 1966-1976, the section concerning the circumstances under which his father divorced his mother cover the Antirightist Campaign very well.

MacFarquhar, Roderick. *The Hundred Flowers Campaign and the Chinese Intellectuals*. New York: Octagon Books, 1974. Useful documents and helpful commentary are provided.

Solomon, Richard H. *Mao's Revolution and the Chinese Political Culture*. Berkeley: University of California Press, 1971. Chapter 17 covers Mao's theory on "contradictions" and permanent revolution. Mao's reactions to destabilization and the Hungarian rebellion, and his motives for the Hundred Flowers Campaign, are well done.

Spence, Jonathan D. *The Gate of Heavenly Peace: The Chinese and Their Revolution 1895-1980*. Viking Books, 1981. Chapter 12 provides very good examples of famous intellectuals who suffered under the Hundred Flowers Campaign. Ding Ling's ordeal, humiliation, and punishment are well described.

*Peng-Khuan Chong*

## Cross-References

Students Demonstrate for Reform in China's May Fourth Movement (1919), p. 276; Khrushchev Implies That Stalinist Excesses Will Cease (1956), p. 952; Mao's Great Leap Forward Causes Famine and Social Dislocation (1958), p. 1015; The Chinese Cultural Revolution Starts a Wave of Repression (1966), p. 1332; China Publicizes and Promises to Correct Abuses of Citizens' Rights (1978), p. 1983; Demonstrators Gather in Tiananmen Square (1989), p. 2483.

# EGYPT ATTEMPTS TO NATIONALIZE THE SUEZ CANAL

*Category of event:* Civil rights
*Time:* October, 1956
*Locale:* Egypt

*Colonial and Western-superiority attitudes reasserted themselves when Great Britain and France, in concert with Israel, invaded Egypt in the wake of Nasser's nationalization of the Suez Canal Company*

*Principal personages:*

GAMAL ABDEL NASSER (1918-1970), the president of Egypt who nationalized the Suez Canal Company

ANTHONY EDEN (1897-1977), the prime minister of the United Kingdom who led his country into a tripartite attack against Egypt

DWIGHT D. EISENHOWER (1890-1969), the president of the United States who pressured the British into stopping military action against Egypt

DAVID BEN-GURION (1886-1973), the prime minister of Israel who agreed with the British and French to invade the Egyptian Sinai Peninsula

GUY MOLLET (1905-1975), the prime minister of France who aspired to use the nationalization of the Suez Canal Company as a reason to attack President Nasser

NIKITA KHRUSHCHEV (1894-1971), the Soviet leader who threatened retaliation for the attack on Egypt

JOHN FOSTER DULLES (1888-1959), the U.S. secretary of state who originated the Suez Canal Users Association (SCUA) plan

## Summary of Event

On July 26, 1956, Gamal Abdel Nasser, president of Egypt, announced that Egypt was nationalizing the Suez Canal Company. His declaration that evening, during a speech in the port city of Alexandria, surprised the world. It also set in motion a train of events that soon led to a coordinated British, French, and Israeli attack on Egypt that some saw as a last hurrah for British and French colonialism. The repercussions were widespread, and many people were deprived of life, freedom, home, property, or country as events unfolded.

The nationalization of the French, but substantially British-owned, Suez Canal Company twelve years before it would, in any event, have become Egyptian property was not simply a quixotic act by a military dictator. There is evidence that a takeover had been discussed within the Egyptian government. Nevertheless, it is generally accepted that the move at that time had clearly defined antecedents. Egypt, whose main enemy was Israel, had been seeking arms in the face of a U.S.-U.K.-French accord to limit the flow of arms into the Middle East. The turndown that Egypt received led Nasser to turn to the Soviet Union, although ostensibly his agreement was with Czechoslovakia. The opening up of the Middle East to Soviet arms upset the Western triumvirate and prompted the United States, followed by the British, to back away from financing the Aswan high dam, the centerpiece of Egypt's socioeconomic development program. Only a few days after that decision was announced, Nasser delivered his riposte, stating that the revenues from the Suez Canal would be used to finance the high dam project.

Major nationalizations of foreign holdings are not everyday events. They are not, however, uncommon, and normally are not considered cause to let blood. Why, then, in this case? Several rationales were offered by British and French officials, such as the protection of world maritime commerce. It is widely held, however, that the real reason was to punish Nasser. To the French, who initially were the most belligerent, Nasser was anathema because he was a major source of support for the Arab revolt in Algeria. The British seemed concerned that Nasser could interfere with their close relationships with the royal governments of Iraq and Jordan. Probably, also, there was British rancor that Egypt under Nasser no longer was amenable to British influence.

There is no denying that the Suez Canal at that time was a vital support system for Western Europe. Any interference with maritime traffic through the canal would create an economic crisis. The closure of the Canal brought on by British, French, and Israeli actions demonstrated that. Taken literally, however, the nationalization of the canal did not change the world role or maritime characteristics of the canal. It merely moved the canal's administration from a private French company to the Egyptian government. The Egyptians wanted the revenue from the Canal, and so had a vital interest in keeping the canal open and operating it at maximum capacity. Subsequent events also showed that the Egyptians could successfully run the canal. They did so in the face of efforts by the dispossessed company to scuttle canal operations by enticing the canal pilots to quit their jobs. Egypt, not the Suez Canal Company, had exercised sovereign control over the canal before it was nationalized, just as it did after nationalization. Egypt can be said substantially to have provided for freedom of transit in accordance with the Constantinople Convention of 1888, the treaty that established international rules for use of the canal. What changed was the political climate surrounding the canal, exacerbating an already extremely distrustful attitude toward Nasser. Accordingly, the events of the Suez Canal crisis were built around the psychologies of the leaders and their perceptions of circumstances, rather than around some objective reality inherent in what had happened. It is in these terms that the events following the nationalization need to be understood.

On July 30, 1956, a few days after nationalization was declared, Sir Anthony Eden, British prime minister, declared that single-power control of the canal was totally unacceptable. On August 16, at a meeting in London, U.S. secretary of state John Foster Dulles advanced a proposal for a users organization to run the canal, clearly implying that control of the canal would be taken out of the hands of the Egyptians. A plan was adopted later for a Suez Canal Users Association (SCUA), with eighteen nations supporting this approach. The SCUA actually never did anything of consequence. Even so, its creation amounted to endorsement of the propositions that the canal was too important to be left in the hands of an apostate like Nasser and that the Egyptians were incompetent to manage the canal. Turning the canal over to the SCUA was not an acceptable option to Egypt. The whole plan simply exacerbated an already tense situation.

Even while the SCUA was prominent in the news, military preparations were under way. British reserves were called up. French troops arrived at a British military base on Cyprus. Despite repeated warnings by U.S. President Dwight D. Eisenhower that military force could not be countenanced by the United States, these moves did presage military action. When the attack came, it was evident that a combined operation had been agreed upon by Britain, France, and Israel.

Israeli involvement is not directly attributable to nationalization of the Suez Canal Company. Israeli ships and cargoes were not allowed to transit the canal, but that had been true before nationalization. What worried Prime Minister David Ben-Gurion and his associates were Palestinian guerrilla raids that the Israelis regarded as supported by Egypt and that, from a point on Sinai, Egypt could and did interdict ships traveling to and from the Israeli southern port of Eilat.

On October 29, 1956, Israel launched an attack on the Sinai Peninsula of Egypt, to the east of the Suez Canal. The Israelis were supported by British and French air attacks on Egyptian airfields. The following day, the British and French issued an ultimatum to Israel and Egypt, which really was an ultimatum to Egypt only, that both countries remove their forces to ten miles from the Suez Canal and that Anglo-French troops occupy the Canal Zone, including the three principal cities of Port Said, Ismailia, and Suez. On rejection of this ultimatum by Egypt, British and French military units attacked from the air and by sea. In the few days necessary to get troops ashore, Egypt sank a number of vessels related to canal operations in the canal. This contributed to blocking the canal for months after the military phase was terminated.

Very shortly after landing, Anglo-French forces stopped their advance 23 miles down the length of the 101-mile canal. Accordingly, the European nations never attained their stated objective of occupying the Canal Zone. Soviet leader Nikita Khrushchev had made threats against the three aggressors, but informed observers tended to think that it was a combination of American moves that could have undermined a fragile British financial system and negative world opinion that caused the European powers to stop. What ensued was a complicated series of maneuvers that led to a United Nations peacekeeping force in the Sinai, the withdrawal of British, French, and Israeli troops, and ultimately the reopening of the canal near the end of March, 1957. For her part, Israel got essentially what she wanted—the end of Palestinian attacks from the Gaza strip and freedom of navigation to Eilat.

This was not a highly destructive war, but many were killed or wounded in action. Egypt was defeated in the Sinai and essentially decided not to defend Port Said. It did, however, give guns to civilians in that area. Those who used their weapons were, of course, no match for trained British and French soldiers. The British and

French seaborne invaders took measures to minimize casualties of the landing operation, but many Egyptians living on the coast lost their homes. A number of foreigners living in Egypt lost what they possessed because their properties were seized and they were forced to leave. Some British and French were imprisoned.

Probably the main innocents to suffer were the Jews and Greeks in Egypt. Essentially, Egyptians previously had distinguished between the Zionists who founded Israel and Jewish worshipers. There was no tradition of anti-Semitism in much of the Arab-Muslim world, such as there had been in Eastern and Western Europe. This affair, particularly the association of Israel with France, changed attitudes. Not only Egyptian Jews but also other Jews in the North African Arab countries bore the brunt of the anti-Jewish sentiment to which these events gave rise. The surge of antiforeign sentiment also affected the Greeks. Egypt had harbored Greek populations for some time. These never integrated into Egyptian society and tended to be better off than the Egyptians, leading to ill will against Greeks. Greece did what it could to be on the right side of this affair. When other pilots left at the instigation of the Suez Canal Company, Greece persuaded its nationals who were canal pilots to stay. These few people were an important element in making it possible for Egypt to keep the canal going until more pilots could be recruited. This did not save Egypt's Greeks. Laws were passed that required Egyptian majority ownership of businesses in which foreigners were involved. Having seen wholesale nationalizations, Greeks began to take out of the country the property that they could, and many eventually left Egypt themselves.

## Impact of Event

The circumstances recounted above are the most direct outcomes of the events of the Suez Canal crisis. The Jews who left North Africa often had to go as unwilling immigrants to Israel. Under the concept of the return, all Jews are welcome to Israel. The saga of the absorption of the Sephardic or Oriental Jews by Israel, however, and the problems that such peoples have encountered in an Israel dominated by Jewish populations from Europe has not been one of the happier chapters in the short history of Israel.

Europe, for its part, lost much of the oil coming through the canal by tanker and, when the military action started, a pipeline bringing oil to the Mediterranean was cut. It was a cold winter in Europe that year. Despite efforts by the United States and other countries to make up the shortfall, a number of Europeans working in industries fired by oil were unemployed during this time and houses were not as warm as they might have been.

The Suez Canal crisis may also have been one of the events that ultimately caused the end of the already dying colonialism and the attitudes represented thereby. The British government fell as an outcome of this affair. The French government did not, but ultimately France did reconcile itself to granting independence from control to Vietnam and Algeria. The United States, despite its role in the SCUA, was widely credited with halting the invasion and enjoyed a reception in Arab lands, for a while, that belied its close association with Israel. The United States soon dissipated this good will by trying to turn its popularity into a device for lining up Arab nations in the fight against the Soviet Union and communism. The Arab nations, by and large, did not see the threat in the same way as the United States did and most were reluctant to sign up on the U.S. team. One of Nasser's sins, in the eyes of the United States, was his role as a major leader in the so-called nonaligned movement, which United States leaders at that time regarded as misguided and even immoral. By the next U.S. administration, being a neutralist developing nation no longer was a cardinal sin.

In retrospect, it is possible to say that Suez should never have happened. To explain what seemed like a wild venture, some analysts have resorted to using the fact of British Prime Minister Anthony Eden's ill health during this period. It is impossible to predict what would have occurred if events had been different, but the great fault of Suez seems to be that it happened at all. Some contend that Suez made the Soviet suppression of the Hungarian revolt more feasible. Whatever the merits of this argument, Suez certainly reduced the credibility of the West in its attempt to portray Hungary's situation as a massive suppression of human rights reflective of the ways of an "evil empire."

## Bibliography

Adams, Michael. *Suez and After: Year of Crisis.* Boston: Beacon Press, 1958. A British reporter's account of this time in the Middle East, part of it reported from Egypt. While not systematic in coverage, it does address a number of issues that tend to be overlooked in more formal studies of these times. He is sympathetic to the Arab side.

Calvocoressi, Peter. *Suez Ten Years After.* New York: Pantheon Books, 1966. Based on ten British Broadcasting Corporation (BBC) programs that drew on the memories of participants in the Suez Canal crisis and on the expertise of persons who had studied the event, this book is one of the best sources of information on the major facets of the affair.

Louis, William R. and Roger Owen, eds. *Suez 1956: The Crisis and Its Consequences.* Oxford, England: Clarendon Press, 1989. A scholarly work resulting from a collaborative effort between the University of Oxford in England and the Woodrow Wilson Center in Washington, D.C., this book contains chapters on many aspects of the crisis. A good source for those who want to understand better the lessons of Suez.

Robertson, Terence. *Crisis: The Inside Story of the Suez Conspiracy.* New York: Atheneum, 1965. A detailed recounting of the Suez Canal crisis, this work includes sections on the tripartite conspiracy and the role of the United Nations in bringing this adventure to a conclusion.

Thomas, Hugh. *Suez.* New York: Harper & Row, 1967. A well-documented and opinionated detailed critical review of the Suez crisis, this is an almost day-by-day recounting of the events that made up the Suez Canal story.

Troen, Selwyn, and Moshe Shemesh, eds. *The Suez-Sinai Crisis 1956: Retrospective and Reappraisal.* New York: Columbia University Press, 1990. This edited work on the Suez Canal crisis, while fundamentally academic in nature, includes chapters by authors who were practitioners at the time of the affair. Subjectively, rather than chronologically, organized. This is a basic source for reviewing certain facets of the crisis and its aftermath.

*Thomas I. Dickson*

## Cross-References

The French Quell an Algerian Nationalist Revolt (1945), p. 651; The United Nations Creates an Agency to Aid Palestinian Refugees (1949), p. 814; Israel Enacts the Law of Return, Granting Citizenship to Immigrants (1950), p. 832; A Hungarian Uprising Is Quelled by Soviet Military Forces (1956), p. 969; The Nonaligned Movement Meets (1961), p. 1131; Algeria Gains Independence (1962), p. 1155.

# A HUNGARIAN UPRISING IS QUELLED BY SOVIET MILITARY FORCES

*Category of event:* Revolutions and rebellions
*Time:* October-November, 1956
*Locale:* Hungary

*The Hungarian people demanded political freedom and the withdrawal of Soviet military forces from their country, but these demands were forcibly suppressed*

*Principal personages:*

IMRE NAGY (1896-1958), the popular Hungarian national communist who led the Hungarian independence movement

MATYAS RAKOSI (1892-1971), the Stalinist leader of Hungary whose dismissal in 1956 paved the way to the uprising

JANOS KADAR (1912-1989), the leader of the Hungarian Communist Party who took power during the Soviet intervention and ruled Hungary until 1988

NIKITA S. KHRUSHCHEV (1894-1971), the first secretary of the Soviet Communist Party who introduced de-Stalinization in the Soviet Union and Eastern Europe

ANASTAS MIKOYAN (1895-1978), a high-ranking Soviet Communist Party official

## Summary of Event

Hungary, defeated in World War I, fought on the side of Nazi Germany during World War II hoping to regain lost territories. The conquest of Hungary by the Red Army of the Soviet Union in the winter of 1944-1945 marked the beginning of nearly five years during which Hungary was a single-party communist state led by Matyas Rakosi. Freedoms of speech, assembly, press, and religious expression were severely curtailed. A state security organ was created, accountable only to the ruling Council of Ministers. Over 300,000 informers reported to this security apparatus, which established files on more than ten percent of the population. Although a new constitution was declared in 1949 that allegedly protected individual rights, there was, in fact, no independent judiciary in Hungary, and scant attention was paid to due process of law. Instead, the Communist Party, under Rakosi, reigned supreme. Rakosi patterned his rule on that of Joseph Stalin of the Soviet Union.

Stalin's death in 1953 was followed by a period of collective leadership in the Soviet Union, from which Nikita Khrushchev ultimately emerged as the most powerful figure. The states of Eastern Europe were urged to follow the Soviet lead. In Hungary, Rakosi was forced to share power with Imre Nagy. Nagy explicitly criticized the abuses of individual rights by state authorities and sought to restore a measure of legality to the lives of Hungarians. By 1955, however, Nagy had been politically outmaneuvered by Rakosi and was expelled from the Communist Party. Nagy remained, however, an immensely popular figure in Hungary because of his advocacy of a more tolerant, national form of communism.

In February of 1956, Khrushchev startled the world with a harsh critique of Stalin's rule. He also promised more autonomy to the communist states of Eastern Europe as long as they remained committed to following the path of socialism. Khrushchev's words led to increasing demands for political and economic freedoms in Eastern Europe, particularly in Poland and Hungary. In March, Hungarian writers and other intellectuals created the Petofi Circle, a forum for debate and discussion that quickly became intensely critical of the government. Rakosi attempted to disband the Petofi Circle, planned to arrest Nagy and other dissident communists, and introduced other repressive measures against the growing freedom of expression. On July 17, Anastas Mikoyan, a member of the Soviet Union's ruling Party presidium, arrived in Budapest with word that Rakosi would have to step down as leader of Hungary's Communist Party in favor of Erno Gero. Additional appointees to the Party leadership included Janos Kadar, who had been a victim of an earlier Rakosi purge.

Rakosi's departure and the other personnel changes were insufficient to stem the rising tide of demands for reforms in Hungary. Central to these was that Nagy should be returned to power. On October 13, Nagy's Party membership was restored, but opposition groups and manifestos continued to proliferate. The opposition was inspired by the increasingly successful efforts of the communist leadership in Poland to win concessions from the Soviet Union. Among the most important of the Hungarian reform proposals was a list of demands drawn up on October 22 by students from the Technical University in Budapest. These included the following: the immediate withdrawal of all Soviet troops from Hungarian territory; the reorganization of the Communist Party along democratic lines; a new government, to be led by Nagy at first, with free multiparty elections; extensive economic reforms; complete recognition of freedom of opinion, expression, press, and radio; and removal of Stalin's statue from one of Budapest's main squares.

On the evening of October 23, a crowd of students attempted to gain access to Budapest's radio headquarters in order to broadcast these demands. They were fired on by members of the Hungarian security police. Demonstrations began occurring throughout Budapest. These multiplied and reached new levels of intensity as a result of an inflammatory speech by Gero accusing the demonstrators of being enemies of the working class. Responding to public pressure, the government then reorganized itself, naming Nagy as premier, but also requested assistance from Soviet military forces already stationed in Hungary. This initial Soviet intervention was limited and rather halfhearted, emboldening rather than discouraging the protestors. Meanwhile, Mikoyan returned to Hungary with Mikhail Suslov, another high-ranking Soviet official. Gero and other Hungarian party leaders were compelled to resign, and Kadar was appointed the new party chief.

Despite leadership changes in Budapest, events in the Hungarian provinces were developing a momentum of their own. Revolutionary councils of workers, students, and peasants were being formed and, although some of their specific goals varied widely, their common objectives included the withdrawal of Soviet troops and the creation of a pluralistic political order in Hungary. Nagy, his good intentions notwithstanding, found himself trapped between the forces demanding radical change and the political reality of having to deal with the Soviet Union. Nagy's difficulties were further exacerbated by foreign radio broadcasts, particularly from Radio Free Europe, which harshly questioned his motives and encouraged opposition groups to press their demands.

Nagy continued to seek a way out of his dilemma and, on October 30, it appeared that he might succeed. Mikoyan and Suslov had returned to Budapest carrying a Soviet declaration from Moscow that called for negotiating the question of Soviet troops in Hungary along with other issues of mutual concern. On the same day, Nagy announced on Hungarian radio that a multiparty political system would be restored and that negotiations would begin on the withdrawal of Soviet military forces. Even this momentous development was insufficient to silence many in the opposition who demanded that Hungary withdraw from the Warsaw Pact and unequivocally declare its neutrality.

The apparent willingness of the Soviet Union to negotiate with Hungary on these issues masked a furious Kremlin debate over how to deal with a direct challenge to Soviet political hegemony in Eastern Europe. If Hungary were permitted to pursue a course of complete independence, what impact might this have on Czechoslovakia, East Germany, and other satellite states? By November 1, there were ominous hints that the Soviets intended to resolve the issue by force rather than by compromise. On that date, Nagy received reports that Soviet troops were entering Hungary, not withdrawing, and his efforts to clarify the situation with the Soviet ambassador to Hungary, Yuri Andropov, were unavailing. Nagy went on Hungarian radio to announce that Hungary was, in fact, intending to leave the Warsaw Pact and become a neutral state. Nagy also informed the Secretary-General of the United Nations, Dag Hammarskjöld, of Hungary's intention. Simultaneously, Kadar, along with several other party leaders, mysteriously disappeared from the Hungarian capital.

By the morning of November 4, Soviet intentions became clear. The Red Army began a massive military intervention that was to result in approximately three thousand Hungarian deaths. Half of those killed were under thirty years of age and many were teenagers. The mystery surrounding Kadar's disappearance was solved when it was revealed, also on November 4, that he and several other party leaders had fled to the Soviet Union, from where they declared that Hungary was threatened with counterrevolution, requiring the formation of a new government. In the face of the Soviet intervention, Nagy was compelled to seek refuge in the Yugoslav Embassy. When he left the embassy, he was arrested. In 1958, Nagy was executed. The United States and the United Nations, caught up in the events of the simultaneously evolving Suez crisis, vigorously protested the Soviet invasion but failed to intervene. Hungary's dramatic effort to achieve political self-determination had been crushed.

## Impact of Event

The massive intervention of Soviet military forces in Hungary was condemned internationally as a blatant violation of Hungarian sovereignty and of the human rights of its citizens. Thousands throughout the world, including many in the United States, resigned their memberships in the Communist Party. The role of communism as a champion of human rights, already greatly damaged by Stalin's crimes, was irreparably destroyed.

In Hungary itself, the casualties caused by the military invasion were compounded by additional widespread repression. Over the following year, twenty thousand were arrested, two thousand were executed, and thousands were deported to the Soviet Union. Over 200,000 became refugees, most of these fleeing across the border to Austria. Workers' councils were abolished, and the recently acquired freedoms of press and intellectual expression were severely curtailed.

Kadar faced a formidable challenge of reconstruction in Hungary. He was widely disliked and distrusted, and the country was in political and economic chaos. Surprisingly, however, Kadar was able to effect a policy of gradual reconciliation which was to heal some of the wounds inflicted in 1956. Although the Communist Party retained its monopolistic hold on political power, some reforms were initiated, notably the New Economic Mechanism (NEM) introduced in 1968. The NEM strengthened the role of market forces in the economy and created a less centrally controlled structure of prices. In other spheres of activity, such as culture and religion, the regime displayed increasingly tolerant attitudes. The result was that, during the decades of the 1970's and 1980's, the reputation of Hungary was that of the most liberal of the Soviet-bloc East European states.

Despite the fact that Hungary's human rights record was somewhat better than that of some of its neighbors, Romania for example, the legitimacy of the political system was still weak. By the mid-1980's, Kadar was losing his grip on power. He was finally removed as party leader in May, 1988. In a development of enormous significance, Nagy was at last given a public funeral on June 16, 1989. Nagy's reburial as a national hero was attended by more than 100,000 citizens. The same year, Hungary began moving toward a multiparty system. In June, 1991, at least some of the ghosts of 1956 were laid to rest when, in the wake of the dissolution of the Warsaw Pact, the last Soviet troops left Hungary.

## Bibliography

Barber, Noël. *Seven Days of Freedom: The Hungarian Uprising, 1956.* New York: Stein & Day, 1974. Competently researched, this account is also based on the author's eyewitness accounts of events he observed as a journalist present in Hungary during the revolution. The book offers a day-by-day description of events, some valuable maps and appendices, a bibliography, and an index.

Gati, Charles. *Hungary and the Soviet Bloc.* Durham, N.C.: Duke University Press, 1986. A scholarly description and analysis of the relationship between Hungary and the Soviet Union, beginning with World War II and covering the entire period up until the mid-1980's. The book is a valuable resource for placing the Hungarian uprising in the broader context of regional and international politics. Included is a chapter on American policy toward Eastern Europe. Extensive footnotes, bibliography, and an index are provided.

Kovrig, Bennett. *Communism in Hungary: From Kun to Kadar.* Stanford, Calif.: Hoover Institution Press, 1979. One of the few English-language surveys of the history of Hungary in the twentieth century. Rich in detail, loaded with sources, but very readable. Index and bibliography are included. For the best discussions of United States and United Nations reactions to the Hungarian uprising, see also Kovrig's *The Myth of Liberation: East Central Europe in U.S. Diplomacy and Politics Since 1941* (Baltimore: Johns Hopkins University Press, 1973).

Lasky, Melvin, ed. *The Hungarian Revolution: The Story of the October Uprising as Recorded in Documents, Dispatches, Eye-Witness Accounts, and World-wide Reactions.* Freeport, Conn.: Books for Libraries Press, 1957. The title is self-explanatory. The book is a gold mine of information on the Hungarian revolution, presented in chronological fashion. Included is a historical overview by Hugh Seton-Watson, a leading scholar of East European history and politics.

Meray, Tibor. *That Day in Budapest: October 23, 1956.* Translated by Charles Lam Markmann. New York: Funk & Wagnalls, 1969. One of several books on the Hungarian revolution written by Meray, a close associate of Imre Nagy. Meray's descriptions are detailed and vivid, and his insights quite valuable. Among the very best of the detailed accounts of the events of October and November.

Zinner, Paul E. *Revolution in Hungary.* New York: Columbia University Press, 1962. Political scientist Zinner's study was sponsored by the Columbia University Research Project on Hungary. The study relies on extensive interviews as well as documentary sources. It successfully explains the origins and antecedents of the revolution. The book is one of the best analytic, as opposed to purely descriptive, studies of the Hungarian rebellion.

*Scott McElwain*

### Cross-References

Soviets Take Control of Eastern Europe (1943), p. 612; Khrushchev Implies That Stalinist Excesses Will Cease (1956), p. 952; The Brezhnev Doctrine Bans Acts of Independence in Soviet Satellites (1968), p. 1408; Soviets Invade Czechoslovakia (1968), p. 1441; Poland Imposes Martial Law and Outlaws Solidarity (1981), p. 2152; Gorbachev Initiates a Policy of *Glasnost* (1985), p. 2249; Hungary Adopts a Multiparty System (1989), p. 2421; Poland Forms a Non-Communist Government (1989), p. 2500; The Berlin Wall Falls (1989), p. 2523; Ceausescu Is Overthrown in Romania (1989), p. 2546; Soviet Troops Withdraw from Czechoslovakia (1990), p. 2570.

# THE SCLC FORMS TO LINK CIVIL RIGHTS GROUPS

*Categories of event:* Civil rights; racial and ethnic rights
*Time:* January-August, 1957
*Locale:* Atlanta, Georgia; New Orleans, Louisiana; and Montgomery, Alabama

*The formation of the Southern Christian Leadership Conference (SCLC) in 1957 was the first Southwide grass-roots movement dedicated to racial desegregation in the United States*

*Principal personages:*

MARTIN LUTHER KING, JR. (1929-1968), the first president of the SCLC (1957-1968)

RALPH DAVID ABERNATHY (1926-1990), one of the cofounders of the SCLC and successor to King as its president (1968-1977)

FRED SHUTTLESWORTH (1922-    ), the leader of the Alabama Christian Movement for Human Rights (ACMHR), the principal SCLC affiliate in its early days

BAYARD RUSTIN (1912-1987), an influential civil rights leader who contributed to the formation of the SCLC

STANLEY DAVID LEVISON (1912-1979), a white Jewish attorney and benefactor of the SCLC in its formative period

CHARLES KENZIE STEELE (1914-1980), the principal leader of desegregation efforts in Tallahassee, Florida, and a seminal figure in the formation of the SCLC

ELLA JO BAKER (1903-1986), an activist who helped plan the SCLC and served as its executive director (1959-1960)

CORETTA SCOTT KING (1927-    ), the wife of Dr. Martin Luther King, Jr., involved in the planning discussions that led to the SCLC

## Summary of Event

When the Southern Christian Leadership Conference was formed in 1957, black Americans faced many obstacles to economic and political equality despite decades of piecemeal reforms. The National Association for the Advancement of Colored People (NAACP), the National Urban League, the Congress of Racial Equality (CORE), and other advocacy organizations had achieved significant gains, but black Americans in many parts of the country were prohibited from voting and blocked by lack of education and segregationist barriers from advancing economically and socially. Particularly in the southern states, black Americans faced formidable barriers that had stood firmly and even intensified in spite of significant legal victories against segregation in interstate transportation and education. The major advocacy organizations began and operated chiefly in the North and had comparatively little impact on southern blacks, who lived in perennial poverty and social ostracism.

The SCLC was the first Southwide civil rights organization. Its distinctive role as the political arm of many black churches gave it the ability to lead direct action campaigns with the kind of massive grass-roots support that had eluded the NAACP and other older advocacy organizations. Under the leadership of Dr. Martin Luther King, Jr., from 1957 to 1968, the SCLC worked with other organizations in many desegregation campaigns. Its nonviolent direct action efforts were on a scale unparalleled in previous campaigns.

By 1957, numerous local desegregation campaigns had been launched without the benefit of a connecting framework. "Movement centers," as Aldon D. Morris called them, included Tallahassee, Mobile, Nashville, Birmingham, Baton Rouge, and several other cities where local leaders applied interorganizational cooperation to effect changes, usually desegregation of public transit systems. What they lacked was an organizational framework to link their efforts with those in other cities and thus achieve a broader impact on behalf of integration and racial equality. Several black leaders, notably the Reverend T. J. Jemison of Baton Rouge, the Reverend Charles Kenzie Steele of Tallahassee, and the Reverend Fred Shuttlesworth of Birmingham, expressed the need for such a larger connecting framework, especially after the important bus boycott in Montgomery, Alabama, during 1955 and 1956.

The 381-day Montgomery boycott, triggered by the bold defiance of segregated seating by a black seamstress, Rosa Parks, was the catalyst in bringing these various reform centers together. The "Montgomery way," as many termed it, had demonstrated the effectiveness of mass direct action without violence. Furthermore, it underscored the value of pooling ideas and resources to challenge laws and traditions that supported segregated public facilities such as restaurants, movie theaters, and hotels. Transportation was a particularly significant area needing attention, because many blacks depended upon public transit to get to their jobs.

Several informal groups began in late 1956 to plan a broad organization for enlarging the civil rights struggle. One of these groups included Ella Jo Baker, a perennial supporter of direct action reform, white attorney Stanley David Levison, and civil rights advocate Bayard Rustin. In New York, they formed a small group known as "In Friendship" and began to contact civil rights leaders across the South. Meanwhile, Martin Luther King, Jr., and the Reverend Ralph David Abernathy, along with others like Joseph E. Lowery, Charles Kenzie Steele, and T. J. Jemison, met periodically in Montgomery to brainstorm on a possible southern direct action organization.

It would be a mistake to attribute this interest entirely to the Montgomery campaign or to contextual factors such as urbanization and its related tensions. The historical setting of the origins of the SCLC included these things as well as the impact of the *Brown v. Board of Education* case of May, 1954, that declared unconstitutional "separate but equal" schools, based on the 1896 *Plessy v. Ferguson* decision. The *Brown* case was a particularly encouraging factor because it showed that the Supreme Court could be a valuable ally of black reform leaders.

In early 1956, Rustin suggested to King in Montgomery the concept of a broad organization to link the various reform centers. By the end of the year, the discussions had advanced sufficiently to attempt an organization meeting. Rustin contacted Steele and others, and round-robin invitations went out from Steele, King, and Shuttlesworth to dozens of southern activists. The foundational meeting took place at the Ebenezer Baptist Church in Atlanta on January 10 and 11, 1957, with approximately sixty people, mostly black pastors, attending.

The discussions covered a wide range of topics, mostly from working papers provided by Rustin. It was agreed that the movement would be nonviolent in method and outlook and that all Americans' rights under the Constitution would be supported in order "to redeem the soul of America." The fact that many participants were ministers added to the emphasis upon faith and ethics. This basic reality of the Atlanta meeting was important in shaping the ethos of the emergent SCLC. The conference also cabled President Eisenhower, requesting that he or Vice President Richard Nixon travel to the South and take a strong stand in favor of civil rights. Eisenhower had already sent a civil rights package to Congress in 1956, but the administration's proposals fell short of the Atlanta delegates' expectations.

Later meetings in New Orleans on February 14, 1957, and in Montgomery in August of the same year completed the organizational process. After experimenting with various names, the new conference arrived at its permanent name, the Southern Christian Leadership Conference, during the Montgomery meeting. Some SCLC leaders feared that adding the word "Christian" might alienate Jews such as Stanley Levison, but King supported the new name, believing that it reflected the true nature of the organization. Levison agreed. Some of the organizers thought that the word "Christian" would lessen the likelihood that the organization would be considered radical or communist.

The Southern Christian Leadership Conference focused chiefly on basic rights for minorities and poor people. Its first major undertaking was a Crusade for Citizenship. Its goal was to at least double the number of registered black voters in the South. Voting rights thus became one of the major emphases of the new organization. Working in conjunction with the NAACP and other organizations, the SCLC added thousands of black voters to the voting rolls in several states. It also continued to work on behalf of ending segregated transportation, desegregating schools, and gaining broader access by blacks to public facilities such as hotel and lunch counters.

The SCLC's loose organization was important to its distinctive role in the Civil Rights movement. Without formal individual membership, it was based on affiliates, such as local churches and activist groups like Fred Shuttlesworth's Alabama Christian Movement for Human Rights (ACMHR). Operating at first in eleven states, it linked hundreds of such entities in a way that facilitated guidance from the central headquarters while maintaining considerable local autonomy. The SCLC came into cities and towns for campaigns when invited by local leaders. As the SCLC became more experienced and efficient, these invitations were carefully planned. The Birmingham campaign of 1963, which was a highpoint of the SCLC's history, began on the basis of an invitation from Shuttlesworth's organization.

The SCLC's focus was primarily on securing rights that were based on the United States Constitution. It was also interested, from the beginning, in economic advancement of minorities and perennially poor people. This aspect of the SCLC's history had not been recognized adequately. The fact that its focus on social and economic gains increased after the Selma campaign and the Voting Rights Act of 1965 should not be taken as an indication that the SCLC came to this emphasis only in the middle 1960's. Poverty was viewed by the SCLC as a seminal cause of the political powerlessness of many black Americans, and from the beginning the organization was interested in the elimination of poverty. At the same time, King and his associates recognized that the right to vote would bring the ability to help determine political leaders and hold them accountable for such needs as jobs and housing. King sounded this note as early as the Prayer Pilgrimage of May, 1957, marking the third anniversary of the *Brown* decision. In his speech, which propelled him higher in public visibility, he gave rhythmic repetitions of the phrase "Give us the ballot," noting that if blacks had the vote they could nonviolently eliminate many barriers to progress.

## Impact of Event

Thus began an important new organization dedicated to racial justice and advancement in the United States. It was quite different in key ways from the older NAACP and CORE, both of which began in the North and historically operated chiefly outside the South. The NAACP did have a strong presence in the South in 1957, but it was under attack by various groups and governments. Its distinguishing feature had always been litigation through the court system. The SCLC provided a framework for mass direct action, which many felt was urgently needed in the South. Furthermore, the SCLC was not a membership organization. It was structured around loosely linked "affiliates," such as the ACMHR, rather than individual membership.

The advent of the SCLC marked a new chapter in the history of racial and ethnic rights in the United States. Strongly grounded in local churches, it sought to bring their moral strength and organizational resources to bear upon the problems of minorities. With King as its president, it had an articulate spokesman who was increasingly drawing media interest. This was both an asset and a liability. King's visibility helped the young SCLC but at the same time hindered the organization's achievement of an identity apart from him. On balance, the SCLC was very significant in the continuance of the momentum gained in Montgomery and other cities in the early and middle 1950's. For more than a decade under King, it would be a major force in massive campaigns in Birmingham, Selma, and other cities, and after 1965 would venture into the northern United States.

Nonviolence was the most characteristic mark of the SCLC's campaigns. At times it had remarkable results, not only for public policy but also for individual experiences of both blacks and whites. During the Birmingham campaign of 1963, for example, a group of marchers who were walking to a prayer vigil were confronted by

Eugene "Bull" Connor's police and fire fighters, who were wielding water hoses to stop marchers. Despite Connor's orders, those in charge of the hoses would not turn them on the unarmed and nonviolent group. They were, as Coretta Scott King later observed, disarmed by the nonviolent spirit of the demonstrators. Not hitting back, not hating, and not giving cause for increased violence were the salient features of the SCLC's new mass-based direct action.

## Bibliography

Abernathy, Ralph David. *And the Walls Came Tumbling Down: An Autobiography.* New York: Harper & Row, 1989. This memoir by King's close friend and successor is disappointing on the formation and early development of the SCLC, but Abernathy's closeness to King and the early campaigns makes this a useful source for the context. Its chief value lies in giving one a firsthand view of what it was like to live through the Civil Rights movement in its heyday. Includes index and illustrations.

Branch, Taylor. *Parting the Waters: America in the King Years, 1954-1963.* New York: Simon & Schuster, 1988. This massive study focuses on the period from the *Brown v. Board of Education* case to the March on Washington in 1963. Its chief value lies in examining the setting in which Martin Luther King, Jr., became the leading spokesperson for racial liberation and equality. Elaborately documented and sympathetically approached, it is the first of a planned two-part series on the King years. Coverage of the founding of the SCLC is marginal, but the book is very strong on the SCLC's early campaigns. Contains notes, select bibliography, and index.

Fairclough, Adam. *To Redeem the Soul of America: The Southern Christian Leadership Conference and Martin Luther King, Jr.* Athens: University of Georgia Press, 1987. A detailed account of the early development of the SCLC and its historical context. A major focus is the changing role and attitudes of black clergy who played a pivotal role in the formation of the SCLC. Coverage of religious views and ideology is comparatively thin, but the book has valuable information on the internal dynamics of the SCLC. Contains detailed notes, chronologies, and index.

Garrow, David J. *Bearing the Cross: Martin Luther King, Jr., and the Southern Christian Leadership Conference.* New York: William Morrow, 1986. This Pulitzer Prizewinning account is thoroughly researched and elaborately documented. Although essentially biographical, Garrow's study deals with far more than King's life. It examines the campaigns, the role of the national and local governments, and the controversial personal details of King's relations with women. Although thin on the inner spiritual struggles of King and his associates, Garrow's is nevertheless the most detailed account to date of King's public career. Treatment of the SCLC's beginnings is relatively thin but useful. Contains detailed notes, illustrations, and index.

Morris, Aldon D. *The Origins of the Civil Rights Movement: Black Communities Organizing for Change.* New York: Free Press, 1984. An excellent study of the historical and institutional foundations of the Civil Rights movement. Morris examines several local centers, such as the Montgomery Improvement Association, that converged to bring about a strong southern cooperative movement. He also explores the emergence of black ministers as pivotal figures in the new activism. His coverage is basically from 1955 to 1965. The SCLC appears as the "decentralized political arm of the black church" that translated moral principles into political activism. Includes elaborate notes, bibliography, appendices, and index.

Peake, Thomas R. *Keeping the Dream Alive: A History of the Southern Christian Leadership Conference from King to the Nineteen-Eighties.* New York: Peter Lang, 1987. The first comprehensive history of the SCLC from its founding to the 1980's, this work focuses on the motivations, programs, and training methods of the SCLC. It contains much biographical and institutional information as well as analysis of the SCLC's religious and political concepts. Detailed notes, bibliography, illustrations, and an index.

Robinson, Jo Ann Gibson. *The Montgomery Bus Boycott and the Women Who Started It: The Memoir of Jo Ann Gibson Robinson.* Edited by David J. Garrow. Knoxville: University of Tennessee Press, 1987. A short but valuable account of the Montgomery bus boycott. Robinson, involved in the Women's Political Council that helped to organize the boycott, underscores the personal dimensions: the emotions, the hope, and the excitement of participating in these events.

*Thomas R. Peake*

### Cross-References

The Congress of Racial Equality Forms (1942), p. 601; Truman Orders Desegregation of U.S. Armed Forces (1948), p. 777; *Brown v. Board of Education* Ends Public School Segregation (1954), p. 913; Parks Is Arrested for Refusing to Sit in the Back of the Bus (1955), p. 947; The Civil Rights Act of 1957 Creates the Commission on Civil Rights (1957), p. 997; Eisenhower Sends Troops to Little Rock, Arkansas (1957), p. 1003; The Council of Federated Organizations Registers Blacks to Vote (1962), p. 1149; Meredith's Enrollment Integrates the University of Mississippi (1962), p. 1167; Civil Rights Protesters Attract International Attention (1963), p. 1188; Martin Luther King, Jr., Wins the Nobel Peace Prize (1964), p. 1257; Martin Luther King, Jr., Leads a March from Selma to Montgomery (1965), p. 1278; Congress Passes the Voting Rights Act (1965), p. 1296.

# GHANA GAINS INDEPENDENCE

*Category of event:* Political freedom
*Time:* March 6, 1957
*Locale:* Accra, Ghana

*The people of Ghana, under the leadership of the Convention People's Party and Kwame Nkrumah, were the first to achieve political independence in sub-Saharan Africa*

*Principal personages:*

KWAME NKRUMAH (1909-1972), the leader of the Convention People's Party and first prime minister of independent Ghana, overthrown in a military coup in 1966

J. B. DANQUAH (1895-1965), a leader of the United Gold Coast Convention, remained a major opponent of Nkrumah and died in detention

CHARLES ARDEN-CLARK (1898-1962), the last British governor of the Gold Coast; helped bring about the transition to self-government

HAROLD MACMILLAN (1894-1986), the prime minister of Britain who granted the Gold Coast independence

## Summary of Event

The Portuguese explorations along the coast of West Africa in the fifteenth century were quickly followed by English, Dutch, Swedish, Danish, and German traders, who named areas of the coast after the products they found there: The Grain Coast (modern Liberia), the Ivory Coast, the Slave Coast (between the Volta River and Niger delta), and the Gold Coast (modern Ghana). Trade in gold and ivory was surpassed by the slave trade after 1650, and European competition along the Gold Coast, which had been fierce (forty-one forts were built there), declined considerably, leaving the Dutch, British, and Danes vying for coastal supremacy.

Trade among African peoples, which had been intense since the fourteenth century, and increased trade between Europeans and Africans affected state formation and development within the boundaries of present-day Ghana. For example, Bono, the earliest Akan state (the Akan are the largest ethnolinguistic group within Ghana), was founded in 1295 and was succeeded by the states of Akwamu and Akyem in the seventeenth and eighteenth centuries, respectively. The most powerful and impressive Akan state was the Asante Confederacy, which emerged at the end of the seventeenth century and was governed from Kumasi, the capital. The Asante Confederacy was an elaborate and decentralized system of state authority, consisting of the *asantehene* (king of the confederacy) and subordinate chiefs in outlying towns, villages, and settlements. The formidable military organization established by the Asante enabled the confederacy, by 1824, to conquer both northern states, such as Donga, and Fante states along the southern coast. Antagonism between the Asante and Fante (they went to war nine times during the nineteenth century) led to intensified British involvement in the Gold Coast. The British sided with the Fante against the Asante in order to lessen the latter's immense political authority and to enable the British to gain undisputed control over trade routes. The British, in alliance with the Fante and other southern peoples, carried out wars against the Asante in 1824, 1826, 1863, and 1874, the year in which the Asante were decisively defeated.

The withdrawal of the Danes and the Dutch in 1850 and 1872, respectively, and the presence of the Council of Merchants (headed by George Maclean from 1829 to 1843), helped pave the way for further developments in British colonial rule. Although Maclean was not a governor-general, and therefore did not officially represent the British government, his activities in the southern part of Ghana went beyond commercial activities and included the exercise of judicial authority and collaboration with burgeoning missionary societies. After Maclean's death in 1847, the British government decided to establish direct jurisdiction over the southern part of Ghana and did so through the establishment of a legislative council (with no African representation) and a poll tax, established in 1852.

African resistance to British rule was fierce. After the defeat of the Asante in 1874, the British created the "Gold Coast Colony" in the area south of Asante. Colonial rule was officially established in Asante itself in 1901. One of the first challenges to British colonialism came from Chief John Aggrey, the mission-educated king of the Cape Coast, who challenged the legal basis of British rule and portrayed the issue as one of fundamental human rights. He complained of British attempts to impose what amounted to martial law and of British efforts to create disunity among the indigenous peoples.

Other protests, particularly from but not limited to the elite of the colony, were carried out during the late nineteenth century against both taxation and the usurpation of indigenous authority. The most noteworthy protest organization of the nineteenth century was the Aborigines Rights Protection Society (ARPS), which was formed in 1897 and for thirty-five years agitated for reforms, fought land dispossession by Europeans, and attempted to educate Africans about the actions taken by colonial authorities.

The scramble for Africa that resulted in the drawing of Ghana's contemporary boundaries began in the 1880's. In response to German and French strategic moves east of the Volta River and north of the Asante states, the British set out to move beyond the Gold Coast Colony. Between 1890 and 1900, the British established juridical and territorial control over modern Ghana through various wars and skirmishes with Africans, the French, and the Germans.

Twentieth century African resistance to British rule took place in three major waves. The ARPS, composed of the largely mission-educated elite of Ghana, agitated for constitutional reform and greater land equity until 1930. Its work was superseded by the pan-Africanist National Congress of British West Africa, which was active from 1920 to 1930. That group passed resolutions demanding reforms in all areas of colonial life: education, sanitation, representation, medicine, and agricul-

ture. Finally, in the 1930's, various interest organizations representing a new generation (often called the "young men," which referred to nonchiefly status rather than
age) emerged to challenge both chiefly authority and colonial rule. As many scholars
have pointed out, the young men were affected by the spread of and greater access to
Western education, their experience in World War I, and the effects of urbanization,
which attenuated ties to traditional authorities in the rural areas.

The first organization actually to demand independence rather than reforms within
the existing system was the West African Youth League, which was formed in 1934.
Although it was disparaged by many chiefs and its leader was deported, its appeal to
the young men of Ghana was taken advantage of by the Convention People's Party in
1949.

World War II ushered in demands for independence all over Asia and Africa. The
United Nations Charter, weakened colonial economies, and the extensive modernization and urbanization that accompanied the war combined to produce new organizations and leaders whose demands went beyond reform to independence. The British responded to demands for self-government with the Burns Constitution, which
united the Gold Coast Colony and Asante and provided for greater African representation in the legislative council. These and a number of other reforms were viewed as
inadequate by Africans, and in 1947 the United Gold Coast Convention (UGCC)
was formed to demand more far-reaching reforms. The leadership opposed chiefly
authority but nevertheless was reformist rather than radical, and only reluctantly
agreed to make Kwame Nkrumah the secretary of the UGCC. Nkrumah, thirty-nine
years old at the time, had been studying in the United States and Great Britain for
twelve years and returned to remarkably changed conditions in Ghana. Economic
conditions had worsened after the war, and a whole generation of lower-class Ghanaians was ready for mobilization into a more militant nationalist organization. Riots in early 1948 provided the precipitant that led Nkrumah and others to break away
from the UGCC to form the Convention People's Party (CPP), which demanded
"Self-Government Now." When the Coussey Committee, formed in response to the
riots, initially recommended both indirect elections and continued chiefly control
over thirty-three of the seventy-five seats in the legislature, Nkrumah ordered massive resistance. The colonial government responded with the imprisonment of Nkrumah and other CPP leaders, which had the unintended effect of increasing the popularity of the CPP. Elections were held in February, 1951, and the CPP won thirty-four
of the thirty-eight popularly contested seats, enabling it to form the government until
elections were scheduled again in 1954 and 1956.

Between 1951 and 1954, the CPP was able to embark upon significant reforms.
Dramatic increases in social spending took place. Nevertheless, opposition to the
CPP increased from a number of sources, including the older generation of middle-
class professionals, who formed the Ghana Congress Party in 1953; chiefs in the
North, who formed the Northern People's Party in 1954; and the National Liberation
Movement, formed by the Asante in late 1954. The CPP campaigned on the pledges
of support for the common man and the promise of continued material rewards. The

CPP won the 1954 and 1956 elections, and on March 6, 1957, it assumed the mantle of government of the first African country to achieve independence. The new name of the country was taken from the Sudanic trading state that had been powerful in the eleventh century.

## Impact of Event

Reporting on Ghana's independence, the magazine *Africa* wrote: "The event is regarded in many quarters as potentially one of the most significant to take place in Africa in modern times and its impact is already being felt elsewhere in the continent." As a sovereign state, Ghana immediately acted to hasten the move toward independence for other African states. Nkrumah declared that "the independence of Ghana is meaningless unless it is linked up with the total liberation of the African continent." Nkrumah was active in organizing various conferences to promote independence and cooperation among Africans. Numerous conferences were held in Accra, the capital of the new nation, which were attended by nationalist leaders from all over Africa. These conferences helped to make nationalism a force to be reckoned with by all colonial powers.

Nkrumah was also active in attempting to convince other leaders of the necessity for pan-African political and territorial unity. In 1958, Ghana and Guinea formed a political union, and in 1961 Mali joined the association. When Ghanaians approved the Republic Constitution in 1960 (which made Nkrumah president), they also approved the president's decision to surrender Ghana's sovereignty if the country ever joined a United States of Africa. Nkrumah was also involved in the formation of the Organization of African Unity (OAU) in 1963, although he was disappointed that most African leaders resisted full-blown unity.

Although Nkrumah's first years in power were marked by significant domestic and foreign policy achievements, his increasingly harsh authoritarian rule and frustration in achieving regional or continental unity brought forth increasingly vocal dissent from many groups and leaders who had opposed him in the preindependence elections. After assassination attempts in 1962 and 1964, Nkrumah attempted to increase security by dismissing several high-ranking police and military officials. With Nkrumah out of the country, the military staged a coup on February 23, 1966. Nkrumah spent the rest of his days in Conakry, Guinea, where he died in 1972. The military initiated a parliamentary government in 1969. Another military takeover followed, in 1972.

## Bibliography

Austin, Dennis. *Politics in Ghana, 1946-60.* London: Oxford University Press, 1964. This is a classic and detailed work on the politics of Ghanaian independence. The author deftly chronicles the emergence of the nationalist movement, the growth of opposition to the Convention People's Party, and the first three years of independence. The author was present during much of this period and is able to provide credible firsthand accounts of the nationalist movement.

Boahen, Adu. *Ghana: Evolution and Change in the Nineteenth and Twentieth Centuries.* London: Longman, 1975. This is a highly readable account of the major actors and events in Ghanaian history in the past two centuries. The author is a well-known Ghanaian historian, and this book is actually a compilation of lectures he prepared for secondary schools and colleges in Ghana. It provides an excellent overview and a good bibliography for those who want to read in more detail on the various topics covered in the text.

Crowder, Michael. *West Africa Under Colonial Rule.* Evanston, Ill.: Northwestern University Press, 1968. A comprehensive account of British, French, and German colonialism in West Africa from 1885 until the end of World War II. The best section of the book is the last, which discusses the emergence of nationalist organizations and the changed social and economic conditions wrought by World War II.

Fitch, Robert Beck, and Mary Oppenheimer. *Ghana: End of an Illusion.* New York: Monthly Review Press, 1966. This is an excellent, short account of the struggle for independence in Ghana and an explanation for the coup in 1966. The authors, writing from a Marxist perspective, contend that Nkrumah was hardly a revolutionary and in fact worked closely with British colonial authorities to ensure continuing neocolonial status for Ghana. They conclude that Nkrumah was easily overthrown because he lacked a firm base of support among the working class and peasantry.

Nkrumah, Kwame. *Ghana: The Autobiography of Kwame Nkrumah.* New York: Thomas Nelson and Sons, 1957. This is probably the best of Nkrumah's writings, which are fairly numerous. The autobiography provides an account of his early years, the chief thinkers who influenced his own political thought, the importance of pan-Africanism, and the struggle for independence.

Zolberg, Aristide. *Creating Political Order: The Party-States of West Africa.* Chicago: Rand McNally, 1966. This is an outstanding work which puts the independence of Ghana in context by comparing it to pre- and postindependence politics of four other West African states: Mali, Senegal, Guinea, and the Ivory Coast. The book's explanations for the emergence of dominant nationalist parties, the move toward one-party states, the sources of opposition to one-party rule, and Zolberg's characterization of these states as patrimonial remain timely and insightful.

*Catherine V. Scott*

## Cross-References

The Atlantic Charter Declares a Postwar Right of Self-Determination (1941), p. 584; The United Nations Adopts Its Charter (1945), p. 657; Algeria Gains Independence (1962), p. 1155; The Organization of African Unity Is Founded (1963), p. 1194; Nigeria Expels West African Migrant Workers (1983), p. 2180.

# THE UNITED NATIONS ADOPTS THE ABOLITION OF FORCED LABOR CONVENTION

*Categories of event:* Workers' rights and civil rights
*Time:* June 25, 1957
*Locale:* Geneva, Switzerland

*The Abolition of Forced Labor Convention encouraged countries affiliated with the International Labour Organisation (ILO) to outlaw forced labor as punishment for political dissent*

*Principal personages:*
> DAVID A. MORSE (1907-      ), the director-general of the International Labour Organisation
> TRYGVE LIE (1896-1968), the first secretary-general of the United Nations (1946-1952)
> DAG HAMMARSKJÖLD (1905-1961), the secretary-general of the United Nations (1953-1961)
> PAAL BERG (1873-1968), a member of the first ILO ad hoc Committee on Forced Labor
> SIR RAMASWAMI MUDALIAR (1887-1976), a member of the first ILO ad hoc Committee on Forced Labor
> FELIX FULGENCIO PALAVICINI (1881-1952), a member of the first ILO ad hoc Committee on Forced Labor
> ENRIQUE GARCIA SAYAN, a member of the first ILO ad hoc Committee on Forced Labor
> PAUL RUGGER, a member of the second ILO ad hoc Committee on Forced Labor
> CESAR CHARLONE, a member of the second ILO ad hoc Committee on Forced Labor
> T. P. B. GOONETILLEKE, a member of the second ILO ad hoc Committee on Forced Labor

## Summary of Event

Since the eighteenth century, human rights advocates have denounced human labor bondage and called for its abolition. Although slavery has been the most conspicuous form of bondage through the years, a new type of bondage known as forced labor has been widely practiced and widely condemned in the twentieth century. Slaves are considered chattel property, usually of individuals. Forced labor has been used as a punishment for the expression of political opinions which are not favored by existing authorities and for economic exploitation which benefits the state. Compulsory employment of indigenous peoples in colonial mines, so-called "correctional labor" for enemies of the people in revolutionary Russia, labor camps associated with Stalin's five-year plans in the 1930's, and the compulsory employment of conquered peoples of Europe to serve the Nazi war machine are examples of this type of bondage. Shortly after World War II, concerted efforts were made to outlaw forced labor throughout the world.

In November, 1947, the American Federation of Labor (AFL) proposed that the United Nations Economic and Social Council (ECOSOC) request that the International Labour Organisation (ILO) conduct a thorough survey of forced labor in U.N. member states and recommend a program to end it as part of the effort to foster human rights and to improve employment conditions. The AFL request pointed to the progress made in suppressing slavery and the slave trade and to the actions of the Nuremberg Tribunal in holding prominent Nazis accountable for abuse inflicted on hundreds of thousands of Europeans during the war. Although progress had been made, the AFL also noted that there were a number of similar cases which were cause for concern. Emphasis was placed on the detention of millions of prisoners of war as forced laborers. In addition, some members of the United Nations operated corrective labor camps that amounted to a form of state slavery where people were punished, often without due process, for expressing political opinions. The AFL resolution was passed.

On February 14, 1949, the ECOSOC took up the AFL resolution amid considerable controversy. The United States charged that the Soviet Union was the world's chief practitioner of forced labor, benefiting from the work of an estimated eight to fourteen million prisoners. The United States introduced a draft resolution calling on the ILO to look into the matter and report its findings to the ECOSOC. Predictably, the Soviet representative, S. K. Tsarapkin, took issue with these assertions and with the AFL resolution. He accused both the AFL and the United States of slandering the Soviet Union by adopting the tactics of the Nazi master propagandist, Joseph Goebbels, who used the frequently repeated "big lie" to distract his audience from the truth. Tsarapkin argued that forced labor was the basis of the capitalist economy and pointed to the discriminatory nature of the AFL report, which made no mention of U.S. penal labor, forced labor imposed on displaced persons, especially in Great Britain's occupation zone in Germany, or practices in Latin America, other capitalist countries, or colonies.

After rejecting a Soviet-sponsored draft resolution to establish an international commission to study worldwide working conditions, the ECOSOC invited the ILO to investigate the problem of forced labor and to determine its extent and instructed the secretary-general of the United Nations to cooperate closely with the ILO. In August, 1949, the United States presented a resolution to set up a commission of inquiry, but the majority of the ECOSOC decided that pursuing the investigation would be useless unless all governments, especially the major powers, were willing to cooperate. The Soviet Union and its allies made it very clear that they would not cooperate with this investigation, which they assumed was politically motivated and aimed primarily against them. After lengthy debate, the ECOSOC asked the secretary-general to ask member governments to agree to cooperate in an inquiry. By the end of 1949, thirty governments had issued statements pledging cooperation.

In 1950, the question of investigating forced labor was postponed once more. The Soviet Union was boycotting U.N. activities in protest of the denial of China's U.N. seat to the Chinese Communists after their ouster of the Chinese Nationalists from the mainland. The ECOSOC decided not to pursue the forced labor issue in the absence of the Soviet delegation. The ILO did begin discussions on establishing a commission of inquiry into the nature and extent of forced labor. A year later, on June 27, 1951, U.N. Secretary-General Trygve Lie and ILO Director-General David A. Morse jointly announced the formation of an ad hoc Committee on Forced Labor.

In October, 1951, the committee members began their work in Geneva. They announced their plans to formulate and distribute to all governments (not only United Nations and ILO members) a questionnaire asking about the use of punitive, educational, or corrective labor as well as other cases of compulsory work in each country. An April 1, 1952, deadline was set for the questionnaire's return. The committee announced its hopes to complete its work by the end of 1952 or early 1953.

On May 27, 1953, the committee presented its report to the ILO and the ECOSOC. Its investigation led it to the conclusion that systems of forced labor did exist in twenty-four countries or territories. Forced labor was used as a form of political coercion to "correct" political opinions and to promote the state's economic prosperity. This report was not discussed at the ECOSOC's summer, 1953, session. The United States called for its inclusion on the agenda for the fall session, arguing that the issue harmonized with the United Nations' determination to promote social and economic progress, to achieve international cooperation in solving problems, and to further human rights. The committee's report discussed not only isolated examples but systemic government action which produced wholesale suppression of human rights. The Soviet Union was identified as the chief culprit, using forced labor as political coercion and to promote its national economy. Georgi F. Saksin, the Soviet ECOSOC delegate, denounced the committee's work as a refusal to consider real forced labor, as it was content to slander the Soviet Union through errors, mistranslations, omissions, and other grave mistakes. After further heated exchanges, the ECOSOC delegates voted in favor of the United States' proposal to have the committee's report presented to the Third (Social, Humanitarian, and Cultural) Committee.

The next step in the slow process came a year later, when the Third Committee approved a resolution condemning forced labor and calling for continued efforts to end it. The resolution also called on the U.N. General Assembly to endorse an ECOSOC condemnation of systems of forced labor used as political coercion or punishment for holding or expressing political views. This resolution passed on December 14, 1954. Consideration of the forced labor issue seemed substantially intertwined with Cold War politics, as the working definition of forced labor was given as Soviet practice. Prompted by the Third Committee's resolution, the ECOSOC and the General Assembly condemned systems of forced labor and urged governments to reexamine laws and administrative practices to find the means to end this threat to basic human rights. U.N. Secretary-General Dag Hammarskjöld and the ILO director-general were asked to prepare a further report, to include any new information that had come to light since the 1953 report. The new report was to be completed by December, 1955, so that the director-general could present it to the ILO governing body and to the delegates to the 1956 and 1957 ILO Conference. In the meantime, the ECOSOC issued a condemnation of all forms of forced labor on the grounds that it contradicted the principles of the U.N. Charter and the Universal Declaration of Human Rights. The condemnation urged action to stop forced labor wherever it existed.

In June, 1956, delegates at the Thirty-ninth General Conference of the ILO heard the ad hoc committee's report. Delegates representing member governments, employers' organizations, and workers' organizations decided that there was sufficient cause to revise the 1930 Convention on Forced Labor. Subsequently, the ILO voted unanimously to draft a new convention to outlaw forced labor, concentration camps, and deportation of national minorities for political or other reasons. The new convention was scheduled for inclusion on the 1957 conference agenda. On another closely related front, on September 4, 1956, the United Nations adopted a supplement to the 1926 antislavery convention to abolish serfdom, debt bondage, bride price, inheritance of widows, and abuses linked to the adoption of children.

Finally, on June 25, 1957, the Abolition of Forced Labor Convention was ready for a vote at the Fortieth General Conference in Geneva. The ILO adopted three new international conventions: forced labor, weekly rest in commerce and offices, and protection of indigenous populations. The forced labor convention was approved 240-0, with the Soviet Union, which had joined the ILO in 1954, abstaining. The terms of the Abolition of Forced Labor Convention called on ratifying states to suppress and to eschew future use of forced labor for political reasons, economic development, labor discipline, punishment for participation in strikes or other labor disputes, or as a means of discrimination. Since the ILO pursued this convention on behalf of the United Nations, the June 25, 1957, vote committed the United Nations to work to end forced labor. The convention took effect on January 17, 1959.

## Impact of Event

The United Nations' moral power had been marshaled once more against those who would abuse their own populations. World "public opinion" has contributed to the increase in pressure on governments and agencies to end various forms of abuse. The United Nations, through its General Assembly and affiliated organizations, has done admirable work in assembling people from many lands and cultures ready to pass judgment on which actions are abusive. Theoretically, the Abolition of Forced Labor Convention was a landmark in human rights, but in practical terms the impact of the convention has been less clear.

In the late 1950's, the Soviet Union began to shut down its infamous "gulag" system. That action seems to be more domestically motivated than the result of world opinion. In 1956, Nikita Khrushchev delivered the famous "Secret Speech" to the Twentieth Party Congress. By denouncing some of the crimes of the Stalinist era, Khrushchev took a giant step toward a different Soviet society. Further steps were taken as prisoners were released and rehabilitated and as camps were closed. The Soviet Union has shown a capacity to brush off its critics' condemnations, but during the Khrushchev era there was a short period when some Soviet policies harmonized with the worldwide drive for human rights.

Given the energetic American promotion of the forced labor issue in the late 1940's and the 1950's, one might erroneously conclude that the United States would be one of the first states to ratify the Abolition of Forced Labor Convention. For a variety of reasons, the United States consistently opposed most international human rights agreements. In 1963, President John F. Kennedy changed the decade-old policy against ratification of human rights conventions when he sent three conventions to the Senate for consideration. The three were the Supplementary Convention on the Abolition of Slavery, the Slave Trade, and Institutions and Practices Similar to Slavery (opened for signature on September 7, 1956), the Abolition of Forced Labor Convention (signed June 25, 1957), and the Convention on the Political Rights of Women (opened for signature on December 20, 1952). Four years elapsed before the Senate held the first hearing on any of the three conventions; on the recommendation of the American Bar Association, it ratified only the slavery convention.

Although more than one hundred states had ratified the Abolition of Forced Labor Convention by the early 1970's, the convention has not been the final word on forced labor or produced its complete abolition. One of the byproducts of the 1948 Universal Declaration of Human Rights was a charter outlining states' obligations regarding human rights. In 1966, the U.N. General Assembly approved the final text for a Covenant on Civil and Political Rights which asserted, among other rights, the right to life, freedom from torture and cruel punishment, and freedom from slavery and forced or compulsory labor.

International agreements remain valid only so long as the parties restrain themselves. Several examples show that while forced labor became less prevalent, it did not completely vanish. Forced labor was a crucial feature of the Cambodian "killing fields." After unification in 1975, Vietnam confined some of its opponents in reeducation camps that featured compulsory work designed to instruct people in the errors of their political and social thinking. In the fall of 1991, United States Secretary of State James Baker used language reminiscent of the 1950's disputes between the United States and the Soviet Union to characterize Chinese forced labor policies for punishment of political dissidents and for the economic benefit of the state.

## Bibliography

Barros, James, ed. *The United Nations: Past, Present, and Future.* New York: Free Press, 1972. This collection of seven essays analyzes the various components of the United Nations, emphasizing the international body's capacity for survival and its superiority over the League of Nations.

Commission to Study the Organization of Peace. *The United Nations and Human Rights.* Dobbs Ferry, N.Y.: Oceana, 1968. A sympathetic report on the theory and practice of the pursuit of human rights through U.N. auspices from 1945 to the mid-1960's.

Coyle, David Cushman. *The United Nations and Its Works.* New York: Columbia University Press, 1969. A structural account of the United Nations' agencies and actions through the formative years and the years of dramatic expansion.

Fernbach, Alfred. *Soviet Coexistence Strategy: A Case Study of Experience in the International Labor Organization.* Washington, D.C.: Public Affairs Press, 1960. Very useful in sorting out the various Soviet stances through the 1950's.

Jacobson, Harold K. "The USSR and the ILO." *International Organization* 14 (September, 1960): 402-428. Compares nicely with Fernbach, although it does not offer similar detail.

Jenks, C. W. *Social Justice in the Law of Nations: The ILO Impact After Fifty Years.* Oxford, England: Oxford University Press, 1970. An informative and engaging account of ILO efforts to shape labor and human rights policies from the end of World War I.

Robertson, A. H. *Human Rights in the World.* 2d ed. New York: St. Martin's Press, 1982. Astonishing in its scope, this volume surveys and appraises the human rights efforts of the United Nations and various regional organizations. Very good for providing fundamental bases for those beginning to explore human rights questions.

Rubinstein, Alvin Z. *The Soviets in International Organizations: Changing Policy Toward Developing Countries, 1953-1963.* Princeton, N.J.: Princeton University Press, 1964. A useful supplement to a study of Soviet foreign policy, very detailed but short on historical perspective on motivation.

Sohn, Louis B., and Thomas Buergenthal. *International Protection of Human Rights.* Indianapolis: Bobbs-Merrill, 1973. Massive tome developed as a textbook but very useful as a source for detailed discussion of specific human rights cases.

*Larry Thornton*

## Cross-References

Reformers Expose Atrocities Against Congolese Laborers (1903), p. 13; The International Labour Organisation Is Established (1919), p. 281; The League of Nations Adopts the International Slavery Convention (1926), p. 436; Nazi Concentration Camps Go into Operation (1933), p. 491; Stalin Begins Purging Political Opponents (1934), p. 503; Ethiopia Abolishes Slavery (1942), p. 607; Nazi War Criminals Are Tried in Nuremberg (1945), p. 667; The United Nations Adopts the Universal Declaration of Human Rights (1948), p. 789; The United Nations Amends Its International Slavery Convention (1953), p. 902; The United Nations Sets Rules for the Treatment of Prisoners (1955), p. 935; Khrushchev Implies That Stalinist Excesses Will Cease (1956), p. 952; The United Nations Issues a Declaration Against Torture (1975), p. 1847.

# THE WOLFENDEN REPORT RECOMMENDS DECRIMINALIZING HOMOSEXUAL ACTS

*Categories of event:* Gay persons' rights and civil rights
*Time:* September 4, 1957
*Locale:* London, England

*The growing public belief after World War II that the state should not legislate morality led the British parliament to decriminalize consensual sexual activity in private between adults*

*Principal personages:*

SIR JOHN WOLFENDEN (1906-1985), chair of the Home Office's departmental committee on homosexual offenses and prostitution

LEO ABSE (1917-    ), a Labour member of Parliament (1958-1987) who sponsored the Sexual Offences Act of 1967

OSCAR WILDE (1854-1900), a popular playwright and short-story writer whose trials for homosexual offenses in 1895 produced a public sensation

RADCLYFFE HALL (1883-1943), an English novelist and poet whose novel *The Well of Loneliness* (1928) was the first major work of English fiction to deal openly with lesbianism

ALFRED KINSEY (1894-1956), an American zoologist and author of influential studies of human sexuality

HAVELOCK ELLIS (1859-1939), a pioneer in the scientific study of sexuality, an English physician who wrote many widely read books

EDWARD, THIRD BARON MONTAGU OF BEAULIEU (1926-    ), a nobleman whose trial for homosexual acts in 1954 led to the creation of the Wolfenden Committee

JAMES ANDERTON (1932-    ), the chief constable of the Greater Manchester Police Force; the leading exponent of a narrow interpretation of the British homosexuality laws

## Summary of Event

The Wolfenden Report of 1957, which recommended that homosexual activities between adults in private should be decriminalized, was the result of a gradual change in public attitudes about whether the state should legislate private morality and about whether homosexuality was a sin, a sickness, or a regular facet of human behavior. The report reflected the broad change in sexual morality that occurred during the twentieth century and that began in the 1890's.

In England, public acts of indecency between males had always been punishable in common law, and church law had forbidden "the abominable vice" of buggery or sodomy (anal intercourse between man and woman, man and man, or man and beast). During the Reformation, Parliament transferred buggery from ecclesiastical jurisdiction to that of the state and made it punishable by death. Executions were rare, however, and in 1861, as part of a general reform of the criminal statutes, imprisonment for between ten years and life replaced the death penalty. In the 1880's and afterwards, the law against homosexuality was tightened. The Criminal Law Amendment Act of 1885 provided up to two years' hard labor for acts of indecency between men in private as well as public. The Vagrancy Act of 1898, which forbade importuning for immoral purposes, was applied exclusively against homosexuals. Although these laws were less severe than the sodomy law, which carried a maximum sentence of life imprisonment, they were routinely enforced to the hilt, while the sodomy law usually was not.

During the same period, partly as a reaction to these legal developments, the idea of homosexuality began to take shape. Oscar Wilde's trials of 1895 were of crucial importance in developing the homosexual image. Wilde, famous as a wit, playwright, and poet, was caught in a homosexual relationship and was sentenced to two years at hard labor under the Criminal Law Amendment Act of 1885. Although his treatment was intended to demarcate acceptable and unacceptable behavior and to discourage others from similar behavior, it also prompted men attracted to members of the same sex to think about their own desires and to come to a clearer understanding of their own identity as homosexuals. It had been thought that some men were inclined to a greater or lesser degree to sodomitical acts and that such acts were sins. Attitudes were changing toward the belief that some men were by nature exclusively attracted to their own sex and that their sexual attraction was the center of a homosexual life-style. The very word "homosexual" had been invented by a Hungarian physician in 1869 and popularized by the English sex researcher Havelock Ellis in the 1890's. Ellis stressed the ideas that homosexuality was a personality condition rather than a sin and that there was a continuum between normal and abnormal sexual behavior. Ellis' dispassionate writings brought respectability and objectivity to the study of nonstandard sexual activities.

This change of attitude toward homosexuality resulted on one hand in a greater degree of sympathy. A few secret organizations were founded in the 1890's to help homosexuals in trouble with the law, and the British Society for the Study of Sex Psychology was started in 1914 to work for legal reform and a more tolerant attitude. During the 1920's, British reformers, including Havelock Ellis, participated in the World League for Sexual Reform, which espoused a platform of liberal reforms including gender equality, the reform of marriage, divorce, and abortion laws, improved sex education, and the decriminalization of consensual sex acts between adults. On the other hand, other pressure groups and reform societies such as the Alliance of Purity, the White Cross, and the Public Morality Council used the existing laws to repress behavior that they considered immoral or degenerate. They enrolled young men in youth clubs, published purity literature, censored plays and films, and patrolled the streets in order to catch prostitutes and homosexuals soliciting sexual partners. As a result, female prostitution became more discreet, and male homosexuals were more likely to be arrested, especially because the Public Morality Council focused increasingly on catching homosexuals. At the same time, more voices calling for greater tolerance and freedom for homosexuals began to be heard.

In contrast, the criminal statutes ignored lesbianism. When it was proposed in 1921 to legislate explicitly against lesbian activities, the legal establishment convinced Parliament that to do so would only teach otherwise ignorant women that such sexual acts were possible. Not until the publication and banning of Radclyffe Hall's novel *The Well of Loneliness* in 1928 did lesbianism receive widespread publicity. Hall, herself a lesbian, dealt with the subject in an open and sympathetic manner. The novel was declared obscene and its publication forbidden. Intended, like the Wilde case, to discourage homosexuality, the Radclyffe Hall case brought much publicity to the novel, informed women of theretofore unknown options, and failed to suppress the work itself, since it was easy to smuggle into Britain editions published in Paris.

The temper of the times changed after World War II. The British public in 1945 voted to create a welfare state, and concern with family, procreative, and sexual matters was a large part of welfare. Social workers, anthropologists, and psychologists investigated numerous aspects of sexual life, including homosexuality. The studies of the American researcher Alfred Kinsey, *Sexual Behavior in the Human Male* (1948) and *Sexual Behavior in the Human Female* (1953), continued Havelock Ellis' work of undermining the idea that homosexuality was unnatural or abnormal. Simultaneously, the number of homosexual offenses increased between 1938 and the middle 1950's, a rise caused partly by the postwar emphasis on domesticity, partly by Home Secretary Sir David Maxwell-Fyffe's extreme antihomosexual beliefs, and partly by the antihomosexual fears raised by Cold War McCarthyism. (The last concern related to the fact that several spies who defected to the Soviet Union were homosexuals.) These feelings came to a head in 1954 with the sensational trial for homosexual acts of Lord Montagu of Beaulieu and Peter Wildeblood, diplomatic correspondent of the influential *Daily Mail* newspaper. The trial convinced many that what the men had done had harmed no one and that existing legislation could not prevent homosexual activity.

In response to the debate that the trial had sparked, the government created a committee in 1954, chaired by Sir John Wolfenden, a distinguished university vice-chancellor, to study the entire question of legal sanctions against prostitution and homosexuality. Its charge was to examine how the laws operated, not how to liberalize them, but its report, published in 1957, proposed bringing the law of homosexuality into congruence with the changed conditions of postwar society. The basic position of the Wolfenden Report was that the purpose of the criminal law was to preserve public order and decency and to protect the weak from exploitation, rather than to interfere with private life in the interests of imposing a specific code of moral behavior. Thus it distinguished between private and public behavior. The state could, and indeed should, regulate public behavior such as solicitation for prostitution and street offenses, but should decriminalize private behavior such as homosexual activity between consenting adults.

The committee's clinical, objective, and pragmatic approach to a controversial topic was persuasive. Public opinion polls at the time indicated that between 40 and 50 percent of those asked approved of the recommendations relating to prostitution. Leading newspapers such as *The Times* and the *Daily Telegraph* endorsed the report, as did religious leaders of the Church of England and the Free Churches. The *Daily Mirror*, which had the largest circulation of any newspaper in the world, proclaimed "Don't Be Shocked by this Report. It's the Truth. It's the Answer. IT'S LIFE." The strongest reservations had to do with the report's recommendations about homosexuality. A substantial body of public opinion feared that relaxation of the law would encourage homosexuals to convert people away from heterosexuality.

## Impact of Event

The Wolfenden Report's recommendations on prostitution were implemented in the Street Offences Act of 1959, which increased fines and imprisonment for street solicitation but which permitted private prostitution agencies. Its recommendations about decriminalizing homosexual acts, however, had to wait for a decade. British medical thinking viewed homosexuality as a sickness, and there was considerable popular opposition to homosexuals; in a 1965 public opinion poll, more than 90 percent of the sample viewed homosexuality as an illness. Nevertheless, attitudes began to swing towards decriminalization. The Homosexual Law Reform Society was founded in 1958 to lobby for implementation of the Wolfenden recommendations, and public opinion came to favor reform. Only 25 percent favored homosexual reform in a 1957 opinion poll, but 63 percent favored it in 1965. The changing political climate also contributed to the eventual coming of reform. The Labour Party under Prime Minister Harold Wilson, which was in power from 1964 to 1970, was willing to allow its supporters to vote their consciences, and thus a cross-party coalition of reformers emerged.

Labour politician Leo Abse took the lead in the parliamentary pressure to modify the law. Abse, who had deep interests in both the human psychological makeup and the varieties of human sexual behavior, sponsored legislation that Parliament passed as the Sexual Offences Act of 1967, which wrote into law the Wolfenden Report's ideas about decriminalizing private adult male activities. It did not legalize homosexuality but merely exempted some activities from criminal penalties. Both the armed forces and the merchant navy, which punished homosexuals in their ranks, were excluded from the measure's purview. Behavior deemed to be against public decency, such as solicitation in public lavatories and cruising areas, remained illegal, as did the publishing of homosexual contact advertisements. Much, then, depended upon local police attitudes. Although what men did in private became their own business, the number of prosecutions for public indecency tripled between 1967 and 1976. James Anderton, chief constable of Manchester, was a leading exponent of the view that the Sexual Offences Act should be interpreted narrowly and enforced strictly. Anderton later charged that the spread of the AIDS virus was the result of "degenerate conduct."

Thus the Wolfenden Report of 1957 and its implementation in 1967 represented a relatively limited reform. The reform only freed consensual behavior among adults in private from the threat of legal prosecution, thereby relieving homosexuals from fears of blackmail. The reform certainly reflected the fact that public opinion generally had become much more tolerant of such activity. The increase in prosecutions for public indecency, however, together with the example of the gay rights movement in the United States, led to the creation of the British gay rights movement in the early 1970's. Yet the full, open equality that activists in the gay rights movement wished for still remained unreached. Section 28 of the Local Government Act of 1988 reflected the limited status that homosexuals had under the law in Great Britain. That measure, passed as part of Prime Minister Margaret Thatcher's policy of reducing the influence of the central government in molding behavior, made it unlawful for local government to "intentionally promote homosexuality" and to treat homosexual relationships as the equivalent of stable, married family life. The Wolfenden Report and its implementation thus legalized private homosexual acts, but British law and society still denied that lesbian and male homosexual life-styles had public merit.

## Bibliography

Bartlett, C. J. *A History of Postwar Britain, 1945-1974.* London: Longman, 1977. This impartial account of Great Britain's history since the end of World War II focuses on political and economic history, not social developments, but includes an extensive bibliography.

Havighurst, Alfred F. *Twentieth-Century Britain.* Evanston, Ill.: Row, Peterson, 1962. Like Bartlett's, this book is political and economic history rather than social history. It provides the context necessary to understand the events of the period.

Hopkins, Harry. *The New Look: A Social History of the Forties and Fifties in Britain.* Boston: Houghton Mifflin, 1964. Written by a journalist, this chatty, impressionistic study of social history describes the changing attitudes toward sexual mores after World War II.

Hyde, H. Montgomery. *The Other Love: An Historical and Contemporary Survey of Homosexuality in Britain.* London: Granada, 1972. A historical survey, written for a popular audience and focusing mainly on personalities.

_____, ed. *The Trials of Oscar Wilde.* New York: Dover, 1962. Based on the transcripts of Oscar Wilde's three trials for homosexual offenses, this well-written and fascinating work covers Wilde's own life and experiences in the late Victorian homosexual underworld, the legal background to the laws governing homosexuality, and the social and political attitudes of the times that the trial revealed. Essential reading for an understanding of the subject.

Pearsall, Ronald. *The Worm in the Bud: The World of Victorian Sexuality.* London: Weidenfeld & Nicolson, 1969. A well-written study of Victorian attitudes and practices related to sexual behavior. One of the first attempts to deal seriously and in a scholarly way with the topic, this book is anecdotal rather than analytical, but it is definitely worth reading.

Weeks, Jeffrey. *Coming Out: Homosexual Politics in Britain from the Nineteenth Century to the Present.* London: Quartet, 1977. A survey of homosexuality as a legal and political issue.

——————. *Sex, Politics, and Society: The Regulation of Sexuality Since 1800.* 2d ed. London: Longman, 1989. Solidly documented, clearly written, thorough, and impartial. Surveys social attitudes about several topics relating to sexuality, such as marriage, women's roles, prostitution, homosexuality, and sexual morality, and analyzes the changing political responses to those topics. This book is the beginning point for any historical study of the topic.

Wildeblood, Peter. *Against the Law.* London: Weidenfeld & Nicolson, 1955. The story of the crucial legal case that precipitated the commissioning of the Wolfenden Report, told from the viewpoint of one of the participants.

*D. G. Paz*

### Cross-References

The American Civil Liberties Union Is Founded (1920), p. 327; The Civil Rights Act of 1957 Creates the Commission on Civil Rights (1957), p. 997; Riots Against Police Harassment Launch the Gay Rights Movement (1969), p. 1479; A NIMH Task Force Recommends Legalizing Homosexual Behavior (1969), p. 1497; Homosexuality Is Removed from the APA List of Psychiatric Disorders (1973), p. 1741; The Civil Service Decides That Gays Are Fit for Public Service (1975), p. 1801; The U.S. Court of Appeals Affirms the Navy's Ban on Homosexuality (1981), p. 2124; Government Mandates Collection of Data on Crimes Against Homosexuals (1988), p. 2364.

# THE CIVIL RIGHTS ACT OF 1957 CREATES THE COMMISSION ON CIVIL RIGHTS

*Category of event:* Civil rights
*Time:* September 9, 1957
*Locale:* Washington, D.C.

*Congress, with bipartisan support, voted to create a Commission on Civil Rights with power to investigate and issue reports on violations of voting and other constitutional rights*

*Principal personages:*

LYNDON B. JOHNSON (1908-1973), the Senate majority leader
DWIGHT D. EISENHOWER (1890-1969), the president of the United States (1953-1961)
RICHARD M. NIXON (1913-     ), the vice president of the United States
HERBERT BROWNELL (1904-     ), the attorney general of the United States (1953-1958)
RICHARD RUSSELL (1897-1971), a Democrat from Georgia who led opposition to the bill
JACOB JAVITS (1904-1986), a Republican senator from New York
SAM RAYBURN (1882-1961), the Speaker of the House of Representatives

## Summary of Event

For its first three years, the administration of Dwight D. Eisenhower was silent on the civil rights issue. The president believed in limiting the powers of government and did not support integration. Even after the Supreme Court ruled in *Brown v. Board of Education* (1954) that legal segregation violated the Fourteenth Amendment's guarantee of equal protection of the law, Eisenhower argued that he should not force change upon the South. He believed that white attitudes in the South could not be changed by Supreme Court decisions and that he, as president, should not enforce laws that did not reflect majority opinion. Few members of the White House staff appeared aware of conditions in the southern states. Eisenhower, for example, expressed surprise when he was told only seven thousand out of nine hundred thousand African Americans in Mississippi were qualified to vote under that state's registration requirements.

The 1956 presidential election changed Eisenhower's mind. He received almost half of the votes of African Americans, a higher share than any Republican presidential candidate since 1932, and saw a chance to increase his party's electoral support from that community in succeeding elections. In his 1957 State of the Union address, he called for passage of a voting rights package that included creation of a bipartisan commission on civil rights. On March 9, Attorney General Herbert Brownell presented a four-point program to Eisenhower's cabinet that outlined the commission's responsibilities and structure, added an assistant attorney general for civil rights to the Justice Department, authorized the attorney general to seek injunctions from federal judges to prohibit civil rights violations, and allowed the attorney general or aggrieved individuals to sue in federal court if voting rights were denied. Recognizing that white southerners would not be likely to vote to condemn their own, Brownell's proposal called for trials without juries for defiance of the law. The cabinet agreed to send this proposal to Congress.

The House of Representatives quickly passed the four-point program by a vote of 282 to 226. The Senate had not passed a civil rights bill since 1875, and southerners stood prepared to filibuster yet another proposal to death. Obstructing passage was Rule 22, calling for a two-thirds vote of the entire Senate to vote to end any debate. A bipartisan attempt to change the rules failed, though proponents argued that the new Senate was not bound by old rules. Vice President Richard Nixon supported this view, suggesting that any rule by one Congress that tried to bind a future Congress was unconstitutional. The Senate voted fifty-five to thirty-eight not to change Rule 22.

Getting the bill to the floor required the adroit leadership of Democratic majority leader Lyndon Baines Johnson. Normally, a voting rights bill would have ended up in the Senate Judiciary Committee, chaired by Mississippi Democrat James Eastland, an enemy of civil rights legislation. To avoid certain death in that committee, Johnson allowed the House bill to be brought directly to the floor for debate and amendments. To gain Southern support, he argued that some bill was necessary and that a weak bill, such as the one offered by the Eisenhower Administration, was preferable to a more radical one that might be proposed if the current legislation were defeated.

Southerners in the Senate tried to weaken the House bill still further. Richard Russell led the opposition. He attacked the section of the bill authorizing the government to seek federal court injunctions to enforce equal rights under the Fourteenth Amendment. Russell said this would allow use of military force to integrate public schools, a question very much on the minds of southerners after the Brown decision. Russell met with Eisenhower to discuss his views. He raised the issue of local control of education and the threat to that American tradition posed by the 1957 legislation. Eisenhower apparently found Russell's argument compelling, as he later told a news conference that he would like to see that part of the bill removed. Some Senate liberals, led by Jacob Javits (R-N.Y.), fought the change. Javits argued that all the bill would require was federal enforcement of constitutional rights being denied by states. The Senate voted fifty-two to thirty-eight to drop this provision and weaken the legislation.

To soften the House proposal even more, Southern senators presented an amendment demanding jury trials for individuals charged with contempt of court in civil rights cases. Republican supporters of the original bill objected, pointing out that jury lists were usually compiled from voting registration lists, producing virtually all-white juries. Few white southerners, it was thought, would convict one of their own in a civil rights case. Judges on the federal bench would more likely be objective in their decisions. This section had to stand unchanged or the law would be meaningless. In an unusual coalition, northern liberals who believed that the right to a jury trial was as important as the right to vote supported their conservative colleagues from the South and defended the amendment. Lyndon Johnson voted for the change, arguing that Americans would demand jury trials. Republican leader William Knowland of California denounced the amendment after consultation with the White House, saying it would kill the voting rights bill. With support from Democratic senators from all sections of the country, the Senate voted to accept the amendment.

At the legislation now read, jury trials would be allowed in criminal contempt cases where large fines or jail sentences were possible. In cases of civil contempt where the court was not asked to punish but only to order compliance with federal law, a judge could convict a defendant without a jury. The Senate approved the amended bill on August 7 by a margin of seventy-two to eighteen, despite a twenty-hour filibuster by Senator Strom Thurmond (D-S.C.). Thurmond's speech was not supported by any other southerner and had no effect on the result, though it did earn for him the record for making the longest single speech in the history of the Senate.

Because of major differences in the House and Senate versions, a conference committee made up of members of both houses was appointed to negotiate a compromise. Both sides agreed to minor changes as Speaker of the House Sam Rayburn (D-Tex.) used his great influence to convince colleagues to accept the much weaker Senate version. The conference agreement gave federal judges the right to decide whether a jury trial would be needed in cases concerning voting rights infractions. A maximum penalty of three hundred dollars and forty-five days in jail was imposed in nonjury cases. If there was a jury trial, the maximum penalty was increased to one thousand dollars and six months in prison. The only sections remaining from the original bill were the creation of a commission on civil rights and establishment of a civil rights division in the Justice Department. On August 29, both the House and the Senate passed the conference bill and sent it to the president for his signature.

Some civil rights leaders called upon Eisenhower to reject the weak bill, but the National Association for the Advancement of Colored People and the Leadership Conference on Civil Rights, the two largest and most-respected civil rights groups, argued that any bill was better than none. Martin Luther King, Jr., who had recently achieved prominence as leader of the Montgomery bus boycott in Alabama, talked with Vice President Nixon and urged him to encourage his boss to sign the legislation. On September 9, in the midst of the school crisis in Little Rock, Arkansas, when white mobs rioted to prevent integration of the public school system, Eisenhower signed the bill and the Commission on Civil Rights came into existence.

## Impact of Event

The Commission on Civil Rights had power to study complaints and issue reports on violations of voting rights but could not force states to change registration procedures. Hence, two years after Congress passed the law, most African Americans in the southern states were still unable to vote. Still, the five-person commission played a valuable role in exposing racist practices used by southern states to maintain a segregated society. Armed with the responsibility of appraising federal authority in promoting equal protection of the laws in education, housing, employment, public transportation, and the administration of justice, the commission issued a series of key reports outlining methods used to discriminate by race. Information developed by staff investigators was later used to promote passage of major civil rights laws such as the Public Accommodations Act of 1964 and the Voting Rights Act of 1965.

The commission issued several key reports between 1959 and 1965. The first study called for major changes in voting registration laws. It called for public inspection of all voting records, necessary since many local registrars in Mississippi and Alabama refused to allow anyone to see registration lists. The commission asked for power to issue subpoenas when records were denied to investigators, a power never granted, and called upon Congress to make it a federal crime for states to refuse to fulfill their registration responsibilities, a suggestion adopted by Congress in 1965. A fourth point, that the president be given power to appoint registrars who would register voters until states could show their procedures were nondiscriminatory, also became part of federal law. In education, the commission called for an annual school census to show the race of each student and offered to provide help to communities developing desegregation plans.

In 1961, the commission presented a massive five-volume report on voting rights, education, employment, housing, and justice. It called for a ban on any voter qualifications other than age and length of residency and for the elimination of literacy tests, the major obstacle to voter registration. Instead of demanding that registrants pass difficult examinations based on knowledge of the Constitution, the commission recommended that a sixth-grade education be recognized as proof of literacy. Concerning education, the commission's main advice was for Congress to cut 50 percent of federal aid to schools in states refusing to end segregation. The commission also recommended that Congress establish a permanent committee on equal employment opportunity to enforce nondiscriminatory hiring practices for the federal government, the armed forces, and all businesses receiving government contracts and grants. To encourage equal opportunity in housing, the commission asked the president to issue an executive order outlawing discrimination in the sale of homes built with federal mortgage insurance or loan guarantees. On the administration of justice, the report asked Congress to consider federal grants to local police departments to raise the racial sensitivity and professional quality of police officers.

All the above recommendations, except for the last, were put into effect by 1965. Even the last proposal ultimately became part of federal law, though not until 1969, after four years of urban riots which cost the lives of more than three hundred people. Despite its limited powers, the commission deserves credit for exposing many illegal practices by southern states and for suggesting remedies to discriminatory treatment that found expression in significant civil rights legislation.

## Bibliography

Ambrose, Stephen E. *The President.* Vol. 2 in *Eisenhower.* New York: Simon & Schuster, 1984. This lengthy biography contains an analysis of Eisenhower's racial views and provides a detailed account of his changing attitude toward voting rights and the 1957 bill. There is a detailed bibliography and an index.

Congressional Quarterly. *Congress and the Nation, 1945-1964.* Washington, D.C.: Congressional Quarterly Service, 1965. A useful reference to the legislative history of the 1957 civil rights bill and ensuing laws. It has summaries of major compromises, an analysis of House and Senate voting, and a guide to legal terms. Contains summaries of reports issued by the Commission on Civil Rights. No bibliography, but has an index.

Conkin, Paul K. *Big Daddy from the Pedernales: Lyndon Baines Johnson.* Boston: Twayne, 1986. One of the most objective Johnson biographies. Describes his changing racial views and their effect on his political career. Has a brief discussion of his influence on the compromises necessary to achieve passage of the 1957 law. Shows the difficulty of persuading southerners to accept a bill. Has a detailed bibliography and an index.

Evans, Rowland, and Robert Novak. *Lyndon B. Johnson: The Exercise of Power, A Political Biography.* New York: New American Library, 1966. A behind-the-scenes view of Johnson's great abilities and effectiveness as Democratic majority leader. Has a complete description of the compromises involved in attaining passage of the 1957 act. An interesting summary of the legislative debate, providing information on reasons for Johnson's final victory. No bibliography.

Lewis, Anthony. *Portrait of a Decade: The Second American Revolution.* New York: Random House, 1964. Assesses the decade from 1954 to 1964. Has a brief discussion of the 1957 debate and the influence of the Commission on Civil Rights. Provides some information on the commission's reports. Index and brief bibliography.

Sundquist, James L. *Politics and Policy: The Eisenhower, Kennedy, and Johnson Years.* Washington, D.C.: Brookings Institution, 1968. One of the few books to discuss all the civil rights legislation of the era. Looks at the views of all the participants, analyzes their contributions, and assesses the value of the laws passed by Congress. A unique look at how things get done in Washington. Has a bibliography and an index.

White, William S. *The Professional: Lyndon B. Johnson.* Boston: Houghton Mifflin, 1964. A journalist's account of Johnson's Senate career. The last chapter tells the story of Johnson's involvement in achieving passage of a weakened but still important civil rights bill. No bibliography or index.

*Leslie V. Tischauser*

## Cross-References

*Brown v. Board of Education* Ends Public School Segregation (1954), p. 913; Parks

# EISENHOWER SENDS TROOPS TO
# LITTLE ROCK, ARKANSAS

*Category of event:* Racial and ethnic rights
*Time:* September 25, 1957
*Locale:* Little Rock, Arkansas

*Integration of Central High School became the first major test of civil rights after the 1954 Supreme Court decision banning segregation*

*Principal personages:*
DWIGHT D. EISENHOWER (1890-1969), the thirty-fourth president of the United States (1953-1961)
EARL WARREN (1891-1974), the chief justice of the United States Supreme Court
ORVAL FAUBUS (1910-     ), the governor of Arkansas during the Little Rock school integration crisis in 1957
HERBERT BROWNELL (1904-     ), the United States attorney general in the Eisenhower Administration
WOODROW WILSON MANN, the mayor of Little Rock during the crisis who called for federal intervention

## Summary of Event

Dwight D. Eisenhower was president during one of the most critical events concerning school integration in the South. Eisenhower was not a strong advocate of civil rights and neither stressed it in his presidential campaign in 1952 nor emphasized it in his domestic policies as President of the United States. His predecessor, President Harry S. Truman, was responsible and best known in civil rights circles for integrating the armed forces by executive order during World War II. African Americans had fought for the United States in the past but had to do so in segregated units of the military. In addition, while African Americans were allowed to be first-class citizens on the battlefield, they were second-class citizens in segregated units and at home after they returned from the battlefield. In the South, they could not vote and were confronted with a host of segregation laws that denied them basic citizenship rights guaranteed under the Fourteenth Amendment to the U.S. Constitution.

In the 1952 presidential campaign, the civil rights platform of the Republicans was similar to that of the Democrats, which called for limited civil rights. Eisenhower, a Republican, was not a strong proponent of racial desegregation in schools. Several factors suggested the reasons that Eisenhower had this attitude toward racial desegregation. First, Eisenhower's popularity as a general in the war carried over into the presidential campaign and election of 1952, in which he garnered 55 percent of the popular vote and 442 electoral votes, of which 57 were from the South. African

Americans were not considered a critical constituency, since only 27 percent of them voted for Eisenhower. In 1956, Eisenhower received a larger percentage of the African-American vote, although he remained fairly passive in the area of civil rights and racial equality.

Second, Eisenhower believed that southern states should voluntarily promote racial equality, and that federal intervention should only be used as a last resort. This explained, to some extent, his hesitancy to intervene in state matters. Eisenhower believed that the use of federal law and its imposition on southern states would set back the cause of improved race relations.

Third, Eisenhower believed that support for a civil rights bill emphasizing voting rights for African Americans was more important than one imposing racial desegregation on southern schools. The president took the position that if African Americans had the right to vote, the quality of life in other areas would eventually improve as well. Emphasizing suffrage also reinforced Eisenhower's incremental philosophy on racial equality, rationalizing this facet as a precursor for civil rights. Consequently, it is somewhat easier to understand Eisenhower's support for the Civil Rights Act of 1957, since this act contained strong voting-rights provisions. His support for this act had political motivations as well, in light of the Republican Party's inroads with the African-American vote in the 1956 presidential election.

Notwithstanding these reservations in the area of civil rights generally and racial desegregation of public schools in particular, officials in the Eisenhower Administration were put under increasing pressure to take action regarding racial equality as the result of two events. One was the 1954 decision of the U.S. Supreme Court in the case of *Brown v. the Board of Education of Topeka, Kansas*. The Court, headed by Chief Justice Earl Warren (ironically an Eisenhower Republican appointee), ruled that separate facilities for whites and African Americans were "inherently unequal" and ordered racial integration of public schools "with all deliberate speed." This landmark case was a challenge to the "separate but equal" doctrine that was legitimized in the 1896 Supreme Court case of *Plessy v. Ferguson*. This case had rationalized racial segregation by reasoning that it was perfectly legal to have separate facilities for whites and for African Americans as long as the facilities were "equal." This meant that African Americans had an inferior legal and social status in every facet of civil and human rights.

The second event that put additional pressure on Eisenhower to act was the crisis brewing in Little Rock, Arkansas, in the wake of the Brown decision on school integration. The school board of Little Rock was in the process of voluntarily complying with the Brown decision but met local political resistance and a court challenge. After a Federal District Court judge ordered integration plans of Central High School to proceed, resistance mounted and tension increased as a result of actions of white segregationists and threats of mob violence as the opening day of school on September 3, 1957, approached. The mayor of Little Rock, Woodrow Wilson Mann, called the White House on one occasion and telegraphed a message on another, urging President Eisenhower to take immediate action by sending federal troops to quell the rising racial tensions surrounding the imminent integration of Central High School. Arkansas Governor Orval Faubus contributed to this tension and helped to appease segregationists by noting an increase in the number of gun sales in Little Rock, associating such sales with imminent violence. This reasoning was used by a Pulaski County court to issue a temporary injunction to halt the desegregation of the high school. School officials, in conjunction with the National Association for the Advancement of Colored People (NAACP), urged the District Court to issue an injunction against all parties attempting to interfere with the desegregation plan. A federal judge concurred and ordered desegregation plans to proceed. Not to be out-flanked, the governor then mobilized segments of the Arkansas National Guard to block physically the entrance of African-American children on school day. To avoid a violent confrontation between opposing forces, the school board rescinded its plans to integrate Little Rock schools, seeking further instruction from the District Court judge.

Although he was sympathetic to the governor's predicament, it was Eisenhower's position in this continuing crisis that Faubus eventually would have to comply with the orders of the federal court. A meeting was set up between Faubus and Eisen-hower, with Eisenhower requesting advance assurances that Faubus would comply with federal court orders. Faubus gave assurances that he would not resist further attempts at desegregation but later betrayed the president. Faubus publicly disavowed any statements attributed to him that he would comply with the president's wishes regarding removal of the troops from the high school or changing their orders to allow African-American children to enter and integrate the school. Faubus went even further on September 19, 1957, by requesting the removal of the federal judge who ordered the desegregation plan to proceed. This occurred a day before Faubus was to appear before the same judge for contempt in obstructing the court's desegregation plans. The request for the judge's removal was based, paradoxically, on the judge's "prejudice" in the case.

It soon became clear that Faubus had no intention of complying with either Presi-dent Eisenhower's request or the order of the federal judge and District Court. Faubus went on statewide television several days later and proclaimed that the troops would be removed from the high school but also stated his continued opposition to desegre-gation through the legal process. Further, he disavowed any responsibility for law and order in the city if there was violence as the result of further integration efforts. He abruptly left the state to go to the Southern Governors' Conference.

Violence erupted on September 23, 1957, when an unruly white crowd received word that African-American children had been admitted to the school through a side door. Mayor Mann urgently requested White House assistance. At this point, the president had no choice but to send federal troops to restore order. On Septem-ber 25, 1957, these troops escorted nine African-American children to school. Faubus further incited the situation by claiming that the federal government had shed the blood of patriotic Americans. This charge stemmed from an incident in which one of the troops' bayonets had cut one of the protesters in a scuffle.

## Impact of Event

Eisenhower's cautious approach to racial integration set a pattern that was to be repeated by future presidents. Eisenhower was patient and slow in pushing a full civil rights agenda, setting a pattern to be followed by southern governors such as George Wallace of Alabama and Ross Barnett of Mississippi. The use of an executive order (10730) would be repeated by Johnson and Kennedy in the struggle for civil rights for African Americans in the United States. Racial integration of public schools in Arkansas once again brought to the surface the tension in a federal structure of government in which power and authority is divided between a central government and states' governments. In the end, it also suggested that Eisenhower was more concerned with the direct challenge to his presidential authority and the constitutional crisis created by a state than with civil rights.

The Little Rock crisis also demonstrated that, in the absence of any strong political or ideological philosophy in the appointment of judges, Eisenhower had selected a number of Republican judges who favored racial integration. This would be reflected in other court decisions involving civil rights in a number of southern states. Part of the legacy of the Eisenhower Administration, however, was the persistence of racial segregation over a longer period of time because of Eisenhower's concern for southern sensitivity over integration. This persistence moved Congress to pass two important bills that became law. The Civil Rights Acts of 1957 and 1960 were part of a determined effort of the federal government to secure civil and racial rights, for African Americans in particular.

The integration of Little Rock was also an important incentive to the Civil Rights movement in the United States. Armed with this victory, civil rights advocates continued their struggle in almost every southern state in the continuing challenge against racial segregation.

## Bibliography

Amaker, Norman C. *Civil Rights and the Reagan Administration.* Washington, D.C.: Urban Institute Press, 1988. Begins with a historical overview of the struggle for civil rights from the case of *Plessy v. Ferguson* in 1896 to *Brown v. Board of Education* in 1954. While the focus of this book is primarily on the Reagan Administration and hostility toward civil rights, it provides an excellent analysis of the retreat from the dream of racial equality, including the area of education, in the 1980's by the federal government.

Brownell, Herbert. "Eisenhower's Civil Rights Program: A Personal Assessment." *Presidential Studies Quarterly* 21 (Spring, 1991): 235-242. This article presents an insider's view of civil rights during the Eisenhower Administration. Brownell, the author, was the attorney general during the crisis in Little Rock. The article provides the reader with the philosophy and attitude of Eisenhower on civil rights and the various legal measures and maneuvering that were part of the process of implementing those rights.

Burk, Robert Fredrick. *The Eisenhower Administration and Black Civil Rights.* Knoxville: University of Tennessee Press, 1984. This work points out Eisenhower's passive and reluctant approach to enforcing constitutional guarantees regarding civil and human rights with regard to African Americans. The president's eye was on the political gauge with respect to every move that he made in this direction.

Lawson, Steven F. *Running for Freedom.* Philadelphia: Temple University Press, 1991. In this book, the author provides a detailed account of the struggle for civil rights and human dignity for African Americans since 1941. Of particular interest in the beginning of the book is a detailed description of how different presidents, beginning with Roosevelt, wrestled with attempts to ensure rights for African Americans as guaranteed in the Bill of Rights.

Meier, August. "Negro Protest Movements and Organizations." In *Conflict and Competition: Studies in the Recent Black Protest Movement*, edited by John H. Bracey, Jr., August Meier, and Elliott Rudwick. Belmont, Calif.: Wadsworth, 1971. A number of civil rights organizations are discussed as part of the broader struggle of racial integration and equality in the south in the 1950's and 1960's. Tactics, strategies, and the effects of protest movements, which cut across class lines in the African-American community, are cogently and succinctly summarized here by Meier.

Walton, Hanes, Jr. *When the Marching Stopped.* Albany: State University of New York Press, 1988. Walton pursues the next logical step in the examination of civil rights in the United States after the marches of the 1960's. Whereas most works have focused on various aspects of the struggle for civil and human rights in America, this analysis examines the various agencies that have been set up to enforce civil rights and the politics involved in such enforcement.

Wilhoit, Francis M. *The Politics of Massive Resistance.* New York: George Braziller, 1973. This study examines white southern attitudes, beliefs, myths, values, and the manipulation of politics and governmental institutions to resist the 1954 Supreme Court decision on school integration. Wilhoit provides a critical discussion of the origins and ideology of white resistance to the black quest for full racial equality.

*Mfanya Donald Tryman*

## Cross-References

Black Leaders Call for Equal Rights at the Niagara Falls Conference (1905), p. 41; The Congress of Racial Equality Forms (1942), p. 601; CORE Stages a Sit-in in Chicago to Protest Segregation (1943), p. 618; *Brown v. Board of Education* Ends Public School Segregation (1954), p. 913; The Civil Rights Act of 1957 Creates the Commission on Civil Rights (1957), p. 997; Greensboro Sit-ins Launch a New Stage in the Civil Rights Movement (1960), p. 1056; Meredith's Enrollment Integrates the University of Mississippi (1962), p. 1167; Civil Rights Protesters Attract International Attention (1963), p. 1188; Martin Luther King, Jr., Delivers His "I Have a Dream" Speech (1963), p. 1200; Three Civil Rights Workers Are Murdered (1964), p. 1246; Congress Passes the Civil Rights Act (1964), p. 1251; Martin Luther King, Jr., Leads a March from Selma to Montgomery (1965), p. 1278; The Civil Rights Act of 1968 Outlaws Discrimination in Housing (1968), p. 1414; The Supreme Court Endorses Busing as a Means to End Segregation (1971), p. 1628; Southern Schools Are Found to Be the Least Racially Segregated (1975), p. 1786.

# PAPA DOC DUVALIER TAKES CONTROL OF HAITI

*Category of event:* Political freedom
*Time:* October 22, 1957
*Locale:* Haiti

*In 1957, François (Papa Doc) Duvalier established his authoritarian regime in Haiti, building it on a pattern and legacy of violence, corruption, and underdevelopment*

*Principal personages:*

FRANÇOIS DUVALIER (1907-1971), the medical doctor who established the most resilient and bloody dictatorship in Haitian history

DUMARSAIS ESTIMÉ (1900-1953), a political leader and former chief of state in Haiti who led a revival of the revolution of the black middle class

LOUIS DEJOIE (1896-1967), a chief political rival of Papa Doc Duvalier, involved in several attempts to overthrow him

CLEMENT BARBOT (?-1963), an ally of Duvalier in the early years who created the infamous Tonton-macoutes secret police organ

CLÉMENT JUMELLE (1915-1959), a family friend turned political rival of Papa Doc Duvalier

DANIEL FIGNOLÉ (1913-?), the founder of the Worker-Farmers Movement Party (MOP) who later became a rival of Duvalier

TOUSSAINT LOUVERTURE (1743-1803), the black revolutionary hero of Haiti in the 1790's to whom Duvalier liked to compare himself

JEAN JACQUES DESSALINES (1758-1806), the revolutionary leader and first chief of state of Haiti after independence

## Summary of Event

On October 22, 1957, François (Papa Doc) Duvalier was inaugurated as the president of Haiti. This story neither begins nor ends on this date. Duvalier inaugurated one of the most brutal authoritarian systems of the twentieth century, but the tendency toward dictatorship was already firmly rooted in the history and political culture of Haiti. The unique aspect of Duvalierism was that the system which evolved was so resilient and far-reaching in its impact on Haitian society.

The former French colony of Haiti was the first land in the Caribbean or Latin America to achieve political independence. Haiti emerged from a plantation-based slave society in 1804, led by revolutionaries Toussaint Louverture and Jean Jacques Dessalines. From the outset, Haiti was beset by problems created by its unique circumstances. To begin with, the revolution was one of national independence, but it also had definite racial overtones. Not only was there an emphasis on black culture but also differences between black and mulatto (mixed ancestry) society in Haiti became immediately apparent. Moreover, the traditional folk religion of Voodoo played a prominent role in Haitian politics from the time of the independence movement until Papa Doc Duvalier's obvious manipulation of it in his own regime. Finally, Haiti was very poor because of semifeudal land distribution practices, illiteracy, and outright corruption among elites.

Such conditions were prevalent long before Duvalier's rise to power but were instrumental in his election and in the style and character of his regime. Duvalier espoused black nationalism, a reverence for Voodoo, and populist sympathies reminiscent of his revered predecessor Dumarsais Estimé. In truth, he fulfilled none of the promise his 1957 campaign embodied.

The years preceding the election of François Duvalier were marked by chronic political and economic instability. Haiti had been one of the richest colonies in the New World, largely based on sugar exportation. Independence had destroyed the plantation system and brought a pattern of redivision of the land among individual small holders. Each generation reduced the size of these lands among its heirs. Land-use practices and management deteriorated with the increasing parcelization of land holdings. In time, the countryside was left in poverty. Soil erosion, loss of profitability, and a host of other problems left the people in the countryside on subsistence farms or as sharecroppers, and living in poor and unsanitary conditions.

The problems of the countryside were evidence also of the increasing gulf between the provinces and the cities, especially the capital, Port-au-Prince. The cities were the political centers. Because of the narrow base of the economy, there emerged few tracks to upward mobility. To be successful in Haitian society, one needed to be born of great wealth, educated in a profession, or lucky in a political career. In fact, a political career was a key to advancement and personal enrichment. Graft and corruption became endemic to Haitian political culture.

The poor conditions in the countryside and the gulf between it and city culture were exacerbated by class competition based on race. Mulatto elites competed bitterly with the black majority but were often excluded from the mainstream in terms of wealth and status. Moreover, as opportunity declined in the provinces, people migrated to the cities. Teeming slums developed, underscoring both class and racial divisions in Haitian cities and increasing the squalor and instability of the nation.

Populist appeals to the poor and black culture in Haiti were commonplace, but the result of plans to benefit them seemed always to enrich a narrow band of elites instead. Haiti had a series of in-and-out presidents from the time of Dessalines to the election of Duvalier. Of twenty-eight presidents since 1843, the average term in office was just over three years. The key factor in the term of a Haitian president was the support of the army. Haiti has been the victim of foreign intervention and was occupied by the United States Marines from 1915 to 1934. A president of Haiti was required to promise economic reforms, conquer multiple social and racial cleavages, gain the support of the United States but also stand up to it, be sensitive to Voodoo and folk culture, respect the Catholic Church, and hold the support of a factionalized military machine. This enormous task was hampered by the fact that the major incentive to be president of Haiti was personal gain.

A chaotic political environment prevailed in Haiti in 1957. François Duvalier was a medical doctor known for his involvement in the treatment of yaws, a contagious tropical disease. He entered politics as a follower of Daniel Fignolé's party and was named director of public health under the presidency of Dumarsais Estimé. When Paul Eugene Magloire succeeded Estimé as president, Duvalier's star declined. For a time, he was forced into hiding, and is said to have read voraciously. His favorite book was *The Prince*, by Niccolò Machiavelli.

Magloire had been moderately successful and popular, but as time approached for him to step down for elections, he stubbornly resisted. It was necessary for a military junta to force Magloire out before the 1957 elections. Duvalier found himself running for president with the support of Estimé. His three opponents were Fignolé, Clement Jumelle, and Louis Dejoie. Although the others were better known, Duvalier received key support from a powerful faction of the military led by General Antonio Kebreau.

In an atmosphere of violence and internecine squabbling, Duvalier presented the image of a docile, dull doctor. He spoke of government honesty and a new deal for the rural masses, and he reminded the people of his humanitarian work in eradication of yaws. Duvalier was widely known as a follower of Voodoo. He claimed the support of the United States and promised to follow in the footsteps of Estimé. Even so, the truly decisive element was the support of a barely organized group of paramilitary thugs who later became the Tonton-macoutes.

In 1957, a premium was placed on the faction which could control the polls. Mobilizing the electors included intimidation, tampering, and an array of power plays among the many political factions. Each candidate had his mob supporters, but the Duvalierists went further, using provocative and disruptive acts of terror to undermine the other candidates. Clement Barbot arose as a leader in these endeavors, in which the overriding goal was to make sure that Duvalier could not be personally blamed. Duvalier played the role of befuddled but committed doctor while his thugs terrorized electors and opponents. François Duvalier achieved the presidency in October, 1957, but his hold on power appeared as tenuous as that of many of his predecessors.

## Impact of Event

François Duvalier did not wait for his people to give him a title. He chose to be called "Papa Doc." This was the first of a series of unique characteristics of his leadership which gave Duvalierism its longevity in an unstable political world. Even before his inauguration, Duvalier survived several attempts to knock him out of power. He realized that to remain president he would need specialized support.

Duvalier was never an efficient manager nor particularly creative, but he assembled the institutional support necessary to destroy his enemies. In effect, he modernized his authoritarianism and became more than a petty dictator. Duvalier institutionalized a terror apparatus which neutralized political opposition and atomized the

Haitian masses. Many observers have likened Duvalierism to a form of fascist total-itarianism.

Duvalier enhanced the strength of his palace guards and politicized elements of the army as protectors of his national security state. This project was facilitated by the Cold War environment. Although Duvalier had a stormy relationship with the United States, he was able to manipulate several U.S. administrations as an opponent of communism. In the Cold War worldview of American foreign policy, Duvalier's dictatorship was preferable to communist insurgency. Hence, the United States became an implicit accomplice in supporting his regime and helped legitimize domestic terror against the Haitian people.

Duvalier's greatest innovation was an auxiliary structure of secret police, or death squads, known as the Tonton-macoute. This organization was put together by Barbot after the 1957 election. The name epitomized Duvalier's emphasis on the dark side of Voodoo. Tonton-macoute literally means "Uncle Knapsack." Taken from Voodoo legend, Uncle Knapsack goes about at night stuffing naughty little boys into his pack and whisks them away. This was virtually the task of the Tonton-macoute: to make people disappear. The arbitrary nature of the terror made it more effective. Ironically, Barbot, leader of the Tonton-macoute, eventually lost his position and was himself killed in 1963 in an abortive attempt to assassinate Duvalier.

The Tonton-macoute generated an antipolitical culture. Anyone suspected of opposition was brutally repressed. For example, the bodies of murdered suspects were often put on public display. In one case, a family was made to walk down a street stripped naked as Tonton-macoutes shot the children from the arms of their mothers. Women and children were often hacked to death with machetes in the presence of their husbands. Executions by firing squad were transmitted by radio and television, broadcast like football games. Even the friends of a son-in-law were executed, to impress the young man entering the Duvalier family. No one may ever know the extent of the carnage, but Haitian society was stigmatized by a pathological pattern of violence.

Duvalier institutionalized the politics of violence. Total violence becomes anti-politics and destroys the ability of people to think and act politically. The Duvalier regime became a classic *kleptocracy*, or rule of the "rip-off" artist, yet it utilized some of the most modern instruments of repression. These instruments were the key to the longevity of Duvalier's system. In its wake was left a legacy of poverty, disease, and corruption which bars the path to healing the wounds which have persisted since Haitian independence.

## Bibliography

Bellegarde-Smith, Patrick. *Haiti: The Breached Citadel*. Boulder, Colo.: Westview Press, 1990. This text provides an excellent study of Haiti. History and culture are carefully analyzed to characterize the context of Haitian development and under-development. The role of *Vodun* or Voodoo and the pattern of autocracy are examined as integral to understanding Haiti.

Diederich, Bernard, and Al Burt. *Papa Doc: Haiti and Its Dictator.* London: Bodley Head, 1969. This book is an excellent and engrossing depiction of the rise to power and first ten years of dictatorship of Papa Doc Duvalier. The authors are journalists who saw at first hand the predatory nature of the regime. The account is written in exacting detail.

Dupuy, Alex. *Haiti in the World Economy: Class, Race, and Underdevelopment Since 1700.* Boulder, Colo.: Westview Press, 1989. The value of this text lies in its careful analysis of the connection between the patterns of Haitian economic development to race and nationalism in Haitian political history. The text charts Haitian development from French colonialism and slave society to current patterns of black nationalism and U.S. economic intervention.

Fass, Simon M. *Political Economy in Haiti: The Drama of Survival.* New Brunswick, N.J.: Transaction Books, 1988. The author analyzes the economic and social exigencies of living in Haiti and provides the reader with concrete evaluations of the living conditions, including food, water, housing, schooling, international credit, and the domestic market in contemporary Haiti.

Logan, Rayford W. *Haiti and the Dominican Republic.* London: Oxford University Press, 1968. Although somewhat dated, this book is a helpful country study and comparison of the two nations which share the island of Hispaniola. It capably compares the histories and relations of Haiti and the Dominican Republic from colonial times to the 1960's.

Perlmutter, Amos. *Modern Authoritarianism: A Comparative Institutional Analysis.* New Haven, Conn.: Yale University Press, 1981. This is a first-rate effort to analyze modern authoritarian regimes according to a model based on structures, functions, and institutions. The analysis places Duvalierism within an appropriate context which highlights the specific structural character of such regimes. Perlmutter avoids value judgments in an effort to maintain objective analysis.

Rotberg, Robert I., and Christopher K. Clague. *Haiti: The Politics of Squalor.* Boston: Houghton Mifflin, 1971. The analysis in this work is somewhat dated, but it presents an excellent discussion of the political, economic, and cultural context of Duvalier's rise to power. The authors predict a grim future based on the effects of Duvalierism. The historical research and focus on issues relevant to human life and dignity are valuable.

Trouillot, Michel-Rolph. *Haiti, State Against Nation: The Origins and Legacy of Duvalierism.* New York: Monthly Review Press, 1990. Trouillot presents an absolutely indispensable analysis of the long-term political effects, both economic and structural, of the Duvalier regime on the politics and culture of Haiti. The author defines Duvalierism as a form of totalitarianism.

*Anthony R. Brunello*

## Cross-References

Castro Takes Power in Cuba (1959), p. 1026; The Inter-American Commission on

Human Rights Is Created (1959), p. 1032; Indonesia's Government Retaliates Against a Failed Communist Coup (1965), p. 1305; Brazil Begins a Period of Intense Repression (1968), p. 1468; The Inter-American Court of Human Rights Is Established (1969), p. 1503; The Amin Regime Terrorizes Uganda (1971), p. 1600; An Oppressive Military Rule Comes to Democratic Uruguay (1973), p. 1715; The United Nations Issues a Declaration Against Torture (1975), p. 1847; The Argentine Military Conducts a "Dirty War" Against Leftists (1976), p. 1864.

# MAO'S GREAT LEAP FORWARD CAUSES FAMINE AND SOCIAL DISLOCATION

*Category of event:* Political freedom
*Time:* Spring, 1958
*Locale:* Henan Province, People's Republic of China

*The Great Leap Forward was Mao Tse-tung's policy of forming communes to boost agriculture and to increase industrial production; natural disasters and mismanagement brought on famine and social dislocation*

*Principal personages:*

MAO TSE-TUNG (1893-1976), the chief political leader and theorist of Chinese communism

PENG DEHUAI (1898-1974), the minister of defense who challenged Mao's economic policies

ZHOU ENLAI (1898-1976), the premier of China, in favor of material incentives to encourage peasant production

CHEN YUN (1905-    ), an economic planner who helped China's recovery from the economic fiasco of the Great Leap

LIU SHAOQI (1898-1969), the vice chair of the Chinese Communist Party, listed as Mao's probable successor in the early 1960's

## Summary of Event

The People's Republic of China's First Five-Year Plan (1953-1957) was coming to a close by June, 1957. The Chinese representatives at the National People's Congress were jubilant upon hearing of an economic growth rate averaging 11 percent per year. China's top leaders, Mao Tse-tung, Zhou Enlai, Peng Dehuai, Liu Shaoqi, and Chen Yun, were worried, however, about a statistical imbalance: Industry had grown 18.7 percent while agriculture had a growth rate of 3.8 percent. What was most disheartening to the leaders was that grain production had increased only 1 percent over the year while the population had grown 2 percent. The Chinese people already had to endure rationing in certain food items and other essentials. Now they would have to receive smaller rations because of low production in agriculture and the further need for China to repay the loans from the Soviet Union with agricultural products.

In order for industry to sustain its growth rate and for agriculture to improve considerably during the Second Five-Year Plan, more would have to be extracted from the Chinese population, which was 80 percent peasantry. According to Premier Zhou Enlai and the brilliant economist Chen Yun, this could be accomplished only by offering the peasants more material incentives, with the chance of being able to buy more consumer goods. Such incentives would have to be accompanied by availability of modern agricultural machinery and chemical fertilizers.

Mao disagreed with such a model because it would merely reflect the Soviet Union's development plan. Ideologically, Mao had contempt for the Soviet model because he interpreted it as a step backward from socialism and lacking in revolutionary zeal. Mao's program was based on reorganizing the social structure of the peasantry and cultivating its altruistic qualities. In short, the Chinese peasant could be exhorted to greater production by good leadership in an environment which encouraged selflessness. If Mao could achieve this, he could take the place of Soviet leader Nikita Khrushchev as leader of the Third World.

From late 1957 to January 1958, 100 million peasants were mobilized to tackle gigantic projects such as building irrigation canals and dams, resulting in 7.8 million hectares of land being opened up for agriculture. This enormous task of moving millions of peasants to work on gigantic projects disrupted the normal routine of farming. There was a shortage of peasants, made up by encouraging women to work in the fields as replacements while men worked away from home. In order to increase peasant productivity, certain industries were relocated in rural areas so that peasants could be gainfully employed during the slack periods of the farming cycle. This mass mobilization took women away from their historical role of domestic work, so attempts were made to centralize children and meal preparations. To expedite the process, 2 million urban party cadres were encouraged to visit the countryside to learn from the peasants and to lead them with the slogan, "More, faster, better, cheaper."

This frenzy of cheerleading and propaganda resulted in the establishment of the people's communes in Henan Province by April, 1958. Private farms were abolished, and twenty-seven cooperatives with 9,369 households were absorbed into one large commune. By the summer of 1958, people's communes had sprouted throughout China. Party leadership attributed the good harvest to the "Great Leap" in agricultural technique and political reforms. By December, 1958, 99 percent of the peasant population, or 120 million households, formed twenty-six thousand communes.

Morale was very high within the ranks of the Chinese Communist Party (CCP). Chairman Mao directed the creation of a new journal for the Party, called the *Red Flag*, which provided the vehicle for espousing the socialist reconstruction that was taking place and the theoretical framework for the Great Leap toward communism.

Some striking features of the Great Leap Forward were the massive entry of women into the work force, the twenty million increase in the number of clerical and industrial workers, and the need for about three million mess halls to feed 90 percent of the rural population because women had been liberated from home kitchens. Mao's Great Leap was a scheme to transform people socially, to make them selfless and able to overcome all obstacles through sheer will. Mao believed that with correct leadership and encouragement, the Chinese could be directed toward economic transformation by "walking on two legs" to achieve both industrial and agricultural development.

With the establishment of communes, rural labor could be mobilized to work on more gigantic projects, especially irrigation, flood control, and land reclamation. Agricultural productivity could also be raised by employing more hands to plant, weed, and harvest. Light industry could then be established locally to produce consumer goods with local material and equipment. This transformation and production would breed the altruistic person who would be both "red and expert"—the communist. "Redness" would be reflected in belief in Mao's leadership, and "expertise" would come from practical application rather than dependence on the knowledge of the bureaucrats and intellectuals, who were being persecuted in the Antirightist Campaign of 1957-1958.

To reinforce the Great Leap belief that the Chinese people could achieve miraculous productivity the Chinese way, as opposed to the outmoded Soviet way, monumental showpieces were erected in Beijing, around Tiananmen Square. The People's Hall was built in ten months by shifts of workers from all over China. The building has an area of 1,853,568 square feet. The foyer is paved with red marble and can hold ten thousand people. The walls are of green marble and are illuminated by twelve chandeliers weighing one ton each. The auditorium has ten thousand seats, the banquet hall can seat five thousand, and the kitchen has the facilities to serve ten thousand diners. At roughly the same time, a three-thousand-loom and 100,000-spindle textile factory was built. A railway station that could accommodate 200,000 passengers a day was also completed. The effect of all these gigantic projects was to give the impression that the Chinese people could accomplish anything if they were well led, well organized, and encouraged to practice altruism.

The commune system, which eliminated most private ownership except the house and a small plot for gardening, was supposed to provide the environment for the ending of private gain and the atmosphere for practicing altruism. It was meant eventually to produce in such great quantities that the communist dream of "from each according to his ability, to each according to his needs" could be accomplished. Thus, free from all personal wants and greed, the communist would work only for the good of all. Mao had this deep faith in "selflessness" because his personal experiences were of giving for the betterment of China. He believed that he had wanted nothing of his country and that all Chinese could be like him when they were shown the way. He saw the people's commune as the foundation of altruism and communism.

In an unprecedented campaign, Mao urged the people to produce iron everywhere. With a great surplus of iron, he thought, China could industrialize rapidly and even catch up with Great Britain in fifteen years. Backyard furnaces sprung up everywhere; in villages, in back streets, and in front of offices. Peasants, workers, officials, doctors, and other professionals found time to smelt iron day and night. Outrageous production quotas were set in a wild frenzy of competition. To meet them, kitchen utensils, iron beds, and even farm tools were smelted.

## Impact of Event

In one year—1958—more than one half billion peasants were shorn of private property and organized into a new social organization, the commune. Men and women were formed into production teams and brigades, and with military precision were exhorted to work in huge farms, dam sites, factories, and backyard iron-making furnaces. Slogans, street opera, and the media were used to urge people to work around the clock and to increase production 300 percent or more. To keep up this frenzy of production, food, child-care, and even haircuts were provided free, as if to show the Soviet Union that China was leaping over it toward communism.

As slogans and songs blared, peasants were told to plow as deep as four feet and to plant three times more seedlings in the same area of land. When harvesting was completed, farmers were urged to join students, factory workers, teachers, and other professionals to produce iron and steel. Much of the iron and steel was of such low quality that it could not be used, yet pride kept production at a high level. Much of the farmland was also ruined by deep plowing and inappropriate irrigation. Many delicate machines and engines were ruined by overheating because many factories ran nonstop. Because communes were in competition, many commune officials inflated production statistics. This encouraged the setting of higher production quotas by the government, which furthered the falsification of statistics. All such setbacks were compounded by three consecutive years of bad weather. China produced only 150 million tons of grain in 1960. This equaled the grain production of 1952, but China had 100 million fewer mouths to feed in 1952. Consequently, even as close as fifty miles outside the capital, Beijing, there were signs of famine. The lack of food was remedied with harsh rationing. This would cause malnutrition and illnesses which eventually killed twenty million people.

As the initial euphoria of the frenetic pace of production faded because of overwork, machine breakdowns, or impossible quotas, the Chinese became disillusioned and cynical. As hunger became a reality, the people reverted to what the CCP labeled as "rightist tendencies." The cure was to identify the criminals—the misguided and the lazy—and apply appropriate punishment. Millions were "sent down" to the countryside and to distant provinces. The more unfortunate were purged from the CCP, driven to suicide, or executed for state crimes.

The CCP faced an internal struggle to seek the appropriate ideology for development. Mao's model would be put aside temporarily until its resurgence in the Cultural Revolution that began in 1966.

## Bibliography

Hsiung, James C. *Ideology and Practice: The Evolution of Chinese Communism.* New York: Praeger, 1970. This book covers the historical and ideological perspectives of Chinese communism. Chapters 9 and 10 provide very perceptive analyses of ideology and practice, with emphasis on the Great Leap Forward and its aftermath.

Karnow, Stanley. *Mao and China: From Revolution to Revolution.* New York: Viking Press, 1972. Chapter 5 covers Mao's motives for the Great Leap. It also gives some firsthand accounts of the backyard iron-making attempts and the failures of the Great Leap. Chapter 6 shows the struggles between Mao and Defense Minister Peng that resulted in the latter's purge and Mao's mistrust of party moderates.

Portisch, Hugo. *Red China Today.* Chicago: Quadrangle Books, 1966. Chapter 11 covers the Great Leap and provides a good summary of the positive and negative effects of the social experiment.

Schurman, Franz, and Orville Schell, eds. *Communist China: Revolutionary Reconstruction and International Confrontation, 1949 to the Present.* New York: Random House, 1967. This reader consists of articles by some of the best writers on China. Michel Oksenberg's contribution on the effects of the Great Leap and Kang Chao's insightful analysis of its aftermath are most valuable.

Solomon, Richard H. *Mao's Revolution and the Chinese Political Culture.* Berkeley: University of California Press, 1971. Chapter 18 covers the political conflict and social change of the Great Leap Forward.

Spence, Jonathan D. *The Search for Modern China.* New York: W. W. Norton, 1990. Chapters 20 and 21 have comprehensive accounts of the First Five-Year Plan and the Great Leap Forward. Good government budget statistics are also given.

*Peng-Khuan Chong*

## Cross-References

Mao Delivers His "Speech of One Hundred Flowers" (1956), p. 958; The United Nations Adopts the Abolition of Forced Labor Convention (1957), p. 985; The Chinese Cultural Revolution Starts a Wave of Repression (1966), p. 1332; China Publicizes and Promises to Correct Abuses of Citizens' Rights (1978), p. 1983; Demonstrators Gather in Tiananmen Square (1989), p. 2483.

# PIRE IS AWARDED THE NOBEL PEACE PRIZE

*Category of event:* Refugee relief
*Time:* December 10, 1958
*Locale:* Oslo, Norway

*Father Dominique Georges Pire was awarded the Nobel Peace Prize in recognition of his work to improve the lives of displaced persons in Europe*

*Principal personages:*
GEORGES PIRE (1910-1969), the founder of Europe of the Heart
EDWARD F. SQUADRILLE, an American serviceman who provided the inspiration for Europe of the Heart
OTTO KILDAL, the Norwegian ambassador to Belgium who met Pire and invited him to speak in Oslo
GUNNAR JAHN (1883-1971), the chairman of the Nobel Committee of the Norwegian Parliament
HANS ERNST, the German merchant who helped Pire establish the European Village at Aachen

## Summary of Event

On December 10, 1958, in Oslo, Norway, the Nobel Peace Prize was awarded to a little-known Belgian priest, Father Dominique Georges Pire. Father Pire, at age forty-eight, was one of the youngest people to receive the prize and one of the few recognized for work with refugees. He was born Georges Charles Clement Ghislain Eugene François Pire on February 10, 1910, in Dinant, Belgium. In 1914, with the outbreak of World War I, the young Pire saw his grandfather murdered by German soldiers and his house set on fire. His family was displaced to France to live until the war's end in 1918. These experiences cultivated a sensitivity which would direct the course of his life.

Pire had an early love of classics and philosophy, and decided at the age of sixteen to become a priest. He entered the Dominican monastery of La Sarte in Huy, Belgium, took his final vows and the name Henri Dominique Pire in 1932, and was ordained in 1934. During the next decade, he continued his studies toward a doctorate in theology and taught moral philosophy and sociology at the Huy monastery.

In 1938, Pire founded the Service d'Entr'aide Familiale (Mutual Family Aid Service) to help indigent families and the Stations de Plein Air de Huy (Open Air Camps of Huy), a program providing vacations for city children. With the outbreak of World War II in 1939, the Open Air Camps were converted to missions that fed thousands of French and Belgian children. After meeting Gerard Tremerie, a member of the Air Cadets Association and a secret agent of the Belgian Resistance, Pire became a chaplain and operative in the movement. Sitting along the river Meuse with a little boy and a fishing pole, Pire secretly kept track of traffic along the Liège-

Namur road. He helped to organize an escape network for downed Allied airmen to return to their forces. After the war, Pire was recognized for his service to the Resistance and Allied efforts with the Belgian Military Cross with Palms, the Resistance Medal with Crossed Swords, the 1940-1945 War Medal, and the Medal of National Gratitude. In 1946, he was appointed Curé of the La Sarte Monastery.

Pire's life work, and the work for which he received the Nobel Peace Prize, began in 1949. On February 27 of that year, he attended a speech by Edward Squadrille, an American colonel, regarding the work of the United Nations Refugee Relief Agency and the International Refugee Organization (IRO). Pire was fascinated with Squadrille, and the two men became close over the following months. Pire immersed himself in the current refugee situation, realizing that thousands of Europeans displaced after World War I were still living in temporary camps; that the 1935 racial laws in Germany and the Spanish Civil War of the mid-1930's had dispersed thousands more; that nations contributing to the IRO welcomed healthy, educated refugees but were not interested in the orphaned, the old, or the infirm; and that the Soviet subjugation of Eastern Europe had created swarms of refugees. Pire and Squadrille drafted a plan of action that involved propaganda, adoptions, and the establishment of homes for elderly refugees. Pire developed a sponsorship plan to connect refugee families in Eastern and Southern Europe with "godparent" families who would send them letters, gifts, and money. Over the next ten years, the sponsorship plan matched up more than fifteen thousand sets of private and refugee families in more than twenty countries.

In April of 1949, Pire journeyed to witness the refugee situation firsthand. Based at IRO headquarters in Salzburg, Austria, he visited twenty-four refugee camps, including those at Lagersparch, Attersee, Kufstein, Spital, Klagenfurt, and Villach-Sankt Marten, two hospitals, an orphanage, and more than twenty-five thousand refugees. He saw people living in huts, caves, and ruined buildings. He was most affected by those whose age or health left them little hope, the so-called "hardcore" cases. A report from the general director of the IRO in late 1949 estimated the number of hard-cores across Europe at 161,000.

After seeing the camps, Pire became determined to establish homes for elderly refugees. He founded L'Aide aux Personnes Déplacées (Aid to Displaced Persons), through which he raised funds from municipal and private sources to rent a vacant house in Huy. Squadrille traveled to Germany and Austria to find elderly refugee couples to bring to the new home. By 1954, four homes, at Huy, Esneux, Artselaer, and Braine-le-Comte, provided hard-core refugees with shelter, clothing, food, medical care, and a place to live and die in peace. Pire himself went to the Trieste region to select residents for the Artselaer home.

While establishing the homes, Pire envisioned a more ambitious project that would offer displaced persons fuller lives and greater self-sufficiency. He proposed buying land on the outskirts of industrial European cities and establishing refugee communities whose residents would have space, jobs, and civic and economic structures. In 1955, he traveled to Aachen, Germany, an industrial city near the French and Belgian borders, to inspect it as a prospective site for the first European Village. There he met a local market owner named Hans Ernst who took a strong interest in the project. Ernst helped locate land, arrange transactions, obtain government permits, and combat community skepticism. Frau von Wussow, a wealthy woman from Munich, heard about the proposed community, met with Pire, and generously provided funds for the purchase of the land. In May of 1956, construction of buildings was begun, and by November the community received its first inhabitants, including refugees fleeing the recent Soviet invasion of Hungary. Meanwhile, with von Wussow serving as the president of Aid to Displaced Persons and Ernst continuing to play a major role in the organization, more European Villages were established. The second was begun in Bregenz, Austria, on September 23, 1956, and the third at Augsburg, West Germany, on May 4, 1957. By 1957, seven European Villages, each designed for a community of 150 people, had been founded or planned, including sites at Berchem-Sainte-Agathe in Belgium and Besseringen, Wuppertal, and Euskirchen in West Germany.

Finances were perpetually difficult. The Albert Schweitzer Village, named for the 1952 Peace Prize winner, benefited from the generous support of the people and government of Besseringen and the Saar. Funding was insufficient for the village at Wuppertal, which was to be dedicated to Anne Frank, the Dutch girl whose diary documented her life in hiding in Amsterdam before she was sent to her death in a German concentration camp. Pire unsuccessfully sought grants from the Ford and Rockefeller foundations. He then applied to the Nobel Committee, but was told that grants were awarded only with the prizes themselves. The committee noted that the Peace Prize had been awarded for refugee work in the past, to Fridtjof Nansen in 1922 and to the Nansen Office for Refugees in 1938. Pire sent the committee a booklet describing Aid to Displaced Persons, under a cover letter by the secretary-general of the European Council, his friend Count Benvenuti. Pire was not selected as the Peace Prize winner but was urged to seek resubmission the following year.

On March 30, 1958, at the opening ceremony of the Fridtjof Nansen Village in Berchem-Sainte-Agathe, Pire met Otto Kildal, the Norwegian ambassador to Belgium. Kildal was impressed with Pire and invited him to Brussels to discuss his work. There he met Rolf Stranger, the burgomaster of Oslo. Through Stranger, he was invited to speak in Oslo on October 21, 1958, as a guest of the Norwegian branch of the European Movement, an organization promoting European unity. He was received by Norway's King Olaf V in the afternoon, and the king was at the well-attended and enthusiastically received address that evening. Pire spoke of his work simply and directly, stressing his humanitarian viewpoint and his refusal to adopt a particularly religious or nationalistic agenda.

Weeks later, the Nobel Committee sent a telegram to Belgium to inform Pire that he had been chosen for the Peace Prize. Ironically, the telegram had the wrong address, and as Pire was not well known in Brussels, the telegram was returned to Oslo unopened. On November 10, a reporter from the Belga News Agency called Pire's mother with the news; Pire himself first learned of his award from his brother-in-law Abel Berger, a newspaper reporter, who found him at a retreat at the monastery. On December 10, 1958, Pire returned to Oslo to accept the Nobel Peace Prize from Gunnar Jahn, chairman of the Nobel Committee, and to deliver his Nobel lecture.

### Impact of Event

The most immediate and tangible effect of Pire's Nobel Peace Prize was the cash award of approximately $41,250 that accompanied the prize. Although more than ten million dollars had been spent through Pire's refugee relief activities by 1958, the prize money was sorely needed for completion of the Nansen Village and construction of the Anne Frank Village. In addition, the Peace Prize brought Pire instant international recognition; greater notoriety and visibility facilitated Pire's constant fundraising activities.

Pire considered the Nobel Peace Prize both an honor and a challenge, and it spurred him personally to continue and broaden his work. He began to travel widely, lecturing on his beliefs and activities, and served as a consultant to various European governments on refugee issues. In 1957, Aid to Displaced Persons became l'Europe du Coeur au Service du Monde (Europe of the Heart Serving the World), a movement devoted to increasing unity and goodwill among people across national, social, religious, and linguistic barriers. Europe of the Heart incorporated Pire's previous projects—the sponsorship service, the homes for the elderly, the European Villages—under one title.

In June of 1959, Pire established Coeur Ouvert au Monde (Heart Open to the World), a geographical and intellectual extension of Europe of the Heart. Pire's previous efforts had been confined to the European continent, but Heart Open to the World sought to help people in other parts of the world. Pire conceived the Fraternal Dialogue, a philosophy of social interaction that stressed mutual understanding of thought and feeling. Amitiés Mondiales (World Friendships) was a correspondence network established to spread the Fraternal Dialogue. Parainages Mondiaux (World Sponsorships) was developed on the model of the European sponsorship plan, linking individuals and families in Europe with refugees in distant places such as Rwanda, Angola, and Tibet for correspondence, gifts, and financial support.

On April 10, 1960, Pire founded the Université de la Paix (University of Peace) at Tihange-lez-Huy, Belgium. This institution was devoted to peace studies and development of the Fraternal Dialogue. More than five hundred individuals from approximately forty nations attended courses in peace during the university's first five years. Another program of Heart Open to the World was the creation of Iles de Paix (Islands of Peace), international communities devoted to the Fraternal Dialogue. The first was founded in Gohiri, East Pakistan, in February of 1962 and was followed by a second in Kalakad, India, in 1968. By the end of the decade, Pire's influence was felt by individuals across the globe.

The announcement of Pire's Peace Prize in 1958 also sparked discussion about the prize itself. The Eastern European press was critical of the selection, primarily because Pire's activities sought to help many refugees fleeing repressive Soviet bloc regimes. Other observers objected that refugee relief was not what Alfred Nobel had intended when he created the Peace Prize. Many, while acknowledging Pire's intentions, questioned whether his modest accomplishments truly merited the Nobel Peace Prize. Pire was barely known, and though he had worked arduously to build homes and communities, those directly affected numbered several thousand at best. Critics thought that the Nobel Committee could have recognized a statesman or peace worker whose accomplishments were more far-reaching, if less dramatic.

Jahn countered such criticism implicitly in his presentation speech by asserting that it was the quality and not the quantity of work that mattered in the selection. Pire's work, while statistically small, was spiritually monumental; it could provide an example and inspiration to all. Thus, his Nobel Peace Prize affirmed the value of individual effort and initiative in a world where individuals all too often felt impotent to effect meaningful change. It set a precedent for such future choices as Mother Teresa, the social worker among Calcutta's impoverished who was the Peace Prize recipient in 1979. The Nobel Committee's recognition of Pire validated such grassroots enterprises and, in a sense, expanded the scope of the Nobel Peace Prize and the definition of peace.

## Bibliography

Holborn, Louise W. *Refugees: The Problem of Our Time.* Metuchen, N.J.: Scarecrow Press, 1975. This massive, two-volume, fifteen-hundred-page work examines all aspects of the refugee issue from 1951 through 1972, with an emphasis on the work of the U.N. High Commissioner for Refugees. Extensive charts and statistics make this an excellent reference work. The latter two-thirds consists of nation-by-nation analyses.

Houart, Victor. *The Open Heart: The Inspiring Story of Father Pire and the Europe of the Heart.* London: Souvenir Press, 1959. This is an imaginatively dramatized narrative of Pire's work through Europe of the Heart. The focus is on Pire, but Houart interweaves personal histories of individual refugees Pire encountered. Picturesque and poetic, this account is easy to read and includes more than thirty pictures of Pire and his projects.

Marrus, Michael R. *The Unwanted: European Refugees in the Twentieth Century.* New York: Oxford University Press, 1985. Marrus combines historical detail, political theory, statistical analysis, and specific anecdotes to portray both the causes of the refugee problem since the late nineteenth century and the solutions that have been attempted. The book is very accessible.

Pire, Dominique. *The Story of Father Dominique Pire as Told to Hugues Vehenne.* Translated by John L. Skeffington. New York: Dutton, 1961. Vehenne, a friend and colleague of Pire, provides an inside view of Pire's activities and the development of his beliefs and strategies. The anecdotal information provides a clear character profile.

Schechtman, Joseph B. *Postwar Population Transfers in Europe, 1945-1955.* Philadelphia: University of Pennsylvania Press, 1962. Schechtman views postwar migration in terms of minority groups, primarily in Eastern and Southeastern Europe, and both home and host government policies. This book maintains objectivity and avoids sensationalism.

Zellerbach Commission on the European Refugee Situation. *Refugees in Europe, 1957-1958.* New York: Crown-Zellerbach, 1958. The commission was a private group of individuals who traveled to Europe in late 1957 in response to the Hungarian refugee situation. They released this analytical, businesslike report, full of statistics, documents, photos, and practical recommendations. Staying clear of generalization or broad philosophy, it is specific and timebound but very applicable to the situation Pire was trying to remedy.

*Barry Mann*

### Cross-References

Nansen Wins the Nobel Peace Prize (1922), p. 361; Nazi Concentration Camps Go Into Operation (1933), p. 491; The Marshall Plan Provides Aid to Europe (1947), p. 706; The United Nations Adopts the Universal Declaration of Human Rights (1948), p. 789; Hundreds of Thousands Leave East Germany for the West (1949), p. 795; The United Nations High Commissioner for Refugees Statute Is Approved (1950), p. 855; The U.N. Convention Relating to the Status of Refugees Is Adopted (1951), p. 867; The United Nations Drafts a Convention on Stateless Persons (1954), p. 918; A Hungarian Uprising Is Quelled by Soviet Military Forces (1956), p. 969; Mother Teresa Is Awarded the Nobel Peace Prize (1979), p. 2051.

# CASTRO TAKES POWER IN CUBA

*Category of event:* Revolutions and rebellions
*Time:* 1959
*Locale:* Cuba

*Cuba was an economic appendage of the United States when Fidel Castro's revolution ended this dependent relationship and thrust the island nation into massive social change*

*Principal personages:*
FIDEL CASTRO (1927-     ), the Cuban revolutionary who took power in 1959
RAÚL CASTRO (1930-     ), a collaborator in the revolution, Fidel's brother
FULGENCIO BATISTA (1901-1973), a Cuban soldier who was the nation's most powerful politician until his overthrow by Castro in 1959
CHE GUEVARA (1928-1967), an Argentine-born revolutionary who was essential to Castro's triumph
JOSÉ MARTÍ (1853-1895), a Cuban intellectual who led his nation's nineteenth century anti-imperialist struggle
HUBER MATOS (1918-     ), a Cuban rebel leader from 1956 to 1959; broke with Castro because of the growing influence of communists in the revolution

## Summary of Event

Fidel Castro's meteoric rise as a worldwide symbol of social revolution originated in the economic and political imbalances of his native Cuba and in his own unusual personal qualities. Born into a nation dominated by foreign-owned corporations, young Fidel became politically active while in college and law school. He admired the struggles of Latin American nationalists, such as Argentina's Juan Perón, against external economic domination. The United States dominated the Cuban economy with heavy investments in land, sugar mills, and mining. Cuban society was divided into a prosperous wealthy elite connected with United States interests, a hard-working but insecure middle class of urban professionals, and an impoverished majority of laborers, most of whom depended on the sugar industry for employment.

Castro threw himself into an attempt to overthrow Fulgencio Batista (a strong ally of the wealthy elite and the United States), who had seized control of the Cuban government by unconstitutional means in 1952. Castro's failure to take the Cuban army's Moncada barracks in the city of Santiago in 1953 resulted in his arrest and trial. Speaking in his own defense, the tall, articulate rebel summoned the revolutionary heritage of the Cuban patriot José Martí in his "History Will Absolve Me" speech. This speech did not prevent his conviction but did establish him as a champion of the poor and of many members of the middle class. Released in a general amnesty in 1955, Castro went to Mexico, where for the next seventeen months he studied that nation's revolutionary experience and planned the overthrow of Batista with his brother, Raúl, and a new acquaintance, Che Guevara.

The seven years after Batista's seizure of power seemed prosperous on the surface, but the underlying frustrations associated with endemic poverty and political repression soon erupted. Nearly one Cuban worker in four had no job or only seasonal employment. While luxury hotels and gaudy casinos stimulated Havana's prosperity, Cuban cane cutters endured low wages for back-breaking work during the sugar harvest and then faced a longer season of minimal or zero income. Cuba's main sugar market, the United States, was saturated by the late 1950's. As a result, the island's sugar industry stagnated. The prospects of cane workers and other agricultural laborers were dim. Labor unions had made some progress in the organization of the rural working class, but their powerful adversaries—large multinational corporations backed by the Batista government—allowed them very few gains at the bargaining table.

Batista's government became increasingly dictatorial as the decade wore on. It faced no serious organized opposition within the island's political system because the traditional parties had become factionalized and ineffective. Therefore, the frustrations of lower- and middle-class Cubans had no outlet in the political system at a time when the growing anger of Cuban workers was matched by the disillusionment of the middle class. The Batista government subsidized the tourist industry and allowed organized crime syndicates from the United States to move into the lucrative hotel and nightclub businesses. Young Cubans were outraged by official corruption and extravagance in the midst of poverty. Some urban dissidents engaged in acts of violence, including an unsuccessful raid on the presidential palace. Batista's brutal campaign against his opponents brought him a few moments of respite but in the long run drove more Cubans to oppose him.

Castro took advantage of this political unrest. His movement struggled for survival in the mid-1950's, but by 1958 he had established a revolutionary base in the rugged Sierra Maestra of eastern Cuba. Much of Castro's reputation came as the leader of an underdog guerrilla campaign against Batista's much larger army. As Batista's army advanced into the rebel-held area, its platoons and companies became isolated from each other. The rebels, concealed in heavy vegetation and the rugged terrain, attacked these small units with rifles, machine guns, and mortars. Unaccustomed to guerrilla combat, the army units retreated in disarray. This pattern of engagement, designed and perfected by Che Guevara, demoralized the army. Faced with the Castro-Guevara campaign in the east and unrest in Havana and central Cuba, the Batista administration collapsed. On December 31, Batista fled to the Dominican Republic.

Castro's enthusiastic welcome in Havana on January 8, 1959, was both a celebration of the defeat of the old regime and a large step in his establishment of a personal relationship with the Cuban masses. He posed rhetorical questions for the huge crowd assembled at Camp Columbia on Havana's outskirts and used its answers to reinforce his authority. For example, he asked if he should take control of and reform the old Batista-run military. The crowd responded overwhelmingly in the affirmative. A gifted orator, Castro laced his revolutionary pronouncements with utopian idealism, the nationalist vision of José Martí, and references to precedents for social reform from the Christian tradition. His use of Cuban television even as early as 1959 brought him and his program to a large audience. Castro's charismatic appeal to the downtrodden and marginal people elevated his yet unformed government to an unprecedented level of public acceptance. The impoverished sugar cane worker caught a glimpse of a better day and the disillusioned urban college student saw an end to corruption and repression.

Castro's power was based on more than military prowess and personal charisma. His 1959 speeches seemed rambling to observers who attempted to determine if he had committed his revolution to communism, but, to the lower strata of Cuban society—workers, peasants, unemployed, and underemployed—as well as to many segments of the middle class, the energetic national leader offered a chance for a new life. The Agrarian Reform Law of May 17, 1959, was an indication that Castro intended to redistribute large quantities of property from the vast sugar estates to peasants and agricultural workers.

Castro's actions in the area of individual rights were often controversial. The new government, as do those of most revolutionary states, conducted trials of ex-officials of the old regime. These highly publicized trials drew sharp criticism from observers in the United States, but the proceedings seemed to be generally respectful of the rights of the accused. The prosecution of Huber Matos was another matter. Matos was a rebel leader during the most difficult months of the movement but objected to the growing influence of communists in the government. Both Castro and Guevara spoke against him at this trial, which opened in December of 1959. The conviction and incarceration of Matos for antirevolutionary activities was based on dubious evidence introduced in a politicized court.

At the end of 1959, the long-term impact of Castro's seizure of power remained unclear for middle- and lower-class Cubans. Both the urban school teacher and the rural cane worker saw Castro as a dynamic leader who had vanquished the Batista dictatorship, but the fundamental restructuring of the nation's economy remained more a promise than a reality. Castro consolidated power in his own hands, power that could be exercised for the benefit of the Cuban masses but that also held the possibility for the erection of another dictatorship.

## Impact of Event

One of the purposes of Castro's movement was to bestow political and economic benefits on previously disadvantaged peoples. Land reform resulted in the transformation of the nation's primary economic activity: The sugar industry moved from foreign-dominated private ownership to government control under the revolutionary state. This change brought better working conditions and an increased sense of pride for laborers. Impoverished cane cutters and other agricultural workers saw an end to unemployment and enjoyed a broadly based increase in wages. Public health campaigns and the extension of primary medical care into rural areas marked significant gains in the lives of the common people. Agricultural workers moved into small but modern houses equipped with electricity and television. All Cubans had access to education, and the Castro government developed a mass-participation sports program and an impressive training system for Olympic athletes. Baseball, a longtime favorite sport among working-class Cubans, continued to provide opportunities for exercise and popular diversion. The government set up day care centers for children, opening new opportunities for women. Women took advantage of these opportunities, making large strides in political leadership roles, medicine, and education.

From a critical perspective, however, Castro's transformation of Cuba had adverse effects. After initial improvements in their daily lives, Cuban workers began to experience difficulties. Shortages of manufactured goods became common, and Cubans improvised to keep automobiles and other essential equipment operational. Food supplies, especially meat, were inadequate, and the government resorted to rationing. The bureaucracies responsible for economic planning and the distribution of resources were often inefficient.

The same Cuban government that offered opportunities for workers, teachers, and women also imposed limitations on national life. The regime's political opponents who remained in Cuba often found it difficult to express their points of view. The eventual exodus of disappointed middle-class Cubans deprived the nation of vital technical and professional skills. Government expropriation of foreign-owned businesses widened the split between Cuba and the United States and contributed to the loss of the North American market for sugar and other exports.

Although the 1959 revolution freed Cuba from the economic control of the United States, Castro's dependent and often subservient relationship with the Soviet Union continued the island nation's external domination. The events of 1959 marked the beginning of the end of six decades of United States preeminence in Cuba, altered the course of Cuban domestic history, and raised the living standards of the working class. Even the determined, resourceful leadership of Fidel Castro could not, however, create an independent economy that brought an enduring sense of security and material well-being to the island's people.

## Bibliography

Benjamin, Jules. *The United States and the Origins of the Cuban Revolution.* Princeton, N.J.: Princeton University Press, 1990. A succinct interpretation of Cuba's history from the 1890's. Benjamin emphasizes that the imbalances in the relationship between Cuba and the United States created an environment in which Castro's nationalistic-populistic revolution triumphed.

Bonachea, Ramón, and Marta San Martín. *The Cuban Insurrection, 1952-1959.* New Brunswick, N.J.: Transaction Books, 1974. A detailed military and political history of the rise to power of the Cuban revolutionaries. The authors use interviews with participants on both sides of the struggle to broaden their coverage beyond the customary focus on Fidel Castro.

Domínguez, Jorge I. *To Make the World Safe for Revolution: Cuba's Foreign Policy.* Cambridge, Mass.: Harvard University Press, 1989. A comprehensive study of Cuba's foreign relations, with emphasis on overseas efforts to promote and defend revolutionary movements. Domínguez discusses Cuba's frustrated quest for an independent foreign policy in the face of its continued economic dependence on the Soviet Union.

Mesa-Lago, Carmelo. *The Economy of Socialist Cuba: A Two-Decade Appraisal.* Albuquerque: University of New Mexico Press, 1981. A careful, nonpolemical study of the first two decades under Castro. While the distribution of income and public services broadened, the productivity of the economy lagged in spite of subsidies from the Soviet Union. Castro's policies have not ended the island's dependence on sugar.

Morley, Morris H. *Imperial State and Revolution: The United States and Cuba, 1952-1986.* Cambridge, England: Cambridge University Press, 1987. An analysis of the complex relationship between Cuba and the United States during and after Castro's rise to power. Morley emphasizes the importance of politics and ideology in the formulation of United States policy toward Cuba but concludes that multinational corporations had a powerful, often decisive, influence

Pérez, Louis A. *Army Politics in Cuba, 1898-1958.* Pittsburgh: University of Pittsburgh Press, 1976. A crucial study for understanding the victory of the revolutionaries. The Cuban army lacked popular support because of its origins under the tutelage of the United States in the early decades of the twentieth century and lacked professionalism because of political influences in the officer corps. One of several valuable historical studies of Cuba by Pérez.

Ruíz, Ramón Eduardo. *Cuba: The Making of a Revolution.* New York: W. W. Norton, 1970. A well-written account of the political, social, and economic background of the revolution. Readable style makes this book suitable for introductory students.

Szulc, Tad. *Fidel: A Critical Portrait.* New York: William Morrow, 1986. A biography that includes much on Castro's early years and his personal life. Szulc emphasizes the military and political battles from 1952 to 1963 and provides a narrative of the crucial year of 1959. He also claims that Castro was a Marxist before the 1953 Moncada revolt.

Thomas, Hugh. *Cuba: The Pursuit of Freedom.* New York: Harper & Row, 1971. A massive volume that combines factual depth and insightful analysis. Covers Cuban history from the Spanish colonial past to the solidification of the Castro regime in the 1960's.

Welch, Richard. *Response to Revolution: The United States and the Cuban Revolution, 1959-1961.* Chapel Hill: University of North Carolina Press, 1985. A survey of the responses of United States government officials, politicians, journalists, and academics to the revolution. Welch analyzes many of their books and articles written in the 1960's and lists them in a useful bibliography of more than three hundred entries.

*John A. Britton*

## Cross-References

U.S. Marines Are Sent to Nicaragua to Quell Unrest (1912), p. 137; The Mexican Constitution Establishes an Advanced Labor Code (1917), p. 196; Lenin and the Communists Impose the "Red Terror" (1917), p. 218; Lenin Leads the Russian Revolution (1917), p. 225; El Salvador's Military Massacres Civilians in *La Matanza* (1932), p. 464; Ho Chi Minh Organizes the Viet Minh (1941), p. 573; Perón Creates a Populist Political Alliance in Argentina (1946), p. 673; The Nationalist Vietnamese Fight Against French Control of Indochina (1946), p. 683; Papa Doc Duvalier Takes Control of Haiti (1957), p. 1009; Cubans Flee to Florida and Receive Assistance (1960's), p. 1044; Allende Is Overthrown in a Chilean Military Coup (1973), p. 1725; Somoza Is Forced Out of Power in Nicaragua (1979), p. 2035; Marcos Flees the Philippines (1986), p. 2286.

# THE INTER-AMERICAN COMMISSION ON HUMAN RIGHTS IS CREATED

*Category of event:* Civil rights
*Time:* August 18, 1959
*Locale:* Santiago, Chile

*The Inter-American Commission on Human Rights developed authority to promote human rights and monitor violations by members of the Organization of American States*

Principal personages:

JOSÉ A. MORA (1897-1975), the secretary-general of the OAS, who requested that the Inter-American Commission on Human Rights be involved in the 1965 Dominican Republic crisis

GONZALO ESCUDERO (1903-    ), the Ecuadoran representative who worked, unsuccessfully, to give the new commission authority to take individual petitions

MANUEL BIANCHI, the chair of the commission who first went to the Dominican Republic on behalf of the commission to establish its active role

DURWARD V. SANDIFER (1900-1981), a United States member of the commission during the Dominican Republic crisis

## Summary of Event

The Ninth Inter-American Conference, held in Bogotá, Colombia, in 1948, adopted the Charter of the Organization of American States (OAS), which introduced a regional political and military framework for the Americas. One of the areas addressed was human rights, as the charter advocated "a system of individual liberty and social justice based on respect for the essential rights of man." It contained some specific human rights provisions, most significantly Article 5(j): "The American States proclaim the fundamental rights of the individual without distinction as to race, nationality, creed or sex." The same meetings also produced the American Declaration on the Rights and Duties of Man, an extensive listing of twenty-eight "rights" and ten "duties."

Nevertheless, the Inter-American Juridical Committee subsequently turned down the assignment of creating a human rights court after concluding that the OAS charter and the American Declaration on the Rights and Duties of Man could not be entwined to create a binding legal obligation on the states. Hence, no institutional framework to oversee human rights existed within the OAS until the creation of the Inter-American Commission on Human Rights at the Fifth Meeting of Consultation of Ministers of Foreign Affairs in Santiago, Chile, August 12-18, 1959. The meeting's eighth resolution directed the OAS council to elect seven persons to serve as individuals (rather than as representatives of their states) on an Inter-American Commission on Human Rights, which was charged with "furthering respect for human rights" and carrying out other "functions which the Council assigns to it."

By June, 1960, the council of the OAS had approved a statute for the new commission. According to the statute's Article 9, the commission was authorized "to develop an awareness of human rights"; to recommend "progressive . . . domestic legislation" to the states; "to prepare such studies and reports" on human rights as were appropriate; to urge the states to give the commission information on human rights matters within their domestic jurisdictions; and to be an "advisory body" to the OAS on human rights.

The debates surrounding the adoption of Article 9 revealed that states wished both to support the concept of human rights and at the same time to sustain the principle of nonintervention in domestic affairs. Most of these states already had human rights provisions in their individual constitutions. In reality, however, non-democratic regimes and large-scale poverty throughout Latin America made the realization of human rights problematic, at best.

Nevertheless, the subsequent history of the commission was one of steadily expanding activity and authority resulting from its aggressive interpretation of the mandate and the resulting perception among OAS members of a solid record of success.

The most disputed issue regarding the statute was whether the commission should be entitled to receive petitions alleging human rights violations from states, groups, or individuals. Despite the vigorous efforts of Ecuador's Gonzalo Escudero (who was later a member of the commission), this option was defeated in all forms. The commission, however, subsequently interpreted its mandate to include the right to receive "information" from individuals. This was embellished by its accompanying assertion of the need to interrogate witnesses and carry out on-site investigations when appropriate. The commission also began making recommendations to individual states, thereby identifying the human rights record of each state.

Reports were completed in the early 1960's on human rights matters in Haiti, Cuba, and the Dominican Republic. A vital turning point for the commission came with the 1965 crisis in the Dominican Republic. Amid civil strife, José A. Mora, secretary-general of the OAS, informed the Tenth Meeting of Consultation of Ministers of Foreign Affairs that he considered "essential and urgent the presence in Santo Domingo of [the] Inter-American Commission on Human Rights" to represent the OAS. The United States had already sent in military forces, which the OAS transformed into an "Inter-American Peace Force" in May.

On June 1, 1965 the commission's chair, Manuel Bianchi, arrived in the Dominican Republic. Subsequently, individual members, each with full authority, took turns representing the commission on two-week tours of duty. The commission proceeded to throw itself into the fray by mediating between the two sides, defending the rights of prisoners taken on each side, and saving nonparticipants caught in the crossfire. The commission continued as an "action body" for the OAS in the Dominican Republic for a full year, verifying the legitimacy of its June 1, 1966, elections.

The United States member, Durward V. Sandifer, noted that during the crisis the commission was literally on the "firing line" for human rights—not confining itself to studying and reporting from the sidelines, but "using its resources and prestige to help . . . end the excesses and the violations of human rights."

This episode led to a favorable review of the commission's performance at the Second Special Inter-American Conference, in 1965. The conference used the commission's record since 1959 to justify granting it additional powers. The most important of these was the right to receive petitions from individuals alleging complaints, not merely as "information." Revised Article 9 of the commission's statute also authorized the commission to request information from governments, make recommendations to them, and report on their compliance—all functions the commission had "interpreted" for itself under the previous mandate in Article 9. The commission was also directed to focus its activities upon the most fundamental rights of the American Declaration on the Rights and Duties of Man.

No less important for the future of the commission was the Third Special Inter-American Conference, held in 1967 in Buenos Aires, Argentina, which revised the OAS charter and ended the commission's dubious status as an "autonomous entity" in the OAS. Thereafter, Article 51 of the revised OAS charter anchored the Inter-American Commission on Human Rights on a firm constitutional basis as a "principal organ" within the OAS. Article 112 spelled out its functions: "to promote the observance and protection of human rights and to serve as a consultative organ of the organization in these matters." The revised OAS charter entered into force in February, 1970.

The human rights to be protected were identified and created in a significant sense by the commission itself, which had worked for several years on a draft treaty based on the American Declaration on the Rights and Duties of Man. The Second Special Inter-American Conference (which also enhanced the commission's authority) requested in 1965 that a final draft be prepared by the commission and sent to the OAS council. In April, 1966, the commission's review of the draft culminated in significant revisions, including the removal of numerous social and economic rights because they were less suited to legal enforcement and more dependent on a government's resources.

The Inter-American Specialized Conference on Human Rights convened in San José, Costa Rica, in November, 1969, and was attended by representatives of nineteen of the twenty-four OAS members. Its fruition, put forward on November 22, 1969, was the American Convention on Human Rights (ACHR). It listed twenty-three human rights, created an Inter-American Court of Human Rights, and redesigned the Inter-American Commission on Human Rights to give it additional authority through a mechanism to take complaints on violations of the ACHR from individuals and to give it authority over state-to-state complaints. The ACHR entered into force with the necessary eleventh ratification on July 18, 1978. By 1990, twenty of the thirty-two OAS states had ratified the ACHR.

## Impact of Event

The Inter-American Commission on Human Rights, in a profound sense, created the inter-American system for the protection of human rights. None of the participants at its creation in 1959 anticipated its swift emergence as a vigorous advocate for human rights, as it had been set up quickly with no well-thought-out role or procedure. Numerous observers echoed the view that the commission skillfully and imaginatively expanded its powers and thereby transformed itself.

As noted, there was a substantial gap between the reality of human rights in most OAS states in 1959 and the ideal espoused by governments in public and official forums. The commission had to deal with numerous arbitrary arrests, systematic torture, hundreds of "disappeared persons," and other flagrant human rights violations. The idea of a regional organ promoting human rights appeared to be an exercise in futility. It is to the credit of the commission that it managed, with few tools but publicity in the hands of its tenacious and dedicated personnel, to find points of leverage that could be brought to bear on its own clients.

A review of the commission's work reveals that smaller states received the bulk of critical attention in the early years. For example, no attacks were directed on the system of segregation still in place at the time in the United States. Using the credibility stored up from its astute management of these circumstances, it proceeded to take on the more politically formidable larger states, some of which were further protected by political connections with the United States.

Once the commission attained the right to receive individual petitions in 1965, it adapted this mechanism to cope more effectively with its particular social and economic context. Receiving a flood of petitions—more than a thousand new cases were opened in 1978 alone—the commission decided to "assume" the facts as alleged in a petition if an accused government failed to respond within 180 days. Moreover, the commission used individual petitions to identify "serious and repeated violations of human rights." Its country reports were the means by which the commission publicized gross, systematic violations discovered in its "general case" examinations.

The commission not only found a way effectively to promote human rights in the absence of a formal treaty document legally binding on the states but also essentially drafted that vital document—the American Convention on Human Rights—in three intensive years of work before the San José Conference. The Inter-American Commission on Human Rights has been a clear success. It has provided a more useful and relevant model than the European system for many areas of the Third World in which similar regimes—feudalistic, militaristic, or totalitarian—have had to be goaded and shamed into honoring their citizen's human rights.

## Bibliography

Blaustein, Albert, Rogers Clark, and Jay Sigler, eds. *Human Rights Source Book.* New York: Paragon House, 1987. All the major international and regional human rights documents are provided. Contains the American Declaration on the Rights and Duties of Man, the statute and regulations of the commission, and the statute and rules of procedure of the Court of Human Rights as well as other documents and judicial decisions. Index and bibliography.

Buergenthal, Thomas, Robert Norris, and Dinah Shelton, eds. *Protecting Human Rights in the Americas: Selected Problems.* Strasbourg, France: International Institute of Human Rights, 1990. This first English-language textbook on the Inter-American Human Rights system was written by a judge on the Court of Human Rights. Its first edition won the 1982-1983 Book Award from the Inter-American Bar Association. Includes cases and materials, index, and bibliography.

Farer, Tom J., ed. *The Future of the Inter-American System.* New York: Praeger, 1979. Farer was a member of the commission; the book was a special project for the American Society of International Law. Excellent background of the multiple aspects of the Inter-American system, including economics and development, trade, military issues, and nuclear proliferation as well as human rights. Includes a chapter on "Human Rights in the Inter-American System." Index but no bibliography.

Farer, Tom J., and James P. Rowles. "The Inter-American Commission on Human Rights." In *International Human Rights Law and Practice*, edited by James Tuttle. Chicago: American Bar Association, 1978. Explanation of the commission's composition, the authority of the commission, and the process of bringing a complaint before the commission. Contains a model complaint form. An appendix contains the commission's regulations regarding the communication of complaints.

Goldman, Robert K. *The Protection of Human Rights in the Americas: Past, Present, and Future.* New York: New York University Center for International Studies, 1972. A thoroughly footnoted, comprehensive summary of the origins of the Inter-American system. Offers a sustained focus on the role of the commission through its redesign under the American Convention on Human Rights. United States participation is also examined. No index or bibliography.

Gros Espiell, Hector. "The Organization of American States." In *The International Dimensions of Human Rights*, edited by Karel Vasak. Vol. 2. Westport, Conn.: Greenwood Press, 1982. Gros Espiell's chapter highlights the commission, the American Convention on Human Rights, the Inter-American Commission on Women, and the Inter-American Children's Institute. Index. Superb fifty-page bibliography on international human rights law.

Laqueur, Walter, and Barry Rubin, eds. *The Human Rights Reader.* New York: Meridian Books, 1989. Four essays on human rights introduce the documentary compilation—two on the concept of human rights, one on the politics, and one on the development of human rights in international law. Sections are excerpts from writings and documents on the philosophy of human rights, various constitutional provisions, important speeches and letters, and human rights treaties. No index. Massive twenty-six-page bibliography of commentaries on the materials included in the text, broken down by topics and time periods.

Medina Quiroga, Cecilia. *The Battle of Human Rights: Gross, Systematic Violations and the Inter-American System.* Dordrecht, The Netherlands: Martinus Nijhoff,

1988. The book, a comprehensive study of the origin and development of the inter-American system in the face of gross violations, is the Chilean author's doctoral dissertation. Includes two chapters on the commission, pre- and post-ACHR. Her concluding chapter on "Lessons of the Inter-American Experience" focuses on the commission's role. Index. Bibliography includes secondary references as well as an elaborate thirteen-page citation of all OAS documents used.

Robertson, A. H. *Human Rights in the World.* New York: St. Martin's Press, 1982. Robertson, a former director of human rights for the Council of Europe, has a chapter on the American Convention on Human Rights that contains sections on the inter-American commission and court. The author presents enormous amounts of information yet retains a lucid text. Index, no bibliography.

Schreiber, Anna P. *The Inter-American Commission on Human Rights.* Leiden, The Netherlands: A. W. Sijthoff, 1970. Perhaps the best single source on the early years of the commission. Excellent, in-depth examination of the debate over the commission's initial mandate and its evolution. Covers the general development of the inter-American human rights system and gives detailed case studies of the crucial episode in the Dominican Republic. Index. Extensive bibliography, including both primary and secondary material. Appendix includes the American Declaration on the Rights and Duties of Man.

*Nancy N. Haanstad*

## Cross-References

The Declaration on the Rights and Duties of Man Is Adopted (1948), p. 755; The United Nations Adopts the Universal Declaration of Human Rights (1948), p. 789; The European Convention on Human Rights Is Signed (1950), p. 843; The European Court of Human Rights Is Established (1950), p. 849; The Organization of American States Is Established (1951), p. 879; The U.N. Covenant on Civil and Political Rights Is Adopted (1966), p. 1353; Brazil Begins a Period of Intense Repression (1968), p. 1468; The Inter-American Court of Human Rights Is Established (1969), p. 1503; Allende Is Overthrown in a Chilean Military Coup (1973), p. 1725; The Argentine Military Conducts a "Dirty War" Against Leftists (1976), p. 1864; Indigenous Indians Become the Target of Guatemalan Death Squads (1978), p. 1972; The National Commission Against Torture Studies Human Rights Abuses (1983), p. 2186; Argentine Leaders Are Convicted of Human Rights Violations (1985), p. 2280; Voters in Chile End Pinochet's Military Rule (1989), p. 2540; Sandinistas Are Defeated in Nicaraguan Elections (1990), p. 2564.

# THE UNITED NATIONS ADOPTS THE DECLARATION OF THE RIGHTS OF THE CHILD

*Category of event:* Children's rights
*Time:* November 20, 1959
*Locale:* United Nations, New York City

*On November 20, 1959, the General Assembly of the United Nations adopted the Declaration of the Rights of the Child in recognition of the special needs of children throughout the world*

*Principal personages:*
CHARLES W. ANDERSON (1934-      ), the United States representative to the United Nations
DAG HAMMARSKJÖLD (1905-1961), the Swedish statesman who was elected secretary-general of the United Nations in 1953
EGLANTYNE JEBB (1889-1978), helped formulate the League of Nations Charter of Children's Rights, a precursor to the United Nations Declaration of the Rights of the Child

## Summary of Event

It has been said that until the twentieth century children were frequently thought of as miniature adults. People gave little or no thought to children as individuals with rights of their own. The concept of children's rights began to develop early in the twentieth century, with one of the highlights of this development being the adoption of the Declaration of the Rights of the Child by the United Nations General Assembly in 1959. This event brought before the members of the United Nations for the first time the idea that, just as adults had human rights simply by virtue of being human, so children had special rights simply by virtue of being children, over and above any civil rights that a government might give them.

The plight of children throughout the world was becoming better known because children's advocates were rising up to demand changes to benefit children. In some agricultural societies, children were expected to contribute to household and agricultural chores almost from the time they could walk. Many children were not strong enough for this exhausting and difficult work and died at an early age.

In urban societies, the Industrial Revolution brought different but equally harsh conditions for children. They worked long hours in mines and factories at difficult and strenuous work, often under unsanitary and dangerous conditions. Additionally, many children endured neglect, exploitation, and physical and sexual abuse. Some ended up in orphanages, prisons, or other institutions that provided little improvement in their lives. European children also suffered untold misery because of World War I, which left many with no one to care for them.

The prevalence of these conditions paved the way for laws to protect children. The

International Labour Organisation (ILO) was the first to adopt an international law on children's rights in 1919. Titled the Minimum Age (Industry) Convention, it prohibited the employment of children under the age of fourteen in industry. During this same year, Eglantyne Jebb, an English woman who was especially concerned about the effects of the war on children, founded the Save the Children International Union (SCIU) with strong support from the Red Cross and the Swiss Committee for the Protection of Children. Jebb believed strongly that all children caught in the ravages of war, regardless of country, should be helped; she maintained that there was no such thing as an "enemy child."

In 1923, the SCIU drafted and adopted a charter of children's rights, the first such document of its kind. In the following year, it was presented to the League of Nations, where it was officially adopted on September 24 and became known as the Declaration of the Rights of the Child, or the Geneva Declaration.

This first declaration was a simple document of only five principles and a brief preamble that stated that mankind owes to the child the best it has to give. The principles stated that children must have the means necessary for natural, moral, and spiritual development; that hungry, sick, orphaned, and disabled children were entitled to help; that children must be the first to receive relief in times of distress; and that children deserved training to earn a living, protection from exploitation, and an upbringing that would instill a sense of service to others.

Partially because the world was plunged into World War II, almost nothing was done about children's rights until after the founding of the United Nations in 1945. Children's advocates pressed to have the United Nations officially adopt the Geneva Declaration, but it was much more concerned about drafting the Universal Declaration of Human Rights in those early years, when it seemed proper, after such a devastating war and the Nazi atrocities involved in the Holocaust, to make a statement declaring the rights of all human beings. After the Universal Declaration was adopted in 1948, however, children's advocates pointed out that a number of the articles did not really apply to children and that the Geneva Declaration was now somewhat outdated. The SCIU, which had merged with the International Association for the Protection of Child Welfare to form the International Union of Child Welfare, was one of the strongest groups to exert pressure on various committees of the United Nations. In 1946 it had already added three principles to the original five of the Geneva Declaration—one, that children should be protected regardless of race, nationality, or creed; another, that the family of a child must be respected; and a third, that children should enjoy full benefits of social security and welfare programs. Even with the pressure exerted, however, it was not until the years between 1957 and 1959 that the U.N. committees involved gave their full attention to the question of children's rights.

During this time, the U.N. Social Commission, Economic and Social Council, and Commission on Human Rights all worked on a draft of a declaration based on the eight principles of the earlier Geneva Declaration. The final draft of ten principles, approved by the three groups, was submitted to the General Assembly's Third

Committee, where it was discussed extensively over a period of three months. One of the discussions related to the document's being a declaration rather than a convention, which would have included provision for implementation of the principles. The United States delegate, Charles W. Anderson, pointed out that the history of the Universal Declaration of Human Rights proved that a document did not have to be legally binding to be effective. The Universal Declaration had not only served well as a goal for all countries but had also been incorporated into the constitutions of several new countries and had become a model for national legislation. He believed that the Declaration of the Rights of the Child would also serve as a model for legislation and a guide for action on the local and national levels with respect to the well-being of children. Several countries agreed, and the document remained a declaration until it was revised twenty years later.

During the discussion, a number of more substantive questions were raised. One was whether the declaration should state in more positive terms the needs of the unborn child for special protection. Italy recommended that the phrase "from the moment of his conception" be added to the statement, noting that children need special safeguards, including legal protection. Those opposed to this amendment pointed out that countries with legalized abortion would find this difficult to accept, and, since it was such a controversial issue, the amendment could not be included if the declaration was to be universally acceptable. In place of the proposed amendment, a compromise suggested by the Philippines—the phrase "the child, before as well as after birth, needs special safeguards"—was substituted.

Another question dealt with the role of the state and the family in taking primary responsibility for the child's welfare. The Soviet Union argued that only the state could guarantee many of the rights set forth in the declaration and proposed that all states should bring their legislation into conformity with the principles of the declaration. The majority argued that the family should take the primary responsibility for the child's welfare, so the proposal was rejected, as were several similar proposals made by the Soviet Union. The group did, however, broaden the responsibility for the child's welfare by calling on parents, individuals, voluntary organizations, local authorities, and national governments to recognize children's rights and strive for their implementation.

Another proposal that was discussed was one to include the right to grow up in the religious faith of one's parents, a proposal supported primarily by Guatemala and Israel. This was not approved, because many of the delegates believed that it might pose difficulties in states of many religions and might also present problems in the case of parents of different religions.

One proposal that was not adopted, though many expressed sympathy with it, related to maladjusted and delinquent children. Italy recommended that, even though the problems presented by these children were becoming increasingly serious in many countries, the children should be treated humanely and reunited with their families whenever possible, rather than being punished. The proposal was rejected on the grounds that it was too general to permit universal application and that it was dealt with to some extent in principle 5, which concerned the care of physically, mentally, or socially handicapped children.

On a more positive side, Mexico, Peru, and Romania proposed adding to principle 7 on the child's right to education a paragraph stating that the child should have a right to play and recreation. This was unanimously approved.

All ten principles, with some additions and changes, were adopted by the Third Committee of the General Assembly on October 19, 1959, by a vote of seventy to zero, with two abstentions; the vote was confirmed by the plenary session of the General Assembly on November 20, 1959. A resolution proposed by Afghanistan, that the declaration be given the widest possible publicity, was also unanimously approved.

## Impact of Event

The impact of a declaration, as opposed to a convention, which has the force of law in countries where governments have signed the document, is difficult to assess. Although much acclaim was given to the Universal Declaration of Human Rights, it is probably safe to say that the Declaration of the Rights of the Child did not have the same impact, partly because its rights were applicable to a smaller group. The declaration was not incorporated in new constitutions, most likely because the new constitutions being formulated by Third World countries concentrated on incorporating the principles of the Universal Declaration, which were more generally applicable than were the principles of the Declaration of the Rights of the Child. Also, some of the provisions in the latter, such as the right to free elementary education, were not possible for many Third World countries.

If the literature following the promulgation of the Declaration of the Rights of the Child is any indication, one would have to say that there was little impact. After a few articles on the declaration following its approval in 1959, very little was written about it. Most books on children's rights mention the Declaration of the Rights of the Child and some describe the events leading up to it, but few throw any light on what, if any, impact it had.

UNICEF (originally the United Nations International Children's Emergency Fund, but since 1953 the United Nations Children's Fund), which was not involved in voting for the adoption of the Declaration of the Rights of the Child, did make a conscious effort to implement its principles, primarily in the fields of health, nutrition, and welfare. UNICEF was, however, heavily involved in these areas anyway and would probably have continued to be involved regardless of the adoption of the declaration.

The most positive impact of the Declaration of the Rights of the Child was that it paved the way for the Convention on the Rights of the Child. The International Year of the Child in 1979 provided an opportunity for a reevaluation of the declaration, and people became aware of the shortcomings of a document that expressed lofty ideals but had no mechanism for enforcement. Even though there had been some movement, particularly in Poland, to prepare a convention for adoption in 1979, it was only the beginning of the long, arduous work for the adoption of a thoroughly revised declaration, which finally came to fruition in 1989, during the thirtieth anniversary of the original declaration's signing.

## Bibliography

Boulding, Elise. *Children's Rights and the Wheel of Life.* New Brunswick, N.J.: Transaction Books, 1979. Convinced that the Declaration of the Rights of the Child focuses on those under fourteen and deals primarily with protection from harm, Boulding attempts to present children as actors, shapers, and contributors to society, comparing their rights, responsibilities, and opportunities to those of the elderly.

_____. "The Silenced Majority." *UNESCO Courier* 32 (January, 1979): 4-8, 34. Presents a case for children's rights, including more autonomy for children and greater opportunity to take initiative in actions that concern them. Argues that the evaluating and policy-making processes of society should be open to young people.

Cohen, Howard. *Equal Rights for Children.* Totowa, N.J.: Rowman & Littlefield, 1980. Discusses human rights in general and the rights of children in particular. Calls into question the emphasis on protectionist rights in the Declaration of the Rights of the Child; recommends extending all rights adults enjoy to children when they are applicable.

Greaney, Vincent, ed. *Children: Needs and Rights.* New York: Irvington, 1985. Presents the views of ten children's rights advocates from a multidisciplinary perspective. Includes chapters on how children's rights developed in the United States and in European countries and on the rights of children with special needs. The chapter on "The United Nations and Children's Rights" contains a copy of the text of the Declaration of the Rights of the Child and proposed revisions of it.

"The Rights of the Child: Draft Declaration Approved." *United Nations Review* 6 (November, 1959): 20-21. Explains the process of how the draft of the Declaration of the Rights of the Child came to be adopted and gives in summary form the content of the preamble and the ten principles. Makes some comparisons of the draft to the Universal Declaration of Human Rights.

"The U.N. Declaration of Rights of the Child." *Parents Magazine* 34 (December, 1959): 74, 107. Simply presents the text of the Declaration of the Rights of the Child with no comment on it. This magazine is generally available in public libraries.

Vittachi, Anuradha. *Stolen Childhood: In Search of the Rights of the Child.* Cambridge, England: Polity Press, 1989. Based on a British television series, this book reviews the plight of children all over the world whose rights have been abused. The poignant illustrations, many in color, serve to highlight the excellent text. Offers hope that the new convention will accomplish more than the declaration was able to do.

Wilderson, Albert E. *The Rights of Children.* Philadelphia: Temple University Press,

1973. Children's human and civil rights are discussed by experts in various fields. The text of the Declaration of the Rights of the Child is the first chapter. Contains a good explanation of human rights as opposed to civil rights for children. Includes extensive discussion of legal rights as they relate to social welfare.

*Lucille Whalen*

## Cross-References

Students Challenge Corporal Punishment in British Schools (1911), p. 109; The International Labour Organisation Is Established (1919), p. 270; Supreme Court Rules That States Cannot Compel Flag Salutes (1943), p. 629; The United Nations Children's Fund Is Established (1946), p. 689; Head Start Is Established (1965), p. 1284; Parents Anonymous Is Established to Treat Abusive Parents (1971), p. 1639; The United Nations Declares Rights for the Mentally Retarded (1971), p. 1644; Congress Passes the Child Abuse Prevention and Treatment Act (1974), p. 1752; Congress Enacts the Education for All Handicapped Children Act (1975), p. 1780; The United Nations Adopts the Convention on the Rights of the Child (1989), p. 2529.

# CUBANS FLEE TO FLORIDA AND RECEIVE ASSISTANCE

*Category of event:* Refugee relief
*Time:* The 1960's
*Locale:* Florida

*In the wake of the Castro revolution, hundreds of thousands of Cuban refugees fled to the United States, most of them initially to Florida*

*Principal personages:*
DWIGHT D. EISENHOWER (1890-1969), the thirty-fourth president of the United States, in office at the outset of the Cuban refugee flow
FIDEL CASTRO (1927- ), the premier (later president) of Cuba and instigator of the revolution that spawned the refugee flow
JOHN F. KENNEDY (1917-1963), the thirty-fifth president of the United States, who substantially broadened federal participation in the Cuban refugee program

## Summary of Event

The story of the Cuban refugee flows of the 1960's begins inside Cuba, which, during the late 1950's, experienced a revolutionary change in regimes. After several years of guerrilla operations, Fidel Castro vaulted from his position as the leader of a small ragtag army to the unquestioned leadership of Cuba, toppling former dictator Fulgencio Batista in January of 1959. Within months, Castro reorganized the Cuban army, arrested and executed members of the former Batista government, suspended elections for four years, and initiated an agrarian reform that saw millions of acres of land expropriated from its previous owners by the government. During 1960, Castro gradually and more openly embraced Communist ideology. He established diplomatic relations with the Soviet Union, nationalized all private schools, stamped out the free and critical press, expropriated foreign-owned oil refineries and American sugar holdings in Cuba, and began to purge Cuba's judicial system.

The revolutionary changes that swept Cuba during this time were generally perceived as having benefited the lower classes at the direct expense of the propertied elites of the nation. Given the generally high level of political repression and the rapid and sustained attacks against the wealthy, many of Cuba's professional and business elites fled the country. By the middle of 1960, some 87,000 Cubans had sought asylum in the United States, chiefly in the Miami, Florida, area. Within three years, another 170,000 followed them, and the numbers continued to mount throughout the 1960's to a total for the decade of about 500,000. That total continued to climb in several waves. By the end of the 1980's, the United States had accepted more than 800,000 Cuban refugees onto its shores since the inception of the Castro revolution.

Although refugees' motivations for flight from Cuba have changed over the years, some persistent patterns explain why large numbers chose to flee. In the early waves, imprisonment and the threat of imprisonment motivated some to flee, while others objected to the intrusiveness of the revolutionaries and their followers who joined Castro's neighborhood Committees for the Defense of the Revolution. Formed by Castro in 1960, these committees encouraged Cubans who supported the Communist revolution to perform surveillance functions on their neighbors and to report those who spoke out against the revolution or failed to show enthusiasm for it. Apart from these more direct forms of political persecution, many of the early escapees fled because they had lost their jobs or property and thus could no longer earn a livelihood in Cuba. Others were simply opponents of Communism or of the tactics employed by Castro's revolutionaries. A substantial number of the earliest escapees were professionals, doctors, lawyers, and educators. As time passed, family reunification and economic betterment became major factors motivating flight, and larger numbers from the middle and lower-middle classes joined in the exodus.

Relations between Cuba and the United States deteriorated during 1960. President Dwight D. Eisenhower responded to the perceived threat of growing Communism by halting imports of Cuban sugar and embargoing exports to Cuba. In January of 1961, the United States broke diplomatic relations with Cuba. Moreover, with growing numbers of militant Cuban exiles pressing for U.S. assistance to topple the Castro regime, Eisenhower initiated plans for the Bay of Pigs invasion, plans that were carried out in April of 1961, several months after President John F. Kennedy took office. The invasion was a colossal failure, and, far from toppling Castro, cemented his hold over Cuba.

As U.S.-Cuban relations deteriorated, the number of exiles from Cuba to the United States increased. By the end of his administration, Eisenhower had concluded that the United States should pursue an open-door policy toward Cuban exiles, essentially admitting all Cubans who sought refuge in the United States. Politically, this policy was seen as a way to deprive Castro of his most educated and productive subjects and to embarrass his regime. From a humanitarian perspective, the upshot was that thousands of potential persecutees found safe haven in America.

After a brief downturn in 1963 and 1964, during which time the number of exiles fleeing Cuba amounted to little more than fifteen thousand in each year, the number of exiles shot back up to an annual level of fifty thousand. This resumption of high exile rates was directly related to Castro's decision in 1965 to promote exile rather than hinder it. He invited Cubans in the United States to come to the port of Camarioca to pick up their relatives by boat. Thus began the Camarioca exodus, which was later mimicked by Castro during the Mariel boatlift exodus of 1980. During and after 1965, large numbers of Cubans, many of whom already had families in Florida, opted to leave Cuba by boat or air with the sanction of the Castro regime. Indeed, by November of 1965, the United States and Cuba had formally entered into an agreement that eventually saw more than 350,000 Cubans transported to the United States through governmentally sponsored and safe, rather than clandestine and hazardous, means.

The fact that a substantial Cuban community existed nearby in Southern Florida even prior to the refugee movements contributed to the decision of many Cubans to seek asylum in the United States. The local Cuban community and civic leaders in Southern Florida were generally responsive to the assistance needs of these refugees. When it became apparent that the flow could persist indefinitely at a high rate, however, state and local officials began to agitate for a more substantial federal role in both assistance and relocation to take the pressure off local resources. Federal involvement began under Eisenhower, who sought congressional approval for admittance of the Cuban exiles and special programs for admission of unaccompanied children under the Cuban Children's Program. In December of 1960, federal money began to flow from Washington into the Cuban Refugee Emergency Center in Miami.

Kennedy built on Eisenhower's policies by formally announcing the creation of the Cuban Refugee Program in the early months of his administration. This program was placed under the stewardship of the Department of Health, Education, and Welfare. It substantially expanded federal involvement in providing assistance for health, welfare, and education services to local governmental authorities and private voluntary organizations for the benefit of Cubans. Also initiated as part of this program was a highly successful relocation program designed to take the pressure off Florida by resettling Cubans in other parts of the United States. By the end of 1972 alone, this program saw nearly 300,000 of Miami's 450,000 Cuban refugees resettled in virtually every state in the union. In 1962, the federal government pumped nearly $40 million into the Cuban Refugee Program. Ten years later, the total approached $140 million annually.

There can be little doubt that the generous federal assistance, combined with state and local resources and the ceaseless efforts of countless private voluntary organizations, speeded the integration of the Cuban exiles into the American economy. The resettlement program, often implemented by private organizations and churches, saw Cubans settled in communities throughout the United States. Thus, although most early Cuban exiles left their homeland with the expectation that they would soon return, many found that their new lives in the United States were quite comfortable. As a second and third generation was born and reared in the United States, many original exiles eventually took American citizenship. This process was further abetted by the realization that the Castro regime was well ensconced and unlikely to reform its policies. The failure of the Bay of Pigs invasion, the consolidation of Castro's power in Cuba, and the longevity of his regime further contributed to the assimilation of many Cuban exiles in the United States.

## Impact of Event

The flight of Cuban exiles had several significant effects both in Cuba and in the United States. Cuba lost most of its highly educated and professional classes during the first year or so of the exodus. The loss of brainpower and skills had two different but related effects. First, Cuba's economic development was no doubt set back by decades, especially when the refugee loss was coupled with the imposition of socialist economic policies. Second, the flight of these classes made it possible for Castro to consolidate his hold over Cuba and to initiate his revolutionary programs without what would have been predictable resistance from educated elites. The exodus, then, simultaneously facilitated the implementation of Communism and deprived the country of its most talented people. The gradual decline in economic productivity and in the standard of living in Cuba was a predictable long-term consequence of the refugee exodus, of Communist economic policy, and of Western economic retaliation. On the other hand, more positive aspects of Cuba's revolution could be seen in the increased rates of literacy and the broader access of poor Cubans to basic, if limited, health care.

The effects of the Cuban migration on the United States were various and considerable. Local health, education, and welfare services in Florida were overwhelmed by Cuban arrivals. To offset the pressure on local and state agencies, the federal government spent more than a billion dollars in refugee assistance and resettlement programs. This intergovernmental cooperation was accompanied by cooperation between government and private voluntary agencies, thus contributing to the further development of institutional mechanisms for responding to later refugee situations. More than eight hundred thousand Cuban exiles benefited from this assistance. They settled throughout the United States, although the highest concentrations remained in Florida. Cubans have proved in the long run to be highly productive members of American society, although frictions are to be found between Cubans and other minority populations, especially in the Miami area, where competition for blue-collar and low-skill employment is often intense. These social tensions, however, are largely offset by the substantial contributions Cubans have made over time to their new country.

The Cuban refugee flow of the 1960's should not be seen as an isolated or temporary event. Cuban support for and American opposition to revolutionary movements in Latin America have precipitated or exacerbated conflicts in the region, most notably in Central America and Grenada. Many of these contests have in turn generated large numbers of refugees and displaced persons while endangering the human rights of thousands. Nor was the effect of the original Cuban exodus during the 1960's limited to that decade alone. Cuban migration to the United States has been a long-term phenomenon with occasionally intense periods of exodus. In 1980, some 125,000 Cubans took flight during the Mariel episode. This sudden outflow of refugees, which was actively encouraged by Castro and which he exploited to rid his country of criminals and mental health cases, immediately challenged the effectiveness of the newly adopted U.S. Refugee and Migration Act of 1980. President Jimmy Carter ultimately allowed Cubans into the United States through the use of his parole power rather than through the quota provisions included in the act, although many refugees suspected of having criminal records were detained indefinitely. Thus, even thirty years after Cubans first began in large numbers to seek asylum in the United States, the legacy of flight and asylum continued to be a major factor in relations between Cuba and the United States.

## Bibliography

Fagen, Richard R., Richard A. Brody, and Thomas J. O'Leary. *Cubans in Exile: Disaffection and the Revolution.* Stanford, Calif.: Stanford University Press, 1968. This book chronicles the political context of the Castro revolution and assumption of power and the refugee exodus precipitated by it. Based on extensive fieldwork and interviews, it is especially insightful in identifying the factors that prompted Cuban exiles to flee from their homeland. Includes notes, appendices, and an index.

Gallagher, Patrick Lee. *The Cuban Exile: A Socio-Political Analysis.* New York: Arno Press, 1980. This interesting case study, a reprint of the author's Ph.D. dissertation of 1974, explores the impact of Cuban exiles in the Miami area as well as the social, political, economic, and psychological experience of Cubans in exile. It focuses on the 1960's experience of Cubans in Florida. Includes appendices and a bibliography. No index.

Larzelere, Alex. *The 1980 Cuban Boatlift: Castro's Ploy—America's Dilemma.* Washington, D.C.: National Defense University Press, 1988. Although this extensive treatment of the Mariel boatlift does not provide much historical context of the earlier refugee movements of the 1960's, it does describe and assess one of the later phases of the Cuban refugee flow. Contains extensive references, a bibliography, an index, and appendices.

Loescher, Gil, and John A. Scanlan. *Calculated Kindness: Refugees and America's Half-Open Door, 1945-Present.* New York: Free Press, 1986. This sometimes overly critical and partial account of American refugee policy nevertheless provides useful insights into the domestic politics of refugee admission policy. The Cuban case is dealt with in chapters 3, 4, and 9, principally in an effort to show how an admissions double standard evolved: Cubans received preferred treatment, while other migrants from non-Communist regimes were handled restrictively. Includes a bibliography and an index.

Masud-Piloto, Felix Roberto. *With Open Arms: Cuban Migration to the United States.* Totowa, N.J.: Rowman & Littlefield, 1988. An excellent, brief, highly readable and balanced treatment of the Cuban migration to the United States, this book sets the refugee exodus in a broad historical context. Well documented. Includes tables, bibliography, and index.

Zolberg, Aristide, Astri Suhrke, and Sergei Aguayo. *Escape from Violence: Conflict and the Refugee Crisis in the Developing World.* New York: Oxford University Press, 1989. Chapter 7 of this excellent work devotes substantial attention to the Cuban revolution and the exile phenomenon. It also treats some of the consequences of these events for the United States and the region. Extensive notes and an index are included.

*Robert F. Gorman*

## Cross-References

The United Nations High Commissioner for Refugees Statute Is Approved (1950), p. 855; The U.N. Convention Relating to the Status of Refugees Is Adopted (1951), p. 867; Castro Takes Power in Cuba (1959), p. 1026; The Inter-American Commission on Human Rights Is Created (1959), p. 1032; The Inter-American Court of Human Rights Is Established (1969), p. 1503; Allende Is Overthrown in a Chilean Military Coup (1973), p. 1725; Indigenous Indians Become the Target of Guatemalan Death Squads (1978), p. 1972; Somoza Is Forced Out of Power in Nicaragua (1979), p. 2035; Race Riot Breaks Out in Miami, Protesting Police Brutality (1980), p. 2101; A Helsinki Watch Report Proposes Reform of Refugee Laws (1989), p. 2494.

# THE IRAQI GOVERNMENT PROMOTES
# GENOCIDE OF KURDS

*Category of event:* Atrocities and war crimes
*Time:* The 1960's
*Locale:* Iraq

*The Kurds, one-fifth of Iraq's population, have struggled ceaselessly for their rights; successive Iraqi governments have responded with repression*

   *Principal personages:*
   MULLA MUSTAFA AL-BARZANI (1904-1979), the Kurdish leader from 1943 to 1979
   ABDUL KARIM KASSEM (1914-1963), the prime minister of Iraq, 1958-1963
   ABDUL SALAM ARIF (1921-1966), the president of Iraq, 1963-1966
   ABDUL RAHMAN ARIF, the president of Iraq, 1966-1968
   AHMAD HASAN AL-BAKR (1914-1982), the prime minister of Iraq, 1963, and president of Iraq, 1968-1979
   SADDAM HUSSEIN (1937-    ), the deputy to the president of Iraq, 1969-1979, and president of Iraq, 1979-
   ABDUL RAHMAN AL-BAZZAZ (1912-    ), the prime minister of Iraq, 1965-1966
   JALAL AL-TALABANI (1933-    ), a Kurdish leader
   IBRAHIM AHMAD (1914-    ), a Kurdish leader

## Summary of Event

The history of the Kurds is tragedy incarnate. Their constant sufferings and ceaseless burdens in the 1960's in Iraq represent the imposition of diabolism. The Kurds' story records the utmost cruelty inflicted by national dictatorships and international abandonment.

The invocation of their history contributed to the Kurds' desire to survive the persecution of countless adversaries in the Middle East. Claiming descent from the Medes, destroyers of Balshazzar's Babylon, Kurds fought repeatedly against aggressors in ancient and medieval eras. The Kurds found inspiration in recalling the deeds of their greatest hero, Saladin. In early modern times, the Kurds were caught between two juggernauts, the Ottoman and Persian empires.

The Ottomans' defeat in World War I and the long Persian decline provided a golden opportunity for the creation of an independent Kurdistan. In 1920, the victorious Allies imposed on the Ottoman Empire the Treaty of Sèvres. This stated that in eastern Anatolia there would be established the autonomous state of Kurdistan, which might become independent. The vast bulk of the Kurdish people, however, lay outside the proposed state and were relegated to France, Syria, Persia, and Armenia. In 1923, the Ottoman Empire's successor, the Republic of Turkey, renegotiated the Treaty of Sèvres in the Treaty of Lausanne. This omitted any mention of Kurdistan. Indeed, Turkey moved swiftly to eradicate any manifestation of Kurdish nationalism, baldly labeling Kurds as "Mountain Turks." In Persia, Reza Shah Pahlavi, who assumed power in 1923, also worked to destroy Kurdish nationalism.

Aspirations for freedom after World War I loomed large among the Kurds of northern Mesopotamia, once a part of the Ottoman Empire. The British, however, with the acquiescence of the League of Nations, placed all of Mesopotamia in the newly created Kingdom of Iraq. Thus the Kurds, one-fifth of Iraq's population, were placed under an Arab-dominated regime. A Kurd, General Bakr Sidqi, dictatorially ruled monarchical Iraq in 1936 and 1937, but he did not help his fellow Kurds. Several Kurdish rebellions occurred against the Iraqi monarchy. The last, beginning in 1943 and led by Mulla Mustafa al-Barzani, was crushed in 1945 by Great Britain's air force. Kurdish tribal differences had undermined al-Barzani.

In 1958, Brigadier General Abdul Karim Kassem overthrew the Iraqi monarchy and proclaimed the Republic of Iraq. At first the Kurds welcomed Kassem, because his constitution accorded equal weight to Kurds and Arabs, and Kassem permitted Mulla Mustafa al-Barzani and the hundreds who had followed him into exile to return. Soon, al-Barzani suspected Kassem of giving lip service to Kurdish demands for autonomy. In 1961, al-Barzani demanded Kurdish autonomy. Kassem then bombed Barzan village, whereupon al-Barzani, joined by the Kurdish Democratic Party, revolted. Kassem inflicted heavy casualties on al-Barzani's forces. Nevertheless, the heavily outnumbered Kurds fought on, badly sapping Kassem's strength and contributing to his overthrow in 1963.

In February, 1963, the Ba'thists, Arab nationalists, seized Iraq's government. The Kurds suffered even more than they had under Kassem. Nevertheless, the Kurds recovered by winter 1963, and the Ba'thists' inability to deal with the Kurds contributed to the Ba'thists' downfall in 1963.

Field Marshal Abdul Salam Arif then dominated the Iraqi government. In February, 1964, Arif and Mulla Mustafa al-Barzani agreed to a cease-fire, calling for recognition of Kurdish national rights in the Iraqi constitution, general amnesty, and a reinstatement of Kurds in the civil service and the military, but there was no mention of autonomy. This agreement, however, led to a deep split in the Kurdish movement. Jalal al-Talabani and Ibrahim Ahmad of the Kurdish Democratic Party demanded a proclamation of Kurdish autonomy. Al-Barzani persuaded a congress of the Kurdish Democratic Party to expel al-Talabani, Ahmad, and fourteen other members from that movement. Al-Barzani received the support of the Iranian Kurdish Democratic Party. Moreover, he received large shipments of arms from Iran's government. Al-Barzani controlled 13,500 square miles and one million inhabitants in Iraq. He also controlled the Turkish and Iranian borders.

The cease-fire soon broke down. By June, 1964, Arif and al-Barzani had serious difficulties. In October, these intensified when al-Barzani demanded autonomy for the Kurds and the transformation of his forces (*peshmergas*) into a regular frontier force. In January, 1965, Arif stated that there would be no further negotiations until the Kurdish army was dismantled, and he pronounced Kurdish autonomy nonnegotiable. In April, 1965, the Iraqi regime and al-Barzani's movement clashed. Iran backed al-Barzani, leading to fighting between Iraq and Iran.

Strife continued in the 1960's, notwithstanding Arif's accidental death in April, 1966. His elder brother, Major General Abdul Rahman Arif, succeeded him as president of Iraq and proved to be weak. In May, 1966, conditions strongly favored the Kurds. They won the fiercely fought Battle of Handrin, thereby preserving their actual autonomy. That battle and President Arif's delegation of power to Prime Minister Abdul Rahman al-Bazzaz, whom the Kurds trusted, produced the June 29 Declaration.

The June 29 Declaration was the most liberal recognition of Kurdish rights up to that time. The Iraqi government explicitly recognized the national rights of the Kurds; the accord admitted that the Iraqi homeland included two main nationalities, Arabs and Kurds. The rights of the Kurds were to be clarified in the permanent constitution upon its promulgation. Thus, for the first time an Iraqi government recognized the binational character of the Iraqi state. The declaration also promised the Kurds decentralization to give them freedom to deal with their own affairs; Kurdish provinces, districts, and subdistricts were to enjoy a recognized corporate personality; and free elections for administrative councils were to occur.

The 1966 declaration devoted special attention to the Kurdish language and culture. Kurdish received recognition as an official language and was to be the medium of instruction in schools in the Kurdish areas, together with Arabic. The University of Baghdad was to give special attention to the study of the Kurdish language, including its literature and ideological and historical traditions; a university was to be established in Iraqi Kurdistan when funds were available. The declaration promised the Kurds their own political and literary press in the Kurdish region, in Arabic, Kurdish, or both, according to the wishes of the people concerned.

The declaration proclaimed equality between Kurds and Arabs in all spheres in Iraq in grants, ministries, public departments, and the diplomatic and military services. Only Kurds were to hold posts in the Kurdish regions as long as the number required was available.

The declaration pledged the government to spend funds on the reconstruction of Kurdistan. Institutions and departments were to be created to develop and improve the Kurdish region. The government was to compensate all those who had suffered damages and would resettle Kurds who had been evacuated back to their own regions.

The declaration also contained secret clauses. One acknowledged the Kurdish demand for the creation of a new all-Kurdish province out of Mosul province. Another permitted public operation for the Kurdish Democratic Party. The final secret clause declared a step-by-step general amnesty.

The 1966 declaration brought peace to Iraqi Kurdistan. The military, however, thought that the declaration humiliated it. In July, 1966, it forced Prime Minister al-Bazzaz's resignation. His replacement would not implement the declaration and encouraged the Talabani-Ahmad group to attack al-Barzani's forces. President Arif attempted to appease al-Barzani, but the army and the Ba'th Party overthrew Arif in July, 1968.

Field Marshal Ahmad Hasan al-Bakr then took Iraq's presidency. His cousin, Saddam Hussein, became deputy to the president. The government tried to undermine al-Barzani by favoring the Talabani-Ahmad faction and by implementing certain sections of the 1966 declaration. In the fall of 1968, Iraq's army and al-Barzani's clashed. Iran gave massive aid to al-Barzani. In March, 1970, Saddam Hussein and al-Barzani agreed to terms: Kurdish autonomy, proportional representation of Kurds in a national legislature, appointment of a Kurdish vice president at the national level, expenditure of an equitable amount of oil revenue in the autonomous region, and recognition of Kurdish and Arabic as official languages in Kurdish territory. Al-Barzani agreed to integrate his forces into the Iraqi army, but the government was to withdraw support from the Talabani-Ahmad clique. The agreement was to take effect after the fourth anniversary of its signing. It failed in its goals, however, and ultimately Saddam Hussein would seek to smash the Kurds.

## Impact of Event

The Kurds present a most interesting story in the history of human rights. Numbering almost twenty million persons in 1990, the Kurds were a Middle Eastern people without independence. They were most numerous in Turkey, Iran, and Iraq. Smaller numbers existed in Syria and the Soviet Union, and the smallest Kurdish communities were in Afghanistan and Lebanon. The Kurds continued to be subject to abuse in practically every country they inhabited, particularly Turkey, Iran, and Iraq.

Iraq's treatment of the Kurds features violence joined to broken promises. This applies to one Iraqi regime after another. The Hashemite monarchy of 1921 to 1958, a creation and perpetual satellite of the British, repressed the Kurds, causing revolts. The Republic of Iraq easily outdistanced the monarchy in viciousness. The enormity of the governmental crimes is highlighted by the fact that both monarchy and republic were controlled by Sunni Muslims who committed atrocities on the Kurds.

Prime Minister Abdul Karim Kassem, founder of the Republic of Iraq, fought the Kurds from 1961 to 1963. By January, 1962, his air force had indiscriminately bombed five hundred Kurdish villages, killed fifty thousand people, and rendered eighty thousand homeless. Momentarily, Kassem attracted some Kurds whom he used against al-Barzani's rebellious Kurds: Kassem's quislings burned crops, slaughtered livestock, demolished houses, and looted. The number of Kurds going over to Kassem declined drastically, however, and al-Barzani's revolt survived.

Kassem's executor, the Ba'th Party, intensified the fight against the Kurds in 1963. Prime Minister al-Bakr's forces bombarded Kurdish villages with tanks and heavy artillery and from the air. In the Kurds' beloved city of Suleymanieh, the Iraqi army massacred 280 civilians and buried them in a mass grave. Al-Bakr's forces also bulldozed Kurdish villages under their control and began "arabization" of strategic areas. They made massive deportations, including most of the Kurdish population of 150,000 in Kirkuk. The Soviet Union and the United Arab Republic protested these atrocities, but the Iraqi government had support from Great Britain and the United States. Nevertheless, Kurdish resistance outlived the Ba'th's fall in November, 1963.

Between April, 1965, and his death a year later, President Abdul Salam Arif fought al-Barzani's Kurds. His methods duplicated those of his predecessors in the republican regime. Again, al-Barzani continued the Kurdish cause.

In April and May, 1966, President Abdul Rahman Arif sought to crush al-Barzani's Kurds. Again the Iraqi army waged total warfare against both the military and civilians. Al-Barzani's victory at the Battle of Handrin on May 11-12, 1966, however, forced Arif to end the war.

In the fall of 1968, President al-Bakr resumed the war against al-Barzani. Abetted by Saddam Hussein, his cousin and deputy, al-Bakr repeated the harsh methods he had employed in his war of extermination in 1963. An example was the burning alive of sixty-seven women and children in a cave where they had sought refuge. Al-Barzani fought on and obtained favorable terms in the 1970 peace agreement.

Like its predecessors, the Iraqi government repudiated the peace. In 1974, al-Bakr and the increasingly powerful Saddam Hussein warred against al-Barzani's Kurds. The government would perpetrate even greater horrors. Saddam Hussein would continue these abominations in the 1980's and beyond.

## Bibliography

Chaliand, Gerard, ed. *People Without a Country: The Kurds and Kurdistan.* London: Zed Press, 1980. A fine collection of articles about the Kurds in various countries. Maps, chronology, annotated bibliography, index. Excellent notes.

Ghareeb, Edmund. *The Kurdish Question in Iraq.* Syracuse, N.Y.: Syracuse University Press, 1981. Strong concentration on the perennial Kurdish question in Iraq by a recognized scholar. Presents the Iraqi nationalist point of view. Excellent documentation, including interviews. Good print, maps, index.

Ghassemlou, Abdul Rahman. *Kurdistan and the Kurds.* London: Collet's Holdings, 1965. A Kurd writes fervently on behalf of his oppressed people. Invocation of Karl Marx's and Vladimir Ilich Lenin's writings to buttress the Kurdish cause. Documentation from sources in several languages. Interesting statistics. Bibliography, index.

Jawad, Sa'ad. *Iraq and the Kurdish Question, 1958-1970.* London: Ithaca Press, 1981. Comprehensive treatment of Iraqi Kurdistan since the establishment of the Republic of Iraq. Critical of the Kurdish leadership. An appendix includes the program of the Kurdish Democratic Party. Largely based on interviews and publications of the Iraqi government and various political parties. Bibliography, index.

Al-Khalil, Samir. *Republic of Fear: The Politics of Modern Iraq.* Berkeley: University of California Press, 1989. Admirable inquiry into the meaning of the Ba'th regime established in 1968. First-class footnotes. Useful chronology and appealing appendix discussing purges of high-ranking officers, Ba'thist old guard, and important politicians. Excellent index.

Kimball, Lorenzo Kent. *The Changing Pattern of Political Power in Iraq, 1958 to 1971.* New York: Robert Speller and Sons, 1972. Places the Kurds within the context of the twin forces of nationalism and militarism and the resulting series of coups d'état that have racked Iraq. Extensive bibliography. Index and valuable documents.

Marr, Phebe. *The Modern History of Iraq.* Boulder, Colo.: Westview Press, 1985. A well-informed, straightforward history of modern Iraq. Reliable treatment of Kurds. Amply documented. Splendidly annotated bibliography. Helpful tables and glossary. Name and subject indexes.

O'Ballance, Edgar. *The Kurdish Revolt: 1961-1970.* Hamden, Conn.: Archon Books, 1973. Excellent objective history based on the author's visit to Kurdish territory and interviews with Arab Iraqis and Kurds. Interesting treatment of Mulla Mustafa al-Barzani. Maps and a good chronological summary.

Pelletiere, Stephen C. *The Kurds: An Unstable Element in the Gulf.* Boulder, Colo.: Westview Press, 1984. Attempts to analyze the significance of the Kurds in the Persian Gulf through an overall perspective. The author has known most of the Kurdish leaders. Map, extensive documentation, a useful index, and an appendix containing the Twelve Point Program of 1966.

Schmidt, Dana Adams. *Journey Among Brave Men.* Boston: Little, Brown, 1964. An American reporter's firsthand account of the Kurdish movement and the Kurdish war during the early 1960's. Sympathetic to the Kurds. Fascinating interviews with Kurdish leaders. Map, chronology, illustrations, index.

*Erving E. Beauregard*

## Cross-References

China Initiates a Genocide Policy Toward Tibetans (1950), p. 826; China Occupies Tibet (1950), p. 837; The European Convention on Human Rights Is Signed (1950), p. 843; The Sudanese Civil War Erupts (1955), p. 941; The U.N. Covenant on Civil and Political Rights Is Adopted (1966), p. 1353; The Proclamation of Teheran Sets Human Rights Goals (1968), p. 1430; Conflicts in Pakistan Lead to the Secession of Bangladesh (1971), p. 1611; Burundi's Government Commits Genocide of the Bahutu Majority (1972), p. 1668; Khmer Rouge Take Over Cambodia (1975), p. 1791; Palestinian Civilians Are Massacred in West Beirut (1982), p. 2164; Iraq's Government Uses Poison Gas Against Kurdish Villagers (1988), p. 2397; Iraq Invades and Ravages Kuwait (1990), p. 2600.

# GREENSBORO SIT-INS LAUNCH A NEW STAGE IN THE CIVIL RIGHTS MOVEMENT

*Categories of event:* Racial and ethnic rights; civil rights
*Time:* February-July, 1960
*Locale:* Greensboro, North Carolina

*Sit-ins by black college students in Greensboro, North Carolina, led to the integration of variety-store lunch counters and inspired similar direct-action tactics across the South*

*Principal personages:*

EZELL BLAIR, JR. (1942-    ), a freshman at North Carolina A & T, one of the "Greensboro Four" who started the sit-in

FRANKLIN MCCAIN (1943-    ), a freshman at North Carolina A & T, one of the "Greensboro Four"

JOSEPH MCNEIL (1942-    ), a freshman at North Carolina A & T, one of the "Greensboro Four"

DAVID RICHMOND (1942-    ), a freshman at North Carolina A & T, one of the "Greensboro Four"

EDWARD R. ZANE (1899-    ), a Greensboro city council member who chaired the committee seeking a negotiated settlement

RALPH JOHNS (1916-    ), a white clothing store owner who urged the black college students to act against segregation

## Summary of Event

Despite court decisions, limited integration of public schools, and events such as the Montgomery bus boycott, much of American life remained racially segregated as the United States entered the 1960's. This was especially true in the southern and border states, where the Jim Crow system of legally imposed racial separation remained largely intact. One symbol of the discrimination suffered by southerners of African descent was the fact that while they could shop in variety stores, they were not allowed to sit down and eat at the lunch counters often found in such establishments.

In 1960, Greensboro, North Carolina, was a rapidly growing city of 120,000 that prided itself on the progressive nature of its race relations. Segregated conditions were as characteristic of Greensboro, however, as they were of cities with reputations for racial violence and intimidation. Despite the fact that Greensboro had been one of the few southern cities to accept publicly the Supreme Court's 1954 decision in *Brown v. Board of Education* that overturned the doctrine of "separate but equal" in public education, the city had permitted only token integration of its schools. Its lunch counters would serve blacks only if they stood, and the color line was effectively maintained in most areas of the city's life.

The prevailing order was unexpectedly challenged on February 1, 1960, when four college students from the all-black North Carolina Agricultural and Technical College (A & T) entered the Woolworth's variety store in downtown Greensboro. To illustrate the illogical nature of the system, the four first bought toothpaste and school supplies, carefully collecting their receipts as proof that the store would sell them merchandise. They then took seats at the lunch counter, to the amazement of store employees and other patrons. They were refused service and, after asking why Woolworth's would sell them toothpaste but not coffee, they left the lunch counter. There was no confrontation with the police, although a reporter did arrive and news of the sit-in was reported by the local press.

The four freshmen—Ezell Blair, Jr., Franklin McCain, Joseph McNeil, and David Richmond—had not launched their protest as part of an orchestrated campaign. Rather, they were encouraged to undertake a public act of protest against segregation by Ralph Johns, the white owner of a clothing store who employed A & T students. Johns provided the students with the money for the items they purchased at Woolworth's and was also responsible for tipping off the newspaper. The students, however, acted on their own initiative and decided to challenge the Jim Crow system the night before the sit-in. During an animated discussion that night, triggered by Franklin McCain's recent experience with segregated bus travel, they dared one another to act. The four later acknowledged the influence of Mohandas Gandhi's example of nonviolence but stressed that their primary motivation derived from their own Christian convictions and sense of justice. Although all four had been youth members of the National Association for the Advancement of Colored People (NAACP), neither it nor any other civil rights organization was involved in the initial sit-in.

News of the protest by the four freshmen spread rapidly over the A & T campus and throughout the city. A Student Executive Committee for Justice was quickly formed, with the four at the center. The next day, February 2, twenty-three additional students accompanied the original quartet to Woolworth's. What had begun as a small protest began to grow, eventually becoming a mass movement. Soon the demonstrators were working in shifts, and the sit-in spread to Kress's, the other downtown variety store. The demonstrators invariably were well dressed and emphasized their commitment to nonviolence. The stores refused to serve them but did not ask the local police to arrest them. White hecklers, one of whom tried to set the coat of a demonstrator on fire, created some tension.

By the end of the week, the sit-ins had grown through the support of students from Bennett College, a black women's college in town, as well as through some participation by students from Greensboro's white colleges. Tensions ran high, however, and on February 6, a bomb scare prompted the closing of both the Woolworth and Kress stores. By this time, a well-organized student protest movement was in place, one that enjoyed wide support from Greensboro's black community as well as national assistance from the Congress of Racial Equality (CORE), which began to organize boycotts of Woolworth and Kress in some northern cities. On February 8, sit-ins began in the neighboring city of Winston-Salem, and from there the phenomenon quickly spread.

In the wake of the bomb scare, the students agreed to a two-week truce, which was subsequently extended as efforts began to negotiate an end to the protests. Edward R. Zane, a city council member who had strong ties to the local business community, pressed for action from Greensboro's mayor, George Roach. The latter eventually agreed to create a committee to seek a negotiated settlement and named Zane to head it.

The mayor's committee was appointed at the end of February and spent all of March gathering information and attempting to mediate between the students and the stores. The committee's mail showed that many in the community sympathized with the students' position. Managers of the two stores, however, believed that they were being singled out unfairly and were unwilling to desegregate without other eating establishments doing the same. The city's restaurants were unsympathetic to the variety stores' plight, however. At the end of the month, the committee announced that it had failed to achieve a settlement.

The sit-ins resumed on April 1. The next day, the two stores closed their lunch counters. Greensboro's black community responded with an economic boycott and street demonstrations that demanded an end to segregated eating facilities. The picketing soon attracted counterpickets organized by the Ku Klux Klan, and the generally peaceful confrontations between the two groups became a feature of life in downtown Greensboro. Kress's reopened its lunch counter later in the month but roped it off to allow store personnel to control access. When students peacefully moved into the restricted area, some forty-five of them were arrested, including three of the "Greensboro Four." This was the only mass arrest during the sit-in campaign. The students were released without bail.

As the stand-off continued, downtown stores found that their business was falling off; Woolworth's sales fell by twenty percent. The economic boycott was directly effective, and in addition many whites stayed away to avoid whatever trouble might occur downtown. In these circumstances, pressure for a settlement mounted. The local newspapers had for some time been sympathetic to the demonstrators' aims, if not always with their methods. Civic leaders and businesspeople not only worried about lost revenue but also feared the loss of Greensboro's progressive image. In June, Zane's committee undertook further negotiations. Finally, the stores agreed to the committee's recommendation that they desegregate their lunch counters, although they waited until school was out in order to avoid the appearance of giving in to the students. Without public announcement, the lunch counters desegregated on July 25, 1960. The first black patrons served were the stores' own employees.

## Impact of Event

The Greensboro sit-ins marked the opening of a major new phase in the civil rights movement, one characterized by large-scale, grass-roots protests against segregated conditions in public accommodations. Such direct action tactics, rather than protracted legal battles in the courts, would mark the civil rights movement of the first half of the 1960's. It was after Greensboro that the struggle for civil rights truly became a mass movement.

The sit-ins in Greensboro were neither the first sit-ins nor the first protests against segregated lunch counters. Facilities in Oklahoma City and Wichita had been desegregated by similar tactics in 1958. It was the Greensboro sit-ins, however, that touched off the tidal wave of direct, confrontational protest that marked the early 1960's. Sit-in protests spread from Greensboro to other cities in North Carolina, then to Nashville and on to dozens of other southern cities as well as a number in the North. By the end of 1960, approximately one hundred southern cities had experienced sit-ins and roughly one-third of them had desegregated their lunch counters. More would follow in subsequent years. Approximately seventy thousand people participated in the sit-ins, making the movement the most massive expression of discontent with the racial status quo that the country had yet seen. Blacks and sympathetic whites were inspired to confront other forms of segregation, and it became increasingly difficult for other whites to maintain that southern blacks were basically content and were only being stirred up by outside agitators. In cities where lunch counters were desegregated, white patrons quickly adjusted, casting further doubt on the proposition that southern race relations were impervious to change.

For Greensboro, the sit-ins marked the beginning of a decade of periodic protests and change. The spring of 1963 would see more than one thousand arrests as demonstrators sought to desegregate a range of public accommodations. Out of this later round of protests would emerge Jesse Jackson, then a student at A & T. In 1969, another period of demonstrations resulted in violence in which an A & T student was killed and several police officers injured.

The Greensboro sit-ins also marked something of a generational shift in the civil rights movement. Although they had received endorsement by the local NAACP chapter and some organizational support from CORE, the sit-ins had not been initiated by any of the major civil rights organizations but by four college students. In part, they grew out of the impatience of the younger generation of southern blacks with the pace of change in race relations. It was largely the young who answered the call, first in Greensboro and later in other cities.

While the sit-ins were still going on in Greensboro, Ella Baker of the Southern Christian Leadership Conference organized a meeting of black student leaders from throughout the South at Shaw University in Raleigh, North Carolina (April 15-17, 1960). Martin Luther King, Jr., and other civil rights leaders addressed the students, who decided to set up their own organization. Out of their efforts was born the Student Non-Violent Coordinating Committee (SNCC). It quickly became one of the most active and militant civil rights organizations of the 1960's and was involved in most of the major civil rights campaigns of the decade. In a broader context, the student activism embodied in the sit-ins and the SNCC helped to inspire the organization of the Students for a Democratic Society later in 1960, as well as contributing to the more general campus unrest of the decade.

Nationally, the sit-in movement that spread from Greensboro helped to push civil rights onto the nation's political agenda. Ultimately, the campaign against segregated facilities that began in Greensboro would help to secure passage of the Civil Rights Act of 1964, a measure that outlawed racial segregation in eating places and other public accommodations.

## Bibliography

Carson, Clayborne. *In Struggle: SNCC and the Black Awakening of the 1960's.* Cambridge, Mass.: Harvard University Press, 1981. The standard history of the Student Non-Violent Coordinating Committee, the most prominent organization to arise from the sit-in movement. Illustrates one of the major organizational effects of the Greensboro sit-ins. Bibliography and index.

Chafe, William H. *Civilities and Civil Rights: Greensboro, North Carolina, and the Black Struggle for Freedom.* New York: Oxford University Press, 1980. The definitive study of the civil rights movement in Greensboro. Contains a chapter on the sit-ins. Especially effective at bringing out the differences between black and white perspectives. Indispensable for seeing the sit-ins in their local context. Includes an informative "Note on Sources" and an index.

Goldfield, David R. *Black, White and Southern: Race Relations and Southern Culture, 1940 to the Present.* Baton Rouge: Louisiana State University Press, 1990. Good overall treatment of race relations that places the civil rights movement within the overall context of southern culture. Provides a useful picture of the racial etiquette that underpinned the Jim Crow system. Sees the Greensboro sit-ins as pivotal in extending the civil rights movement across the South. Bibliography and index.

Morris, Aldon. *Origins of the Civil Rights Movement: Black Communities Organizing for Change.* New York: Free Press, 1984. A combination of history and sociology that explores the civil rights movement through 1963 by focusing on the organizations involved. Its account of the sit-ins differs from others in the importance it places on pre-existing organizations, both in providing a background and in facilitating the movement's spread. Bibliography and index.

Oppenheimer, Martin. *The Sit-In Movement of 1960.* Brooklyn: Carlson Publishing, 1989. Originally written as a doctoral dissertation in sociology in 1963. Provides a nearly contemporary perspective on the sit-in movement as a whole. Useful for placing events in Greensboro in overall context. Bibliography and index.

Raines, Howell. *My Soul Is Rested: Movement Days in the Deep South Remembered.* New York: Penguin, 1983. An oral history of the civil rights movement. Includes an interview with Franklin McCain that provides a firsthand account of the original Greensboro sit-in. Other interviews show how quickly the sit-in movement spread. Index but no bibliography.

Wolff, Miles. *Lunch at the 5 and 10.* Rev. ed. Chicago: Ivan R. Dee, 1990. First published in 1970, this is a highly readable account of the Greensboro sit-ins based in part on interviews with the major participants. Contains an interesting epilogue that provides accounts of the subsequent careers of the Greensboro Four. Also contains a useful introduction by August Meier. Lacks a bibliography but includes an index.

Zinn, Howard. *SNCC: The New Abolitionists.* 2d ed. Boston: Beacon Press, 1965. Though less comprehensive than Carson's work listed above, this is a contemporary account written by a historian who served as an adviser to the SNCC. Vividly brings out the student context in which the sit-in movement began and spread.

*William C. Lowe*

## Cross-References

*Brown v. Board of Education* Ends Public School Segregation (1954), p. 913; Parks Is Arrested for Refusing to Sit in the Back of the Bus (1955), p. 947; The SCLC Forms to Link Civil Rights Groups (1957), p. 974; The Civil Rights Act of 1957 Creates the Commission on Civil Rights (1957), p. 997; Eisenhower Sends Troops to Little Rock, Arkansas (1957), p. 1003; Meredith's Enrollment Integrates the University of Mississippi (1962), p. 1167; Civil Rights Protesters Attract International Attention (1963), p. 1188; Martin Luther King, Jr., Delivers His "I Have a Dream" Speech (1963), p. 1200; Three Civil Rights Workers Are Murdered (1964), p. 1246; Congress Passes the Civil Rights Act (1964), p. 1251.

# THE INTERNATIONAL ORGANIZATION OF CONSUMERS UNIONS IS FOUNDED

*Categories of event:* Consumers' rights; health and medical rights
*Time:* April 1, 1960
*Locale:* The Hague, The Netherlands

*Consumer organizations in five nations created the International Organization of Consumers Unions to coordinate, augment, and expand the consumer movement*

*Principal personages:*
> ARTHUR KALLET (1902-1972), the first director and a founder of Consumers Union of the United States
> COLSTON E. WARNE (1900-1987), the first president of the International Organization of Consumers Unions
> FLORENCE MASON, the staff member of the International Organization of Consumers Unions who, with Warne, led early efforts to assist consumer groups in developing countries

## Summary of Event

The exigencies of capitalism understandably focus suppliers of goods and services on creating profits. By necessity, such suppliers are generally well organized and articulate when it comes to protecting their interests. Individual consumers, however, are not. They are alone in the marketplace and are often ill-equipped to balance competing claims and make optimal decisions. Consumer organizations were created to alter the informational imbalance between consumers and producers. Independent and noncommercial, their purpose is to speak up for consumers and safeguard consumer interests. They publish unbiased information about goods and services gathered through comparative testing that considers such factors as safety, price, quality, and environmental concerns. In these ways, consumer organizations promote the right of individuals to make wise and safe choices.

During the first half of the twentieth century, consumer organizations were established in many countries. One of the first and most successful was Consumers Union of the United States. Formed in 1936, the organization has been an integral part of the American consumer movement and has become an internationally respected institution.

Organizations in Europe also began testing products and publishing information about their quality and safety. Despite common goals and activities, however, these national consumer movements were isolated. There was no coordination to prevent the duplication of specific activities, to push for common product, health, and safety standards, or to spread the consumer movement to other countries. In an attempt to correct these deficiencies and advance consumer rights, five organizations from Australia, Belgium, The Netherlands, the United Kingdom, and the United States founded what is now known as the International Organization of Consumers Unions (IOCU) on April 1, 1960.

The IOCU is a nongovernmental, nonprofit international foundation that as of 1991 links the activities of more than 170 consumer organizations in some sixty countries. The group, originally named the International Office of Consumers Unions, has central aims of promoting consumer movements and consumer rights worldwide. The IOCU organizes information networks, sponsors international conferences and workshops, conducts research, collects and disseminates information, and represents consumer interests in other international organizations. It has international headquarters in The Hague and regional offices worldwide.

Independent consumer organizations compose IOCU membership. Associate members with full voting privileges must be nonprofit groups which act exclusively in the interest of consumers and do not accept financial or other support from corporations, industry groups, or political organizations. Consumer groups that do not qualify as associate members or choose not to pay dues may still participate in IOCU activities as supporting members or correspondents.

The formal organization of the IOCU is composed of a general assembly containing one voting delegate from each associate organization. The assembly selects a twenty-member governing council, which in turn designates a six-member executive committee that handles administrative matters. The IOCU also convenes triennial world congresses which gather multiple representatives from member organizations. IOCU activities are financed primarily through members' dues, but funds also come from grants and publication sales. The budget, set by the council, is small but growing, rising from $100,000 in 1970 and $190,000 in 1975 to $1,026,000 in 1990.

The IOCU advances consumer rights through a wide variety of activities and interorganizational relationships. As set out in a new constitution adopted in 1968, IOCU objectives and functions include assisting consumer groups and genuine government efforts in promoting consumer rights; fostering international cooperation in comparative testing of goods and services; collecting and disseminating information relating to consumer interests, laws, and practices; providing a forum for national consumer organizations to discuss consumer problems and possible solutions; representing consumer interests in United Nations agencies and other international bodies; and providing assistance and encouragement to consumer education and protection programs in developing countries.

From its inception in 1960 until 1968, IOCU was almost exclusively an organization promoting international cooperation in the comparative testing of consumer goods and services, facilitating exchange of test methods and plans, and furthering the dissemination of product information based on comparative tests. The expansion of its chosen portfolio was first clearly seen, and criticized by some as overly political and contentious, in the 1972 United Nations Conference on the Human Environment, during which IOCU representatives emphasized broad consumer and environmental issues and criticized multinational corporations.

The original goals of producing and disseminating information remained, however, a vital part of the organization. Activities in this area include maintaining working groups on product testing, consumer education, medical issues, air transport, and other matters. The IOCU library in Penang, Malaysia, collects and distributes legislative, technical, and educational data relevant to consumer interests. The IOCU supports and conducts studies on a variety of consumer issues, including the dumping of dangerous drugs in developing countries, pesticides, and baby food production and marketing. The organization led development of an international warning system to alert individuals and consumer organizations of products that have been banned, recalled, or controlled in any part of the world.

The IOCU both publishes its own material and acts as a distribution center for materials produced by member organizations. IOCU publications as of 1991 include two major monthlies, the flagship *IOCU Newsletter* and *Consumer Currents*, a global news digest. Among the dozens of titles appearing regularly are many that focus on specific issues. These include *The Consumer Protector*, providing current information on consumer laws in the Asia-Pacific region, the *Pesticide Monitor*, and the *Tobacco Action Pack*. Other notable publications include *Consumer Interpol Focus*, *HAI News*, and the biannual *Consumer's Directory*, a global register of consumer organizations. More than two hundred books, special publications, and monographs have also been produced and published by the IOCU. Prominent topics include tobacco, pesticides, infant formula, consumer laws, food, and medicine.

The IOCU is also active in creating new information networks to promote information exchange for the advancement of consumer rights. It regularly organizes seminars, workshops, training programs, and regional conferences which allow consumer groups to exchange experiences and build specific skills in areas such as research, lobbying, and community organizing. These programs often include participation by both government officials and nongovernmental organizations in an attempt to develop common goals and strategies. Special efforts have been made to use these networks to stimulate and assist consumer groups in developing countries.

The IOCU maintains important relationships with numerous international governmental and nongovernmental organizations. The IOCU has consultative status with the United Nations Economic and Social Council, one of six major organs of the United Nations and an important international policy-making body. The IOCU also has official relationships with a number of the specialized agencies of the United Nations, including the World Health Organization, the Food and Agriculture Organization, and the United Nations Children's Fund. These relationships enable the IOCU to represent consumer issues during international negotiations and policy-making. Finally, the IOCU is a leader in several citizen and consumer action organizations, most notably the International Baby Food Action Network, Health Action International, and Pesticides Action Network.

## Impact of Event

The IOCU has played an important role in advancing consumer interests, particularly in the Third World, by coordinating and augmenting the efforts of national consumer organizations. The organization's impact is seen through its distinctive capacity to promote consumer interests in international forums, sponsor international conferences and workshops, and produce and distribute information.

IOCU's formal relationship with the United Nations and several specialized agencies enabled consumer interests to be represented at the international level to a degree impossible before its creation. In 1985, the organization successfully completed a decade-long campaign to secure approval for the United Nations Guidelines on Consumer Protection. This standard embraced the concept of consumer rights and established a framework for strengthening consumer protection policies. In a variety of other international forums and negotiations, the IOCU has argued for consumer interests on a wide range of issues including safety standards, pesticide control, and the regulation of transnational corporations.

The IOCU's special interest in assisting disadvantaged and vulnerable consumers has led to a number of successes. The organization plays an important role in stimulating and assisting consumer groups in developing nations. This effort is particularly important and, when effective, of great relative impact because consumers in developing countries are among the least educated, have little buying power, and often do not enjoy effective government protection. IOCU activities have also been instrumental in assisting the fledgling consumer movement in Eastern Europe. As a result, a growing number of IOCU members are now located in Eastern Europe and the Third World.

The IOCU has significantly increased the amount of consumer information produced and disseminated around the world. In addition to testing products and publishing, the information and organization networks established by the IOCU play other important roles. The Pesticides Action Network and International Baby Food Action Network have been instrumental in advancing safeguards for those without adequate information to judge the quality or potential dangers of particular products. Consumer Interpol supplies more than three hundred groups and individuals concerned with environmental and consumer issues with information on emerging hazards to consumer health. The Consumer Protection Advisory Service provides lawyers worldwide with information on consumer laws, while the Consumer Educators Network promotes the introduction of consumer education into classrooms.

Perhaps most significant, the IOCU has been instrumental in the increasing formalization and recognition of the concept of consumers' rights. These include the right to basic needs—adequate food, clothing, shelter, health care, education, and sanitation; the right to protection from hazardous products or production processes; the right to make an informed choice between products; the right to advocate consumer interests; the right to redress grievances against sellers or manufacturers of poor-quality or dangerous goods and services; the right to consumer education; and the right to a healthy environment. Consumer rights form the basis for IOCU activity and unify the actions of member organizations. The IOCU's advocacy of consumer rights has also served to help legitimize its actions as ongoing attempts to secure and protect important individual rights. More important, consistent articulation of a strong set of consumer rights has provided individuals and consumer groups a standard against which to measure the level of consumer protection in their own countries. Through a wide variety of activities, the IOCU has strengthened national consumer movements and international individual rights by steadfastly supporting each consumer's ability to make informed decisions.

## Bibliography

Aaker, David A., and George S. Day, eds. *Consumerism: Search for the Consumer Interest.* 3d ed. New York: Free Press, 1978. This large and generally strong collection of essays gives the reader a broad understanding of consumerism as a social movement and its impact on the marketplace. Among the issues considered are historical and current perspectives on consumerism; advertising; safety and liability; and government and industry responses. Includes references and index.

Silber, Norman Issac. *Test and Protest: The Influence of Consumers Union.* New York: Holmes & Meier, 1983. A well-written examination of the history and influence of Consumers Union of the United States. Includes general histories of consumer protest and scientific consumer reform as well as case studies of three critical battles: smoking, automobile design safety, and food contamination by radioactive fallout. Outstanding references, bibliographic essay, and index.

*Testing: Behind the Scenes at Consumer Reports, 1936-1986.* Mount Vernon, N.Y.: Consumers Union of the United States, 1986. This book offers a fascinating photographic history of Consumers Union and the issues it has examined. Each topic is addressed through a one-page essay and an often beautiful and always interesting photograph from Consumers Union's archives. Unique and informative.

Thorelli, Hans B., and Sarah V. Thorelli. *Consumer Information Handbook: Europe and North America.* New York: Praeger, 1974. A detailed but dry and somewhat dated study of forty consumer information programs in fifteen countries. This is the descriptive companion to their more analytic 1977 volume. Includes a very short chapter on the IOCU. Many tables and figures. Selective bibliography, references, index, and lists of consumer agencies, organizations, and journals.

_____. *Consumer Information Systems and Consumer Policy.* Cambridge, Mass.: Ballinger, 1977. The last and best of the three-volume International Consumer Information Survey, a seven-year research project. This comprehensive text provides an integrated and comparative analysis of the history, purpose, content, and impact of consumer information systems in North America and Western Europe. Excellent references, tables, figures, bibliography, and index.

*David Leonard Downie*

## Cross-References

The Pure Food and Drug Act and Meat Inspection Act Become Law (1906), p. 64; The International Labour Organisation Is Established (1919), p. 281; Consumers Union of the United States Emerges (1936), p. 527; The World Health Organization

Proclaims Health as a Basic Right (1946), p. 678; Nader Publishes *Unsafe at Any Speed* (1965), p. 1267; The Motor Vehicle Air Pollution Control Act Is Passed by Congress (1965), p. 1310; Congress Passes the Occupational Safety and Health Act (1970), p. 1585; The World Health Organization Adopts a Code on Breast-Milk Substitutes (1981), p. 2130; New York State Imposes the First Mandatory Seat-Belt Law (1984), p. 2220; Manville Offers $2.5 Billion to Victims of Asbestos Dust (1985), p. 2274.

# RIOTS ERUPT AS KATANGA PROVINCE
# SECEDES FROM THE CONGO

*Categories of event:* Revolutions and rebellions; political freedom
*Time:* July, 1960
*Locale:* The Congo

*The Congo crisis was a product of unplanned and halfhearted Belgian decoloni-
zation and uncompromising Lumumbist nationalism*

> *Principal personages:*
> PATRICE LUMUMBA (1925-1961), the first prime minister of the Congo
> JOSEPH KASAVUBU (1917-1969), the first president of the Congo
> MOISE TSHOMBE (1917-1969), the president of Katanga province; declared
> Katanga's independence at the expense of the larger interest of the
> Congo
> JOSEPH MOBUTU (1930-       ), an early supporter of Lumumba, who later
> sent Lumumba to his death; he set up a one-man rule after eliminat-
> ing rivals
> DAG HAMMARSKJÖLD (1905-1961), the secretary-general of the United Na-
> tions at the time of the Congo crisis

## Summary of Event

The Belgian Congo became the Republic of the Congo upon independence in
1960. In 1964, it changed its name to Democratic Republic of the Congo. To dis-
tinguish it from a northern neighbor with the same name, it was variously referred to
as "Congo-Leopoldville" and as "Congo-Kinshasa" after 1966, when its capital city
changed from Leopoldville to Kinshasa. In 1971, the official name of the country
became Zaire.

The Belgian Congo became independent in 1960. Unlike other African countries
that gained independence the same year, the Congo immediately began to slip into a
severe civil disorder that degenerated into superpower political confrontations. Less
than two weeks after independence, Congo's wealthiest region, Katanga province,
announced its secession. The Belgians, the former colonial rulers, returned with
force without the invitation of the Congo's national government. The Congolese
army mutinied after independence because its officer corps remained predominantly
Belgian. With political independence, the Congolese expected but did not get rapid
Africanization of the army's officer corps. Because the army constituted the primary
instrument of government coercion at the time, Belgian control of its officer corps
meant that the Congo did not have real political independence.

On their part, the Belgians were determined to retain some economic and political influence even after their reluctant return of self-government to the Congolese.
The region of Katanga was the economic hub of the independent Congo, but the

economy of Katanga was controlled by Belgian nationals. It was these Belgian businesspeople who engineered Katanga's secession in order to escape political control of the new African leaders of the Congo. When African leaders of independent Congo resisted this economic sabotage by Belgians resident in Katanga, the government of Belgium intervened with force, ostensibly to save Belgian lives. Thus, in only two weeks the coercive power of the new government, the primary source of its revenue, and the national sovereignty regained after seventy-five years (1885-1960) of colonial subjugation were all in jeopardy.

The crisis appeared first as civil strife between rival ethnic groups (the Bakongos and Bakavas) on the first day of July, only one day after Congo's independence was declared. Fifty people were injured and two hundred were arrested in the cities of Leopoldville and Luluabourg before a curfew that ended independence celebrations was imposed. Four days later, in the city of Thysville, the Congolese army mutinied against the Belgian-dominated officer corps. The mutiny quickly spread to other cities, including Elisabethville, in the province of Katanga, and the capital city of Leopoldville, where the mutineers refused to take orders from Belgian officers. On July 10, without permission of the central government of the Congo, Belgian paratroopers attacked the city of Elisabethville. Twenty-five people were reportedly killed before the Belgians reestablished control. The next day, Belgian naval forces heavily bombarded the city of Matadi after the evacuation of European residents. Nineteen Congolese casualties were reported, although some accounts claimed a generalized massacre with hundreds of deaths, exacerbating the atmosphere of panic, distrust, and fear between Europeans (especially Belgians) and Congolese. On that same day, under the protection of Belgian troops, Moise Tshombe, the president of the province of Katanga, declared Katanga an independent state.

The secession of Katanga internationalized the Congo crisis. In 1960, 25 percent of Congo's foreign exchange earnings, 50 percent of its national budget, and 75 percent of its mining production came from Katanga. To Patrice Lumumba's central government, therefore, successful secession by Katanga meant national economic death. On July 12, after fifty Congolese mutineers were shot by Belgian troops in Katanga, Congo's national government, fearing the disintegration of the country and its recolonization by Belgium, appealed to the United States for military intervention. The United States, preferring to get involved through the United Nations, denied the request for bilateral military assistance to the besieged republic. That night, the president of the Congo, Joseph Kasavubu, and Prime Minister Lumumba cabled the United Nations (U.N.) for military assistance to end the Belgian-supported Katanga secession and continuing Belgian violations of Congo's sovereignty. The United Nations was quick to act. On July 14, its Security Council adopted a resolution calling on the Belgian government to withdraw from the Congo. Belgium ignored the resolution and proceeded instead to extend its military reconquest and political influence to all of the Congo. The authority of Lumumba's government was undermined with impunity by the superior military force of the Belgians. As a result, the rule of law was replaced by disorder and by violations of human rights and fundamental freedoms—not that Africans in the colonial Congo had enjoyed widespread human rights in the first place.

The colonial rule of the Belgians and Portuguese, the poorest Europeans in colonial Africa, is generally noted for deprivation of basic rights to colonial subjects. Racial discrimination was as rigid and ferocious as in the height of South African apartheid. Africans had no rights to employment and were forced by law to work in the public sector for sixty days per year without pay. In the private sector, they were bound to their European employers by "contract of work" rather than "contract of employment." This distinction denied Africans the protection of trade unions enjoyed by their employed European counterparts. Even the right to spend their meager incomes freely was denied to the Africans by the colonial government. Until 1955, it was illegal to sell liquor to an African and all Africans were subjected to a severely enforced nightly curfew, with no freedom of movement in their immediate neighborhoods.

Political and economic rights were nonexistent. The right of Africans to own land was prohibited by law even though most were peasant farmers. Education was allowed only to the extent that it served the administrative needs of colonialism. Even then, Africans were denied access to the well-equipped schools paid for by their labor but preserved for Europeans. Thus, at independence in 1960, after seventy-five years of Belgian rule, there were only thirty Congolese with a university education. The humiliation of colonial paternalism and the injustice of denial of human rights were the bitter realities fundamental to uncompromising Lumumbist nationalism. The Congolese were not willing to see the Congo recolonized behind the smokescreen of secessionist Katanga.

In desperation, therefore, Lumumba sent a telegram to Moscow requesting the Kremlin to keep an eye on events in the Congo. That same day, July 15, the first detachments of U.N. troops arrived in the Congo. Thus began the first Cold War clash in Africa.

The principal actors in the Cold War, the Soviet Union and the United States, had different views regarding the core of the Congo crisis, the secession of Katanga. Lumumba's government wanted the United Nations to end Katanga's secession by any means, including force. The East, led by the Soviet Union, took a similar position. The United States and the West initially held the view that the incorporation of Katanga into the Congo would increase disorder, and in any event, they were against the use of force to end the secession. Moise Tshombe, the president of Katanga, and the government of Belgium, his main financial, technical, political, and military supporter, both announced their readiness to use force to prevent the United Nations' presence in their "sovereign" state of Katanga. The United Nations was against the use of force and advocated diplomatic and political means. The internationalization of the Congo crisis finally settled along the lines of the dialectics of the Cold War.

For the Soviet Union, it was a new opportunity to bring communism into the heart of Africa. For the United States, it became another front in the war to contain communism. The Soviet Union began to support factions which in turn supported

Lumumba. The United States began to support factions seeking the overthrow of Lumumba. The Belgians sought the same goals as did the United States, but pursued them through control of Katanga and influence on Kasavubu.

Kasavubu overthrew Lumumba's government and had Lumumba arrested by Colonel Joseph Mobutu, chief of staff of the Congolese National Army. Lumumba was transferred to Katanga, where he was humiliated, tortured, and finally murdered on the night of January 17-18, 1961, in a farmhouse belonging to a Belgian settler. The United Nations' failure to prevent the political assassination of Lumumba brought its impartiality in the Congo crisis into question. At the Security Council meeting in February, a bitter Soviet Union called for the dismissal of U.N. secretary-general Dag Hammarskjöld, accusing him of being a participant in and organizer of Lumumba's assassination. Six months later, Hammarskjöld was killed in a mysterious air crash in Katanga.

After the deaths of Lumumba and Hammarskjöld, catastrophic political confrontations in the Congo continued. Indiscriminate political assassinations increased until January 14, 1963, when Tshombe terminated Katanga's secession. The Congo became a single country again, although constitutional crises continued until November 25, 1965, when Mobutu (by then a general) assumed power through a military coup. Mobutu remained in power as of mid-1991, as president of the country that had renamed itself Zaire.

## Impact of Event

In general, the Congo crisis concerned the collective human rights of a people to political self-determination. The underlying struggle was between powerful European mining interests resident in the Katanga province of the Congo and uncompromising Lumumbist nationalism. Indeed, the idea and implementation of Katanga's secession, the root cause of the crisis, were inspired and supported by Belgians who had substantial financial and industrial interests in Katanga. The bulk of the human cost was borne by ordinary Africans.

About one year into the crisis, a U.N. refugee camp in the city of Elisabethville sheltered an estimated 50,000 to 100,000 Africans. According to one expert on the Congo crisis, Jules Gérard-Libois, the camp "was a running sore, a center of misery, of banditry and of violent opposition to established authorities." Camp conditions constituted an effective denial of the basic human right to freedom, pursuit of happiness, and decent life. Africans, however, were not the only victims of the crisis. Ordinary Belgians who worked in the Congo suffered from the crisis as well. Families were separated. Many were forced by fear to ship wives, children, and property back to Belgium in the face of the virulent appeals to racial hatred.

On the whole, the situation in the Congo, marked by administrative breakdown, military chaos, and political fragmentation, was not conducive to the rule of law. In this sense, few people, irrespective of race, enjoyed any kind of human rights. Order, due process, and economic and social advance promised in preindependence election platforms were replaced by uncertainty and insecurity, suspicion and fear, and arbitrary arrests and killings. Such events were not part of the hopes raised in the minds of the Africans by the prospect of independence. Independence was conceptualized as freedom from humiliating European domination, a return to full citizenship with all of its fundamental rights. Instead, independence became a more dehumanizing life in refugee camps.

In the 1960's, Cold War imperatives, not patriotism, determined who got what rights. Had Lumumbists understood this reality, there may not have been a crisis in the Congo. For that matter, Mobutu may never have been able to implement his dictatorship, under which, according to Amnesty International, many citizens of Zaire still live without significant human rights.

## Bibliography

Dayal, Rajeshwar. *Mission for Hammarskjöld: The Congo Crisis.* Princeton, N.J.: Princeton University Press, 1976. This book is a participant's account of the Congo crisis. Dayal was head of the U.N. operation in the Congo. The book is authoritative but subjective. It is a useful account of the United Nations' perspective on the crisis.

Epstein, Howard M., ed. *Revolt in the Congo: 1960-1964.* New York: Facts on File, 1965. This is a very useful documentation of relevant dates and corresponding events in the Congo crisis. The author volunteers little analysis. In a sense, this is the strong point of the book. Very informative.

Gérard-Libois, Jules, and Rebecca Young, trans. *Katanga Secession.* Madison: University of Wisconsin Press, 1966. Gérard-Libois' account of the special interests and politics behind Katanga's decision to secede is by far one of the best histories of events, personalities, and organizations connected with the crisis. The book is largely impartial, leaving the reader to form his or her own opinion about the forces behind the rupture. The book includes useful original documents related to the crisis.

Lefever, Ernest W. *Crisis in the Congo: A United Nations Force in Action.* Washington, D.C.: Brookings Institution, 1965. This book does relatively little to aid in understanding unique Congolese experiences that were fundamental to the crisis. Relying primarily on documents and interviews, the book rehashes the Cold War thinking of the West and appraises the role played by the United Nations. This book is useful for those interested in an opinionated account of the roles played by the United States and the United Nations in the crisis.

Young, Crawford. *Politics in the Congo: Decolonization and Independence.* Princeton, N.J.: Princeton University Press, 1965. This is a scholarly analysis of the challenges of nation building in the Congo. The book contains informative historical facts necessary for understanding the crisis. It is objective and will arm the reader with an appreciation of internal and external factors that finally pushed the Congo from the devastation of colonialism to the catastrophy of self-rule.

*Ebere Onwudiwe*

## Cross-References

Reformers Expose Atrocities Against Congolese Laborers (1903), p. 13; The Mau Mau Uprising Creates Havoc in Kenya (1952), p. 891; The Sudanese Civil War Erupts (1955), p. 941; The United Nations Intervenes in the Congolese Civil War (1960), p. 1074; The Organization of African Unity Is Founded (1963), p. 1194; Zimbabwe's Freedom Fighters Topple White Supremacist Government (1964), p. 1224; Civil War Ravages Chad (1965), p. 1273; The Secession of Biafra Starts a Nigerian Civil War (1967), p. 1365; Burundi's Government Commits Genocide of the Bahutu Majority (1972), p. 1668; Revolution Erupts in Ethiopia (1974), p. 1758; Biko Is Murdered by Interrogators in South Africa (1977), p. 1887; Hunger Becomes a Weapon in the Sudanese Civil War (1988), p. 2354.

# THE UNITED NATIONS INTERVENES IN THE CONGOLESE CIVIL WAR

*Categories of event:* Political freedom; revolutions and rebellions
*Time:* July, 1960
*Locale:* The Congo

*The Congo crisis in the wake of the country's independence from Belgium in 1960 was marked by a complex civil war involving intervention by the United Nations*

Principal personages:
PATRICE LUMUMBA (1925-1961), the first prime minister of the Congo
JOSEPH KASAVUBU (1917-1969), the first president of the Congo
MOISE TSHOMBE (1917-1969), the president of the secessionist province of Katanga
DAG HAMMARSKJÖLD (1905-1961), the secretary-general of the United Nations
JOSEPH MOBUTU (1930-    ), an army colonel who overthrew Lumumba and later became the undisputed strongman in the Congo

## Summary of Event

Immediately on achieving its independence in June of 1960, the Congo lapsed into a prolonged and politically complicated civil war. With the former Belgian colonial administration no longer in control, the politically unstable character of the Congo state became painfully obvious. Consisting at the time of independence of nearly fifteen million people divided into some two hundred ethnolinguistic groups, the Congo was wholly unprepared to govern itself. It had been a Belgian colony since 1885, when the Berlin Conference on West Africa divided the continent among the European colonial powers. The Congo was awarded to King Leopold of Belgium as a personal possession, but in 1908, after scandalous reports on the inhumane treatment of Congolese labor in the mineral-rich country, the Belgian government assumed direct administration over the colony. In the late 1950's, faced with increasing economic and political pressure, including the Leopoldville riots of early 1959, Belgium moved rapidly to divest itself of the colony and grant its independence.

The potential leadership of the Congo at this time was badly divided along ethnic, geographical, and ideological lines. There was little agreement on whether the Congo should be a federal or unitary state, nor was there agreement about what the ongoing relationshp with Belgium should be. Ten political parties, several explicitly based on ethnic foundations, sprouted up in the two years preceding independence and had little time to forge a nationwide consensus on anything, other than that independence should be sought. To complicate matters, the once dynamic economy of the Belgian Congo had fallen on leaner times, a fact that influenced Belgium's decision to allow independence to be so rapidly, and perhaps imprudently, effected. Furthermore, the country's most valuable resources were located in the south, especially in secession-minded South Kasai and Katanga provinces. The Katanga province party (the Conakat party), headed by Moise Tshombe, sought to retain close ties with Belgium, in contrast to the positions of other parties and individuals. As the country gradually descended into civil war, the safety of foreigners and indigenous people alike was threatened. These threats, together with actual attacks on foreigners, triggered immediate intervention by Belgian troops, and this eventually precipitated involvement of the United Nations.

The postindependence history of the Congo, then, is a study in personal rivalries, geographical factionalism, political intrigue, high-stakes maneuvering by conflicting Congolese government officials, U.N. intervention, and Cold War politics. It is also the story of assassination, political executions, racially motivated conflict, secessionist rebellion, intertribal and interclan rivalry, and interregional animosity. It is not surprising that it is also a story of war, displaced persons, terrorized populations, refugees, and human suffering. Before the conflict was over, the Congo had lost its first prime minister, Patrice Lumumba, who was murdered while in the captivity of Katanga secessionists, and the United Nations had lost its secretary-general, Dag Hammarskjöld, in a plane crash while he was en route to negotiations intended to resolve the Katanga revolt.

Unlike most other newly independent African nations, the Congo experienced no political honeymoon free of political conflict. Virtually from the day of independence, mutinies in the armed forces, turmoil, and tribal violence erupted. Belgian military forces intervened to protect foreigners and presumably to restore order in the mineral-rich Katanga province, which remained an important commercial resource for Belgium. The chief political figures in the Congo vied from the start to gain favorable treatment for their separate constituencies. The tenuous compromises between Patrice Lumumba, who was elected premier of the Congo, and Joseph Kasavubu, who had competed for Lumumba's post but settled for the position of the presidency, began to break down over how to deal with the Belgian military intervention, which Kasavubu welcomed but Lumumba condemned. In Katanga, Tshombe, going even further than Kasavubu, not only welcomed a strong Belgian presence but also declared independence from the Congo.

The spreading disorder prompted Kasavubu and Lumumba to ask for U.N. intervention. Less than two weeks after independence, forces from the United Nations Operation in the Congo (UNOC) arrived. They did not leave until four years later, after losing more than two hundred troops to battle deaths or accidents and incurring about $430 million in expenses. Once in the Congo, UNOC forces became a source of dissension among Congo leaders even though Hammarskjöld attempted to ensure U.N. neutrality. Lumumba distrusted Hammarskjöld and the U.N. presence, although these very forces later helped to shield him from arrest by his political adversaries, and Tshombe refused to allow UNOC forces into Katanga. Hammarskjöld nevertheless secured a withdrawal of Belgian troops, even as Kasai province joined Katanga in secession and mutual recriminations between Lumumba and Kasavubu led to a complete break between them. Lumumba's appeals for direct Soviet assistance ran counter to the U.N. operation and Hammarskjöld's objectives. A few weeks later, Colonel Joseph Mobutu, who sided with Kasavubu, engineered a coup and had Lumumba arrested only to see him escape and remain under U.N. protection in his Leopoldville residence.

In time, four distinct governments contested for control over parts or all of the fragmented Congolese state. The Western-backed government of Kasavubu, Mobutu, and Cyrille Adoula in Leopoldville held sway in the western part of the country and eventually won the contest. In the East, a Lumumbist government headed by Antoine Gizenga maintained periodic control over Stanleyville and the surrounding areas. In the South, two secessionist governments in Kasai and Katanga held out against attacks by U.N. contingents as well as forces under Mobutu, on one hand, and Gizenga, on the other. The fragmentation of the Congo reflected traditional geographical and ethnic divisions as well as more modern ideological concerns.

Gradually Kasavubu, working with Mobutu, was able to gain U.N. recognition for his government, which took the Congo's seat at the United Nations. Having been largely outmaneuvered on the international scene, Lumumba escaped from Leopoldville in a desperate effort to reach his supporters in the East, only to be captured again by Mobutu forces before attaining his objective. Following this, Lumumba forces, led by Gizenga, proclaimed independence for the government in Stanleyville. Within two months, Patrice Lumumba had been murdered after having been transferred into Katangan custody. East Bloc countries promptly recognized Gizenga's Stanleyville government. Civil war with both Gizenga in the East and Tshombe in Katanga preoccupied the Leopoldville regime during most of 1961, although a compromise federal regime under Cyrille Adoula held out promise for an end to the civil conflict. These hopes were short-lived. Katanga province quickly reverted to open rebellion, and Gizenga returned to Stanleyville to reorganize opposition to the central government. Fighting in Katanga was especially difficult, and it was while on his way to obtain a cease-fire there that Hammarskjöld was killed in a plane crash, in September of 1961. The Katanga secession was successfully suppressed in 1964, and UNOC forces were able to quit the country. By that time, the central government had gained sufficient strength to ensure the integrity of the nation, although internal dissent and turmoil persisted, if at a more manageable level.

This brief account of some of the salient events in the Congo crisis provides only the barest outline of an infinitely more complicated series of events. The United Nations operated under the very difficult constraint of opposition from the Soviet Union. It also faced politically entrenched interests inside the Congo that perpetuated the civil war. Measured in human terms, thousands of Congolese died during the hostilities, many as a result of spontaneous tribal disputes that the central government was powerless to prevent. Hundreds more died in clashes between the forces of the vying governments. Thousands of people were displaced and became refugees. Having passed through this terrible four-year trial during its infancy, the Congo emerged scarred but whole.

## Impact of Event

The Congolese civil war underscored the tremendous difficulties facing new states in Africa whose colonially inherited borders did not conform with demographic realities and whose people had too little time and too few of the skills needed to prepare for self-government. The Congo crisis helped to underscore for other African governments the importance of reaffirming the legitimacy of colonial boundaries and the need of peoples residing within them to build genuine nations where only juridical states existed in many instances.

Within the Congo itself, the crisis led to the ascension of Joseph Mobutu (who later adopted the name Mobutu Sese Seko) to the presidency in 1965. He took control of the central government and ruled the country with a firm hand, often with little regard for human rights, while accumulating a considerable fortune of his own from the nation's wealth. In the 1970's, Katanga, earlier renamed Shaba province, on two occasions experienced renewed separatist violence. On the other hand, the Congo, which came to be known as Zaire, has to a large extent avoided, since the early 1960's, the bloodier and more brutal paths taken by many other African countries. The Shaba incidents were mild in comparison to the civil wars in Ethiopia, Chad, Mozambique, Rhodesia, Angola, Somalia, and the Sudan.

The Congo civil war had significant international as well as domestic consequences. The involvement of the U.N. peacekeeping forces was controversial from the beginning. That these forces were eventually authorized to use force against Katangan secessionists was a controversial milestone in U.N. peacekeeping. Although the U.N. Charter clearly permitted the use of force by the United Nations where threats to the peace or acts of aggression required international action, many argued nevertheless that this was still inconsistent with the spirit of the organization. The Soviet Union used the occasion of the U.N. Operation in the Congo to challenge the authority of the secretary-general. Soviet leaders were particularly incensed at the decisive role Hammarskjöld played in the early months of the crisis and proposed diluting the secretary-general's authority with their famous "troika" proposal, which would have divided the office among three persons. In addition, the recalcitrance of the Soviet Union in paying its fair share of peacekeeping expenses in the Congo led to a major financial crisis in the United Nations. The Soviet Union succeeded in its refusal to pay for UNOC but failed to gain support for its troika proposal. Thus, UNOC provided another case in which the United Nations showed an ability to take action to promote long-term peace and regional stability. United Nations peacekeeping efforts have since drawn on many of the lessons learned in the Congo operation. This institutional machinery has since proved invaluable in regional conflict resolution, much to the benefit of populations whose lives are disrupted or lost by prolonged international or civil conflict.

## Bibliography

Burns, Arthur, and Nina Heathcote. *Peace-Keeping by UN Forces: From Suez to the Congo.* New York: Praeger, 1963. This book contains extensive treatment of political background of the Congo crisis and the context of U.N. involvement. Footnotes and appendices are included. No bibliography or index.

Dayal, Rajeshwar. *Mission for Hammarskjöld: The Congo Crisis.* Princeton, N.J.: Princeton University Press, 1976. Written by a controversial U.N. official involved in the Congo peacekeeping operation, this book explores in great detail the events of 1960 and 1961 that saw the United Nations gradually and more deeply implicated in the crisis. Includes a bibliography and an index.

Epstein, Howard M., ed. *Revolt in the Congo: 1960-1964.* New York: Facts on File, 1965. A useful chronology of events from 1960 to 1964, with commentary on the evolution of the crisis. Described by the author as an "interim history." The journalistic tone of this source makes for easy reading, but the work lacks a bibliography or footnotes. Index included.

Harrelson, Max. *Fires All Around the Horizon: The U.N.'s Uphill Battle to Preserve the Peace.* New York: Praeger, 1989. This contemporary source, written by a respected longtime U.N. official, describes the general history of U.N. peacekeeping operations. A very good chapter treats the Congo case, providing a brief but useful account of the evolution of the crisis from the perspective of U.N. headquarters. Contains endnotes, a selected bibliography, and an index.

Lefever, Ernest W. *Crisis in the Congo: A United Nations Force in Action.* Washington, D.C.: Brookings Institution, 1965. This dispassionate treatment of the Congo crisis and of U.N. involvement provides an interesting contrast to the Dayal and Harrelson books, written by U.N. insiders with perhaps less distance from the events and more of a stake in how they are interpreted. Contains notes, a bibliography, and an index.

Young, Crawford. *Politics in the Congo: Decolonization and Independence.* Princeton, N.J.: Princeton University Press, 1965. Written by a highly respected American Africanist, this extensively documented book is a detailed historical treatment and political analysis of Belgian colonial rule, independence movements, and the postindependence crisis in the Congo. Includes an exhaustive bibliography and an index.

*Robert F. Gorman*

## Cross-References

Reformers Expose Atrocities Against Congolese Laborers (1903), p. 13; The Mau Mau Uprising Creates Havoc in Kenya (1952), p. 891; The Sudanese Civil War Erupts (1955), p. 941; Riots Erupt as Katanga Province Secedes from the Congo (1960), p. 1068; The Organization of African Unity Is Founded (1963), p. 1194; Zimbabwe's Freedom Fighters Topple White Supremacist Government (1964), p. 1224; Civil War Ravages Chad (1965), p. 1273; The Secession of Biafra Starts a Nigerian Civil War (1967), p. 1365; Burundi's Government Commits Genocide of the Bahutu Majority (1972), p. 1668; Revolution Erupts in Ethiopia (1974), p. 1758; Hunger Becomes a Weapon in the Sudanese Civil War (1988), p. 2354.

# GREAT EVENTS
# FROM
# HISTORY II

# CHRONOLOGICAL LIST OF EVENTS

## VOLUME I

# VOLUME II

## VOLUME III

## VOLUME IV

## VOLUME V

# CHRONOLOGICAL LIST OF EVENTS

CHRONOLOGICAL LIST OF EVENTS